Isaiah

Through the Centuries

Wiley Blackwell Bible Commentaries

Series Editors: John Sawyer, Christopher Rowland, Judith Kovacs, David M. Gunn
Editorial Board: Ian Boxall, Andrew Mein, Lena-Sofia Tiemeyer

Further information about this innovative reception history series is available at
www.bbibcomm.info.

Forthcoming

Isaiah
Through the Centuries

John F. A. Sawyer

WILEY Blackwell

This paperback edition first published 2020
© 2018 John Wiley & Sons Ltd

Edition history: John Wiley & Sons Ltd (hardback, 2018)

All rights reserved. No part of this publication may be reproduced, stored in a retrieval system, or transmitted, in any form or by any means, electronic, mechanical, photocopying, recording or otherwise, except as permitted by law. Advice on how to obtain permission to reuse material from this title is available at http://www.wiley.com/go/permissions.

The right of John F. A. Sawyer to be identified as the author of this work has been asserted in accordance with law.

Registered Offices
John Wiley & Sons, Inc., 111 River Street, Hoboken, NJ 07030, USA
John Wiley & Sons Ltd, The Atrium, Southern Gate, Chichester, West Sussex, PO19 8SQ, UK

Editorial Office
The Atrium, Southern Gate, Chichester, West Sussex, PO19 8SQ, UK

For details of our global editorial offices, customer services, and more information about Wiley products visit us at www.wiley.com.

Wiley also publishes its books in a variety of electronic formats and by print-on-demand. Some content that appears in standard print versions of this book may not be available in other formats.

Limit of Liability/Disclaimer of Warranty
While the publisher and authors have used their best efforts in preparing this work, they make no representations or warranties with respect to the accuracy or completeness of the contents of this work and specifically disclaim all warranties, including without limitation any implied warranties of merchantability or fitness for a particular purpose. No warranty may be created or extended by sales representatives, written sales materials or promotional statements for this work. The fact that an organization, website, or product is referred to in this work as a citation and/or potential source of further information does not mean that the publisher and authors endorse the information or services the organization, website, or product may provide or recommendations it may make. This work is sold with the understanding that the publisher is not engaged in rendering professional services. The advice and strategies contained herein may not be suitable for your situation. You should consult with a specialist where appropriate. Further, readers should be aware that websites listed in this work may have changed or disappeared between when this work was written and when it is read. Neither the publisher nor authors shall be liable for any loss of profit or any other commercial damages, including but not limited to special, incidental, consequential, or other damages.

Library of Congress Cataloging-in-Publication Data

Names: Sawyer, John F. A., author.
Title: Isaiah through the centuries / by John F.A. Sawyer.
Description: Hoboken, NJ : John Wiley & Sons, 2018. | Series: Wiley Blackwell
   Bible commentaries | Includes bibliographical references and index. |
   Description based on print version record and CIP data provided by
   publisher.
Identifiers: LCCN 2017031787 (print) | LCCN 2017044589 (ebook) | ISBN
   9781119441182 (pdf) | ISBN 9781119441168 (epub) | ISBN 9780631219637
   (hardback) | 9781119673910 (paperback)
Subjects: LCSH: Bible. Isaiah–Commentaries. | Isaiah (Biblical prophet)
Classification: LCC BS1515.53 (ebook) | LCC BS1515.53 .S29 2018 (print) | DDC
   224/.107–dc23
LC record available at https://lccn.loc.gov/2017031787 LC record available at https://lccn.loc.gov/2017044589

Cover Design: Wiley
Cover Image: Life of William Blake (1880), Volume 2, Job illustrations by Cygnis insignis is licensed under CC BY-SA

Set in 10/12.5pt Minion by SPi Global, Pondicherry, India

Printed and bound by CPI Group (UK) Ltd, Croydon, CR0 4YY

10 9 8 7 6 5 4 3 2 1

For Jean

Contents

The Wiley Blackwell Bible Commentaries series, the first to be devoted primarily to the reception history of the Bible, is based on the premise that how people have interpreted, and been influenced by, a sacred text like the Bible is often as interesting and historically important as what it originally meant. The series emphasizes the influence of the Bible on literature, art, music and film, its role in the evolution of religious beliefs and practices, and its impact on social and political developments. Drawing on work in a variety of disciplines, it is designed to provide a convenient and scholarly means of access to material until now hard to find and a much-needed resource for all those interested in the influence of the Bible on Western culture.

Until quite recently this whole dimension was for the most part neglected by biblical scholars. The goal of a commentary was primarily if not exclusively to get behind the centuries of accumulated Christian and Jewish tradition to one single meaning, normally identified with the author's original intention.

The most important and distinctive feature of the Wiley Blackwell Commentaries is that they will present readers with many different interpretations of each text, in such a way as to heighten their awareness of what a text, especially a sacred text, can mean and what it can do, what it has meant and what it has done, in the many contexts in which it operates.

The Wiley Blackwell Bible Commentaries will consider patristic, rabbinic (where relevant) and medieval exegesis as well as insights from various types of modern criticism, acquainting readers with a wide variety of interpretative techniques. As part of the history of interpretation, questions of source, date, authorship and other historical-critical and archaeological issues will be discussed, but since these are covered extensively in existing commentaries, such references will be brief, serving to point readers in the direction of readily accessible literature where they can be followed up.

Original to this series is the consideration of the reception history of specific biblical books arranged in commentary format. The chapter-by-chapter arrangement ensures that the biblical text is always central to the discussion. Given the wide influence of the Bible and the richly varied appropriation of each biblical book, it is a difficult question which interpretations to include. While each volume will have its own distinctive point of view, the guiding principle for the series as a whole is that readers should be given a representative sampling of material from different ages, with emphasis on interpretations that have been especially influential or historically significant. Though commentators will have their preferences among the different interpretations, the material will be presented in such a way that readers can make up their own minds on the value, morality and validity of particular interpretations.

The series encourages readers to consider how the biblical text has been interpreted down the ages and seeks to open their eyes to different uses of the Bible in contemporary culture. The aim is to write a series of scholarly commentaries that draw on all the insights of modern research to illustrate the rich interpretative potential of each biblical book.

John F. A. Sawyer
Christopher Rowland
Judith Kovacs
David M. Gunn

Acknowledgements

Over the twenty years that have passed between the publication of *The Fifth Gospel* (1996) and the completion of this volume, an enormous number of people have given me advice, ideas, suggestions and encouragement, colleagues, students, friends – too many to mention by name. I am extremely grateful to you all. But I would like to say a special word of thanks to Martin O'Kane, Francis Landy, Miriam Talisman, Stuart Leyden, Jimmy Russell, Bernhard Lang, Max Sussman, Howard Clarke, Karen Langton, Siobhán Dowling Long and Jean Sawyer.

I would also like to thank the library staff at the Warburg Institute in London, the Pontifical Biblical Institute in Rome, the Bill Bryson and Palace Green Libraries in Durham, Newcastle University Library and the University and New College Libraries in Edinburgh, and a special word of thanks to Rebecca Harkin at Wiley Blackwell for all she did for the whole series, not just this volume.

Earlier versions of parts of Chapters 5, 6 and 21 were published in *Poets, Prophets, and Texts in Play: Studies in Biblical Poetry and Prophecy in Honour of Francis Landy*, ed. E. Ben Zvi et al. (London: Bloomsbury Press 2015), pp. 161–174 and parts of chapters 1, 14, 15–16, 37 and 65 in *Reading the Sacred Scriptures: From Oral Tradition to Written Documents and their Reception*, ed. F. Long and S. Dowling Long (London: Routledge 2017), 249–262.

List of Illustrations

Introduction

A text has more than one meaning, depending as much on who is reading it as on what the original author intended. This is not a new idea – already the rabbis and the Church Fathers distinguished between literal and allegorical or mystical meanings – and it was particularly true of ancient texts where, before the revolution in eighteenth-century scholarship, we knew next to nothing about the original author. But over the last 250 years, archaeological discoveries, comparative philology, palaeography, textual criticism and the like, have made it possible to draw ever nearer to the original author's intention, and historical-critical commentaries were designed to present one meaning for every text, the

Isaiah Through the Centuries, First Edition. John F. A. Sawyer.
© 2018 John Wiley & Sons Ltd. Published 2020 by John Wiley & Sons Ltd.

correct meaning, the one nearest to the original author's intention. The many other meanings the text has had down the centuries in the church and the synagogue, in sermons, hymns, liturgy, literature, art and music, were simply ignored by biblical scholars. Later meanings were considered irrelevant because 'that is not what the original Hebrew meant.' In a modern critical commentary on Isaiah it was inappropriate to mention the sacrament of Baptism (Isa 1:16) or the Trinity (6:3) or Lucifer (14:12) or Muhammad (21:7) or the Lamedvavniks (30:18) or China (49:12) or the Holocaust (56:5) because such material usually has little or nothing to do with the 'original meaning.'

The Wiley Blackwell Bible Commentary series was created to redress the balance and enable us to hear some of the voices of readers from the beginning down to the present. It is increasingly being realized that, whether you are trying to get back to the original meaning or whether you are interested in how medieval and modern readers have interpreted it in literature or music or worship or politics, the story of how it has been understood down the centuries can be a source of scholarly interest and inspiration. What Jerome or Rashi or Luther or Milton or William Blake or Charles Wesley or Martin Buber or Benjamin Britten or Bob Dylan made of a text can be exegetically interesting. The Bible is a text sacred to many people and institutions, and what people believe it means may often be more important, historically and theologically, than what it originally meant. What is equally important, is that this way we learn how to listen to other people's interpretations, however odd they may appear at first, however different from our own, and, when deciding which meaning or interpretation is best, we can try to avoid generalizations and dogmatism. It may be less a matter of what it originally meant or which interpretation is more beautiful or more convincing: what matters 'at the other end of the hermeneutical process is how many spirits are impoverished and how many filled' (Boyarin 2000: 246).

The Reception of Isaiah

The book of Isaiah has always had a particularly high profile in both Jewish and Christian tradition, while in medieval Islam, Isaiah takes pride of place among the biblical prophets in foretelling the coming of Muhammad and the spread of Islam (Adang 1996: 146). Already in the Kings narrative, Isaiah is far more prominent than any of the other Writing Prophets (2 Kgs 19–20), and, apart from Psalms and Deuteronomy, there are more quotations from the Book of Isaiah in Second Temple Jewish literature, including the Dead Sea Scrolls, than from any other book in the Bible (Lange and Weigold 2011). At Qumran, evidence of at least twenty manuscripts of Isaiah was found, as well the famous 7.3-metre long Isaiah Scroll.

In the New Testament, not only is Isaiah more often quoted than any other part of scripture, again apart from Psalms, but New Testament writers often give his name when they quote him, and Paul introduces quotations with phrases like 'Isaiah cried out …' (Rom 9:27) or 'Isaiah is so bold as to say …' (Rom 10:20), a further indication that Isaiah held a special position in Paul's heart as he clearly did in the hearts of other first-century Jews as well. He is far more often quoted in the Mishnah than any other prophet, as he is in at least one large anthology of rabbinic literature (Montefiore and Loewe 1963), and in Jewish lectionaries more haftarot (readings from the Prophets) come from Isaiah than from any other prophet. He is also the subject of a popular martyr-dom tradition according to which he was 'sawn asunder' (Heb 11:37), recorded in a first- or second-century BCE Jewish text and an elaborately developed Christian version known as the *Ascension of Isaiah* (Knibb 1985: 143–176) (Isa 1:10).

Cited already by Clement of Rome to provide scriptural authority for bishops (Isa 60:17) and by Justin Martyr in his attacks on the blindness of the Jews (Isa 6:9–10), Isaiah soon became a mainstay of patristic exegesis. Origen wrote a huge commentary on the first thirty chapters, now lost, while com-mentaries that have survived include those of Eusebius of Caesarea, Cyril of Alexandria and John Chrysostom in Greek, and Ephrem the Syrian in Syriac. Jerome introduces his massive eighteen-volume commentary in Latin by explaining that Isaiah is more an evangelist than a prophet since he often uses past tenses: 'For to us a child is born (9:6) … he was wounded for our trans-gressions (53:5)'. This is how Isaiah has been interpreted by Christian writers and artists right down to the present. 'Behold a virgin shall conceive …' (Isa 7:14 LXX; cf. Matt 1:23), in Greek, Latin and other languages rapidly became the text most frequently associated with him. Matthew stands on Isaiah's shoulders (Cowan 1979: 14–15), but all four Gospels begin with 'the voice of one crying in the wilderness' (Isa 40:3; cf. Matt 3:3; Mark 1:3; Luke 3:4; John 1:23). Isidore of Seville in his polemical work *De Fide Catholica* found in Isaiah an allusion to almost every detail in the gospel narrative, from the mys-tery of the birth of Christ (Isa 53:8; cf. 66:7–9) to his resurrection (Isa 33:10), Ascension (Isa 52:13) and Second Coming (Isa 49:14). Images of the Good Shepherd (Isa 40:11) and Alpha and Omega (Isa 44:6; cf. Rev 1:8; 21:6) were common in early Christian iconography, as were the ox and the ass (Isa 1:3) and the camels (Isa 60:6) from the nativity story. The wolf and the lamb (Isa 11:6) appear too but more rarely.

The patristic exegetical tradition continued into the medieval period in works like the *Glossa Ordinaria*, the *Bible Moralisée* and the *Biblia Pauperum*.

A new interest in the Passion is evident in Christian iconography, so that Isa 7:14 is sometimes replaced as Isaiah's motto by 'truly (he bore) our weaknesses' (Isa 53:4) or 'like a lamb before its shearers' (Isa 53:7). The wine press imagery in Isaiah 63, interpreted as a reference to the crucifixion, becomes common, and the wood of the Jesse Tree (Isa 11:1, 10) is occasionally transformed into the wood of the cross. Thomas Aquinas and Nicholas of Lyra for the most part follow patristic exegetical tradition, with occasional historical, theological or other insights of their own.

In Judaism down the centuries, Isaiah is first and foremost the prophet of consolation. Already in Ben Sira he is remembered as the one who 'comforted those who mourned in Zion' (Sir 48:24), and, according to the Talmud, Ezekiel's consolation is like the speech of a villager, Isaiah's like that of a courtier (bHagigah 14a). In Jewish lectionaries seven passages, beginning with chapter 40, are known as the 'consolation readings' read on the seven Sabbaths after the Fast of 9th Ab commemorating the Destruction of the Temple, and in the orthodox Jewish prayer book, the prayer to be recited in a house of mourning ends with three verses from Isaiah (Isa 66:13; 60:19; 25:8).

There is also a legend that Isaiah was rebuked by God for calling his people 'unclean' (Isa 6:5), and chapter 1 contains some of the strongest language used by any prophet to criticize his people. The passage was used by Jews to explain why the Temple had been destroyed, but Christians used such passages as scriptural authority for anti-Jewish polemic, which was a persistent feature of Christian interpretations of Isaiah right down to modern times (e.g. Isa 1:15; 65:2–3). The great medieval Jewish commentators Rashi, Ibn Ezra and Kimḥi occasionally refer to such hostile gentile attitudes towards them (Isa 53:3–4), and Isaiah provided the poet Ephraim of Bonn with the image of angels weeping (Isa 33:7) when they saw the suffering of the Jews at the hands of the Crusaders. The Book of Isaiah was a battleground for Jewish–Christian debate, notably in the great Disputation in Barcelona in 1263 (Isa 2:4; 41:8–9).

In the sixteenth century, Renaissance scholarship, the Reformation and vernacular translations of the Bible led to a break with medieval tradition evident in Luther's *Lectures on Isaiah* and Calvin's commentary on Isaiah. Anti-Judaism is joined by anti-papism in a fresh quest for the true, literal or historical meaning of scripture, aided by philology and largely unencumbered by ecclesiastical tradition. Vitringa, Lowth, Matthew Henry and others followed this new direction, but the medieval tradition continued in the poetry of John Donne, George Herbert, Milton, Byron and Tennyson, motets by William Byrd, cantatas by Bach, Handel's *Messiah* and Brahms' *German Requiem*, and in paintings by Grünewald, Mantegna and Rubens.

In the modern period historical-critical concerns about date, authorship and literary form became ever more prominent and led to the identification of more than one author (Döderlein) and the four 'Servant Songs' (Isa 42:1–4; 49:1–6; 50:4–9; 52:13–53:12) (Duhm), but the book continued to play a significant role in Judaism and Christianity. In the twentieth century there were Jewish translations of Isaiah into Yiddish (Yehoash in 1910; Orlinsky in 1941), German (Buber/Rosenzweig in 1934) and English (JPS in 1917, 1978). The language and images of Isaiah crop up very frequently in journals (8:6), organizations (2:5) and place names (40:9; 41:27) associated with Zionism and the establishment of the State of Israel. Isaiah has inspired numerous Hebrew songs and dances (Isa 12:3; 41:19; 52:7) as well as larger compositions including Robert Starer's cantata *Ariel* (1963) and has made important contributions to the language and theology of post-holocaust Judaism (Isa 43:12; 45:15; 56:5) and the iconography of world peace (Isa 2:4; 11:6–9). He also played an important role in the Church's seventeenth- and eighteenth-century missionary enterprise (54:2–3; 60:9), Hindu–Christian dialogue (*Ghose* 1982: 644–647, 651), ecumenism (32:18) and liberation theology (Isa 32:17; 61:1–2), as well as more recently in both Jewish and Christian feminism (Isa 34:14; 66:13).

Reception Exegesis

'Reception history' and *Wirkungsgeschichte* (impact history) (Gadamer 1975) are concerned with the afterlife of the text as an end in itself. *Rezeptionsästhetik* (reception criticism) (Jauss 1982) shifts attention somewhat away from history to critical analysis, but here again the focus is often more on the literature, music, works of art and the like where the text has been contextualized, than on the biblical text itself. 'Reception exegesis', a term first coined by Paul Joyce and Diana Lipton in their Lamentations volume (2013), is concerned primarily with the biblical text and how the history of its reception helps us to appreciate what it has meant in all kinds of different contexts. In a commentary motivated by an interest in reception exegesis, reception history is the handmaid of exegesis and is not an end in itself. Both are concerned with the *Wirkungsgeschichte* of the text over time, but the method of handling, selecting and arranging the material is different.

In other words, while *The Fifth Gospel: Isaiah in the History of Christianity* (Sawyer 1996) gave a historical account of how Isaiah was used and interpreted in the early Church, medieval art, the Reformation, English literature, Church music and so on, the present volume uses the reception history to write an exegetical work, a commentary, not a history, working though the text, verse by verse, chapter by chapter, illustrating how each phrase or passage has been used and interpreted in all kinds of different contexts from its earliest context down to the present day. A historical context is given for every use or interpretation discussed, and essential background information on authors, artists, musicians and the like is provided in the Glossary and Brief Biographies at the end of the volume. But historical details are kept down to a minimum to leave as much room as possible to discuss exegetical matters. The material is arranged thematically rather than historically. Discussion of a passage may begin, for example, with a comment about where the passage features in the lectionaries (Isa 40) or a reference to a piece of music (Isa 45:8) rather than with its most ancient context. Jerome, Rashi, Luther and Childs are grouped together if they all interpret a text in the same way (Isa 3:13), rather than in chronological order, which could lead to repetition, and no attempt is made to cite all the sources for any one interpretation: theoretically one authority is sufficient for exegetical purposes, and the relative frequency of a particular interpretation is not always discussed.

The biggest problem facing anyone attempting to write such a commentary is the sheer volume of the material – in literature, art, music, liturgy, theology, politics, popular culture, etc. over two thousand years. Thanks to the Internet, which of course was not available to me when I was working on *The Fifth Gospel*, texts, visual images and musical interpretations are now easily accessible online. I have beside me, on my computer, the commentaries of Eusebius, Jerome, Cyril of Alexandria, Theodoret, Thomas Aquinas, Nicholas of Lyra, Calvin, Oecolampadius, Vitringa, Matthew Henry, Ibn Ezra, Luzzatto and others. I also have a small library of printed commentaries of my own including those of Martin Luther (*Lectures on Isaiah*) and Bishop Lowth, as well as Rashi, Kimḥi and David Altschuler ('Metzudat David,' 'Metzudat Zion') in my *Miqraʾot Gedolot*, and many of the modern commentaries from Cheyne (1895), George Adam Smith (1888–1890, 1.408) and Duhm (1892) to Clements (1980), Childs (2001) and Roberts (2015).

The Isaiah volumes in the *Ancient Christian Commentaries* Series (McKinion 2004; M. W. Elliott 2007) and *The Church's Bible* (Wilken 2007) are valuable resource, as is *Isaiah through the Ages* (Manly 1995), an interesting Eastern Orthodox commentary with an English translation of the Greek text and a selection of examples from patristic, modern and Judaic literature. A very useful ground-breaking article, 'Isaiah, Book and Person', has recently been published in Volume 13 of *EBR* (2016). Many works of reference have valuable indexes of biblical texts, including the *Blackwell Companion to the Bible and Culture* (Sawyer 2006), *The Bible in Music* (Dowling Long and Sawyer 2015) and the *New Cambridge History of the Bible* (4 vols., 2012–2016). Other important works with indexes of biblical references include Danby's *Mishnah*, the Soncino translation of the *Babylonian Talmud* and Montefiore and Loewe's *Rabbinic Anthology*.

Often it is from a kind colleague in another discipline that I have discovered some new aspect of the reception history of Isaiah. This is a decisively interdisciplinary project, involving cooperation with literary critics, art historians, musicians and the like. As the authors of the Lamentations volume put it, 'here in reception exegesis is a model for two-way interdisciplinary interaction in which biblical scholars do not merely give but also receive' (Joyce and Lipton 2013:19). At one time, not so long ago, biblical scholarship was a highly specialized discipline, closely allied to ancient history and archaeology, having little or no contact with English literature, art history, music and other disciplines where the Bible has often had a significant, not to say, crucial role to play. Thankfully, this is rapidly changing as can be seen from the increasing number of interdisciplinary projects such as *Between the Text and the Canvas: The Bible and Art in Dialogue* (Exum and Nutu 2007), *Biblical Art from Wales* (O'Kane and Morgan-Guy 2010) and *The Oxford Handbook of the Reception History of the Bible* (Lieb, Mason and Roberts 2011), where many of the contributors are specialists in other fields.

There remains the question of whether it is desirable, or indeed possible in practice, to let the interpretations speak for themselves without privileging any particular ones. The eighteen authors of the Blackwell Bible Commentaries published so far have tackled the problem in different ways. Most aim at no more than a 'representative sampling' and acknowledge at the outset that they have approached their task from a particular perspective. I gladly acknowledge that I am white, male, old and Scottish Presbyterian and that this may have influenced my judgement in ways of which I am not always aware. I make no apology for occasionally describing interpretations as beautiful or ugly, convincing or far-fetched. I struggled with the special issue of how to handle the anti-Jewish polemic in so many Christian inerpretations of Isaiah, and decided that, like other interpretations, it should be allowed to speak for itself as an integral part of Christian biblical interpretation and a monument to the appalling attitude that persisted till comparatively recently in the Church towards the Jewish people.

Constraints of space made it impossible for me to include more than a relatively small selection of examples from the two thousand years' reception history of Isaiah in Judaism, Christianity and Islam, ancient, medieval and modern, worldwide. I have tried to focus on interpretations and uses of the text that are exegetically interesting or that have been historically important or influential in some way. The place of each passage in the liturgy, and especially in the lectionaries, is given some prominence, not only because it throws light on how a passage has been traditionally interpreted in Judaism and Christianity but also because it can sometimes explain why a particular verse is better known and more often quoted in religious literature and other social and political contexts than other texts. Western European and North American culture has had the lion's share of my attention, mainly because it is easier to access and I am better able to handle it. I am well aware how much I have neglected in the Eastern Orthodox tradition and how little space is given to Isaiah in postcolonial Christianity despite the pioneering work of scholars like Musa Dube, Gerald West and R.S. Sugirtharajah. There is much more to say on what the 'Prophet of Consolation' has given to Jews through the centuries worldwide, and the 'Fifth Evangelist' to Christians. I hope this commentary, along with *The Fifth Gospel* (1996), will encourage others to fill in the gaps.

The Title (Isa 1:1)

Verse 1 implies that the whole book of Isaiah is a single prophecy, described as a 'vision' seen by the prophet during the reigns of Uzziah, Jotham, Ahaz and Hezekiah, kings of Judah. In this way the human element in the process is minimized: the prophets' 'words are divine oracles and their writings have come down from heaven' (Chrysostom)[1]. Jewish tradition compares Isaiah's vision to

---

[1] References to verse-by-verse commentaries, listed separately in the Bibliography, are by author's name only.

Isaiah Through the Centuries, First Edition. John F. A. Sawyer.
© 2018 John Wiley & Sons Ltd. Published 2020 by John Wiley & Sons Ltd.

that of Abraham (Mann 1971: 1, 112–113). Prophets are called 'seers' (1 Sam 9:9), a word denoting weakness and humility: the prophet sees; the people hear (cf. John 3:11) (Luther). In the 'vision' we confront not Isaiah but the speech of God (Seitz 1988: 117–118).

The use of the word 'vision' (Heb. *ḥazon*) to refer to a collection of visions, however, is without parallel, and it may be that it originally referred only to chapter 1 (Lowth) or chapters 1–12 (Duhm; cf. Rev 1:1), with the more usual title reserved for the beginning of chapter 2 (cf. Hos 1:1; Joel 1:1; Mic 1:1; Zeph 1:1). Some traditions have 'against Judah and Jerusalem' (LXX, Eusebius), and there is a rabbinic tradition that of all the Hebrew words for 'prophecy', *ḥazon* is the harshest (cf. Isa 21:2) (Rashi); and this certainly applies particularly to chapter 1. The book includes prophecies about Babylon, Moab, Damascus and other places (13–19), not only Jerusalem and Judah (Rashi), but Ibn Ezra points out that the greater part of Isaiah's prophecies do refer to Jerusalem and the cities of Judah. Indeed one of the most distinctive themes running through the whole book is 'the larger sweep of God's dealing with Zion in both judgement and mercy' (Williamson 1994: 242).

Since Ibn Ezra, major stylistic and historical differences between 1–39 and 40–66 have been noted (U. Simon 1985). Aquinas divides the book into two parts, and since the late eighteenth century there has been widespread agreement that the whole book cannot be by the same author. Large sections were probably composed during and after the Babylonian exile. But the literary fiction implied by verse 1 that the whole book is made up of Isaiah's prophecies reflects numerous signs of continuity evident throughout the book and has increasingly been appreciated by modern scholars (Jones 1955; Rendtorff 1984; Vermeylen 1989; Tull 2006: 279–314). References to the deaths of Uzziah (Isa 6:1) and Ahaz (Isa 14:28) imply that most of the prophecies were delivered in Jerusalem during the 'Golden Age' of Hezekiah (2 Chron 29–32), after which the prophet was put to death by the evil king Manasseh (see commentary on Isa 1:10; 50:4–9) (Rashi).

The Ox and the Ass Have More Sense (Isa 1:2–9)

Isaiah's first prophecy is one of his bitterest attacks on the people of Judah. In Jewish tradition, part of this chapter (vv. 1–27) is the haftarah read on the Sabbath before the Ninth of Ab, the fast commemorating the destruction of the Temple. Known as 'the Sabbath of (Isaiah's) vision' (*shabbat ḥazon*), it is intended as a day to reflect on why the Jewish people lost their land and the holy city of Jerusalem and is followed by the seven 'Sabbaths of consolation' when the *haftarot neḥamah* (readings of consolation) from chapters 40–66 are read, beginning with Isaiah 40:1–26 (Elbogen 1993: 145, 425–426). In Christian tradition too verses from chapter 1 are read in churches at the beginning of Lent (*ORM*, RCL), supplemented in Orthodox tradition in the following weeks with some equally bitter judgement oracles from chapters 2–14 (*OSB*).

Many of these verses were cited by Justin, Chrysostom, Isidore of Seville and others as scriptural authority for the use of all manner of anti-Jewish rhetoric hurled at a 'sinful nation' (v. 4): they did not recognize the Messiah in the manger (v. 3), their beloved city had been left by alien invaders 'like a booth in a vineyard' (vv. 7–9) and they have blood on their hands (v. 15; cf. Matt 27:25) (Sawyer 1996: 109–115). Of course Isaiah was addressing the people of ancient Judah, not the Jews of Christian Europe, and in modern times the Churches have made strenuous efforts to disown such anti-Semitic interpretations of scripture (cf. Rom 11:11–32; Flannery 1975: 741).

Isaiah's preface is in the form of a trial-scene (Smith). Heaven and earth are summoned as witnesses (v. 2), recalling Moses' words when he prophesied that his people would 'soon utterly perish from the land' (Deut 4:26; cf. 32:1) (Ibn Ezra; cf. Luther, Calvin). The story of how God brought up his people like children, freeing them from slavery in Egypt and leading them to safety through the wilderness (v. 2b), is cited to condemn their ungrateful, rebellious behaviour: 'the fuller and more abundant the grace of God which has been poured out on us, the higher will be the ingratitude of which it shall convict us … and the severer the punishment we shall deserve' (Calvin). Recent commentators with ecological concerns find in the involvement of heaven and earth here, a reference to the divinely ordained world order which Israel had chosen to ignore (Marlow and Barton 2009:210).

Even the ox and the ass have more sense (v. 3): John Chrysostom compares this with Jeremiah's 'even the stork in the heavens knows her times' (Jer 8:7) and Solomon's 'Go to the ant, thou sluggard' (Prov 6:6). The ox and the ass are valued domestic animals who, in recognizing the hand that feeds them, show more sense than the people (Jerome). But it is also uncannily appropriate that the 'Fifth Gospel' should begin, like Matthew and Luke, with a reference to the Nativity of Christ: the ox and the ass 'at their master's crib' have been present in Christian representations of the nativity scene from patristic times down to the present day, despite the scornful comments of Calvin ('an absurd fable … by which they have shown themselves to be egregious asses') and the consensus of modern historical-critical scholarship.

Isaiah's reference to the ox and the ass adoring the baby Jesus, along with a prophecy of Habakkuk (Hab 3:2 LXX) (Coggins and Han 2011: 75–76), appears in the eighth-century apocryphal Gospel of Pseudo-Matthew (14:2), and in the thirteenth century, St Francis of Assisi invented the popular custom of recreating the humble nativity scene at Christmas time, showing the child in a manger, complete with hay and an ox and an ass standing by (Bonaventure 2010: 86).

PLATE 1   'The ox knows its owner and the ass its master's crib' (Isa 1:3). Fourth-century sarcophagus in Milan.

But the tradition goes back much earlier. From the fourth century the ox and the ass appear in Christian iconography, sometimes standing alone by the manger without any human figures in the scene (Schiller 1971: 59) (Plate 1). Some identify the ox as the Jews, bearing the burden of the law, and the ass as the gentiles tainted by idolatry (Jerome): thus all humanity, Jews and gentiles, 'all came to the one manger and found the fodder of the Word' (Augustine, *Sermon* 375.1). Augustine calls upon Christians to identify with the ass: 'Don't be ashamed of being the Lord's donkey. If you carry Christ, you won't go astray' (Augustine *Sermon* 189.4). Sometimes the ox represents Christian faith and obedience, while stubbornness, disobedience and materialism, usually Jewish, are represented by the ass. Botticelli's *Mystic Nativity* (*c*.1500) in the National Gallery, London, is a good example, where the quiet obedience of the kneeling ox is contrasted with the behaviour of the ass who is standing up and disrespectfully chewing a mouthful of straw.

The two animals, without any ethical or political associations, are frequent in Christmas literature. Christina Rossetti's 'Before the Paling of the Stars' (Rossetti 1904: 217) contains a typical nineteenth-century English example:

> Let us kneel with Mary maid,
> With Joseph bent and hoary,
> With saint and angel, ox and ass,
> To hail the King of Glory.

Rudyard Kipling in his poem 'Eddi's Service' imagines a midnight service in seventh-century pagan England attended only by a priest and the two animals

(Kipling 2013: Vol.2, 689f). They also figure in a good many Christmas carols from the anonymous thirteenth-century French 'Entre le boeuf et l'âne gris' (*SNOBC* 289) to 'Good Christians All Rejoice' where 'ox and ass before Him bow' (*CH4* 322, *AM* 65; cf. *CH2* 58; *GtG* 132), and 'The Little Drummer Boy' (1941), popularized in the film *The Sound of Music* (1955), where they keep time to the drumbeat.

The prophet angrily describes the people as 'sinful … laden with iniquity … they have forsaken the Lord … they are utterly estranged' (v. 4). 'Seed of evil-doers' (v. 4 AV) is taken literally by some to refer to Israel's pagan ancestry condemned by Ezekiel (cf. Ezek 16:23) (Ibn Ezra), and by others to imply that they have been disowned by their ancestors and can no longer claim to be the 'seed of Abraham' (Isa 41:8; cf. 61:9) (Eusebius; cf. Calvin). The term 'Holy One of Israel', which occurs very frequently in the Book of Isaiah, is especially appropriate in this attack on God's 'holy people' (Deut 7:6) (Rashi): their rebelliousness against the source of their holiness is all the more ungrateful and 'barbarous' (Calvin). Patristic commentators take the 'Holy One' in this context to be referring to Jesus (Chrysostom, Jerome), and in the fourteenth-century *Biblia Pauperum* the words 'they have blasphemed against the holy one of Israel' (v. 4 Vg) accompany illustrations of the crowd mocking Christ (Matt 27:27–31; 26:67) (*BP* 94).

Verses 5 and 6 envisage a disobedient slave beaten repeatedly by his owner (Childs) or a rebellious son disciplined by his father (Blenkinsopp; cf. Prov 10:13; 13:24). Applied to the 'sinful nation', the words 'from the sole of the foot even to the head' may be interpreted as referring to the whole people, from the poorest at the very bottom of the social scale to those with wealth and authority at the top, all equally deserving punishment (Rashi, Cyril). The image of an unnamed individual, bruised, wounded and bleeding, is developed later in the book, notably in the 'Man of Sorrows' poem in 53 (Duhm), and was used by Christian interpreters to add some gruesome details to representations of Christ's Passion. In one example from late mediaeval iconography, verse 6, coupled with Job 2:7, is illustrated by a scene of Christ's tormentors working 'from the sole of the foot even to the head', so that they could see that every inch of his body had been beaten before it was covered with blood (Marrow 1979: 48).

Some commentators see a glimmer of hope in verses 7–9. Paul finds prophetic authority here for his teaching on 'the remnant' of the Jewish people, saved by the grace of God (Rom 9:29; cf. Isa 11:10–11). On the size of the remnant ('few survivors' RSV), Calvin cites the words of Christ (Luke 12:32) and admits that the number of the godly may be small: it is only hypocrites that are 'proud of their numbers' (cf. Henry). Of course the bare survival of Jerusalem in 701 BCE is interpreted as a miracle later in the book (Isa 36–37). In the present context, however, there is little sign of hope, and most commentators take it as a description of the situation referred to in Sennacherib's Annals where Hezekiah was shut up 'like a bird in a cage' (Childs), and Judah was utterly devastated like the cities of Sodom and Gomorrah (Gen 19; cf. Deut 29:23; Isa 13:19; Matt 10:15).

Blood on Your Hands (Isa 1:10–20)

The next prophecy begins where the previous one ends, by comparing the sins of the people of Judah to those of Sodom and Gomorrah, defined elsewhere as 'pride, surfeit of food and the oppression of the poor and needy' (Ezek 16:49; cf. Isa 3:9) (Kimḥi; Miranda 1977: 96). There is a tradition first recorded in the *Martyrdom and Ascension of Isaiah* that it was this particularly bitter attack on Judah's leaders, in which he calls 'Jerusalem Sodom … and the princes of Judah Gomorrah', that was the main reason for his execution under Manasseh (*OTP* 1.160). His condemnation of ritualism and hypocrisy (vv. 11–15) is followed by an appeal for repentance and social justice (vv. 16–20).

For the rabbis the key to this apparent wholesale rejection of the Temple cult is to be found in the references to 'iniquity' and 'evil' in the speech itself (vv. 13–17), and in statements from elsewhere in the Bible such as 'the sacrifice of the wicked is an abomination' (Prov 22:27) (Rashi). They also deduced from the array of religious practices listed by Isaiah (vv. 11–15) that 'prayer, which comes last in the list, is superior to sacrifice' (*RA* 357). The Church Fathers also argued that 'prayer alone conquers God' (Tertullian, *On Prayer* 29) and true sacrifice is 'giving alms and kindness to the poor' (Augustine, *Sermon* 42,1). Calvin understood the passage as saying that 'our actions are of no value in the sight of God, when they do not proceed from a good conscience'. Some Christian commentators noted that the Sabbath is included (v. 13) and deduced from this that the passage advocates the total abrogation of the old Covenant, not just the Temple cult (EpBarn 15:8–9; Tertullian, *Against Marcion* 12), while others, including many Protestant scholars with a historical-critical interest, used passages like this to show that the spirit of eighth-century prophecy demanded an alternative to the ritualism and sacrifice-based religion of the Pentateuch (cf. Amos 5:14–15; Mic 6:8) (Smith, Gray). From the same period, the old beggar Edie Ochiltree in Sir Walter Scott's novel *The Antiquary* (1816) quotes part of verse 13 as a comment on the 'grand parafle o' ceremonies' that used to fill the churches before the Reformation (Moffatt 1924: 238).

The reference to bloodstained hands (v. 15) is normally understood as referring to murder and blood-guilt in general, perhaps intended to include the intention to kill as well (Henry), but the Church Fathers saw here an explicit reference to the Jews' killing of the prophets sent to them time and time again

(Matt 23:29–39) (Jerome), and also to their willingness to accept the blame for Christ's death: 'his blood be upon us and on our children'(Matt 27:25) (Chrysostom, Cyril). Tertullian distinguishes the scarlet blood of the prophets from the crimson blood of Christ, which is brighter (*Against Marcion* 4:10). Taken with Isaiah 66:2–3 it has also been applied to the blood of animals (v. 11) and interpreted as a scriptural recommendation of vegetarianism (Skriver 1990:100).

The appeal for repentance in verses 16–20 (cf. v. 27) is rare in Isaiah (Sommer), but much commented on. Jewish tradition found in the passage explicit allusions to the Day of Atonement. Thus the ten imperatives ('wash yourselves, make yourselves clean, remove the evil …') correspond to the 'Ten Days of Repentance' between Rosh Ha-Shanah and Yom Kippur (Rashi), while verse 18 is cited as biblical authority for a tradition recounted in the Mishnah that on Yom Kippur a thread of crimson wool tied to the door of the temple turned white when the scapegoat reached the wilderness. This was a signal for the high priest to start reading from the Torah (Lev 16; 23:26–32) and then pronounce the eight blessings with which the atonement ritual concluded (m*Yoma* 6:8; cf. m*Shabbat* 9:3). Clement of Rome, paraphrasing Ezekiel with words from Isaiah 1:18, points out that the repentance of a sinner is what God wants, not his death (cf. Ezek 33:11–20) (*Letter to the Corinthians* 8:1–9:1).

The appeal to 'Wash yourselves, make yourselves clean', alongside the images of bloodstained hands and scarlet sins becoming 'white as snow' (vv. 15–18), is cited by the Church Fathers, along with Ezekiel 36:25–27, as scriptural author-ity for the sacrament of baptism (Justin, *First Apology* 61; Jerome). The popular evangelical notion of being washed in the blood of the Lamb (Rev 7:14) also finds biblical expression here, as in the refrain 'I've washed my robes in Jesus blood / And he has made me white as snow' (*SBSA* 359), and in the popular hymn 'Rock of Ages':

> Let the water and the blood,
> From thy riven side which flowed,
> Be of sin the double cure,
> Cleanse me from its guilt and power. (*CH2* 413; *GtG* 438) (*NCHB* 4,731–2)

Some modern commentators argue that verse 18 does not follow on from the preceding verses but begins a new section with a question, challenging the audience to an argument and asking them ironically whether they think a seri-ous sin can just disappear: 'if your sins are coloured scarlet, can they become white like snow?' (Blenkinsopp; cf. Clements): 'a murder is a murder even when it is forgiven' (Duhm). The heretic Pelagius, on the other hand, quoted verses 19–20 to prove that divine forgiveness is not unmerited (Augustine, *Perfection in Righteousness* 40.42) but a response to a prior decision by the sinner, while, according to Calvin, the papists twisted the passage to support their doctrine of free will. Thomas Aquinas in his commentary on the verse, also separates it from what precedes, and he observes that the verse is about sins, not sinners. He interprets it as an analysis of two different types of sin and how they can be cured: 'scarlet' sins caused by burning desire (*amore incendente*), which can be cured by putting snow on them (cf. Job 9:30), and those that are 'crimson' (L. *vermiculus* 'worm, crimson dye'), caused by mortifying fear (*timore mortificante*), which can be cured by applying pure wool to them (cf. Dan 7:9).

In a short poem entitled 'Beyond Knowledge' (1901) the English Catholic writer and suffragist Alice Meynell (1847–1922) notices that the passage is not about washing away sins and making the believer white as snow or about challenging sinners to face up to their responsibilities. On the contrary, what the words actually say is that, however scarlet the sin, it can be changed into something white and pure, although unlike Aquinas, she envisages this as something that happens after death. Perhaps thinking of Paul's description of the resurrection of the dead, when 'we shall all be changed' (1 Cor 15:51), she imagines a time when what is an abomination in this world will be transformed into a thing of great beauty in the next. There will be no hell where evil is disposed of but rather a new heaven and a new earth where even sins can be 'rescued' (Meynell 1927: 93).

But the passage begins by addressing the 'rulers' (v. 10) and later directs the main thrust of the speech towards 'princes ... judges ... and councillors' (vv. 21.26; cf. 10:1–2), and the obvious inference, although little noticed until the late twentieth century, is that this is not about individual morality but an attack on corrupt government institutions, the law courts and property owners. Ordinary people, like widows and orphans, are their victims (vv. 17, 23). This is how the liberation theologians of the 1970s and 1980s understood such passages (Miranda 1977; Lohfink 1987; Tutu 1991: 21–22).

The Faithful City (Isa 1:21–31)

The prophet's attack continues in the form of a lament (cf. 2 Sam 1:19–26; Lam 1), and again commentators have ignored the fact that it is about corrupt 'princes' (v. 23) and 'judges' (v. 26), not individual morality: Jerome, for example, interprets 'the faithful city that has become a harlot' (v. 21) as an individual, formerly righteous, but now inhabited by murderous demons. 'The faithful city' (vv. 21, 26) is a striking phrase, recalling the golden age of David and Solomon (Luther) as well as prophecies about the role of Zion in the future (Isa 2:2–4; 40:9; 66:20). The Septuagint actually adds the word 'Zion' in both verses. More specifically, in Hebrew, the choice of a poetic word for 'city' (*qiryah*) recalls passages like 'Ho Ariel, Ariel, the city [*qiryah*] where David encamped' (Isa 29:1) and the so-called Zion songs in the Psalter (e.g. Ps 48:2). 'Faithful' in Hebrew no doubt refers to 'firmly established' as well as to a 'city of righteousness' (cf. v. 26), 'faithful in conduct and piety' (cf. Isa 7:9; Clements), although Calvin interprets it more precisely as 'chaste', applying it to the 'spiritual chastity' of the Church as well as of the Jewish people: 'once faithful to the marriage contract, she has now become an harlot'. The radical feminist writer Mary Daly cites this verse as a good example of the biblical prophets' 'tiresome propensity for comparing Israel to a whore' (Daly 1973: 162: see comm. on Isa 47:2–3).

The details of her behaviour are spelled out in graphic language and imagery. She is accused of murder, robbery, bribery and corruption at the highest level and the neglect of orphans and widows. What had once been as pure and bright as silver has become dross, and what had promised to be a good wine has been spoilt by the addition of water. Jerome and Cyril see here a reference to the wrong interpretation of scripture, citing a Psalm where 'the promises of the Lord are pure ... as silver refined in a furnace' (Ps 12:5), and they identify the 'innkeepers mixing water with wine' with scribes and Pharisees. For Luther dross is a worthless metal that looks like silver and so provides an image of hypocrisy, familiar among the bishops and political leaders of his own day. For many English-speaking Christians 'dross' in this passage (vv. 22, 25) came to be synonymous with human sin and, no doubt partly because it rhymes with Cross, figures regularly in evangelical hymns such as John Wesley's 'O Thou to whose all searching sight' (1738), which contains the lines 'Wash out its stain, refine its dross / Nail my affections to the Cross'.

The 'faithful city' poem, however, which starts as a dirge bemoaning the seemingly irredeemable wickedness of Jerusalem, ends with the return of good judges and counsellors and the restoration of the 'city of righteousness' (v. 26). The turning point is the intervention of 'the Lord of hosts, the Mighty One of Israel' who promises he will avenge himself on his enemies and, in another metalworking metaphor, smelt away the dross and produce pure, fine quality silver again (vv. 24–25). Some Christian writers since Jerome follow the Greek version of the text of verse 24, which has 'Woe to the mighty of Israel' instead of the 'Mighty One of Israel', and interpret these verses as addressed to Israel's leaders in New Testament times, recalling Christ's words 'Woe to the Scribes and Pharisees' (Matt 23) (Eusebius). Verse 26 is cited in the weekday *Amidah* (*ADPB* 84–85) and in modern times Zionist extremists have used it as scriptural authority for the reconstitution of the Sanhedrin: 'I will restore thy judges as at the first' (Ravitzky 1996: 91–92).

In the description of Jerusalem as 'full of justice' (v. 21), the word 'full' is spelled in a slightly unusual way in Hebrew (*mele'ti*), and, by gematria, provided scriptural authority for a rabbinic tradition that there were 481 synagogues in Jerusalem in which 'righteousness lodged' (Rashi). Many Christian commentators apply the poem about the decline of the 'faithful city' (vv. 21–26) to Jerusalem in the first century CE, highlighting prophetic references to the treachery of Judas (v. 23), the corruption of the authorities (v. 23), the emergence of the apostles (v. 26) and the faith which created the Church after the Passion (v. 26) (Eusebius, Cyril, Jerome). The 'faithful city', or 'the city of the righteous one' (*civitas justi* Vg), like 'the city on a hill that cannot be hidden' (Matt 5:14), is obviously the Church (Jerome). In a sermon on verse 21, entitled 'Hypocrisy in Oxford', John Wesley applied the poem to the current state of the Church, specifying the sins of the clergy and divinity students in great detail, including wearing immodest clothing, frequenting taverns and not studying Hebrew: 'how is the faithful city become a harlot!' (*Sermons* 4.392–407).

Verses 27–31, are written in a very different style from the preceding poem, although continuing the theme of the redemption of Zion. A striking new element in these verses is the addition of the worship of idols to the long list of the city's crimes (see comm. on Isa 2:6–22). The passage also anticipates later chapters by separating the sheep from the goats when judgement comes (cf. Isa 65:13–14). It is as though a remnant has heeded the calls to 'wash yourselves: make yourselves clean' earlier in the chapter (vv. 16–17) and shall be rewarded, while the 'rebels and sinners … and those who forsake the Lord' shall be destroyed (v. 28) (Eusebius, Jerome). The city will be saved not be divine intervention but by people who practise righteousness (Rashi), that is, by the spirit and by faith (Luther). As we have already noted, repentance is rare in Isaianic tradition, and the word translated 'those who repent' (RSV), 'converts' (AV) or 'the repentant ones' (Childs) in verse 27 is taken by some to refer to 'those who return', that is to say, the returning exiles (Calvin). The verse was quoted by Chaim Weitzmann, the first President of the State of Israel, at the opening of the first Israeli parliament in 1948: 'Zion shall be redeemed by justice and those who return by righteousness' (v. 27).

Isaiah 2

A Second Title (Isa 2:1)

The relationship of the title (v. 1) to the longer title at the beginning of chapter 1 has already been mentioned. A widely held view among modern scholars is that, after chapter 1, which has a certain independence within the overall structure of the book, it has been inserted to introduce the next literary unit, whether this is the famous prophecy in verses 2–5 or a longer unit (Isa 2–4 or 2–12 or 2–39) (Kaiser, Childs). The Greek Fathers, noted with approval by Jerome,

Isaiah Through the Centuries, First Edition. John F. A. Sawyer.
© 2018 John Wiley & Sons Ltd. Published 2020 by John Wiley & Sons Ltd.

follow the Septuagint in contrasting the prophecy '*against* Judah and Jerusalem' in chapter 1 with the 'word which Isaiah saw *concerning* Judah and Jerusalem' in chapter 2: the one is a description of the plundering of Judah in Isaiah's own day, the other a prophecy about the future when 'Zion, the city in Judah that sits on a mountain, will be rebuilt' (Cyril).

Swords into Ploughshares (Isa 2:2–5)

The famous vision of a world without war (vv. 2–4) appears in another collection of eighth-century BCE prophecies (Mic 4:1–4), and is alluded to in a cruel parody in a later apocalyptic text: 'they shall beat their ploughshares into swords' (Joel 3:10). The plain meaning of the text is that there is to be a miracle on Mount Zion greater than the miracles performed on Sinai, Carmel and Tabor (Rashi). 'In the last days' (LXX, Vg, AV, NJB), that is, when the Messiah will come (Ibn Ezra), all the peoples of the world will say, 'Come let us go up to the house of the God of Jacob and he will teach us his ways and we will walk in his paths'. In the synagogue, the words 'for out of Zion shall come forth Torah and the word of the Lord from Jerusalem' are recited as the ark is opened and the Torah Scroll brought out (*ADPB* 120–121). For many it means that the promise was given above all to the Jews: Luther cites Paul (Rom 1:16; 2:9) to make the point. Modern Jewish writers like Ben Gurion believe that the Jews were the first to see the vision of a new human society (Hertzberg 1997: 607) and their mission is to ensure that its benign influence reaches to the ends of the earth (Sicker 1992:19). *Torah Mitziyon* (Torah from Zion) was the title of a journal published in Jerusalem at the end of the nineteenth century, as well as the name of several modern organizations based in Jerusalem and elsewhere promoting Jewish education. The words also provide the climax to a selection of biblical verses on the 'Restoration of Zion', mostly from Isaiah, appended to a High Holiday Prayer (*Maḥzor* 856–857).

For Christians down the centuries every phrase in this short prophecy, and its parallel in Micah 4:1–4), is rich in theological associations. 'The last days' refers to what Paul describes as 'the fullness of time' (Gal 4:4; Eph 1:10), when the Lord will 'pour out his spirit on all flesh' (Joel 2:28; Theodoret). The 'mountain of the house of the Lord' cannot be literally the Temple Mount in Jerusalem since, as is well known, 'Zion was a little hill of no extraordinary height' (Calvin). The 'highest of the mountains … raised above the hills' must refer to the invincible strength of the Church (Chrysostom), and the flow of people to it will be like water 'flowing by its own effort … for when the Gospel is heard hearts grow soft, rejoice and come running' (Luther). Catholics applied the verse to Rome (Plate 2). For Augustine the 'house of the Lord' in the vision is

PLATE 2 'All the nations shall flow to it' (Isa 2:2). Coin of Pope Clement X showing St Peter's Basilica, Rome (1674). Reproduced with kind permission of the Warburg Institute, London.

the body of Christ destroyed and raised up after three days (cf. John 2:19): 'Christ is your mountain of refuge ... approach the mountain, climb the mountain ... there you will be safe' (*Sermon* 62A).

Some Christian interpreters take the verse as speaking about the historical origins of Christianity, since Jesus taught in the Temple at Jerusalem (Matt 13; Jerome) and 'salvation is of the Jews' (John 4:22; Aquinas). Others see in it a reference to the Word, that is, the voice of the apostles, 'going out into all the earth' (Rom 10:18), no longer from Sinai but from Jerusalem (Luther; cf. Theodoret). More explicitly anti-Jewish is the view of some of the Church Fathers that the verse is about the rejection of the Jews: 'the law has left Zion ... grace has crossed over from those choosing not to believe to those called through faith' (Cyril; cf. Chrysostom).

The vision of world peace in verse 4, with its famous image of beating 'swords into ploughshares' (cf. Micah 4), is nowadays, after two world wars and the subsequent East–West arms race, among the most universally familiar biblical images. At least two US presidents had the Bible open at this passage when they were sworn in (*NCHB* 2: 407). In 1959 the Soviet Union presented a huge bronze sculpture entitled *Let Us Beat our Swords into Ploughshares* to the United Nations Building in New York, where it stands to this day, and Gorbachov quoted the verse when the Russian army withdrew from Afghanistan in 1989. In the cardinals' pronouncement on 'The Church in the Modern World' at the Second Vatican Council (*Gaudium et Spes* 1965), the section on 'The Nature of Peace' ends with the 'swords into ploughshares' text (Isa 2:4) (Flannery 1981: 986). In the 1980s and 1990s it appears in the titles of numerous publications such as *Disarmament: Nuclear Swords or Unilateral Ploughshares* (1987) by the

Catholic peace campaigner Bruce Kent, and *Hammering Swords into Ploughshares: Essays in Honour of Archbishop Desmond Tutu* (1987) (Sawyer 1996: 233). A more recent example is *Isaiah's Vision of Peace in Biblical and Modern International Relations: Swords into Plowshares* (Cohen and Westbrook 2008). In Israel the 'swords into ploughshares' text is inscribed in Hebrew and Arabic on a 'Monument of Peace' erected in Jerusalem after the Six Day War in 1967 (Plate 3), and it is the inspiration for a huge stained glass window by Mordecai Ardon in the National and University Library in Jerusalem (1980–1984). There is a popular Scottish paraphrase of the passage beginning 'Behold the mountain of the Lord' (1781) (*CH4* 715) as well as a well-known American spiritual, 'Down by the Riverside', which has the chorus 'I aint gonna study war no more' (v. 4; cf. Isa 9:6).

PLATE 3   'Swords into Ploughshares' (Isa 2:4). Sculpture overlooking the Old City of Jerusalem (1967). Photograph by the author.

Christian interpreters argued that the prophecy had been fulfilled in Christ by interpreting the 'swords into ploughshares' image spiritually as a metaphor for the Church's mission to break through the hardness of human hearts by preaching the word (Tertullian, *Against Marcion* 3.21). Calvin argued against those who say this passage means it is unlawful for Christians to use the sword, citing Jesus words (Luke 22:36) and suggesting that the prophet was speaking metaphorically. Others take it literally and point to the *pax romana* under the Emperor Augustus (Theodoret) or the relatively peaceful conditions that accompanied the persecution of Christians under Diocletian (Aquinas). In *Pier's Plowman* (1367–1370), Conscience, quoting Isaiah, envisages a kingdom where anyone who carries a sword will be put to death and men will pass their time digging and ploughing because there will be nothing else to do (Langland 1959: 91). A seventeenth-century Scottish writer claimed that the prophecy was fulfilled in his own day, during the reign of King James VI of Scotland, who in 1603 became king of England (Moffatt 1924: 131).

Apart from such conspicuous examples of wishful thinking, most interpreters view the prophecy as a vision for the future. In the popular medieval pictorial commentary *Biblia Pauperum*, for example, verse 4 along with Ezekiel 7:3, John 5:26–28 and Revelation 4:3; 21:3–8, refers to the Last Judgement (*BP* 122), and according to widespread Christian custom, Isaiah 2:2–5 is read on the first Sunday in Advent at which the Second Coming is as much in mind as the First. The idea that it had been fulfilled already was called into question by the great Jewish rabbi Moses ben Nahman (Nahmanides) of Gerona in his debate with the Dominican friar Pablo Christiani at the court of King James I of Aragon in 1263. He could not believe that the Messiah had come, he declared, because, as the prophecy says, the messianic age is to be characterized by global peace 'yet from the days of Jesus till now, the whole world has been full of violence and plundering, and the Christians are greater spillers of blood than all the rest … and how hard it would be for you, my lord king, and for your knights if they were not to learn war any more' (Maccoby 1982: 121).

One day the nations of the world will say to the House of Jacob, 'Come, let us walk in the light of the Lord' (v. 5), and Jews and gentiles will live in harmony together (cf. John 10:16; Rom 11:25–26; Aquinas). Micah's version of this prophecy ends with a very different scene (Mic.4:5). Jerome sees the prophet turning to his own people and calling on them to walk in the light of Christ (John 8:12), and this is how it is sometimes portrayed in medieval Christian iconography, where the prophet is leading his people out of the darkness of idolatry to which there are some colourful references in the following passage (vv. 7, 8, 18, 20) (*Bible Moralisée*). Augustine goes further by using verse 6 to prove that Isaiah's call in verse 5 is not addressed to the Jews at all, as they have been rejected, but to the Church, which has taken their place as the 'New Israel' (*In Answer to the Jews* 8,11).

The vision of good relations between Jews and gentiles is also absent from the Jewish Targum, which takes the House of Jacob as subject of both verses 5 and 6: thus it is the Jews who say, 'Come let us walk' and 'the House of Jacob' who have forsaken their God, not the other way round, as in the Hebrew text. In nineteenth-century Eastern Europe, the Biluim, a group of secular pioneers in the early days of Zionism, interpreted this verse in a similar way. Their name, Bilu, is an acronym derived from the first four Hebrew words in the verse: *bet ya'akov lekhu ve-nelekhah*, and for them 'house of Jacob, come on let's go' is a call to their fellow Jews to leave Europe and join the flow of immigrants to Palestine. It stops short of the words *be-or YHWH* (in the light of the Lord) but picks up the theme of a mass movement of population in the direction of 'the house of the God of Jacob' from verse 3 (Sawyer 2003: 253). A choral setting of the whole verse forms the finale of Starer's cantata *Ariel* (1959).

Haughtiness Shall Be Humbled (Isa 2:6–22)

In verses 6–22 we move from the sublime vision of a new world order (vv. 1–5) to the first in a series of prophecies of judgement that make up much of the early chapters of Isaiah. The main themes of the passage are idolatry (vv. 8, 18, 20), the humbling of the haughty (vv. 9, 11, 12–17) and the terrible 'day of the Lord' (vv. 11, 12, 17, 20). In Hebrew, verse 6 apparently refers to the country being overrun by people from the East ('Aramaeans') and intermarriage with the 'children of foreigners' (cf. LXX, Rashi), with references to 'soothsayers' and 'Philistines', to which the Targum adds 'idols'.

Many Christian commentators assume that the object of this tirade is the Jewish people, referred to as 'the house of Jacob (LXX Israel)' in verse 6, and try to identify periods in their history to which the prophet refers. For some, reading 'as at the beginning' (LXX, Vg) for 'from the east' (Heb. *miqqedem*), attacks on idol-worship must refer to an earlier period in their history, since idol worship was unknown among the Jews by the time of Christ: indeed 'they waged many wars with the Romans because of images' (Luther 35). Allusions to 'soothsayers like the Philistines' (v. 7) and the 'ships of Tarshish' (v. 16) prompted speculation about the political and religious situation in eighth-century BCE Judah (Eusebius, Jerome) and John Chrysostom identi-fied 'the man in whose nostrils is breath' (v. 22) as Hezekiah before the defeat of Sennacherib (Isa 37). Other commentators point out that similar moral criticisms could be applied to the Greek and Roman ruling classes, thinking, for example, of the decadence of the Emperor Hadrian in contrast to the reign of Constantine when 'in the light of the Gospel of Christ immorality was removed' (Jerome).

Cyril of Alexandria looks for a spiritual context rather than a historical one: in verse 7 the prophet is attacking avarice and pride, recalling the Mosaic law against the king accumulating silver and gold and horses (Deut 17:14–17), and verse 20 is about those who 'admit idols into their mind … and become nests for bats, that is, unclean spirits' (cf. James 1:14–15). A similar spiritual interpretation of verse 20 appears in William Cowper's famous hymn 'O For a Closer Walk with God' (1769):

> The dearest idol I have known,
> Whate'er that idol be,
> Help me to tear it from Thy throne
> And worship only Thee. (*EH* 445; *CH2* 457; *GtG* 739)

For Calvin, on the other hand, quoting Jer 10:14, the references to the worship of idols, things made by human hands (v. 8), can be taken literally and applied by 'the same reasoning' to contemporary Catholic practice. Luther also applies the passage to his contemporaries, interpreting it as an attack on all forms of religion apart from the worship of Christ, and he compares the abolition of idols in verse 18 to the change of 'monks into laymen, etc. through the Gospel'. Recent postcolonial comments on this and other passages in Isaiah (Isa 30:22; 40:18–20; 44:9–20; 46:1–7) question the out-and-out rejection of idol-worship, especially in the Indian context where it is a normal and venerated religious practice (Soares-Prabhu 1995).

'On that day' (vv. 11, 17, 20) according to most commentators, Jewish and Christian, refers to the Day of Judgment (e.g. Rev 6:15–16; Eusebius, Rashi, Luther), although this does not necessarily rule out its application to historical events as well, such as the destruction of Judah by the Babylonians or the Romans (Cyril, Jerome) and the coming of Christ (2 Thess 1:9; Fekkes 1994: 137). As in the Tower of Babel story (Childs), it is a day when haughty godless human beings, compared to the cedars of Lebanon, mountains, high towers and tall ships, will be brought low (vv. 11, 17) 'before the terror of the Lord and the glory of his majesty' (v. 19, 21). To expand on the identification of sin with 'haughty looks', Rashi cites a psalm (Ps 101:5) and Luther a Gospel: 'for what is exalted among human beings is an abomination to God' (Luke 16:15). Others focus on the virtue of humility: 'God opposes the proud but gives grace to the humble' (James 4:6, cf. Prov 3:34; Cyril).

The image of sinners trying to hide from the wrath of God in 'the caves of the rocks and the holes in the ground' (v. 19; cf. vv. 20–21) appears again in the Apocalypse (Rev 6:15–16) and is alluded to by Shakespeare, Christopher Marlowe, Charles Wesley and others (Kovacs and Rowland 2004: 89–93). Best known is the African American spiritual immortalized by Nina Simone on her album *Pastel Blues* in 1965: 'Sinnerman, where you gonna run to? ... I run to the Rock, please hide me, Lord, All on that day'.

There is evidence that verse 22 was not in all the earliest manuscripts (Jerome, Theodoret), but its relevance as a comment on what goes before is unmistakeable: in the words of the Psalmist, 'put not your trust in princes, in mortals in whom there is no help. When their breath departs they return to the earth and that very day their plans perish' (Ps 146:3–4; Theodoret, cf. Rashi). Calvin uses the verse to emphasize his theology of unmerited grace while Luther, by contrast, following an earlier tradition (Jerome, Aquinas), interprets the verse as referring to Christ on the Day of Judgment, comparing the 'breath in his nostrils' to Saul 'breathing threats and murder' (Acts 9,1; Luther 38f.).

Isaiah 3

In chapter 3 Isaiah continues his ferocious attack on his people. The chapter is in two parts: the first targets a situation of anarchy in which 'mighty men' are replaced by 'babes' and 'women' (vv. 1–15), and the second tells how the proud 'daughters of Zion' in all their finery will be humiliated and led into slavery, and their menfolk slain in battle (vv. 17–26).

Isaiah Through the Centuries, First Edition. John F. A. Sawyer.
© 2018 John Wiley & Sons Ltd. Published 2020 by John Wiley & Sons Ltd.

Anarchy in Jerusalem (Isa 3:1–15)

The absence of priests from the list of leaders has been noted, and also the additional detail of the leadership crisis highlighted in verses 6–7, namely, reluctance to stand for office. The inclusion of 'doctor' (Heb. *ḥobesh*, lit. 'bandager') in verse 7 has puzzled some commentators, and maybe LXX, Targum and Rashi are right to read 'leader'. Some suggest that references to children (v. 4) and women (v. 12) are not to be taken literally: they just means weakness, as illustrated by verses 16–26 (Rashi) or Leviticus 26:36 (Calvin). The child oppressors and women rulers are absent from the Septuagint, which has 'tax-collectors and cheats' (cf. Tg, Jerome).

Commentators are not agreed on what historical situation was originally referred to in this chapter: Sennacherib's invasion because of the reference in verse 8 to 'stumbling' rather than falling (Blenkinsopp), or unrest early in the reign of Ahaz (Wildberger, Clements) or the Fall of Jerusalem in 586 (Kaiser). In a famous sermon castigating the Catholic royal family, John Knox applied verse 4 to the situation in 1565 when Queen Mary married the young Darnley, glancing perhaps at the callow youth as he read the words 'babes shall rule over them' (Percy 1937: 401). On verse 12 Jerome castigates his Church leaders for allowing women too much influence, and Luther compares the bishops in his day to women who 'give themselves up to pleasures and have their minds on dancing'.

A rabbinic commentary identifies eighteen curses in verses 1–4: Jerusalem and Judah are going to be deprived of the eighteen things they need most to survive, all related to Torah scholarship (bḤagigah 14a). The list includes masters of the Torah ('stay'), masters of the Talmud ('stay of bread'; cf. Prov 9:1), masters of traditions ('mighty man'), experts at intellectual warfare ('the soldier') and students who make their teachers wise (v. 3 'skilful craftsman'; RSV 'magician'). Rashi adds that, in rabbinic tradition, an 'expert in charms' (v. 3 RSV; 'eloquent orator' AV) is someone fit to be entrusted with the secrets of the Torah, and that means an expert in the two branches of Jewish mysticism, Creation (Gen.1) and Merkabah ('Chariot') (Ezek 1). 'Boys' are those who do not obey the commandments (Rashi), but 'babes' (Heb. *ta'alulim* cf. Jer 6:11 Ibn Ezra) has been interpreted as 'delusions' (cf. Isa 66:4 AV) or 'scoffers' (LXX Rashi; cf. 2 Pet.3:3). The mention of insolent behaviour on the part of the young toward their elders and 'the base towards the honourable' (v. 5) completes Isaiah's curse of his people.

Verses 13–15 remind us that this chapter is also about the Day of Judgement, in language reminiscent of Daniel 7, Ezekiel 34 (Aquinas) and Psalm 82 (Calvin), and can refer as much to the Coming of Christ at the beginning of the Christian era as to his Second Coming (Luther). In the Hebrew, the Lord's judgement is against 'peoples', that is, the nations of the world (v. 13), who 'crush my people and grind the faces of the poor' (cf. Vg, NRSV; Jerome, Rashi, Luther, Childs), while the Septuagint, followed by most of the Church Fathers, Aquinas, Calvin and many modern commentators (cf. AV, RSV, NJB, Lowth, Kaiser, Clements), reads 'his people', and in so doing turns Isaiah's words on the Jews.

The Greek Fathers, working for the most part with the Septuagint rather than the original Hebrew text, found several anti-Jewish references in the passage which have a long history in the Christian Church. Cyril maintains that the references to bread and water in verse 1 must be interpreted figuratively because the Jews do not lack bread and water. Bread refers to scripture which they have, while what they lack is 'strength from bread' (LXX), that is to say, the spiritual nourishment that comes from understanding the true meaning of scripture: 'to this day whenever Moses is read a veil lies over their minds' (2 Cor 3:15; cf. Jerome). They also lack the spiritual nourishment that comes from the two sacraments, the bread of the Eucharist, which is the Body of Christ, and the water of baptism (cf. Isa 12:3; Cyril, Jerome, Chrysostom). The literal interpretation of the verse is proposed by Thomas Aquinas, who quotes Ecclesiasticus: 'the essentials of life are bread and water and clothing' (Sir 29:21). But the anti-Semitism remains in the 'broken staff' in the hand of 'Blind Synagogue', an image all too familiar in Christian iconography (Seiferth 1970: 95–109) and the title of a modern study of Judaism through Christian eyes (Manuel 1992).

Verse 8 is repeatedly quoted in Christian tradition to explain the fall of Jerusalem in 70 CE by reference to what Jews said and did 'against the Lord' in the Passion Narrative, shouting 'Crucify him! Crucify him!' and 'His blood be on us and on our children!' (Matt 27:25) (Isidore, *De Fide Catholica* 1. 27, 2; Eusebius, Jerome). In the Septuagint, verse 10 reads 'For they said, "Let us bind the righteous one"' (cf. Wisd 2:12), and this refers to the treachery of Judas, while, as both Cyril and Jerome point out, citing Paul (Gal 6:7), the next verse refers to his fitting end (Matt 27:5). In the medieval *Biblia Pauperum*, verse 11 is quoted to illustrate the scene of Judas' kiss (*BP* 90).

The Daughters of Zion are Haughty (Isa 3:16–26; 4:1)

In Isaiah's famous reproach against the 'daughters of Zion' (vv. 16–26), some suggest that 'women' refers to men behaving like women, and is therefore no more than a colourful elaboration of the first part of the chapter (cf. Ezek 16:8–13; Eusebius, Cyril, Rashi). John Chrysostom suggests that this 'rare passage' is due to the fact that haughtiness and arrogance are worse among women. Many just take it for granted that Isaiah should castigate 'brazen and wicked women' (cf. Prov 7:11; Eccl.7:26; Cyril), their 'haughtiness and lasciviousness' (Aquinas) and the 'shameless lust in their eyes' (v. 16; Calvin). Thomas Aquinas cites as an example Solomon's love of many foreign women and what he suffered as a result. Rashi describes them as adulteresses, and on verse 16 quotes a rabbinic tradition according to which 'a tall girl would walk between two short ones in order to appear to be floating over them' (b*Shabbat* 62b). On the identification of the ornaments and garments listed in verses 18–23, some commentators reckon there is no need to specify (Theodoret): just take note of how 'superfluous … excessive … unchaste' they are (Calvin). Others devote considerable space to discussing the details (Jerome, Aquinas), and in the Zohar they are interpreted as the twenty-four books of the Bible with which the Shekinah, Israel's bride, is adorned on the night before the Feast of Weeks (*Zohar* 1, 8a; 3, 98a; Scholem 1965: 138).

There is a painting of the scene by the nineteenth-century Jewish artist Solomon Solomon (1860–1927), and around the same time Elizabeth Cady Stanton quotes the passage in full in her *Woman's Bible* (1895). It is the only passage from Isaiah she refers to, using it partly to focus on men's treatment of women as symbols and not as human beings in their own right but also to condemn the bad taste of women in her own day going to church in 'bonnets trimmed with osprey feathers' (Stanton 1985: 102). The wantonness of the daughters of Zion with their mincing steps and tinkling ornaments is the theme of the third movement of Robert Starer's cantata *Ariel: Visions of Isaiah* (1960), a mordant *scherzo* followed by 'Fear and the Pit and the Snare' (Isa 24:17). There may be a chilling allusion to the horror of the Aqedah story in the Greek version of verse 25: 'and your most beautiful son whom you love will fall by the sword' (cf. Gen 22:2) (Baer 2006: 42–46).

Verse 1 appears to continue the description of the fall of Jerusalem and the fate of her citizens so graphically described in chapter 3. It envisages a situation in which so many men have been killed in battle that women will give up their right to food and clothing laid down in the law (Exod 21:10) if only they can find someone to marry them. Rashi, citing a midrash (LamR V.11), explains that Nebuchadnezzar commanded his soldiers not to have relations with married women, and this made the women of Jerusalem all the more desperate to be nominally married. Bishop Lowth compares their situation with that of a

Isaiah Through the Centuries, First Edition. John F. A. Sawyer.
© 2018 John Wiley & Sons Ltd. Published 2020 by John Wiley & Sons Ltd.

woman in ancient Rome who, according to Lucan, craved at least the empty name of marriage (*nomen inane connubii*) (*Pharsalia* 2:342).

The Pride and Glory of the Survivors (Isa 4:2–6)

The traditional chapter division takes verses 1 and 2 together, perhaps partly because the phrase 'in that day' is common to both. Joseph Kara (twelfth century) says this pairing where 'a rebuke is followed by a consolation' is a conventional literary device (Harris 2006: 185). Christian commentators from the time of Origen devised a different way of reconciling the two verses. The 'one man' in verse 1 and the 'branch of the Lord' in verse 2 are one and the same, Christ, and the seven women are the seven gifts of the spirit which, according to a more famous messianic prophecy, rested upon him (Isa 11:1–2; cf. John 1:32–34) (Eusebius, Jerome, Aquinas). The *Bible Moralisée* shows the spirit descending upon Christ at his baptism (John 1:32). According to another ancient Christian interpretation, the seven women are the seven churches (Rev 1:4, 11), nourished by the bread of the Holy Spirit and clothed in the garments of immortality (1 Cor 15:53). Such interpretations are rejected by Cyril and Luther, and not even mentioned by Calvin and subsequent commentators, who ignore the chapter division.

Jewish and Christian interpreters understand the 'branch of the Lord' as a reference to the Messiah, especially the new growth that will arise on the family tree of David after destruction (cf. Jer 23:5; 33:15; Zech 6:12) (Tg, Luther). Bede applied verse 2 to the day when Elizabeth greeted the Virgin Mary with the words 'Blessed are you among women' (Luke 1:42): in her the 'branch of the Lord shall be beautiful ... and the fruit of the earth shall become sublime' (Vg) (*Homily on Luke* 40). The verse also figures on Isaiah's scroll beside the image of Christos Pantocrator in the great eleventh-century dome mosaic of the Byzantine church at Dafni near Athens.

The word 'branch', however, is not present in the Septuagint, and many interpreters focus on the restoration and exaltation of a righteous remnant, 'the glory of the survivors of Israel' (v. 2 RSV). Ibn Ezra notes that the Targum translates the 'branch of the Lord' as the 'Messiah of the Lord', interpreted by some as a reference to Hezekiah, but he too prefers to understand it as a reference to the righteous remnant. This is also how Rashi interprets it, picturing a community whose beauty is embodied in the teaching of the sages, rather than the discarded ornaments listed in the previous chapter, and whose children are all students of the Torah. Modern scholars interpret the verse in a similar way since the emphasis is on the fertility of the land in which the survivors are to settle (cf. Isa. 35) rather than on the intervention of a messianic figure (cf. 9:1–7; 11:1–9) (Kaiser, Childs). Several scholars find an illuminating parallel in Isaiah 45:8, where righteousness and salvation spring up out of fertile soil (Calvin, Lowth, Blenkinsopp). The verse features in 'The Sun Goeth Down', a beautiful nocturnal interlude sung by Mary (soprano) at the end of scene 4 of Elgar's oratorio *The Kingdom* (1906) (*BiM* 134).

Verse 3 goes on to describe the survivors as those that are 'written for life', a phrase picked up by most commentators as a reference to those listed in the book of life (cf. Dan 12:1; Mal 3:16; Rev 5–8) and mentioned already by Moses (Exod 32:32). Cyril of Alexandria identifies them as the apostles whose 'names are written in heaven' (Luke 10:20). For John Chrysostom they are the chosen few, 'set apart, marked with a seal' (cf. Ezek 9:4), like the homes protected from the destroying angel in the Passover story (Exod 13; Calvin). Rashi stresses that they will be picked out of the nations from all over the world.

The holiness of this remnant of God's people is explained as the result of divine cleansing and burning which will purge away the filth and bloodstains that had led to the destruction of Jerusalem (v. 4). Ibn Ezra compares the process to the treatment of a rebellious son prescribed by law to 'purge the evil from your midst' (Deut 21:21). The Church Fathers, quoting John the Baptist, saw this as a reference to baptism 'with the Holy Spirit and with fire' (Matt 3:11; Luke 3:16; cf. Mal 3:1–3; Jer 6:29) (Jerome; cf. Irenaeus, *Against Heresies* 4.22.1), while some, quoting Peter (Acts 3:19), applied the words specifically to Jews who repent (Cyril). Didymus saw here a distinction between 'filth', which he said was due to involuntary transgressions, and 'bloodstains', which are the mark of deliberate crimes (*Homilies on Job 9:30–33*,), while Origen cites Isaiah 1:6–7 and Jeremiah 2:22 to prove that some sins cannot be cleansed even by the lye and the soap of the Word but only by the spirit of burning (*Homilies on Jeremiah* 2:2–3).

The prophecy ends with a description of the protection that God will provide for his people in Jerusalem (vv. 5–6). Many commentators pick up an allusion to the 'pillar of cloud by day and the pillar of fire by night' in the wilderness (Exod 13:21–22; Cyril, Jerome, Calvin, Childs). Luther interprets the pillar and the cloud as Christ 'our Mediator, Leader, Teacher, Priest … who leads us through unknown ways … a fire by night and our shade by day'. Rashi counts seven *huppot* 'shelters, canopies' in verse 5: cloud, smoke, splendour, fire, flame, shelter and the presence of God (Shekinah). Verse 6 recalls the 'coals of fire and brimstone' that rain down upon the wicked (Ps 11:6), but from which Jerusalem will be sheltered (Rashi). Others note a parallel in the Psalms: 'the sun shall not smite thee by day, nor the moon by night' (Ps 121:6) (Jerome, Calvin). For Luther the heat and the rain are the internal and external pressures that beat relentlessly upon the faithful in times of prosperity and adversity alike, while those who look to Christ are safe inside a pavilion which is the Word of God.

Many note parallels with the creation (v. 5 Heb. *bara*) of a New Jerusalem in Isaiah 65:18 and the 'holy city, a new Jerusalem coming down from heaven like a bride adorned for her husband' in Revelation 2:2 (Childs). The AV highlights the parallel by the choice of the word 'tabernacle' (v. 6 Heb. *sukkah*; cf. Vg; LXX, RSV 'shade') both here and in Rev 21:3 (Gk *skene*; cf. Kaiser). The apocalyptic language and imagery of the prophecy ensured it a place in Advent liturgies (BCP, *ORM*, RCL).

The Fate of God's Vineyard (Isa 5:1–7)

The prophet's choice of a love song for the next part of his prophecy has been much discussed. John Chrysostom compares it to the Song of the prophet Moses at the end of Deuteronomy (Deut 32) and suggests that it is easier to teach virtue with a memorable melody, while Luther imagines the prophet saying, 'My prose rhetoric has failed to convince them – maybe they will take my song to heart!'. Several commentators discuss its relationship to Isaiah's other

Isaiah Through the Centuries, First Edition. John F. A. Sawyer.
© 2018 John Wiley & Sons Ltd. Published 2020 by John Wiley & Sons Ltd.

'Song of the vineyard' (27:2–6) 'read as a radical revision or eschatological abrogation' (Blenkinsopp; cf. Aquinas). In both passages agricultural imagery is used to illustrate the message that Yahweh's protection of his people is conditional on their willingness to uphold his divine order in the world (cf. Ps 80:8–16: Marlow and Barton 2009: 214–221). In 2015 Isaiah's 'parable of the vineyard' was depicted on an Israeli postmark celebrating the award of the 'Green Globe' to the Dizengoff Centre in Tel Aviv for its contribution to environmental protection.

The Targum glosses 'a very fertile hill' (RSV; Heb. *qeren ben shamen*) as a 'lofty mountain in a fruitful land', a clear reference to Mount Zion; the watchtower is the Temple and the wine vat 'my altar to make atonement for their sins'. The 'choice vines' (Heb. *soreq*) (v. 2) are the Torah, by gematria a reference to the 606 Commandments (that is, 613 minus the 7 Noachic commandments). Verses 5–6 become 'I will take away my Shekinah from them … I will break down their sanctuaries …' and 'I will command the clouds that they rain no rain on it' is interpreted as a reference to the end of prophecy (Tg; cf. Rashi). A Qumran commentary also interprets the chapter as referring to the fate of the corrupt establishment in Judah, described as the 'Scoffers in Jerusalem' (*DSSE* 498–499), but it also contrasts this with God's true vineyard, which resembles the Garden of Eden (4Q433a) where the righteous, 'his pleasant planting' (v. 7: cf. 60:21; 1QS 8:5), will possess the land forever (Blenkinsopp 2006:108–109). There is also a popular rabbinic interpretation that the vineyard is the Garden of Eden, originally cleared of stones, that is, of temptation, but which later produced wild grapes, that is, Adam 'reviled and blasphemed' (GenR XIX. 12). 'I will break down its wall' (v. 5) refers to the expulsion of Adam and Eve, and 'I will command the clouds' (v. 6) to the angels guarding the way to the tree of life (Gen 3:24) (GenR XXI.8; cf, Ibn Ezra, Rashi).

The Parable of the Vineyard in the New Testament (Matt 21:33–46; Mark 12:1–12; Luke 20:9–19), based directly on the Isaiah passage, identifies the tenants with the Jews responsible for killing the owner's son and, like Isaiah, implies that the owner had no choice but to remove them from the vineyard (Matt 21:40–41; Luke 20:15–16; cf. Isa 5:3–4). This is how the Church Fathers understood it, some of them finding in the text more specific allusions to Jewish involvement in the Passion story like Isidore's application of the 'briars and thorns' to the crown of thorns (Isidore, *De Fide Catholica* 1.31,2), and Cyril of Alexandria's identification of the 'loud cry' in verse 7 as their shouts of 'Crucify him' (John 19:15).

For many the 'beloved' in verse 1 is Christ (cf. Matt 3:17; Isa 42:1; Eusebius, Theodoret, Cyril, Jerome), and, as the passage about Christ weeping over Jerusalem shows (Jerome; cf. Matth 23:37), that love made the destruction of his vineyard all the more painful for him (cf. Hos 9:10; Chrysostom). The true vinedresser built a fence around us (v. 2 LXX), with heavenly precepts and the angels standing guard (cf. Ps 34:7) to liberate us from the burden of earthly anxieties, and built a tower of apostles, prophets and teachers to defend the peace of the Church (Ambrose, *Hexameron* 5.12.50). Jesus is the True Vine (John 15), and 'we should hold fast to our neighbours with love ... and reach the greatest heights of lofty teachings like climbing vines' (Basil, *Homilies on Hexaemeron* 5:6). 'There must be more than buds and blossoms ... there must be fruit, a good heart and a good life ... which is the fatness of the vineyard' (Gal 5:22, 23; Henry; cf. Augustine, *Sermon* 376A 2).

Calvin reminds us that, although the passage originally referred to the Jews, it can be applied equally to the Church in his own day. A painting by Cranach the Elder (1472–1553) in the church at Wittenberg shows Luther and his Protestant followers at work in the vineyard, protected by a high fence from the serried ranks of Catholic princes, bishops and clergy (Plate 4). In a sermon preached fourteen times between 1748 and 1788, John Wesley identifies the vineyard with the Methodist Church and applies verse 4 to current evils: 'it

PLATE 4 'The Vineyard of the Lord' (Isa 5:1–7). Oil painting by Lucas Cranach the Younger, in the Stadtkirche, Wittenberg (1569). Reproduced with kind permission of Bridgeman Images.

brought forth wild grapes, fruit of a quite contrary nature, error in ten thousand shapes … enthusiasm, imaginary inspiration … pride … prejudice … anger, hatred, malice, revenge, and every evil word and work' (*Sermons* 3.505–517). The Vineyard Movement, founded in 1982, a network of over 1500 churches worldwide, also takes its name from Isaiah 5 and its New Testament parallels referred to above (Labanow 2009). Sinead O'Connor's hauntingly beautiful song 'If You Had a Vineyard', based on Isaiah 5, highlights the depth of God's sorrow at the wicked behaviour of his people (*BiM* 108).

The effect on the audience when the singer tells them who the parable is about (v. 7) has been compared to the prophet Nathan's 'Thou art the man!' at the end of his parable (2 Sam 12; Duhm, Marti, Blenkinsopp). Many commentators also note the striking play on words in verse 7: instead of justice (*mishpaṭ*) there is bloodshed (*mispaḥ*), and instead of *ṣedaqah* (righteousness) there is *ṣeʻaqah* (a loud cry) (e.g. Rashi, Calvin, Lowth, Blenkinsopp). The word *ṣeʻaqah* in verse 7, which is most often the cry of the oppressed (Gen 18; Exod 3, 22:21–22; cf. Miranda 1977: 88–90), highlights the theme of social justice which is the subject of the first of the 'woe oracles' immediately following it (cf. Gorringe 2006: 416–418).

Woe to Those Who Are Wise in Their Own Eyes! (Isa 5:8–30)

The literary connection between the Song of the Vineyard and the rest of the chapter (vv. 8–30) has often been obscured by modern commentators who identify differences in genre and date. The repetition of a refrain five times (Isa 5:25, 9:12, 17, 21;10:4) suggests that the material has been rearranged (Kaiser, Blenkinsopp). But in addition to the first of the six 'woe oracles' just referred to, three others continue the theme of vine cultivation (vv. 8–10) and wine consumption (vv. 11–12, 22) (Goulder 2004: 26), and the two prophecies of divine judgement on the land, introduced by 'therefore' (vv. 13:17, 24–30), clearly take up the theme of the destroyed vineyard from vv. 1–7. As one nineteenth-century commentator puts it: 'The wild grapes which Isaiah saw in the vineyard of the Lord, he catalogues in a series of Woes' (vv. 8–12, 18–24; Smith). The measurements of desolation (v. 10) are reversed in Enoch's vision of plenty (1 Enoch 10:19; *OTP* 1.18). But the passage is interpreted literally in a dramatic chorus, punctuated by cries of 'Woe' and ending with 'the thunder of many peoples' (Isa 17:12), in Randall Thompson's choral work *The Peaceable Kingdom* (1936) (*BiM* 185).

The attack on drunkenness (vv. 11–12), like the first 'woe', is a frequent theme in eighth-century prophecy (Hos 4:11; 7:5; Amos 2:8; 4:1; 6:1; Mic 2:11) and is aimed at people in power whose judgement is impaired by strong drink, not drinking wine in general, which can be beneficial (Prov 31:4–7; Luther). They do not regard 'the work of the Lord' which, according to a traditional Jewish interpretation refers to the Torah (Tg, Rashi), nor do they see his hand in the wonders of creation (Childs) or in the history of the human race (cf. Gen 6–9) (Nicholas). In Alfred Hitchcock's film *The Birds* (1963) verse 11 is quoted by a waitress in response to some biblical comments uttered by a drunken guest.

In his *Babylonish Captivity of the Church* (1520), Luther applied 'want of knowledge' (v. 13) to the starving of the laity of proper education by the bishops and clergy of his own day (*LW* 36, 116–117). Eusebius explains that the dramatic language of verse 14 refers not only to the physical destruction of Jerusalem in 70 CE (v. 14) but also to the spiritual exile and starvation of the Jews because they had rejected the 'Author of life' (Acts 3:14–15). According to a Jewish midrash 'in justice … in righteousness' here (v. 16) refers to the righteous acts of God's people by which his holiness dwells among them, and by which God is exalted and they will be redeemed (Isa 56:1) (DeutR V.6). For many, especially Protestant scholars, the association of holiness with justice and righteousness in the verse epitomizes the 'ethical monotheism' of the eighth-century prophets, particularly Isaiah, and signals a high point in Old Testament theology (Bright 1981: 286–287).

Three of the four remaining 'woes' in the chapter (vv. 18–23) can be applied to different human situations. Justin Martyr confidently applies the first two (vv. 18–20) to the Jews responsible for Christ's death (*Dialogue with Trypho* 17) and in the medieval *Biblia Pauperum* the scene depicting the Jews condemning Christ (Matt 27:11–26) has the caption 'Cursed be those who call evil good and good evil' (v. 20) (*BP* 91). Augustine uses verse 18 to illustrate the interconnectedness of sin since what starts out as a simple theft can end up, after other more serious crimes, in a heretical sect: 'the rope is growing. Beware of the rope' (*Tractates on John's Gospel* 10.5.2). There is a similar comment in a Jewish midrash: 'the beginning of sin is like the thread of a spider's web: its end is like a cart rope' (*RA* 63–64). In an extraordinary work for soprano, reciting voice and instrumental ensemble entitled *Strophes* (1959) by the Polish composer Krzysztof Penderecki, which explores the mystery of death and the human condition, Isa 5:20 and Jeremiah 17:9 are recited in Hebrew, beside texts in Greek and Persian (*BiM* 227–228).

The attack on 'those who are wise in their own eyes' (v. 21) reminds John Chrysostom of Paul's comments on the pagan philosophers (Rom 1:22), while Gregory the Great, also citing Paul (Rom 12:16), takes it as a call for humility: 'knowledge is a virtue, but humility is its guardian' (*Forty Gospel Homilies* 7:4). Verse 22 returns to the theme of heavy drinking and once again stresses the social consequences of such behaviour on the part of a country's leaders 'who acquit the guilty for a bribe' (Eusebius). In *Piers Plowman* (1367–1370) the verse is quoted in reaction to the sight of a Master of Divinity greedily gulping his wine (Langland 1959: 191).

The last section of the chapter (vv. 24–30) concludes the account of divine judgement with imagery drawn from the Exodus story as well as from vivid descriptions of an invading army, possibly eyewitness reports. No historical details are given, and commentators have proposed the Assyrians, the Babylonians and the Romans in the role of invaders. In favour of the Roman invasion of 70 CE is the phrase 'nations from afar' (plural in Hebrew), which would describe the allies of Vespasian and Titus fighting under one standard (v. 26) (Cyril). The 'signal' was interpreted by Isidore of Seville and others as a reference to the sign of the cross (cf. Isa 66:19; 55:13); (Isidore, *De Fide Catholica* 2.26.3), which played a significant role in the military history of Constantine the Great. Some have suggested that the whistle mentioned (cf. Isa 7:18) alludes to a beekeeper's whistle, which summons the bees from their hives in the morning and calls them back from the fields in the evening (Cyril, Theodoret). Modern scholars argue that this is one of the passages dateable to the eighth century, and that the swarm of invaders here (cf. Isa 7:18–19 and 10:27–32) 'unmistakeably' refers to the Assyrian invasions of 732–701 (Clements; cf. Blenkinsopp).

Isaiah 6

The reception history of chapter 6 begins within the book of Isaiah itself, where there is at least one direct quotation (Isa 57:15), to which we may add the heavenly court scene in chapter 40 and the recurrence throughout the book of the Isaianic title 'Holy One of Israel' (Otto 1950: 76–77; Williamson 1994: 38–45). The Sanctus (v. 3; Gk *Trisagion*) appears already in Revelation (Rev 4:8) and in the popular Latin hymn *Te Deum*. It also plays a significant role in the Roman Mass and the celebration of the Eucharist in virtually every other Christian tradition (Spinks 1991). In the 'Reproaches' (*Improperia*), traditionally sung on Good Friday, the refrain consists of the *Trisagion* sung in Greek followed by a

Isaiah Through the Centuries, First Edition. John F. A. Sawyer.
© 2018 John Wiley & Sons Ltd. Published 2020 by John Wiley & Sons Ltd.

Latin translation (Otto 1950: 71). The *Qedushah* (from Heb. *qadosh* 'holy') features three times in Jewish daily prayer: in the Blessings leading up to the recitation of the *Shema* (*ADPB* 64–65); in the *Amidah*, the 'summit of prayer when we enter the holy of holies' (*ADPB* 74–79); and, with a brief Aramaic commentary, in the final prayer at the conclusion of the morning service (*Qedushah de-Sidra*) (*ADPB* 36–37). In the annual lectionary the whole chapter is in the haftarah accompanying the story of the commissioning of God's people at Sinai (Exod 18:1–20:26) (*JSB*), Isaiah's response 'Here am I, send me' (Isa 6:8) echoing the people's 'All that the Lord has spoken we will do' (Exod 19:8).

The impact of Isaiah's vision goes far beyond Jewish and Christian liturgical tradition, however, not only in music and the arts, as we shall see, but in the history of religion. The passage plays a crucial role, for example, in Rudolph Otto's famous description of the numinous: 'the capital instance of the mutual interpenetration of the numinous with the rational and the moral is Isaiah … we meet it in an unsurpassable form in the sixth chapter of Isaiah … and for a true understanding of the experiences bearing on the Resurrection, we would refer … to the nature of spiritual revelation as recounted in Isaiah vi' (Otto 1950: 63, 75, 228).

Holy, Holy, Holy (Isa 6:1–3)

In Jewish tradition the 'death' of Uzziah (v. 1) was not taken literally but understood as a reference to the tale of how Uzziah's reign ended when he was 'smitten' with leprosy, and how his son Jotham reigned in his stead until his death many years later (2 Chron 26:16–23) (Tg, Rashi). The implication that the vision took place while Uzziah was still alive (cf. Isa 1:1) then leaves open the possibility that this was the initial call and commissioning of the prophet, even although it is not placed, like those of Jeremiah and Ezekiel, at the beginning of the book. Ibn Ezra takes the words literally but solves the problem by suggesting that Isaiah's call took place 'in the year that King Uzziah died', but some months before his death. Many commentators, in view of the reference to the vision 'which he saw … in the days of Uzziah, Jotham, Ahaz and Hezekiah' (1:1), assume that it was not his first vision, and that chapters 2–5 date from the reign of Uzziah (Lowth). Modern calculations conclude that the date of the vision was 736 BCE, and that consequently the earliest prophecies in the book of Isaiah are to be dated to the reign of Ahaz (7:1–9:1; cf. 14:28) against the background of the Assyrian invasions beginning with that of Tiglath Pileser III in 734 (cf. 2 Kgs 16) (Clements).

The patristic commentators discuss the significance of the event rather than its chronology. The end of the reign of the wicked king Uzziah means the end of a reign of sin. Isaiah could not have had visions while King Uzziah was alive because 'as long as Uzziah is alive, we will not be able to see the glory of God' (Origen, *Homilies on Isaiah* 1.1–2; cf. Theodoret; Jerome). Others note that the end of the long reign of Uzziah marked the end of a period of stability and material prosperity (2 Chron 26:1–15) (Smith, Clements), and the beginning of the Assyrian threat, which is reflected in the changed tone and content of Isaiah's prophecies: 'chapter 6 depicts a new stage in Isaiah's career' (Sommer), and 'offers a massive new theological grounding' (Childs).

On why the prophet's call does not appear at the beginning of the book, a number of solutions have been proposed. Calvin rejects the suggestion that it is a scribal error and urges us not to think it strange that Isaiah was 'so completely overpowered by this extraordinary vision as to forget that he was a prophet'. He also reminds us that this would not be the only time that God's apostles have received two calls, citing Matthew 10 and Acts 2. Matthew Henry suggests that either Isaiah had previously been on probation, so to speak, and only now is properly 'ordained', or else he had hitherto had so little success that he was thinking of giving up when this vision inspired him to greater efforts. Literary critics argue that the positioning of the vision after chapters 1–5, is a literary device designed to provide a background for the vision and emphasize the enormity of the task confronting him: the 'woe oracles' in the preceding chapters describe the kind of people Isaiah is to address – 'a people of unclean lips' (v. 5) (Conrad 1991: 122–130).

The text does not tell us where Isaiah was when he received this vision. He may have been asleep or he may have been conducted into the Temple or it may have happened in his own home or in a field, as in the case of other prophetic visions (Calvin). In a fresco on the ceiling of the Palazzo Patriarcale in Udine, Tiepolo has him sitting on his own in the open country with the angel on a cloud above him (1726–1729) (Plate 5), while in Benjamin West's famous painting *Isaiah's Lips Anointed with Fire* (1782), the prophet is sitting on a chair with a scroll in his hand, perhaps suggesting he was at home in his study at the time. Some commentators envisage the prophet in the Temple 'actively worshipping' (Childs) or 'looking through the entranceway into the main *aula*' (Clements; cf. Wildberger), where he sees God enthroned above the ark in the holy of holies (cf. Jer 17:12; Ezek 43:7), the veil having been removed (Lowth). In an illustration of the scene in the Wittenberg Bible (1534), attributed to Lucas Cranach the Elder, he is standing in a field within sight of the Temple (Plate 6).

Wherever he was at the time, what he saw was taking place in heaven, and the scene has its closest biblical parallel in the book of Kings (cf. 1 Kgs 22:19–23; Ibn Ezra, Duhm). Already in the Targum the words 'in the highest heavens' are inserted to make this more explicit, and Kimḥi also suggests it may refer to 'the

PLATE 5   "The Prophet Isaiah" (Isa.6:6). Fresco on the ceiling of the Palazzo Patriarchale in Udine by Giovanni Battista Tiepolo (1726–29).

PLATE 6   Isaiah's vision (Isaiah 6, with Isa 5 and 53). Woodcut by Lucas Cranach's workshop for Martin Luther's first complete German Bible (Wittenberg 1534). Reproduced with kind permission of David Gunn.

heavenly regions' rather than the Temple in Jerusalem. The word translated 'temple' (Heb. *hekhal*) in verse 1 came to be associated in Jewish mystical writings with the heavenly palaces where choirs of angels sing the *Qedushah* round the throne of God (3 Enoch; Alexander 1983; 240, 245), and the liturgical notion of human choirs joining with the angels and archangels in the singing of the Sanctus further demonstrates that Isaiah is here given a glimpse into 'the throne room of God' and a chance to hear the voices of his divine attendants (Brueggemann, Blenkinsopp).

A major difference between seraphim (v. 2) and angels, cherubim and other divine beings, is that the Hebrew verb *saraph* means 'to burn', and many commentators cite Psalm 104:4 to explain the word: they are the 'flaming ones' (Jerome, Luther), characterized by speed, agility and energy (Chrysostom). Some connection with the 'fiery serpents' (Heb. *nehashim seraphim*) in the wilderness (Num 21:6, 8; Deut 8:15) and winged cobras in Egyptian iconography has also been suggested (cf. 1 Enoch 20:7; *OTP* 1.24) (Gray, Kaiser, Blenkinsopp, Roberts). The Targum has 'servants' (cf. Heb. *shamash*) and omits the reference to 'smoke' in verse 4 (cf. Rashi). Their position 'above it' (i.e. 'the temple' Vg, AV) is explained by Rashi and others as 'in heaven'. Ibn Ezra explains the phrase as 'on his left and on his right' (cf. 1 Kgs 22:19) while the Septuagint has 'around him', no doubt to avoid the implication that anything or anyone could be above the Lord (Lowth; cf. RSV).

The seraphim had six wings: with two they covered their eyes to protect themselves from the lightning flashes of God's glory (Chrysostom) and with two they covered their feet. In biblical Hebrew 'feet' may be a euphemism for private parts (cf. Judg 3:24; 1 Sam 24:3; Ibn Ezra), translated 'bodies' (Tg) or the like. But in a society where men wore long garments down to the feet, it may have been thought immodest to appear in public and on solemn occasions with the feet uncovered (Rashi, Lowth). According to Luther, 'feet' here means conduct: 'their walk and their endeavours … which are not worthy to be seen in God's presence', and this reminds believers that they will have no intercourse with angels till they raise themselves high and are no longer fastened to the earth (Calvin). Heavenly creatures with six wings reappear in Revelation (4:8) and play a prominent part in Christian iconography down to the present.

Many writers, Jewish and Christian, discuss how it is possible that Isaiah could have seen God when it states so clearly elsewhere in scripture that 'you cannot see my face: no one can see God and live' (Exod 33:20). According to the *Martyrdom of Isaiah* (3:8–10), he was accused of lying because no man can see God and live and was punished for claiming to have seen God's face, but other patristic commentators explain that it was God's face and feet that the seraphim covered with their wings, not their own, so that, like Moses on Sinai, he saw

God but not his face (Exod 33:23) (Eusebius). Others cite John 12:41 to prove that it was Christ enthroned that Isaiah saw (Jerome, Eusebius).

The number of seraphim is not given, whether two or two thousand (Luther; cf Calvin). Most assume that it is a vision of the Lord surrounded by his heavenly court (cf. Daniel 7:10; I Kgs 22:19; Ibn Ezra) and that there are many (Eusebius), perhaps in two choirs singing antiphonally (cf. Exod 15:20, 21; Ezra 3:11; Lowth). But many Christian commentators maintain that there were only two, and that they represent Christ and the Holy Spirit who, together with the Lord 'sitting upon a throne', make up the three persons of the Trinity celebrated in their cry of 'Holy, Holy, Holy' (Origen, *On First Principles* 1.3.4; Cyril). This interpretation is rejected as 'impious' by Jerome because the Lord Jesus is the one sitting on the throne (cf. Luther). In Revelation, which draws on Ezekiel (Ezek 1) as well as Isaiah, there are four living creatures with six wings singing the Sanctus (Rev 4:6–8), as there are in 3 Enoch, a work strongly influenced by Isaiah 6 (3 Enoch 26:9; Alexander 1983: 246). In an elaborate allegory, Luther interprets the seraphim as the apostles and preachers of the word, flying with two wings which are the Old Testament and the New Testament or the testimonies of the Law and the Prophets, and veiling their faces and feet to signify that 'the life of the godly is hidden in Christ'. The fiery coal is the gospel, whereby those put to death by sin are revived and shaken like the lintels of the temple during an earthquake.

The threefold repetition of the word 'Holy' (v. 3) may be just for emphasis (cf. Jer 7:4; 22:29; Ibn Ezra). Calvin says he would personally choose a more convincing scriptural text to use in a theological argument about the Trinity, while Luther conspicuously omits all reference to it in his comments on the passage as do most historical-critical commentators (e.g. Duhm, Gray, Clements, Childs, Blenkinsopp). In the Targum it refers to three aspects of God's holiness: 'Holy in the highest heavens, where his Shekinah dwells, Holy upon earth, the work of his might, Holy for endless ages is the Lord of hosts.' In Revelation it means 'the Lord God Almighty who was and is and is to come' (Rev 4:8).

The most common traditional Christian interpretation, which goes back to the Church Fathers, sees in these words 'the mystery of the Trinity in the one Deity' (*mysterium Trinitatis in una Divinitate* Jerome; cf. Cyril, Ambrose *On the Holy Spirit* 3.16.110). Gregory the Great compares Isaiah's articulation of the doctrine of the Holy Trinity with those of David (Ps 67:6–7) and Paul (Rom 11:36) (*Morals on Job* 29.70). In the Byzantine Trisagion, 'Holy God' refers to the Father, 'Holy and Strong' to the Son and 'Holy and Immortal' to the Spirit (Wybrew 1989: 79). To confirm the trinitarian interpretation, some point to the first person plural in verse 8: 'who will go for us?' (Henry). The trinitarian interpretation still continues in many Christian traditions where Isaiah 6 is read on Trinity Sunday (RCL, BCO) and Bishop Heber's famous hymn is sung – 'Holy, Holy, Holy! Lord God Almighty!' (1826) with its refrain 'God in Three Persons, Blessed Trinity' (*EH* 162; *CH4* 768; *HON* 215; *GtG* 1).

The second part of the hymn of the seraphim – 'the whole earth is full of his glory' – is interpreted by some Christian writers as a deliberate rejection of Jewish claims that God's glory is restricted to their Temple or their land (Jerome) and as a reference to the coming of Christ: 'for now the whole world is indeed filled with His glory' (cf. Cyril, Eusebius). Luther concludes from the mention of smoke filling the house (v. 4), as it did when the Temple of Solomon was dedicated (1 Kgs 8:10), that the Lord and the seraphim were seen and yet cannot be seen, like the Body of Christ in the bread of the sacrament. Recital of the Sanctus unites human worshippers with 'Angels and Archangels and all the company of heaven' (BCP): 'in this way earthly things imitate the heavenly, transcendent, the spiritual order of things' (Wybrew 1989: 127). There is a tradition dating back to the fifth century CE that when the people of Constantinople sang the Trisagion, they were miraculously rescued from an earthquake (Mango and Scott 1997: 145).

The voices of the seraphim made the lintels shake (v. 4) 'to show it was not a human voice' that Isaiah heard (Calvin). Some see here an allusion to the earthquake that shook Judah during the reign of Uzziah (Amos 1:1; Zech.14:5; cf. Rashi), but most interpret the shaking of the foundations and the smoke as typical cosmic responses to the appearance of God (cf. Exod 19:16–19; Judg 5:4–5; Ps 18:7–15; Kaiser, Blenkinsopp). In place of 'smoke' the Targum has 'thick darkness', alluding to the events at Sinai (Exod 20:21; Deut 5:22). According to a Jewish mystical tradition, when the *Qedushah* is sung by the seraphim in heaven, the pillars of the heavens shake and the foundations of the earth shudder 'because of the thunder of their voices' (3 Enoch 38; *OTP* 1.290–292; cf. Ps 77:18). In an anonymous medieval Hebrew poem beginning 'He wraps himself in a cloak', all eight stanzas end with a phrase from verses 4–6 (Carmi 1991: 251–252).

There are numerous musical interpretations of the heavenly hymn, many of them now heard as often in secular performances as in the liturgy (*BiM* 103, 212–213). In his beautiful *Duo seraphim clamabant* from the *Vespers of the Blessed Virgin* (1610), Monteverdi follows the tradition that there were only two seraphim. Mendelssohn's setting in *Elijah* (1846) is a heavenly dialogue between a quartet and the chorus, inserted into the story of the 'still small voice' (I Kgs 19:11–18), while Verdi's thrilling fugal setting for two choirs in his *Requiem* (1874) portrays the multitude of a heavenly host. Bach's sublime choral setting of the Sanctus in his B Minor Mass (1748) is based on the number six (six voices, recurring sixths), recalling the six wings of the Seraphim. Britten's 'Sanctus' in the *War Requiem* (1962), set for soprano solo and chorus, is coupled with a setting for baritone solo of Wilfred Owen's poem 'The End' (1918), beginning 'After the blast of lightning from the East, / The flourish of loud clouds, the Chariot Throne'. One of the most popular compositions to have been inspired by the text is Schubert's exquisitely simple setting of a German 'Sanctus' from his *Deutsche Messe* (1827), now sung in Latin, English and other languages all over the world

Here Am I: Send Me! (Isa 6:4–8)

Isaiah describes his reaction to all this in the words 'Woe is me! For I am lost!' (Heb. *nidmeti*) (v. 5). Some take the verb to mean 'reduced to silence', that is, unworthy to join in the singing because of his unclean lips (Jerome, Lowth; cf. Sir 15:9). Others take it as 'dumbfounded' (*Pesh*, Ibn Ezra). The Targum has 'Woe is me for I have transgressed'. But many believe that it means Isaiah thought he was about to die (Rashi: cf. Ps 49:13–20) or that, in his sinful mortality, he had already died, reduced to nothing before this vision of perfect holiness (Luther). The Septuagint, perhaps to emphasize the lethal precariousness of the situation, divides the phrase 'I am a man of unclean lips' into two parts: 'I am mortal and I have unclean lips'.

Ancient Christian commentators mostly see in the touching of Isaiah's lips and the forgiveness of sins a prefiguration of the Eucharist. The burning coal 'taken from the altar with tongs' is the food of the holy sacrament, first laid on the altar as bread and wine, then transformed into the body and blood of Christ which blots out the sins of those who partake of it (Theodore of Mopsuestia, *Comm. on the Eucharist* 6:118–119; cf. Chrysostom). It is Christ who, as 'a coal according to the flesh, burnt up our sins' (Ambrose, *On the Holy Spirit* 1.10.113). Others stress that it was not on his own merits that Isaiah was chosen but because he had first been cleansed by the grace of God (Jerome). According to Luther, Isaiah was a different man after he had risen from the dead, strengthened by the burning coal, ready to hazard his life for God's sake, while Calvin suggests that God's words 'Whom shall I send?' indicate that God deliberated carefully before deciding and chose not any prophet but one who is eminent among the prophets. In his Ode 'On the Morning of Christ's Nativity' (1629) Milton refers to the prophet's lips 'from out his secret Altar toucht with hallow'd fire' (1998: 1–9).

According to a Jewish tradition Isaiah's lips were burnt (v. 6) because he had spoken ill of his own people (v. 6) (*CantR* I.6; cf. Rashi), but there is no doubt about the appropriateness of his appointment as God's prophet after his sins were forgiven (v. 7). According to another midrash, when he offered himself to God with the immortal words 'Here am I. Send me' (v. 8), God said, 'My children are wearisome and rebellious. If you will take it upon yourself to be despised and beaten by them, then go forth on this mission, but if not, accept it not'. And Isaiah said, 'Upon this condition I go forth namely my back I give to the smiters, my cheeks to them that pluck out my hair [cf. Isa 50:6], and even so I am not worthy to go forth on thy mission to thy children' (LevR X.2; Uffenheimer 1971: 236–238). Christians also noticed a connection between this scene and later chapters of the book, where they saw Christ's passion foreshadowed (Plate 6; cf. Isa 53).

The phrase 'Here I am' (Heb. *hinneni*) is familiar from the stories of Abraham, Joseph, Moses, Samuel and other Old Testament characters, to whom we may add the Virgin Mary's more deferential 'Behold the handmaid of the Lord' (Luke 1:38) and Ananias' 'Here I am, Lord' (Acts 9:10). But of all the human examples in the Bible, only Isaiah offers himself without being first called by name. Calvin adds the ethical corollary that this remarkable instance of obedience ought to produce such an effect on our minds that we shall be ready to 'undertake any task which he may be pleased to enjoin, however difficult we may imagine it to be'.

Hinneni became a symbol of commitment, loyalty and courage in both Jewish and Christian tradition. It has an important role in the Jewish liturgy in a prayer recited before God on Rosh ha-Shanah and Yom Kippur by the cantor as representative of the community (*sheliaḥ ṣibbur*), beginning 'Here I am, deficient in good deeds' (*hinneni he'ani mi-ma'as*) (*Maḥzor* 279, 609), and the Jewish philosopher Levinas replaces Descartes' 'I am' with the biblical *hinneni* 'Here I am' of ethics and subjectivity (Eskenazi, Phillips and Jobling 2003:13). Today there are several organizations in New York, Sydney and elsewhere with websites containing *hineni* (e.g. www.hineni.org; www.hineni.org.au) and *Here I Am Send Me* or *Here Am I Send Me* is the title of quite a number of autobiographies and CDs, both Jewish and Christian. It has also played a significant role in contemporary Christian worship. In Italian, for example, where 'Here I am' is one word, *Eccomi*, as it is in Hebrew, there's a popular setting of Psalm 40 with the refrain *Eccomi ... Si compia in me la tua volontà*: 'Here I am ... Be it unto me according to thy word' (Luke 1:38). In English there are numerous settings, of which the best known today is probably the hymn beginning 'I the Lord of sea and sky', written by the American Jesuit Dan Schutte, with the refrain 'Here I am, Lord. Is it I, Lord?' 'Isaiah 6' is a popular song on the album *Smash* (2005) by the Christian band 'One Bad Pig' with the chorus:

> Here am I – send me
> Here am I – take me
> Here am I – use me
> Here am I – spend me
> Send me, take me, use me, spend me, I am not my own. (*BiM* 113)

In the Second World War film *Fury* (dir. David Ayer, 2014) verse 8 is quoted by an American soldier waiting with his mates in a tank for the SS to attack.

Go and Say to this People, 'Hear, But Do Not Understand' (Isa 6:9–13)

The 'incredible message about blinding the Jews' (Calvin 163) (vv. 9–10) is cited no less than five times in the New Testament and was much quoted in early Christian literature (Evans 1989). Jewish commentators refer to Israel's wilful disregard for God's commandments and the hardening of their hearts, like Pharaoh's (Exod 7–14), and explain the prophecy as an intensification of their punishment and a means of ruling out the possibility of repentance and forgiveness (Rashi, Kimḥi). The New Testament quotations follow the Septuagint, which deviates from the Hebrew at the end, making it more explicit that God is the subject ('lest they repent and I heal them'). The quotations in Matthew, Mark and Luke are all in the context of a discussion of the parable of the sower (Matt 13; Mark 4; Luke 8) and are intended to explain why it is that the disciples can understand the 'secrets of the kingdom of heaven' and other people cannot. John couples the quotation with another verse from Isaiah (Isa 53:1) and highlights the role of the Jewish authorities among those who reject Jesus' teaching (John 12:37–44). But it is at the very end of the Book of Acts that the prophecy is quoted in full by Paul to explain the rejection of the Jews and the new favoured role of the gentiles (Acts 28:25–28). The Isaiah passage was no doubt in Paul's mind also when he wrote elsewhere about Israel's blindness (Rom 11:7–10; 2 Cor 3:12–16).

A number of commentators suggest that the prophecy does not necessarily mean that it was God's purpose, or that the prophet was being literally asked to 'make the heart of this people fat' (cf. Jer 1:10; Ezek 43:3; Lowth; cf. Ibn Ezra). This has nothing to do with predestination (Luther). But the fact that Isaiah's prophecy seemed to the early Christians and Church Fathers to have been so spectacularly fulfilled in the blindness of the Jews makes this theologically less significant. Jerome takes the passage literally but argues that it was a sign of God's mercy that 'one people should perish so that all might be saved'. Their fate was due to their own 'impassioned evil and enthusiastic perversity' (Chrysostom, *Homilies on Matthew* 13:10–11). Their maladies were not the work of nature but of deliberate choice (Theodoret; cf. Augustine, *Tractate 53 on John 12:37–35,* 4–6). 'Ungodly men have no right to blame the word for making them worse after having heard it' (Calvin). The image of *synagoga caeca* 'blind synagogue' became all too common in medieval literature and art: in the words of an eleventh-century plainsong sequence, *nunquam tamen desinit / esse caeca* 'but she never stopped being blind' (Terry 1932: 65–66). The 'Tree of Jesse' in the twelfth-century Lambeth Bible (Isa 11:1) shows Isaiah trying to drag her to Christ (Bevan and Singer 1927, and there is a fifteenth-century example on the cover of a volume entitled *The Broken Staff: Judaism through Christian Eyes* (Manuel 1992) (see on Isa 3:1; 29:9).

The scene of desolation and depopulation that follows (vv. 11–12) is interpreted by most of the early Christian commentators as referring to the campaigns of Vespasian and Titus that resulted in the destruction of Jerusalem (Eusebius, Jerome). This was taken as proving the reliability of the rest of Isaiah's prophecies. Modern historians are divided between the Assyrian invasion of the Northern Kingdom, culminating in the destruction of Samaria in 722, and the Babylonian conquest of Judah in 586, both events involving major deportations of the population into exile.

The Septuagint finds hope in verse 12: 'after this God will remove the men far off, and they that are left upon the land shall be multiplied' (*ATWAT* 36–38). 'Yet in it shall be a tenth' (v. 13) can also be interpreted as a ray of hope. The Targum has 'like a terebinth or an oak which appears to be dried up when its leaves fall but retains moisture to preserve the seed within it: so the exiles of Israel shall be gathered together and shall return to their land; for a holy seed is their plant'. Some find a reference in the phrase 'when it is felled' (RSV; Heb. *be-shalleket*) to a city gate (1 Chron 26:15) and suggest it refers to rebuilding in the time of Ezra (Rashi). A medieval mystical interpretation identifies the 'tenth' with the Shekinah 'the Divine Presence', tenth of the Sefiroth (*Zohar* 1:15a). The Isaiah Scroll from Qumran scornfully rejects this: 'How could the stump be the holy seed?' (Sawyer 1964), and this is how some of the Church Fathers interpret it: 'it is very ugly with its dry twigs … without blossom … like an acorn when it falls to the ground, it resembles what is fed to cattle' (Cyril). Luther points out that it cannot refer to the returning exiles after the Babylonian Captivity because the same sort of ungodly people returned as they were before. The holy seed must therefore be a spiritual remnant, men born of God, the Church of Christ: 'a little branch … finally growing and filling the world' (Luther). In the Jewish liturgy the messianic hope in the reference to 'the holy seed' (v. 13) is highlighted by reading two verses from chapter 9 at the end of the haftarah (Isa. 6:1–7:6; 9:6–7; MT 9:5–6).

Between the autobiographical narratives of chapters 6 and 8, there is a short narrative account in the third person about Isaiah's involvement in events in Jerusalem 'in the days of Ahaz'. Jerusalem is under siege from the armies of Syria and Ephraim (Israel) and the king and his people are panicking (vv. 1–2). The prophet is instructed to go to King Ahaz and assure him there is nothing to fear from these two little kingdoms (vv. 4–9): a much greater threat will shortly become apparent in the form of a series of invasions by the mighty Assyrian army, which will sweep through Syria and Israel, leaving a trail of destruction 'on that day' (vv. 18, 20, 21, 13) (cf. 2 Chron 28).

Isaiah Through the Centuries, First Edition. John F. A. Sawyer.
© 2018 John Wiley & Sons Ltd. Published 2020 by John Wiley & Sons Ltd.

Faith and Reason (Isa 7:1–9)

Jewish and Christian commentators on the chapter mostly focus more on the character of Ahaz and the words of Isaiah than on the history. On the basis of 2 Kgs 16, Ahaz is universally condemned both as 'an idolater, abominable and profane' and as a traitor who robbed the Temple to bribe the Assyrian king (Cyril). Rashi asks why the royal lineage is given (v. 1) and explains it as the author's way of stressing that Jerusalem's survival was for the sake of the Davidic dynasty, not for Ahaz himself, just as the expression 'House of David' in verses 2 and 13 is employed to avoid using his name. 'His heart and the heart of his people shook' (v. 2) because during the siege the king of Syria had slain '120,000 men of valour in one day' because 'they had forsaken the Lord, the God of their fathers' (2 Chron 28:5) (Luther).

Isaiah takes his son Shear Yashub and meets the king at the pool (v. 3) where people do their washing 'to humiliate Ahaz' (Rashi). The name of Isaiah's son means 'a remnant shall return' and is understood by Jewish commentators to refer to Isaiah's disciples (Rashi), 'the remnant that have not sinned' (Tg). The phrase appears in another of Isaiah's prophecies (10:20–23; cf. 11:11; 37:32) and evidently had a strong appeal to the Qumranites (Blenkinsopp 2006: 114–116). Several patristic commentators follow the Septuagint, which has 'Jashub who is left', and interpret the name Jashub as 'converted, repentant' (Jerome, Chrysostom). This suggested to Cyril of Alexandria that the 'upper pool' prefigures the baptismal font where we are washed by the 'spiritual fuller … who expunges every stain of ours and rids us of defilement'. The name Tabeel (v. 6) is unknown, possibly originally an Ammonite (Blenkinsopp): the Targum has 'whoever we please' and Aquinas suggests the invaders planned to set up an idol in Jerusalem rather than a king.

The reference to sixty-five years from the current crisis until the fall of Samaria in 722 BCE is chronologically problematic, considered a late insertion by most scholars and bracketed in the RSV (v. 8). According to a Jewish tradition it may refer to a final Assyrian deportation of Israelites, along with Manasseh in 674 BCE (2 Chron 33:11) (Kimḥi, Lowth). To solve the problem, Rashi, Eusebius, Jerome and others suggest that it refers to sixty-five years after the earthquake mentioned in Amos 1:1.

The prophet uses powerful language to try to persuade Ahaz to 'take heed, be quiet, do not fear and do not let your heart be faint' (v. 4): 'who would not take courage in response to these exhortations?' (Luther). But the king refuses to listen and his obduracy provides the occasion for two of the most often quoted Isaianic statements. The first of these is a kind of wordplay on two Hebrew verbs which have the same root (v. 9). Most commentators take the first verb in the sense of 'believe' and the second as 'be sure, established' (cf. 22:23, 25): 'If you will not *believe* (Heb. *ta'aminu*) [the words of the prophet], you will not be *established* (Tg, RSV; Heb. *te'amenu*) or *remain* [in your land]' (Jerome, Aquinas, Lowth). Some, perhaps because the kingdom is safe even if Ahaz does not believe the prophet, take the second verb as the passive of the first: 'If you will not *believe*, you will not be *believed* – there is no truth in you' (Rashi: cf. Ibn Ezra).

The Greek Fathers, by contrast, following the Septuagint, have: 'If you do not believe, you will not understand', a text which is then cited frequently by them in discussions of the relationship between faith and reason. Eusebius applies it to the immediate context and explains that the reason why the Jews don't understand Isaiah's words is that they do not believe in Christ. Augustine quotes it more than once to explain Christian understanding of the mysteries of their faith: 'if you are not able to understand, believe, that you may understand: faith goes before, understanding follows after' (*Sermon* 68.1; 76:1; *Contra Faustum* 12:46; 22:53). Anselm of Canterbury and Nicholas of Cusa also used it to prove that faith always precedes understanding (J. Hopkins 2006: 67–68).

The Immanuel Prophecy (Isa 7:10–17)

The other much quoted text from this chapter is introduced in a brief dialogue between the prophet and the king (vv. 10–17). The king is invited to ask for a sign from God 'as deep as Sheol or as high as heaven': that is, 'anything from bringing someone back from the dead to a heavenly portent' (Rashi). Luther notes that Paul approves the use of signs to accompany the Word (2 Cor 12:12). But the king stubbornly continues to disobey God's word, sarcastically quoting the Mosaic law (Deut 6:16), and chooses instead, according to one commentator, to 'busy himself with necromancy and the flight of birds and seek help from the demons' (Cyril). The prophet angrily responds, once more avoiding the use of the king's name (cf. v. 2), and tells him what the 'sign' is going to be: 'Behold a young woman (Heb. *'almah*, LXX *parthenos*, L. *virgo*) will conceive and have a child and call his name Immanuel' (v. 14).

According to one modern commentator this verse has generated 'more commentary than any other single verse in the OT' (Wildberger), and it is also true to say that in Christian tradition, including iconography, few other texts are so closely associated with Isaiah (cf. 9:6; 11:1) (Réau 1956: 366; Kirschbaum 1970: col. 356). It is in two parts, one applied to the doctrine of the Virgin Birth, the other, the name Immanuel, to teaching about the Person of Christ. Neither of these doctrines has any relevance in Jewish tradition and indeed they have little to do with the original Hebrew.

The 'young woman' (Heb. *'almah*) is a not named, and the Hebrew word used does not describe her as a 'virgin' (Heb. *betulah*: cf. Isa 37:22; 62:5) (Kimḥi). Ibn Ezra and Rashi both assume it refers to the prophet's wife and the birth of a third son alongside Shear Jashub (v. 3) and Mahershalalhashbaz (Isa 8:1–4). The miracle was that, although not a prophet herself, she was enabled by divine inspiration to utter the words *'immanu'el* 'God is with us': that is the meaning and purpose of the sign (Rashi). Like the three children of the prophet Hosea (Hos 1:2–9), their names embody the prophet's teaching, and later in the book it may be relevant that, as Ibn Ezra points out, the prophet's own behaviour is described as 'a sign and a portent' (Isa 20:3). Jewish writers also reject the theory that the verse could refer to Jesus, not only because the 'young woman' is not a virgin but also because the context makes it clear that it refers to something in the immediate future, not many centuries away (Ibn Ezra).

Much has been written on the identity of Immanuel (Laato 1988). Some people claim that the Immanuel prophecy refers to the wife of King Ahaz and to his son Hezekiah, who was to rule in Jerusalem when the Assyrians invaded Judah thirty years later. To show that 'Immanuel' was an appropriate name for Hezekiah, the rabbis cited a verse from the Chronicler's account of Sennacherib's invasion: 'with him is an arm of flesh; but with us (*'immanu*) is the Lord our God' (2 Chron 32:8; ExodR XVIII.5). Rashi and others rule it out because Hezekiah was born nine years before his father began to reign (2 Kgs 16:2; 18:2). Many modern scholars, however, favour a royal, dynastic interpretation despite the chronological problem (Lindblom, Clements, Wildberger, Blenkinsopp). Other proposals for who the 'young woman' might be include a mythical being (Gressmann 1929; Wolff 1959), a woman seen by the prophet in a vision (Schmidt 1925), and perhaps more convincing, any young woman who has a son in the near future and calls it 'Immanuel' (Duhm, Kaiser). The significant fact would then be not who she was or whether she was a virgin, but simply that, within a year she will be celebrating her country's escape from the Syro-Ephraimite threat by naming her son Immanu-El 'God is on our side' (Sawyer 2008).

The role of this famous verse in Christian tradition begins at the very beginning of the New Testament, where it is quoted in relation to the story of the Virgin Mary's miraculous conception of a son who will be called Immanuel (Matt 1:22–25). The Greek has *parthenos* 'virgin', and it is this version that has been almost universally adopted in Christian translations right down to the modern period. The Church Fathers defend it against Jewish claims that the original Hebrew (*'almah*) does not refer to a virgin: the Septuagint is older and more reliable than the translations of the Jewish scholars (Eusebius, Theodoret; cf. Justin, *Dialogue* 43; 71). Furthermore the text does not say that the young woman was not a virgin (Cyril, Eusebius, Jerome), and 'what sort of a sign would it be if a young woman who was not a virgin bore a son?' (Origen, *Against Celsus* 1:34–35; cf. Justin, *Dialogue with Trypho* 84; Chrysostom; Luther). The view that the young woman was the wife of Ahaz is also dismissed: 'who ever called Hezekiah Immanuel?' (Cyril). The virgin birth is the fulfilment of Isaiah's prophecy (cf. Matt 1:23) (Augustine, *Sermon* 370.3; Leo the Great, *Sermon* 23.1). Ambrose suggests that the Virgin Mary had read the prophecy and realized it was fulfilled in her (*Commentary on Luke* 2:15). For others, such as Gregory of Nyssa, it is more than a prophecy: it is the formulation of a doctrine (*On the Birth of Christ*). Adolf Harnack even suggested that the doctrine of the Virgin Birth originated as 'just a postulate' of this verse (Harnack 1893: I, 113; cf. *ChDogm* I.2, 178).

In the original Hebrew it is the young woman who calls her son 'God is with us', implying that 'God is with her people'. The Greek 'you [singular] will name him' in some of the manuscripts, presumably refers to Ahaz (Isa 7:14) and has the same restrictive sense (Eusebius). But most Christian commentators from Jerome onwards follow a different manuscript tradition that has 'they will call him' or 'he will be called' (cf. Matt 1:23), referring to the gentiles who appreciate the true meaning of the Immanuel sign, missed by the Jews. For many the name signifies the two natures of Christ as both divine and human (Eusebius, Cyril; cf. Bede, *Homilies on the Gospels* 1:5). Perhaps it is not a personal name at all but, rather, 'describes what kind of a person he will be … "God with us", therefore both God and man' (Luther 84). Karl Barth describes the name Immanuel as the solution to the theological problem raised by the Virgin Birth: the child conceived and born in such a miraculous fashion is 'God with us', that is, 'the Word made flesh' (John 1:14) (*ChDogm* I.2, 178; cf. Augustine, *Sermon* 370.3). The Immanuel sign gives us scriptural authority to call the Son 'God' (Chrysostom; cf. Ps 83:18).

The 'curds and honey' in verse 15 are not the 'milk and honey' of the promised land (Exod 3:8, 17) and can be understood to mean bare subsistence, the only thing left after vineyards, orchards, cornfields and cattle have been destroyed (Kaiser) or, in some cultures, the customary food for a newborn baby (Calvin). Some commentators believe that it refers to rich nourishing produce (Rashi), and even the food of the gods, appropriate for the child born to be the Messiah (Lowth). According to the Church Fathers the fact that the child eats normally proves he is truly human, while his ability to distinguish between good and evil when still a child, proves he is also divine, the 'one who is to be our Saviour' (Eusebius; cf. Jerome, Cyril). The prophet continues to try to persuade King Ahaz that he has nothing to fear from the 'two kings': their land will be destroyed before the child knows the difference between right and wrong (v. 16).

In many respects Isaiah 7:14 defines the prophet's central role in the history of Christianity from the beginning (Matt 1:23). It accompanies the Annunciation scene in the *Biblia Pauperum* along with Ps 72:6, Ezek 44:2 and Jeremiah 31:22 (*BP* 50), and in medieval English drama it is quoted by the Magi to King Herod (Beadle and King 1999: 73). A painting of the Annunciation by Raffaellino del Garbo (c.1510) shows Isaiah, opposite Jeremiah (Jer 31:22), pointing excitedly at the Virgin Mary with the words *Ecce virgo...* (There she is...) on his scroll (Plate 7). Another, by Matthias Grünewald, shows Mary reading the Bible, open at Isaiah 7, just as the archangel Gabriel addresses her.

In the Western liturgy *Ecce virgo concipiet* is a communion motet to be sung at the Mass of the Blessed Virgin during Advent and at the Feast of the Annunciation; it was set to music by William Byrd (*c*.1540–1623), Jan Sweelinck (1562–1621) and others. Cristobal de Morales (1500–1553) in his setting combines 7:14 with 9:6, substituting 'Wonderful Counsellor' for 'Immanuel'. In Handel's *Messiah*, 'Behold a virgin shall conceive' is a recitative before the alto aria 'O thou that tellest good tidings to Zion', and more recently the Swiss composer Willy Burkhard, in his oratorio *The Face of Isaiah* (1933–1935), like

PLATE 7   'Behold a virgin will conceive and bear a son' (Isa 7:14). Painting by Raffaellino del Garbo in St Francis' Convent, Fiesole (*c*.1510).

de Morales, links it with 9:6–7, and interprets it as a ray of hope in a context of deep darkness and despair, beginning with the chorale 'Out of the Depths' (Ps 130) (Berges 2012: 126–127).

The name Immanuel appears as a messianic title already in the third-century Greek Testament of Solomon (*TSol* 6:8; 11:6; 15:11; *OTP* 1.968, 974, 976), and it becomes very frequent in Christian tradition alongside other titles. It figures as one of the seven Great O Antiphons, sung at vespers in Advent since the early Middle Ages (*EH* 734; *BiM* 171), and translated into English as the Advent hymn 'O come, O come, Immanuel' (1853) (*EH* 8; *CH4* 273; *HON* 384; *GtG* 88). The plainchant provided the inspiration for James MacMillan's percussion concerto entitled *Veni Veni Emmanuel* (1992).

The King of Assyria (Isa 7:18–25)

The 'king of Assyria' is a far greater threat, a reference to two Assyrian invasions of Judah, the first in the days of Ahaz when Tiglath Pileser 'afflicted him instead of strengthening him' (2 Chron 28:20) and the more famous invasion of Sennacherib in 701 BCE in the days of Hezekiah when 'the miracle was performed' (Rashi; cf. Isa 37:36). 'The day when Ephraim departed from Judah' (v. 17) refers to the schism that divided the Kingdom of David into a northern kingdom (Israel or Ephraim) and a southern kingdom (Judah) when Solomon died (1 Kgs 12:16), 'the worst kind of calamity' (Calvin; cf. Jerome). The Qumran sect interpreted the verse in a very different way, identifying themselves with Ephraim who escaped from Judah 'to the land of the north', while the apostates in Jerusalem were given up to the sword (*CD* VII.10–15; *DSSE* 134–135; Blenkinsopp 2006: 94–95). Christian interpreters, rejoicing in the birth of their saviour foretold in verse 14, also refer the scenes of devastation to divine judgement on the obdurate Jews, whether at the hands of the Egyptians, the Assyrians, the Babylonians or the Romans (Eusebius, Cyril, Aquinas, Luther).

Armies will come from Egypt like flies attracted by the blood (Eusebius), warriors from Assyria that sting like bees (v. 18) (Rashi), and they will settle everywhere, eating and contaminating everything (v. 19) (Luther). The Lord will take up the king of Assyria in his hand like a sharp razor (v. 20; cf. Isa 10:5) and shave the land of Judah, its leaders ('the head'), the ordinary people ('the feet') and the king, the high priest ('the beard'): the eastern people have always held a man's beard in the highest veneration (Lowth). But God will bless those who survive with abundant milk, curds and honey, although each person will have only one cow and two sheep (v. 21), so they will have time to engage in the study of Torah instead of getting drunk on wine (v. 23; cf. b*Sanhedrin* 94b): this refers to the generation of Hezekiah (Rashi).

The prophet continues his own account of events during the Syro-Ephraimite siege of Jerusalem with the birth of another son, Mahershalalhashbaz, the 'waters of Shiloah' prophecy, another Immanuel prophecy, and then another call from God to hold fast to his faith amid an unbelieving people, doomed to destruction.

Isaiah Through the Centuries, First Edition. John F. A. Sawyer.
© 2018 John Wiley & Sons Ltd. Published 2020 by John Wiley & Sons Ltd.

The Waters of Shiloah (Isa 8:1–10)

Some commentators believe that the son born here is the same as the one foretold in the previous chapter (Isa 7:14) because the 'prophetess' could not have had two babies in one year (Rashi). The boy is given a new name, Mahershalalhashbaz, which means 'Speed the spoil, hasten the prey' (vv. 3–4), and the 'Immanuel' sign is transformed from one of hope into one of terror and destruction as the invading army floods the land (vv. 8, 10). To explain verse 3, which apparently states that the child was called Mahershalalhashbaz, not Immanuel, and his mother was a prophetess, not a virgin, the Church Fathers argued that the new name (LXX 'spoil quickly, plunder speedily') was just as appropriate since Christ 'plundered Satan and rescued from his knavery all those in thrall to him through sin' (Cyril). Damascus and Samaria (v. 4) are symbols of the idolatry and wizardry of Satan destroyed by Christ (Justin, *Dialogue with Trypho* 78; cf. Jerome, Cyril). Luke 1:48 proves that Mary was a prophetess (Jerome).

The word translated 'tablet' (v. 1 RSV, NJB) is not normally applied to writing materials and appears in a description of women's garments and jewellery (Isa 3:23). Accordingly it must refer to a 'scroll' (Rashi) or a 'sheet' (of papyrus) (Kaiser), or, even, as Ibn Ezra suggests, a piece of cloth with the inscription embroidered on it. The Church Fathers follow the Septuagint, which has a 'large new volume' instead of 'tablet' or 'scroll', and suggest it refers to a revised or parallel version of what precedes rather than the birth of another son (Blenkinsopp).

The 'waters of Shiloah that flow gently' refer to the modest canal which, before Hezekiah's tunnel was built (2 Chron 32:30), carried water round the eastern side of Jerusalem from the spring of Gihon (1 Kgs 1:33, 38, 45) to the pool of Siloam (Greek for *Shiloah*; John 9:7, 11). The word is related to Hebrew *shalah* 'send' (John 9:7), and commentators speculate on its meaning: it suggests trees sending out 'shoots (Heb. *shelahim*) in a garden of pomegranates' (cf. *CantR* 4:13; Ibn Ezra), and the saviour 'sent' to redeem us (Cyril). The waters of Shiloah are that 'spring of living water welling up to eternal life' (John 4:14) (Eusebius). Here they are contrasted with the mighty waters of the river Euphrates that runs through Assyria, and Luther eloquently cites a famous verse from later in the book to explain this contrast: 'in quietness and in trust shall be your strength' (30:15).

Some note an allusion to Zion in the Psalms: e.g. 'there is a river whose streams make glad the city of God' (46:4) (Calvin), and Milton alludes to the verse at the beginning of *Paradise Lost*:

> Or if Sion's Hill
> Delight thee more and Siloah's brook that flowed
> Fair by the oracle of God, I thence
> Invoke thy aid to my adventurous song. (1998: i. 10–13)

They were also the inspiration for Bishop Heber's famous hymn beginning 'By cool Siloam's shady rill' (1812) and the Quaker John Greenleaf Whittier's description of heaven:

> The flowers of Eden round thee blowing,
> And on thine ear the murmurs blest
> Of Siloa's waters softly flowing. (*To the memory of Thomas Shipley*, 1836)

The Jewish writer Aḥad Ha'Am (Asher Ginsberg) gave the title *Ha-Shiloaḥ* to his influential literary journal, first published in Berlin in 1897, because he was opposed to the political Zionism of Theodore Herzl and others and believed in slow steady progress rather than precipitate revolutionary change (L. Simon 1960: 131).

The second Immanuel prophecy (vv. 7–10) has been interpreted in various ways. For Rashi 'Immanuel' is the tribe of Judah, as named by the prophetess (Isa 7:14), and the reference is to the miraculous survival of Jerusalem when Sennacherib invaded Judah (cf. Isa 36–37). The Targum translates 'waters' (v. 7) and 'wings' (v. 8) as 'armies' and removes the name 'Immanuel' entirely, substituting 'O Israel' in verse 8 and 'for our God is our help' in verse 10. For Christians the 'peoples ... countries' (v. 9) are all who reject Christ, whether Greeks or Jews (Eusebius) or the armies of Satan (Luther). Calvin pictures the prophet on a watchtower (cf. Isa 21:8): 'refreshed by the name and the sight of Christ, he forgets all his distresses, as if he had suffered nothing' (cf. (Ps 46:10–11). The array of nine imperatives addressed to 'far countries' (vv. 9–10) anticipates the global rhetoric of later chapters (e.g. 41, 51) and also perhaps some of the Jerusalemite fervour of the early Second Temple period, reflected in chapters 56–66 (Kaiser, Blenkinsopp). In the Greek Orthodox liturgy Isa 8:1–4, 8–10 is read at vespers on the Feast of the Nativity (*OSB*), and 'God is with us' (vv. 8,10) is the refrain in a hymn based on the passage (Isa 8:9–10, 12–14, 17–18; 9:2, 6), beginning 'God is with us, understand, O ye nations, and submit yourselves' (v. 9 LXX) (Manly 1995: 165).

The Strong Hand of the Lord (Isa 8:11–22)

The second part of the chapter gives us another account of the private experience of the prophet, warned to dissociate himself from 'this people' (cf. Isa 6:9–10). The 'strong hand of the Lord' describes the fire burning in the bones of biblical prophets like Jeremiah (Jer 20:9) and Ezekiel (3:14; 8:1; 37:1) (Rashi). The hand of God also guides the prophet on the right path (Calvin) and protects him from danger (Luther). The conspiracy referred to is identified by some with those supporting King Ahaz's pro-Assyrian policy (2 Kgs 16:7–9) (Ibn Ezra), by others with events in Jerusalem associated with Shebna the scribe (cf. Isa 22:15–25; Rashi). There is no hope for the two 'houses of Israel', ensnared, fallen and broken (v. 14), whether this refers to 'Pekah son of Remaliah and his company or to Shebna and his company' (Rashi), or more generally to unbelieving Israel as the Targum implies by adding the words 'if you will not hearken'. In the Targum the 'sanctuary' (Heb. *miqdash*) is replaced by God's punishing word, the Memra, as the seal of his divine presence (Chilton 1987: 59–60). The verse is given an eschatological interpretation at Qumran (4QFlor = 174: *DSSE* 526).

Ancient Christian commentators following the Septuagint interpret these verses as referring to Jews and other disbelievers who conspire against the Lord (v. 12; Eusebius, Cyril, Jerome). Modern scholars suggest that the reference is to Isaiah himself, clashing with authority as Amos (Amos 7:10) and Jeremiah did (Jer 32) (Kaiser). Others, puzzled by references to sanctification and the sanctuary in this context emend the Hebrew text of verse 13: 'but Yahweh of the hosts, with him you shall conspire [*taqshiru* for *taqdishu* 'sanctify'] … he shall be your co-conspirator' [*meqasher* for *miqdash* 'sanctuary'] (Blenkinsopp). Verse 13 as it stands contrasts the misguided conspirators with the holiness of the Lord, a central theme in the Book of Isaiah, with ethical implications, and urges Isaiah and his disciples (plural) to 'sanctify him', that is, to 'worship and trust him' (Luther), to 'exalt his power highly' so as to remember that 'he holds the government of the world' (Calvin), and fear him as 'the fear of the Lord is the beginning of wisdom' (Prov 1:7) (Eusebius).

According to most Christian interpreters down the centuries, verses 14–15 continue the contrast between those who fear the Lord and those who reject him: he will be a sanctuary to the faithful and a stone of offence, a rock of stumbling, to 'both houses of Israel … many shall fall and be broken'. The Septuagint has 'if you trust him, he will be a sanctuary for you' and the Church Fathers, like the Targum, interpret this spiritually as the presence of God (cf. Ezek 11:16), a benign power intervening on behalf of the faithful and punishing the unbelievers. The 'double-edged' prophecy (Childs) also plays on the familiar associations of the words 'stone' (cf. Isa 28:16: 'precious cornerstone') and rock (cf. Isa 26:4; 30:29; 44:8). The stone motif (Gk *petra*) is elaborated in 1 Peter 2:4–8, no doubt with the author's name in view (cf. Matt16:18) (Calvin): Christ is the 'cornerstone chosen and precious' (Isa 28:16) and 'the stone that will make men stumble' (Isa 8:14). Luke ends his version of the Parable of the Vineyard with an allusion to verse 14 (Luke 20:18).

But it is Paul who, with 'great sorrow and unceasing anguish' (Rom 9:2), applied the words of Isaiah most poignantly to his fellow Jews. They have 'stumbled over the stumbling stone … because they tried to fulfil the law through works not faith' (Rom 9:32–33) … 'Christ is a stumbling block to Jews and folly to Gentiles' (1 Cor 1:23). The Church Fathers understood the verse to be primarily about belief in Christ and, to make the application of the prophecy to the Jewish people in the time of Christ more explicit, some even suggested that the mention of two 'houses of Israel' in verse 14 refers to the two schools of rabbinic tradition, the 'House of Hillel' and the 'House of Shammai' (Jerome). Aquinas thinks rather of the scribes and Pharisees. By contrast both Luther and Calvin maintain that the prophet includes all the ungodly, including the papists, not just the Jews, while modern scholarship, like Rashi, seeks to contextualize the reference in the history of ancient Judah (Clements).

The narrative account of the prophet's activity during the reign of King Ahaz concludes with a mention of the writing down and careful preservation of the prophet's words by his disciples (v. 16), anticipating two somewhat problematic references to prophetic books later (Isa 29:11–12; 30:8). In his comments on the two Hebrew terms translated 'testimony' (*te'udah*) and 'teaching' (*torah*) Rashi understands the first as referring to the prophet's teaching as a 'warning' and the second as the law (Heb. *torah*) of Moses (cf. Prov 6:21). The Targum explains that the Torah has to be sealed and hidden from those who do not wish to learn. The Septuagint also has 'law' (Gk *nomos*), both here and in verse 20, and reads, 'Then those will be revealed who seal up the law so as not to learn … He gave the law, however, as a help' (vv. 16, 20). The Greek translators thereby turned Isaiah into an advocate of Torah obedience for the benefit of Jews living in Alexandria who had escaped from the godless hierarchy in Jerusalem (Berges 2012: 92). The ancient Christian commentators by contrast assume that the verse (in Greek) refers to a time when people will no longer study the law of Moses but obey the commandments of the gospel (Jerome, Cyril, Eusebius).

The idea of sealing up the prophecies in a form that no one but his own disciples can understand is another popular reading of the passage. To illustrate this Luther cites Christ's words to his disciples: 'To you it has been given to know the secrets of the kingdom of God' (Luke 8:10). Calvin speaks of the need for the Holy Spirit to unlock the meaning of the Word, a motif developed in the apocalyptic tradition: Daniel is instructed to 'shut up the words and seal the book until the time of the end' (Dan 12:4; cf. Dan 8:26; 9:24), and, at the very end of the Apocalypse, the angel says to John, 'Do not seal up the words of the prophecy of this book because the time of the end is near' (Rev 22:10). This passage, along with Isa 29:11–12 and 34:16, is where Joseph Blenkinsopp found the title for his study of the early afterlife of the book of Isaiah, *Opening the Sealed Book* (2006:1–27).

The hidden face of God (v. 17) is a theological theme much discussed in post-holocaust Jewish literature and we shall return to it again later (Isa 45:15). On this verse Rashi comments, 'There is no harsher prophecy than that time when Moses said, "And I will surely hide my face on that day"' (Deut 31: 18). Calvin focuses on 'waiting for the Lord' and labels the verse a 'remarkable passage … by meditating continually on it, we must be greatly encouraged'. For Cyril the prophet's words 'I will wait for the Lord' recall those of David (Ps 40; cf. 130:6), for Aquinas those of Micah (7:7), and for Luther the Letter to the Hebrews: here, as in Hebrews 2, there is contained the sum of the whole Christian doctrine: 'I will put my trust in Him' (Heb 2:13). In verse 18 not only the prophet's sons with the three ominous names are described as 'signs and portents in Israel' but also the prophet himself, an allusion, no doubt, to chapter 20 (Aquinas). The words 'I and the children whom God has given me' are quoted in Hebrews to prove that Christ is of the same flesh and blood as his disciples (Heb 2:13) and recall Peter's description of Christians as dependent on the Word as 'newborn babes' are wholly dependent on their mother's milk (1 Pet 2:2) (Luther).

Verses 19–22 are rather different in style and content from what precedes them, and the last words of verse 18 may be a conclusion to the original narrative in chapters 6–8 (Blenkinsopp). According to a rabbinic tradition, verses 19–22 were originally the words of Beeri, the father of Hosea (Hos 1:1) but were attached to Isaiah as they were not enough to make a whole book (Rashi). The repetition of the terms 'teaching' and 'testimony' from verse 18 ensures some continuity of thought: 'don't be tempted to consult the spirits of the dead – remember the words of the prophet' (Rashi). Jewish tradition identified the 'teaching' (*torah*) with the Law of Moses 'given to us as a testimony' (Tg). Christian commentators interpreted it as the gospel of Christ and even suggested that the words were spoken by Immanuel (Cyril).

Luther understands the 'law' as Scripture and the 'testimony' as preaching: the 'morning light' is the Word of God, an 'opening through which the light of dawn appears', a light of which blind unbelievers such as 'Pharisees and Sadducees, papists and heretics', are deprived (v. 20) (*LW* 33. 92). Similarly John Wesley cites verses 16–20 to illustrate that the will of God must be sought out, not 'by dreams and visions, particular impressions or sudden influences, but in the 'law and the testimony', that is in scripture (*Sermons* 2.54).

In Christian Bibles the chapter ends with a description of unrelenting darkness and destruction identified by most commentators with the Assyrian invasions of Palestine in the latter half of the eighth century and the exile of the ten northern tribes. Some interpret it as a reference to the fate of blind obstinate Jews, not only in the eighth century BCE (Jerome, Eusebius). Calvin understands the mention of 'turning their faces upwards' (v. 21) as a reference to the conversion of the Jews, facing such a fate that they finally turn to heaven (v. 21). Jewish commentators, on the other hand, reckon that, when this happens, God will not listen to them 'for the verdict will have been sealed' (Rashi; cf. Tg) and, in the Hebrew Bible, chapter 8 continues for another verse (9:1 in English versions), which completes the blow-by-blow account of national suffering with some explicit geographical details.

Galilee of the Nations (Isa 9:1)

In one of the earliest interpretations of this verse, where it is applied to the arrival of Jesus in Galilee (Matt 4:12–16), verse 1 (MT 8:23) is read along with the famous messianic prophecy beginning 'The people who walked in darkness' (vv. 2–7), and this is followed in modern versions, although ignored in many lectionaries. It is in prose and continues the description of 'thick darkness' from the previous chapter (Isa 8:22), and it is considered by Jewish commentators and modern scholars to have little directly to do with the poem that follows. It apparently refers to two

Isaiah Through the Centuries, First Edition. John F. A. Sawyer.
© 2018 John Wiley & Sons Ltd. Published 2020 by John Wiley & Sons Ltd.

enemy invasions into the Northern Kingdom, identified with some certainty as a Syrian invasion under Hazael or Ben Hadad (cf. Isa 7:1–2; 2 Kings 13:3), and then the more substantial and well-documented Assyrian invasion under Tiglath Pileser III in 732 BCE (2 Kgs 15:29). The later one resulted in the establishment of three Assyrian provinces, closely corresponding to the regions listed in the text: Duru (Dor, 'the way of the sea'), Gal'azu (Gilead, 'the land across the Jordan') and Magidu (Megiddo, 'Galilee of the nations') (Kaiser, Clements, Childs). Earlier commentators, including Ibn Ezra and Calvin, assume the reference was to Assyrian invasions in both cases. Rashi takes the first words of the verse, which are difficult, as referring to the Assyrians, 'for there is no weariness for the one who oppresses her' (cf. Tg), but suggests that 'Galilee' (Heb. *galil*) means the entire land of Israel, admired and envied by the nations (cf. Jer 3:19).

Christian interpreters by contrast found signs of hope for the future in verse 1. Modern translations begin 'But there will be no gloom for her that is in anguish' (RSV; cf. Clements, Blenkinsopp) and, instead of 'did more grievously afflict' (AV Heb. *hikbid*), several commentators read 'will make glorious' (Luther, Duhm, Kaiser, Brueggemann; cf. RSV, NJB), contrasting God's action 'in the former time' with what he will do 'in the latter time'. This appears to be how verse 1 was understood in Matthew 4:15, where the verbs are omitted. In the York Mystery Plays Isaiah comes on stage to tell us 'he preached in Naphtali, that land, and Zebulun … and said a light should on them land … now see I God this same has sent. This light comes all of Christ' (Beadle and King 1999: 239). The Septuagint diverges from the Hebrew and reads 'Drink this first, do it quickly, O country of Zebulon and Naphthali', and the Church Fathers readily applied this to Christ. When he was among the people of Galilee, he 'gave them the cup of salvation and wine which rejoices the heart of man, the gospel of Christ' (Cyril). This is what Isaiah meant when he said the 'people that walked in darkness have seen a great light', for Jesus Christ is the Light of the World (John 8:12; Jerome).

For Unto Us a Child Is Born (Isa 9:2–7)

The prophecy celebrating the birth of a Davidic prince (vv. 2–7; MT vv. 1–6) may have been associated with the birth of Hezekiah. Jewish commentators note the appropriateness of the name 'prince of peace' (v. 6) since 'there will be peace and security in his days' (2 Chron 32:22). The 'great light' (v. 2) refers to the miraculous defeat of Sennacherib and the 'yoke of his burden' (v. 4) to the heavy Assyrian tribute which had oppressed Hezekiah (Rashi). 'You have aggrandised the nation' (v. 3) refers to the respect Israel will gain among the nations witnessing the miracle, and 'increased its joy' to the celebrations in Jerusalem, although a negative in the Hebrew text (Kethib *lo* 'not' AV; Qere *lo* 'for it, its' RSV) reminds us that Hezekiah's joy was not complete since he knew that 'everything in his palace would be carried off to Babylon' (Isa 39:5) (Rashi).

Jewish interpreters, concerned to maintain the distinction between the Messiah and God, interpret most of the names in verse 6 (MT v. 5) as referring to God, not the king (Rashi, Kimḥi; cf. Tg) (Chilton 1987: 21), and modern Jewish translations differ strikingly from the Christian tradition: He has been named 'The Mighty God is planning grace, the Eternal Father, the peaceable ruler' (JPS). Ibn Ezra, on the other hand, carefully demonstrates the appropriateness of each name to Hezekiah. 'From this time forth and for ever' is not to be taken literally (cf. 1 Sam 1:22; Rashi), or else implies that, thanks to Hezekiah, the line of David will last for ever (Ibn Ezra). Today *pele yoʻez* appears in a street name in Jerusalem (Plate 8).

Christian interpretations of the prophecy go back to the beginning, although, perhaps surprisingly, the rich messianic imagery is not developed in the New Testament (Matt 4:15–16; cf. Luke 1:79). It seems likely that the passage was quoted in Matthew for apologetic reasons, the emphasis being primarily on

PLATE 8   *Reḥov Pele Yoʻez* (Isa 9:6) 'Wonderful Counsellor Street' in the Yemin Moshe district of Jerusalem.

Christ's mission to the gentiles ('Galilee of the nations') (Gundry 1982: 59–61; W.D. Davies 1988: 379–386). The Church Fathers found here one of the most explicit predictions of the Nativity of Christ (Eusebius), and from early on it has held an important place in the Christmas lectionary (*ORM, RCL, OSB*). It begins with the coming of the light of the Risen Christ into the world to take away the blindness of ignorance (Leo the Great, *Sermon* 25.3) or to bring hope to the 'people who dwelt in the land of the shadow of death' (MT, LXX, Vg, AV; 'deep darkness' RSV) (Origen, *Commentary on John* 13.134; Ambrose, *On Paradise* 5:29). In the Gospel of Nicodemus it describes the Harrowing of Hell (J. K. Elliott 1993: 186) and in *Piers Plowman* the moment when Lucifer was blinded and 'the people that sat in darkness sang 'Behold the Lamb of God' (John 1:36) (Langland 1959: 114, 264). It also inspired the fifth of the 'O Antiphons' sung in Advent (cf. Isa 60:1–2; see comm. on Isa 7:14).

For some the breaking of the 'rod of the oppressor' (v. 4) refers to the end of the reign of Satan (Cyril), for others, to the end of the tyranny of the law (1 Cor 15:56) (Luther). 'The government will be upon his shoulder' (v. 6) refers to Christ bearing the cross of our salvation (Justin, *First Apology* 35: Cyril); the symbol of his dominion is a cross carried on his back rather than 'a crown on his head or a sceptre in his hand or some royal apparel' (Tertullian, *Against Marcion* 3.19). The prophet then announces, for a third time, the birth of a son (cf. 7:14–15; 8:3–4) (Eusebius), both a 'child' with reference to his age and a 'son' with reference to the 'fullness of the godhead' (Ambrose, *On Satyrus* 1.12; cf. Calvin).

The Septuagint version of the rest of this verse differs strikingly from the Hebrew. As in the Jewish Targum, none of the names in the Hebrew text is given to the child: 'his name is called the messenger of great counsel: for I will bring peace upon the princes, and health to him.' God, who gives wondrous counsel, is a mighty God and an everlasting Father, while "the prince of peace" is Hezekiah's name. This was a problem for Augustine since Christ is God, not an angel (*Sermon* 7.3), but Cyril explains the name by reference to John 3:34. Jerome found six names in the Hebrew text by separating the first two: 'Wonderful, Counsellor, God, Mighty, Everlasting Father and Prince of Peace', but most commentators treat 'Mighty God' as one name, giving a total of five (Calvin, Henry, Lowth; cf. AV). Modern scholars on linguistic grounds treat 'wonderful counsellor' as a single name (RSV, NJB), giving a total of four, but detect the remains of a fifth in two as yet unexplained letters at the beginning of verse 7 (Roberts). This would then give a possible parallel with Egyptian royal protocol where the king was given five royal names at his enthronement (Kaiser, Clements).

The miraculous birth of a 'Wonderful Counsellor' (*pele yo'ez*) is described in a hymn found at Qumran (1QH 11:7; *DSSE* 265) and the 'Prince of Peace' was a title given to Hezekiah because 'peace and truth will be in his days' (Rashi). Although the names do not appear in the New Testament, there have been numerous christological interpretations. He was called 'Wonderful' (Heb. *pele* 'a wonder') because it is a wonder that God should show Himself as a Babe (Ephrem, *Hymns on the Nativity* 1). The 'Mighty God' justifies the Virgin Mary's title 'Mother of God' (Theodoret, *Letter* 152). The 'Prince of Peace' came to be so closely associated with Jesus in English that modern Jewish translations avoided it with 'the Ruler of Peace' (JPS 1917) and 'a peaceable ruler' (JPS 1978).The claim that he will bring endless peace into the world (v. 7) is much commented on. According to John Chrysostom it refers to the peace of Christ (cf. John 14:27) (*Demonstration against the Pagans* 2:8–10). Bede argues that the prophecy was fulfilled because Christ was born during the Pax Romana, which made it possible for preachers of the gospel to travel wherever they wished (*Four Books on 1 Samuel* 4.24). For Luther we are the 'government of Christ whom he carries on his shoulders' and the names 'wonderful ... mighty ... peace' refer as much to his kingdom on earth as to Christ himself (Rom 5:1; Phil 4:7; cf. Calvin). Since the Second Vatican Council, the title 'Prince of Peace' and Isaiah's vision of universal justice and peace have been interpreted more literally as a call to fight for social justice throughout the world (Miranda 1977: 172–173).

Puer natus is the introit for Christmas Day (v. 6; Ps 97:1; *MR* 29) and the refrain in William Dunbar's macaronic poem 'On the Nativity' (see comm. on *Rorate* Isa 45:8). Musical settings include the Christmas Mass *Puer nobis natus est* (A boy is born to us) by Thomas Tallis (1554), a William Byrd motet (1607) and a Bach Cantata composed for Christmas Day in 1712 or 1713 (*BWV* 142). Probably the best known is Handel's setting in his *Messiah* (1742). Following a bass recitative ('For behold darkness shall cover the earth' (Isa 60:2)) and the aria ('The people that walked in darkness' (Isa 9:2)), the choral fugue 'For Unto Us a Child is Born' emphasises that this birth is for us by accenting the beats 'us ... born ... us ... given ... us ... given' (A. Davies 2007: 481–484), and concludes with the five royal names sung fortissimo in unison. The title 'Prince of Peace' figures in numerous songs and hymns, including Charles Wesley's 'Hark the Herald Angels Sing' (1739) and the gospel song 'Ain't Gonna Study War No More', which contains the words 'Gonna talk with the Prince of Peace – down by the riverside' (cf. 2:4). A popular verse translation of the whole prophecy by John Morison, beginning 'The race that long in darkness pined', is sung to a variety of melodies (*EH* 43; *CH4* 290).

Verse 6 is one of three texts most commonly associated with Isaiah in Christian art (cf. 7:14 and 11:1). In the *Presentation of the Child Jesus at the Temple* (Luke 2:22–38), by Lorenzo Costa (1502), the prophet Anna in the foreground holds a tablet on which texts from Isaiah (53:8; 9:6) and Psalms (105:1, 5), are inscribed in Hebrew, with the word *zeh* (this) inserted twice: '*this* is the child born to us, *this* is the son given to us!' (Haitovsky 1994; Sawyer 2011a: 366–367). Other examples include the early twelfth-century Klosterneuburg Altar (Schiller 1971: 110), the *Biblia Pauperum* (*BP* 51) and a recent Christmas piece from the Lindisfarne Scriptorium (Plate 9). An image of the Infant Jesus as *Imperator Mundi* (emperor of the world) in a painting by Mantegna (*c*.1430–1506) may have been inspired by verse 7 (*multiplicabitur euis imperium*) (Lightbrown 1986: 148) (Plate 10).

PLATE 9   'And his name will be called Wonderful Counsellor … Prince of Peace' (Isa 9:6). Painting by Mary Fleeson (2016), www.lindisfarne-scriptorium.co.uk. Reproduced with kind permission of www.lindisfarne-scriptorium.co.uk.

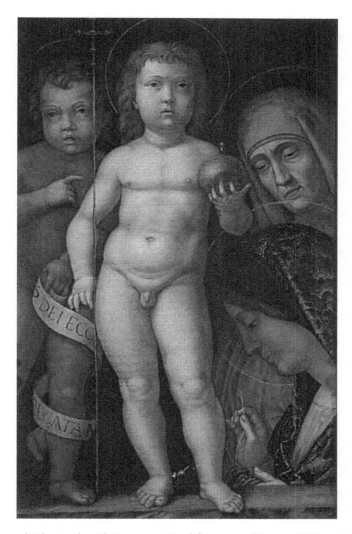

PLATE 10 'Holy Family with *Imperator Mundi* [emperor of the world]' (Isa 9:6–7). Painting by Andrea Mantegna (*c.*1500) in the Musée du Petit Palais, Paris.

Wickedness Burns Like a Fire (Isa 9:8–21)

The rest of chapter 9 (vv. 8–21; MT 7–20), picks up where chapter 5 left off and consists of three stanzas of a poem on the wickedness and arrogance of Judah's northern neighbours, Ephraim and Samaria, each ending with the same refrain about God's unrelenting anger (vv. 12, 17, 21; cf. 5:25). The first refers to a prophetic warning (v. 8), perhaps that of Amos (Blenkinsopp), and to a disaster that has already struck, perhaps the earthquake referred to at the beginning of the Book of Amos (1:1). Rashi explains 'the adversaries of Rezin', king of Syria (7:8), in verse 11 (MT 10; cf. AV) as a reference to the king of Assyria, incited by the Lord, along with forces from Syria and the coast (vv. 11–12), to invade Israel. The people's defiance is expressed in terms of rebuilding what has been destroyed even more strongly and expensively than before (v. 10). The Targum interprets this as a metaphor for finding new leaders and purchasing new possessions even finer than those taken into exile, while Pachomius compares this to the arrogance of the Tower of Babel story (*Letter* 3.10). Calvin draws a parallel with the 'luxury ... lawless passions ... and profligacy' of his own day and people's refusal to learn from the disasters that have afflicted Europe.

Some of the Church Fathers, including Gregory the Great, applied the first words of this prophecy (v. 8) to the rejection of Christ (the 'Word') by the Jews ('Jacob') and his acceptance by the gentiles (the 'new Israel'); Gregory also identifies the rebuilding after destruction as the 'Holy Church built from square stones' (v. 10) (*Homilies on Ezekiel*, 2.9.5). Similarly the second stanza (vv. 13–17) was interpreted by Christian writers as referring to the Roman destruction of Jerusalem, the 'head' signifying the priests and elders, and the 'tail' the mass of the Jews who blindly followed their lead (Cyril). The young people, widows and orphans are as guilty as their leaders and are shown no mercy (v. 17). The word translated 'godless' (Heb. *ḥaneph*) is rendered 'hypocrite' by Jerome and reminded Luther of Christ's words to the scribes and Pharisees: 'you brood of vipers' (Matt 23:29–36).

The third stanza (vv. 18–21) further spells out the horrors of war and the monstrous behaviour human beings are capable of (Calvin). The Hebrew text reads 'each devours the flesh of his arm' (v. 19; cf. LXX, Vg), which is 'extraordinary' enough (Cyril), but parallels elsewhere in the Bible (Jer 19:9) and the ancient Near East suggest that the correct reading should be 'the flesh of his neighbour' (RSV). This is understood metaphorically by some (Tg, Luther, Blenkinsopp), but according to others as a literal reference to cannibalism (Lowth, Duhm). Luther compares Manasseh joining forces with Ephraim against Judah (v. 21) to Pilate and Herod becoming friends (Luke 23:12).

After the poem on the anger of God directed at Samaria (9:8–21), a chapter beginning with a 'woe oracle' (vv. 1–4) and ending with the same refrain (5:25; 9:12, 17, 21) is addressed to the leaders of Judah. Scholars suggest it was originally the first of the 'woes' and locate it immediately after the Song of the Vineyard (5:1–7) (Barth 1977; Clements, Blenkinsopp). The rest of this very long chapter attacks the arrogance of the Assyrian king (vv. 5–19) and offers hope that a remnant of Israel will survive (vv. 20–27). It ends with the graphic account of an advancing army, halted within sight of Jerusalem (vv. 28–32), and the dramatic metaphor of mighty trees being cut down with an axe (vv. 33–34).

Isaiah Through the Centuries, First Edition. John F. A. Sawyer.
© 2018 John Wiley & Sons Ltd. Published 2020 by John Wiley & Sons Ltd.

Woe to Those in Power! (Isa 10:1–4)

The prophet attacks the country's leaders for using their authority to deprive defenceless women and children of their legal rights (Rashi; Calvin). Some interpret the verse as referring to the scribes and Pharisees who distorted scripture and exploit the poor and needy (Cyril). Jerome applied it to those who in his own day were writing heretical books, and this is how it was understood throughout medieval Europe. Luther cynically quotes Solomon's words 'Of making many books there is no end' (Eccl 12:2), and adds, 'This is as true now as it was then'. Modern political activists have applied this prophecy to present-day governments and policymakers (Gutiérrez 1974: 293) and have noted that women are explicitly mentioned among the victims of such institutionalized oppression (Ruether 1983: 32). The punishment for such abuse of power will be severe (vv. 3–4). There will be no escape even for those who try to survive by hiding among the corpses and pretending to be dead (Ibn Ezra). Verse 3 inspired a poem by Francis Quarles ending,

> How will your eyes endure this day?
> Hills will be dead and mountains will not hear;
> There be no caves, no corners there
> To shade your souls from fire, to shield your hearts from fear. (1777: 80–81)

The refrain about the unremitting anger and outstretched hand of God is repeated one final time (v. 4; cf. Isa 5:25; 9:12, 17, 21).

Woe to Assyria! (Isa 10:5–19)

The next prophecy begins with the same word as is used in verse 1, and some commentators take it as 'Woe to Assyria' (Rashi; cf. LXX, Vg, Tg, NJB), a continuation of the 'woe oracle' (vv. 1–4). Others prefer the more neutral 'O' (AV) or 'Ah' (RSV) and take it as the beginning of a separate prophecy about Assyria (vv. 5–19). It is a dramatic illustration of the prophetic view of history: 'these things don't happen by chance' (Calvin) and God sometimes uses evil agents to achieve his aims (Theodoret). There are indications in the Septuagint that the translator understood the passage as referring to events in the Hellenistic period (van der Kooij 1981: 34–38), but the Hebrew is usually dated to the reign of Hezekiah. The cities listed in verse 9 were conquered by Shalmaneser V and Sennacherib, although the reference to graven images in Jerusalem (vv. 10–11) must go back to the reign of Ahaz because Hezekiah removed them (2 Kgs

18:4) (Cyril). The Assyrian's blasphemy (vv. 10–11) is all the greater because he puts Israel's God on the same level as the false gods of the heathen (Calvin).

God's overall control of events (v. 12) and his limitation of the Assyrian king's power (vv. 15–19) anticipate the comfort soon to be spelled out in more detail (vv. 20–27) (Eusebius, Luther). The words of the king rise to a hysterical climax (vv. 13–14), making him into the archetype of doomed human pride: 'none of my might is from the Holy One Blessed be He' (Rashi). He is like the worshippers of the Golden Calf (cf. Ps 106:19–23) (Ibn Ezra). Christian commentators compare him to Satan (Jerome) or a dragon to be 'drawn with a hook by the Saviour' (cf. Job 41:1) (Athanasius, *Life of St Antony* 24). The dramatic image of a human leader threatening to conquer the world and to treat its inhabitants like eggs in an abandoned nest (v. 14) is quoted by a number of writers in various contexts (John Cassian, *Institutes* 12.8; Theodoret, *On Divine Providence* 10.54).

But the Assyrian king is a mere instrument in God's hands (vv. 15–19) and, when his task is complete, he will be cast aside 'as a father commonly breaks or throws away the rod with which he chastised his son' (Calvin). The mention of a disease (v. 16) is taken by most commentators, Jewish and Christian, to refer to the miraculous defeat of Sennacherib (cf. Isa 37:36). Ibn Ezra says the 'light of Israel' (v. 17) is merely an expression for God or his angel, but Rashi takes it to be a reference to the Torah, which, in the hands of Hezekiah, became fire for Sennacherib. For Christian commentators the verse shows that the Holy Spirit is not only light but fire: 'for God is a consuming fire' (Deut 4:24). The conflagration that decimated the Assyrians, is taken literally by some as a reference to the burning of the corpses (Luther), but the destruction of a forest of great trees is also a graphic metaphor for the downfall of the arrogant (cf. vv. 33–34). According to an ancient Jewish tradition there were only ten survivors, because 'a child can write them down' (v. 19) and 'there is no small child who cannot write a Yodh' (the smallest Hebrew character; cf. Matt 5:18) which denotes the number '10' (Rashi).

Be Not Afraid of Assyria, My People (Isa 10:20–34)

The next passage on the 'remnant of Israel' (vv. 21–22) is seen by some as an early interpretation of the Shear Jashub narrative (7:3), dated by some to the time of Josiah (Clements), but for most recent commentators it is post-exilic (Wildberger). A parallel to verses 22–23 ('destruction is decreed') in the Book of Daniel (9:26–27) has been noted (Blenkinsopp 2006: 229–230), and a fragmentary commentary on the passage found at Qumran identifies the sect as the 'remnant' who had survived the exile and who are the true inheritors of the promise to Abraham (v. 22; cf. Gen 12:1–3; 22:17) (*DSSE* 498; Blenkinsopp 2006: 113–119). Isaiah's prophecy that a time of destruction is still to come and the final act of judgement (vv. 22–23) in a very short time (v. 25) was applied by the sect to their apocalyptic belief that, under the leadership of the messianic Prince of the Congregation, they would soon throw off the yoke of the Assyrians, that is, the Romans (cf. Isa 31:8), and make their final assault on Jerusalem.

Jewish interpreters explain the change in Israel's fortunes as due to Hezekiah's righteousness: Shear Jashub ('the remnant that shall repent') shall wash away with righteousness the decreed destruction (v. 22) (Rashi). The last words of verse 27 in Hebrew read 'the yoke shall be destroyed because of oil' (cf. AV, Vg), which 'yields no sense' (Gray), but is taken as a reference to the 'anointed one' in the Targum, and elsewhere is explained as a reference to 'Hezekiah's oil which burnt in the synagogues and in the study-halls' (cf. Prov 25:1) (Rashi). Verses 28–34 describe Sennacherib's advance on Jerusalem, some of the place names identifiable, others perhaps descriptive terms like *gebim* (pits) (Ibn Ezra). They will be cut down like tall trees 'with an axe ... by a mighty one' (v. 34 MT, AV, NJB), that is, by the hand of the angel of the Lord (cf. Isa 37:36) (Ibn Ezra). 'By a mighty one' is interpreted by Rashi as 'through the merits of Hezekiah'. Modern experts point out, however, that the route of the advancing army, described here as passing through Aiath, Migron, Michmash and Geba (vv. 28–29), does not correspond to Sennacherib's well-documented route, and the text probably refers to the much earlier Syro-Ephraimite campaign of 734 BCE (2 Kgs 16:5; Isa 7:1–9) (Roberts).

The earliest Christian interpretation is Paul's application of the passage to the tragedy of the rejection of the Jews: 'Isaiah cries out concerning Israel ... only a remnant will be saved' (Rom 9:27–28). In the same context he quotes other verses from Isaiah comparing the fate of Israel to Sodom and Gomorrah (cf. Isa 1:9) and saying that this is because they have 'stumbled over the stumbling stone' (Rom 9:32; cf. Isa 8:14). The Church Fathers identified the remnant with Jews who believed in Christ, starting with the twelve apostles (Augustine, *City of God*, 17.5). The Greek version of verse 23 has a variation suggesting that the word of the Lord will be cut short (cf. L. *abbreviationem*), and Christian commentators have suggested that this refers to Christ's summary of all the law and the prophets in two commandments (Matt 22:35–40) (Tertullian, *Against Marcion* 4:16) or the Lord's Prayer as a summary of all prayers (Cyprian, *The Lord's Prayer* 28). They found a reference in verse 27 to the 'oil of anointing' and interpreted it either as the oil of the Holy Spirit by which we are liberated from the bondage of our slavery (Gregory, *Morals on Job* 4.19.24), or as Christ since 'anointing is the name given to his kingdom' (Ps 45:7; 89:20; Isa 61:1) (Calvin).

The Greek version of verses 31–32 adds the word *parakaleite* 'comfort' twice, anticipating the more famous passage immediately following the Hezekiah narrative later in the book (Isa 40:1 LXX; cf. 13:2). The future destruction of the forest (vv. 33–34) is interpreted by many as the miraculous death of the Assyrians in 701 (Isa 37:36) (Aquinas, Luther, Lowth, Clements), but others take 'Lebanon' as the 'usual' term for the Temple (cf. Zech 11:1–2; Eusebius) and take the passage as a threat against Judah (Kaiser, Wildberger) executed both by the Babylonians in 586 BCE (Calvin) and by the Romans in 70 CE (Jerome). Bob Marley's song 'Small Axe' on the album *Burnin'* (1973), takes up the 'remnant' theme and tells the 'big trees' in the world who boast and play smart that 'we are the small axe ready to cut you down' (vv. 33–34) (*BiM* 222–223).

Isaiah 11

The messianic prophecy at the beginning of this chapter foretells the coming of a king to the throne of David on whom the spirit of the Lord will rest and who will establish a reign of peace and justice over the whole earth (vv. 1–9). Parallels with Davidic prophecies from a later period (e.g. Jer 23:5–6; 33:14–22; Ezek 37:24–28) and verbal correspondences with Isaiah 56–66 (e.g. 'holy mountain' v. 9; cf. 56:7; 57:13; 65:11, 25; 66:20) have led many modern scholars to date the passage to the reign of Josiah (Vermeylen) or the post-exilic period (Clements), though some assign it to Isaiah in his old age as his 'swan song' (Duhm; cf. von Rad 1965; Wildberger). More recently it has been argued that,

Isaiah Through the Centuries, First Edition. John F. A. Sawyer.
© 2018 John Wiley & Sons Ltd. Published 2020 by John Wiley & Sons Ltd.

unlike the prophecies in chapters 7 and 9, where a historical background is identified, this 'messianic promise transcends the initial eighth-century setting' so that precise dating of the passage is less important (Childs; cf. Blenkinsopp). Despite obvious linguistic and thematic differences between verses 1–5 and verses 6–9 (Barth 1977: 60–63), few commentators now question the literary unity of the passage. The power of the spirit of Yahweh both to establish justice and righteousness in human society (vv. 3–5; cf. 32:15) and to influence animal behaviour (vv. 6–9; cf. Isa 34:16) has also been noted (Marlow and Barton 2009: 241).

The Noble Stem of Jesse (Isa 11:1–5)

The image of new growth appearing on the tree of Jesse, David's father (Ruth 4:22; Matt 1:6), against the background of the giant trees cut down at the end of the previous chapter (cf. Isa 6:13), denotes a new king who would bring hope to the people of Israel, whether already in exile in Assyria (Rashi) or faced with the threat of Assyrian invasion (Ibn Ezra). Many Jewish commentators see a reference to Hezekiah in these verses, his wisdom and strength (v. 2), according to Ibn Ezra, recalling that of Joshua (Josh 1:6–7; cf. 2 Chron 32:7–8), and his girdle of righteousness (v. 5) referring to the fact that he will be surrounded by righteous people, clinging to him like a girdle (Rashi; cf. Tg). For some it recalls the story of the unusual wisdom of Joseph (Gen 41:38–42:17) (Mann 1971: 1, 313–315). For others the prophecy goes beyond eighth-century politics (cf. 1 En 49:3; TLev 18:7): the rod symbolizes the royal power of the Messiah, yet to come, while the reference in verse 2 to the spirit of God resting upon him suggests that the 'King Messiah was born at the creation of the world' (cf. Gen 1:2) (*PesR* 33.6). In the annual Jewish lectionary the passage, beginning at 10:32 and continuing to the end of the Song of Thanksgiving in chapter 12, is read on the last day of Passover (*JSB*).

In Christian tradition from the beginning verses 1–2 have played a central role, starting with Paul (Rom 15:12), where Christ is referred to as the 'root of Jesse' (cf. Rev 5:5; 22:16). Some also believe that the prophecy referred to in Matthew 2:23 that 'He shall be called a Nazarene' (Heb. *noṣri*) is another, since the Hebrew word for 'branch' is *neṣer*. The linguistic evidence for this was questioned already by Jerome, but Bede maintains that the verse refers to the 'Redeemer who would be conceived in Nazareth' (*Homilies on the Gospels* 1.6), and modern commentators on Matthew 2:23 still refer to this famous Isaiah passage. The passage figures in the Advent lectionary of some Churches (*ORM*, RCL) and in the Christmas Eve liturgy of others (*OSB*). A choral setting in the cantata *Flight into Egypt* (1986) by the American composer

John Harbison brings together verse 1 and 'like a root out of dry ground' (Isa 53:2) (*BiM* 83–84).

At first both terms, 'rod' (AV) or 'shoot' (RSV) and 'branch' are taken as references to Christ as the Davidic Messiah descended from the tree of Jesse (Tertullian, *Against Marcion* 3:17). Justin connects the verse to the 'star prophecy' (Num 24:17): 'A star shall arise from Jacob and a blossom from the root of Jesse' (*First Apology* 32). The 'rod' suggested to Cyril of Alexandria the rod and staff that comfort the Psalmist (Ps 23:4) and the shepherd that lays down his life for his sheep (John 10:11), but also the discipline meted out to those who disobey him (cf. v. 4; Isa 10:5; Ps 2:9; Prov 13:24). In Greek the second term is translated *anthos* 'flower' and is compared by many of the Church Fathers to the language of the Song of Solomon where 'the Lord and Saviour says, "I am the blossom of the field and a lily of the valleys"' (Cant 2:1 LXX) (Ambrose, *On the Holy Spirit* 2.5.38; cf. Jerome, Cyril). This is what Paul is referring to when he speaks of Christians as spreading the fragrance of the knowledge of Christ everywhere (2 Cor 2:14) (Cyril).

Struck by the similarity between the two Latin words *virga* 'rod' and *virgo* 'virgin', however, Christian commentators traditionally interpret the first part of the verse as referring to the Virgin Mary: 'the root is the family of the Jews, the rod is Mary and the flower is her Christ' (Ambrose, *On the Patriarchs* 4:19–20; cf. Jerome, Leo the Great, *Sermon* 24.1). Like Aaron's rod that miraculously blossomed without being watered (Num 18:8), so the rod 'signifies the Virgin and the blossom the Virgin Birth' (Bernard of Clairvaux, *Homilies in Praise of the Virgin Mother* 2.5). A medieval Latin composition, arranged for a capella choir by Bruckner (1885), puts it this way: *Virga Jesse floruit: Virgo Deum et hominem genuit* (the Rod of Jesse blossomed; the Virgin gave birth to God and Man). The fifteenth-century German poem *Es ist ein' Ros' entsprungen* beautifully develops this interpretation and is today a well-known Christmas carol in a setting by Praetorius (1609) (*SNOBC* 100–104). The 'root of Jesse' features in the third of the 'O Antiphons' (see comm. on Isa 7:14).

The prophecy that 'the spirit of the Lord shall rest upon him' (v. 2; cf. Isa 61:2) is fulfilled in Christ (John 1:32–33) (Jerome) and the apostles (1 Pet.4:14). The Spirit could find no place to rest among human beings … until the Word of God became man (Cyril; cf. Origen, *Homilies on Numbers* 6.3). In the original Hebrew, verse 2 defines the Spirit of the Lord in a list of six spiritual gifts, to which 'fear of God', repeated at the beginning of verse 3, may be added, giving a total of seven. The Septuagint ensures that this is how the passage should be understood by translating the 'fear of God' at the end of verse 2 as 'piety' (*eusebeia*). The Church Fathers then found in this verse scriptural authority for their doctrine of the seven gifts of the spirit developed by Augustine, Gregory the Great, Thomas Aquinas and many others. Already in the Book of Revelation the 'seven lamps of fire burning before the throne are the seven Spirits of God' (Rev 4:5). Ambrose pictures the Holy Spirit as a river dividing into seven channels (*On the Holy Spirit* 1.16.159). Augustine attempted to correlate them with the Beatitudes (Matt 5:3–9; *On the Sermon on the Mount* 1.4.11), while Gregory compares them to the seven steps on the way to heaven from the fear of God to wisdom, listed in reverse order by the prophet who 'reasoned from heavenly realities to the lower things' (*Homilies on Ezekiel* 2.7.7). Bede contrasts this description of Christ, receiving the fullness of the spirit, with Paul's discussion of the saints each allocated one specific spiritual gift (1 Cor 12:8–11; cf. Rom 12:6–8) (*Homilies on the Gospels* 1.2). Luther makes no mention of the number seven but rather stresses that these are the spiritual weapons of Christ's kingdom, while Calvin rejects the papists' application of this verse to their doctrine of sevenfold grace both as a numerical blunder and as a limitation of the manifold gifts of the Spirit.

Mendelssohn combines verse 2 with Isa 41:25 and 42:1 in one of the final choruses of his oratorio *Elijah* (1846), and verses 1–2 are set as a soprano solo in Otto Goldschmidt's choral work *Ruth* (1867) (*BiM* 201). Liberation theologians used these verses, along with verses from Numbers 11, Isaiah 28 and Micah 3, to prove that 'the spirit of Yahweh is the spirit of interhuman justice – definitive total justice' (Miranda 1974: 220). The Latin technical term *sacrum septenarium* 'seven gifts of the Spirit, sevenfold sacramental grace' appears in a hymn for Pentecost beginning *Veni Sancte Spiritus*, attributed to Archbishop Stephen Langton and set to music by many composers (*BiM* 255). The tradition also figures in Bishop Cosin's popular hymn, based on a ninth-century Latin composition, 'Come Holy Ghost, our souls inspire ... Thou the anointing spirit art who dost thy sevenfold gifts impart' (*EH* 153 *CH4* 586 *GtG* 278).

In Christian art the Jesse Tree, derived from these two verses and the genealogies of Christ in the Gospels (Matt 1:1–17; Luke 3:23–38), typically shows Jesse, David's father, lying on his side, a tree emerging from his body, recalling Eve coming out of Adam's side (Gen 2:22) (A. Watson 1934; Schiller 1971: 14–22). In the branches are the ancestors of Christ with the Virgin Mary at the top and Christ enthroned with seven doves symbolizing the seven gifts of the spirit. No doubt influenced by medieval preoccupation with ancestry, royal lineages and heredity, it appears most frequently in stained glass windows and illuminated manuscripts from the eleventh to the sixteenth centuries (Plate 11). Among the earliest are the illuminated initial letter of the Book of Isaiah in the twelfth-century Lambeth Bible, and a magnificent lancet window in Chartres Cathedral where the 'melody of the branches ascends in beautiful arabesques to explode in the seven gifts of the spirit' (Lee, Sedden and Stephen 1976: 37). Several of the great medieval cathedrals, including Chartres, Rheims and Amiens, have a Jesse Tree built into the architecture of their façades, showing

PLATE 11   'Tree of Jesse' (Isa 11:1). Oxford Psalter *c*.1200. Reproduced with kind permission of the Bavarian State Library.

various heralds of Christ, including Isaiah, each clutching a branch of the tree, on either side of the West Door, with the Virgin Mary, to whom the building is dedicated, enthroned above them. A fourteenth-century English example shows the tree in stone and the ancestors in stained glass (Plate 12).

Among many significant variations is the portrayal of Christ crucified at the top instead of the Virgin Mary or Christ enthroned, the wood of the tree of Jesse becoming the wood of the cross (Schiller 1972: 135–136), as for example in the Brougham Triptych, a sixteenth-century Belgian carved wooden altar-piece now in Carlisle Cathedral. This striking image also inspired Victor Hugo's

PLATE 12   'Tree of Jesse' (Isa 11:1) window in Dorchester Abbey, Oxfordshire (1330).

poem 'Booz endormi' (1859), in which Boaz dreams of an oak tree coming out of his belly, reaching up to the sky with a long line of people on it, David at one end and Christ crucified at the other: 'Un roi chantait en bas, en haut mourait un dieu' (Lucas 1957: 355–358).

After the Jesse Tree passage the prophecy describes the kind of government the new king will impose on his subjects (vv. 4–5). He will govern with exemplary justice, showing particular concern for the poor and ruthless in his punishment of the wicked. According to Bede, this is what Christ was referring to when he said: 'Blessed are the poor for yours is the kingdom of heaven' (Luke 6:20) (*Four Books on 1 Samuel* 1.7.6). In the phrase 'with the rod of his mouth' the Hebrew has a different word for 'rod' from the term used in verse 1, but the Latin has *virga* in both cases and the powerful overtones of this 'rod of Jesse', which punishes the wicked and establishes justice in the world, sometimes drown the gentler image of the Jesse Tree, as in the famous Advent hymn *O come, O come, Immanuel*: 'O come thou rod of Jesse, free thine own from Satan's tyranny'. The Greek omits the word 'rod' here and Jerome recalls that the words 'by the breath of his lips he shall slay the wicked' (v. 4) are applied by Paul to the way Christ will dispose of Satan (2 Thess 2:8), while for others they recall the image of a two-edged sword issuing from his mouth in the Apocalypse (Rev 1:16; cf. Matt 10:34; Eusebius). Calvin tells us that the gospel is 'sharper than a two-edged sword' (Heb 4:12) and that Isaiah refers as much to preachers of the word as to Christ (cf. Luke 10:16). For princes and rulers a belt (v. 5) is an emblem of authority (cf. Isa 14:5; Calvin), but Isaiah tells us the belt of Christ the king will be adorned with righteousness and truth (LXX) rather than gold and precious stones (Eusebius). Some cite Paul (2 Cor 10:4; Eph 6:10–17) and stress that Christ's kingdom is a spiritual kingdom, unlike any other, and the weapons we need to win the 'victory that overcomes the world' (1 John 5:4) are righteousness and faithfulness (Vg, RSV) (Luther).

The Peaceable Kingdom (Isa 11:6–9)

Many compare this prophecy with visions of a new creation going back before the Fall when 'wild beasts should obey and be subject to human beings and return to the diet that God originally gave them' (Irenaeus, *Against Heresies* 5.33.4; cf. Calvin). This is how the passage is interpreted in a later chapter of Isaiah (Isa 65:25) and in the Sibylline Oracles (*Sib.Or.* 3:788–795; *OTP* 1.379). Parallels are often quoted from classical texts about a future 'Golden Age' (Jerome), especially the Fourth Eclogue of Virgil, but all 'fall short of the beauty and elegance and variety of imagery' in the Isaiah passage (Lowth), and Alexander Pope's 'sacred eclogue' entitled *The Messiah* (1712) was inspired more by Isaiah than by Virgil. The scene is alluded to by Blake, Shelley, Henry James and others (*DBTEL* 456).

Other commentators favour an allegorical reading of the passage in which the wild beasts represent wicked oppressors tamed by Christ and able to live in harmony with the poor and weak (Chrysostom, *Demonstration against the Pagans* 6.8; cf. Calvin), an interpretation which nicely picks up the theme of verses 3–4. Others understand the wild beasts as referring to the barbarians and Greeks (Eusebius) or Jews (Cyril) transformed by the teachings of Christ.

Jerome applied the image of the 'wolf' to Paul the Benjaminite (Rom 11:1), 'a rapacious wolf' before his conversion (cf. Gen 49:27), and a lamb to Ananias who baptized him (Acts 9:11–18): perhaps it refers as much to Peter, to whom Christ said, 'Feed my lambs' (John 21:15). The prophecy is fulfilled in the Church where all will come together under one 'chief shepherd' (1 Pet 5:4; Cyril): 'behold the kind of charity that … melds and reforms such a diversity into one species of gold' (Gregory, *Homilies on Ezekiel* 2.4.3).

The 'little child' leading seven animals (v. 6) may be referred to in the striking expression 'shepherd of the seven' (*ro'eh shiv'ah*) in some versions of the medieval Jewish poem 'Ma'oz Tzur', sung at Hanukkah (Melamed 2016). For many Christian commentators 'a little child shall lead them' refers to Christ, already mentioned in Isaiah 9:6 (Jerome) and frequently described as a shepherd (Henry), but Calvin thinks instead of communities so obedient that their leaders will not need force or violence to restrain them (Calvin: cf. Cyril). Several commentators cite Jesus' words to his disciples as fulfilment of verse 8: 'Behold I have given you authority to tread upon serpents and scorpions and over all the power of the enemy and nothing shall hurt you' (Luke 10:19) (Jerome; Eusebius).

The final verse of this famous prophecy (v. 9), quoted in the Book of Habakkuk (2:14) and in the Testament of Levi (TLev. 18:5; *OTP* 1.794), predicts that 'the earth will be filled with the knowledge of the Lord as the waters cover the sea' and Christian commentators from all ages relate it to New Testament texts about the disciples going forth to all nations (Matt 28:19; cf. John 6:45) (Athanasius, *Against the Arians* 1.13.8) and predictions that 'at the name of Jesus every knee shall bow' (Phil 2:10) (Cyril). John Wesley's sermon entitled 'The General Spread of the Gospel' (1783) is an exposition of this verse (*Sermons* 2.481–499). It also provided the refrain for the hymn 'God is Working His Purpose Out', substituting 'glory' for 'knowledge' (cf. Hab 2:14) (see comm. on Isa 41:1).

Pictures showing beasts of prey consorting happily with their vulnerable victims are nowadays among the most familiar biblical images, but this was not the case before modern times. An interesting exception is a series of mosaics from late antiquity. Derived from pagan themes relating to the Golden Age, especially Orpheus, fifth-century Christian examples have been found in Jordan, Asia Minor and Corsica, including a leopard grazing peacefully beside a kid (v. 6) (Russell 1987: 70–74) (Plate 13), and an ox and a lion facing a table piled high with straw (v. 7) (Moracchini-Mazel 1967: 24–29). A kontakion by the sixth-century Greek poet Romanos contains a charming variation: 'a lamb carries a lion, a swallow an eagle and the servant her master' (*Romanos*; trans. Lash 1995: 17). Medieval examples include the thirteenth-century *Bible Moralisée*, which illustrates verses 6–9 in some detail but is strictly limited to

PLATE 13   'The leopard shall relax with the kid' (Isa 11:6 LXX). Mosaic floor of church in Anemurium, Turkey (*c*.500 CE). Reproduced with kind permission of Österreichische Akademie der Wissenschaften, Vienna.

Jerome's interpretation and portrays none of the global or political aspects of the scene so familiar to us today, and a sixteenth-century woodcut by the French Calvinist artist Georgette de Monteney, entitled *foedere perfecto* (the covenant complete), showing a lion, a lamb and a wolf eating together.

It is not until the early nineteenth-century that the passage gains its popularity, thanks to the paintings of the Quaker artist Edward Hicks. Over a period of about twenty years he painted nearly a hundred versions of 'The Peaceable Kingdom', of which about twenty-five have survived. The title was derived from a Bible illustration by the English artist Richard Westall, (Westall and Martin 1835: 141). This was as much an illustration of verse 1 as of verses 6–9, and the focus is on the little child holding a grapevine in his hand as a symbol of the Eucharist. In Hicks' paintings the emphasis gradually switched away from the child and away from Christian theology to the animals, seen as the warring elements in human nature coming together in perfect harmony. In some versions, for example, the child is a little girl, sometimes holding an olive branch instead of the sacramental vine, and the title becomes 'The Peaceable Kingdom with Liberty'. Another group entitled 'The Peaceable Kingdom of the

Lion' makes this interpretation even clearer, while in the background of several explicitly political versions, he depicts William Penn signing the peace treaty with the Native Americans in 1681. The American poet Daniel Hoffmann wrote a penetrating analysis of how Hicks handled 'Isaiah's verses' in 'To the maker of "A Peaceable Kingdom"' in *Brotherly Love* (New York 1981).

The influence of Hicks' 'The Peaceable Kingdom' has been profound. It is the title of a choral work by the American composer Randall Thompson (1936) (*BiM* 185–186), a novel by Jan de Hartog (1972), a collection of poems by Jon Silkin (1975) and a Christian ethics primer by Stanley Hauerwas (1983). The popular gospel song 'Peace in the Valley', written for Mahalia Jackson (1937), and frequently performed at funerals, is loosely based on verse 6 and Revelation 21 (*BiM* 185). The choral work *Children of God* (2004) by the American composer Daniel Kellogg focuses on the 'little child' (cf. Matt 18:3–4; Gen 22:1–19; 1 Sam 1–3) (*BiM* 46), while one of Emma Lou Diemer's *Four Biblical Settings* (1933) for organ is a musical interpretation of chapter 11 with allusions to Bach's motet *Jesu Meine Freude* (*BiM* 85). One of Stanford's six *Biblical Songs* (op.113 1909) for baritone and organ, entitled 'A Song of Peace', is a musical setting of verses 1–6 and 9–10 (*BiM* 33), and 'Isaiah the Prophet Has Written of Old' is a modern paraphrase of verses 6–9 and Isa 55:11–13 sung to an American folk melody (*CH4* 241; *GtG* 77).

The bronze Menorah presented by Britain to the young State of Israel in 1948, now standing opposite the Knesset, has a panel portraying Isaiah surrounded by wild beasts grazing peacefully with lambs, gazelles and other small animals (Plate 14). Three postage stamps showing scenes from verses 3–8 were issued in 1962 to celebrate the Jewish New Year (Plate 15). Vegetarians quote the passage, along with Isaiah 66:2–3, in defence of a 'peaceable kingdom' where the slaughter of animals for food will cease for ever (Skriver 1990: 108).

The Messianic Age (Isa 11:10–16)

Verses10–16 are an expansion of the preceding prophecy, picking up the themes of the 'root of Jesse' and the spread of his royal power to 'the four corners of the earth' (v. 12), as well as the 'remnant' of Israel from chapter 7 (v. 11, 16). The striking new term 'ensign, banner' (Heb. *nes*) is introduced (vv. 10, 12), and there is a Jewish tradition that this is a reference either to the solar miracle in the reign of Hezekiah which attracted the attention of the Babylonians (2 Chron 32:31; cf. Isa 38:8) or to the miracle of Sennacherib's defeat (Isa 36–37) (Ibn Ezra). Whatever the 'sign', in the world to come it is the gentiles who will be summoned to Jerusalem ('his dwelling' v. 10), not Israel, because Israel will no longer need the teaching of the Messiah (GenR XCVIII.9). The effect of the

PLATE 14   The prophet presiding over the Peaceable Kingdom (Isa 11:6–8). Panel on bronze menorah presented to the State of Israel by the British Government in 1956.

Lord's intervention in world history 'a second time' (v. 11) is that the remnant of the people of Israel will be able to return in safety to their homeland from Assyria, Egypt, Ethiopia and elsewhere. Rashi interprets 'the coastlands of the sea' as a reference to the Roman Empire. In modern times *nes 'ammim* (a banner to the peoples) (v. 10) is the name of an international and ecumenical kibbutz founded in northern Israel in 1963 to encourage dialogue between Israeli Jews and Arabs.

The earliest Christian interpretation of the passage is in Romans 15:9–12, where Paul picks up the theme of the Davidic ancestry of Christ in the words 'root of Jesse' (cf. Rom 1:3) and the transparent allusion to the resurrection in the Greek word *anistamenos* (the one who rises) (LXX) and portrays the gentiles joining together with Israel to praise Israel's God: 'Rejoice, O gentiles, with his people' (Deut 32:43). He follows the Greek 'in him shall the gentiles

PLATE 15 'The wolf shall dwell with the lamb...' (Isa 11:3–8). Israeli postage stamps celebrating Rosh Ha-Shanah (1962). Reproduced with kind permission of Israel Philatelic Society, Israel Postal Company.

hope' (Heb. 'seek') (v. 10 LXX) but significantly omits 'in that day', clearly because he believes the day when 'the root of Jesse ... will rise to rule the gentiles' has already arrived (Wagner 2006: 100–103).

For the Church Fathers the 'root of Jesse' in verse 10 is Christ who will be 'an ensign to the nations' (cf. John 12:32). The Septuagint reads 'his rest will be glorious', and some commentators take this as a reference to the death and resurrection of Christ, referring to his words in John 17:5 (Eusebius, Cyril). Others take it as a reference to his tomb (*et erit sepulcrum eius gloriosum* Vg), venerated since the time of Constantine in the Basilica of the Holy Sepulchre in Jerusalem (Jerome). The verse accompanies the scene of the Entombment (Matt 27:57–60) in the *Biblia Pauperum* (*BP* 102) and elsewhere (Schiller 1972: 184). Calvin believes it refers to the Church where 'God is pleased to dwell continually though this may not always be seen by men'. The 'remnant of Israel' refers to the Jews who believed in Christ, first the twelve apostles, then the seventy (Luke 10:21), one hundred and twenty (Acts 1:15), five thousand (Acts 4:4) (Jerome). Verses 11–12 were cited as evidence for the presence of Jews in Ethiopia in the First Temple period and therefore fundamental to Falashas' demand for the right to Israeli citizenship (Kessler 1982: 161).

There will be peace between Judah and Ephraim (v. 13): the Messiah, son of David, and the Messiah, son of Joseph (Gen 41:50–52), shall not envy each other (Rashi). The purpose of the utter destruction (Heb. *heḥrim* cf. Lev 27:29) in verse 15 is the building of a highway (v. 16; cf. Isa 35:8; 40:3) from Assyria for a new Exodus (Ibn Ezra). One commentator identified the 'tongue of the Egyptian Sea' (v. 15) with the tongue of Leviathan, that is, the superstition of the mathematicians ... 'the false wisdom of the world', forever silenced when the Lord 'bound the tongue of Leviathan with the cord of the incarnation' (Gregory, *Morals on Job* 6.33.18–19). Luther also interprets the passage allegorically, referring to the power of the gospel to establish Christ's kingdom all over the world: 'wherever there are seas and rivers, there will be passageways for the Word; the Spirit and the Wind of the Lord will accomplish this'.

With Joy Shall You Draw Water from the Wells of Salvation (Isa 12:1–6)

The first part of the Book of Isaiah concludes with a jubilant hymn of thanksgiving, written in a very different style from what has gone before, but picking up 'on that day' (vv. 1, 4) from chapter 11 (v. 10, 11) and 'your anger turned away' (v. 1) from the refrain repeated five times in chapters 5, 9 and 10. The chapter is in the haftarah read in synagogues on the last day of Passover (10:32–12:6). Verses 1–3 are recited at the beginning of the weekly *Havdalah*

Isaiah Through the Centuries, First Edition. John F. A. Sawyer.
© 2018 John Wiley & Sons Ltd. Published 2020 by John Wiley & Sons Ltd.

service at home marking the end of the Sabbath (*ADPB* 608–611), and verse 3 is cited in the Talmud in relation to the joy experienced during the water libation ritual on the last day of the Feast of Sukkot (b*Sukkah* 48b, 50b). Jewish interpreters understand the 'water' drawn from the wells of salvation as 'new teaching' (Tg; cf. Rashi) implying that, when the Messiah comes, some of the laws will become obsolete (*RA* 669). There is another Jewish tradition associating the chapter with the scene of Rebecca at the well (Gen 24) (Mann 1971: 1, 191–194). *Ma'yanei ha-yeshu'ah* (wells of salvation) is the title of a commentary on the book of Daniel by Abravanel (Borodowski 2003: 6–7), and the words of verse 3 are set to music in a popular Israeli song, 'Mayim be-sason' (water with joy), frequently accompanied by dancing: it was composed in 1937 for a festival celebrating the discovery of water in the desert (*BiM* 155).

The Church Fathers, following the Septuagint 'God is my saviour' (MT 'my salvation' v. 2) and 'the wells of the saviour' (MT 'salvation'), interpreted the 'wells' in verse 3 as the Holy Spirit described by Jesus as 'rivers of living water that flow from the heart' (John 7:37–39) or the evangelical teaching of Christ 'springing up to eternal life' (John 4:13–14; cf. Ps 68:26) (Jerome, Eusebius). For Ambrose the 'wells' recalled the wounds of Christ (*Explanation of the Twelve Psalms* 37.31–2). For others they are the scriptures (Theodoret) or 'the Gospel, sermons about Christ in various places, or even the preachers of the Gospel' (Luther). Calvin tells us the fountain is Christ from whom the mercy of God flows and which 'satisfies … refreshes … and revives'. The reference in the last verse to the Holy One being 'exalted in your midst' (LXX) is applied by the Church Fathers to the crucifixion (cf. John 8:28; John 3:14; Theodoret).

The chapter is one of the canticles recited at morning prayer (Mearns 1914:51), and there is an eight-part setting of the piece by the Italian renaissance composer Andrea Rota. An illustration of the passage in the ninth-century Utrecht Psalter relates it to the Transfiguration (Matt 17:1–9, Mark 9:2–8, Luke 9:28–36; cf. 2 Pet 1:16–18), depicting Christ in a mandorla at the top, flanked by Moses and Elijah, with Peter standing at the foot of the mountain looking up and James and John lying prostrate. Beneath is the 'well of the saviour', from which streams flow out through the gate of a city wall, while people drink from it, bringing cups and jars and singing praises (v. 3 Vg) (de Wald 1933: 65–66).

Another medieval illustration of verse 3 appears in the illuminated initial C in the eleventh-century St Albans Psalter showing the prophet looking up to God, enthroned above him (Isa 6), and pointing to a well (Isa 12:3) at the foot of the cross, which has branches sprouting out of it (Isa 11:1) and a lamb on the crosspiece (Isa 16:1Vg; 53:7) (Dodwell 1960: 268). The same verse accompanies an illustration of the Baptism of Christ in the *Biblia Pauperum*, along with Psalm 68:26 (Vg), Ezek 36:25 and Zechariah13:1 (*BP* 66). The Dominican painter Fra Bartolommeo in his painting of Isaiah in the Uffizi, chose the words

PLATE 16   'Behold God is my saviour' (Isa 12:2 Vg). *The Prophet Isaiah*, oil painting
by Fra Bartolommeo (*c.*1516) in the Galleria dell'Accademia, Florence.

ECCE DEUS SALVATOR MEUS (v. 2 Vg) for the prophet's scroll, interpreted
perhaps as a statement about the divinity of Christ: 'My Saviour is God'
(Plate 16). It is one of the 'spirituall songes, and holy hymnes of godly men,
patriarckes and prophetes, all sweetly sounding, to the glory of the highest'
paraphrased by the Elizabethan poet Michael Drayton in his earliest work *The
Harmonie of the Church* (1591), and verses 5–6 feature in a joyful chorus at the
end of Philip Armes' short oratorio *Hezekiah* (1878) (see comm. on Isa 38:1–8).

Isaiah 13

Chapters 13–23 contain a collection of prophecies concerning the foreign nations (cf. Amos 1–2; Jer 46–51; Ezek 25–32). Most modern commentators are agreed that, while some passages may reflect an original eighth-century BCE context (e.g. 14:29–32; 20), the collection includes material from later periods, such as references to the Medes in the account of the fall of Babylon (13:17) and a thriving Jewish community in Egypt (19:18–25). In their present context they are intended to comfort the Jews (Jerome; cf. Cyril) and others suffering defeat or oppression: 'Do not lose hope ... Even if there were a hundred Babylons to be destroyed ... if you have faith, God will deliver you' (Luther). There is also

Isaiah Through the Centuries, First Edition. John F. A. Sawyer.
© 2018 John Wiley & Sons Ltd. Published 2020 by John Wiley & Sons Ltd.

the implication that, if God punishes unbelieving gentiles with such severity, how much more severe will the punishment of his own rebellious people be (Calvin).

The term 'oracle' (RSV; Heb. *massa*) (v. 1; cf. 13:1; 15:1; 17:1; 19:1; 21:1, 11, 13; 22:1; 23:1), translated as 'vision' in the Septuagint and 'burden' in the Vulgate (AV; cf. L. *onus*), has been much discussed. According to the rabbis *massa* was the severest of the ten names for prophecy (*CantR* III.4), and the Targum explains it as 'a cup of cursing to give Babylon to drink'. The Church Fathers also understood it as a 'burden', whether the burden by which Babylon is threatened (Jerome) or the 'eternal punishment with which the wicked will be burdened' (Aelred, *Burdens of Isaiah*, Homily 2). Modern scholarship distinguishes two Hebrew words, one meaning 'burden' (Ps 38:5; Jer 17:21–2) and another, in the present context, meaning 'lifting up [of the voice], utterance' (cf. Isa 42:2, 1) (*DCH* 5, 495–499). The first and by far the longest of the 'oracles' envisages the fall of Babylon (13:1–14:27). It follows the miraculous defeat of Assyria celebrated in a previous chapter (cf. 11:11–16) because Babylon destroyed Assyria (Ibn Ezra) and is the first because the Babylonians were the cruellest and most savage of Judah's enemies (Cyril). Babylon (Heb. *babel*) was the embodiment of all that is evil, arrogant and oppressive, epitomized in the Tower of Babel story (Gen 11:1–9) and remembered above all for its destruction of the Temple in 586 BCE and the Babylonian exile (Ps 137). For later writers, especially Christians, the image was applied to Rome, the 'great whore who corrupted the earth with her fornication' (Rev 19:2) and traded in all kinds of fine goods, 'horses, chariots, slaves and human souls' (Rev 18:11–13). Luther entitled one of his most effective attacks on the Church of Rome *The Babylonian Captivity of the Church* (1520). Today, for Rastafarians, biblical traditions about exile in Babylon are applied to the United States, Jamaica and Western culture in general (*CELR* 85).

Howl, For the Day of the Lord Is at Hand! (Isa 13:1–22)

The prophecy is in two parts, the first described by an eighteenth-century writer as 'one of the most beautiful examples of elegance of composition, variety of imagery and sublimity of sentiment and diction, in the prophetic style' (Isa 13), and the second as an 'ode of supreme and singular excellence' (Isa 14) (Lowth). The prophet first envisages the enemies of Babylon being summoned to execute God's anger. The signal (AV 'banner') raised on a hill recalls the 'ensign to the peoples' from a previous chapter (11:10) (Rashi, Jerome), and it was interpreted allegorically by Christians as the sign of the Lord's Cross, raised by the apostles and teachers of the church in their fight against paganism (Jerome). The AV inspired the American missionary hymn 'Fling out the banner' (1848) (*EH* 546; *CH2* 383).

For most commentators, Jewish and Christian, 'my consecrated ones' (v. 3) are the Medes and Persians, led by Cyrus 'the Lord's anointed' (Isa 45:1) (Rashi, Jerome, Luther), and parallels with Jeremiah's account of the fall of Babylon (50:25; 51:12, 27–28) are often noted. For others references to 'giants' (LXX; cf. Gen 6:2; RSV 'mighty men') and 'hosts … from the farthest heavens' (vv. 4–5), suggest a battle involving an angelic host 'sent out with a loud trumpet call' (Matt 24:31; Eusebius, Nicholas). 'The weapons of his wrath come from the end of heaven' (v. 5) was cited by the rabbis as proof that 'only the angels of mercy and peace stand in the presence of God; the angels of wrath stand far off' (*RA* 237). A tempting modern proposal, anticipated by the rabbis (Rashi), reads 'draw your swords' (NEB; cf. Pss 37:14; 55:22) for 'enter the gates' (RSV) in verse 2. On the other hand, the translation 'from the far horizons' (NJB) removes any suggestion of angelic intervention here (cf. Ibn Ezra).

Apocalyptic imagery associated with the 'day of the Lord' (vv. 6, 9) becomes more explicit as the account continues (vv. 4–16). The call to 'Howl, therefore, for the day of the Lord is at hand!' (v. 6 AV; cf. 14:31) is addressed to the citizens of Babylon (Jerome, Calvin). 'Howl ye, howl ye …', with words from Isaiah's prophecy to Hezekiah (Isa 39:7), features in the dramatic opening chorus of William Walton's oratorio *Belshazzar's Feast* (1931) (*BiM* 30), and also in a double chorus in Randall Thompson's *Peaceable Kingdom* (1936) (*BiM* 185–186). 'The whole land' (AV; Heb. *ha'aretz* vv. 5, 9, 11, etc.) refers to the land of Babylon (AV, Jerome, Rashi, Ibn Ezra) or to the whole Babylonian Empire described as 'the world' like the 'Roman world' (Lowth). But the Septuagint version ('the whole earth' RSV) and quotations from the passage in the Gospels (Matt 24:29; Mk.13:24) and Revelation (Rev 6:12; 8:12; 18:2), suggest that the global interpretation was already in vogue by the first century CE.

This is the only occurrence in the prophetic literature of the divine name 'Almighty' (Heb. *shaddai*) (v. 6; cf. Exod 6:3), perhaps selected here to show the Babylonians by their own 'destruction' (Heb. *shod*) how appropriately God is called Shaddai, that is 'strong and powerful to destroy' (Calvin). The graphic image of a woman in childbirth (vv. 7–8) is used elsewhere to describe the effect on a community of the arrival of very bad news (cf. Isa 26:17–18; Jer 50:43). Here as elsewhere it applies to the birthpangs of a new age (vv. 9–16; cf. Rom 8:22; Rev 12:2; *CGL* 5, 446). Isaiah adds a comment on the expressions on their faces showing 'panic' (Aquinas, Luther) or 'amazement' (Rashi) or 'intense grief' (Calvin) or 'shame' (Henry).

The arrival of the 'day of the lord' is accompanied, as it is elsewhere, by the darkening of the sky (v. 10) and the quaking of heaven and earth (v. 13; cf. Joel 2:10; Rev 9:2). Orion (LXX) and the other stars will withhold their light from the ungodly (Eusebius). The whole world (Heb. *tevel*) will be punished for its evil, particularly the arrogant and the haughty (v. 11), and destruction will be so total that almost no human beings will be left alive (v. 12): no one will be spared, men, women or children (vv. 15–16). Rashi draws a parallel between the weighing-up of the value of human beings against the value of the 'gold of Ophir' (v. 12), and the writing on the wall at Belshazzar's Feast on the night when the king of Babylon was slain (Dan 5:24–30). The image of a 'hunted gazelle' used to describe the few defenceless victims that survive (v. 14) caught the imagination of several commentators (Jerome, Cyril), and the reference to children being murdered in the presence of their parents (v. 16) recalls the notorious final verse of Psalm 137 (Cyril, Jerome, Calvin). The Targum substitutes 'young men' for 'infants', and modern commentators compare the scene to the First World War (Oswalt) and to what Hegel called 'the slaughterhouse of history' (Blenkinsopp).

The tradition that the Medes and Persians did not accept bribes (v. 17) is confirmed in a speech made by Cyrus to his army (Xenophon, *Cyropaedia* 5:20) (Lowth). The final ignominious end of Babylon, 'the glory of kingdoms', is compared to the fate of Sodom and Gomorrah (vv. 19) where no human habitation survived (v. 20) (cf. Rev 18:2) and all manner of wild beasts and evil spirits took up their residence (vv. 21–22) (cf. Rev 18:2). Attempts to identify these creatures range from monsters and demons (LXX) to ostriches and goats (NJB) in

PLATE 17   'And their houses will be filled with owls' (Isa 13:21 JPS). Israeli postage stamps (1987). Reproduced with kind permission of Israel Philatelic Society, Israel Postal Company.

verse 21, and from satyrs and hedgehogs (LXX) to hyenas and jackals (RSV) in verse 22. A series of Israeli stamps issued in 1987 found references to an eagle owl (L. *bubo bubo*) and a scops owl (L. *otus Brucei*) in verse 21 (cf. Deut 14:6; Isa 34:14) (Plate 17). LXX has 'sirens' for 'ostriches' (RSV), which in classical mythology were birds with woman's faces that lured sailors to their death on a rocky Italian shore, and in Christian tradition became symbols of worldly temptation (Eusebius). For 'wild beasts of the islands' in verse 22 (AV) Ibn Ezra suggests 'vultures', and Jerome has 'sirens in the temples of pleasure' for 'jackals in the pleasant palaces'. The prophecy ends with a warning that the wicked shall be punished in God's good time, not when we wish it (Calvin).

The Lord Will Again Choose Israel (Isa 14:1–3)

The second part of the 'oracle concerning Babylon' is introduced by a short prose introduction on God's compassion and Israel's return to their homeland (vv. 1–3). The notion of a second election ('he will again choose Israel' v. 1) became a central concern both at Qumran and in early Christianity (Blenkinsopp 2006: 196). 'The nations will take them and bring them to their place' (v. 2) is clearly a reference to the role of Cyrus (2 Chron 36:22–23), and the mention of 'aliens' (RSV;

Isaiah Through the Centuries, First Edition. John F. A. Sawyer.
© 2018 John Wiley & Sons Ltd. Published 2020 by John Wiley & Sons Ltd.

LXX 'proselytes') joining the returning exiles is explained by Ibn Ezra as follows: 'when the nations see that Cyrus is honouring Israel, they will seek to become their servants'. The verse was cited by the rabbis to prove that proselytes can serve as priests in the Temple since this is how the rare word 'cleave' (Heb. *sapaḥ*) is used elsewhere (1 Sam 2:36; ExodR XIX.4). Christian commentators, while appreciating the original historical background of the passage, applied the verses to the return of God's people to a spiritual Jerusalem where an increasing number of people were brought under the rule of Christ by the preaching of the apostles (Cyril). For Calvin this is a prophecy about the call of the gentiles. The promise of 'rest' in verse 3, with Isa 25:8, is set as a meditative chorus a capella in Robert Starer's cantata *Ariel: Visions of Isaiah* (1959) (*BiM* 19).

How Art Thou Fallen from Heaven, O Lucifer! (Isa 14:4–23)

The poem is described as a 'taunt' in some modern versions (v. 4; RSV), picking up on the reference to 'lording it over those who had once oppressed them' (v. 2). The Hebrew word *mashal* normally means 'parable' (Jerome) or 'wise saying, proverb' (Prov 1:1; 10:1), but in this context it is applied to a poem that is clearly in the form of a lament (LXX *threnos*; cf. 2 Sam 1:19–26; Lam 1, 2, 4) and can perhaps be understood as a satirical lament (cf. NJB) or 'a song suited to the events' (Cyril). At the same time it implies that the 'ruin of Babylon will become a proverb' (Calvin), a 'byword' among the nations (cf. 2 Chron 7:20; Oecolampadius).

The poem celebrates the extraordinary change in the fortunes of the world's most powerful tyrant, 'how the oppressor has ceased, the insolent fury ceased!' (v. 4 RSV). The Hebrew word translated 'insolent fury' (*madhebah*) is otherwise unknown and has been much discussed. One popular suggestion was 'golden city' (AV), from the Aramaic *dahaba* (gold) (Dan 5:2,3,4) (cf. Ibn Ezra, Lowth, Henry). Some of the ancient versions have 'taskmaster' (LXX; cf. Tg). 'Onslaught', reading *marhabah* with Isaiah ScrollA from Qumran (cf. Isa 3:5; Cant.6:5), has also been proposed (Roberts). 'The king of Babylon' (v. 4) is not named: most commentators assume it is Nebuchadnezzar (Jerome, Cyril, Rashi, Ibn Ezra, Luther) but Sargon (Childs), Nabonidus (Duhm) and others have also been proposed, but none of them fits all the details in the poem. The Septuagint translators may have had Antiochus IV Epiphanes in mind (van der Kooij 1981: 99–101). The poem, which prompts Luther to describe Isaiah at this point as a 'disciple of Calliope', the muse of epic poetry, contains a striking personification of Hades (LXX; Heb. *she'ol*) and the sarcastic welcome the 'bloodstained murderer' (Cyril) receives from his victims. Former world leaders are described as 'giants' (LXX) or 'ghosts' (NJB; Heb. *repha'im*), whose dead bodies now lie unattended, eaten by worms and maggots (cf. vv. 9–11). Chaucer's Parson cites verse 11 to instil the fear of death into his listeners (Chaucer 1980, *Parson's Tale*, line 198) (cf. Isa 66:24).

Equally poetic is the famous description of the 'fall of the day-star (Heb. *helel*; Vg *lucifer*), son of dawn' (Heb. *ben shaḥar*) that follows (vv. 12–23) (cf. Ezek 28; Matt 11:23–24). A parallel with the Greek myth of Phaeton, son of the sun god Apollo (or Helios), who fell from the sky to his death, has been suggested (Duhm, Sommer). There is evidence in the Ugaritic texts that both Helel and Shaḥar were Canaanite astral deities, but little is known about them. The 'morning-star' is Venus, which is brighter than all the other stars, and the king of Babylon is compared to it, not because he was greater than all the other kings of the world, but because he thought he was (Cyril, Theodoret, Calvin). Unlike all the other 'kings of the nations' (v. 18), he is now an unburied corpse, dragged out of its tomb and hidden away like an aborted foetus (v. 19; Tg, RSV). Ibn Ezra tells us there was a tradition that this is what happened to Nebuchadnezzar. Out of context the striking words 'the man who made the earth tremble, who shook kingdoms' (v. 16) were applied to a famous second-century CE miracle-working rabbi, Shimon ben Yohai (*Zohar* 14:16).

Despite objections from the Reformers (Luther, Calvin) and modern scholars (Clements, Childs), verse 12 has regularly been applied to Satan, a fallen angel, who got his Latin name 'Lucifer' from this passage (cf. Ps 110:3; Vg, Jerome). Satan applies it to himself in the first-century BCE Jewish text known as the *Life of Adam and Eve* (12–17; *OTP* 2.262; cf. 2 Enoch 29:3–5; *OTP* 1.148), and Jesus probably alludes to it too: 'I saw Satan fall like lightning from heaven' (Luke 10:18; cf. Rev 12:7–9). Origen cites the passage to explain how the devil, 'a being of darkness', came to be called 'light-bearer' (L. *lucifer*; Origen, *On First Principles* 1.5) and asks how this verse could refer to any human being (Origen *On First Principles* 4, 3, 9). Augustine quotes the devil's behaviour here to explain what robbery means in Philippians 2:6–7 (*Expositions on the Psalms* 68). By an ingenious pun on the word *edammeh* 'I will make myself like' (v. 14), the kabbalists showed how Adam could be at the same time a man of the earth (Heb. *adamah*) and made in the likeness of the Most High (Scholem 1965: 160).

Many interpret the passage as being capable of both interpretations, one with reference to Nebuchadnezzar and the other with reference to the devil (Jerome, Theodoret, Aquinas). It was one of the biblical sources for the tale of the 'Fall of the Angels', which begins all the medieval English cycles of mystery plays (Beadle and King 1999: 2–7; Twycross 2006: 346). For Dante, the creature that 'fell like lightning from the sky' (1995: *Purg*.11:25–26) was Nebuchadnezzar, not Satan, but Milton certainly had Isaiah 14 in mind when he described how Satan was 'hurl'd headlong flaming from th'ethereal sky' at the beginning of *Paradise Lost* (1998: i. 43), as had Gustav Doré in his famous engraving of the

'Fallen Angel' (1866) (Plate 18). There is a dramatic dialogue motet scored for bass (Devil), soprano (God) and continuo by Carissimi, entitled *Lucifero, Caelestis Olim* (1693) (*BiM* 151), and Victor Hugo's unfinished epic *La Fin de Satan* (1886) ends with the words 'Satan est mort; renais, ô Lucifer céleste!' (Satan is dead, be born again, O heavenly Lucifer) (*DBLF* 330).

The king's sons and heirs (vv. 20–23) are identified by most commentators as Belshazzar and his children, whose kingdom was given to the Medes (Dan 5:31) (Rashi, Cyril, Jerome, Luther). Nothing will remain of them, not even

PLATE 18   'The Fall of Lucifer' (Isa 14:12). Illustration by Gustav Doré for Milton's *Paradise Lost* (1866). Reproduced with kind permission of David Gunn.

their name (v. 20). Babylon will be a ruin inhabited only by hedgehogs ('bitterns' AV, *JSB*) 'to this day' (Jerome, Lowth), swept clean by the Lord (v. 23). Rashi notes that the Hebrew word for 'broom' (Heb. *maṭ'ateh*) was unknown to the rabbis till they overheard a maidservant using it.

Prophecies against the Assyrians and the Philistines (Isa 14:24–32)

The last part of the 'oracle against Babylon' (vv. 24–27) is about God's treatment of the Assyrians, in particular the miraculous defeat 'in my land ... upon my mountains' (v. 23) in the fourteenth year of Hezekiah (Isa 36; Eusebius). It is addressed to Nebuchadnezzar to convince him that no one can frustrate the words of the prophets of Israel, not even the Assyrians (v. 26; Ibn Ezra; cf. Rashi). Isaiah also had in mind the 'wavering hearts and jittery faith' of his own people, weighed down by the yoke of the Assyrian king, as he spoke these words to encourage them (Luther). The prophecy ends with another allusion to a familiar refrain (cf. Isa 5:25; 9:12, 17, 21; 10:4).

The date of the oracle concerning the Philistines is given as 'the year that King Ahaz died' (14:28). A new chapter should begin here (Calvin), and Jerome points out that this means that all the prophecies that follow (Isa 14:29–66:24) were given during the reign of Hezekiah. The Philistines are told to refrain from celebrating the death of Judah's king, whose father had defeated them (2 Chron 26:6) and with whom they were still at war (2 Chron 28:18), because Hezekiah the son of Ahaz was going to 'smite them as far as Gaza, from watch-tower to fortified city' (2 Kgs 18:8 Rashi, Eusebius, Jerome).

In a biting parody of Isa 11:1, the prophet compares Hezekiah to a snake that will come forth from the serpent's root, more venomous than its parent (Rashi). Jerome describes the serpent (L. *regulus*; Gk *basiliskos*) as a creature so terrifying it kills by its look and by the breath from its mouth. Luther notes the oddness of comparing the Lord's anointed to such a creature, but he explains that the more ferocious it is, the more easily it can kill their enemies and points out that Christ is compared to a serpent (John 3:14) and a lion (Hos.5:14). Nicholas of Lyra recalls that Dan, ancestor of Samson who fought the Philistines, is described as 'a serpent in the way, a viper by the path' (Gen 49:17; cf. Heb 11:32). Calvin understands the adder and fiery serpent to refer more generally to God's people, first the Jews, and subsequently the Church, which 'will always rise again ... and pierce the eyes of the ungodly'. Contemporary Assyrian records confirm that there were a number of Assyrian campaigns in the region before and during the reign of Hezekiah (Blenkinsopp, Roberts), and 'smoke from the north' (v. 31) may refer to an Assyrian attack on the Philistines, rather than Judah (Cyril). At all events, like Babylon, Philistia will be destroyed and all survivors ('the remnant' v. 30b) killed. On musical interpretations of 'Howl' (v. 31 AV), see comm. on Isa 13:6.

In the middle of these scenes of destruction and wailing, there is a brief glimpse of a land free from war and famine, where the children of the poor have plenty to eat and the 'needy lie down in safety' (v. 30a). 'Out of place', according to most modern scholars, this half-verse nonetheless reassures the Jews, who were not far from despair (Calvin): 'there is need here of faith and hope'. These are the words of the Spirit (Luther). The prophecy ends with another scene of peace and security, attracting the attention of the 'messengers of the nation'. According to some, the 'nation' is Assyria and it refers to them sending messengers to find out why only Jerusalem was spared (Jerome). The Septuagint has 'the kings of the nations' (plural) and this would point rather to those who came to congratulate Hezekiah on his victory over Sennacherib (2 Chron 32:23) and acknowledge the superiority of the God of Israel (Aquinas, Lowth). The chapter ends with a return to a favourite Isaianic theme, 'one of the interpolated Zion passages' (cf. Isa 2:2–4, 4:2–6; 10:12, 20–27a; 11:10; 14:1–2), which provide a 'vantage point from which events can be viewed and interpreted' (Blenkinsopp). Zion is where the afflicted find refuge because it is built, 'not of lime or stones, but of the gracious promises of eternal life' (Calvin).

My Heart Cries Out for Moab (Isa 15:1–14)

Next is an 'Oracle concerning Moab' in the form of a lament, describing the destruction of another of Judah's neighbours (15–16). Similar in many respects to a long prophecy 'concerning Moab' by Jeremiah (48:1–47), the description of Moab's fate contains some difficult Hebrew and some obscure place names. Ar was a Moabite city (Num 21:15; Deut 2:9) identified by the Church Fathers with the Hellenistic Areopolis (Jerome, Eusebius). Kir was apparently also known as

Isaiah Through the Centuries, First Edition. John F. A. Sawyer.
© 2018 John Wiley & Sons Ltd. Published 2020 by John Wiley & Sons Ltd.

Kir-Hareset (16:7; 2 Kgs 3:25) to distinguish it from a Syrian city of the same name (Amos 9:7), while Dibon, Nebo, Medeba and Heshbon are all familiar names from the region beyond Jordan (Num 21:27–30; Jer 48). The scene of refugees fleeing with all their possessions across the 'Brook of the Willows' (Vg; Heb. *'arabim*) (v. 7) sounds like a reference to the southern border of Moab (modern Wadi el-Ḥesi). Others take it as a reference to Arabia or the Arabs (LXX, Eusebius). The meaning of some of the other names may be more important than their location: Eglath (v. 5) and Eglaim (v. 8) from Hebrew *'egel* 'calf' remind us that the Moabites were idol worshippers (Jerome, Cyril). Nimrim (v. 6), recalls wild leopards (Heb. *nemerim*) and the river Dimon (v. 9 MT, AV; Vg, RSV 'Dibon') suggests blood (Heb. *dam*) (Rashi).

It is impossible to relate the prophecy with any certainty to a specific historical event, though there have been many attempts to do so (Lowth, Duhm, Kaiser). Rashi suggests that Isaiah was predicting another Assyrian invasion in three years' time (Isa 16:14), and that later Nebuchadnezzar and the Babylonians would come like a lion for 'those who escape' (v. 9). Eusebius points out that it does not matter whether it refers to Assyrians, Babylonians or Arabs (15:7, 9 LXX) since nothing is left of ancient Moab today. What is remarkable about this prophecy, and the Jeremiah parallel (cf. Jer 48:36), is that the prophet is moved to sympathy by the plight of the Moabites (v. 5; Jerome). The prophet wept like Jesus weeping over Jerusalem (Luke 19:41; cf. Isa 22:4): 'God desires not the death of sinners' (cf. Ezek 33:11; Henry). Luther thinks this is 'prophetic irony', but Rashi and others maintain that this distinguishes Israel's prophets from 'gentile prophets', recalling the king of Moab's attempt to induce Balaam to curse Israel (Num 22–24).

Verse 6, beginning 'the waters of Nimrim shall be a desert, the grass withers', recalls a better known comment on the transience of human existence (Isa 40:6–8), and is quoted in full, along with Ecclesiastes 9:12, by the Argentinian writer Eduardo Mallea at the beginning of his novel *Todo Verdor Perecerá* (1941). This is a deeply pessimistic study of a woman's isolation, her vain search for happiness and her ultimate despair, in which the last words of Isa 40:8 ('but the word of the Lord shall stand for ever') are conspicuous by their absence, as they are in this Moabite lament.

Hide the Fugitives, Do Not Betray the Refugees (Isa 16:1–14)

The abrupt change of style and more difficulties in the Hebrew text have prompted many different interpretations of the first passage (vv. 1–5). The simplest is to read it as a call to the Moabites to 'Send the lambs of the ruler' (MT) to Jerusalem, in the hope of buying help against the invader. Rashi points out that the king of Moab was a sheep-breeder (2 Kgs 3:4). 'It is about obstinate men … who fearlessly despise God until they are visited by his judgements'

Isaiah Through the Centuries, First Edition. John F. A. Sawyer.
© 2018 John Wiley & Sons Ltd. Published 2020 by John Wiley & Sons Ltd.

(Calvin). The plight of the Moabite women is highlighted in a graphic simile (v. 2; cf. Isa 3:24–26) in contrast to the 'Daughter of Zion' addressed in verse 1. The Moabites' request for protection from Jerusalem ends with a vision of the establishment of the throne of David in steadfast love and faithfulness (vv. 3–5). According to Rashi, Theodoret and others this is a reference to Hezekiah, who showed exceptional generosity towards refugees from other lands (2 Chron 30:24–25). In the Syriac version verse 1 reads 'I will send the son of the ruler', an even more desperate attempt to get help from Judah (Lowth). Other suggestions include 'They have sent lambs' (RSV) or 'They will send tribute' (Tg).

The Vulgate of verse 1 stays closer to the original Hebrew than most modern versions: 'Send forth a lamb, a ruler of the earth, from a rock in the desert to the mountain of the daughter of Zion'. Jerome tells us that this prophecy was to bring comfort to the suffering Moabites: for out of you will come a Lamb that will take away the sins of the world, from a rock in the desert, that is, descended from Ruth the Moabitess, to Mount Zion, whether literally when the Virgin Mary brought Jesus to the Temple in Jerusalem (Nicholas), or, in a spiritual sense, to the Church (Jerome, Eusebius). The imagery recalls a passage from later in the book: 'Look to the rock whence you were hewn … look to Abraham … and Sarah' (Isa 51:1–2; cf. Deut 32:18). *Emitte Agnum Domine* 'Send forth the Lamb, O Lord' features in one of the Great Antiphons, sung like the *Rorate* during Advent, as well as in a prayer recited by Isaiah in John Bale's religious drama *God's Promises* (1538) (see comm. on Isa 45:8).

In the late twentieth-century, liberation theologians found in the prophecy a succinct expression of their concerns for good counsel, justice and the protection of the rights of immigrants and refugees, aspects of social justice highlighted in more familiar passages elsewhere (Isa 1:17; 11:3–5) but present here in a very distinctive context. In the eyes of the Moabites, Jerusalem and the Davidic Messiah are a source of 'steadfast love, interhuman compassion' (Heb. *ḥesed*) as well as 'justice and righteousness' (Miranda 1977: 47). This is one of the few places in Isaiah where 'steadfast love' is mentioned (cf. 54:10; 55:3; 63:7) and is cited by the rabbis to show that not only the world (Ps 89:2) but also the throne of God is founded on it (*MidrPs* 89:2).

The rest of the chapter assumes that Moab's request was refused and their land devastated (vv. 6–13). Like Babylon, Moab is condemned for her arrogance and empty boasting (v. 6). The wailing of Moab reappears like a refrain in verse 7 (cf. Isa 15:2). Much is made of the fate of her wine trade, starting with an apparent reference to 'raisin cakes' (Heb. *ashish*), a delicacy for which the Moabite city Kir was apparently noted (Ibn Ezra; cf. 2 Sam 6:19; Cant. 2:5). Others read 'the foundations or walls of Kir' (Tg; Rashi, Luther, AV) or the 'men of Kir' (cf. Jer 48:31; Lowth). The fate of her great vineyards is then graphically described, once the source of joy and singing, now fallen silent and deserted (vv. 7–10).

The language and imagery in these two chapters is striking, not least in regard to the prophet's response to Moab's fate. Dante appears to allude to verse 9 (Vg *inebriabo lacrima mea*) in his description of his eyes as so 'intoxicated' (*inebriate*) that they made him weep when he recognized someone he knew among the tortured souls in Hell (*Inf.* 29:1–3). Again in verse 11 the prophet is physically sickened by what he sees, reading 'my bowels' with AV (Heb. *me'ay*; Vg *venter* 'belly'; cf. Rashi, Tg) rather than 'my soul' (RSV). Again Luther says the prophet is 'putting on an act', but Jeremiah uses similar language (Jer 48:36) while Isaiah's reaction to his vision of the destruction of Babylon (Isa 21:2–4) is perhaps the closest parallel. A final comment reminds us that it is not the prophet who is speaking, but the Lord, and that the downfall of Moab will be in exactly three years' time: hired workers are 'very punctual in observing the time for which they are hired' (Wesley).

An Oracle Concerning Syria and Ephraim (Isa 17:1–3)

The short 'oracle concerning Damascus' is about the kingdom of Israel on Judah's northern border as well as Syria, recalling the Syro-Ephraimite alliance referred to in chapter 7 (Rashi). This is made clear by the references to Aroer (v. 2), which was in the territory of Gad (Num 32:34) and Ephraim (v. 3). Some omit 'Aroer' and read 'her cities' (Heb. '*areha* Tg, LXX, RSV, NJB), but it makes good sense applied, albeit ironically, to the ten tribes of Northern Israel who are

Isaiah Through the Centuries, First Edition. John F. A. Sawyer.
© 2018 John Wiley & Sons Ltd. Published 2020 by John Wiley & Sons Ltd.

already in exile (2 Kgs 16:9; 17:4–6): they are 'the remnant' (Heb. *she'ar*) (v. 3; cf. Isa 7:3) (Rashi). They applied to the Assyrians for help in the first place (Isa 7) (Calvin). Damascus was destroyed by the Assyrians (Isa 10:9–10; 2 Kgs 16:19), but the prophecy can be applied to the Babylonian invasion (Jer 49:23–27) and later to the city's changed status (v. 1) under the Romans (Eusebius).

The Glory of Jacob Will Be Brought Low (Isa 17:4–14)

Three prophecies beginning 'in that day' continue the attack on the Northern Kingdom (vv. 4–6; 7–8; 9). The first represents the downfall of Israel in the image of the patriarch Jacob, at one time blessed with the 'fatness of the earth and plenty of grain and wine' (Gen 47:28), now stripped of his fine raiment ('glory') and reduced to skin and bone (v. 4; cf. Aquinas). This is followed by a graphic description of what is left after the harvest, when the gleaners and fruit-pickers have done everything they can to ensure that as little as possible has been missed (vv. 5–6). Perhaps the mention of the Valley of Rephaim, which is near Jerusalem (Josh 15:8), suggests that the 'remnant' here could be Hezekiah and his company, sole survivors of the Assyrian invasions (cf. Isa 6:13; 11:11) (Rashi). The Church Fathers understood the fourteen surviving 'olives' (LXX, Vg; MT, RSV 'berries') left in the branches, to be the twelve apostles, plus Paul and James, brother of Jesus (Eusebius, Jerome). 'The gleanings' (v. 6; AV) were a consolation in a time of crisis: 'some remnant will always remain, though frequently it is not visible to our eyes' (Calvin). Horrifying parallels elsewhere (Isa 1:9; 14:22; 15:9; 16:14; e.g. Amos 3:12), however, point to an originally more pessimistic interpretation of the remnant theme (Theodoret, Lowth, Childs).

The second 'in that day' prophecy (vv. 7–8) envisages a change of heart among the people of Israel, 'driven by the scourge of chastisements' (Calvin). The specific references to Asherim (LXX 'trees') and Hammanim (LXX 'abominations'), idols of female and male deities respectively (2 Chron 34:4), do not help us to identify any particular historical context. For some it recalls Hezekiah's reformation (2 Chron 29–31), although this affected only the people of Judah in the south (Jerome). The word 'a man' (v. 7 AV; Heb. *adam*) suggests that the prophet is looking beyond any one historical example (Duhm) and recalls Paul's statement that those who were once 'strangers to the covenants of promise', through Christ became 'fellow citizens with the saints and members of the household of God' (Eph 2:11–21) (Eusebius).

The third 'on that day' prophecy (vv. 9–11) introduces a quite different image, apparently comparing the fate of Syria and Ephraim to that of the ruined cities conquered by the Israelites in the days of Joshua when 'one of you put to flight a thousand' (Josh 23:10; cf. Lev 26:8; Deut 32:30; Calvin, Rashi). The mention of the Amorites and the Hivites (RSV; cf. Josh 9:1–2) comes from the Septuagint: MT has 'forests and branches' (Rashi) or 'woods and heaths' (NJB), perhaps connected with the images of planting and growth in what follows. Verses 10–11 are addressed to a female devotee or 'sorceress' (cf. Isa 57:3) accused of having abandoned true religion and doomed to a life of 'grief and incurable pain'. Her careful observance of pagan rituals, practised in her garden, will be of no avail. An explicit reference to the popular Hellenistic deity Adonis, known as Na'aman in Syria and Tammuz in Babylon (Ezek 8:14), is identified as 'the alien god' by many scholars in the phrase translated 'pleasant plants' (AV, RSV; Heb. *niṭ'e na'manim*) (Duhm, Blenkinsopp). Rashi applies it to the history of God's people, who had corrupted the original pleasant planting of the Lord (Ezek 20:5–8). LXX has 'you will plant an unfaithful plant and an unfaithful seed', and the passage recalls the Parable of the Sower, where the kingdom of heaven is compared to a 'man who sowed good seed in his field' (Matt 13:24) (Eusebius). The Greek, ignoring the second person feminine singulars in the Hebrew and taking *nahalah* ('grief' AV, RSV) in its normal sense of 'inheritance', creates a happy ending in the passage: 'as a man's father, you shall obtain an inheritance for your sons' (v. 11) (Eusebius).

The final part of this chapter is in a very different style, reminiscent of some of the Psalms where God's triumph over worldly powers is compared to the 'thunder of the sea ... the roaring of mighty waters', blown away overnight at his rebuke like chaff or specks of dust (vv. 12–14). Like other Isaianic images (Isa 27:1; 51:9–11), this is probably derived from ancient Canaanite mythology (Kaiser, Clements), but, according to most commentators, it also reflects the story of the angel of the Lord slaying the Assyrian army overnight (cf. Isa 37:36) (Jerome). According to Rashi it refers both to Sennacherib and to the armies of Gog and Magog, including Cush (Ethiopia) (Ezek 38:5), the subject of the next 'oracle' (Isa 18). Calvin applies it generally to the fate of all the enemies of Israel and of the Church, likened to the waves of a tempestuous sea, and reminds us of the Psalmist's image of the Lord stilling the tempest and bringing the faithful 'to their desired haven' (Ps 107:30). Luther also cites a Psalm as a comment on the final verse: 'Weeping may tarry for the night, but joy comes in the morning' (Ps 30:5). There is a dramatic a cappella choral setting of verse 12, accompanied by cries of 'Woe!' from chapter 5 (see comm. on 5:8), in Randall Thompson's *Peaceable Kingdom* (1936).

A Prophecy Concerning Ethiopia (Isa 18:1–7)

Ethiopia (Heb. *kush*) (18) and Egypt (19), the subject of the next two prophecies, are grouped together here and elsewhere (Isa 20:3–5), not only because of their geographical location but also because during Isaiah's lifetime Egypt was ruled by an Ethiopian (Nubian) dynasty (Isa 37:9). Opinions have been much divided since ancient times both on the meaning of the passage and on possible historical references. Most nowadays believe the people described as 'tall and smooth'

Isaiah Through the Centuries, First Edition. John F. A. Sawyer.
© 2018 John Wiley & Sons Ltd. Published 2020 by John Wiley & Sons Ltd.

at the beginning and end of the passage (vv. 1, 7; RSV) are the Ethiopians although it is surprising that there is no mention of the colour of their skin (cf. Jer 13:23). Sudanese Christians have argued that it refers to their own land, a land divided by rivers (v. 2), where the Nuer and Shilluk are among the tallest people on earth (v. 2), and the 'whirring wings' (v. 1) are those of the pervasive tsetse fly: it is a prophecy of judgement predicting the violence and destruction of post-independence Sudan (vv. 5–6), but also the hope that Christians will have the faith to bring gifts to a new Zion, to be built one day in the Sudan (v. 7) (LeMarquand 2006: 563–570). Several recent commentators have suggested that the prophecy is directed at Judah, doomed to destruction for choosing alliances with foreign nations instead of quiet trust in God (cf. Isa 8) (Marti, Sweeney, Childs).

The 'wings' in verse 1 are interpreted by most modern scholars as the whirring wings of locusts (NJB; cf. Deut 28:42), but by Rashi as the wings of great birds and by others as the sails of ships (LXX, Tg; Luther). A recent commentator suggests that 'smooth' here means 'slippery' in the sense of 'untrustworthy' (Lavik 2001: 97). The word translated 'mighty' (RSV; Heb. *qav-qav*) is unusual and interpreted by some modern commentators as 'gibberish', that is, a nation speaking a strange foreign language (Sommer; cf. 28:11). Another suggestion is that the terms 'long and smooth' refer, not to the people of Egypt, but to the land, which is '750 miles in length ... and made smooth by the overflowing Nile' and the word *qav-qav* (cf. Heb. *qav* 'a line') refers to the surveying skills developed in ancient Egypt (Lowth). The messengers (v. 2) appear to be from Judah, seeking military assistance against the Assyrians from Egypt and the Ethiopians, a strategy explicitly criticized elsewhere by the prophet (cf. 20:1–6; 31:1–9) (Cyril, Jerome). For others the verse recalls Christ's words to his disciples to 'go rather to the lost sheep of the house of Israel' (Matt 10:6) (Eusebius). The tradition that many nations brought gifts to Hezekiah in Jerusalem after the destruction of the Assyrian army (2 Chron 22:32), explains the reference at the end to Ethiopians bringing gifts to Mount Zion (v. 7).

But the adjectives translated 'tall and smooth' (RSV) are actually the passive participles of verbs meaning 'pull' and 'tear', and there is an important alternative interpretation of these verses (cf. AV; Calvin). The reference is to a people 'robbed and plundered' (Tg), 'pulled and torn' (Rashi), plucked out of the flock like a lamb to be slaughtered (Ibn Ezra). The term translated 'mighty', literally 'a line for a line' (Heb. *qav-qav*), refers to the appropriate punishment received by the people, a 'nation punished in kind' (Rashi), and 'conquering', literally 'trampling' (Heb. *mebusah*) to the trampling underfoot suffered by Israel when their land was invaded by the Assyrians, compared to a river (cf. Isa 8:7–8) (Ibn Ezra). This is then the description of God's people suffering the consequences of their disobedience, and the 'messengers' are ambassadors of the nations sent to see what has happened and learn of the true power of Israel's God (Rashi). The people are 'a strange and harsh people ... without hope and trodden down', recalling Paul's 'strangers to the covenant of promise' (Eph 2:12) (Eusebius). Calvin also sees this as a prophecy about the state of God's people, applied to the church in his own day, 'not far from despair, being plundered, scattered, and everywhere crushed and trodden under foot', and a call for faith in God's power to rescue it.

Verse 3 is another call to the nations of the world, this time no messengers are needed because they will see the signal on the mountains and hear the sound of the shofar (AV; RSV 'trumpet'; NJB 'rams horn') summoning the exiles home (Rashi). In the Jewish liturgy this is one of the verses cited at the blowing of the shofar on New Year's Day (*Maḥzor* 276, 323). The Cross will be raised high above the mountains and the gospel will be heard like a trumpet call by all the nations, even distant Ethiopia (v. 3) (Eusebius). For others the trumpet is a call to battle, proclaiming war against the enemies of Israel, conquerors of Egypt (Aquinas) or, for some Christian interpreters, the enemies of the Church (Henry).

The prophet again hears a voice, as he did during the Syro-Ephraimite crisis (Isa 7:9), urging him to trust in the Lord and oppose alliances with Egypt which are unnecessary and wrong (vv. 4–6; cf. 31:1–9). God has now ceased from punishing his people and is looking down with favour on his dwelling place, the Temple in Jerusalem (LXX, Rashi). He will give them light ('clear heat') and life ('dew'), and Israel's enemies will be destroyed, their remains left to birds of prey and wild beasts (vv. 5–6). The light of the gospel lights up the Church like the noonday sun, and the Holy Spirit protects us like a 'cloud of dew in the heat of the harvest' (Eusebius).

The scene of approaching harvest time (cf. John 4:35), normally a time of joy (cf. Isa 9:3), is here transformed into a prophecy of judgement in which useless branches, 'like the traitor Judas' (Eusebius), are mercilessly cut off and the fields abandoned to wild beasts (vv. 5–6). But in the end these strange foreign people, who had been beaten and trodden down, will turn to God and bring gifts to Mount Zion 'the city of the living God, the heavenly Jerusalem' (vv. 7–8; Heb 12:22) (Jerome). Commentators have noted a parallel in the Psalms: 'Let bronze be brought from Egypt, and let Ethiopia hasten to stretch out her hands to God' (Ps 68:31), and according to some the passage finds its fulfilment in the story of the Ethiopian eunuch who came to Jerusalem to worship (Acts 8:27; cf. 2:5) (Luther, Henry).

The apparent reference to Jews bringing gifts from Ethiopia (cf. Isa 11:11) has an interesting parallel in the Book of Zephaniah (3:10), who is known among Africans and African Americans as the 'black or African prophet of the Old Testament' (Coggins and Han 2011: 101–112). According to a modern American reading of the passage the 'land shadowing with wings' (v. 1 AV) is taken as a reference to the bald eagle, America's national symbol, or to the US aircraft industry, while 'a nation scattered and peeled' (v. 2 AV), that is, 'clean-shaven', refers to the fact that the US army was the first to issue a razor to every soldier, and a 'nation meted out and trodden down' (AV) is a reference to the comprehensive Washington geographic surveys (Boyer 1992:245–246).

Isaiah 19

An Oracle Concerning Egypt (Isa 19:1–15)

The long 'oracle concerning Egypt' (cf. Jer 46; Ezek 29–32; Zech 14:18–19) begins with a description of divine judgement in terms of civil unrest, a cruel dictatorship, natural disaster and economic ruin (vv. 1–15). Natural disasters in Egypt and periods of civil unrest were so common that it would be impossible to date the passage on this alone (Clements). Some identify the 'hard taskmaster'

Isaiah Through the Centuries, First Edition. John F. A. Sawyer.
© 2018 John Wiley & Sons Ltd. Published 2020 by John Wiley & Sons Ltd.

(v. 4) with an Assyrian king in the time of Isaiah (cf. Isa 20:4; Rashi, Ibn Ezra; cf. Luther), but there were more significant invasions of Egypt by the Persians under Cambyses two hundred years later and by the Greeks under Alexander the Great in the fourth century (Lowth). The Septuagint has plural 'cruel lords' (cf. Heb. *adonim*) and some of the Church Fathers identified these with the Ptolemaic and Roman rulers who 'enslaved the Egyptian nation' (Eusebius, Cyril; cf. Nicholas).

The image of the Lord entering Egypt 'riding on a swift cloud' (v. 1) recalls the night when he passed through the land of Egypt to execute punishment upon all their gods (Exod 12:12) (Rashi). Commentators note other parallels with the Exodus story, such as the contest between the Lord of hosts and the Egyptian magi (vv. 2–3) and the drying up and fouling of the Nile (vv. 5–8; Blenkinsopp). The rabbis cited vv. 11–13 in accounts of how Israel's God ridiculed the wisdom of Egypt (*Tanḥ*. Exod 2.8).

In Christian tradition verse 1 was applied to the flight of the Holy Family into Egypt (Matt 2:13–15). The Lord 'riding on a swift cloud' is Christ entering Egypt (cf. Ps 104:3; Matt 17:5; Acts 1:9) (Bede, *Homilies on the Gospels*, 2.15). For some Christ is himself the cloud in which God is incarnate, 'high above the earth ... pure and free of all earthly impurities' (Cyril, Theodoret). For others the cloud is a symbol of the Virgin Mary, carrying Christ, but 'not made heavy by the weight of any human seed' (Jerome; cf. Romanos, trans. Lash 1995: 201). The shaking of the idols, which is the climax and 'final miracle' in the story of the Flight into Egypt, as told in Pseudo-Matthew 17–25, is based on this verse (cf. Ezek 30:13) (Eusebius, Jerome, Theodoret) and is frequently depicted in Christian art (Schiller 1971: 117–122; O'Kane 2007: 73–79) (Plate 19).

The author's knowledge of Egyptian life in vv. 5–10 has been commented on, as well as literary parallels with Egyptian literature (Marlow 2007: 229–242). Most agree that vv. 6–7 refer to plant-life: 'reeds and rushes' (LXX 'papyrus') (AV, cf. LXX, Rashi, Duhm). The 'paper reeds by the brooks' (AV) is set as a lament sung by the survivors in Randall Thompson's *Peaceable Kingdom* (1936) (see on Isaiah 13:6) (*BiM* 185–186). The difficult Hebrew phrase '*arot 'al-ye'or* (v. 7) is understood by many as 'bare places by the Nile' (RSV, cf. Vg Lowth). Some find a reference to 'weavers' (Aram. *shatah* 'to weave') in verse 10a (cf. v. 9) and 'brewers of beer' (LXX) and 'drunkenness' (Heb. *sheker*) in verse 10b (Eusebius, Theodoret, Blenkinsopp). Others take verse 10 as a description of collapsing dams (Heb. *seker*; cf. Gen 8:2) and the destruction of fishponds (Rashi, Ibn Ezra, Tg Jerome, Calvin, AV, *JSB*); or alternatively envisage the plight of 'pillars of the land' in the sense of wealthy employers, and 'wage-earners' (Heb. *seker* 'wages') (Luther, Duhm, Childs; cf. NRSV, NJB), all meeting with the same fate.

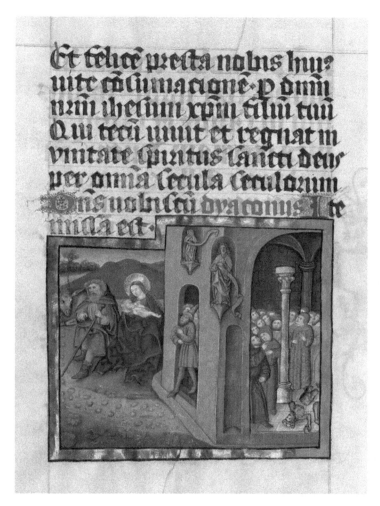

PLATE 19 'The idols of Egypt will tremble at his presence' (Isa 19:1). 'The Flight into Egypt' from the Salzburg Missal (fifteenth century). Reproduced with kind permission of Bavarian State Library, Münich.

Blessed Be Egypt, My People! (Isa 19:16–25)

The second part of the chapter is a series of five 'on that day' prophecies, mainly about Judah and the Jews in Egypt. The first (vv. 16–17) continues the prophecy of doom begun in the first part of the chapter, adding the detail that it will be 'the land of Judah' that strikes terror into the Egyptians. Rashi suggests that this refers to their reaction on receiving the news of Sennacherib's miraculous destruction in Judah, terrifying evidence of the power of Israel's God. The Church Fathers interpreted the verses as referring to the conversion of the Egyptians to Christianity: they learnt to fear God either when they saw how the Jews' land was destroyed by the Romans in 70 CE because they had been disobedient (Cyril) or from the 'knowledge of Scripture', scriptures written in the 'land of Judah' (Jerome, *Glossa*). Modern commentators have seen a possible reference here to the period of relative peace and prosperity in Judah after Egypt had been invaded and conquered by Cambyses in 525 BCE (Wildberger).

Commentators are agreed that the five cities in Egypt which speak the language of Canaan (Hebrew) and swear allegiance to the Lord of hosts (v. 18) are five of the Jewish communities known to have existed in Egypt from the sixth century BCE. Evidence for these comes both from the Bible (e.g. Jer 43:8–44:1; cf. Isa 49:12) and from discoveries at Elephantine and elsewhere. The prophecy describes the setting up of an altar at one of these centres, where both Jews and Egyptians will come to worship the Lord (v. 19), and the coming of a saviour to defend them (v. 20). People will then be free to travel between Mesopotamia and Egypt, and all three nations will be blessed (vv. 23–25). According to Josephus the prophecy in verses 18–21 was fulfilled when the High Priest Onias IV was forced out of Jerusalem by the Syrians around 170 BCE, and went to Egypt, where he built a temple at Leontopolis 'after the pattern of the Temple in Jerusalem'. He tells us that the Egyptian king supported the project, being at war with the Syrians and impressed that the prophet Isaiah had long ago predicted that 'there should be an altar in Egypt to the Lord God' (v. 19) (*Antiquities* 13.62–73).

Leontopolis was in the district of Heliopolis ('city of the sun' Heb. *ḥeres* v. 18; Vg, RSV, NJB). This is the reading found in the Qumran Isaiah Scroll A. The Septuagint has *polis-asedek*, 'the city of righteousness' (cf. Heb. *ha-ṣedeq*), with the addition in several manuscripts of the word *heliou* 'sun', clearly reflecting a connection perceived between Isaiah's prophecy and the Temple at Leontopolis. If the name *polis ased*, a variant reading in Codex Sinaiticus, contains the Arabic word *asad* 'lion', then the connection with Leontopolis 'city of the lion', is even closer (Sawyer 1986: 27). The reference in the Septuagint to the saviour 'judging' (Gk *krinon*) may suggest another possible allusion to Onias since on two occasions he passed judgement in favour of the Jews (Hayward 1982: 441). The temple of Onias at Leontopolis, however, was condemned as heretical by the Judaean establishment. The rabbis declared that sacrifices offered there were illegitimate (m*Menaḥot* 13:10), and this is reflected in the MT 'city of destruction' ('*ir ha-heres*; cf. *Pesh*, AV, Calvin). Tg has both: the 'city of Heliopolis (*qarta bet shemesh*) which is about to be desolate'. Rashi quotes Jeremiah 43:13

as proof that the verse refers to Heliopolis in Egypt and, on the reference to the sacred 'pillar' (Heb. *maṣṣebah*) in verse 19, points out that Jeremiah predicted the destruction of the 'pillars' (RSV 'obelisks') there.

Christian commentators from patristic times refer to Josephus' account of Jewish worship at the Temple of Onias in Heliopolis but reject the suggestion that Isaiah's prophecy refers to it (Cyril, Jerome, Theodoret). It proves that the Jewish law prohibiting the offering of sacrifices anywhere other than at the Temple in Jerusalem (Deut 12) is wrong (Jerome). Onias was a 'wicked and ambitious priest' who maliciously used this prophecy of Isaiah to authorize the building of an altar in Egypt (Calvin; cf. Henry). They interpret the passage with reference to the coming of Christianity to Egypt. The five cities (v. 18) are the five senses and the change of language from Egyptian to 'the altered language of Canaan' represents the move from works of darkness to the 'fragrance of Christ' (2 Cor 2:15) (Bede, *Exposition of Luke* 5.19,17–19). The 'altar' in verse 19 is the Church and the 'pillar' is the cross (Cyril), or the 'pillar set up beside the altar of Christ' is the New Testament, the Old Testament having already come from the 'land of Judah' (v. 17) (Eusebius). When the Egyptians cry to the Lord, he will send them a 'saviour' (v. 20; Heb. *moshia*'), that is, Jesus, whose name in Hebrew means 'he saves' (Jerome; cf. Ambrose, *Letter* 44, 15.7), though Jesus saved not only the Egyptians but the whole world (Cyril). 'The Lord will smite them and heal them' (v. 22) refers to the persecution of the faithful which in the end earns them a victor's crown for 'the Lord punishes those whom he loves' (Prov 3:12) (Jerome; cf. Eusebius, Cyril, Calvin). World peace symbolized by the highway linking Egypt and Assyria (v. 23) recalls one of Isaiah's earlier prophecies (2:4) and refers not only to the peace of Christ when all nations will be under one spiritual ruler but also to the Pax Romana which facilitated the spread of the gospel to the ends of the earth (Cyril).

The blessing of Israel's worst enemies, Egypt and Assyria (vv. 24–25), is by any standards very remarkable, and commentators find it hard to accept at face value. Rashi takes the 'blessing' in verse 24 as referring to prominence and greatness in general, with Israel coming third chronologically after the miraculous defeat of Sennacherib and his army. In verse 25 he follows the Targum in implying that the prophecy refers to 'my people in Egypt' and 'my people in Assyria', not to the Egyptians and Assyrians themselves (cf. LXX, *Pesh*). An eighteenth-century Jewish commentator even suggests that 'third' in verse 24 (Heb. *shelishiyyah*) should be translated as 'government, authority' (from *shalish* 'officer'; cf. Exod 14:7) and the verse translated 'Israel will be a ruling power over Egypt and Assyria' (*Metzudat David*). But according to Ibn Ezra the text means what it says: 'God has blessed all three nations' (cf. Kimḥi). Christian interpreters welcome the universalistic tone of the passage (Eusebius, Aquinas,

Henry). Jerome cites the Song of the Sea (Exod 15:1) to celebrate the fact that Christ achieved in Egypt what Moses failed to do, and Luther comments that, with the abolition of the Law, gentiles as well as Jews will receive the gospel: all will be equal 'and there will be one fold' (John 10:16).

Without reference to such Christian appropriations of the passage, many commentators agree that this is some kind of a highpoint in Old Testament theology: 'in an extraordinarily venturesome manoeuvre … the enemies are named as fellow members of the covenant … it is the world that turns out to be God's chosen people' (Brueggemann; cf. Lowth, Duhm, Kaiser). As to dating, the unusually generous attitude towards Egypt and Assyria recalls other sixth- and fifth-century BCE texts such as Isaiah 49:6 and 66:18–23, Jeremiah's letter to the exiles (Jer 29) and the Book of Jonah (Wildberger, Clements, Blenkinsopp).

Put Not Your Trust in Egypt and Ethiopia (Isa 20:1–6)

The last in the series of prophecies (Isa 18–20) is a short narrative account of an episode in the life of Isaiah intended to warn his people against putting their trust in the Egyptians and Ethiopians. The prophet is instructed to walk about the streets of Jerusalem naked and barefoot for three years, as a 'sign and a portent' that the Egyptians and the Ethiopians will be defeated and led away captive, naked and barefoot, by the king of Assyria (vv. 2–4), just as the

Isaiah Through the Centuries, First Edition. John F. A. Sawyer.
© 2018 John Wiley & Sons Ltd. Published 2020 by John Wiley & Sons Ltd.

Syro-Ephraimite coalition had been twenty years earlier (7:1–9). The account ends with his people's dismay and despair when they see what happens to those in whom they had placed their faith (vv. 5–6). The date is given as the year of an Assyrian campaign against the Philistine city of Ashdod, that is, according to contemporary records, 711 BCE. Egypt was not involved in the Ashdod campaign, but the collapse of a relatively strong city in the region would have provided an appropriately frightening background for a prophecy about the deadly power of the Assyrian army. Ashdod was one of the five great Philistine cities (1 Sam 6:17–18) and, according to Herodotus (2:157), held out against the Egyptians under Psammetichus for twenty-nine years (Lowth).

The prophet's behaviour for three years is extraordinary, even in comparison with other acted parables (e.g. 1 Kgs 22:11; Jer 13:1–7; 19; Ezek 4; 12:1–16), and commentators have questioned some of the details. According to the Targum, he is told to 'put on' sackcloth, not take it off (v. 2), because there is no reason why he should have been wearing sackcloth at the time, and thus he was not totally naked, but 'in torn and worn out clothing' (Rashi). There is no question about the nakedness of the Egyptian and Ethiopian captives: 'young and old, naked and barefoot, their buttocks uncovered' (v. 4). For Rashi Egypt's 'shame' (Heb. *'ervah*) recalls the crime of Ham, who saw his father's nakedness (Heb. *'ervah*) and did not cover him up (Gen 9:20–25). This punishment of Ham's African descendants is therefore most appropriate.

Some argue that Isaiah's symbolic action lasted, not for 'three years', but for three days, citing a parallel in which 'a day stands for a year' (Ezek 4:6), so that the prophet's three days' eccentric behaviour symbolized the three-year-long Assyrian siege of Ashdod (Aquinas, Nicholas, Henry). The Church Fathers, on the other hand, saw great virtue in the prophet's behaviour: Isaiah was an example of frugal living, like John the Baptist and Elijah (Clement of Alexandria, *Paedagogus* 2.10.113), 'surpassing every ascetic practice when he went naked and barefoot for three years' (Origen, *Against Celsus* 7.7). It was a demonstration of the prophet's obedience and faith that such a 'wise, decent and virtuous man' should let himself be ridiculed like that (Jerome, Cyril; cf. (Henry). The godly would be moved by the sight of his nakedness and 'fix their attention on the word … in the same manner as, in the visible sacraments, we ought to behold those things which are invisible' (Calvin).

The prophecy concludes with cries of despair from 'the inhabitants of this island' (LXX, Vg, AV) (v. 6). Some Christian commentators thought this must refer to Egypt (Cyril, Eusebius, Luther), but it is assumed by most to be a description of the people of Judah. Judah is described as an island because it is situated between the Mediterranean and the Dead Sea, or because it is like an island separated from other nations by a wall of hostility (Eph 2:14), a wall finally thrown down by Christ (Calvin; cf. Nicholas, Henry). Jerome points out that it is a good description of God's people, the Church, 'beaten and buffeted by waves of persecution' (Jerome). Modern scholars note that the Hebrew word translated 'island' (Heb. *'i*) in the old versions includes coastal regions ('coastlands' RSV) such as Lebanon and Palestine as well as islands (cf. Isa:11:11; 66:19), and it could therefore be a correct geographical description of Judaea as the Jewish commentators assume.

This chapter figured in the 'great Quaker debate' of 1672 in which the English clergyman and founder of the first Baptist church in the USA, Roger Williams (*c.*1604–1683), in attacking the principles and practices of the Quakers, cited an incident in which some women had run about naked in the streets (Williams 1963: 5, 61). Such behaviour may have been a result of the treatment Quaker women received from the Massachusetts authorities, which at times was so brutal and severe that it drove some to mental breakdown (Lowenherz 1959: 164, note 9). But the antinomian William Blake regarded nudity as a representation of primeval innocence (Ackroyd 1995: 158), and he records how Isaiah once told him he went about naked and barefoot for three years for the same reason as 'our friend Diogenes the Grecian' (Blake 1966: 153–154). In 1986 a young Sudanese Christian named Paul Kon Ajith began a three-year ministry as a wandering preacher, naked like Isaiah, except for a waist belt, and carrying a cross, a bell and a drum. He frequently preached on Isaiah 18 (LeMarquand 2006: 564–565).

Babylon is Fallen! (Isa 21:1–10)

The chapter contains three more 'oracles concerning foreign nations' (vv. 1, 11, 13).
Verse 9 'Fallen, fallen is Babylon' makes it clear what the first one is about
(vv. 1–10), although it has a different title from the earlier, much longer and
more elaborate 'oracle concerning Babylon' (13–14). It must be assumed that
'the wilderness of the sea' (v. 1) must refer to Babylon, perhaps the echo of an
Akkadian name for the region: *mat-tamtim* (the land of the sea) (Blenkinsopp).

Isaiah Through the Centuries, First Edition. John F. A. Sawyer.
© 2018 John Wiley & Sons Ltd. Published 2020 by John Wiley & Sons Ltd.

Jewish commentators take it to mean the 'western desert' since the Hebrew word for 'sea' (*yam*) can also mean 'west' (e.g. Gen 12:8; Isa 11:14), and this would be a natural way for the Elamites and Medes (v. 2) to describe Babylon (Ibn Ezra; cf. Rashi). Some point out that the name is appropriate because Babylon was situated in well-watered land in the valley of the Euphrates, citing another prophecy against Babylon: 'I will dry up her sea' (Jer 51:36; Jerome; Lowth). Others interpret it metaphorically as a land that is densely populated (Cyril, Theodoret, *Glossa*) or invaded by armies 'coming from the wilderness like the waters of the sea' (Tg). For Aquinas it recalls the image of the roar of nations 'like the thundering of the sea' (Isa 17:12). The Septuagint has 'the vision of the desert', which would apply to the other two oracles in the chapter as well, concerning Dumah (v. 11) and Arabia (v. 13), although less appropriate for Babylon.

The 'whirlwinds in the Negeb [desert]' are the approaching Elamite and Median armies according to most commentators (Theodoret, Aquinas, Rashi, Henry, Childs). It may be that it is an image of the onslaught of the 'hard vision' (v. 2), a reference to the frightening experience of the prophet to be elaborated in the next verses (LXX, Eusebius). Calvin suggests that the 'terrible land' from which the vision comes is Judah, because it was there, in the history of his chosen people, that God demonstrated to the nations his terrifying power. The Targum and the Peshitta have 'the robbers are robbed, the destroyers destroyed' (v. 2). This is implied by the Hebrew (Rashi; cf. Eusebius, Jerome) and can be achieved by a simple emendation recommended by many modern commentators. 'All her sighing' means the sighing and the suffering she (Babylon) had caused in many countries, including Judah, and which will now be ended by God's intervention (Kimhi; cf. Tg; Rashi). The Septuagint reads 'the Elamites are upon me … I will groan and console myself', and Jerome believed these are the words of the frightened people of Babylon.

According to a rabbinic tradition, the description of the prophet's anguish and mental turmoil that follows (vv. 3–4) shows that he had compassion even for the Babylonians (Rashi: cf. Isa 16:11; *Tanḥ.* Num 1.1; cf. Jerome, Aquinas). Some compare it to similar passages in the account of the experiences of Jeremiah (4:19) and Habakkuk (3:16) and argue that the extreme reaction of the prophet in this case to the news of a Babylonian defeat suggests an eighth-century date when Babylon was an ally of Judah (Isa 39; Childs). Rashi interprets it as the prophet imagining the Babylonians lamenting their fate (cf. Cyril; Cassel 2006: 155–156), while, according to Luther, the prophet is ridiculing them. For many commentators the references to 'twilight' (v. 4) and the preparing of a banquet ('prepare the table … spread the rugs' v. 5 RSV) recall Belshazzar's Feast (Dan 5) (Jerome, Cyril, Nicholas, Calvin, Henry). In the medieval tradition verse 5 out of context was used as an instruction to preachers: 'prepare the table', that is holy scripture; 'watch in the watchtower' (AV, Vg), that is, study it diligently; and, nourished by its goodness, arm yourselves for service in Christ's army (*Glossa*).

The prophet is asked to appoint a watchman to look out for the approach of riders and chariots (vv. 6–7). Many commentators, both Jewish and Christian, have taken this to be a reference to the prophet Habakkuk (cf. Hab 2:1), said to have been a disciple of Isaiah, who complained that Isaiah's prophecy about the fall of Babylon was delayed (Rashi, *Glossa*, Aquinas). He too stations himself on a tower (Hab 2:1), and the numerical value of his name by gematria equals that of the word 'lion' (Heb. *arieh*) in verse 8 (MT, Tg, Vg, AV) (Rashi). The riders and chariots in verse 7 (cf. v. 9) have been much discussed, not least because the Hebrew word *rekeb*, which occurs three times, can refer both to horses and chariots, both singular and collective. Rashi envisaged a single chariot with two riders, one on a donkey and one on a camel, representing respectively Persia and Media (cf. LXX, Vg, Jerome, *Glossa*). For others one was Cyrus and the other Darius, or one animal was for fighting, the other for carrying supplies (Theodoret, Lowth), while the Arab historian Al-Biruni and other Muslim scholars tell us that this is one of several biblical prophecies about the coming of Muhammad on a camel, with the Messiah beside him on a donkey (Biruni 1879: 22; cf. Déclais 2001: 150) (Plate 20).

Many take the nouns as collectives and imagine a whole army of riders, some on donkeys or mules, some on camels, and note that according to Herodotus (*Histories* 1.80) Cyrus' army rode on camels (Lowth) (Plate 21). The 'horsemen in pairs' (RSV, NRSV, NJB) are quoted by the Latin writer Peter Chrysologus as the prophetic background of Jesus sending out his disciples 'two by two' (Mark 6:7). (*Sermon* 170).

The 'lion' in verse 8 (MT, Vg, AV) refers to Habakkuk according to Jewish sources, as we saw, but is identified by Eusebius and others as the avenging angel Ariel (Heb. *ariel* 'lion of God'; cf. 1 Pet 5:8), ready to destroy Babylon as he destroyed the Egyptians (Exod 13) and the Assyrians (Isa 37:36). The Targum explains it as a reference to the lion on the Persian standard. Modern scholars mostly emend it to *ha-roeh* (the one who saw (RSV); the look-out (NJB)) as 'obviously correct' (Lowth), and this is now supported by the evidence of the Isaiah Scroll A from Qumran. The question still remains, however, as to where the lion came from if it was not in the original Hebrew.

The destruction of Babylon with all her idols is explicitly mentioned (v. 9; cf. 44:9–20; 46:1–2). In verse 10 the dramatic image of threshing and winnowing (v. 10), which is used elsewhere of the fate of Babylon (Jer 51:2, 33; cf. Isa 41:15), is applied by the prophet to his own people. They are 'the stack of wheat which I was commanded by the Holy Spirit to rectify and to lead on the straight path' (Rashi) or those threshed by the Lord 'for the purpose of separating the wheat from the chaff' (Luther). Christians have applied it to the Church 'threshed by

صورة المسيح وصورة المحمد

PLATE 20   'And I saw a rider on an ass and a rider on a camel' (Isa 21:7 LXX), identified as the Messiah and Muhammad. Fourteenth-century Arabic ms. Reproduced with kind permission of Edinburgh University Library.

afflictions and persecutions', like 'God's Israel of old … under the plougher's plough (Ps 129:3) and the thresher's flail' (Henry).

One of Bob Dylan's best known lyrics, 'All along the watchtower' (1967), was inspired by Isaiah 21: the watchtower (v. 8), the princes (v. 5), the two riders (v. 7, 9), the growling wild cat (v. 8) and the howling wind (v. 1) (Gill 1998: 130–131). Perhaps the thief's 'the hour is getting late' was inspired by the watchman's words 'Morning comes but also the night' (v. 12). The main part of the lyric is a dialogue between the joker and the thief, and the setting is not revealed till the end. In Dylan's own words 'Isaiah the prophet, even Jeremiah, see if their brethren didn't want to bust their brains for telling it right like it is – there are my roots I suppose' (Heylin 1991: 370).

Watchman, What of the Night? (Isa 21:11–17)

A short 'oracle concerning Dumah' follows (vv. 11–12). Like Tema and Kedar (vv. 13–17), Dumah was among the Ishmaelite peoples living in north Arabia (Gen.25:13–14), but the reference to the much better known Edomite place

PLATE 21   'A chariot of asses and a chariot of camels' (Isa 21:7 AV). Copper engraving
from Johann Jacob Scheuchzer, *Physica Sacra* (1735). Reproduced with kind
permission of David Gunn.

name Seir in the first line of the prophecy, and the similarity of the two names
in Hebrew (*edom*) and Greek (*Idumaia*), has resulted in most commentators
from ancient times assuming it refers to Edom (cf. Jer 49:17–22; Ezek 35; Obad)
(LXX; Cyril, Eusebius, Aquinas, Rashi). Luther interprets the prophecy as the
threat of an attack on an Arabian region coming from Edom, and modern scholars also take it with the following verses as one of three prophecies 'concerning
Arabia' (vv. 11–17; Childs, Clements) and date it to the time of Nebuchadnezzar

or later (Eichhorn, Duhm, Dillmann; Sweeney 2006: 248, 259). At all events the region is to be reduced to 'silence' (Heb. *dumah*) (Jerome, Aquinas).

The brief dialogue between an unnamed questioner from Seir and a watchman, usually taken to be the prophet himself, has been much discussed. The question 'What of the night?' could mean no more than 'what time is it?' – repeated twice because it is addressed to more than one watchman to check whether they were asleep (Ibn Ezra; cf. Calvin). A more dramatic interpretation would be 'What is left of the night?' in the sense of 'How much more darkness do we have to endure before dawn?' (cf. Ps 30:5) (Brueggemann). The Septuagint has an entirely different text in which the Lord apparently mocks the feeble preparations of the Edomites as an invading army approaches: 'They are calling to me from Seir, Guard the fortifications!' (Cyril, Theodoret).

The prophet's enigmatic reply 'Morning comes and also the night', seems to be about God's justice: light for the righteous and darkness for the wicked (Rashi; cf. Tg). For Aquinas, it recalls the fate of the Egyptians when 'the whole world was illuminated with brilliant light, while over those men alone heavy night was spread' (Wisd 17:20–21), and for Calvin, the fate of the wicked who 'in the morning say, Would it were evening! and in the evening Would it were morning!' (Deut 28:67). Gregory the Great applied it to the Jewish rejection of Christ since, when the light of Christ came into the world, they chose the 'darkness of disbelief' (*Morals on Job* 2.6.34). The prophecy ends with the equally enigmatic 'If you inquire, inquire; come back again'. 'Inquire' is interpreted by most commentators as 'make your requests known to God', and 'come back again' as a call to repentance (Tg, Rashi, Jerome, Aquinas, *Glossa*). Theodotion paraphrases it as 'If you want salvation, come to me', while for Cyril, following the Septuagint 'dwell with me', it recalls the words of Jesus, 'If anyone loves me, he must follow me; where I am, there shall my servant be also' (John 12:26).

'What of the night' inspired a personal reflection on living in the shadow of Auschwitz. It is with these words that the Anglican priest Alan Ecclestone began his book *The Night Sky of the Lord* (1980) on the horrific culmination of centuries of Christian anti-Semitism. In Jewish lectionaries it accompanies a reading from the Exodus story (Exod 12:29–51) (Mann 1971: 1, 411), and it features in a poem by the Jewish poet Yannai printed in most Passover Haggadahs where 'what of the night? is the cry of those waiting for the black night of exile to end' (Birnbaum 1976: 138–139). A very different interpretation is to be found in the Christmas carol 'Watchman, tell us of the night' (1825) by John Bowring, in which the watchman explains to a traveller the events of Christmas Eve, ending with 'Traveller, lo! the Prince of Peace, Lo! the Son of God is come!' (*GtG* 97). It has been suggested that an illustration in the tenth-century Paris Psalter showing Isaiah standing between a grey-clad woman representing Night and a small child labelled 'Dawn' beside a flourishing tree (cf. Isa 11:1), is a messianic interpretation of verse 12 (Berges 2012: 122).

The prophecy concerning Arabia is also difficult to follow (vv. 13–17). According to the Jewish commentators, it envisages a time when the Arabs dwelling in Dedan, Tema and Kedar will be punished for failing to give water and bread to the people of Israel when they were passing through their territory (cf. Deut 23:4) (Rashi, Ibn Ezra). By contrast verse 14 expresses sympathy for refugees fleeing through the desert (cf. Isa 58:7; Aquinas), whether they are victims of an invasion by Sennacherib in Isaiah's day (Rashi) or a campaign by the Babylonians in the middle of the sixth century BCE (cf. Jer 49:29–31) (Jerome). Some take Dedanites as 'cousins' (cf. Heb. *dodim*) and point to the ancient family ties between Israel and the desert-dwelling 'sons of Ishmael' (Gen 25) (Rashi, Jerome). The Hebrew title translated 'concerning Arabia' (RSV; Heb. *ba'arab*) in verse 13 is unusual. It is rendered by the Septuagint Vg and *Pesh* as 'in the evening' (Heb. *ba'ereb*) and in some modern versions as 'concerning the wasteland' (NJB) or 'desert plain' (NRSV), which suggestively recalls the mysterious title with which the chapter began (Roberts).

Let Me Weep Bitter Tears (Isa 22:1–14)

The inclusion of Jerusalem among the nations castigated in these chapters demonstrates God's justice and recalls the words of Amos: 'Are you not like the Ethiopians to me? says the Lord' (Amos 9:7) (Jerome, Eusebius). The 'valley of vision' (v. 1; cf. v. 5) must refer to Jerusalem (Rashi; cf. vv. 4, 10): LXX has 'the valley of Zion' and the Targum 'the city which lies in the valley'. Some say the term applies to the city after it had been destroyed by the Romans (Theodoret).

Isaiah Through the Centuries, First Edition. John F. A. Sawyer.
© 2018 John Wiley & Sons Ltd. Published 2020 by John Wiley & Sons Ltd.

Luther says it is a deliberate slur on the holy city, once the most famous mountain on earth, now brought low and reduced to nothing (cf. Eusebius). According to Jerome, Zion, that is, the Church, has its valleys and its mountains: 'Let us flee from the valleys of Zion ... and go up to the mountains' (*Homilies on the Psalms* 45). Calvin thinks it refers to the whole of Judaea, surrounded on all sides by hills (Ps 125:2). The 'valley of vision' is also reminiscent of the name Abraham gave the place (Gen 22:14 AV) (Aquinas), which became 'the seedbed (*seminarium*) of the prophets' (Jerome; cf. Rashi, Luther, Calvin, Lowth).

Many believe the situation envisaged is Sennacherib's invasion in 701, in view of references to the building works of Hezekiah (vv. 8b–11: cf. 2 Chron 32:5; 2 Kgs 20:20) and his palace officials Shebna and Eliakim (vv. 15–25; cf. Isa 36–37). Others argue that references to the destruction of Jerusalem (vv. 4, 8a) point to Nebuchadnezzar in 586 BCE (Rashi, Jerome) or the Romans in 70 CE (Theodoret), while modern critical scholars identify an original eighth-century BCE core (vv. 1–3, 12–14) with later additions reflecting events in the sixth century (vv. 4–8a) or later, and the prose style of the Deuteronomistic historian (vv. 8b–11) (Clements, Childs).

The prophecy begins with a rebuke aimed at the crowds going up on to the rooftops of Jerusalem to celebrate victory (cf. v. 13) when they should be mourning the destruction of most of their territory, the cowardice of their leaders and the fate of Judaean prisoners of war (v. 3). This resembles the contemporary Assyrian account of events, which is very different from the biblical narrative (Isa 36–37) (Blenkinsopp). Rashi says they went up on to their roofs 'to see the army and to fight' (cf. Calvin), but he does not explain why the prophet rebukes them, although he quotes a rabbinic tradition that the people of Jerusalem were haughty (cf. Tg), and others note that the roof was a place for pagan rituals (Ibn Ezra, Aquinas). Jerome cites this passage in an explanation of the meaning of Gog and Magog (Ezek 38:1–23): we shall understand 'roof' (Heb. *gag*) as the leaders of the heretics and 'from the roof' (Heb. *mi-gag*) as their followers (*Comm. on Ezekiel* 11.38:1–23). The Church Fathers also understood 'slain but not by the sword ... dead but not in battle' (v. 2) allegorically as referring to the death of sinners, not caused by military weapons, but by the 'sharp sting of death, which is grievous sin' (1 Cor 15:56; Basil, *Letter* 44; cf. Eusebius, Jerome). The fleeing 'rulers' in verse 3 recall the futile attempt of King Zedekiah and his retinue to escape by night from the Babylonian siege (2 Kgs 25:4–7) (Cyril, Rashi).

The prophet's poignant outburst of grief over the destruction of Jerusalem, 'Look away from me, let me weep bitter tears' (v. 4), accompanies medieval representations of Christ weeping over Jerusalem (Luke 19:42) alongside Jeremiah (Lam 1:1) and the exiles in Babylon (Ps 137:1) (Heitz and Scheiber 1903) (Plate 22). The prophet's words are evidence of his compassion for the

PLATE 22 'Let me alone: I will weep bitterly' (Isa 22:4). Christ weeping over Jerusalem (Luke 19:41–2; Lam.1:1) from a *Biblia Pauperum* (Netherlands 1480–1485). Reproduced with kind permission of Warburg Institute London.

victims of war, and a source of comfort to the grieving (Chrysostom, *Homilies on the Statutes* 18.8). Rashi says that it is God who is weeping: 'Leave Me alone!', he says to the ministering angels. In Starer's *Ariel* (1960), a tender lament, sung by a soprano solo, begins 'Look away from me' (Isa 22:4) and is followed by raucous voices from the chorus singing 'Let us eat and drink, for tomorrow we shall die' (v. 13) (*BiM* 19). The poem ends with the Lord God removing 'the covering (Heb. *masak*) of Judah' (vv. 8a), a word elsewhere applied to a screen for the door of the tabernacle (Exod 35:15, 17) and the cloud that protected Israel in the wilderness (Ps 105:39). But Rashi suggests that here it refers to the whole Temple, which had protected Jerusalem until it was destroyed by Nebuchadnezzar (cf. Jerome, Aquinas).

Up to this point the prophet has been addressing the city as a woman (vv. 1–7). Now a detailed description of the city's preparations for a siege, is addressed to a masculine audience. The 'House of the Forest' (v. 8) was where Solomon stored three hundred shields of beaten gold (1 Kgs 10:17; cf. 1 Kgs 7:2–5), and the Targum appears to allude to Pompey's victorious entry into the Temple treasury in 63 BCE (Chilton 1982: 43–44). Hezekiah's famous building works (cf. 2 Kgs 20:20; 2 Chron 32:3–4, 30) were all to no avail since they 'did not look to the One who made it all' (vv. 9–11). For Calvin, Jerusalem here is a 'lively image of the Church: What madness is it to think of defending the city when you despise him who made it!'. Modern visitors to Jerusalem can still walk through 'Hezekiah's tunnel', discovered in 1838, that takes water from the spring of Gihon to the pool of Siloam (v. 11; cf. Isa 8:6; John 9:7).

The climax of this prophecy (vv. 13–14) returns to poetry and to its first theme (vv. 1–3). According to a rabbinic comment, verse 12 implies that God takes up the position of a mourner and joins in their uncontrollable weeping (LamR *Proem* 24; Linafelt 2000:104–108). But the people who should be in mourning are defiantly feasting and celebrating: the prophet tells them 'this iniquity will not be forgiven you till you die' (v. 14). The Targum takes this as a reference to the second death, that is, in the world to come (Rashi, cf. Rev 2:11; 20:6, 14; 21:8). The Church Fathers found in this verse criticism of those who enjoy eating and drinking too much, citing Paul: 'the kingdom of God is not food and drink but righteousness and peace and the joy of the spirit' (Rom 14:17) (Cyprian, *To Quirinus* 3.60; cf. Athanasius, *Festal Letter* 7.2). But, as Calvin and others point out, this is not a criticism of eating meat and drinking wine, but of the revellers' mockery of God and his prophets. Rashi says that those who say 'Let us eat and drink for tomorrow we die' have no share in the world to come, while Luther cites Paul's letter to the Corinthians to prove that they are mocking the resurrection of the dead (1 Cor 15:32).

The Key of David (Isa 22:15–25)

The second part of the chapter begins with a personal attack on a palace official called Shebna (vv. 15–19). Prophecies against named individuals are rare (cf. Amos 7:16–17; Jer 20:1–6; 28:12–17) and the reason for this one is not entirely clear. He is described as a 'steward' (RSV) or 'treasurer' (LXX), 'in charge of the household' (v. 15), and is referred to elsewhere as a high-ranking official (Isa 36–37), and, according to many, a priest (Jerome, Aquinas). Isaiah is instructed to go and tell him he is to be 'hurled like a ball into a wide land' where he will die, a disgrace to his master's household (vv. 17–18). At first sight his crime seems to be pride and self-importance exemplified in the tomb he had planned for himself (v. 16; Jerome, Luther). But others find a different meaning in the rare Hebrew word, translated 'steward' (Heb. *soken*). It is applied to the young woman sent to comfort King David on his deathbed (1 Kgs 1:2), and the rabbis describe Shebna as 'pleasure loving' and 'lustful' (b*Sanhedrin* 26b; cf. Rashi), while Calvin suggests he was 'cunning' and 'treacherous', engaged in secret negotiations with the enemy behind Hezekiah's back in order to save his own skin (Calvin).

His fate is described in colourful language (vv. 17–18), interpreted in various ways from being shaken like an old garment (NEB; Heb. *beged*) to being whirled round like a cockerel (Heb. *geber*) (Jerome; cf. Rashi) before being let go and flying off into 'a vast space' (NJB). There is a rabbinic tradition that he was dragged to his death behind the horses of Sennacherib's army (Rashi). However that may be, Shebna is to be removed from his high office (v. 19), a dramatic fall from grace perhaps alluded to in the Parable of the Unjust Steward (Luke 16) (Myers 2012: 61). Calvin tells us that the story of Shebna reminds him of Thomas More, who planned a vast and expensive tomb for himself but was then found guilty of treason and executed: 'and thus he had a gibbet for his tomb'.

The prophet goes on to humiliate Shebna even further by telling him that Eliakim, son of Hilkiah, will put on the sacred garments and carry the key of David (vv. 20–25). His promotion may be further described in Isa 33:16–17 (Nicholas). Elsewhere Shebna and Eliakim are mentioned as working together (Isa 36–37), but here they appear opposed to each other. Two striking images of Eliakim's authority are introduced, both conspicuously absent from the main Greek versions. First, he will carry 'the key of the house of David' on his shoulder. The Targum explains that this means that the 'key to the Temple and the authority of the house of David' will be upon his shoulder (cf. Isa 9:5; cf. Duhm). More prosaic commentators discuss the dimensions and weight of keys in ancient Israel (Lowth; Gray).

In the other, somewhat more domestic image, Eliakim is compared to 'a peg in a sure place' on which all his responsibilities will be safely hung (vv. 23–24). These include responsibility for his family and household, the 'small vessels and cups' being the weakest and most in need of his support (Rashi, Calvin), and also, in some versions, his responsibility for music taking the last word in the verse as 'lyres' rather than 'flagons' (Heb. *nebalim*; Vg, Tg, Rashi, Nicholas, Luther, Calvin). Such concentration of power in one man, perhaps suggesting nepotism, with the abrupt announcement of his death, has been interpreted by modern scholars as evidence that the last two verses were added by another hand after the fall of Jerusalem in 586 BCE (Clements, Blenkinsopp). An ultra-orthodox, anti-Zionist newspaper published in Israel since 1985 took its title *Yated Ne'eman* ('a secure peg') from verses 22–23.

The Church Fathers interpret Shebna allegorically as presiding over the Jewish Temple, now destroyed, and Eliakim, which they tell us in Hebrew means 'risen God', as embodying the truth of the gospel (Cyril, Jerome, Eusebius). The 'key on his shoulder' foreshadows the cross on Christ's back (*Glossa*) and became a messianic symbol, used already in the Book of Revelation with reference to the power of the 'holy one' to open the way to eternal life (Rev 3:7–13; Henry). Another New Testament allusion was found in Christ's giving of the 'keys of the kingdom of heaven' to Peter (Matt 16:19). Later the Latin *Clavis David* 'key of David', with Isa 42:7, is the fourth of the messianic titles in the 'O Antiphons' and in the popular Advent hymn: 'O come, Thou Key of David, come, and open wide our heav'nly home' (*EH* 8; *CH4* 273; *HON* 384) (see comm. on Isa 7:14). A dramatic elaboration of the image, 'sad instrument of all our woe', appears in Milton's *Paradise Lost* (1998: ii. 872).

Howl Ye Ships of Tarshish! (Isa 23:1–18)

The climax of the series of oracles concerning the foreign nations (13–23) is directed at the great Phoenician cities of Tyre and Sidon, whose wealth and international reputation were proverbial (I Kgs 9:11; Ps 45:12; 2 Esd 1:11; Matt 11:21–22). Ezekiel devotes three chapters to Tyre (26–28; cf. Jer 25:22; 27:3; 47:4; Amos 1:9–10; Joel 3:4–8; Zech 9:2–3). The first part announces their destruction (vv. 1–14) and most commentators, following Ezekiel (26:7–14;

Isaiah Through the Centuries, First Edition. John F. A. Sawyer.
© 2018 John Wiley & Sons Ltd. Published 2020 by John Wiley & Sons Ltd.

cf. Jer 27:1–7), locate this in the Babylonian period (Jerome, Cyril, Aquinas, Calvin, Lowth, Childs). For others the reference to Assyria (v. 13) supports an Isaianic context (Eusebius, Rashi, Rudolph, Erlandson, *JSB*), while many also note the relevance of the dramatic conquest of Tyre after a long siege by Alexander the Great in 332 BCE (Jerome, Luther, Duhm, Wildberger).

The dramatic opening of the prophecy envisages the news of Tyre's destruction reaching its seafaring citizens wherever they are. 'Ships of Tarshish' may mean no more than 'sea-going vessels' (cf. 2:16; 60:9; Ps 48:7; Rashi) but probably alludes to a Phoenician colony in Spain (Gk *Tartessus*) (Lowth). The Septuagint translators identified Tarshish with 'Carthage' in North Africa, another Phoenician colony (cf. Jerome, Theodoret) and apparently interpreted the whole prophecy as being fulfilled in their own day when Carthage was destroyed by the Romans in 146 BCE (v. 10 LXX; cf. van der Kooij 1998).

'The Kittim' (vv. 1, 12 MT, LXX, AV) are often identified with the Romans (Rashi; cf. Dan 11:30), sometimes also the Greeks and Macedonians, including Alexander the Great (cf. 1 Macc 1:1; Jerome, Aquinas, Calvin), but here the term is understood by modern commentators as a name for Cyprus, derived from *Kitium*, one of its main ports (cf. Jerome, Theodoret). The mention of an 'island' in verse 2 (Heb. '*i*; cf. LXX, Vg, AV) prompts discussion of Alexander's siege of Tyre, which had been an island until he built a mole connecting it to the mainland in 332 BCE (Katzenstein 1997:15). The term is normally interpreted, however, as a collective noun 'islands' (Calvin) or 'coast' (RSV; cf. 11:11; 41:1, 5), not as a reference to Tyre. Shihor (v. 3) is a name for the Nile (cf. Josh.13:3; Jer 2:16) (Rashi, Jerome). In his comments on these verses, Calvin compares Tyre with Venice or Antwerp: what happens to a great seaport will have inevitable consequences for trading partners all over the world.

The text of verse 4 is difficult but appears to say to Sidon, 'Be ashamed because the sea, source of all your wealth, has lost everything.' She is like a desolate widow. She used to bring shiploads of young people to Tyre to be trained in trade and business: 'now all that is finished' (Rashi; Henry). Others take it as a speech by Tyre described as 'the sea, the stronghold of the sea' because it was 'as if she reigned alone in the midst of the sea' (Calvin; cf. Cyril). The Church Fathers cite the first words of the verse 'Be ashamed, O Sidon, said the sea' (*Erubesce Sidon, ait mare*) in more than one context, representing the sea as a source of great blessing (Theodoret, *On Divine Providence* 2.18, 20) – 'great and vast, where there are creatures without number and animals both small and large. Ships navigate there with the dragon whom you formed to play in it' (Ps 104:25–26; Jerome) – or as a metaphor for the chances and changes of this world (Gregory, *Morals on Job* 1.5). Thomas a Kempis cites it as a warning to anyone tempted away from the way of humility and obedience by the blandishments of this world (*Imitation of Christ* 23.4). The comment on Egypt's reaction to the news (v. 5) suggests to Rashi that the plagues of Tyre shall be like those of Egypt. Then the taunts continue with a reference to the former glory of this ancient city and the global achievements of her citizens (vv. 6–7).

The reason for Tyre's downfall is given in a typically Isaianic theological comment referring to the Lord of hosts and his outstretched hand (vv. 8–12; cf. Isa 5:25; 9:17). There is a brief reference to the Tyrians' sins (v. 9), greatly expanded in Ezekiel 27 (Jerome), and further allusions to their fate both at home and abroad. The mention of what the Lord did in Egypt and Canaan (vv. 10–11) is interpreted by some as illustrating the kind of fate the Phoenicians can expect (Luther; cf. Calvin), not least because Tyre and Sidon were in Canaan (cf. Gen 10:19; Matt 15:21–22; Jerome; Rashi). There is no escape even for those who flee to Cyprus – or Macedonia or Rome (see on Kittim in v. 1) (v. 12). Mention of the Chaldeans (that is, Babylonians) (v. 13) has been interpreted in two very different ways. The Hebrew text as it stands appears to reject any involvement by the Chaldeans described as 'a people that never was' (AV, NJB) or a people that God regretted ever having created (b*Sukkah* 52b; Rashi; cf. Hab 1:6). Assyria then takes full responsibility for the destruction of Tyre. Alternatively a small change in the punctuation of the Hebrew blames 'the Chaldeans … this is the people; it was not Assyria' (RSV; cf. Lowth). In fact Tyre was destroyed both by the Assyrians and the Chaldeans: either way 'she will undoubtedly be made to feel the hand of God, and her power will be of no avail to her' (Calvin). The passage ends as it began 'Wail, O ships of Tarshish…!' (v. 14). D. H. Lawrence uses the words 'Howl, ships of Tarshish' as the title of his discussion of the Bible as a 'book of roaming, more than Herodotus or the Odyssey … the wideness of its contact and the bigness of its intelligence and its secret sympathy' (1974: 1.157–158).

The second part of the oracle promises that Tyre will be restored after seventy years (vv. 15–18), a remarkable prophecy, comparable to the 'blessing of Egypt and Assyria' a few chapters earlier (19:24–25). The parallel with the duration of the Babylonian exile (Jer 25:11; 29:10) suggests that this refers to rebuilding under Cyrus (Jerome, Cyril, Theodoret, Henry). Scholars have also noted that there was a period of rebuilding in Tyre in 274 BCE under Ptolemy II, fifty-eight years after the siege of Alexander, which appears to be alluded to in the Septuagint (van der Kooij 1998; cf. Childs).

The image of the harlot recalls Isaiah's lament over the decline and fall of his own city (Isa 1:21), but here she represents a city coming to life again, taking up her harp and going about the city, singing and plying her trade as she had done in the old days. Israel's traditional attitude towards her as a symbol of wickedness and idolatry continues into the New Testament, where verse 17 is applied to Rome, described as 'the great harlot seated upon many waters, with whom the kings of the earth have committed fornication' (Rev 17:1–2) (Fekkes 1994: 280–282).

But Isaiah breaks with that tradition in a very striking way and envisages a time when 'her merchandise and her hire will be dedicated to the Lord'. Rashi says that this must refer to when the Messiah comes. But other commentators point out that Tyrian currency was used in the Temple (Chilton 1987: 47; Jeremias 1969: 36) and have little difficulty in finding other examples of Tyrian involvement in the affairs of Judah and Jerusalem in the Second Temple period, including those who 'brought in fish and all kinds of wares and sold them on the Sabbath' (Neh.13:16) and crowds coming from Tyre and Sidon to hear Jesus (Luke 6:17; cf. Mk 3:8).

Later Christian commentators apply it to the presence of Christians in Tyre (Acts 21:2–6; Nicholas, Lowth) and see it as proof that the goodness of God 'can penetrate even into this abominable brothel' (Calvin). An illustration of verse 16 in the medieval *Bible Moralisée* contrasts the harp-playing harlot with King David singing about her (Ps 45:12) while the penitent sing God's praises 'with the spirit … and the mind' (1 Cor 14:15; Aquinas; cf. Jerome, *Glossa*).

After the long series of prophecies concerning Babylon, Moab, Egypt and the other nations of the world (13–23), chapters 24–27 contain very few specific geographical and historical references and appear to be concerned with the end of the world. For the Church Fathers the section recalled passages in the New Testament about the Last Judgement (John 12:31–32; Rom 2:16) and the resurrection of the dead (1 Thess 4:16–17) (Cyril, Eusebius, Jerome, Theodoret), and since the nineteenth century it has often been described as the 'Isaiah Apocalypse', closer in style to Daniel and the Book of Revelation than to anything in the prophetic literature. More recently commentators have stressed

Isaiah Through the Centuries, First Edition. John F. A. Sawyer.
© 2018 John Wiley & Sons Ltd. Published 2020 by John Wiley & Sons Ltd.

continuity with the rest of the book of Isaiah and the absence of some of the chief characteristics of Jewish apocalyptic, such as elaborate angelology, patterns in history and visionary experiences.

The End of the World (Isa 24:1–13)

Chapter 24 was interpreted by many as a horrifying description of the destruction of the land of Judah (cf. 5:1–6; 7:18–25) at the hand of the Assyrians (Rashi) or the Seleucids (Vitringa) or an unnamed enemy (Lowth), while Luther interpreted it as another prophecy about the 'devastation of the land of Judaea and the synagogue that does not accept the Gospel'. The survival of a righteous remnant (Isa 24:14–16; 26:1–4; 27:6) was identified with Hezekiah and the miraculously rescued citizens of Jerusalem (Rashi), or the Jews in the diaspora (Lowth) or the 'apostles proclaiming the Gospel' (Luther). The global perspective and developed eschatology, however, including the defeat of death (Isa 25:8) and the resurrection of the dead (Isa 26:19) are unique, and probably reflect developments in third-century BCE Judaism (Sweeney; Blenkinsopp).

The word translated 'the earth' (Heb. *haʾareṣ*: v. 1; cf. vv. 1, 3, 4, 5, 6) can also mean 'the land' (cf. 27:13), especially the 'land of Israel' as Rashi believes, but 'the earth ... the world (Heb. *tevel*) ... the heavens' in verse 4 make the global perspective hard to miss (cf. Ps 24:1) (Eusebius, Calvin). Rashi resorts to an ingenious linguistic argument to prove that here 'world' (Heb. *tevel*) refers to the land of Israel (cf. Lowth). In death all are equal (v. 2; cf. Job 3:19; Rom 2:6–10) (Jerome, Eusebius, Aquinas); and the 'heights' in verse 4 are taken by many to refer to the high and mighty, brought down like everyone else (LXX, Vg, Jerome, Eusebius, Rashi, Luther, AV, Lowth, NJB, *JSB*). Modern commentators take it as a reference to the heights of heaven (cf. 21–23): 'the heavens languish together with the earth' (RSV; cf. Isa 33:5; 57:15; Blenkinsopp, Roberts).

'The everlasting covenant' (v. 5) or the 'covenant of the universe' applies to all humanity (Ibn Ezra), like 'the natural, law' written in the souls of Greeks and barbarians alike (Rom 2:15) (Eusebius), and God's promises concerning Christ (Luther). The whole earth is 'polluted' (RSV; 'defiled' AV) by their crimes which include murder (cf. Gen 9:6), as the story of Cain and Abel makes clear (Gen 4:10) (Jerome; cf. Origen, *Homily on Ezekiel* 4.1), but the prophecy can be applied to environmental pollution as well: the fertility of the land is cursed (v. 6) by human wickedness as it is elsewhere in biblical teaching (Deut 28; Jer 23; Marlow and Barton 2009: 200). The assonance in this chapter has been commented on by several commentators: for example, verse 5 contains 'one of those bitter puns where cause (*ḥalap* 'transgress') and effect (*ḥanap* 'pollute') audibly echo each other' (Buber 1994: 31–32). Others see in this powerful imagery an 'analogy between the world natural and the world politic' (Newton 1733: 17; cf. Lowth).

The graphic description of a 'city of chaos' follows (RSV) in which every house is boarded up, people go about the streets wailing, there is no laughter or music or singing and the city gates are lying in pieces. Commentators have identified the city as Jerusalem, either in the time of Sennacherib (Rashi) or after the Romans had finished with it in 70 CE (Luther). The prophet's words about no longer drinking wine with a song (v. 9) were applied by the rabbis to the end of the custom of singing at wedding feasts when the Temple was destroyed (m*Sotah* 9:11). Jerome has 'city of vanity', citing Ecclesiastes, and compares it to Babylon, symbol of human iniquity in the Book of Revelation (Rev 18:22). The word 'chaos' (Heb. *tohu*) recalls the first chapter of Genesis (Gen.1:2) and suggests a return to a time before there were cities (Gen 4:17) and wine (Gen 9:20–21) and people (Gen 1:26–27): in a word, a return to primeval chaos when 'the world was empty' (Oecolampadius). The passage ends with the dramatic image, already familiar from an earlier prophecy, of someone shaking the last few olives off a tree or looking for the last few grapes on a vine after the vintage is over (v. 13; cf. Isa 17:6).

The Last Judgement (Isa 24:14–23)

Although this is not specified in the Hebrew, it must be the survivors that 'shout ... sing ... cry aloud from the sea' in the next passage (vv. 14–16) (Sommer). The Septuagint inserts 'they that are left on the land'. Commentators stress the minute size of the remnant: 'there would be few or almost none left, and yet their shouting would be heard everywhere' (Calvin; cf. Jerome, Eusebius, *Proof of the Gospel*, 2,3). The reference is to synagogues in Egypt, Asia Minor, Greece and elsewhere in the Hellenistic world (Lowth), and later, for Christian commentators, to the establishment of churches all over the world like islands in a sea of polytheism (cf. Ps 104:25; Cyril, Jerome, Aquinas, Luther). The Septuagint has 'the water of the sea will be troubled' (v. 14), that is, the peoples of the earth will be disturbed by the knowledge of the truth (Cyril). The sea figures in other visions of the Last Judgement: 'the sea gave up the dead in it ... and all were judged' (Rev 20:13; cf. Dan 7). Some commentators understand the reference to the sea in verse 14 as comparative and suggest that their shouts will be louder than the sea (Blenkinsopp) or louder than the (Song of the) Sea sung by Moses and the people of Israel when they escaped from Egypt (Exod 15) (Rashi; cf. Tg). Jerome notes that the word translated 'cry aloud' (AV Heb. *sahal*) or 'shout' (RSV) is associated with the neighing of horses enjoying themselves (cf. Jer 5:8; 50:11).

The word translated 'from the sea' (LXX, Vg, Tg, AV; Heb. *mi-yam*) can also mean 'from the west' as Kimḥi and most modern commentators take it (cf. RSV, NJB), corresponding to 'in the east' in verse 15 (RSV, NJB). But the Hebrew *ba-urim*, literally, 'in or with the fires, lights', is not found elsewhere with the meaning of 'in the east, i.e. towards the fires of dawn'. The Targum explains 'glorify the Lord with lights' (*JSB*) as 'when the light comes to the righteous', and Rashi tells us this refers to the lights ('beacons?') bringing good news, news of redemption from Babylon and news of redemption from Edom (i.e. Rome). A very different suggestion is 'even in the fires of persecution' recalling Paul's words 'for your sake we are killed all the day long' (Rom 8:36) and the Song of the Three Children (Dan 3) (Henry; cf. AV). Other possibilities include 'in the holes and crevices' (Rashi) or 'in the valleys' (Luther), while Jerome deduces from the priestly Urim and Thummim (Exod 28:30) that it refers to the teaching (*doctrina*) of the Church (cf. Aquinas).

In verse 16 we hear the voice of the prophet, as we do in Daniel (8:27; 10:15–17) and Revelation (1:17), reacting to his vision of the end of the world: 'My secret is with me! My secret is with me! Woe is me!' (Vg, Tg, Rashi; Heb. *razi li razi li oi li*). Jerome paraphrases it as follows: 'it is too terrible to describe – I cannot tell you everything I have seen' (cf. Aquinas). Eusebius and Theodotion compare the passage to Paul's account of the 'secret and hidden wisdom of God … revealed to us through the Spirit' (1 Cor 2:6–13; cf. Isa 4:4). Some interpret the double secret as a reference to the fate of the righteous and the fate of the wicked (Tg, Rashi), although Calvin doubts whether there is anything about the fate of the righteous here. There was a Rabbinic tradition that 'the end of the earth' (Heb. *kenaph ha'areṣ* 'wing of the earth') refers to the Temple in Jerusalem (Tg cf. Rashi).

An illuminated letter at the beginning of Book 8 in a twelfth-century manuscript of Jerome's twelve-volume commentary, has a beautiful illustration of his interpretation of verse 16b (Sawyer 1996: 1–2; Fig. 1). It shows the prophet at the top carrying a scroll in each hand, one with *Ecce virgo …* (Isa 7:14), the other with the words *Secretum mihi …* (Isa 24:16). Looking up at him is Jerome, and on his scroll are the words *Dic tu Isaias dic testimonium Christi* (Go on Isaiah – tell them about Christ!). What is particularly interesting about this miniature is that it functions as the title of the 'Isaiah Apocalypse' (Isa 24–27): here more than anywhere else, he says, in the difficult and often frightening language and imagery of Isaiah's vision of the end of the world, are we to learn the truth about Christ.

The word 'secret' (Heb. *raz*) is an Aramaic loan word occurring several times in the Aramaic part of the Book of Daniel (Dan 2:18; 4:6) but not elsewhere in the Hebrew Bible, and many writers prefer to read it as 'my leanness, my leanness' (AV) or 'I pine away' (RSV) (cf. Ezek 34:20; Zeph 2:11), indicating the physical effect the vision had on the prophet, or 'to express the feeling of poignant grief which torments the Church inwardly' (Calvin). The verse ends with a remarkable sequence of five Hebrew words all from the same root (*bgd*), meaning 'treacherous', 'treachery', 'deal treacherously' and the like, prompting the rabbinic suggestion that they refer to five different acts of treachery directed at God's people, those by Babylon, Media, Persia, Greece and Edom (that is, Rome) (b*Sanhedrin* 94a; Rashi).

The language and imagery of the description of final judgement in the next few verses is also striking: 'Terror and the pit and the snare (Heb. *paḥad va-paḥat va-paḥ*) are upon you!' (v. 17). The alliteration of the three terms, employed by Jeremiah as well (Jer 48:43), appealed to the authors of the Damascus Rule at Qumran, who applied them to the three nets of Satan – fornication, riches and profanation of the Temple – with which he will catch Israel (*CD* 4.13; *DSSE* 132). Rashi interprets the three hazards as the sword of the Messiah son of Joseph, the sword of the Messiah son of David and the 'trap of the Wars of Gog': there can be no escape for anyone (v. 18). For Calvin and others the picture of people frantically trying to escape recalls an even more graphic image in Amos (5:19) and the oracle concerning Moab (Isa 15:9), while Aquinas compares it to being caught between Scylla and Charybdis. The 'windows of heaven' are signs and portents (Tg), or 'the prophets in whom the Lord showed concern for human-kind before he himself would descend to earth' (Ambrose, *On Isaac or the Soul* 4.32–33). According to Luther and others the 'foundations of the earth' (v. 18) are world leaders (cf. *Glossa*).

Some, like the Qumran community, envisaged this scene of judgement as restricted to the 'inhabitants of the land [of Judah]' (cf. Rashi, Luther, Lowth), but most interpret the prophecy as applying to the inhabitants of the whole earth. It is the whole planet that is 'utterly broken … rent asunder … violently shaken … staggering like a drunk … swaying like a hut' (vv. 19–20) (AV, RSV; Calvin). The reason is that it is collapsing under the weight of human sin (cf. Ps 38:4): 'what is heavier than lead? A fool. Sand, salt and a lump of iron are easier to bear than a stupid man' (Sir 22:15) (Aquinas). Modern commen-tators on this passage note recent awareness of the global damage that human activities have inflicted on the planet including pollution, a steady increase in the number of endangered species and climate change (cf. Isa 24:1; Blenkinsopp).

Burkhard's oratorio 'The Face of Isaiah' (1936) contains a dramatic setting of verses 1, 5, 8, 16b, 19 (Berges 2012: 126) and the first of *Two Motets 'In Diem Pacis'* (1945) by Wilfrid Mellers entitled 'The City of Desolation' (v. 10) is a set-ting of verses 4–14 (AV). The second movement of Robert Starer's *Ariel: Visions of Isaiah* (1960) was also inspired by this chapter (v. 4), while the fourth reaches a dramatic climax in the chorus 'Fear, and the Pit, and the Snare' (v. 17) (*BiM* 19).

The last part of the chapter (vv. 21–23) introduces the notion, familiar from the apocalyptic literature of the Second Temple period, of a war in heaven which influences events on earth: 'the kingdom of earthly kings is tied to the kingdom of angels' (cf. Dan 10:13ff) (Ibn Ezra; cf. Eusebius). Verses 21–22 are about the 'eternal fire prepared for the devil and his angels' (Matt 25:41) (Jerome, Aquinas). The host of heaven will be punished along with the nations of the world (cf. Rev 20:3, 7–10; 1 Enoch 90:24 *OTP* 1.70–71) and 'kept in eternal chains in the nether gloom until the judgement of the great day' (Jude 6).

A few commentators interpret the sun, moon and stars in verse 23 as metaphors, 'the sun for the whole species and race of kings, the moon for the body of the common people considered as the king's wife, and the stars for subordinate princes and great men, or bishops and rulers of the people of God when the sun is Christ' (Newton 1733, Ch. 2; cf. Rashi, Ibn Ezra Luther, Calvin, Lowth). Luther adds a psychological interpretation where 'the sun, moon, bells, drums and songs sound and shine sad to the sad, but are joyful to the happy and rejoicing'. The Targum also removes the personification: 'the worshippers of the moon will be ashamed and the worshippers of the sun humiliated'. Theodoret implies that the sun, moon and stars are being punished for their role in pagan worship. The Septuagint omits the moon and the sun altogether and reads 'the brick shall decay and the wall collapse'.

But for many Christian writers this is a description of the active participation of the heavenly bodies in the last battle, recalling the solar eclipse during the crucifixion (Luke 23:45) (Oecolampadius) and the heavenly portents when the Son of Man comes (Matt 24:29–31; Mark 13:24) (Jerome). Then the city will have no need of sun and moon because 'the glory of God is its light' (Rev 21:23; cf. Isa 60:19) (Nicholas; cf. Aquinas), or, as Calvin puts it, the kingdom of Christ will be 'so illustrious that it will darken the sun and stars by its brightness' (cf. Bede, *Exposition of Mark* 4.13.24). The climax of the vision is the enthronement of the Lord on Mount Zion 'before his elders' (cf. Heb 12:22). This prompts Jerome to discuss the merits of old age with reference to Abraham (Gen.25:8), the seventy elders (Num 11) and the Ancient of Days in Daniel's vision (Dan 8:9; cf. Wisd 4:8–9). Others see an allusion to the vision of God granted to Moses and the elders on Mount Sinai (Exod 24:9–11). It too was accompanied by a feast (25:6–8) (Clements, Blenkinsopp).

The Eschatological Banquet

The chapter begins with another song of thanksgiving (vv. 1–5) sung 'by the prophet or by the elders' mentioned in the previous verse (24: 23) (Ibn Ezra), celebrating God's faithfulness to the covenant made of old with Abraham (Rashi, Luther). The language and imagery of verse 1 come from the Psalms (e.g. Pss 77, 78), but 'wonderful things … counsels' (AV) echoes Isaiah 9:6, and 'faithful and sure' (Heb. *emunah omen*) is reminiscent of Isa 7:9 (cf. Isa 1:21, 26; 30:15).

Isaiah Through the Centuries, First Edition. John F. A. Sawyer.
© 2018 John Wiley & Sons Ltd. Published 2020 by John Wiley & Sons Ltd.

The Hebrew wordplay was missed in the Greek and Latin versions, which end with 'Amen' (cf. Deut 27; John 6:54) or 'So be it' (LXX) (Aquinas; cf. Jerome, Cyril).

The 'fortified city' in verse 2, like the 'city of chaos' in the previous chapter (Isa 24:10), is not named and could be Nineveh, Babylon or any other city possessed by the enemies of God (Lowth). Rashi identifies it as Mount Seir, that is, Edom, which was interpreted from as early as the second century BCE, as a coded reference to Rome. Jerome rejects the Jewish interpretation and identifies the city instead with Jerusalem, occupied since 135 CE by non-Jews and never to be rebuilt (van der Kooij 2006: 55), although he points out an 'obvious mistake' in the Septuagint where it has 'in Zion' (*be-ṣiyyon*) for 'in a dry place' (Heb. *be-ṣayon*) (v. 5). Verses 3–5 celebrate the downfall of tyrants and divine protection for the poor and needy. The imagery, again reminiscent of the Psalms (e.g. Ps 18:2), compares the song of the righteous to a thick cloud which everyone enjoys in the summer heat, while 'the song of the ruthless will be silenced' (Rashi).

The feast prepared by the Lord on Mount Zion, unlike the feast on Mount Sinai (Exod 24:9–11), will be 'for all peoples', not just Moses and the elders, and death will be swallowed up for ever (vv. 6–9). Jews and gentiles are here together invited to a 'very splendid banquet' (Calvin), described in two words, each repeated twice: 'fat things' (Heb. *shemanim*) which include meat, fruit and vegetables, rich and full of goodness ('marrow'), and 'dregs, lees' (Heb. *shemarim*), which suggests both unrestrained drinking, as in 'drink to the dregs', and the high alcoholic content and rich flavour of wine made from the lees (Calvin, Lowth). The Septuagint reads 'on this mountain they shall drink joy, they shall drink wine, they shall anoint themselves with myrrh' (cf. Ps 23:5; Aquinas). Nothing will interfere with their joy, not even death; 'the Lord God will wipe away every tear from their eyes' (v. 8). The 'covering that is cast over all peoples' (v. 7), whether a veil worn by mourners (cf. 2 Sam 15:30) or a shroud wrapped round dead bodies (NRSV) or the fetters of death in which all people are enmeshed (Jerome) will never be seen again.

The notion of death being 'swallowed up' (v. 8; cf. I Cor 15:54) was difficult for some: the Targum has 'they will forget death', while the Septuagint turns it round: 'death swallowed them up' (v. 8; cf. Irenaeus, *Against Heresies* 4.9.2; Theodoret; Ibn Ezra). Kimḥi suggests that it refers only to violent death and envisages a world without war and crime. But there is a rabbinic tradition that when Satan hears the shofar (cf. Isa 27:13), he trembles because he knows the time has come for him to be swallowed up (cf. b*Rosh ha-Shanah* 16a–16b; Matt 1983: 232).

A short hymn, introduced separately (v. 9) and sung by Israel (Rashi) or by the 'children of the new age' (Eusebius), contains their joyful response. It begins

with the words 'Lo this is our God ... this is the Lord' (v. 9), described by Calvin
as a 'joyous shout ... the actual test and proof of the experience of the grace of
God', and then applies the emotive word 'salvation' (Heb. *yeshu'ah*; cf, 12:2–3;
26:1) to the 'wonderful things' (v. 1) that have happened. Cyril compares this to
what Zachariah and the aged Symeon sang when they witnessed 'salvation'
(Luke 1:69; 2:30–31).

The apparent universalism of these verses, although characteristic of chapters 24–27, was challenged by many commentators and translators. Jewish
commentators suggest that the 'peoples' and 'nations' are Israel's enemies and
the feast will be a 'feast of dregs' and a 'humiliation' for them like the feast of
Gog and Magog (Ezek 39:17–20; Rashi; cf. Tg), while Christian commentators
maintain that 'all peoples' indicates a shift away from the Jews towards the gentiles, and 'his people' in verse 8 is the Church (Jerome, Eusebius, Nicholas).
Luther on verse 6 envisages a horrific feast in which Judaea is 'devoured and
drained to the last dregs' by her enemies.

The Targum of this chapter differs significantly from MT and appears to
reflect second-century CE Jewish history. In verse 2 it reads 'a temple of the
gentiles will never be built in the city of Jerusalem', an apparent objection to the
Emperor Hadrian's plan to build a temple for Jupiter Capitolinus in Jerusalem
in 130 CE, while the 'covering' in verse 7 is glossed 'the face of the great one who
is master over all the peoples', an obvious reference to the emperor himself
(van der Kooij 2006: 58–60). Jewish opposition to Roman imperial plans for
Jerusalem was a major factor leading to the second Jewish revolt in 132–135 CE.

The Church Fathers interpreted the 'wonderful things, plans formed of old'
(v. 1) as the 'kingdom prepared from the foundation of the world' (Matt 25:34),
the 'mystery hidden for ages' (Eph 3:9; cf. 1:4) and now 'made manifest to his
saints' (Col 1:26; cf. 1 Cor 2:6–13) (Jerome, Cyril, Theodoret). The Septuagint
reads 'fortified cities' (plural) and Cyril argues that these are not real cities but
strongholds of the devil, evil forces finally destroyed 'when Immanuel appeared'
(Cyril). The feast on Mount Zion (v. 6) is the 'festal gathering' (Gk *panegyris*)
described by the Apostle in his letter to the Hebrews (Heb 12:22–23a)
(Eusebius). The wine is the wine of the Eucharist (1 Cor 11:26; Aquinas; cf.
Cyril) and the 'anointing with myrrh' (LXX) refers to those who are 'truly
anointed by the Holy Spirit' (Cyril, *Catechetical Lectures* 11.5–7). There will be
no more weeping, no more mourning because Christ struck down death when
he rose on the third day (Cyril), and sin, the cause of death, will be no more
(Augustine, *Sermon* 155.2)). The foretelling of the defeat of death can be compared to Hosea's words quoted by Paul (Hos 13:14; 1 Cor 15:54–55) (Aquinas).

Verses 7–9, cited already by Paul in his discourse on the resurrection of the
dead (1 Cor 15) and in the Book of Revelation (Rev 7:17), came to have an
important role to play in the context of death and mourning, in both Jewish and

Christian tradition. It is one of three passages from Isaiah read at the conclusion of the Jewish 'Prayer in the House of Mourning' (see comm. on Isa 66:13). The passage is read at Christian funeral services and Masses of the dead (*ORM*) and is one of four passages chosen by Luther as suitable to be used as epitaphs (cf. Isa 26:19; 26:20; 57:2) (*LW* 53.328–329). An early example is the funeral oration by Ambrose on the death of his brother Satyrus in 378 CE, in which, by stressing verse 9, he puts the emphasis on the faith that survives death (*On Satyrus* 1.70). There is a beautiful setting of verse 8 by the Venetian composer Antonio Caldara in *Le profezie evangeliche d'Isaia* (1729), as well as better known versions in Handel's *Messiah* (1742) and Brahms' *German Requiem* (1869). The opening chorus of Stainer's cantata *The Daughter of Jairus* (1878) combines verse 8 with Isaiah 33:2 and 30:19 (*BiM* 57), and, with Isaiah 14:3, it also features in an a cappella chorus in Starer's *Ariel* (1959) (*BiM* 19). Samuel Sebastian Wesley's anthem 'O Lord Thou Art My God' (1839) is a setting of verses 1, 4, 8 and 9, interspersed with verses from Psalm 33 and 1 Corinthians 15 (*BiM* 174).

For some 'the hand of the Lord will rest on this mountain' (v. 10) recalls Psalm 132:14 (Aquinas), but in Isaiah, more often than not, it is the role of 'the hand of God' to strike the wicked (cf. Isa 5:25; 9:12, 17, 21; 10:4; 14:26–27), and the chapter ends with a grotesque prophecy concerning the fate of Moab (cf. Isa 15–16). In an image familiar from the Psalms (Ps 69:1–2; cf. 40:2), they will be like someone drowning in a 'cesspool' (Heb. *madmenah*), perhaps a pun on the name of the Moabite town Madmen (Jer 48:2) (Calvin). The Septuagint and Vulgate have a different image in which the victim is run over by some heavy vehicle, reminiscent of the fate of Gilead (Amos 2:3; cf. Isa 41:15) (Theodoret, Aquinas). Moab is the only place name explicitly mentioned in the 'Isaiah apocalypse' (Isa 24–27), apart from Jerusalem, and the reason for singling out one among Israel's many traditional enemies is unclear. One suggestion is that it refers to the conquest of Moab by Alexander Jannaeus in the second century (Josephus, *Antiquities* 13.13; Duhm). Christian commentators are mostly satisfied with the notion that Moab here stands for the devil (cf. Matt 25:41) (Theodoret; cf. Jerome, Aquinas) or the Antichrist (cf. 2 Thess 2:9) (Nicholas) or 'all the enemies of the Church' (Calvin).

The Resurrection of the Dead (Isa 26:1–21)

The 'Isaiah Apocalypse' continues with another song to be sung by the righteous 'on that day' (cf. Isa 24:14–16; 25:1–5; 27:2–5). Continuity with the preceding chapters is established in the striking images of the 'lofty city … brought low' (v. 5; cf. 24:10; 25:2) and the resurrection of the dead (v. 19; cf. Isa 25:8). Commentators note close parallels with the Psalms: the city of God (cf. Ps 46:4; 87:3), the gates through which the righteous enter Jerusalem (cf. Ps 24; 100:4;

Isaiah Through the Centuries, First Edition. John F. A. Sawyer.
© 2018 John Wiley & Sons Ltd. Published 2020 by John Wiley & Sons Ltd.

118:19–20), the way of the righteous and the fate of the wicked (cf. Ps 1:6), the soul yearning for God (cf. Pss 25:15; 42:1–3; 631–632) and the assurance of final salvation (Pss 22:22–21; 73:21–26) (Jerome). The prophet's words bring comfort to his people by summoning them to 'behold from the lofty watchtower of faith the restoration of Jerusalem' (Calvin; cf. Rashi).

Christians identify the city as the Church: it is a 'strong city' because 'the gates of hell will not prevail against it' (Matt 16:18; Cyril, Jerome). The 'wall and bulwark' (LXX, Vg) protecting it are Christ and the prophets whose words support the faithful (Gregory, *Homilies on Ezekiel* 2.2.5); and its inhabitants are 'the righteous, by faith indeed' (Luther).

In Jewish tradition the gates are to be opened for the 'righteous nation' who have never lost their faith in God (v. 2; Rashi) or who 'have kept the law with a perfect heart' (Tg). This is how the verse is interpreted in the Hebrew inscription above the entrance to the New Synagogue in Berlin, opened in the presence of Bismarck in 1866, destroyed in the Second World War and rebuilt after perestroika in 1993 (Plate 23). The verse is also quoted by the rabbis to prove that a 'righteous gentile is equal to the High Priest' (b*Sanhedrin* 59a), and the phrase 'that keeps faith' (NRSV; Heb. *shomer emunim*), read as 'that

PLATE 23   'Open the gates that a righteous nation may enter in' (Isa 26:2–3).
Inscription on the façade of the New Synagogue, Oranienburger Strasse, Berlin (1866).

says Amen' (Heb. *she-omer amenim*), inspired the tradition that the sinners of Israel and the righteous gentiles in Hell will shout 'Amen' when they hear God's voice, and when God hears them, he gives the keys to Michael and Gabriel and says to them 'Open the gates of Gehinnom and bring them up' (*RA* 558).

Combined with Isaiah 52:1, verse 2 provides the text for Movement 4 of Penderecki's choral *Symphony no.7: The Seven Gates of Jerusalem* (1996) (*BiM* 232), and in Patten's *Isaiah* (1898) a lovely contralto aria beginning 'Thou wilt keep him in perfect peace' (vv. 3–5 AV) features at the middle of the prophet's ferocious attacks on his people (e.g. Isa 1:13,15; 2:10; 3:16; 30:27–28; 58:1; 63:1–9) (*BiM* 112–113). Verse 3 also inspired an anthem by Samuel Sebastian Wesley (*c*.1850) (*BiM* 241) sung at the coronation of Queen Elizabeth II in 1953, as well as the popular hymn 'Peace, Perfect Peace in this Dark World of Sin' by Edward Bickersteth (1875) (*EH* 468; *CH2* 444; *AM* 764). The passage provides the epitaph, written in Hebrew, on a fresco by Raphael, commissioned in 1510 by a senior papal official named Johannes Goritz, who no doubt interpreted the Hebrew term *goy ṣaddiq* as 'a righteous gentile' and applied it to himself (Ettlinger and Ettlinger 1987: 121–123) (Plate 24).

The phrase translated 'everlasting strength' (AV) or 'everlasting rock' (RSV) (v. 4) (Heb. *ṣur 'olamim*) appears as 'rock of ages' in the margin of King James' Authorized Version, Matthew Henry's commentary (1708–1710), the Darby Bible (1890) and several modern commentaries (Blenkinsopp). The phrase inspired the well-known hymn 'Rock of Ages, Cleft for Me' by Augustus Toplady (1740–1778), who applied the image to Christ from whose 'riven side' flowed water and blood, to 'be of sin the double cure' (*EH* 477; *CH4* 554; *AM* 772). In the Jewish Daily Prayer Book verse 4 appears in the *Qedushah de-Sidra* at the end of the morning service (cf. 42:21; 59:20–21; 65:24) (see on Isa 6:3; *ADPB* 138–139).

'The lofty city...brought low' (v. 5) is not named (cf. 24:10; 25:2) and has been identified with Tyre or Rome (Rashi) and Jerusalem (cf. Luke 13:34–35; Jerome; cf. Luther), but the verse can also be interpreted in general terms recalling Mary's words: 'he has put down the mighty from their thrones, and exalted those of low degree' (Luke 1:52; cf. Calvin). Jews identify the 'poor man' (v. 6 singular; Heb. *'ani* Vg *pauper*) as the Messiah 'humble and riding on an ass' (Zech 9:9; cf. Ps 70:5) (Rashi), while for Christians he is Christ, and the 'needy' (plural) are the apostles (Jerome, Aquinas). Luther takes the verse literally and envisages a destruction so complete that cripples can walk over it.

The 'way of the righteous' (v. 7) described as 'level' and 'smooth' is reminiscent of traditional Wisdom teaching (Prov 4:11–12; Ps 23:1–4; 91:12; Wisd 10:10) (Aquinas; cf. Calvin), though many challenge this in the light of human experience (Job 10:3; Fackenheim 1990; Blenkinsopp).

PLATE 24   'Open the gates that a righteous nation may enter in' (Isa 26:2–3).
Fresco by Raphael in the Basilica of Sant'Agostino, Rome (1512).

The 'path of your judgements' (v. 8 AV) means the way God will wreak
vengeance on the wicked (Rashi). 'In the night' (v. 9) refers to the exile (Rashi;
cf. Jerome) where 'other lords' rule over God's people (v. 13): these include the
papacy (Calvin). The prophet prays that the wicked should see God's might and
'his zeal for his people' and be ashamed (v. 11). Then peace will be established
for we have already received fair punishment for our sins (v. 12); and we shall
recite 'Our God alone is god' (v. 13) (Rashi).

Christian writers apply verses 7–13 to the devotional life. Jerome stresses
that according to the prophet, it is the spirit and not the flesh that 'yearns for
God' (vv. 8–9; cf. Ps 63:1; Gal 5:16–24). For Thomas Aquinas the explicit reference to 'in the night' (v. 9) recalls the devotional language of the Song of Songs
(Cant 3:1) and the Psalms (63:6), while Ambrose, following the Septuagint in
verse 9 ('your judgements are a light in the earth'), deduces that 'if you get up

before the sun rises, you will receive Christ shining on you' (cf. Eph 5:14) (*Exposition of Psalm* 118, 19.30). Cyril cites Paul on the relationship between faith and peace (Gal 5:1) and Augustine's comment on peace in verse 12 is that God has given us all the things he promised (LXX) (*Confessions* 13:35.50–52). It also means that whatever goodness we possess, we possess only through the grace of God (Bede, *Three Books on Solomon's Proverbs* 2.20). The 'prayer of Isaiah the prophet' (vv. 9–21) was one of the nine Greek Canticles from as early as the fifth century (Mearns 1914: 7–14).

The 'other lords' (v. 13) are base desires and 'O Lord our God, take possession of us' (LXX) expresses the Christian's desire to be filled with love and free from the slavery of sin (cf. Rom 5:5) (Augustine, *Sermon* 169.15; cf. Henry). The German New Testament scholar Ernst Käsemann records how a political interpretation of this verse was responsible for his arrest by the Gestapo in 1937 (Harrisville and Sundberg 2002: 249–250). The Church Fathers understood seeing the 'glory of God' in verse 10 (LXX, Vg) as a reference to the resurrection of the dead, anticipating verse 19 (Irenaeus, *Against Heresies* 5.35.1; Augustine, *Sermon* 65.8). Augustine illustrates this by citing the beatitude: 'Blessed are the pure in heart: for they shall see God' (Matt 5:8) (*Sermon* 214.9).

But before the optimism of verse 19, there is a desperate cry of pain from a community suffering the chastisement of a righteous God (vv. 16–18). 'They poured out a prayer' (AV, RSV) illustrates how suffering can bring people closer to God: 'before, prayer came drop by drop … but now it comes like water from a fountain' (Henry). The Hebrew word for 'prayer' (*laḥash*) more commonly means 'whisper', perhaps suggesting in secret for fear of persecution (Fouts 1991; cf. Tg). Calvin comments, 'those who are tortured by extreme anguish can hardly speak'. Like a woman in the throes of childbirth, we thought our agony was about to end (cf. John 16:21), but nothing came of it: 'it was wind (Heb. *ruaḥ*) … we cannot prepare salvation for ourselves' (Rashi; cf. Luther, Calvin). The Church Fathers by contrast, following the Septuagint, read 'we have brought forth the spirit of salvation' (Ambrose, *On Cain and Abel* 1.10.47; Augustine, *Sermon* 210.7; Jerome, *Letter* 121.4), an interpretation preferred by some genteel eighteenth-century scholars to the 'unacceptably gross' image of bringing forth wind (Hammond 1982: 148, 151).

The prophet contrasts the fate of the wicked in verse 14 ('they are shades, they will not live') with 'your dead' who shall 'awake and sing for joy' in verse 19, whether in a prayer (Rashi) or an 'oracle of salvation' addressed by the prophet to his suffering compatriots (Kaiser, Childs). 'Your dead' are the righteous, killed for their faith (Rashi; cf. *Tanḥ* Gen 6:19). Jewish commentators speak of 'the dew of the Torah … which shall be for them a dew of light' (Rashi), but also of 'the dew of resurrection'. This is how it was interpreted in Ephraim of Bonn's poem about the Sacrifice of Isaac: 'it fell down up him and he revived' (Carmi

1981: 382; cf. Spiegel 1979: 32; see below on Isa 33:7). Rain and resurrection are connected in the Amidah (*ADPB* 76–79; cf. *Ta'anit* 7a). The divine dew that brings our bodies back to life after we die is mentioned in the *Gospel of Nicodemus* (J. K. Elliott 1993: 188) and frequently by the Church Fathers (Ambrose, *On Satyrus* 2.67–68; cf. Irenaeus, *Against Heresies* 5.34.1; Tertullian, *On the Resurrection* 31). Elsewhere the dew is the life-giving Spirit of God (cf. Ps 104:29–30) (Cyril) or of 'Christ', recalling the effect of the words of Moses 'like gentle rain upon the grass' (Deut 32:2) (Jerome, *Comm. on Hosea* 2.6.5).

Modern scholars are agreed that belief in the bodily resurrection of the dead is not attested in the Bible much before the Hellenistic period and that consequently verse 19 along with others, notably the 'valley of dry bones' passage (Ezek 37), must originally have referred to the 'resurrection' of a community, not individual resurrection (Ibn Ezra). But the belief is clearly expressed in the Hebrew text as it has come down to us in the words '(together with) my dead body (Heb. *nevelati*)' (AV) as well as in the Septuagint 'those in their tombs shall awake' (cf. Dan 12:2) (Kimḥi). Luther includes verses 19 and 20 among his four texts recommended for use as epitaphs (see comm. on Isa 25:7–9). Verse19 features, beside John 3:16 and Job 19:25–26, in a funeral motet by Heinrich Schütz (1636), and verse 20 in a dramatic chorus beginning 'The earth mourneth' (Isa 24:4) in Starer's *Ariel* (1959).

The chambers mentioned in verse 20 are hiding places where 'the children of the earth' will seek to hide from the Great Glory on Judgement Day (1 Enoch 102:3; *OTP* 1.82). Others say they are graves where the dead can hide in safety until judgement day (Clement of Rome, *Letter to the Corinthians* 50:4; Tertullian, *On the Resurrection* 27), or else caves where the righteous can hide (cf. Isa 2:19; Luther), like Noah in the ark (Origen, *Homilies on Genesis* 2.3) or the Israelites on the night of the passover (Exod 12:22; 14:13–14) (Lowth). For Rashi they are schools and synagogues, and the same verse might have been in Jesus' mind when he taught, 'when you pray, go into your chambers and shut the door [Matt 6:6] and pray to your father in secret' (cf. Ps 141:3) (Jerome) (Gundry 1982: 103; Luz 2007: 298).

The last chapter of the 'Apocalypse' contains a variety of images describing the final victory of the Lord, introduced four times by the phrase 'in that day' (vv. 1, 2, 12, 13). Verse 1 takes up the theme of the last two verses of chapter 26 and is taken by some to be the conclusion of the preceding chapter (Eusebius, Duhm, Blenkinsopp).

Isaiah Through the Centuries, First Edition. John F. A. Sawyer.
© 2018 John Wiley & Sons Ltd. Published 2020 by John Wiley & Sons Ltd.

Leviathan (Isa 27:1)

Leviathan is the name of one of the mythical sea monsters or dragons that symbolize the powers of chaos in the Hebrew Bible (e.g. Pss 74:13–15; 89:6–14; Job 26:12–14) as well as in the more ancient Canaanite texts found at Ugarit where there is a close parallel to this description (*CML* 105). Christian artists applied the myth to baptism, where the powers of chaos were conquered and the water sanctified (Schiller 1971: 131–132), and in an apocalyptic vision of a new heaven and a new earth, the destruction of 'the dragon, that ancient serpent, who is the Devil and Satan' (Rev 20:2–3) meant that 'the sea was no more' (Rev 21:1) (Plate 25). The monster's influence on Hermann Melville's *Moby Dick* (1851) has been noted (Kreitzer 1994: 54–55).

Rashi identified Leviathan 'the piercing serpent' (Heb. *nahash bariah*; LXX, Vg, AV) with Egypt, since the Pharaoh was 'like a bar (Heb. *bariah*), a straight, penetrating serpent, that does not coil'; while Leviathan 'the crooked serpent' is Assyria and the 'dragon that is in the sea' Rome (cf. Tg). Luther similarly takes the two serpents, the straight one and the twisted one, as earthly powers that 'fought with each other till Rome swallowed them both'. Calvin identifies in the 'crowbar' a reference to 'open violence' which characterizes Leviathan as much as his wiles and tricks. The Church Fathers interpret the serpent as 'slippery' (RSV 'fleeing'; cf. Heb. *barah* 'to flee'), that is, deceitful and crooked like the serpent in the Garden of Eden (Gregory, *Morals on Job* 4.17.51) or 'that ancient serpent who is called the Devil and Satan, the deceiver of the whole world' (Rev 12:9) (Jerome; cf. Aquinas). The 'hard [LXX 'holy'] and great and strong sword' is the Word of God (cf. Rev 19:21; Heb 4:12) and the victory is the victory of Christ over all evil on Judgement Day (Cyril).

The Lord's Vineyard (Isa 27:2–11)

The prophet returns to the vineyard (vv. 2–6; cf. Isa 5:1–7), this time to describe how, under God's care, his people Israel 'will blossom and put forth shoots and fill the whole world with fruit' (v. 6) (Marlow and Barton 2009: 222–225). 'Thorns and briars' that once led to the vineyard's destruction (5:6; cf. 7:23–24) no longer pose any threat (v. 4) and Israel will be at peace with their God (v. 5), the last sentence repeated twice recalling the 'perfect peace' of Isa 26:3. According to the Hebrew text (MT; cf. 1QIsaᵃ) the vineyard is a 'vineyard of red wine' (Heb. *hemer*; Vg, AV), that is, a vineyard producing good wine (Rashi). But most modern commentators follow LXX, which has a 'pleasant vineyard' (RSV; Heb. *hemed*; cf. Amos 5:11; Isa 32:12). Regular watering clearly contrasts with the fate of the doomed vineyard (Isa 5:6), both literally and allegorically

PLATE 25 'In that day the LORD shall punish Leviathan (Isa 27:1). Illustration by Gustav Doré for *La Sainte Bible* (Tours 1866). Reproduced with kind permission of David Gunn.

referring to prophecy which never ceases even in times of trouble (Ibn Ezra), and to the water of life promised by Christ to his Church (John 7:37; Luther). For Rashi it is water from the 'cup of retribution', little by little so as not to destroy Israel (cf. Isa 51:17).

God's treatment of his people and the other nations in their midst (the 'thorns and briars'), seems to be the subject of verse 4: 'I have no wrath' means I cannot pour out all my wrath on my own people, however badly they behave, because of my promise to their forefathers (Rashi). Did Israel suffer as much as the Egyptians when God smote them 'in the day of the east wind' (cf. Exod 14:21)? Was their punishment not in just measure (vv. 7–8)? Their iniquity will be expiated when they finally clear the land of all traces of idolatry (v. 9), while the unnamed 'fortified city' (cf. Isa 24:10) where the unrepentant hold out till it is razed to the ground and deserted (vv. 10–11), is identified as Samaria (Ibn Ezra; cf. Sir 50:26). Some scholars find a reference to Alexander the Great here (Berges 2012: 21).

For Christian commentators the vineyard is the Church, the peace (v. 5) is the peace of Christ (1 Cor 1:3) and its global outreach (v. 6), the preaching of the apostles (Jerome; cf. Luther, Calvin). God's treatment of his sinful people 'measure by measure' (v. 8) means that he never suffers them to be tempted beyond what they are able to endure (cf. 1Cor 10:13) (Calvin, Henry). The prophecy that Jacob's guilt will be expiated (v. 9) is alluded to by Paul in his discussion of the salvation of the Jews (Rom 11:22; cf. Isa 59:20–21; Wagner 2006: 88). According to many the 'fortified city ... deserted and forsaken' (v. 10) must be Jerusalem, where Christ was rejected (Aquinas, Luther; cf. Duhm). The women referred to in verse 11 recall both the 'daughters of Jerusalem' weeping on the Way of the Cross (cf. Luke 23:27–28) (Jerome) and the witnesses to the resurrection (Luke 24:1–11) (Tertullian, *Against Marcion* 4.43, Rufinus, *Comm.on Apostles' Creed* 30)), elsewhere compared to the prophets Deborah (Judg.4–5) and Huldah (2 Kgs 22:14–20) (Jerome, Aquinas).

The Greek version, followed by Christian interpreters, differs markedly from the Hebrew especially in verses 3–5 where 'a strong city', presumably Jerusalem (cf. 26:1–6), utters a desperate lament: 'I am a strong city, a city under siege ... in vain shall I water her ... she shall be taken by night ... I am burnt up ... those who dwell in her cry, "Let us make peace"'. Ambrose quotes the passage several times, identifying the city as the soul of a righteous person (or the Church) 'defended by Christ and besieged by the devil' (cf. Cant 8:10) (*On Isaac or The Soul* 5.39).

The Sound of the Shofar (Isa 27:12–13)

The 'Isaiah Apocalypse' ends with two more verses beginning 'in that day' (vv. 12–13). The first seems to compare the ingathering of the exiles to an olive harvest when the trees are first beaten and then the olives gathered up (cf. Isa 24:13) (Rashi). Others take it as a reference to threshing grain (RSV). Either way the effect is to reduce a huge multitude, 'one by one', to a small remnant (Ibn Ezra). For Jews the shofar is a call to worship summoning 'those who were lost' back to Jerusalem, thinking perhaps especially of exiles in Egypt (cf. Isa

18:3) and the 'sons of Ephraim' from the Northern Kingdom exiled in Assyria (Ibn Ezra). Others propose that the trumpet call refers to the edict of Cyrus (2 Chron 36:22–23) (Henry) or the edict of the Emperor Hadrian who rebuilt Jerusalem (Nicholas). Christian commentators, citing Paul (Rom 11:5), speak about the 'remnant chosen by grace' (Luther; cf. Cyril, Jerome, Aquinas).

Cyril compares the 'great trumpet' (v. 13) to the sound of the trumpet that the people heard on Mount Sinai, getting louder and louder amidst the fire, smoke, thunder and earthquake (Exod 19:19), but here he says it refers to the sound of the gospel preached by the apostles as they rescue people from idolatry and bring them to the 'holy mountain', that is, the Church, the New Jerusalem (cf. Jerome, Nicholas, Calvin). Jerome ends Book 8 of his commentary at this point and, referring back to the beginning of the Isaiah apocalypse ('Behold the Lord will lay waste the earth' Isa 24:1), compares the conclusion to Paul's account of the resurrection of the dead when 'the trumpet shall sound and the dead will be raised up' (1 Cor 15:52; cf. 1Thess 4:16; cf. Henry). It is the clarion call that proclaims liberty throughout the land (Lev 25:9–10) and strikes terror into the heart of Satan (see commentary on Isa 25:8).

After the 'Oracles against the nations' (13–23) and the 'Isaiah Apocalypse' (24–27), the prophet returns to the internal politics of Judah in a series of prophecies reminiscent of much of Isaiah 1–12 (Isa 28–35). Modern scholars are agreed that much of this section, particularly 28–31, goes back to the original prophet although, apart from one verse (Isa 30:8; cf. 8:16), no biographical details are given. It would be natural to assume that the historical context of these prophecies was the reign of Hezekiah (cf. Isa 16:28) when the Assyrian threat was still real and Judah was again tempted to put their faith in human powers like Egypt rather than in the power of God (Isa 30:15; cf. 7:9).

Isaiah Through the Centuries, First Edition. John F. A. Sawyer.
© 2018 John Wiley & Sons Ltd. Published 2020 by John Wiley & Sons Ltd.

Woe to the Drunken Priests and Prophets! (Isa 28:1–13)

The series begins with a prophecy that divine judgement is about to fall upon the city of Samaria, the 'proud crown of the drunkards of Ephraim' (vv. 1–4) (Exum 1982). This is what happened in 722 BCE when the Assyrian king Shalmaneser V took the city after a three-year siege (2 Kgs 18:9–12), and most commentators confidently date this prophecy to the years leading up to that event (Nicholas, Lowth, Duhm, Childs). The legendary wealth and 'glorious beauty' of Samaria (cf. Amos 6:1–6) are like a 'fading flower' facing hailstorms and floods (v. 2), or the first-ripe fruit on a fig tree at the mercy of passers-by (v. 4). The city was known for the drunkenness of its leaders, drunk with power and arrogance as much as with wine (Amos 6:6). The Septuagint has 'drunk without wine' (v. 1): 'drunk with gall, bitterness, Satan's poison' (Cyril). Jerome interprets these verses as including heretics in general (cf. 1 Tim 4:1–2), while Luther sees in the images of 'the proud crown … and the fading flower' a reference to the costly pomp and self-reliance of 'our pope'.

In a short and very different prophecy introduced by the formula 'in that day', the doomed crown of Samaria is contrasted with the divine 'crown of glory and diadem of beauty' which will bring justice and strength to the remnant of God's people (vv. 5–6). Ibn Ezra combines this with the preceding prophecy against his northern neighbours by adding that part of their punishment will be seeing the reign of God restored in Jerusalem (v. 5). 'A spirit of justice to him who sits in judgement' refers to the establishment of the Sanhedrin (Ibn Ezra) (v. 6), and the 'strength of those who turn back the battle at the gate' is the Torah (Rashi). For Cyril the 'remnant of Israel' means those who believe, Jews and gentiles, 'a crown of glory in the hand of the Lord' (cf. Isa 62:3; 1 Pet 5:4). For others the 'remnant' is the Church characterized by counsel and the strength to 'turn back the battle at the gate', but only if 'the Lord shall direct them' (Calvin).

The prophet now turns to attack the drunken priests and prophets of his own country, Judah (vv. 7–8) (cf. 5:11–12, 22–23). Ibn Ezra adds judges to the list: 'those who stumble in giving judgement' (v. 7). Some take the text literally and condemn the excessive consumption of alcohol (Pachomius, *Instructions* 45), pointing out that priests were supposed to abstain from drink when on duty (Lev 10:9) and 'it is not for kings to drink wine or for rulers to desire strong drink' (Prov 31:4; Henry). Others maintain that the 'madness which he condemns is metaphorical' (Calvin) and recall the fool who is 'like a dog that returns to its vomit' (Prov 26:11) (Aquinas). The best teaching they could offer would hardly be suitable for the education of infants just weaned (v. 9), one simple instruction at a time (*ṣaw laṣaw*), learning to write one line at a time (*qaw laqaw*), little by little (*ze'ir sham ze'ir sham*) (v. 10) (Ibn Ezra). The only people who listen to them are infants who know no better or those deprived of the 'milk of the Torah' (cf. 1 Pet 2:2) who claim 'we have a precept to match your precept and a plumb-line equal to your plumb-line' (Rashi; cf. Calvin). For many verse 10 represents the drunkards' scornful mimicry of the prophet's speech whether as boring and monotonous ('Precept after precept, line after line …') (Jerome, Lowth) or as gibberish like an unknown foreign language (cf. Isa 18:2) (NJB, Nicholas, Luther, Wildberger).

The prophet's response is to say that the Lord will deride them (vv. 11–13; cf. Ps 2:4; Luther), describing them scornfully as 'this people' (vv. 11, 14; cf. Isa 6:9–10; 8:6, 11, 12), and speak to them in 'an alien tongue', thinking perhaps of the language of the Assyrian invaders (cf. Isa 36:11). He had spoken to them in their own beautiful language about 'rest' (*menuḥah*; cf. Deut 12:9; Ps 23:2; Ruth 1:9; 1 Kgs 8:56) and 'repose' (*marge'ah*), a rare word (v. 12), but they would not listen. So he repeats the derided prophecy, word for word, coupling it with an elaborate prediction of their downfall: 'they will stumble, collapse, get trapped in a snare and end up in captivity' (v. 13). The Church Fathers follow the Septuagint translation of the twice repeated enigmatic prophecy: 'Expect affliction upon affliction (reading Heb. *ṣar* for *ṣaw*), hope upon hope (cf. Heb. *qawa* 'hope'), yet a little while, yet a little while.' They saw it as predicting the sufferings of the apostles and all the faithful who remembered Christ's words: 'a little while, and you shall not see me: and again, a little while, and you shall see me … and your sorrow shall be turned into joy' (John 16:19–20) (Cyril; cf. Jerome, *Letter* 130.7; Luther). For Richard of St Victor 'a little here, a little there' suggested human diffidence in God's presence recalling Abraham (Gen 18:1) and Elijah (1 Kgs 19:13) (*NCHB* 2, 699).

There is yet another context in which these verses were quoted. Paul cites vv. 11–12 in his discussion of g*lossolalia* 'speaking in tongues': 'in the law it is written, "by men of strange tongues and by the lips of foreigners will I speak to this people, and even then they will not listen to me, says the Lord" ' (1 Cor 14:21). The people could not understand the words spoken by the Lord: to them it was a foreign language. The text is cited by Augustine and others as scriptural authority for glossolalia, one of the 'gifts of the spirit', noting that Paul introduces it with the formula 'in the law it is written' (Augustine, *On the Trinity* 15.17.30; cf. Chrysostom, *Demonstration against the Pagans* 7.2). The suggestion that the Prophets have the same authority as the Torah appears again in verse 26. For several commentators the verse recalls the story of the apostles at Pentecost when they were filled with the Holy Spirit and spoke languages that people from all over the world could understand as their own (Acts 2) (Cyril). The miracle of Pentecost was that people were able to understand the words of the apostles and it is in this context that verse 11 features in a tenor solo in Scene 3 of Elgar's oratorio *The Kingdom* (1906) (*BiM* 134).

A Covenant with Death (Isa 28:14–29)

The next section is a prophecy of judgement addressed to the people of Judah, described as 'scoffers' (v. 14). It recalls Paul's warning to the Galatians: 'Be not deceived: God is not mocked' (Gal 6:7) (Calvin). Members of the Qumran community applied the epithet 'Scoffers' to the priestly hierarchy in Jerusalem, those who had rejected their teachings (*DSSE* 498–499), and called their leader the 'Scoffer' (*CD* 1:14) the 'Lying Preacher' (*CD* 8:12–13), and, with heavy sarcasm, *ṣaw* 'Precept' (*CD* 4:19), a title probably derived from the drunkards' gibberish in the previous verse (Blenkinsopp 2006: 111). As well as 'scoffers' Isaiah also calls them 'rulers of this people in Jerusalem', where 'this people' is insulting (cf. v. 11), but 'rulers' (Heb. *moshle*) is perhaps unexpectedly neutral in this context, and some commentators have suggested reading the more colourful 'allegorizers, purveyors of riddles or fairy-tales' (Heb. *meshalim*) (cf. Num 21:27) (Ibn Ezra, Rashi).

'We have nothing to fear because we have made a covenant with death … we can shelter behind lies and deceit' (v. 15; cf. 18) is a good example of the kind of fanciful nonsense peddled by such people (Rashi). Perhaps originally this alluded to some ancient Canaanite or Egyptian belief or practice (Ibn Ezra; Aquinas; Wildberger) or to a treaty between Hezekiah and Egypt which was doomed from the start (Clements), perhaps with an allusion to the Egyptian goddess Mut (cf. Heb. *mawet* 'death') (Childs, Roberts). The rare word translated 'agreement' (AV, RSV; Heb. *ḥozeh*) normally means 'prophet', and attempts have been made to recognize this, notably by Ibn Ezra who suggests that it highlights the contrast between this covenant with Death and the Sinai covenant with God, mediated by the prophet Moses. According to some it is a pun: the scoffers have 'substituted Death, self-concealment and mystification for God, prophecy, truth and mystery' (Landy 2001: 227).

Lowth compares the 'covenant' (Heb. *berit*) between the righteous farmer and the stones on his land in Job 5:23 and Lucan's 'truce with death' (*pax … cum morte*) that protected the mythical Psylli from venomous snakes (Lucan 2012, *Pharsalia* 9.894). Contracts with death and the devil became quite common in the Middle Ages, culminating in the contract signed by Faust in his own blood (Nabholz 1958). In a powerful twentieth-century example Wilfred Owen (1893–1918) applied the image to his own and other soldiers' vain efforts to come to terms with their tragic fate:

Oh, Death was never enemy of ours!
We laughed at him, we leagued with him, old chum. (*The Next War*, ll. 9–10; 1994)

There is also a poignant moment in Britten's *War Requiem* (1962) when these words are sung laughingly (*allegro e giocoso*) by the two male soloists at the heart of the *Dies Irae*.

'Therefore thus says the Lord God' introduces the awful consequences of the 'Scoffers'' wicked misjudgement (vv. 16–22). First a 'precious cornerstone, of a sure foundation' is laid in Zion: anyone who believes is safe, for justice and righteousness will prevail (vv. 16–17). According to Jewish tradition this refers to the King Messiah who shall be a tower and fortress in Zion (Rashi), towering above the King of Assyria, perhaps with Hezekiah in mind (Ibn Ezra). The Targum appears to identify this 'strong, mighty and terrible king' with a Roman emperor, perhaps Vespasian (Chilton 1987: 56), and takes it with the following description of the judgement about to fall on the wicked. There is a Muslim tradition that the precious stone referred to in verse 16 is the Kaaba (Lazarus-Yafeh 1992: 95).

For Christians the stone, the precious stone not cut with hands, as foretold by Daniel (Dan 2:34), is Christ (Jerome, Aquinas, Luther). The stone anointed by Jacob at Bethel (Gen 28:10–22) points to this stone, 'the elect and precious stone' which is Christ, the Lord's anointed (Augustine, *Tractates on John* 7.23). He is a 'tested stone', that is, 'distressed and afflicted … polished and hewn by Death and the Cross' (Luther). Christ is the sure foundation of the Church on which Paul urges his brethren to build (1 Cor 3:10–11) (cf. Jerome, Cyril, Theodoret). He is the cornerstone 'in whom the whole structure is joined together' (Eph 2:20–21) and 'who has joined in himself those who came from the gentiles and those who came from Israel to make us one people' (Theodoret). The image appears in the sixth of the 'O Antiphons' sung in Advent (see comm. on Isa 7:14), and it inspired an anonymous seventh-century Latin hymn beginning *Angularis fundamentum lapis* ('corner stone'), familiar today in an English version by John Neale (1851): 'Christ is made the sure Foundation, / Christ the Head and Cornerstone' (*EH* 170; *CH4* 200; *HON* 82). Paul and Peter both use the image of a 'stone' to separate believers from unbelievers, particularly among the Jews: 'to you who believe he is precious, but for those who do not believe … a stone that will make men stumble' (cf. Isa 8:14) (Rom 9:32–33; 1 Pet 2:4–8).

'He that believes will not be in haste' is explained by Paul as 'will not be put to shame' (Rom 10:11) because 'running away is the precise characteristic of a terrified conscience' (Luther). Others take it to mean 'will not be impatient' (Rashi) because, as Jesus said to his disciples when he left them, 'It is not for you to know the times or seasons which the Father has fixed' (Acts 1:7) (Nicholas). However it is interpreted, this became a popular prophecy about the power of faith, repeated twice by Paul (Rom 9:33; 10:11) and frequently elsewhere (cf. 1 Pet 2:6–8; Origen, *Comm. on Romans*, 8.2.8; Augustine, *Sermon* 279.9; cf. Cyril, Luther). Calvin compares it to 'being justified by faith, we obtain peace with God' (Rom 5:1).

'The bed is too short … the covering too narrow' (v. 20). Jewish commentators apply these words to the godless reign of Manasseh who set up an idol in the House of God (2 Chron 33:7): this was like asking God to share his bed with an idol when even 'heaven and the highest heaven cannot contain him' (1 Kgs 8:27) (Rashi). The terrifying power of divine intervention is then illustrated by two rare allusions to the history of ancient Israel (v. 21). The first was at Baal Perazim (Heb. *peraṣim*), where the Lord broke through (Heb. *paraṣ*) David's enemies 'like a bursting flood' (Heb. *pereṣ mayim*) (2 Sam 5:20), and the second at Gibeon, where miraculously 'the sun stood still ... until the nation took vengeance on their enemies' (Josh 12:13). We met the striking phrase translated 'the decree of destruction' (RSV; Heb. *kala ve-neḥraṣah*) earlier in the book (Isa 10:23), where the emphasis is on finality, and it is quoted again dramatically in the Book of Daniel (Dan 9:27). Perhaps originally it was applied to the fate of the 'whole land' (of Judah) but many have taken as a prophecy about the 'whole world' (Jerome, Calvin).

The description of God's work as 'strange ... alien' is sometimes explained by reference to the extraordinary events in the history of Israel just referred to. God treats his enemies in ways so amazing that everyone will be struck with horror (Calvin; cf. Cyril). According to the Septuagint, it means that God acts out of character when he acts with anger and bitterness: 'for his compassion is over all that he has made' (Ps 145:9) (Aquinas; cf. Nicholas, Henry). Jerome says this is about God having to use cruel methods (L. *verberibus et cauterio*) to treat his wayward children (Jerome; cf. Rashi). Gregory the Great applies the words to the suffering of Christ: his 'strange work' was to be flogged, spat upon and crucifed although this is the 'work' of a sinful person who deserved all these things (*Homilies on Ezekiel* 2.4.20). Luther interprets God's 'strange work' (L. *opus alienum*) as the rejection of righteous works by humans in order to raise up their own righteousness: 'the splendour of the flesh, like a rose, must fall away to let the spiritual flower blossom in its place'.

The last passage is written in a rather different style reminiscent of the Wisdom literature (cf. Prov 19:20; 20:4) and presents a peaceful orderly agricultural scene as a way of describing how God works: 'God does not act with bustle or confusion, but knows the times and seasons for doing his work ... the Lord regulates his threshing in such a manner that he does not crush or bruise his people' (Calvin). Details have been interpreted allegorically, like the details in the Parable of the Sower (Matt 13): dill, cumin, barley and spelt, for example, are the gifts of the spirit strategically distributed (v. 25; cf. 1 Cor 14:1–5) (Luther), and the different agricultural implements, threshing sledge, cartwheel, stick and rod (v. 27), correspond to the different punishments meted out to sinners at the Last Judgement (Nicholas). According to Jerome, dill and cumin are the gentiles who have not heard the gospel and who will be corrected with a stick and a rod, while the barley and spelt are the Jews, whose punishment will be severer because they were like the servant who 'knew his master's will but did not act accordingly' (cf. Luke 12:47). The verb 'to thresh' as well as the noun 'threshing sledge' are used figuratively elsewhere (Isa 41:15; Amos 1:3). The image of ploughing is applied to sexual intercourse in the Bible (Judg 14:18), and elsewhere Jerome cites verse 24, rather cryptically, in a discussion of celibacy and the role of virgins in the Church (*Letter* 22.20).

Verse 26 has been interpreted in several different ways. The simplest way is to take it as a comment on the wisdom of the farmer, as a gift from God (AV, RSV, *JSB*). Agricultural wisdom is attributed to the gods in many societies (v. 26; cf. Sir 7:15; Lucretius 2001: 5:14; Lowth; cf. Calvin). The wisdom of the farmer in harmony with divinely appointed methods and seasons, like the wisdom of the ox and the ass (Isa 1:3), is being contrasted with the stubborn 'scoffers' who rule in Jerusalem (v. 14) (Marlow and Barton 2009: 213–214). The closing doxology in praise of God's 'counsel' and 'wisdom' (v. 29; cf. Prov 8:14), is alluded to in the first of the 'O Antiphons' (see comm. on Isa 7:14) and is not restricted to agricultural wisdom (v. 29; cf. Ps 139) (Aquinas). Alternatively the word translated 'instruct' (Heb. *yasar*) frequently means 'chasten' (Ps 118:18; Jer 31:18), and this is how the Jewish commentators have understood it, as a comment on God's chastening of his people 'in just measure' (Rashi). For the rabbis, the last word 'teaches him' (Heb. *yorennu*; cf. *torah*) raises the possibility that the Prophets have halakhic authority like the Torah (cf. 1 Cor 14:21; see above on v. 11), although this was officially rejected (*RA* civ).

Ariel, the City of David (Isa 29:1–8)

The chapter begins with a prophecy about the miraculous survival of Jerusalem after a terrifying siege (vv. 1–8, probably that of Sennacherib; cf. Isa. 36–37) (Rashi, Calvin, Lowth), although some Christian commentators point out that verses 1–4 are equally applicable to the siege of Jerusalem by the Babylonians or the Romans (Cyril, Aquinas, Nicholas). Whether or not the prophecy refers to

Isaiah Through the Centuries, First Edition. John F. A. Sawyer.
© 2018 John Wiley & Sons Ltd. Published 2020 by John Wiley & Sons Ltd.

a historical event, it certainly illustrates the 'strangeness of the purpose of God, who both attacks and defends Jerusalem' (cf. Isa 28:21) (Childs).

The name 'Ariel' (vv. 1–2, 7) is traditionally understood as 'lion of God' (Heb. *arieh* 'lion') and its appropriateness as a name for the city of God is emphasized by many commentators. Jerusalem was 'the head-city of Judah, who is called a lion's whelp' (Gen 49:9) (Henry). Aquinas cites Proverbs 3:30: 'the lion is mightiest among beasts and does not turn back before any'. The rabbis noticed that the Temple building resembled a lion in being 'narrow behind and wide in front' (m*Middot* 4:7; Rashi). Others point out that the word *ar'el* can mean 'altar' (cf. Ezek 43:15–16), which would not only focus on the sanctity of the holy city, but make verse 2 all the more graphic: Jerusalem will be like an altar, that is, a scene of bloodshed and slaughter (Rashi, Nicholas, Calvin). 'The city where David encamped' is a reference to David's siege and capture of Jerusalem from the Jebusites (2 Sam 5:6–10) (Jerome).

'Ariel' is used as an epithet for two 'lion-like' Moabite warriors (1 Chron 11:22) and later becomes the name of an angel (cf. Isa 21:8; 33:7). He figures as an airy spirit in Shakespeare's *The Tempest* (1613), a rebel angel in Milton's *Paradise Lost* (1667) and chief of the sylphs in Pope's *The Rape of the Lock* (1712). Seen as the spirit of poetic imagination, it is the title of André Maurois' biography of Shelley (1935), a set of five Christmas poems by T. S. Eliot (1927–1954) and the best known collection of Sylvia Plath's poems (1965). It is also the name of a large Israeli settlement established on the West Bank in 1978. The opening chorus of Robert Starer's *Ariel* (1960) combines this passage (vv. 1–4) with verses from chapter 1 ('Ah sinful nation …' vv. 4, 7) (*BiM* 19), and in Burkhard's oratorio *The Face of Isaiah* 1936), after a tenor solo summoning heaven and earth to listen (1:1–2a) and a chorus of seraphim (6:1–4), *Weh Ariel* 'Woe to Ariel!' is the first of a series of prophecies condemning human sin (1:4–7, 10–11; 3:16–26; 5:18–25; 29:1,7) (Berges 2012: 126).

The lowest point in the city's fortunes is compared to a loss of voice: gone are their 'proud and idle boastings' (Calvin); 'like the voice of a ghost … your speech shall whisper out of the dust' (v. 4). Perhaps there is a veiled reference to Hezekiah's forced capitulation to the king of Assyria (2 Kgs 17:14): 'then his speech was low, out of the dust' (Henry). The verse is quoted in the Book of Mormon (2 Nephi 26:16–17) and much discussed in the Church of Latter Day Saints (see comm. on vv. 11–12). When the Lord of hosts intervenes with 'thunder and an earthquake', the multitude of the enemies of Jerusalem will be 'like small dust' (v. 5), that is as innumerable as specks of dust (cf. Gen 28:14), or more likely blown away like dust or chaff in a whirlwind (vv. 5–6) (Rashi, Calvin). They will be like 'a dream, a vision in the night', quickly fading away and deceptive (cf. Sir 34:7) (Aquinas).

Having Eyes They See Not (Isa 29:9–16)

The next prophecy is an attack on the 'stupor' and 'blindness' of the people (vv. 9–16), recalling the prophet's mission to 'make his people's ears heavy and shut their eyes' (Isa 6:10) (Rashi). In Jewish tradition the passage is associated with Pharaoh's dream in the Joseph story (Gen 41:1–37) (Mann 1971: 1, 301–304). It was as though God had poured a deep sleep upon them (cf. Gen 2:21; Jon 1:5) (Jerome). They are 'drunk but not with wine' means 'drunk with anger, unseemly desire, greed, vainglory, ten thousand other passions' (Chrysostom, *Discourses Against Judaizing Christians* 8.1.1). A similar image reappears later in the book (Isa 51:14), where it is from the 'cup of staggering' that suffering Israel has been drinking (cf. Matt 26:39) (Lowth). Here too, as in chapter 6, the blindness is a punishment sent by God: 'for judgement I came into this world, that those who do not see may see, and those who see may become blind' (John 9:39) (Aquinas; cf. Augustine, *Tractates on John* 53.5.2–6.2). From the beginning Christian commentators understood these verses as referring to the blindness of the Jews: 'a veil lies over their minds but when a man turns to the Lord the veil is removed' (2 Cor 3:15–16; Chrysostom, *Discourses against Judaizing Christians* 8.1.1; cf. Luther) (Evans 1989:83; Wagner 2006: 99). By contrast, Calvin preached a sermon on these two verses in which he attacks the fanciful excesses of allegorical exegesis in Christian writings and points out that 'in many persons there will now be found no less blindness and obduracy than formerly existed among the Jews, and not more excusable' (Pauw 2006: 214–215).

The silencing in particular of prophets and seers, that is, the 'eyes' and 'heads' of the community (v. 10), refers to 'stargazers', according to Rashi, who will lose their ability to interpret the constellations as though they had become a 'sealed book'. Modern scholars take it as a comment, by a later hand, on the end of the age of prophecy and the increasing reliance on written scripture in the Second Temple period (Wildberger, Roberts). The Church Fathers readily find a reference in the 'sealed book' to the impossibility of understanding scripture without Christ, the 'key of knowledge' (Luke 11:52): 'Behold the Lion of the tribe of Judah … has conquered all and can open the book and break the seal' (Rev 5:5) (Origen, *Homily on Exodus* 12.4; Jerome, *Letter* 53.5–6; cf. Theodoret). Before Christ it was very hard to understand the words of Isaiah (Nicholas): Jews could not understand his prophecies about Christ because there was a veil over their eyes (2 Cor 3:12–16) and so the book was sealed (Isa 29:11) (Isidore, *De Fide Catholica* 2.21.2; cf. Theodoret). Luther applies the images of the veil and the sealed book to his bishops who do not know the Scriptures. Cyril quotes the reference to a 'sealed book' here in support of his belief that the whole Greek Bible was a single integrated work (Cassel 2006:148) and the two apparent references in Isaiah to the writing down of the prophet's words (Isa 8:16; 29:11; cf. 34:16) have been much used in modern historical-critical discussions of biblical prophecy (Williamson 1994: 94–115). Mormons believe verse 11 was fulfilled when learned men said they could not read the Book of Mormon because it is sealed (cf. v. 4; Vogel 1996: 2.253, 328).

A vivid attack on hypocrisy in religion and the shortcomings of human wisdom follows (vv. 13–14). The Targum adds arrogance ('this people exalts itself with their mouth'), and Rashi says that the people are not behaving like this of their own accord but because their teachers tell them to, while Ibn Ezra compares them to 'the untrained calf' in Ephraim's heart-rending confession in Jeremiah (Jer 31:18). The unknown fate that awaits them ('shocking and amazing' v. 14 NRSV) recalls the curse in store for those who break the covenant (Deut 28:59) (Rashi) and the mysterious 'alien work' of God in the previous chapter (Isa 28:21) (Blenkinsopp).

Verse 13 is quoted in full in the Gospels where, in a dispute with the scribes and Pharisees, Jesus introduces the quotation with the words: 'You hypocrites! Well did Isaiah prophesy when he said ...' (Matt 15:8–9 Mk 7:6–7). He 'explains the passage' by adding the words 'in vain' (cf. LXX): 'in vain do they worship me, teaching doctrines, the commandments of men' (Calvin; cf. Berges 2012: 101). It was precisely because the prophecies of Isaiah were a 'sealed book' to the Jews that their hearts out of unbelief were far from the Lord (v. 13) (Origen, *Comm. on Matthew* 15:1–20). Aquinas, citing Jeremiah 17:9–10, notes the evil potential of the human heart, while Chrysostom says we cannot blame our teachers: 'bring me a heart free from worldly tumults so I can write on it what I want to' (*Homilies on Matthew* 11.9).

Christian interpreters apply the 'commandment of men learnt by rote' to the teachings of the scribes and Pharisees (cf. Matt 23:2–4 (Irenaeus, *Against Heresies* 4.12.4), while for Martin Luther the term exactly describes the teachings of the Catholic Church as human teachings elevated above Christ and His Word, so that 'saying anything against the Pope is a greater sin than if it were against God'. The condemnation of the wise (v. 14) is interpreted by many as a reference to the statesmen responsible for the plight in which the country finds itself, allied to Egypt and at the mercy of the Assyrians (cf. Isa 20, 30–31; Jer 8:8–9; Obad 8) (Clements, Roberts). The prophecy can also be taken as an attack on human wisdom in general (cf. 1 Cor 1:18–25; Aquinas, Nicholas) or, for some, the wisdom of contemporary bishops and Church leaders who 'pretend it came from God' (Calvin). The Australian poet Robert Harris wrote a short poem inspired by verses 11–14, entitled 'Isaiah by Kerosene Lantern Light', in which he dissociates himself from the doomed hypocrisy and raucous, senseless culture of 'this generation' (cf. 'this people'; Isa 6:9–10; 28:11,14) (Atwan and Wieder 1993: 392–393).

The 'woe' prophecy (vv. 15–16) is directed at people's misguided attempts to hide their wicked ways from God, like Adam and Eve in the garden of Eden (Gen 3:8) (Jerome) or the 'fool who says in his heart, There is no God' (Ps 14:1; Luther). For Aquinas it recalls Jesus' words: 'everyone who does evil, hates the light' (John 3:20). It is as if a lump of clay should say to the potter, 'Why have you made me like this?' (cf. Isa 45:9; Rom 9:20–21) (Jerome). In the *Biblia Pauperum* verse 16 accompanies the scene of Satan tempting Christ (Matt 4:1–3; cf. Gen 3:1–6) (*BP* 67) and Augustine cites this passage in a discussion of original sin: if we ask, 'Why did God create us like this?' the answer must be because he gave us free will and the first act of disobedience corrupted all humanity (*Letter* 186.18). The word translated here 'the thing formed' (RSV; Heb. *yeṣer*) is elsewhere translated 'imagination' (Gen 6:5; 8:21) and is understood in Jewish tradition to be a reference to the *yetzer ha-ra* 'the evil inclination' in every human being (Rashi).

Jacob Shall No More Be Ashamed (Isa 29:17–24)

The last part of this chapter consists of two prophecies of salvation (vv. 17–24), filled with beautiful language and imagery, much of it 'repealing' what has gone before (Rashi): the sealed book (vv. 11–12) will be unsealed (v. 18); the eyes of the blind (vv. 9–10) will be opened (v. 18); those who challenged the work of the creator (v. 16) will 'stand in awe of him … and accept instruction' (vv. 23–24) (Duhm). This 'revolution' is first described in a proverbial saying (Heb. *mashal*) (Lowth), capable of various interpretations: 'Lebanon shall be turned into Carmel [or 'a fruitful field'] and Carmel shall be regarded as a forest' (v. 17). Thinking of the miraculous revolutions in nature described elsewhere (e.g. Isa 32:15; 35:1–2; 40:4; 41:17–20), perhaps this means that the cedars of Lebanon will bear fruit like vines and fruit-trees, and the vines on Carmel will produce timber like the cedars of Lebanon (Sawyer; cf. Calvin). In Jewish tradition the forests of Lebanon will be turned into fruitful fields and vineyards, while the vineyards will be populated by large cities, crowded like a forest (Tg, Rashi). Christian commentators interpret the image as referring to the Jews as Carmel, 'God's vineyard' (Heb. *karmel*), arid, overgrown and laid waste (Isa 5:7–8), and Lebanon as the gentiles who, with the apostles and disciples, take over the vineyard when the Jews are rejected (Jerome, Aquinas, Nicholas, Luther, Lowth).

Modern authors note that verses 18–19 bracket the poor with the deaf and the blind, all singled out as joyful participants in the 'revolution' (Lohfink 1987: 21; Berges 2012: 97). Those responsible for their suffering, the 'ruthless … the scoffer … all who seek to pervert the course of justice', whether these are false prophets (Rashi) or evil demons (Jerome) or corrupt institutions (Miranda 1977: 144), will be cut off (vv. 20–21). The closing prophecy (vv. 22–24) recalls the origins of the people of God in Ur of the Chaldees where Abraham was redeemed by God (Gen 12), and describes how they will one day be singing God's praises like the three survivors of the burning fiery furnace (Dan 3) (Rashi).

Woe to the Rebellious Children! (Isa 30:1–17)

The chapter begins with a sequence of four short prophecies of doom, which probably go back to the prophet himself (1–5, 6–7, 8–14, 15–17). References to an alliance with Egypt in the first part (vv. 2–3, 7) suggest that it dates from the short period of political unrest in the Assyrian Empire following the death of Sargon II in 705 BCE when Babylon, Judah and others rebelled against his successor Sennacherib (2 Kgs 20:12–19) (Roberts). Isaiah's opposition to such an alliance is evident in several passages (Isa 30:1–7; 31:1–3) and was vindicated

Isaiah Through the Centuries, First Edition. John F. A. Sawyer.
© 2018 John Wiley & Sons Ltd. Published 2020 by John Wiley & Sons Ltd.

by the Assyrian defeat of the Egyptian army in 701. Others suggest the background of this prophecy may have been the revolt of the Philistine city Ashdod some years earlier, when Egypt was involved (cf. Isa 20:1–6) (Wildberger). Rashi favours an even earlier period, in the reign of Ahaz, when Hoshea, king of Samaria in the north, sent messengers to Egypt with disastrous results for Samaria (2 Kgs 17:1–18). The Church Fathers believed Isaiah's prophecy was fulfilled when the people of Judah, against the advice of the prophet Jeremiah, went to Egypt for fear of the Babylonians, a move which led to the fall of Jerusalem in 586 and the Babylonian exile (Jer 42–43; Eusebius; cf. Jerome, Cyril).

The first of the four short prophecies, one of several 'woe oracles' in this section (Isa 29:15–16; 31:1–3; 33:1; cf. 5:8–23; 10:1–4), addresses the politicians as 'rebellious sons', recalling Isaiah's very first words to his people (1:2) and perhaps also the law of Moses (Deut 21:18–21). The Fathers compare them to the tenants in the parable of the vineyard (Matt 21:33–41) (Cyril), while Aquinas cites Jeremiah to make the same general point: 'Cursed is the man who trusts in man' (Jer 17:6). Calvin points out that the prohibition of alliances with foreign nations, especially Egypt, is also made explicit in the law (Exod 13:17; Deut 17:16). The word 'league' (RSV; cf. LXX, Lowth) (Heb. *massekah*) is elsewhere translated 'cover, veil, web' (AV, Vg; cf. Isa 25:7) and suggests furtive behaviour on the part of those who 'endeavour to escape from the eyes of God' (Calvin). 'His princes [Vg, AV; RSV 'officials'] … and envoys' (v. 3) are probably Hezekiah's officials already in Egypt (Rashi), both in Zoan (Gk Tanis) in the Nile Delta and in Hanes (Gk Heracleopolis) south of Memphis in Upper Egypt. LXX refers to 'evil messengers in Tanis', interpreted as bringers of bad news by some (Cyril) and evil demons by others (Eusebius), sure to bring shame and contempt on any who ally themselves with Egypt.

The second prophecy, the 'oracle on the beasts of the Negev' (vv. 6–7), graphically illustrates, on the one hand, the dangers of travelling in the desert – lions, venomous snakes and the legendary fiery serpents that terrorized the Israelites in the wilderness (Num 21:6; cf. Deut 8:15), and, on the other, all the effort and paraphernalia needed for such an operation: 'riches on the backs of asses … and treasure on the humps of camels' (Calvin). Some of the Church Fathers point out that in Egypt wild animals were represented as idols and worshipped like gods, which makes the Judaeans' preference for Egypt all the more shameful (Jerome, Eusebius). Calvin compares this arduous, expensive and pointless journey to the 'long and toilsome pilgrimages to various saints' from which he and his followers have now been excused.

The phrase 'worthless and empty' (Heb. *hebel wa-req*) used to appear in the *Alenu*, a medieval Jewish prayer (*ADPB* 140–143), where it referred to the practices of 'the nations of the earth … for they worship vanity and emptiness

[Isa 30:7], and pray to a god who cannot save [Isa 45:20]'. Denounced as anti-Christian on the grounds that by gematria the letters of the word *wa-req* (and emptiness) have the same numerical value as *yeshu'* (Jesus), it was censored, even though in reciting it, probably very few Jews ever thought of Christians (Elbogen 1993:72; *RA* 366–367).

The last words of the prophecy ('I have called her Rahab') are obscure. There are other cases where a prophet gives a mocking name to the object of his scorn (Jer 46:17), but the precise meaning of this one is unclear. Hebrew *rahab* suggests 'pride, arrogance' (cf. Ps 40:4; Isa 3:5), and this is how it is interpreted by Rashi (Vg, Jerome). Ibn Ezra applies it to Jerusalem, not Egypt: 'their strength is to sit still' (Heb. *hem shabet*), that is, not go down to Egypt (cf. AV; Calvin). 'Rahab' is one of the mythical monsters of the deep (cf. Job 26:12; Ps 89:10), however, more than once applied to the historic enemy defeated at the Red Sea (cf. Isa 51:9–10; cf. Ps 87:4; Ezek 29:3; 32:2), and most modern commentators interpret it in this way: 'Rahab who sits still' (RSV) or 'Rahab the inactive' (reading *ha-moshbat*; Lowth; cf. Wildberger), in the sense of ignoring Judah's plea for help (Luther).

The third prophecy is in the form of a legal judgement, first stating the charge levelled against the accused (vv. 8–11) and then passing judgement (vv. 12–14). The charge is written down ('with a pen of iron, and with the point of a diamond engraven on their hearts'; cf. Jer 17:1) lest anyone imagine their crimes will be forgotten (Calvin). Others take this a reference to the writing down of Isaiah's prophecies, described here and elsewhere as *torah* (cf. 1:10; 5:24; 28:26) at the earliest stage in their transmission (cf. 8:1, 16; Kaiser, Clements). Either way the document will be 'a witness for ever' (Vg, Tg, *Pesh*, RSV; Lowth) reading Heb. *la'ed* for *la'ad* 'for ever' (MT, AV). The silencing of the prophets (vv. 10–11) recalls the treatment Jeremiah received at the hands of his contemporaries (Jer 11:2; 43:2–3; Cyril, Calvin), and the request for them to preach 'smooth things' (Heb. *ḥalaqot*) rather than the truth, left its mark on the Qumran community, who regularly used these words of Isaiah to describe their opponents in Jerusalem, probably the Pharisees (*DSSE* 499; Blenkinsopp 2006:145–146). The fate of those who despise the word of the Lord and trust in oppression, introduced with the conventional 'Therefore' (cf. v. 3; Isa 1:24; 13:13; 28:14), is described in two particularly vivid similes (vv. 12–14): first, it will be like the sudden collapse of a high wall (cf. Ps 62:3 Lowth), weakened by rain seeping into the cracks (Rashi, Calvin), and second like a vessel made of pottery smashed so completely that not a single useful potsherd survives. Potsherds (*ostraka*) had many uses in the ancient world, as scoops, shovels and, of course, writing material.

The last of the four brief oracles begins with a typical reminder of where salvation is to be found – 'in returning and rest ... quietness and trust' (cf. Isa 28:12; 32:17–18) – then spells out the fate of those who seek it else-where. 'Returning' means resting, like the ark of the covenant, and not going down to Egypt (cf. Num 10:36; Ibn Ezra, Rashi). Calvin reminds us of Moses' advice to his people before the defeat of the Egyptians: 'You shall be silent, and the Lord will fight for you' (Exod 14:14). Luther says, 'Patience conquers all things' and quotes Paul's 'overcome evil with good' (Rom 12:21). 'Returning' can also mean repentance (cf. Jer 4:1; Hos 14:1) (Eusebius, Cyril, Nicholas). The second part of the verse, 'in quietness and confidence shall be your strength' is inscribed on a medallion erected in Poet's Corner, Westminster Abbey, in memory of John Keble, and is the motto of the mili-tary section of Reali High School in Haifa, Israeli's oldest private school, founded in 1913.

The oracle ends with another scene of humiliating disaster: those who thought they could ride to safety on horseback, will be running for their lives ('a thousand shall flee at the threat of one') and nothing will remain of them except a tiny remnant 'like a flag-pole on top of a hill' (vv. 16–17). Some envis-age a mast sticking up from the rocks, so that everyone can see where the ship-wreck is (Nicholas, Calvin). The description fits Nebuchadnezzar's destruction of Jerusalem when some of the Judaeans were carried off captive to Babylon, while others tried to escape to Egypt, and only a wretched few survivors remained in the ruins of what had been their homeland.

Blessed Are All Those Who Wait for Him (Isa 30:18–26)

The second part of the chapter switches abruptly from judgement to salvation, beginning with a statement that, although 'the Lord is a God of justice, he is patient and long-suffering and waits to be gracious to you' (cf. 65:1–2; John Cassian, *Conferences* 13.12). Picking up on verse 15, the prophet assures his people that 'everything would turn out all right if only you would wait' (Luther). Rashi and others understand the verse less benignly and take the rather odd 'exalts himself' (v. 18) as withdraws, parallel to 'waits, hesitates': the Lord will not come down from heaven to rescue them until they repent. All the more fortunate, therefore, are the few who wait for him (cf. Isa 40:31). These are the Judaeans who returned to Jerusalem in the days of Zerubbabel (cf. v. 19; Eusebius, Jerome, Aquinas), or, for many others, those who followed Christ when he was exalted on the cross (cf. John 12:32; Jerome). This is how medieval Franciscan preachers interpreted it (*NCHB* 2.686).

The short beatitude with which this verse ends (Heb. *ashre kol-ḥoke lo*) pro-vided scriptural basis for the popular Jewish tradition that the world's existence depends in every generation on Thirty-Six hidden *Tzaddiqim* (righteous ones)

(*RA* 231–232; Scholem 1971: 251–254). By gematria, the two Hebrew letters of the last word *lo* (for him), *lamed* and *vav*, stand for the numerals 30 and 6. No one ever knows who the 'Lamedvavniks' are, though speculation is not discouraged. The tradition, which recalls the story of the destruction of Sodom and Gomorrah when God said, 'For the sake of ten, I will not destroy it' (Gen 18:32), goes back to the Talmud (b*Sanhedrin* 97b; b*Sukkah* 45b) and figures especially in eighteenth- and nineteenth-century hasidic folklore as well as in the novel *The Last of the Just* (1960) by André Schwarz-Bart.

The next prophecy reads like an expansion of verse 18, first applying it specifically to the citizens of Jerusalem, then amplifying it with images of God's grace, evident in their obedience and the fruitfulness of their land (vv. 19–26). The Septuagint begins 'when a holy people shall dwell in Zion', perhaps preferable to the Hebrew 'Yea, O people ...' (RSV; Lowth; cf. Cyril). There will be no more weeping because 'at the sound of your cry, He shall respond to you' (Rashi). Jerome compares it with Christ's 'Blessed are you that weep now, for you shall laugh' (Luke 6:21) and reminds us that 'Moses spoke and God answered' (Exod 19:20).

The 'bread of adversity and the water of affliction' are prisoners' rations according to the Mishnah (m*Sanhedrin* 9:5), or the reference may be to a famine (Ibn Ezra, Calvin). 'But the suffering will soon be over: "your Teacher will no longer hide his countenance from you"' (vv. 20–21) (Rashi). The notion of God as 'Teacher' is elaborated in charming Talmudic stories about him daily studying the Torah and engaging in scholarly debates with other rabbinic teachers (b*Abodah Zarah* 3b; b*Shabbat* 107b). According to others the 'Teacher' is Hezekiah (Ibn Ezra) or the prophet Isaiah (Luther) or Christ (Matt 23:8; Nicholas). Some have argued that 'Teacher' (Heb. *moreh*) here is out of context and read instead 'your rain (Heb. *moreh*) shall no longer be restrained', anticipating verse 23 (Calvin; cf. Clements). 'You shall hear a word behind you' contrasts with those who turn a deaf ear to the prophet's teaching (v. 9) (Rashi). According to the rabbis this refers to the *bat qol*, a voice from heaven by which God informs them concerning anything they are doubtful about (b*Megillah* 32a). Other suggestions include the voice of one's conscience (Henry) and a comforting word addressed to people unsure which way to turn, who hear a voice behind them saying, 'I will support you whichever way you turn'. In Luther's easily misinterpreted words, 'Sin boldly, but believe and rejoice in Christ even more boldly' (*LW* 48: 281–282). In William Sterndale Bennett's cantata *Woman of Samaria* (1867) the words are addressed by the chorus to the woman at the well as she talks to Jesus (*BiM* 270–271).

The first thing the new pupils do is to get rid of all the glittering idols that have come between them and their teacher (v. 22). They are to be treated like sources of ritual uncleanness and avoided with the same religious zeal

(Jerome, Rashi). Luther is reminded of Paul: 'for his sake I suffered the loss of all things and count them as refuse' (Phil 3:8).

There follows an idyllic picture of a land of plenty, rich in grain, with cattle grazing in large pastures, oxen and asses tilling the soil and streams of water on every hill. The animals will be fed on enriched provender (v. 24) and the grain will be twice winnowed, first, by a shovel and then by a fan (Rashi). For Christian interpreters this first recalls the parable of the sower (Matt 13), but it adds the image of the apostles tilling the soil like the animals and streams of living water giving eternal life to those who drink it (John 4): 'Blessed be the Lord from the fountains of Israel' (Ps 68:26 Vg) (Cyril, Jerome, Nicholas; cf. Calvin). This is one of twenty texts cited by Irenaeus to defend the view that the just will reign in a literal earthly kingdom, not in another world (Gorringe 2006: 427).

'In the day of the great slaughter, when the towers fall' (v. 25) may refer to the miraculous destruction of Sennacherib's army (Rashi, Luther, Henry) or to the destruction of Babylon when the Judaeans were able to return to their homeland (Calvin). But for many it is about the last days, the final victory over evil in the days of Gog and Magog (Ibn Ezra), the Last Judgement (Nicholas), the day when 'heaven and earth shall pass away' (Matt 24:35) and a new age will dawn (Jerome; cf. Cyril). The 'towers' are the haughty ones who said, 'Come let us build a tower with its top in the heavens' (Gen 11:3; cf. Isa 14:13–14) (Jerome). Over it all there will be a light, like the light of seven suns, shining day and night (cf. 1 Enoch 91:16; *OTP* 1.73). The rabbis used this verse to explain the two kinds of light in the creation story (Gen 1:3, 16) (b*Hagigah* 12a; Schwartz 1998: 16). Some relate it to the solar miracles in the days of Joshua (Josh 10:12–14) and Hezekiah (Isa 38:7–8), but many interpret it metaphorically, citing 'the sun of righteousness' (Mal 4:2; Cyril) or Christ's saying that 'the righteous will shine like the sun' (Matt 13:43): 'God will enlighten believers with such great brightness that, if "seven" suns were brought together, their brightness would be far inferior to theirs' (Calvin).

The Burning Anger of the Lord (Isa 30:27–33)

The next prophecy seems to be another vivid expansion of the first part of the chapter, this time spelling out the lurid details of what divine judgement on the wicked entails. The Assyrians are mentioned by name (v. 31), and the whole passage is a celebration of the miraculous defeat of Sennacherib in 701 (Rashi, Luther, Calvin, Henry). No doubt there are other events in mind as well, such as the fall of Nineveh in 612, which is celebrated in the Book of Nahum, and the fall of Babylon in 538 (Jerome, Cyril). Others take 'Assyrian' as a term that includes all those who rule like tyrants and arrogantly boast of their conquests (Eusebius) and interpret the passage as a description of Judgement Day and the destruction of Satan (Cyril).

The description begins and ends with the image of a God 'burning with anger ... his tongue like a devouring fire ... his breath like a stream of brimstone'. Jerome traces the image back to Moses (Deut 4:24) but points out that Christ spoke in these terms too: 'I came to cast fire upon the earth; and would that it were already kindled' (Luke 12:49). Mention is made in verse 28 of a 'sieve of destruction, a useless sieve' (Heb. *nafat shav*'; Tg, AV, RSV), that is, a sieve that does not work properly so that nothing is saved (Lowth). Verses 27–28 provide the terrifying words of the opening recitative in Willard Patten's oratorio *Isaiah* (1898) (*BiM* 112–113).

The fate of the Assyrians is described in terms reminiscent of Dante's *Inferno*: from the flame of devouring fire and the hailstones (v. 30) to the great pyre on Tophet 'with fire and wood in abundance' (v. 33). The name Tophet (Vg, AV; RSV 'burning place') has terrible associations: first it was the place where human sacrifices to the god Moloch were made (2 Kgs 23:10), known also as the 'valley of slaughter' (Jer 19:6) and Gehinnom (Neh.1:30) (Lowth); then later, like Gehenna (Isa 33:14 Tg; 2 Esd 2:29), it came to be applied to the fate of the wicked after death: 'the eternal fire prepared for the devil and his angels' (Matt 25:41; Jerome). Verses from Isaiah like this one (cf. Isa 33:14; 66:24) played an important part in the development of the lurid images of hell familiar to us from paintings by Hieronymus Bosch and others. In modern Hebrew *mekonit tofet* is a car bomb.

Alongside the visual imagery the passage describes the sounds that will be heard. The 'majestic voice' (v. 30) of the Lord is interpreted by Rashi as the singing of the fiery creatures surrounding God in heaven (Isa 6), to which the terrified Assyrians will be forced to listen. In Catholic tradition, part of the verse was read (in Latin) at Mass on the second Sunday of Advent (*MR* 5). Most striking is the sound of the righteous triumphantly singing to the sound of the flute, as if they were celebrating a holy feast (v. 29). The verse is set to joyful dance-like music in the final chorus of Randall Thompson's *Peaceable Kingdom* (1936) (*BiM* 185–186) and represented on an Israeli postage stamp in 1956 (Plate 26). The lyres and timbrels keep time with the strokes of punishment as they landed, blow after blow, on the victims (v. 32). Luther envisages the celebrations in Jerusalem in the evening after the destruction of Sennacherib (Isa 37:36), and Calvin notes that the extreme punishment fits the crime, quoting another passage from Isaiah: 'Woe to you destroyer, for you yourself shall be destroyed' (Isa 33:1; cf. Matt 7:2). A cautionary Scottish commentary on the

PLATE 26   'Rejoicing as when they march with the flute' (Isa 30:29). Israeli postage
stamp celebrating Rosh Ha-Shanah (1956). Reproduced with kind permission of Israel
Philatelic Society, Israel Postal Company.

final verse can be found in the following inscription on a house in Dunfermline:
'Since an hour's fire on 25 May 1624 with its fierce flames could work such
damage, O think of the fearful fires which the breath of Jehovah with a torrent
of brimstone will kindle' (Moffatt 1924: 82).

Woe to Those Who Rely on Horses and Chariots! (Isa 31:1–9)

The fifth in the series of 'woe oracles' (Isa 28–31) is the strongest expression of the prophet's conviction that an alliance with Egypt is doomed (vv. 1–3). Scholars are mostly agreed that it dates from the year 701 BCE, possibly after Egypt had been defeated by Sennacherib at Eltekeh, although Rashi, to keep Hezekiah's reputation clean (2 Kgs 18:5), again thinks the reference is to an earlier alliance between Samaria and Egypt (2 Kgs 17:1–9; cf. Isa 30:1–5). The Church Fathers mostly apply it to the time of Jeremiah (Jerome, Cyril).

Isaiah Through the Centuries, First Edition. John F. A. Sawyer.
© 2018 John Wiley & Sons Ltd. Published 2020 by John Wiley & Sons Ltd.

There are echoes of the miraculous destruction of Pharaoh's army: 'the horse and his rider ... the chariots ... the outstretched hand' (Exod 15:1, 4, 12; Eusebius, Jerome, Rashi,). The fragility of the mightiest human army is contrasted with the power of God (v. 3): 'a warhorse is a vain hope for victory' (Ps 33:17; cf. Ps 20:7) (Aquinas). 'Going down to Egypt' is synonymous with descending to a life of depravity (Calvin), to 'a great city allegorically called Sodom and Egypt where the Lord was crucified' (Rev 11:8; Jerome).

To represent God's protection of his people, the prophet uses two images from nature. He will be like 'a lion or a young lion growling over his prey' (v. 4; cf. Hos 13:7). Cyril applies this to Christ who leapt upon the god of this world (2 Cor 4:4) 'like a lion or a young lion' and did away with him by the power of his word. He will also be like 'birds hovering' (v. 5), which recalls the eagle in the Song of Moses that 'flutters over its young, spreading out its wings' (Deut 32:11) and Christ's cry over Jerusalem: 'How often would I have gathered your children together as a hen gathers her brood under her wings...!' (Luke 13:34; Jerome, Aquinas). The emphasis is on the lion-like ferocity (cf. v. 4) and the selfless determination with which a mother defends her chicks from snakes or humans or other birds, by flying around, making a lot of noise and doing whatever she can with her beak and her claws to frighten them off (Cyril, Jerome). The verse appears in an RAF Memorial window in Durham Cathedral, and, at the beginning of Part III of Willy Burkhard's oratorio *The Face of Isaiah* (1936), very different, but effective use of the bird imagery is made in a beautiful setting of verse 5, sung by the chorus in response to the soprano solo 'They will mount up with wings like eagles' (Isa 40:31) (Berges 2012: 126).

The call to the 'people of Israel' to turn back (from Egypt) and throw away the idols they had made there (vv. 6–7) makes good sense in the eighth-century context, but it is ingeniously applied to the sixth century by Eusebius, who claims that 'when the people returned from Babylon and built the Second Temple, there were no longer any idols to be found in Jerusalem'. William Cowper may have had these verses in mind when he wrote the fifth verse of his famous hymn 'O For a Closer Walk with God' (1772) (cf. Isa 2:20) (*EH* 445, *CH2* 457 *GtG* 739 *AM* 132).

The fall of Assyria 'by a sword, not of man' (v. 8), appears to be a reference to 701 BCE (cf. Isa 37:36), although, as we have seen, commentators apply the prophecy to other events such as the fall of Babylon and the defeat of Satan. The verse was interpreted by members of the Qumran community as foretelling the end of Roman rule (1QM 11:11–12; *DSSE* 177; Blenkinsopp 2006: 98,119). The fire burning perpetually in Zion is the fire on the altar of sacrifice (Lev 6:13; Nicholas), or else the fire that awaits the wicked (cf. Isa 30:27–33; Rashi, Jerome). God himself is a consuming fire (Deut 4:24; Heb 12:29): though it may appear as if we are defenceless, he will be 'a fire' to our adversaries (cf. Zech 2:5; Henry). Aquinas, in a more benign reading of the verse, finds a reference to the 'fire of charity' in the Church militant, destined to become a 'furnace' in the Church triumphant. Bede cites the words of Christ's companions on the way to Emmaus: 'Did not our hearts burn within us when he spoke along the way...?' (Luke 24:32) (*Three Books on Ezra and Nehemiah* 3).

A Kingdom of Righteousness and Peace (Isa 32:1–20)

This chapter, a favourite with liberation theologians (Miranda 1977: 173), describes a new society, characterized by justice and peace, where the poor will be protected (vv. 1–8; 15–20). According to Rashi it expresses the people's hopes when Hezekiah came to the throne, the man who 'shall be as an hiding-place' (v. 2 AV) (cf. Aquinas, Luther, Calvin, Henry). Modern scholars believe the prophecy reflects the optimism of the reign of Josiah when the Assyrian Empire was breaking up (cf. Isa 28:23–29; 30:27–33)

Isaiah Through the Centuries, First Edition. John F. A. Sawyer.
© 2018 John Wiley & Sons Ltd. Published 2020 by John Wiley & Sons Ltd.

(Berges 2012: 13; Barth 1977; Clements). The Church Fathers apply it to the coming of Christ: 'a man shall hide his words' (v. 2 LXX) refers to Christ 'speaking in parables' (Matt 13:34; Mk 4:33–34); the 'streams of water in a dry place' are the life-giving water he offers to those who believe in him (John 4:14) and that 'makes glad the city of God' (Ps 46:4), that is, the Church (Cyril; cf. Eusebius, Jerome). Mark Twain points out that 'the shade of a great rock' (v. 2) is best appreciated in the 'blistering naked treeless land' of Palestine (Twain 1980: 382), while for T. S. Eliot it is a refuge from modern secular civilization (*The Waste Land* 1.25–26) (Ricks and McCue 2015: 606).

In an elaborate analysis of the virtues and vices of political leadership, reminiscent of biblical wisdom literature (cf. Prov 8:15–16; 17:7; 21:1), the prophecy describes how blindness, deafness, stupidity and wickedness will be removed, the hungry and the thirsty will be satisfied, and the poor and the needy protected (vv. 3–7). The theme of blindness (cf. Isa 6:10) and its eventual removal runs through those chapters (cf. Isa 29:10, 18; 32:3–4; 35:5) to be developed later in the book (42:7, 16, 18–22; 43:8; 56:10; 59:10; 61:1; Wagner 2006: 99). No longer will there be fools in high places mumbling inarticulately (v. 4; cf. Prov 14:2,15) and practising 'hypocrisy' (Vg, AV: RSV 'ungodliness'), like the scribes and Pharisees (Matt 23:14; Jerome). Commenting on this ideal state of affairs, Luther makes the general observation that 'the ruling office has been set up as an umbrella … to protect us from Satan and his members' and notes that the 'Roman Empire must have been a help to the apostles so that the Gospel might be preached throughout the world'.

The rabbis identified a reference to Hezekiah's son, Manasseh (2 Kgs 21) in verse 7 (Berges 2012: 109) and contrasted him with the senior officials of Hezekiah alluded to in verse 8 (Ibn Ezra). 'He who is noble' (Heb. *nadib*; RSV; Vg 'prince'; cf. Isa 13:2; 1 Sam 2:8) is identified by others as Josiah (Nicholas). The term is interpreted by many, however, as 'pious' (LXX; Cyril, Eusebius) or 'generous, liberal' (cf. Exod 35:5, 22; 1 Chron 28:21; Rashi, Calvin, Henry): 'the liberal deviseth liberal things; and by liberal things shall he stand' (AV). In a sermon preached on this text in the presence of King Charles I in 1628, John Donne notes that *nadib* is a 'royal term' (cf. Ps 51:12) and states that 'the very form of the office of a king, is liberality' (Potter and Simpson 1953–1962: 3.243). Queen Victoria may have had this in mind when she chose the verse as one of four epitaphs in the mausoleum built in memory of her husband at Frogmore, near Windsor Castle (cf. 2 Sam 23:4; 1 Kgs 3:10; Dan 12:3).

The vision is interrupted by a lament when 'the palace is forsaken … and the populous city deserted' (vv. 9–14). Mourning was a professional activity conducted by women in ancient Israel (Jer 9:20), and verse 9 need not suggest suffering on their part. Indeed it is cited by the rabbis to show that women have a special role in Jewish society, equal if not superior to that of men (b*Berakhot* 17a; cf. Ackerman). LXX has 'rich women', perhaps reflecting conditions in Hellenistic Egypt (van der Kooij 2006: 53). They are understood by many to represent provinces and cities, prosperous and complacent like Samaria (cf. Amos 6; Cyril, Jerome, Ibn Ezra, Rashi, Calvin). According to Ibn Ezra, it is a lament over the fall of Samaria 'in the fourth year of King Hezekiah' (2 Kgs 18:9–12). Others believe it refers to the destruction of Jerusalem, whether by the Babylonians in 586 BCE (Luther) or the Romans in 70 CE (Tg, Jerome). The 'joyful city' (v. 13) refers to Jerusalem elsewhere (Lam 2:15; Rashi), and the term 'hill' in verse 14 (RSV; Heb. *'ophel* 2 Kgs 5:24) may be an explicit reference to Mount Ophel (Lowth). It can also mean 'darkness' (Jerome) and the scene of devastation (vv. 13–14) recalls the fate of the vineyard of the Lord (Isa 5:7; cf. Ps 80:8, 12–13) (Cyril, Eusebius). Now it will become a wilderness, 'a joy for wild asses', whether understood as unclean spirits (Cyril) or foreign nations that do not know God (Jerome).

After the destruction of the city the prophecy continues its description of an age of justice and peace (vv. 15–20). The pouring out of the spirit recalls the prophecy of Joel (Joel 2:28; cf. Zech 12:10) (Rashi), which for Christians was fulfilled at Pentecost (Acts 2; cf. John 16:7) (Eusebius, Jerome, Cyril, Nicholas). It is also comparable to Ezekiel's vision, when the Lord said 'I will put my spirit within you and you shall live' (Ezek 37:12) (Aquinas), and the Psalmist's 'send forth your spirit and … you shall renew the face of the earth' (Ps 104:30) (Calvin). 'Justice will dwell in the wilderness and righteousness in the fruitful field' (v. 16), alongside the description of King Solomon's legendary knowledge of the natural world (1 Kgs 4:29–33), nicely makes the point that ecological issues are integral to this vision of the ideal king, whose subjects have a duty to conserve the order of all creation for which we are responsible and answerable to God (Marlow and Barton 2009: 241).

Opus iustitiae pax (v. 17), translated 'justice will bring about peace', was inscribed on a medal minted in 1958 in honour of Pius XII. But the same motto translated rather differently as 'peace is an enterprise of justice', seems to have played a crucial role in the initial formulation of the Vatican 2 pronouncement on justice and peace (*Gaudium et Spes* 78; Flannery 1975: 986). By placing the emphasis on action, the cardinals and bishops found in the verse a definition of justice in terms of this worldly praxis, rather than as an otherworldly messianic hope. Isaiah 32:15–17 is quoted more than once in Miranda's *Marx and the Bible* (1977), where, for example, he defines peace as the 'fruit of justice'(Isa 32:17) and uses the passage as background for Paul's definition of the kingdom of God as 'justice and peace and joy in the holy Spirit' (Rom 14:17; cf. Isa 61:1; Luke 4:18) (Miranda 1977: 51, 224).

'My people will dwell in a peaceful habitation' (v. 18; Heb. *neve shalom*) or 'city of peace' (LXX) was interpreted in the patristic period as a reference to

PLATE 27   'An oasis of peace' (Isa 32:18). Neve Shalom is an ecumenical kibbutz, founded in 1979.

the Church which will take the place of the 'great and splendid city being demolished' (Eusebius; cf. Cyril). In modern times the Hebrew of verse 18 has been set to music in an Israel folk song and Neve Shalom 'Oasis of Peace' (Arab. *waḥat al-salam*) is an ecumenical kibbutz founded in 1979 by the Dominican Bruno Hussar with the object of bringing together Israeli Jews, Christians and Muslims (Hussar 1989) (Plate 27). There are also Neveh Shalom Synagogues in London, New Jersey, Istanbul, Casablanca, Sidney, Calcutta and elsewhere (Slapak 1995: 38–39; Olitzky 1996: 300–301).

The forest battered down by hailstones (v. 19; MT LXX Vg AV) refers to the wicked (Rashi) or 'the armies of the gentiles' (Tg), and the city to be 'utterly laid low' is Nineveh (Aquinas) or Babylon (Lowth) or Jerusalem destroyed by the Roman armies (Nicholas, Luther). For some the images in verse 19 are figurative intended to highlight the contrast between the fate of the arrogant struck down by hailstones like great trees (cf. Isa 10:33–34; 28:17; 30:30) and the peace and freedom of the righteous (Eusebius, Calvin). Some modern scholars consider the verse discordant and remove it (Duhm) or translate it differently (NEB; cf. Clements).

Jewish interpreters take the blessing in verse 20 as a repetition of an earlier prophecy (Isa 30:23–25): 'you who sow beside all waters' are the righteous whose works will prosper and who will be rewarded by plentiful harvests (Tg, Rashi). Some cite it in praise of the study of the Torah (*RA* 133; cf. Isa 55:1): the 'waters' are wisdom (cf. Sir 24:25–31) (Cyril, Aquinas). For many it refers to the spread of the gospel 'beside all waters', that is, to all nations (cf. Ps 29:3) (Gregory, *Morals on Job* 6.31.9). The ritually clean ox and the unclean ass recall Paul's 'to the Jew first and also to the Greek' (Rom 1:16) (Eusebius). Others apply it to the study of scripture: the ploughman's ox, bearing the yoke of the law, represents the Old Testament, and the ass on which Christ rode, signifying the gentiles, the New (Ambrose, *Letter* 74.9). The donkey represents humility (cf. Zech 9:9) (Jerome). The ox and the ass together represent the strong and the weak, the educated and the simple, all receiving the same gospel without discrimination (Nicholas) (see comm. on Isa 1:3).

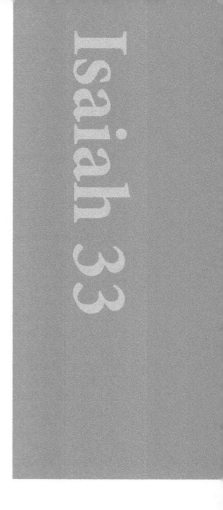

This chapter, 'manifestly distinct from the foregoing … and peculiarly elegant' (Lowth), has a mysterious, dramatic quality about it reminiscent of some of the Psalms (Pss 46, 82). Dubbed a 'prophetic liturgy' by some (Gunkel 1924), it stands at the midpoint of the book and, rather like Job 28, exhibits some of the characteristics of the chorus in a Greek drama (Henry). In the great Isaiah scroll from Qumran there is a distinct gap between chapters 33 and 34, dividing the book into two parts (Brooke 2006: 77), which exactly agrees with the modern view that chapters 34–35 have more in common with Isaiah 40–66 than

Isaiah Through the Centuries, First Edition. John F. A. Sawyer.
© 2018 John Wiley & Sons Ltd. Published 2020 by John Wiley & Sons Ltd.

with 1–33, and chapter 33 serves as a point of connection between Isaiah of Jerusalem and Deutero-Isaiah (Williamson 1994: 238–239).

The Destroyer (Isa 33:1–12)

Verse 1 is a vivid curse on a 'destroyer ... treacherous one', in fourteen Hebrew words corresponding to over forty in English. Assonance and repetition recall descriptions of the destroyer of Moab (Isa 16:4) and the king of Babylon (Isa 21:2), and the appropriateness of his fate recalls Christ's words, 'the measure you give, will be the measure you get' (Matt 7:2) (Aquinas). Traditionally he was identified with Sennacherib (Ibn Ezra, Rashi, Luther, Lowth, Vermeylen) but other suggestions include Nebuchadnezzar (Clements) and the Seleucid king Antiochus Eupator (cf. 1 Macc.6) (Duhm, Kaiser). The Septuagint differs from the Hebrew: 'Woe to those who afflict you, but no one makes you miserable ... for they shall be destroyed like a garment eaten by moths'. These words were understood by the Church Fathers as giving comfort to the saints who suffer for Christ's sake (Cyril, Jerome).

In the psalm-like prayer that follows (vv. 2–6; cf. Pss 46, 51, 56, 86), uttered under the threat of the 'destroyer' (v. 1), the prophet expresses his people's faith in God. Cyril compares the observation that 'salvation comes in the time of trouble' to Christ words, 'my power is made perfect in weakness' (2 Cor 12:9–10) (cf. Theodore, *Instructions* 3.3; Eusebius). The verse is applied to the story of the raising of the daughter of Jairus in Stainer's cantata (1878) (see comm. on Isa 25:8). 'The thunderous noise' (Vg 'voice of the angel') (v. 3) refers to miraculous intervention by God (Rashi), in particular the destruction of Sennacherib's Assyrian army (Isa 37:36) (Jerome), and the looters collecting spoil the morning after (v. 4) are compared to caterpillars and locusts swarming over the dead bodies (cf. Joel 1:4).

The establishment of justice and righteousness is celebrated in two verses that transcend any single historical situation (vv. 5–6). The priority of the 'fear of the Lord' over 'stability [or 'faith' Vg, Rashi; Heb. *emunah*; cf. Isa 7:9] ... salvation, wisdom and knowledge' (v. 6, cf. Prov 1:6; 3:14–15) is commented on both by Christian writers (Jerome, Leo the Great, *Sermon* 92.3; Aquinas) and Jews (Ibn Ezra). The words 'the fear of the Lord is his treasure' are cited more than once by the rabbis to prove that what God prizes in good deeds is not the acts themselves but the religious motivation from which they spring (b*Berakhot* 33b; b*Shabbat* 31a).

The 'valiant ones' (v. 7; AV RSV) in rabbinic tradition are the angels, and the verse is quoted more than once to describe the angels in heaven weeping when Isaac was bound on the altar (GenR LVI.5; Mann 1971: 1, 173; Spiegel 1979: 157), or when the Temple was destroyed and God's covenant with Abraham was apparently broken (v. 8) (LamR, *Proem* 24; cf. EstherR VII.13). The medieval Jewish poet Ephraim of Bonn quotes the verse in 'The Slaughter of Isaac and his Revival' (Carmi 1981: 382). The Venerable Bede identifies 'the messengers of peace weeping bitterly' with Israel's prophets, lamenting the fate of the Jews (*Four Books on Samuel* 3.16.1), because they refuse to believe Isaiah's news of victory (vv. 2–6) and continue to spread reports of national disaster and broken treaties (vv. 7–9) (Tg, Ibn Ezra, Luther). The word 'treaties' (RSV 'covenants') perhaps originally referred to Sennacherib's treaty with Hezekiah (2 Kgs 18:13–16) (Ibn Ezra, Lowth).

The 'valiant ones' (Heb. *ar'elim*; cf. 2 Sam 23:20), however, is an emendation. The Hebrew has *er'ellam* (their altar) (cf. Isa 29:1) and Rashi has 'for their altar they have cried', an allusion to the desecration of the Temple. Other suggestions are 'people of Ariel [Jerusalem]' (cf. 29:1), parallel to 'messengers of Salem' (reading Heb. *shalem*, for MT *shalom* 'peace') (Blenkinsopp). LXX 'they shall be terrified for fear of you' prompts the Greek Fathers to comment on the fate of the Jews, once persecutors of Christians, now that their land is destroyed and the Old Covenant with Moses put away, watching in fear as the Church, the people of the New Covenant, expands and prospers (Cyril). Yet another interpretation is 'I will appear to them' (Heb. *era'eh lahem*; Aquila, Symmachus, Theodotion), nicely anticipating verse 10 which can be applied to Christ's appearance to his apostles (Luke 24:34): even they wept, as Christ did … if only they had known the things that make for peace (Luke 19:41–42) (Eusebius).

It follows then that verses 10–12 are about Christ's resurrection and ascension ('Now I will arise, says the Lord) (Cyril; cf. Isidore, *De Fide Catholica* 1.56.6), or according to some, his Second Coming or the Day of Judgement (cf. Isa 29:6–7; 30:27–33; 66:24) when the wicked will be consumed in the fires of hell (vv. 11, 12, 14; cf. Luke 3:17) (Eusebius). Luther praises Isaiah's faith for being able to laugh at the mighty Assyrian army and describe them as nothing more than stubble and straw. The image of 'the peoples burnt to lime' (v. 12) is used in a rabbinic discussion of the relationship between Jews and gentiles: just as lime without sand will not last, so the gentiles without Israel could not last, as God said to Abraham, 'In your seed will all the gentiles be blessed' (Gen 22:18) (*PesR* 10.5).

A Place of Broad Waters and Streams (Isa 33:13–24)

The next passage begins (vv. 13–16) with something like a 'Torah liturgy' (Clements) or moral catechism (Blenkinsopp) in which worshippers approaching the Temple are challenged: 'who shall ascend the hill of the lord …?' (cf. Pss 15, 24).

Isaiah's version is more dramatic: the wicked will face a 'consuming fire … and everlasting flames', the righteous a vision of God in the beauty of his holiness and 'a land that stretches afar' (vv. 14,17). The prophet calls upon people far and near to listen (v. 13 MT, Vg, Tg), or predicts that people far and near will listen (LXX). Isaiah's universalism is familiar from other passages such as Isa 49:1 (Aquinas; cf. 34:1; 41:1); those from afar are the gentiles and those near at hand are the Jews (Ibn Ezra, Cyril, Jerome). Rashi puts it the other way round: those from afar are those who have believed in God and done his will from their youth, while those nearby are repentant sinners who have recently drawn near.

God is the consuming fire (v. 14; cf. Deut 4:24), both in the Temple (Rashi) and on the battlefield (Ibn Ezra). For the Church Fathers these are the 'everlasting flames' that await the wicked in hell on Judgement Day (Cyril, Jerome) or the baptism of fire foretold by John the Baptist (Luke 3:17; Aquinas). Calvin demythologizes it as 'the inward anguish by which ungodly men are tormented, the stings of conscience which cannot be allayed, the unquenchable burning of crimes which exceeds every kind of torment'.

In answer to the question, 'Which of us can survive the devouring fire?' (v. 14; NJB), the prophet gives us a detailed description of what it means to be righteous (vv. 15–16). Modern scholars suggest a connection with the Temple entrance liturgy (cf. Pss 15; 24) (Clements, Roberts) and a parallel with the so-called negative confession recited by the deceased on Judgement Day in the Egyptian 'Book of the Dead' (cf. Job 31) (Blenkinsopp). The rabbis counted six commandments here (b*Makkot* 23b–24a; cf. Henry), while Aquinas reduces the list of sins to be avoided to three: avarice, cruelty and lust (cf. Matt 5:28; cf. Nicholas). On verse 15 Ibn Ezra cites the example of the adder that stops his ear so 'he does not hear the voice of snake charmers' (Ps 58:4–5). Calvin cites a psalm to prove that no one can be sinless (Ps 130:3) and warns against 'popish doctors, by whom passages of this kind, which recommend works, are abused in order to destroy the righteousness of faith.'

For the Church Fathers the 'strong rock' (LXX v. 16) is the rock on which Christ built the Church, 'and the gates of Hades shall not prevail against it' (Matt 16:18). It provides an everlasting abode for the righteous (Tertullian, *Against Marcion* 4.34). There in safety the righteous shall receive bread and water, supplied from heaven (Rashi), 'the necessities of life' (Calvin), and, for some Christian interpreters, the bread of life and the grace of holy baptism (Cyril).

The change of person ('your eyes', singular) suggests that a new section begins here, but many commentators take verse 17 as the rhetorical climax of the 'liturgy' (vv. 13–17). The 'king in his beauty' and a 'land that stretches afar' may have originally referred to the restoration of King Hezekiah after

Sennacherib had departed (Ibn Ezra, Calvin, Henry). The word for 'beauty' (Heb. *yophi*; Vg *decus*) is not applied elsewhere to God, but both LXX (*doxa*) and Targum (*yeqar*) make it clear that from an early date most believed it goes far beyond that: it is a vision of the Shekinah, seen from afar, and the fate of the wicked descending into the land of Gehenna (Tg; cf. Rashi). For Christians it is a vision of 'the pure in heart for they shall see God ... and the meek for they shall inherit the earth' (Matt 5) (Jerome). Christ promised to manifest himself to those who keep his commandments (John 14:21; Bede, *Homilies on the Gospels* 1.19), and this could refer to the appearance of the risen Christ to his disciples (Adamnan, *On the Holy Places* 1.2.13).

The rest of the chapter fills in details of the new age in a series of striking images (vv. 18–24). Gone are the symbols of Assyrian oppression, tax-collectors and people speaking a foreign language in Judah (vv. 18–19; cf. Isa 28:11; 36:11–13). 'Counting towers' was for tax purposes (Ibn Ezra). The vision of Jerusalem at peace and secure (v. 20) reminds us that 'not since the days of Hezekiah have the children of God had a quiet habitation' (Calvin; Pauw 2006: 205). The 'broad rivers and streams' are a reference to Hezekiah's improvements to the water system (2 Kgs 20:20; Isa 22:8–11) (Nicholas), and verse 23 apparently refers to the booty acquired from the defeated Assyrian army (v. 23), which helps to explain his vast wealth (2 Chron 32:27; cf. Isa 39:2; Lowth). A widely accepted emendation of the words 'prey and spoil' produces 'the blind will divide the spoil, the lame will take the prey' (Tg, cf. 53:12; Duhm), recalling the story of David's capture of Jerusalem (2 Sam 5:6).

The reference to 'scribes and those who count young children (for tax purposes)' (v. 18) comes from the days before Christ's victory, when the Jews were ruled by the scribes and the Pharisees (Cyril, Eusebius). Now the land is a 'place of broad rivers and streams', that is, populated by the evangelists and apostles who 'like a stream of water bedew the minds of the faithful' (cf. Ps 46:4; Cyril). Like a great river the Lord encircles the Church to protect it from all her enemies (Eusebius). The passage ends with a reference to the fall of Jerusalem, like a shipwreck, and the arrival of the lame, that is the gentiles, 'crippled in mind', who come to take the spoil and profit from God's gifts, and whose iniquities are forgiven (vv. 23–24) (Cyril).

John Newton's famous hymn beginning 'Glorious things of thee are spoken' (*EH* 393; *CH2* 206; *AM* 641) was originally entitled 'Zion or City of God. Isaiah xxxiii.20,21' (Moffatt 1927: 75; *BiM* 92), although clearly influenced by Psalm 87 as well. The Mormons derived their term 'stakes' (local congregations) from verse 20 (cf. Isa 54:2) (*EM* 3.141), and it may be that the vision of a land of 'broad rivers and streams where ... no stately ship can pass' (v. 21) inspired the fifteenth-century Christmas carol 'I Saw Three Ships Come Sailing

In (to Bethlehem)' (Blenkinsopp). Verse 22 is alluded to in the second of the O Antiphons (see comm. on Isa 7:14), and inspired a hymn by Scott Holland (1902) (*EH* 423; *CH2* 636; *GtG* 342) (*NCHB* 4.740). It appears in full, in Hebrew and Latin, on the frontispiece of a work published in Vienna in 1559 by Paul Weidner, a Jewish doctor who with his family had converted to Christianity (Sawyer 1996: 100–101).

The Day of Vengeance (Isa 34:1–17)

Chapters 34–35 have more in common with 40–66 than with what precedes them. The wide gap in the great Isaiah Scroll from Qumran, separating 1–33 from 34–66, has already been mentioned (see comm. on Isa 33) and scholars since Torrey (1928) have grouped 34–35 with Deutero-Isaiah. The highway through the wilderness at the end of chapter 35, anticipates the highway at the beginning of 40; and verse 10 is actually repeated in 51:11. The two chapters are

Isaiah Through the Centuries, First Edition. John F. A. Sawyer.
© 2018 John Wiley & Sons Ltd. Published 2020 by John Wiley & Sons Ltd.

sometimes treated as a diptych, the ugly images of slaughter and devastation in 34, corresponding to images of peace, freedom and prosperity in 35 (Lowth, Childs; cf. Miscall 1999). The passage is quoted in Revelation (Rev 6:13–14; 19:3) and sometimes referred to as the 'Little Apocalypse' (cf. Isa 24–27; Duhm; cf. Berges 2012: 21).

The prophet summons all the nations, first Sennacherib's allies (cf. chaps 36–37), then the whole world (v. 1; cf. Isa 49:1) (Aquinas). The Lord is angry (v. 1), about to wield his sword of judgement (vv. 5–6); it is a day of vengeance and the enemies of Zion will pay the penalty for their crimes (v. 8). According to some this is a prophecy fulfilled in the victories of Nebuchadnezzar (cf. Jer 25) (Nicholas, Calvin, Lowth) and composed in the exilic period or later (Clements), although many writers apply the chapter to the Messianic period (Ibn Ezra), or God's final victory over the powers of darkness (Jerome, Henry).

The striking word translated 'doomed' (v. 2 AV 'utterly destroyed'; Heb. *heḥrim*) refers to the grim ancient rules of war (Josh 6:15–21; 7:1) according to which a victorious army kept nothing that survived, but 'put it under the ban' (Heb. *ḥerem*), that is, utterly destroyed it as an offering to the deity (v. 7) (Clements, Blenkinsopp). The victims are described as 'the people of my *ḥerem*' (RSV 'the people I have doomed') (v. 5).

Reference to the 'host of heaven' (v. 4) recalls apocalyptic language about the end of the world when 'the moon will be confounded and the sun ashamed' (Isa 24:23; cf. Rev 6:12–17) or the coming of the Son of Man when 'the stars will fall from heaven' (Matt 24:29; Jerome). The verse is quoted by the rabbis as the climax of a series of cosmic catastrophes, each more cataclysmic than its predecessor, affecting the hills and mountains (54:10), the earth and heaven (51:6), the sun and moon (24:23) and finally the stars and planets (34:4) (b*Abodah Zarah* 17a). Rashi and Ibn Ezra interpret the verse as a reference to the war in heaven where the ups and downs of human history are played out in battles between the angelic 'princes of the nations' (cf. Dan 10:12–14, 20–12). Eusebius also believes the reference is to the 'principalities, powers and world rulers of this present darkness' referred to by Paul (Eph 6:12). Calvin favours a natural explanation according to which the stars are blotted out by great clouds which make it look as though the skies are rolled up like a scroll, and the wicked will be so terrified they will imagine the sky is falling on top of them (Calvin). Walter Scott's brief paraphrase of the *Dies irae* has 'When, shrivelling like a parched scroll / The flaming heavens together roll…' (*EH* 487, *CH2* 161).

The naming of Edom, alone of all the nations of the world, has been explained by reference to contemporary events such as Edomite encroachment on Judaean territory and possible collaboration with the Babylonians in the sixth century BCE (cf. Jer 49:7–22; Ezek 35; Obadiah; Ps 137:7) (Clements).

Calvin compares the bitter hatred that existed between Jacob and Esau and their descendants, Judaeans and Edomites, to his attitude to papists: 'in like manner we have no enemies more deadly than the Papists.' But 'Edom' can also stand for other bitterly hated enemies. In ancient Jewish tradition Edom came to be identified with Rome: 'the streams of Rome will be turned to pitch' (v. 9; Tg; cf. Jerome). Christian commentators, determined to identify Zion with the Church and the wicked with the Jews, argued that Edom (Heb. *'edom*) 'refers to Judah … for being attached to earthly affairs' (Heb. *adamah* 'earth'; Cyril), or was allied to the Jews and therefore suffered the same fate (Luther).

The devastation of the land described in the next few verses (vv. 8–10) recalls the story of Sodom and Gomorrah (Gen 19:24; cf. Ps 11:6) (Aquinas) and provides modern dispensationalists with imagery for their vision of the approaching end of the world (Boyer 1992: 331). Others interpret it as a description of hell (Gregory, *Homilies on Ezekiel* 1.6.18). 'From generation to generation' (v. 10) reminds Rashi of Moses' curse of the Amalekites (Exod 17:16) which means till the Messiah comes. The land to be called 'No Kingdom There' and the mention of princes who 'shall be nothing' (v. 12) recall a parallel in Jeremiah where 'many shepherds destroyed my vineyard … and made it a desolation' (Jer 12:10–11; Cyril) and the 'thorns and thistles' (v. 13) recall what happened to another vineyard when it yielded wild grapes (Isa 5:6; Eusebius). The reference to a measuring line of 'chaos' (NJB Heb. *tohu*) and a plumb line of 'emptiness' (NJB Heb. *bohu*) (v. 11) recalls the time when the 'earth was without form and void (Heb. *tohu wa-bohu*)' (Gen 2:2), and means that any attempt to rebuild Edom will fail (cf. 2 Kgs 21:13; Mal 1:4–5) (Calvin).

The second part of the chapter (vv. 11–17) is about creatures that will find a resting-place in the ruined strongholds and fortresses (v. 13): from hawks (or pelicans NJB), owls, ravens and hedgehogs (v. 11) to jackals, ostriches (v. 13), hyenas (v. 14), the great owl (AV; Heb. *qippoz*) and the kite (Rashi 'vulture'), nesting and bringing up their young in safety (v. 15). A tawny owl (*strix butleri*; Heb. *lilit*; cf. AV, Lowth) (v. 14) is portrayed with her chicks in one of a series of four stamps issued in Israel in 1987 (cf. Isa 13:21; Deut 14:16).

The Septuagint has mammals in verse 15 instead of birds: 'There the hedgehog (Heb. *qippod*; cf. Tg) made its nest and the earth safely preserved her young ones: deer met and saw each other's faces'. For the Church Fathers this refers to Christian believers, rescued from destruction by Christ and thirsting after God like deer (Ps 42:1–2) (Cyril) (cf. Prov 5:19; Cant 2:10) (Jerome). Others take it as a description of a wilderness inhabited by wild beasts, monsters and demons (Aquinas): the hedgehog, able to hide its head and its feet and turn into an innocent-looking ball, symbolizes the duplicity and insincerity of the wicked (Gregory the Great, *Pastoral Care* 3.11). The poet Abraham Cowley's lengthy paraphrase of Chapter 34 is about wild animals getting their revenge on men for having been for so long the victims of ritual sacrifice:

> 'Tis fit at last beasts their revenge should have
> And sacrificed men their better brethren to save. (1967: 2.28–29)

According to one recent interpretation, the chapter describes the destruction of a wicked human civilization in favour of 'an alternative ecology of wild animals and birds' (Marlow and Barton 2009: 227–234).

Among the creatures listed is Lilith, the dangerous seductive female demon of Jewish legend who kidnaps babies and visits men sleeping alone (b*Shabbat* 51b). She appears in a list of 'demons and howlers' in the Dead Sea Scrolls (4Q510; *DSSE* 451) and by the medieval period she is frequently mentioned in childbirth amulets designed to ward off evil spirits. She was Adam's first wife who would not accept his dominant role and asserted her independence by leaving the Garden of Eden (Scholem 2007). She figures in Goethe's *Faust*, poems by Dante Gabriel Rossetti and Browning, and late nineteenth-century writings and paintings (Dijkstra 1986: 306–309). In the Isaiah passage, her name (Heb. *lilit*) has often been translated by a general word like *lamia* 'witch' (Vg) and 'night-hag' (RSV) and both 1QIsa[a] and the Targum have the plural (cf. LXX 'satyrs'). Rashi describes her as 'a female demon', as does Luther who comments that she is rumoured to harm children by suckling them at night-time (cf. Lam 4:3; cf. Oecolampadius).

In modern versions she has reappeared (NRSV, NJB; cf. JPS) and this coincides with a reassessment of her role in contemporary culture. *Lilith* is the title of an 'Independent, Jewish and Frankly Feminist' quarterly published in New York since 1976 (Plate 28). Judith Plaskow's essay 'The Coming of Lilith' in *Womanspirit Rising* (1979) came out soon after, followed by many other publications such as Barbara Hill Rigney's *Lilith's Daughters* (1982), Jacques Bril, *Lilith ou la mère obscure* (1984) and Michelene Wandor, *The Gardens of Eden: Poems for Eve & Lilith* (1984) (Borts 1994: 98–109). This all prompts a fresh look at her role in Isaiah 34. She is the only creature in the passage with a personal name, and in contrast to the predominantly masculine language of the first half of the chapter, the company she keeps is predominantly female: 'for them' (Heb. *lahen*) in verse 17 is feminine. This is, then, a quite remarkable description of the restless outsider, elsewhere feared and despised, finding rest like the wolf and the lamb in the peaceable kingdom (Isa 11:6–9).

'Seek and read from the book of the Lord', which is not in the Septuagint (v. 16), has been described as 'one of the strangest passages in all the prophetic literature' (Duhm). One suggestion is that it is addressed to future generations

PLATE 28 'There too shall Lilith alight and find herself a resting place' (Isa 34:14). Cover of first issue of the 'independent, Jewish and frankly feminist' magazine *Lilith* (1976). Reproduced with kind permission of *Lilith* magazine.

and refers to the book of Isaiah's prophecies (Aquinas, Nicholas; cf. Isa 8:16; 29:11–12; Jer 25:13; Dan 12:4), or to one passage (Isa 13:21–22) (Clements). Other suggestions include the Torah (Calvin); Genesis, where all the animals, of every species, male and female, are rescued – not one of them is missed (Rashi); or Deuteronomy with reference to Moses' long description of the diseases, deprivations, desolation and destruction that await Israel if 'you will not obey the voice of the Lord your God' (Deut 28:15–68). Whatever the precise meaning, the purpose seems to be to claim some kind of scriptural authority for the view that among the consequences of the terrible 'day of vengeance' (vv. 1–12) will be everlasting peace and contentment (vv. 13–17) (cf. Henry).

The Day of Redemption (Isa 35:1–10)

The vision of a peaceful and contented alternative society in the wilderness, after all the wicked human principalities and powers have been destroyed (Isa 34:14–17), leads straight into a vision of the 'desert blossoming like the rose' (AV; RSV 'crocus'; LXX, Vg 'lily') (v. 1). In the nineteenth century it was applied by Jewish settlers to their agricultural achievements in Palestine and by Mormons to their colonizing of the Great Basin of Utah (O'Dea 1957: 90).

Isaiah Through the Centuries, First Edition. John F. A. Sawyer.
© 2018 John Wiley & Sons Ltd. Published 2020 by John Wiley & Sons Ltd.

More recent ecological insights find a 'fundamental interconnectedness within the created order' (Marlow and Barton 2009: 238) when the 'eyes of the blind shall be opened' (v. 5) and 'the ransomed of the Lord shall ... come to Zion with singing ... sorrow and sighing shall flee away' (v. 10; cf. 51:11). Verses 2 and 10 feature in the final chorus of Spohr's oratorio *The Fall of Babylon* (1839–1840) (*BiM* 82–83).

According to Jewish tradition this wonderful prophecy was originally inspired by the miraculous destruction of Sennacherib's army, which is the subject of the following chapters (Isa 36–37): the wilderness refers to Jerusalem, 'Lebanon' is the Temple (Rashi); and the feeble knees, the fearful heart, the blindness and deafness refer to the people's initial disbelief (Ibn Ezra). But it goes beyond any single historical situation and looks forward to the messianic age when God's people will finally be able to return with singing to Zion (Ibn Ezra). A highway will be there so that even a blind person can find their way and a fool cannot become lost (v. 8), protected from uncleanness and from wild beasts like Nebuchadnezzar (v. 9; Rashi). In the midrash verse 5 is quoted as scriptural authority for the belief that 'what God smites in this world is healed in the next' (*Tanḥ.* Gen 11.9). Five Israeli settlements, established in the years 1949–1950 in the Negev by immigrants from Iran, the Yemen and North Africa, took their names from this emotive chapter: Tifraḥ 'blossom', Gilat 'joy', Ranen 'singing' (v. 2), Maslul 'highway' (v. 8), and Peduim 'ransomed' (v. 10).

Christians from the beginning interpreted the chapter as being fulfilled in the life and work of Christ, 'the day of restoration and renovation' (cf. Acts 3:21 NRSV; Calvin). As Matthew Henry puts it, 'We find more of Christ and heaven in this chapter than one would have expected in the Old Testament'. In Christian lectionaries the chapter is prescribed to be read on the third Sunday of Advent (*ORM*, RCL) or the Eve of Theophany (*OSB*), and it has inspired many hymns including several composed since the Second Vatican Council (HNO 280, 522, 698). The Septuagint, used by the Greek Fathers, reads 'the deserts of the Jordan shall blossom' (v. 2), and this is taken as a reference to the baptism of Jesus in the River Jordan, where the waterless desert became the Church of God through the washing of rebirth (cf. Cant 8:5) (Eusebius; cf. Bede, *Six Books on the Song of Songs* 5.8.4–5). The 'lily' (v. 1 LXX) is a figure of the purity that comes about in baptism (Theodoret). The desert is the 'soul that is parched and unadorned' (Gregory of Nyssa, *On the Baptism of Christ*) or the Church watered by the ever-flowing stream of the Holy Spirit welling from above (Eusebius). These two verses also provided the motto for a study of desert spirituality (Louth 2003).

The feminine pronoun in the Hebrew and Greek of verse 2 ('The glory of Lebanon shall be given to her, the majesty of Carmel and Sharon') made it applicable to the Virgin Mary, and the words appear in the medieval *Biblia Pauperum* and elsewhere beside portrayals of the Coronation of the Virgin

(*BP* 119; cf. 1 Kgs 2:19–20, Esth 2:15–20; Wisd 4:1; Ps 45:13; Cant 8:5). 'My people [LXX] shall see the glory of the Lord' (v. 2) points to the coming of Christ (Cyril, Nicholas). As Augustine points out, 'He will come and save you' (v. 4) means 'not just anyone, an angel, an ambassador but Christ himself born in mortal flesh ... a pattern of extreme humility' (*Sermon* 293.5). His glory is here identified with compassion and the power to 'strengthen the weak hands ... He will come and save you' (vv. 3–4; cf. Ps 63; 138; Miranda 1977: 235; cf. Irenaeus, *Against Heresies* 3.20.3; Tertullian, *Answer to the Jews* 9).

Christ's healing ministry is clearly predicted in verses 5–6, as cited in the Gospels (cf. Matt 11:5; Luke 7:22), and frequently by the Church Fathers (Justin, *First Apology* 48; Tertullian, *On the Resurrection* 20; Origen, *Against Celsus* 2.48; Leo the Great, *Sermon* 54.4). Athanasius argues that none of the healing miracles listed ever took place in the Old Testament: so the prophecy must refer to Christ (Matt 9:33; Mark 7:33; John 9:1) (*On the Incarnation* 38). The healing of illnesses of the soul is included, such as deafness to the words of scripture and tongues tied by Satan to keep them from confessing the true God (Eusebius; Calvin). Luther adds lame idolaters to the list who 'limp on one leg and do not walk in an upright faith' until they accept the Word of faith and 'leap for spiritual joy in Christ'. In Handel's *Messiah* (1742) verse 5 provides the words for a short recitative that links the soprano aria 'Rejoice Greatly, O Daughter of Zion' (Zech 9:9) with the alto solo 'He Shall Feed His Flock' (Isa 40:11). 'Burning sand' (Heb. *sharab*) (v. 7) should probably be understood as a 'mirage' (Vitringa, Lowth, Blenkinsopp), and the jackals (Tg, Rashi, RSV; 'dragons' Vg, AV) represent creatures that inhabit dry terrain (cf. Isa 13:22; 34:13; 43:20). For Luther the 'dragons' are teachers of ungodly things, whom Christ called 'brood of vipers' (Matt 23:33).

Christ is the 'Holy Way' (v. 8; cf. John 14:6), the way of insight (Prov 9:4–6; Jerome), the one and only royal and holy way 'smoothed by means of the completely firm Word' (Luther). The threat of the lion and ravenous beasts (v. 9), that is, Satan and his demons (cf. 1 Pet 5:8), will be removed (Cyril). This is the way that leads to the heavenly Jerusalem (cf. Heb 12:22) and the 'everlasting joy upon their heads' (v. 10) recalls the crown of righteousness (1 Tim 4:8) that awaits the faithful in the kingdom of heaven (Eusebius). Luther finds in the words 'redeemed' and 'ransomed', a reference to Christian liberty ('subject to all men but inwardly lord over all things'; cf. John 8:36). Calvin comments that the joy and gladness referred to here are not of this world (cf. Rom 5:3; 14:17; Gal 5:22).

Verse 10 is cited frequently in discussions of death and resurrection: Ambrose, for example, cites it in a funeral oration (*On Theodosius* 37; cf. Tertullian, *On the Resurrection* 58). John Chrysostom comments that the prophet is here speaking of 'the place ... where there is eternal life, unspeakable joy and inexpressible beauty' (cf. 1 Cor 2:9; Isa 64:4) (*Homilies on Matthew* 55.6).

In Brahms' *German Requiem* (1869) the verse comes at the end of the chorus *Alle Fleisch is wie die Gras* ('All Flesh Is Grass') (Isa 40:6–8), as a triumphant comment on the words 'But the word of the Lord stands for ever' (*BiM* 90). The chapter also provides the text of *Part II* of Patten's oratorio *Isaiah* (1898) (*BiM* 112–113), and is one of *Four Biblical Settings* for organ by Emma Lou Diemer (1933) (see comm. on Isa 11).

The Assyrian Invasion of Judah (Isa 36:1–22)

Isaiah 36–39 is written for the most part in prose, and tells the story of three events in the reign of Hezekiah. The Isaiah narrative differs in some ways from the accounts given in Kings and Chronicles: there is no hint that he ever gave in to the Assyrian threats (2 Kgs 18:14–16) and no mention of his religious reforms (2 Chron 29–31), while Hezekiah's Psalm of Thanksgiving (Isa 38:9–20) appears only in Isaiah. The account of Sennacherib's invasion of Judah and miraculous

Isaiah Through the Centuries, First Edition. John F. A. Sawyer.
© 2018 John Wiley & Sons Ltd. Published 2020 by John Wiley & Sons Ltd.

destruction (36–37) is presented here as the fulfilment of Isaiah's earlier prophecies: 'a seal to authenticate the prophecies which might otherwise have been
called in question' (Calvin; cf. Theodoret). Chapter 36 gives historical content
to prophecies about Assyrian arrogance (e.g. Isa 10:12–19) and chapter 37 ends
with the dramatic account of Sennacherib's downfall as foretold earlier (e.g. Isa
30:29–33; 31:8–9; 33:1–4, 10–11, 23–24).

The date of the invasion is given as the fourteenth year of King Hezekiah
(v. 1; cf. 2 Kgs 18:13), that is, 711 BCE, which would be six years before
Sennacherib succeeded Sargon II as King of Assyria. We now know from
Assyrian records written at the time that Sennacherib's forces besieged
Jerusalem in 701 BCE, shutting up Hezekiah 'like a bird in a cage', and then leaving the city intact on receipt of a large tribute (2 Kgs 18:14–16) (Clements,
Childs). It may be that the biblical date is simply an error for the twenty-fourth
year of King Hezekiah, but the relationship between the biblical narrative and
what actually happened in 711 and 701 BCE is certainly more complex. Modern
scholars have suggested that at least two separate sources have been combined
in the text as we now have it (Blenkinsopp). It must also be said that the enemy's
blasphemous speeches (36:4–10; 13–20; 37:10–13), which together with prayers
(37:16–20) and prophecies (37:6–7; 37:21–35) account for most of the narrative, make it clear that these two chapters are as much religious discourse as
historical narrative (Childs). In Luther's words, in these four chapters 'we see
how the attack on faith and its near destruction take shape (cf. Heb 11)'.

The assault on Jerusalem begins with the arrival of an official sent 'with a
great army' to deliver a message from the king of Assyria to Hezekiah (v. 2). The
moment is described in the 'March of Sennacherib's Army upon Jerusalem' in
John Truman Wolcott's oratorio *Hezekiah* (1908) (*BiM* 101). Of the three
officials mentioned in the parallel narrative (2 Kgs 18:17) only the Rabshakeh
appears here. The name means 'chief cup-bearer' in Assyrian and it is doubtful
whether he was a military official: he is presented rather as a clever and eloquent
orator whose mission was to persuade Hezekiah to surrender, and in both
Jewish and Christian tradition, the Rabshakeh became an archetype for the
blaspheming enemy of God. This is his role already in Ecclesiasticus (Sir 48:18;
cf. 1 Macc 7:41; 3 Macc 6:5). In the Talmud he is said to have been an apostate
Israelite (b*Sanhedrin* 60a), and Jerome refers to a Jewish tradition that he was
Isaiah's son, brother of Shear Yashub (cf. Isa 7:3). This would explain his famili-
arity with the language and beliefs of the Judaeans (cf. Theodore, *Comm on Ps*
52:1). Later the term was applied to Julian the Apostate (Gregory of Nazianzus,
Contra Jul 648) and Nestorius (Cyril of Alexandria, *Oratio* 43), while
Bonaventure explains that 'by Rabshakeh is meant the bad Christian who is
sent by a diabolical suggestion to commit sin and thus to blaspheme
God' (*Sermon* 46.3.3). In seventeenth-century London, pamphlets attacking

contemporary political opponents had titles like *Rabshakeh vapulans* (squirming) (London 1691) and *Rabshakeh Rebuked and His railing accusations Refuted* (London 1695).

Greeted by three of Hezekiah's senior officials (cf. Isa 22:20–24), the Rabshakeh delivers the first of three speeches (vv. 4–10) which contain 'the blasphemies of Satan … by means of which … he attacks not the walls but the faith and heart of the king himself' (Luther). This is how the illustration in the *Bible Moralisée* portrays the scene. He starts with the words 'Tell Hezekiah', insultingly referring to the king simply by name without a royal title (Cyril); and then in the words 'Thus says the great king', arrogantly mimics the prophets' formula 'Thus says the Lord', which is intended to show the authority and greatness of the one sending the message (Jerome; cf. Eusebius, Luther). The Rabshakeh challenges the king by ridiculing three possible sources of confidence available to him: his trust in his own strength (v. 5), his trust in Egypt (v. 6) and his trust in God (vv. 7–10) (Calvin). He argues that mere words and prayers are not enough against horses and chariots, you yourself have already condemned 'those who go down to Egypt for help' (Isa 31:1): and it was your own God who commanded me to invade your land (Isa 10:5–6) (Eusebius, Calvin). Jerome and others point out that the Rabshakeh is lying when he says the word of God is not so powerful as horses and chariots (cf. Ps 20:7) and when he claims that Hezekiah sought help from Egypt and had destroyed the altars of his God. On the other hand, he is right when he scornfully contrasts the might of the Assyrian cavalry with that of Hezekiah (vv. 8–9), because according to the law of Moses the king must not 'multiply horses for himself or cause the people to return to Egypt in order to multiply horses' (Deut 17:16; cf. Isa 31:1) (Eusebius). Luther sees in the speech the tactics of the devil making Hezekiah feel guilty: 'these are the fiery darts of Satan' (cf. Eph 6:16; 1 Pet 4:12).

The three officials plead with the Rabshakeh to speak in Aramaic, the international language of diplomacy, rather than Hebrew, the language of Judah, so as to avoid spreading unjustified terror and panic among the people (v. 11) (Jerome). The Rabshakeh's response was to address the people directly in a loud voice, in Hebrew, using even more violent and insolent language: they are all doomed to eat their own dung and drink their own urine (v. 12). The ordinary people, not just their leaders, will suffer the deprivation of a long siege (cf. Deut 28:53–57; Lam 4:4–5, 10), and they should be informed. Luther recognizes here the dangers of entering into a debate with Satan: 'the more we wrestle with him, the more we despair … we play into Satan's hands … they asked for quiet and Satan shouts all the more'. His second speech tells them not to listen to what Hezekiah is saying (vv. 14–20), quoting the words of Isaiah (37:35; cf. 29:5–8; 31:4–5, 8–9), and offers to make peace with them (v. 16). He ends with a list of nations conquered by Assyria, culminating with Samaria, whose gods could do nothing to help (cf. Isa 10:9; Jer 49:23; 2 Kgs 17:31). If these cities were not protected by many gods, what hope is there for lonely Jerusalem, which has the protection of only one God? (Jerome).

This time Hezekiah had told the people not to answer (v. 21), an indication of Hezekiah's exceptional wisdom (cf. Prov 13:10) (Jerome, Eusebius), for he knew that any response might lead to even greater blasphemies: 'Do not kindle the coals of the sinner, in case you scorch yourself in his blaze' (Sir 8:10 NJB; Pss 4:4; 39:1–2; 141:3–4) (Cyril, Luther). But the three officials returned to Hezekiah, their clothes rent as a sign of mourning in anticipation of imminent death and destruction at the hands of the Assyrian army (cf. Judg 11:35; Isa 15:2–3; 22:12; 32:11–12). According to Rashi they rent their garments because they had heard blasphemy against the Name of God.

The Salvation of Jerusalem (Isa 37:1–38)

The chapter division marks a change of focus from the city and its officials to the two characters, Hezekiah and Isaiah, who now take centre stage until the end of chapter 39. The king's response was to tear his clothes and wear sackcloth. It was the custom of the Jews to rend their garments on the occasion of blasphemy as the high priest did during the trial of Jesus (Matt 26:65) (Cyril), and Paul and Barabbas at Lystra (Acts 14:13) (Jerome; cf. Rashi on 36:22).

Isaiah Through the Centuries, First Edition. John F. A. Sawyer.
© 2018 John Wiley & Sons Ltd. Published 2020 by John Wiley & Sons Ltd.

But in this context it has a different significance: Hezekiah 'betakes himself to the protection of God, and thus acknowledges that there is no other remedy for heavy distresses' (Calvin). He tore his clothes and made his way to the Temple dressed in sackcloth (v. 1), to acknowledge his sins and show himself humble before God and worthy of compassion and mercy (Eusebius, Jerome). Then he sent his officials, also dressed in sackcloth, with a message to his prophet, as many others have done including Josiah (2 Kgs 22:11–20) and Zedekiah (Jer 21:1–2).

Their message describes the crisis as a day of 'distress, rebuke and disgrace' (RSV) or 'insults' (Tg) or 'blasphemy' (KJV, Vg) or 'anger' (LXX), and asks Isaiah to pray for them (vv. 3–4). It is introduced modestly by the words 'Thus says Hezekiah ...', not 'Thus says the king ...', which would 'swell with a name of political power' (Jerome; cf. Eusebius). First the plight of the people is compared to the pain, fatigue and powerlessness of a woman during a difficult childbirth (cf. Isa 26:18; Hos 13:13) (Jerome). The situation is portrayed as all the more pathetic by the reference to the Lord as Isaiah's God, as though they were afraid to address him as their own, and in the prayer itself which is not for the whole people but for the remnant who are besieged (Jerome). Calvin also picks up subtleties in the language identifying in the reference to Isaiah's God, for example, an expression of 'praise and commendation of Isaiah's calling', and in the 'lifting up of prayer' a call to 'lift up our hearts to heaven' (Lam 3:41) in such a manner that 'our hearts may not grovel on the earth ... but take a lofty flight'.

Isaiah's reply begins with the prophetic formula 'Fear not', reminiscent of his words of reassurance to King Ahaz thirty years earlier (Isa 7:4) and of many more to come (e.g. Isa 41:10, 13, 14; 43:1, 5; 44:2, 8). Divine intervention on this occasion will take the form of a spirit (Heb. *ruaḥ*) which will enter the heart of the king of Assyria, like the evil spirit that tormented Saul (1 Sam 16:14), and make him return to his own land, where he will be killed (cf. 37:37–38). According to some this was the spirit of cowardice (Cyril, Lowth). Rashi thinks the 'rumour' mentioned here refers to the report concerning Tirhakah, king of Ethiopia, which temporarily distracted Sennacherib from his assault on Jerusalem (v. 9). Commenting on apparent discrepancies between Isaiah 36–37 and the parallel accounts in Kings and Chronicles, Jerome says 'prophecy may be confused with history in the book of the prophet', while Calvin, with similar concerns, ingeniously argues that the reference here is to a strong wind (cf. KJV) sent by the Lord to blow away his enemies like chaff (cf. Ps 1:4). While the Assyrian campaign continued elsewhere in Judah (v. 8) and Egypt (v. 9), Sennacherib sent a letter to King Hezekiah in which, in language similar to the Rabshakeh's, he boasted that the fate of Jerusalem would be no different from that of all the other cities in the regions already destroyed by the Assyrians, whatever his God had promised (vv. 8–13). Things spoken long ago about

Assyrian arrogance (Isa 10:5,7,11) and their ultimate fate (Isa 10:12) were now being fulfilled (Eusebius).

Hezekiah's response on receiving the Assyrian king's letter was once again to go to the Temple (v. 14; cf. v. 1). There he 'spread the letter before the Lord' and uttered a prayer (v. 15). Hezekiah's prayer (vv. 16–20), the first of two in this section (cf. 38:9–20), must have been inspired by his prophet to contain 'such rich theology' (Eusebius). The titles 'Lord of hosts, God of Israel, enthroned above the Cherubim' are employed by Hezekiah for the confirmation of his faith (Calvin). The prayer is written in the same prose style as those of David (2 Sam 7:18–29) and Solomon (1 Kgs 8:3–53), but its explicit monotheism (v. 16) and violent rejection of idols (v. 19) anticipate the poetry of chapters 40–55 (e.g. Isa 40:18–20; 44:9–20; 45:5, 6, 14, 18, 21; 46:9). Verse 19 may have inspired the second verse, now normally omitted, of Bishop Heber's famous hymn 'From Greenland's Icy Mountains' (*EH* 547; *NCHB* 2.736). The prayer is set to music in George Arnold's cantata *Sennacherib* (see comm. on v. 36) and by Orlando Gibbons in a paraphrase by George Wither (1588–1667) to the tune 'Hezekiah' (Moffatt 1927: 72).

Isaiah's second prophecy is much longer (vv. 21–35). The longest part, which is in verse, is an extended personal attack on Sennacherib (vv. 22–29). He begins with the striking image of the 'virgin daughter of Zion' rebuffing a powerful suitor with a scornful toss of her head (v. 22) (Sawyer 1989). Jerusalem is described elsewhere in Isaiah as a young woman overcoming adversity (e.g. 1:21–26; 52:1–2), but here, especially so soon after the agonizing image of a woman going through a difficult childbirth (v. 3), it is a powerful expression of the prophet's faith, laughing at adversity as the Lord laughs at the nations in Psalm 2:4 (cf. Rom 1:17) (Luther). The city is a 'virgin' because of the integrity of her faith, especially under the exemplary rule of Hezekiah (Nicholas).

The rest of the poem is reminiscent of earlier prophecies quoting the arrogant boasts of the Assyrian king (vv. 24–25; cf. 10:8–14) and the Lord's response (vv. 26–29; cf. 10:15–19). Rashi understands 'the heights of the mountains … Lebanon … its tallest cedars' (v. 24) as references to the Temple and Judah's leaders (cf. Tg, Jerome, Luther). Commenting on verse 26, Calvin thinks of Jerusalem, founded long ago (cf. Ps 78:69; Isa 14:2) and the Church ordained before the foundations of the world were laid (Eph 1:4). Vitringa compares the Lord's words to the king of Assyria with those of Christ addressing Saul on the Damascus road: 'Why do you persecute me?' (Acts 9:4). His blasphemy and ferocity must be restrained 'with my hook ['ring' Vg] in your nose and my bit in your mouth' like wild horses (cf. Ps 32:9; Jerome, Nicholas) or camels (Rashi) or bears (Luther).

The poem is followed by two shorter sections in conventional prose, addressed to Hezekiah, not Sennacherib. First there will be a sign (cf. 7:10–14) that, after two years of disruption, normal agricultural processes will be resumed, thereby proving that the Assyrians have gone (vv. 30–32). 'Out of Jerusalem will go forth a remnant ... out of Zion' recalls both the 'remnant' theme (cf. Isa 7:3; 10:19–22; 11:11, 16; 18:5; 46:3) and the role of Zion in wider biblical tradition (cf. Isa 2:3; Joel 3:16; Amos 1:2; Mic 4:2), while the 'zeal of the Lord of hosts' also goes back to an earlier messianic prophecy (Isa 9:7). Rashi comments that the statement implies that God's intervention was not motivated by any merits his people may have (cf. Cyrus).

The last part of Isaiah's prophecy predicts that the Assyrian king will withdraw from the city without a blow being stuck, and it repeats that this is not because of anything his people have done, but 'for my own sake and for the sake of my servant David' (vv. 33–35). 'The Prophet bids Hezekiah and the whole nation turn their eyes towards God ... in like manner, if we now contemplate the power of our enemies, we shall be overpowered by fear ... but we ought to look directly to God, and embrace his promises, by which we are defended as by a shield' (Calvin).

The fulfilment of Isaiah's prophecy, in the famous story of how the angel of the Lord slew 185,000 Assyrians in one night, is described very briefly in one verse (v. 36; cf. 2 Macc 8:19; 15:22; Tob 1:21). Luther observes that this is because the prophet had already provided us with ample details of the event, thinking no doubt of Isa 10:15–19, 30:29–33, 31:8–9, 33:1–4, 10–11, 23–24 and other prophecies understood by him to refer to the defeat of the Assyrians. He also comments that, while historians might have described the slaughter with 'ponderous and great words in the tragic manner', the Holy Spirit is more concerned with perfecting and strengthening our faith than with details of the story (cf. Brueggemann). The details are discussed, however, by many commentators. On the 'angel', for example, several commentators note a parallel with 'the exterminating angel' in the Exodus story (Exod 12:29) (Eusebius, Jerome), and Jewish commentators suggest that Sennacherib's defeat gave Hezekiah a second reason to celebrate Passover (2 Chron 30; cf. Isa 30:29–33). Calvin accepts the possibility that many angels may have been involved (cf. Ps 91:11; Eph 1:21) and like many others rejects the view, found for example, in Josephus' account (*Antiquities* 10,19–21; cf. Duhm), that the slaughter was due to a plague. There is nothing to suggest this in the text and no reference to a plague in the Assyrian records (Childs, Clements). Sennacherib's return home, a 'fugitive' (Luther), and subsequent assassination at the hands of his sons, provide a fitting end to the story of Assyrian arrogance and blasphemy (37:37–38), and we know from the Assyrian records that Sennacherib's reign did end in this way but twenty years later in 681 BCE (Roberts).

Whatever happened in the fourteenth year of Hezekiah (Isa 36:1), the Assyrian records tell of Sennacherib's withdrawal from Jerusalem (2 Kgs 18:14–16) in 701 BCE (the twenty-fourth year of Hezekiah). This survival of Jerusalem, alone of all the cities of Judah, was something of a miracle in itself and, combined with a firm faith in the special divine role of Zion (Isa 2:3; 37:32; cf. Ps 48), probably inspired the story of the miraculous destruction of Sennacherib's army described in Isa 37:36. It is predicted in many passages in the book of Isaiah as Luther pointed out, and Lowth quotes Hosea as a 'plain prediction of this miraculous deliverance': 'I will have pity on the house of Judah. I will save them by the Lord their God. I will not save them by the bow, nor by the sword, nor by battle, nor by horses nor by horseman' (Hos 1:7).

Rubens' dramatic painting *The Destruction of Sennacherib* (1616) depicts 'a wild and raging tumult of flight caused by heavenly apparitions, with men, mostly mounted, fighting against an unearthly enemy; even the horses are beside themselves, and over the whole there pour streams of light and night' (Burckhardt 1950: 84). This is in striking contrast to Byron's equally dramatic poem *Sennacherib* (1815), which makes no mention at all of men on horse-back, either fighting or fleeing from the battlefield. Almost every word, every image comes from a close reading of one verse (Isa 37:36): 'the Angel of Death spread his wings on the blast ...That host on the morrow lay withered and strown ... The tents were all silent, the banners alone, / The lances unlifted, the trumpet unblown ... The might of the Gentile, unsmote by the sword, / hath melted like snow in the glance of the Lord!'. His emphasis on silence captures the chilling atmosphere of the miracle, missed by Rubens. The famous first stanza, beginning 'The Assyrian came down like a wolf on the fold', and references in the last to the 'widows of Ashur' and the broken idols in the Temple of Baal, give the poem a context. But otherwise the poem asks us to focus single-mindedly on verse 36.

Another accurate portrayal of the passage could once be seen in a thirteenth century painting in the Painted Chamber in the Palace of Westminster, destroyed by fire in 1834. A reconstruction by Professor Ernest Tristram (1892–1952) shows the sleeping army at the mercy of the angel of death, with Isaiah on the left on his knees before God and Sennacherib on the right about to be slain by his son Adramelech. The verse is sung as an eery choral recitative by tenors and basses, to the accompaniment of orchestral semiquavers and demisemiquavers, at the end of George Arnold's cantata *Sennacherib* (1883) (BiM 216). There is also an Islamic illustration of the destruction of Sennacherib's army, overlooked by Isaiah, in a sixteenth-century Turkish manuscript of *Zubdat al-tawarikh* ('The Cream of Histories') by Luqman-i 'Ashuri, in the Chester Beatty Library in Dublin (CBL T414, folio 91b).

The Recovery of King Hezekiah from Illness (Isa 38:1–22)

The account of the miraculous defeat of the Assyrian army is followed by the story of how Isaiah made the sun go backwards and lengthened the life of the king by fifteen years (cf. Sir 48:23). According to Jewish tradition, Hezekiah fell sick three days before the downfall of Sennacherib and 'on the third day', the first day of Passover, he went up to the Temple and was healed (Rashi; cf. 2 Kgs 20:5).

Isaiah Through the Centuries, First Edition. John F. A. Sawyer.
© 2018 John Wiley & Sons Ltd. Published 2020 by John Wiley & Sons Ltd.

Cyril cites a proverb to explain why such a pious king should be struck down: 'God disciplines those whom he loves' (Prov 3:12).

Isaiah first rebukes the king (v,1) and then, in response to the king's repentance, prophesies that he will be delivered both from his sickness and from the Assyrian threat (vv. 5–6). When Hezekiah heard Isaiah's words, he 'turned his face to the wall and prayed' (v. 2). This was so that he could pray more devoutly, in secret, without distractions (Nicholas; cf. Calvin, Lowth). Others say the wall must be the wall of the Temple because Hezekiah was too ill to go to the Temple itself (Jerome). But the expression was used by Henry James, Søren Kierkegaard and others to describe a gesture of resignation and the acceptance of death (*DBTEL* 353). 'He wept bitterly' (v. 3), and Isaiah delivers another prophecy to the king, informing him that the Lord has heard his prayer and he will have another fifteen years to live: that is, from the fourteenth year (Isa 36:1), a reign of twenty-nine years (cf. 2 Kgs 18:2; 2 Chron 29:1) (Calvin). Philip Armes' oratorio (1878) ends with Hezekiah's prayer (v. 3), a moving tenor solo, and God's reply (vv. 4–8), sung by a bass, followed by a joyful choral setting of Isa 12:5–6 (*BiM* 101–102).

Like Ahaz (Isa 7:10–14), Hezekiah is given a sign (vv. 7–8). It is not clear exactly what the sign was. It is traditionally interpreted as the shadow on some kind of sundial (Vg *horologium*; Tg 'stone of the hours') going backwards ten 'steps' or 'degrees' or 'hours' (Luther). The sun went back to the east and, incredibly, gave an extra ten hours (Rashi; cf. Eusebius). Nicholas compares the phenomenon to the sun standing still at Gibeon (Josh 10:12–14) and illustrates his commentary with a mathematical diagram. The text has 'the steps of Ahaz', and this could refer to an architectural feature such as a staircase leading to a balcony or upper room (Duhm, Clements). Several commentators highlight the contrast between the wicked Ahaz mentioned here and his pious son Hezekiah (Rashi, Jerome). Cyril contrasts Hezekiah with Christ: for Hezekiah the sun turned back, for Christ it was eclipsed (Luke 23:45) (*Catechetical Lectures*, 2.15).

The story is set to music in a dialogue motet for five soloists, strings and continuo by Carissimi in which the change from despair to joy is dramatically portrayed (*BiM* 81). The scene of the prophet standing over Hezekiah's sickbed, with a sundial and a red sun overhead, also appears in a small medieval stained glass window in Canterbury Cathedral (Plate 29).

The most prominent part of the story is the famous psalm of thanksgiving (vv. 9–20), which does not appear in either of the parallel versions (2 Kgs 20; 2 Chron 32). It is introduced as a composition of King Hezekiah, written after he had recovered from his sickness (v. 9). Writing is traditionally associated with Hezekiah's reign (Prov 25:1): there is even a rabbinic tradition that he wrote the whole book of Isaiah (b*Baba Bathra* 15a). Described as a 'prayer' in the

PLATE 29   'So the sun turned back on the dial ten steps' (Isa 38:8). Stained glass window in Canterbury Cathedral (thirteenth century). Reproduced with kind permission of Sonia Halliday Photography.

Septuagint or a Psalm (Heb. *miktam*; cf. Pss 57–60 RSV) or a 'thanksgiving' (Tg), it expresses the fear and resignation of someone very close to death (vv. 10–15), alongside faith in a God who can restore his people to life and happiness (vv. 16–20). As a theological comment it goes beyond Hezekiah's illness, and as 'Hezekiah's Canticle', has been sung in churches since medieval times.

There are many difficulties and ambiguities in the Hebrew text. The phrase translated 'in the noontide of my days' (RSV, NJB; Heb. *bi-demi yamay*) occurs nowhere else and is explained by reference to the traditional Latin *in dimidio dierum* (at the midpoint of my days). Jerome points out that saints die, like Abraham, 'full of years at an old age' (Gen 25:8) while the wicked 'shall not live out half their years' (Ps 55:23). Others translate the words 'in the desolation of my days' (Rashi), 'in the sorrow of my days' (Tg) or 'in my prime' (lit. 'the height of my days' LXX; Cyril). 'The gates of Sheol' that were such a threat to Hezekiah are those same gates that could not prevail against Peter (Matt 16:18) (Jerome).

The first regret of the dying man is that he will not 'see the Lord' (v. 11), as it is said 'the dead shall not praise the Lord' (Ps 115:17) (Rashi). The repetition of the divine name (MT, Vg, AV; cf. Isa 12:2; 26:4) is ignored by most commentators (Clements, Blenkinsopp; cf. 1QIsaᵃ). He will never again hear the Word or worship God, nor will he ever again see his friends and colleagues: 'he laments leaving both orders, the spiritual and the political realm' (Luther). His life is cut short, as when shepherds pack up their tents and move on, or weavers cut their threads from the loom (v. 12). Luther notes the contrast between Hezekiah's splendid palace in Jerusalem and the humble transportable home of a shepherd.

'I lay quietly (Heb. *shiwwiti*) till morning' (cf. Ps 131:2) (Roberts; cf. Vg, AV). Many read 'I cry for help (Heb. *shiwa'ti*)' (RSV, NJB; cf. JPS) or 'I roared like a lion' (Lowth; cf. Tg). The lion that 'breaks all my bones' is the pain of his illness (v. 13) (Cyril). The birdsong (v. 14) has been interpreted by some as the shrieks of a bird caught in a trap (Tg; Rashi) or unable to find its mother (Aquinas) and by others as imitating the unceasing hymns of praise Hezekiah promises to sing on his recovery (Cyril). Instead of 'I am oppressed' (AV, RSV; cf. Vg), the Hebrew may mean 'contend for me' (cf. Gen 26:20): 'Contend for me, take me out of the hand of the angel of death, and pledge Yourself to save me' (Rashi; cf. Lowth). Verse 15 adds sleeplessness to the list of Hezekiah's symptoms (Heb. *shenah* 'sleep'; Rashi, RSV), but there is an old tradition that the king here reflects on the years he has lived (Heb. *shanah* 'year'): 'I must eke out the rest of my years in bitterness of soul' (NJB; cf. AV, Tg, Vg, Jerome, Lowth).

It is generally agreed that verse 16 marks a shift from despair to hope, but again the Hebrew is difficult: 'O Lord, concerning them [that is, the dead; Tg], they shall live, and before them all is the life of my spirit' (Rashi; cf. Jerome, AV). This is broadly in line with the Greek version commented on by Eusebius who cites parallels from the Psalms (Pss 9:13; 33:19; 56:13). Modern suggestions include 'O Lord, for that reason my heart holds on to you' (Duhm) and 'by such things men live and my spirit finds life in them too' (Childs; cf. RSV). The two verbs at the end of the verse may be future ('you shall make me well' Vg, AV, Rashi) or imperative ('restore me to health' RSV) or past ('you have preserved me alive' Tg, LXX).

Whether a prayer or a statement of faith, it seems the crisis is over and the rest of the psalm is a celebration (vv. 17–20). The juxtaposition of 'peace, welfare' (RSV; Heb. *shalom*) and 'bitterness' (v. 17) is striking. Some take it as a reference to the fact that the Assyrians had been put to flight, peace restored, the city once again secure, while Hezekiah alone was at the gates of hell (Jerome, cf. Rashi). His suffering was all the more unbearable because it afflicted him while 'peace and joy smiled upon him' (cf. Ps 30:6–7; Calvin). The Targum contrasts the peace that awaits the righteous with the bitter fate of the wicked, while some suggest that the king's 'great bitterness' was for his own good (AV, RSV).

He goes on 'You desired (Heb. *ḥashaq*) my soul from the pit' (Rashi, cf. Tg) or 'in love you delivered my life' (cf. AV, Calvin). More prosaically others read 'you held back (Heb. *ḥashak)* my life from the pit' (Lowth, RSV; cf. Vg). Saved from death, the first thing the righteous king does is praise God, something that cannot be done in Sheol. If God wants to be worshipped, then it is in his own interest to rescue the righteous from death (Ps 6:4–5) (Luther). The king's promise to teach his children about God's faithfulness (v. 19) prompts comments about his wicked son Manasseh (2 Kgs 21:16) and the suggestion that the promise might not refer to children but to a choir of young singers which he would institute in the Temple (Cyril). Athanasius cites verse 20 to show that at no time should one praise God more freely than after passing through affliction (*Festal Letter* 10.3).

In a brief reference at the end of the chapter, some further details of the healing miracle are given: there is mention of 'boils' (Heb. *sheḥin*) as one of the symptoms, reminiscent of Job's affliction (Job 2:7), and some kind of fig poultice as part of the treatment (vv. 20–21). Lowth quotes Pliny as evidence that fresh figs were applied to boils in ancient times, but Cyril interprets the king's recovery as a sign of divine intervention and nothing to do with the figs. Either way, the story ends with Hezekiah exclaiming, 'How good and beautiful is this sign!' (cf. Ps 84:1; Isa 52:7; Luther; cf. Rashi) and going up to the house of the Lord. Instead of going down to Sheol, he is able to go up to the temple to sing God's praises with stringed instruments all the days of his life (v. 20).

'Hezekiah's Canticle' (vv. 10–21) (Mearns 1914: 14) features in many illustrated medieval manuscripts, such as the tenth-century Paris Psalter and the twelfth-century St Albans Psalter, where Hezekiah is shown standing at the jaws of hell (v. 10), pointing to his failing eyesight (v. 14). The first line of Dante's *Inferno*, 'Nel mezzo del cammin' di nostra vita', is 'precisely modelled' on verse 10 (Boitani 2011: 281), where the image of Hezekiah at the gates of hell had a particular relevance. In the Office for the Dead section of the beautiful fifteenth-century *Très Riches Heures du Duc de Berry* (folio 103f.) Hezekiah is shown standing naked in a dark scene of black rocks and huge red flames at the entrance to Hell. There are several English poems inspired by Hezekiah's Thanksgiving, including Christopher Smart's 'Hymn to the Supreme Being' (1756), and the fourth of Kuhnau's *Biblical Sonatas* for harpsichord (1700) is a musical interpretation, marked *agonizzante e risanato* (*BiM* 32).

Envoys from Babylon (Isa 39:1–8)

The third part of this lengthy narrative section (36–39) tells the story of a visit to Jerusalem by envoys sent from Babylon (vv. 1–4) followed by a prophecy of judgement (vv. 5–8). The king of Babylon, Merodach Baladan, had heard about Hezekiah's recovery from illness and the astronomical phenomenon that accompanied it (2 Chron 32:31). The Babylonians were skilled observers of the stars (Eusebius, Cyril, Nicholas). Merodach Baladan had also heard of the

Isaiah Through the Centuries, First Edition. John F. A. Sawyer.
© 2018 John Wiley & Sons Ltd. Published 2020 by John Wiley & Sons Ltd.

defeat of the Assyrians by the god of the Hebrews and wanted to make Hezekiah his ally (Calvin; cf. Eusebius). When the envoys arrived, Hezekiah welcomed them and showed them all his treasures, omitting nothing (v. 2), not even the Torah Scroll (Rashi).

Isaiah questions his actions in a way that implies criticism (v. 4). This is made more explicit in the parallel version in Chronicles: he did not repay God for the benefit he had received for 'his heart was proud' (2 Chron 32:25) (Lowth). Instead of telling the Babylonians about God's pre-eminence in creation, he showed them all his own possessions (Cyril). He had only recently promised to praise God continually (Isa 38:20), and now he has forgotten God entirely (Calvin). He boasts to Isaiah that the Babylonians had come a long way to see him, not for the sake of the Lord (Luther). Tertullian compares him to the rich man in the parable (Luke 12:16–21) (*Against Marcion* 4:28).

Isaiah's reaction to Hezekiah's behaviour was to utter a grim prophecy of judgement: all his possessions will be carried off to Babylon and some of his descendants will be made eunuchs there (vv. 6–7; cf. 2 Kgs 20:12–19). Some say this refers to Daniel, Ananiah, Mishael and Azariah (Dan 1:11) (Jerome, Aquinas, Nicholas, Rashi). There is also a tradition that his best known son, the wicked Manasseh, was taken in bronze fetters to Babylon and that it was there that he repented and prayed to God (2 Chron 33:10–13). In a brief comment on the seemingly unreasonable sacking of a city on account of the sin of one man, especially as elsewhere it is due to the collective sin of the people, Calvin points out that every individual has responsibility for the fate of his community as well as for himself. Verse 7 is one of several passages from Isaiah in Osbert Sitwell's libretto for William Walton's *Belshazzar's Feast* (1931) (see comm. on Isa 13:6).

Hezekiah interprets the prophecy as meaning 'there will be peace and security (Heb. *emet*) in my days' (v. 9 RSV). Earlier interpreters have 'peace and truth' (Vg, Tg, AV), recalling Isa 26:2 (Aquinas). Some criticize Hezekiah for rejoicing in his own temporary prosperity, instead of lamenting the future fate of his descendants and praying on their behalf, like Moses (Exod 32:32), for lasting peace (Cyril; cf. Jerome). Calvin, by contrast, defends Hezekiah's response to the prophecy, arguing that 'he unhesitatingly acknowledges his guilt, and confesses that he is justly punished … and thus holds out to us an example of genuine submissiveness and obedience' (cf. Aquinas, Nicholas). Jerome in his defence points out that he prays for his people at the beginning of the next chapter in the words 'Comfort, comfort my people' (Isa 40:1).

Modern scholars point out that, since the Assyrians brought the reign of Merodach Baladan (Babylonian *marduk-apal-iddina*) to an end before 701 BCE, the incident must have taken place before the defeat of Sennacherib and Hezekiah's illness, not after as the biblical story relates. Furthermore, after Sennacherib's invasion, he would have had nothing to show the envoys (v. 2) as his treasuries had been emptied (2 Kgs 18:14–16). It has also been suggested that the historical background of the story was a Babylonian attempt to gain Judah's support against Assyria (Calvin). Isaiah's stern questioning of Hezekiah's actions (vv. 3–4) and the force of his prophecy of judgement, were thus the result of his opposition to this policy (cf. Isa 30:1–3; 31:1–3). As for the date of composition, most are agreed that it was some time after the first Babylonian assault on Jerusalem in 597 (cf. 2 Kgs 24:10–17). The story of the Babylonian visit to Jerusalem was then placed at this point in the Book of Isaiah, both as the last words of chapters 1–39, which mostly have their narrative context in the Assyrian period, and as a link to the rest of the book, which reflects events in the Babylonian period and later (40–66). Its theological function is to form a connection between the 'new things' promised by Second Isaiah and the 'old things' of First Isaiah (Childs; cf. Isa 42:9).

Chapter 40 contains some of the best known and best loved verses in the whole Bible. In Jewish lectionaries it contains the first of the seven 'consolation readings' (*haftarot shel neḥamah*) (Isa 40:1–26; 49:14–51:3; 54:11–55:5; 51:12–52:12; 54:1–10; 60:1–22; 61:10–63:9) read on the Sabbaths following the Fast on the Ninth of Ab, which commemorates the destruction of the Temple (Elbogen 1993: 145, 425–426; *JSB*).

Isaiah Through the Centuries, First Edition. John F. A. Sawyer.
© 2018 John Wiley & Sons Ltd. Published 2020 by John Wiley & Sons Ltd.

'Comfort My People,' Says Your God (Isa 40:1–11)

Verses 1–5 also come first in an anthology of 'consolations' (*Tanḥumim*) (Ps 79:2–3; Isa 40:1–5; 41:8–9; 49:13–17; 43:1–2, 4–6; 51:22–23; 52:1–3; 54:4–10; Zech 13:9) from Qumran (4Q176 *DSSE* 535; Berges 2012: 96). The rabbis say that *naḥamu* 'comfort' is repeated twice to offer consolation for both destructions, the Babylonian in 586 BCE and the Roman in 70 CE (cf. v. 2). In Jewish tradition Isaiah is first and foremost the prophet of consolation. There is a rabbinic tradition that if you see Isaiah in a dream, you can expect consolation (bBerakhot 57b). In the words of Avraham Joshua Heschel 'no words have ever gone further in offering comfort when the sick world cries' (1962: 145).

Christian interpreters from New Testament times have found here, especially vv. 1–11, prophecies pointing to Christ and the Church: 'here the prophet is the most joyful of all, fairly dancing with promises' (Luther). Three of the Gospels start with quotations from the passage (Mark 1:3; Luke 3:4–6; John 1:23). Verse 1 features in the *Rorate* (see on Isa 45:8), while vv. 1–11, in whole or in part, appear in Advent lectionaries (*ORM*, RCL). 'The word of our God will stand forever' (v. 8) was a favourite with the Reformers, and verse 11 inspired an important motif in early Christian iconography. Muslim writers found a reference to the success of Islam in the image of 'a highway across the desert for our God' (Lazarus-Yafeh 1992: 84). An English version of a seventeenth-century German paraphrase of verses 1–5 found its way into modern hymn books (*CH4* 274; *GtG* 87), but the best known musical setting is the opening chorus of Handel's *Messiah* (1741), parodied by George III in Peter Maxwell Davies' poignant music theatre work *Eight Songs for a Mad King* (1969).

Many have noted the apparent discontinuity between 39 and 40, between a scene of 'peace and security' in the days of Hezekiah (39:8) and a call to comfort people suffering the consequences of divine wrath. In the 'second part of the book' (Ibn Ezra) prophecies of consolation are separated from prophecies of retribution (Rashi). There is also the obvious change in historical background from eighth-century Jerusalem threatened by the Assyrians, to the sixth century where Jerusalem has been destroyed by the Babylonians (Isa 44:28) and Cyrus, king of the Medes and Persians, is the 'Lord's anointed' (Isa 45:1). Scholars since the eighteenth-century are mostly agreed that the author of Isaiah 40–55 lived at least 150 years after the death of Isaiah and addressed his contemporaries in language and imagery very different from the author(s) of 1–39. According to Ben Sira, however, Isaiah was 'great and faithful in his vision … and by the spirit of might … he comforted those who mourned in Zion' (Sir 48.22–24). Although he is never mentioned by name again, we are to imagine that in 40–66 Isaiah is addressing the exiles in Babylon whose plight he explicitly predicts in chapter 39 (vv. 6–7). Long before the Lord sent his people into captivity, he sent this prophecy of comfort to them and we can imagine 'how much it helped to dry up their tears by the rivers of Babylon' (Henry).

Exactly who the words 'Comfort, comfort' are being addressed to (v. 1) is not made clear. The Septuagint inserts the word 'priests' and according to some this is Hezekiah ordering his priests to comfort his descendants, doomed to suffer exile in Babylon (Isa 39:6–7) (Jerome; cf. Eusebius, Cyril) (see above on Isa 39:8). The Targum begins 'O ye prophets', and this is how many understand it (Rashi): a multitude of prophets after the silence of affliction (cf. Ps 74; Calvin). Others suggest both prophets and priests (Aquinas) or prophets together with the other great leaders of Israel (Ibn Ezra). The words were later addressed to the apostles enabled by 'the God of all comfort ... to comfort those who are in affliction' (cf. 1 Cor 3:3–7; Eusebius, Luther). There is also a rabbinic tradition that here God is mourning the destruction of his Temple and pleading with his people to comfort him: 'Comfort, comfort me, my people' (*RA* 69).

But there is another interpretation favoured by many modern commentators. This is a second glimpse into the heavenly court (cf. Isa 6:1–13), where the prophet overhears God addressing his angelic courtiers (vv. 1–2), instructing them to intervene on behalf of his people (vv. 1–5). The voice then addresses the prophet himself, and says, 'Cry!' (v. 6), and, as in the first vision (Isa 6:8), the prophet speaks and receives the subsequent prophecies as his answer. This is another account of the call of the prophet, involving a mystical experience in which the prophet sees into heaven like 'First Isaiah' (Isa 6), Micaiah ben Imlah (1 Kgs 22), Daniel (Dan 7) and Paul (2 Cor 12:1–3), but unlike Isa 6:1–13, which 'authorizes the theme of judgement in chapters 1–39, this passage authorizes the theme of deliverance for the remainder of the book' (Brueggemann). A striking parallel to this 'call' (Heb. *qera'*) (vv. 3, 6) appears in one of the early suras of the Quran: 'recite!' (Arab. *iqra'*) (Sura 96:1, 3).

The personal 'your God' is rare in Isaiah (cf. v. 9; Isa 35:4; 59:2), and the phrase 'Speak tenderly' (lit. 'to the heart of' NJB) recalls the happy ending of the story of Joseph and his brothers (Gen 50:21; Ibn Ezra). Modern commentators note in this verse (cf. v. 9) the appearance of the image of Jerusalem as a woman, introduced first in chapter 1 (cf. 37:22) and developed, alongside that of the male Servant of the Lord, in some detail later (Isa 40:9; 52:1–2; 54:1–10; 60:1; 66:7–11) (Sawyer 1989). 'Her warfare (AV, RSV; Heb. *ṣaba'*) is ended' seems to refer to the exile as a period of service in the army (cf. Job 7:1; Num 4:23) (Rashi, Calvin; cf. NRSV, NJB). For Luther the word describes the struggle against the Law ended by Christ the Redeemer. The Targum takes 'her host' (Heb. *ṣaba'*) as a reference to the city once again crowded with the returning exiles. The Church Fathers have 'humiliation' (LXX) or 'wickedness' (Vg), perhaps reading *malitia* for *militia* (Luther).

Jerusalem 'received from the Lord's hand double for all her sins' (v. 2). This raises questions about divine retribution, apparently contradicting another prophet (Nah 1:9 LXX) (Cyril; cf. Aquinas). The Targum has 'as if she had been punished twice' and Lowth has 'double (blessings)'. But Rashi quotes Jeremiah to prove that the text is correct (Jer 16:18), and for many it refers to the fact that Jerusalem was besieged and destroyed twice, first by the Babylonians in 586 BCE and then by the Romans in 70 CE (Eusebius, Jerome). Calvin says it should not be taken literally but interpreted as showing that God understands how severe his people's sufferings have been, like a father who after punishing his son feels sorrowful because he thinks the punishment was excessive (Cyril). Theodoret suggests that apparently disproportionate suffering in this world will be rectified in the world to come, and Luther uses the verse to show that God's boundless mercy bears no relation whatever to what we have done or what we deserve.

'The voice' (v. 3) is the voice of the prophet addressing all nations (Ibn Ezra) or perhaps Cyrus in particular (Calvin). In the Hebrew text, the voice cries, 'In the wilderness prepare the way' (cf. RSV), and this is a command to prepare a way through the wilderness for the exiles to return to Jerusalem (Rashi). For Christians, reading 'a voice of one crying in the wilderness' (cf. LXX, Vg, AV), it is the voice of the gospel, no longer shut in by the Law, in a particular city or temple, but proclaimed to the gentiles (Jerome), 'unrestrained like a wilderness' (Luther). At Qumran it is an instruction to the community, already living in the wilderness, to 'prepare the way of the Lord', that is, to 'study the law in order to act according to all that has been revealed from age to age' (1QS 8.12–16; *DSSE* 109; cf. 1QS 9.9, 16–21; Blenkinsopp 2006: 125). In the Gospels 'the voice of one crying in the wilderness' is that of John the Baptist (Matt 3:1–3; Mark 1:2–3; Luke 3:4–6). The 'way of the Lord' (cf. Isa 30:20–21; John 14:6; Acts 18:25–26) had already almost become a term of self-definition for both the Qumran sect and the Christians (Blenkinsopp 2006:178–185). Bach's cantata *Bereite die Wege* (*BWV* 132 1715) is a musical comment on John 1:19–28, the reading for the fourth Sunday in Advent, and 'Prepare ye the way' is one of the best known lyrics in the musical *Godspell* (1971) (*BiM* 93–95).

The vision beginning 'every valley shall be lifted up' (vv. 3–4) looks like a continuation of what goes before: preparing the way home will be easy, all obstacles will be miraculously removed (cf. Baruch 5:7; Rashi). The Church Fathers apply it to the spiritual way toward piety, made smooth and easy by Christ (Cyril, Jerome). Some of the rabbis and Church Fathers take it as a metaphor for the humbling of the proud and the exaltation of the humble or penitent (b*Erubin* 54a; Eusebius). Luther explains that 'valleys are sinners, fools, lowly. Mountains are presumptuous saints'. Members of a gay community in Brighton noticed that in modern Hebrew the words *kol ge yinnase* (every valley shall be exalted) can be translated 'every gay person will get married', which could then be included in the miraculous reversal of the current state of affairs to be made possible in a new age.

For Christian commentators the prophecy 'the glory of the Lord shall be revealed' refers to Christ, God incarnate, and 'all flesh shall see it together' (v. 5) recalls the heavens opening at his baptism and the pouring out of the Holy Spirit 'upon all flesh' (Joel 2:28; Acts 2:17) (Eusebius, Cyril). Jerome also sees a reference to preachers in his own day going out into the wilderness of the gentiles and making the rough places of our hearts smooth to the glory of God. In Handel's *Messiah* (1742) the words are given a somewhat harsher eschatological interpretation (cf. Hag 2:6–7; Mal 3:1–3), and verses 4–5 were immortalized in Martin Luther King's 'I have a dream' speech in August 1963 (*NCHB* 4.748). Verse 5 figures in the Sabbath morning Torah Service alongside Isa 52:8 (*ADPB* 410–411) and in the Sabbath song 'Lekha Dodi' (see comm. on Isa 52:1–2).

The next prophecy is introduced by a voice saying, 'Cry!', this time addressed to an individual, not a group (v. 6). The prophet, assuming it is addressed to him, asks, 'What shall I cry?', and the answer he receives is one of the most beautiful and best known prophecies in the Bible. 'All flesh is grass' is normally understood to refer to human mortality in general (cf. Ps 90:6) (Ibn Ezra), although many take it as the baser parts of man (Eusebius, Jerome), specifying human arrogance as doomed like the 'flower of the field' (Rashi, Luther). This is apparently how Hieronymus Bosch interpreted it in his famous painting *The Haywain* (1516) (Elsig 2004: 37; see also comm. on Isa 15:6). 'Beauty, grace' (Heb. *ḥesed*) here 'denotes all that is naturally most highly valued among men, but condemned by the Prophet as vanity' (Calvin). The 'spirit of the Lord' (v. 7 Vg, AV) introduces the idea of divine judgement on sinful flesh (Jerome, Calvin). But most read it is a 'wind from the Lord' (Tg, Rashi), a natural phenomenon that affects all grass and flowers equally (Lowth; cf. RSV). The comment 'surely the people is grass' is added by a different hand in 1QIsaᵃ and bracketed in some modern versions (NJB).

'The word of our God will stand for ever' in the second part of the prophecy (v. 8) probably originally referred to the word of prophecy (cf. Isa 55:11), 'the good tidings' that 'emanate from the mouth of Him Who lives forever' (Rashi). Christians since Peter take it as a reference to the gospel, 'the good news which was preached to you' (1 Pet 1:25; cf. Calvin), while for others it is Christ the Word who did not change when he became a man, whatever the Arians say (Athanasius, *Against the Arians* 1.12.48), but dwells in our hearts where he remains forever sustaining and enlivening us (cf. John 8:51; Cyril). For the Reformers the 'Word of God' meant scripture and verse 8 (L. VERBUM DOMINI MANET IN AETERNUM) was one of their favourite texts, the monogram VDMIÆ embroidered on their sleeves (Luther). Luther and others frequently quote it against the misuse of scripture by papists and Anabaptists, right down to the present when it is cited by a Presbyterian writer as a *cri de coeur* on the waning influence of the Bible in Scottish society (Wright 1988:219). It figures as the concluding statement of the Second Vatican Council's *Dogmatic Constitution on Divine Revelation* (*Dei Verbum* 18 November 1965) (Flannery 1981:765).

Brahms' choral setting of the passage at the beginning of his *German Requiem* (1867) beautifully expresses the contrast between the grim inevitability of death in verses 6–7, sung twice slowly and rhythmically, with James 5:7 inserted between, and the statement of faith in the Word of God so dear to Luther (v. 8) (*poco sostenuto*), followed by a joyful fugue on another Isaiah passage familiar to Christians both as an Advent reading and from funeral liturgies (Isa 35:10) (*BiM* 90).

The prophet tells a 'herald of good news' to go up on to a high mountain and say to the cities of Judah 'Behold your God!' (v. 9). The word for 'herald of good news' (Heb. *mevasser*; LXX, Vg *evangelizo*) appears three times in Deutero-Isaiah (cf. Isa 41:27; 52:7), but here uniquely it is in the feminine form, *mevasseret*). Ibn Ezra says we must supply a feminine noun such as 'community' (Heb. *'edah*). Another suggestion is that it was customary in those days for women to announce and celebrate a joyful event (cf. Exod 15:20–21; Judg 11:34; 1 Sam 18:6–7) (Lowth). Handel's alto aria 'O Thou That Tellest Good Tidings to Zion' beautifully combines this interpretation with 'Arise, shine, for thy light is come' (Isa 60:1), while the African American spiritual 'Go Tell It on the Mountain' (cf. Isa 52:7) applies the words to the Christmas story (*HON* 187; *GtG* 136). Both Mevasseret Tzion and Mevasseret Yerushalayim are place names in the modern State of Israel.

The alternative favoured by most modern commentators is to take the feminine singular as applied to Zion and translate 'O Zion, herald of good tidings … O Jerusalem, herald of good tidings' (RSV; Westermann, Childs). Jerome already cited another famous prophecy in favour of this interpretation: 'Out of Zion shall go forth the law' (Isa 2:3). Christian commentators interpret the verse as referring to the Church's mission to preach the gospel (Eusebius, Cyril, Jerome). It recalls another joyful command, 'shout from the top of the mountains' (Isa 42:11) so that as many as possible will hear your voice (Aquinas), although according to some 'the cities of Judah' must refer to those who accept God's word: otherwise you would be casting pearls before swine (Matt 7:6) (Oecolampadius). For Nicholas of Lyra 'Behold your God' recalls the voice of John the Baptist, 'Behold the Lamb of God' (John 1:29).

The image of the Lord 'coming with vengeance … to save you' (v. 10) features before this in Isaiah 35:4 (Aquinas, Childs), and Rashi understands it as retribution upon the nations. The Church Fathers find a reference to the coming of

Christ, his 'reward' being the 'fruit that comes from dying in the flesh' (cf. John 12:24) (Cyril). For Luther it is rather 'the fruit and promotion of the Gospel'. Others see here a prophecy of the Second Coming of Christ 'bringing my recompense' (Rev 22:10; cf. Matt 16:27) (Eusebius, Jerome). Coupled with this image of God's great power is the image of a shepherd tending his flock and, like a mother, carrying the lambs in his arms (v. 11) (Luther, Calvin). This means that God will bring together the exiles, heal those that are suffering and 'feed them with knowledge and understanding' (Jer 3:15; cf. Ezek 34:31) (Aquinas; cf. Ibn Ezra). At Qumran he was the Teacher of Righteousness (Blenkinsopp 2006: 125–126), and for Christians the prophecy was fulfilled in Christ 'the good shepherd' (John 10:14–15) (Theodoret, Eusebius) and his lambs (John 21:15) (Jerome).

The Good Shepherd then became one of Christianity's most familiar symbols, appearing already in a third-century catacomb fresco (Spier 2008: 6, 12–13). Other examples include the fifth-century mosaic in the mausoleum of Galla Placidia in Ravenna and a painting by the Spanish artist Murillo in the Prado, Madrid (*c*.1660). There is also the famous alto aria 'He Shall Feed His Flock' at the end of Part 1 of Handel's *Messiah* (1742), where it is linked to 'Come unto him' and 'His yoke is easy' (Matt 11:28–30). The phrases 'gather with his arm', 'carry in his bosom' and 'gently lead' appealed particularly to nineteenth-century hymn writers such as Fanny Crosby (1820–1915), whose 'Safe in the Arms of Jesus, Safe on His Gentle Breast' became very popular (*EH* 580; *CH2* 707). Another nineteenth-century example is a stained glass window by Edward Burne-Jones and William Morris in St Martin's Church, Brampton (1878), where the Good Shepherd is accompanied by an angel carrying a scroll with Isa 40:11 on it (Plate 30).

Creator of Heaven and Earth (Isa 40:12–31)

To reassure the people that it is well within God's power to do all that he has promised, the prophet urges them to 'raise their minds to heaven and ... fix their whole heart on the power of God' (vv. 12–26) (Calvin, cf. Jerome, Rashi). For some it is the mystery of the universe that prompts our admiration, the incomprehensible and incomparable Wisdom of its Creator (Cyril). This was how Paul interpreted it (Rom 11:33). For others it is the sheer scale of it and the ease with which God 'measured the waters in the hollow of his hand' (v. 12): the small measures listed (handful, span, three fingers) just mean 'easily' (L. *faciliter*) (Aquinas, Nicholas; cf. Tg). Others develop the image of God as an architect measuring the world's volume, length and weight using a compass, scales and other tools (cf. Prov 8:22–31), and this is how artists, inspired by this verse,

PLATE 30   'He shall feed his flock like a shepherd' (Isa 40:11). Stained glass window by Edward Burne-Jones and William Morris in St Martin's Church, Brampton (1878). Reproduced with kind permission of Sonia Halliday Photography.

have depicted him from the eleventh-century Tiberius Psalter (folio 7v) down to William Blake's famous painting 'The Ancient of Days' (1794) (Plate 31). Rashi adds another detail by suggesting that the instrument translated 'measure' (Heb. *shalish*; Vg 'three fingers') was one that 'measured by thirds, one third wilderness, one third inhabited and one third seas and rivers'.

'Who directed the spirit of the Lord…?' (vv. 13–14) refers to the spirit of prophecy (Rashi) or perhaps more generally to the reason or judgement of

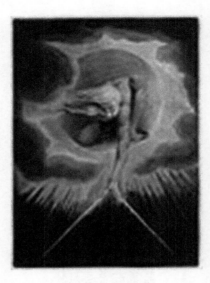

PLATE 31   'He measured the heavens with a span' (Isa 40:12). Etching/Watercolour
by William Blake (1794).

God (Calvin). The Septuagint 'Who has known the mind of the Lord?' is
explained by the Fathers with reference to Paul: 'no one comprehends the
thoughts of God except the Spirit of God' (1 Cor 2:11; cf. Matt 11:27)
(Chrysostom, *On the Incomprehensibility of God* 5.230–250). Modern scholars
suggest that 'the path of justice' (Vg, RSV; Heb. *mishpaṭ*) in verse 14 might better be understood as 'the right path' (cf. Exod 26:30), a reference to the natural
order of the universe rather than to justice in human society (cf. Isa 42:1,4)
(Westermann, Childs).

Worldly powers are as 'less than nothing and emptiness' beside him, like a
drop of water or dust that tips the scales (cf. Wisd 11:22). The Septuagint adds
'spittle' (v. 15 LXX), a striking image quoted twice by the author of Pseudo-
Philo (7:3; 12:4; *OTP* 2.313, 320). Ibn Ezra points out that all living beings are
included here, humans ('nations'), plants ('Lebanon' means forests) and animals
(v. 16) (cf. Aquinas). The idea that nothing in this world is enough for a burnt-
offering has a parallel in the apocrypha (Judith 16:16) (Lowth). According to
Ambrose the prophet does not mean that 'all the nations' are worthless since
God said to Abraham 'in you shall all the nations be blessed' (Gen 12:3; cf. Ps
2:8; 72:11): instead this is about the thousands, tens of thousands, millions of
thousands of angels, archangels, principalities and powers in the universe, in
comparison with which the nations are like a drop from a bucket (*Exposition of
Psalm 12:1*, 49–50). For Luther this was a 'great and mighty text' about 'those

who want to appease God by their own wisdom and righteousness ... let him who wants to become a monk read this text.'

The next passage is the first of several colourful attacks on idolatry (vv.18–20; cf. Isa 41:7, 29; 44:9–20; 48:5). Jerome points out that the ban on idols goes back to Moses (Jerome). But he also suggests a metaphorical interpretation of the passage as a description of heretics creating idols in their hearts, out of silver, that is, by their charming speech, or gold to appeal to the senses, or wood in the case of their baser teachings. Calvin sees a distinction between the gentiles (vv. 18–20) and the Jews who should have known better, having been told in scripture 'from the beginning' how to worship God correctly (v. 21). Idols, especially those associated in their minds with the Church of Rome, were a major preoccupation of sixteenth-century Protestant writers, and this passage, with several others from Isaiah 44–49, figure prominently, for example, in a volume containing *Certain sermons or homilies appointed to be read in churches* (1572) (Sawyer 1996: 139). For a post-colonial interpretation of such passages, see comm. on Isa 2:7–8.

The first word in verse 20 (Heb. *ha-mesukkan*) is unknown elsewhere. Rashi suggests 'he who is accustomed', citing a word used by Balaam's ass (Heb. *ha-hasken* Num 22:30). Ibn Ezra has 'treasurer' (cf. *soken* Isa 22:15). Others have 'the poor man', referring to a much better known word (*misken*; cf. Eccl 4:13; 9:15) (Luther, AV, RSV), while the theory that it refers to a species of tree (cf. Jerome, Tg) has won favour in modern times by the discovery of the Akkadian term *musukkānu* 'mulberry wood' (NRSV, Childs).

The wonders of God in creation beside the frailty of human efforts are then described in another series of images (vv. 22–26; cf. vv. 12–17). God holds up the heavens over the earth like the roof of a tent (cf. Ps 104:2; Calvin, Theodoret, Eusebius), with human beings like grasshoppers feebly whirring about on the floor (Luther). They are like trees uprooted by the wind or withering plants blown away in the storm like chaff (v. 24), or like the cedar of Lebanon in the Psalm (Ps 37:35–36; Jerome).

Finally, there is the magnificent image of the stars in the sky reviewed by God like an army on parade, each called by name (v. 26): 'not one is missing' as in an earlier vision of order and comfort (34:16; Calvin). In the triennial Jewish lectionary, the passage accompanies the reading of Genesis 15 where Abram is invited to 'look toward heaven and number the stars if you can' (v. 5) (Mann 1971: 1,113), though, as Jerome points out, unlike Abraham, God has numbered all the stars and given them names (cf. Ps 147:4). He has fixed the courses both of the stars and of the planets with numbers unknown to the astronomers (Ibn Ezra). The term 'create' (Heb. *bara*), a favourite of Deutero-Isaiah, appears here for the first time (vv. 26,28) (cf. Isa 41:20; 42:5; 43:1; 45:7). Ibn Ezra stresses that it means 'to cut' or 'shape' rather than to create something out of nothing (cf. Isa 41:20), and it was translated into Greek with words like *ktizo* (to found) and *metakosmeo* (to rearrange) (see comm. on 45:7) (Lampe 1961: 782–783).

Confronted by all this evidence, why does Israel say, 'My way is hidden from the Lord' (v. 27)? How can they doubt God's continuing compassion for them even when it seems he is ignoring them for a time (Jerome, Calvin)? Some say it refers to the people's attempts to hide their sinful behaviour from God and escape judgement (Eusebius, Cyril, Ibn Ezra). But the passage goes on to describe how God unfailingly gives power to the faint and how 'those who wait upon the Lord shall renew their strength and mount up with wings like eagles' (vv. 29–31), recalling David's words of encouragement to those in despair (Ps 27:14) (Cyril). In the famous eagle image with which the chapter ends, the prophet may be alluding to the popular belief that eagles moult in their old age and grow new feathers (Ambrose on Ps 103:5; cf. Eusebius, Lowth). The rabbis apply the verse to God's care of the elderly.

In the Jewish lectionary the last five verses of the chapter appear in the third haftarah of the year (Isa 40:27–41:16) accompanying the Torah portion telling the first part of the Abraham story (Gen 12:1–17:27; cf. Isa 41:8). The flight of eagles is 'higher than the vultures' (1 Enoch 96:2; *OTP* 1.76). The passage also inspired one of the Scottish Paraphrases (1781), ending with a beautiful eschatological interpretation (cf. Eusebius):

> On eagles' wings they mount they soar,
> Their wings are faith and love,
> Till, past the cloudy regions here,
> They rise to heav'n above. (*CH2* Paraphrase 22)

George Herbert was probably inspired by this verse, too, in his poem 'Easter Wings' (1633), as was the Scottish athlete Eric Liddell in the film *Chariots of Fire* (1981) (Magnusson 1981: 49). It also features as a soprano aria at the beginning of Willy Burkhard's oratorio *The Face of Isaiah* (1936) (see comm. on Isa 31:5).

The Lord of History (Isa 41:1–7)

Chapter 41 begins with a call to people in distant lands to listen in silence to what God has to say. It is a challenge to the nations to come 'to judgment' (v. 1) and see who is the mighty one (Ibn Ezra). It is like a law court where silence is necessary to give everyone a fair hearing (Calvin) (cf. vv. 21–29; Isa 34:1; 49:1). The 'islands' (LXX, Vg, AV Heb. *iyyim*) are the churches surrounded by a sea of pagan culture (Eusebius, Theodoret). Scholars point out that the Hebrew word

Isaiah Through the Centuries, First Edition. John F. A. Sawyer.
© 2018 John Wiley & Sons Ltd. Published 2020 by John Wiley & Sons Ltd.

has a wider semantic range than the English word 'island' and can be applied to Greece, Tarshish and other places that are not islands (e.g. Gen 10:5). Alternatives include 'coastlands' (RSV) or 'coasts and islands' (NJB; cf. Luther). From the late eighteenth century, references to 'islands' here and elsewhere in Isaiah (Isa 42:4, 10; 49:1; 51:5; 60:9) had special significance for missionaries to Ceylon, the East Indies and the Pacific and feature prominently in hymns such as 'God Is Working His Purpose Out' (1894): 'Give ear to me ye continents, ye isles give ear to me, / That the earth may be filled with the glory of God as the waters cover the sea' (*EH* 548; *CH2* 380 *AM* 646) (cf. Isa 11:9). The 'princes' (LXX) who are to renew their strength (cf. Isa 40:31) are Peter, Paul and the other apostles (Cyril).

'One from the east' whom 'righteousness accompanied' (v. 2) is Abraham, according to many commentators (cf. v. 8) (Tg, Rashi, Nicholas, Aquinas, Calvin, Lowth). Abraham is mentioned again in verse 8, and, in addition to his eastern origins (Gen 11:31–12:3) and his legendary righteousness (Gen 16:6), 'he tramples kings under foot and makes them like dust with his sword' (AV, RSV), a reference to his victory over the five kings (Gen 14). In the triennial lectionary verses 2–13 were the haftarah read with Genesis 14 (Mann 1971: 1, 104–1,106). Verse 3 implies that his feet barely touched the ground because as a man of faith he journeyed joyfully 'as if he were flying' (Luther). Since Abraham did what he did by the grace of God, he is just one example of God's power in the world, and through him all the nations will come to know God (vv. 4–5) (Calvin).

Ibn Ezra suggests that a reference to Cyrus would be more appropriate in this context and most modern commentators agree (Westermann, Oswalt, Childs). As king of the Medes and Persians, he came 'from the east', as God's anointed (cf. Isa 44:28; 45:1) to destroy Babylon, and passed a law permitting the exiles to return to Jerusalem and rebuild the Temple (2 Chron 36:23). Many recommend 'whom victory (Heb. *ṣedeq*) meets at every step' instead of 'righteousness' (cf. v. 10; RSV). Thinking of the great armies of Cyrus, Ibn Ezra proposes an appropriate, if rather far-fetched, interpretation for the last part of the verse (literally, 'he makes his sword like dust …'): 'he makes his sword as numerous as the dust and his arrows to fly like chaff in the wind'. Verse 4 is a powerful statement of the unique power of God in history (Rashi, Ibn Ezra; Luther, Calvin, Lowth): and the Targum adds the comment 'besides me there is no God' (cf. Isa 45:5, 6).

Some of the Church Fathers quote another prophet to prove that the 'one from the east' must refer to Christ, 'the sun of righteousness risen with healing in its wings' (Mal 4:2) (Cyril; cf. Jerome). Origen argues that 'from the east' is metaphorical, not geographical, and refers to 'the east of true light' (*Homily on Isaiah* 5.1). Verse 4 confirms the christological interpretation by anticipating

Christ's words, 'I am Alpha and Omega' (cf. Rev 22:13) (Jerome, Aquinas). The verse also contains one of the divine self-proclamation passages appropriated by Jesus in John's Gospel (cf. Isa 43:10; 46:9) (cf. John 8:24, 28). When the people saw Christ they came from the ends of the earth and joined together in one faith (v. 5); and having tasted the Lord they did not keep the gift for themselves but shared it with their neighbours and brothers (v. 6) (Cyril).

Verse 7 returns to the theme of idolatry, intended to highlight the contrast between God's power and the futility of human endeavours (cf. Isa 40:19–20; 44:9–10), like craftsmen driven by some kind of blind impulse (Calvin). For a postcolonial interpretation of such passages, see comm. on Isa 2:7–8. Aquinas compares it with an even more colourful description (Wisd 13:10–19). Luther enjoys a pun on the name of one of his fiercest opponents, Johannes Faber (L. 'craftsman'), known as the 'hammer of the heretics', and sees the pope as the idol, propped up by arguments and publications as misplaced and ineffectual as the hammer and nails of pagan idolaters.

Fear Not, Israel, My Servant (Isa 41:8–20)

'Now follows a torrent of consolations' (vv. 8–20) (Luther). Verses 8–9 are among the *Tanḥumim* at Qumran (see comm. on Isa 40). The prophet turns to his people and addresses them now directly for the first time, as 'Israel my servant, Jacob whom I have chosen … whom I took from the ends of the earth' (vv. 8–9; cf. Isa 42:1). The passage is cited by Jewish commentators, including Nahmanides during the famous Barcelona Disputation in 1263, to prove that the 'suffering servant' in chapter 53 refers to Israel, not the Messiah (cf. Isa 44:1) (Maccoby 1982: 113). Rashi compares God reaching out and grasping Israel to Moses reaching out and grasping a snake by the tail in the Exodus story (Exod 4:4) and notes that it was at that time that he first called them 'Israel, my first-born' (Exod 4:22). Christian commentators see this prophecy as fulfilled when many Jews, though not all, accepted the word of God: Jesus himself makes the distinction (John 8:31–46) and instructs his followers to 'go to the lost sheep of the house of Israel' (Matt 10:6) (Eusebius; cf. Cyril, Theodoret).

'Abraham, my friend' has been interpreted in a variety of ways. Calvin sees it is an extraordinary honour that God should call him his 'friend' and compares it to Christ calling his disciples his friends, not his servants (John 15:15). Abraham is called the 'friend of God' elsewhere in the Bible (2 Chron 20:7; James 2:23) and in the Qur'an (Sura 4:125): in Arabic Abraham (Ibrahim) is known simply as al-Khalil 'the Friend'. For some it means the one who loved God sufficiently to be prepared to sacrifice his own son (Nicholas; cf. Ibn Ezra, Rashi). The names 'Israel … Jacob … offspring of Abraham' seem to include all

God's people, though Luther takes 'my friend' here as vocative: to hear Christ call us 'friends' should make us leap for joy. Theologians today note the evidence here in Isaiah for another metaphor for God: God as 'friend' alongside 'father' (Isa 63:16), 'king' (Isa 41:21), 'mother' (Isa 42:14) (McFague 1982:177–178).

'Fear not' (v. 10) introduces the first of what modern scholars have called 'salvation oracles' (*Heilsorakel*), short prophecies addressed to an individual in distress (cf. vv. 14–16) (cf. vv. 13, 14; Isa 43:1, 5; 44:2, 8; 54:4). Whether or not these had their origin in a temple ritual as some have suggested, they have a distinctive rhetorical function in Isaiah 40–55 (Westermann, Childs), where they function as the answers to such cries of despair as 'my way is hidden from the Lord' (Isa 40:27) (Calvin). On the phrase 'I am with you', Luther says that 'I' is worth more than 100,000 princes and kings. Verse 10, taken with Isaiah 43:1, inspired one of Bach's motets (*Fürchte dich nicht, ich bin bei dir BWV* 228) (1726) (*BiM* 87). 'My victorious right hand' (RSV) or 'saving right hand' (NJB), like the 'victory' mentioned in verse 2, reflects the fact that the Hebrew word *ṣedeq* is less abstract than 'righteousness' (AV) and implies an act of divine intervention, 'saving justice' (NJB), not just an attitude or a virtue. 'All who are incensed against you ... they shall be as nothing' (v. 11) refers to the fate of the Babylonians punished and destroyed by Cyrus (Ibn Ezra; cf. Nicholas; Calvin). For Luther they are the powers of Satan, including those responsible for the death of the Reformer Jan Hus in 1415.

'You worm Jacob' (v. 14) describes a people subjected to the domination of unbelieving nations (Eusebius). The image recalls words from the Psalm quoted by Christ on the cross (Ps 22:6) (Jerome). The rabbis cited this passage in a rabbinic discussion of prayer as 'the weapon of the mouth' to show that the worm, whose only weapon is its mouth, can fell mighty cedars with it (*RA* 342). The rare expression 'you men of Israel' (Heb. *mete yisraèl;* cf. 'men of iniquity' Job 22:15; 'men of vanity' Ps 26:4) (AV, RSV; Henry) is taken by some as an abbreviation for 'few in number' (LXX; cf. Gen 34:30; Deut 4:27) (Rashi, Luther). Theodotion has 'the dead of Israel' (cf. Isa 22:2 Heb. *met* 'dead') and Jerome suggests 'as good as dead' citing Paul (cf. 1 Cor 15:31) (cf. Calvin). A modern theory, based on the Akkadian word *mutu* 'louse', has found support in some quarters (cf. Oswalt, Brueggemann, Childs) and is represented in some of the versions: 'you maggot Israel' (JPS mg; cf. NRSV, NEB).

No such uncertainty surrounds the word *morag* 'threshing sledge, new, sharp and having teeth' (v. 15), described in detail by many commentators (Cyril, Lowth). References elsewhere to threshing (Isa 28:27–29; Amos 1:3) illustrate the effectiveness of the agricultural process as a metaphor. Here mountains and hills, that is, the Babylonians (Ibn Ezra) or the leaders of the heretics (Jerome) or the elite of the world who rely on their own works (Luther), will be ground to dust and carried away in the wind. It may be that, as the name of an Israeli settlement founded in Gaza in 1972 and evacuated in 2005, 'Morag' suggests power, defiance, even vengeance, but it could also refer to the settlers' determination to exchange pens, typewriters and scalpels for agricultural implements (cf. Isa 2:4) (Sawyer 2003: 267). Verse 19, 'I will plant cedars in the wilderness, acacias and myrtles' (v. 19 JPS; Heb. *etten bamidbar*) provided the words for a popular Israeli song composed by the award-winning musician Dov Seltzer (1957), and also the names of a group of three Moroccan settlements in the northern Negev, Brosh (cypress), Tidhar (plane) and Ta'ashur (pine), founded in 1953 and known collectively as *Moshave Yaḥdav*, the 'together settlements'.

Before this scene of new life and hope, the prophet describes a drought (v. 17): 'not a famine of bread or a thirst for water, but of hearing the words of the Lord' (cf. Amos 8:11). The desert is a place where there is no Torah Wisdom (Rashi). God will not forsake his thirsting people: he will open rivers in the wilderness, even 'on the bare heights' (Ibn Ezra) and plant trees of all kinds (vv. 18–19). The rivers create 'an understanding heart' and the trees produce all kinds of wisdom, goodness and peace (Rashi). God will do the same for the Jews in Babylon as he did in the Exodus, and will pour out his spirit upon the gentiles as he opened rivers and pools in the wilderness (cf. John 7:38–39) (Henry). For Christians, this refers to the spread of the gospel: 'he who believes in me … out of his heart will flow streams of living water' (John 7:38) (Theodoret; cf. Cyril, Jerome).

The Impotence of False Gods (Isa 41:21–29)

Like a judge, the Lord invites unbelievers, including any Israelites who lost their faith in Babylon (Ibn Ezra) or false gods (cf. v. 23) (Jerome, Lowth, Childs) or idolaters ancient and modern (Luther), to present their case and mocks their claims to have knowledge that only he possesses. 'Strong reasons' (AV Heb.'*aṣumot*) (v. 21) is a word later used in rabbinic disputes (e.g. b*Sanhedrin* 31b) (Rashi). He has revealed how things were 'in the beginning' (Gen 1:1) and what it will be like in the end-time (2 Pet 3:13) (Cyril). Calvin adds that Satan 'father of falsehood' (John 8:44; cf. 2 Thess 2:11) has deceived many people with his claims to foreknowledge (1 Kgs 22:22), while Isaiah correctly predicted the coming of Cyrus more than two hundred years into the future. Verse 23 challenges them to add actions to their arguments so that we can see the evidence for ourselves and be 'dismayed' (Tg, AV) or 'amazed' (LXX, Duhm). Modern commentators read 'dismayed and terrified (Heb. *ve-nira*)' (RSV, NJB; cf. Lowth, Brueggemann). Idols are nothing; they can do nothing; anyone who chooses to worship an idol rather than God is an abomination (v. 24) (Rashi). An 'abomination out of the earth' (LXX) refers to idols made out of wood or stone (Cyril). For a postcolonial comment on such passages, see comm. on Isa 2:7–8.

By contrast there is good news for Jerusalem (v. 27) because her God has raised up 'one from the north' who is going to trample on her enemies: no one else has the power to do anything (vv. 25–29). Most commentators take this to be another reference to Cyrus (cf. v. 2): 'he shall call on my name' refers to the edict in which he acknowledges the power of Israel's God (2 Chron 36:23) (Ibn Ezra, Rashi, Nicholas). Others suggest it refers to the Babylonians coming from the north to destroy Jerusalem in 586, as well as Cyrus coming from the east to conquer Babylon in 538 (cf. Isa 13:17–22; Dan 8:4) (Rashi, Calvin; cf. Luther). Christians take it as a reference to Christ, conceived in Nazareth in the north of Judaea, and baptized in the Jordan to the east (*Glossa*; cf. Cyril, Eusebius). This is how the verse is interpreted, along with Isa 11:2 and 42:1, in one of the final choruses of Mendelssohn's *Elijah* (1846).

'First to Zion' (v. 27) refers to Cyrus, who permitted the Jews to return to Jerusalem (Ezra 1:3), and 'Behold them' are the words of a messenger announcing the approach of the first exiles returning home (Rashi). In the Hebrew there is no verb in the first half of the verse, and many commentators insert one: 'the first [shall say] to Zion' (AV) or 'In the beginning [I spoke] to Zion' (Mckenzie). The 'herald of good tidings' (L. *evangelista*) is a reference to the prophet that God promised to send to his people (Deut 18:15) and whose task is continued by the Church (cf. Isa 40:9) (Calvin). Rishon Le-Tzion (First to Zion) is the name of one of the earliest settlements in Palestine, established by Ukrainian Jews in 1882, and now one of the largest cities in Israel.

The chapter ends with a final scathing attack on rival gods and their 'graven images' reminiscent of the golden calf story (Exod 32:4) (Ibn Ezra). They are dismissed in four words, the first of which 'delusion' (Heb. *aven*) is a sinister word best known from the phrase 'evil-doers' (*po'ale aven*) in the Psalms (RSV, Jerome, Childs). Some follow IQIsa[a] and read 'nothingness' (Heb. *ayin*; cf. vv. 24, 26, 28), which is more closely related to the other three terms translated 'nothing', 'wind' and 'emptiness' (NJB; McKenzie, Westermann). The last two terms, 'wind and confusion' (AV; Heb. *ruaḥ va-tohu*), are often taken together as 'empty wind' (RSV; cf. Luther), and recall the chaos before creation (Gen 1:2) (Calvin).

Behold My Servant (Isa 42:1–13)

The first prophecy in this chapter (vv. 1–9) is reminiscent of the messianic language of chapter 11 and some of the Psalms (2, 45, 72, 110, 132). The 'servant' is not named but according to Kimḥi and some good manuscripts of the Targum, he is the Messiah, and that is how the passage has been interpreted by Christians from the Gospels (Matt 12:18–21; Luke 2:32), the Church Fathers (Cyril, Jerome) and Reformers (Luther, Calvin) right down to the present day,

Isaiah Through the Centuries, First Edition. John F. A. Sawyer.
© 2018 John Wiley & Sons Ltd. Published 2020 by John Wiley & Sons Ltd.

where it is the Old Testament reading for Mass on the Feast of Christ's Baptism (*ORM*). Others have identified him as Israel (Rashi; cf. LXX), the prophet (cf. Isa 49:6; Ibn Ezra) and Cyrus (cf. Isa 44:28; 45:1) (Blenkinsopp). For some Muslims, including the ninth-century scholar Al-Bukhari, it refers to Muhammad (Lazarus-Yafe 1992:108; Lambden 2006: 148). Whoever he is, his mission is to 'establish justice in the earth' (vv. 1–4) and be a 'light to the nations' (vv. 5–9). In Latin America 'the notion of the servant as individual does not exhaust the individual, collective, historical, or eschatological aspects' (Dussel 1964: 449; Mesters 1990: 23).

In modern times the passage is widely known as the first of the four 'Servant Songs' (cf. Isa 49:1–6; 50:4–9; 52:13–53:12), a term invented by Bernhard Duhm. Duhm's theory that these passages were by a later author than the rest of Deutero-Isaiah, was widely accepted for many years, both by scholars and in the Church where, for example, in modern lectionaries (*ORM*, RCL) the four passages are read in sequence on Monday, Tuesday, Wednesday and Friday of Holy Week. Nowadays most commentators treat each passage independently, in its own literary context, rather than as part of an artificially constructed group of four (Mettinger 1983).

According to Rashi God refers to Israel as the people whom he chose to be his servant (cf. Ps 135:4; Isa 41:8; 45:4); he poured his spirit on them so that, like prophets, they could teach justice to the nations (cf. Isa 2:3), and they will not have to shout or raise their voices (v. 2) because people will come to learn from them of their own accord (cf. Zech 8:23). The poor and the needy will have hope (v. 3) and 'the earth shall be filled with the knowledge of the Lord as the waters cover the sea' (v. 4; cf. Isa 11:9). Liberation theologians note that when Matthew quotes the passage he changes verse 4 to 'till he brings justice to victory' (Matt 12:20) and then goes on to use the same word three times in the sense of Last Judgment (vv. 36, 41, 42) (Miranda 1977: 128–129).

It is as though the Lord, creator of heaven and earth (v. 5), said, when I formed you, I had this thought that you should be a 'covenant people' (v. 6 Rashi), as it is said 'The Lord will establish you as a holy people' (Deut 28:9) (Kimhi). The Hebrew term *berit 'am* 'a covenant to the people' (RSV) is glossed by Rashi as 'covenant people' ('*am berit*), and he comments that the prophecy is about a God who keeps his promises (vv. 8–9; cf. Isa 49:7) (Rashi). In verse 6 he turns to the prophet Isaiah and calls upon him to bring his people back to the covenant to be a 'light to the nations', and to tell them they shall be delivered from the Babylonian exile (v. 7; Ibn Ezra).

Christians from the beginning have applied the passage to Christ, even though LXX reads 'Jacob my servant … Israel my chosen' (v. 1): he is called 'Jacob' and 'Israel' because he took the flesh of the line of Jacob (Cyril, Augustine, *City of God* 20.30). According to Jerome, the correct reading is to be found in

Matthew's Gospel, where the passage is quoted in full and the names Jacob and Israel are absent (Matt 12:18–21) (cf. Eusebius). These verses came to be so closely associated with the Christian gospel that they were omitted from the Jewish lectionary. Every detail is applied to Christ. The word 'servant' reminds us of his humanity: 'taking the form of a servant being born in the likeness of a human being' (Phil 2:7) (Gregory of Nazianzus, *On the Son, Theological Oration* 4 (30).3; Calvin). 'I have put my spirit on him' refers to his baptism when the spirit 'descended upon him like a dove' and God hailed him as the one 'in whom my soul delights' (Matt 3:16–17) (Cyril, Jerome). In a chorus near the end of his oratorio *Elijah* (1846), Mendelssohn, like several earlier commentators (Eusebius, Aquinas), identifies the spirit of the Lord here (v. 1) with the 'spirit of wisdom and understanding, the spirit of might and counsel' that rests upon the Messiah (Isa 11:2).

The images in verses 2–3 refer to the gentleness and benevolence of Jesus (cf. Matt 11:29) (Eusebius; cf Athanasius, *Life of St Anthony* 35), and the peaceful kingdom where the weak are rescued and the hopeless are supported (Irenaeus, *Against Heresies* 4.20.10). Instead of 'he shall not cry' (v. 2; Heb. *yiṣʿaq*) some take it as impersonal: 'no one will cry for help', a common theme in scenes of justice and peace (cf. Rev 21:4; Jones). For Luther verse 3 is a 'golden text' that sets forth Christ as the 'true Physician, Guide and Pastor', caring for his apostles, whatever their failings, 'not unlike a mother with her child'. In verse 4 Matthew follows the Septuagint where it is the name of Jesus that brings hope to the nations, not his teaching (Heb. *torah*) (cf. Ps 89:16; Cyrus, Theodoret). Jerome defends the Hebrew but interprets the 'law' (Heb. *torah*) as the gospel, that is, the new covenant (Jer 31:31–32), which supersedes the Law of Moses and 'in the last days … will go forth from Zion' (cf. Isa 2:3).

A reference to the creation of life in verse 5 is much discussed. Some draw a distinction between the breath of life (Heb. *neshamah*), common to all living creatures, and the spirit (Heb. *ruaḥ*), which is given only to those who 'tread down earthly desires' (Irenaeus, *Against Heresies* 5.12.2; cf. Tertullian, *On the Soul* 11.3–4; Eusebius). Rashi distinguishes between the breath of life given to all people and the spirit of sanctity given only to those who walk before God, while Ibn Ezra explains that *neshamah* (soul) is common to all humans, while *ruaḥ* (breath) is given to animals. The description of the mission of the servant continues but this time the Lord 'who created the heavens' (v. 5; cf. Isa 40:12–17) addresses him personally (vv. 6–9): 'I have called you … I have taken you by the hand'. This is the prophet's way of telling us not to question the servant's authority (Luther).

He is to be a 'covenant to the people' (LXX, Vg, RSV; Heb. *berit ʿam*), confirming God's promises to Israel (cf. Isa 49:8). A Qumran reading has the more obvious 'everlasting covenant' (*berit ʿolam*; cf. Isa 55:3; 61:8) here, but not in the parallel (Isa 49:8). He is also a 'light to the nations' (v. 6; cf. 49:6), and 'covenant, promise' in this context can be interpreted as a means of redemption (Duhm). Karl Barth cites this passage to show that God's covenant with the people of Israel will transcend their history (cf. Isa 2:2–4; 19:23–25): salvation is of the Jews (John 4:22) (*ChDogm* IV.1.31). For Christian commentators Christ is the new covenant as the 'one mediator between man and god' (cf. 1 Tim 2:5) (Eusebius; cf. Cyril, Luther). This means that Christ is 'the minister of circumcision, to fulfil the promises which were given to the fathers' (Rom 15:8) (Calvin). 'A light to the nations' recalls the words of the aged Simeon (Luke 2:32) (Luther).

Having opened the eyes of the blind and freed them from the bonds of ignorance and error, he will lead them to the light of truth (v. 7) (Theodoret). God's statement that 'I give my glory to no other' (v. 8) confirms the Church's doctrine that Father and Son are of the same nature since the Son manifestly possesses the glory of the Father (Theodoret; cf. Cyril). Luther sees it as a powerful statement that God wants no one to glory except those who have come to know Christ (cf. Gal 6:13). The 'former things' (v. 9) are all the acts of God already performed in history since the promise to Abraham, and the 'new things' are the life of incorruption, holiness and righteousness promised by Christ (Cyril; cf. Eusebius). Modern commentators suggest that the 'former things' refers to the work of judgement that dominates chapters 1–39, and the 'new things' are the work of the servant and the restoration of Israel as described in chapters 40–66 (Brueggemann; cf. Childs). Spurgeon cites verse 9 in an attack on 'sham Christian critics' who invented a 'second Isaiah' (Spurgeon 1856–1916: 25.684–685).

The hymn that follows (vv. 10–12) is the first of what are known as 'eschatological hymns of praise' (cf. 44:23; 45:8; 48:20–1; 52:7–10) (Westermann). Origen comments that a 'new song' is sung by someone who has descended into the water and risen, a new person, cleansed from the filth of their sins (*Homilies on Exodus* 5.5; cf. Cyril). For Clement of Alexandria, Christ is the 'New Song', the Word made flesh (*Exhortation to the Greeks* 1). 'Let the sea roar' is a modern emendation taken from Psalm 96:11 (cf. Ps 98:7; 1 Chron 6:22) (Duhm). The Hebrew has 'those who go down to the sea' (LXX, Vg, AV; cf. Ps 107:23): all the people on the earth, on board ships, living by the sea, in houses built in the sea, as in Venice … all are summoned to join in the celebration (Rashi). The Church Fathers identified 'those who go down to the sea' as the apostles (cf. Mark 1:16–20) and the 'desert' as the wilderness of ignorance and idolatry where they are to preach the gospel from the tops of the mountains (v. 11; cf. 40:9) (Cyril, Jerome). 'Inhabitants of the rock' (Heb. *selaʿ*) (cf. LXX, Vg, NJB) refers to Petra (Heb. Sela), another desert city like Kedar (Cyril, Eusebius; cf. LXX, Vg, RSV). Others say it is a reference to the dead: the Targum has 'the dead shall come forth from their tombs' (Rashi). Luther took it to mean nowhere is beyond the reach of the voice of the gospel.

The description of God's intervention ends with the image of God as a man of war (v. 13), central to the Old Testament idea of the Holy War (cf. Exod 15:3; Ps 24:8) (Hengel 1989: 271). The 'fury' (RSV) or 'jealousy' (AV; cf. LXX, Vg) recalls the 'zeal of the Lord of hosts' mentioned at the time of the destruction of Sennacherib (Isa 37:32; cf. 9:7). It is the jealous fury of a God who sees the Babylonians worshipping other gods (cf. v. 17) (Ibn Ezra) and human beings corrupted by sin and the devil (Jerome; Theodoret). It is also the passion shown by God for his people (Zech 1:14) and by his holy martyrs starting with Paul (Rom 8:35; cf. Phil 1:21) (Cyril).

God as Mother (Isa 42:14–25)

The male imagery of a man of war is followed immediately by the striking image of God as a woman in childbirth (v. 14), rather like the scene of God coming with might followed by the gentle shepherd image in Isa 40:10–11. Ibn Ezra comments on God's longing to rescue his people expressed in cries (Heb. *pa'ah*) and gasps (Heb. *sha'aph*) like a woman in childbirth. Calvin defends the use of this image: 'in no other way than by such figures of speech can his ardent love towards us be expressed … he intended also to intimate that the redemption of his people would be a kind of birth … and in order to exhibit more fully the excellence of his grace in this new birth, he not inappropriately attributes to himself the cry of "a woman in labor"'. Luther points out that this image is not of a person dying, but of a woman giving birth, who after the birth will rejoice again (Luther; cf. John 16:21). It is about God's long-suffering patience and compassion for the people of this world, comparable to the suffering of Christ on the cross (Alexander of Alexandria, *Epistles on the Arian Heresy* 5.5; cf. Luther), and how it finally ended when the 'day of recompense' came (Isa 34:8; 61:2) (Eusebius). For a long time God kept the Word deep within, now he speaks like a woman giving birth (Gregory the Great, *Morals on Job* 10.31): 'like a woman in childbirth I will put all my effort into bringing forth the salvation of my people' (Oecolampadius; cf. Luzzatto, Trible 1978: 22, 64; Gruber 1992: 8–9; Darr 1994: 104–105; Dille 2004: 71–72; Low 2013: 125–133). Another view is that the image simply describes a change from silence to restless and noisy activity (cf. v. 13) without any emphasis on childbirth (Brueggemann; cf. Westermann, Childs), and this is supported by the older versions which read, instead of 'gasp and pant', 'destroy and devour' (AV; cf. Vg, LXX, Tg, Rashi).

There follows another violent, graphic description of God's intervention in human affairs (vv. 15–17): 'the mountains and hills' to be laid waste are kings and leaders, 'herbage' (cf. Isa 40:6–7) refers to their subjects and followers (Eusebius, Rashi, Luther). The 'rivers' to be dried up are pagan scholars and poets whose teaching will be transformed into islands where the Church is founded (cf. Isa 41:1) (Cyril). The blind will be guided, their darkness turned into light (v. 16): according to Rashi this refers to Israel (cf. v. 19). Christian interpreters identify the blind as the saints referred to by Paul: 'once you were in darkness, now you are light in the Lord' (Eph 5:8) (Cyril). Freed from the darkness of ignorance, their way will be smooth along the path of truth (Theodoret). They will walk securely on paths they did not know, with the Word as a lamp to their feet and a light to their path (Ps 119:105; cf. 2 Pet.1:19) (Luther). All who put their faith in idols, ancient like those of the Jews or modern like our own, will be utterly put to shame (Luther).

The last section of this chapter rather surprisingly goes back to the subject of Israel's blindness (vv. 18–19) and disobedience (v. 24) and reminds them that their sufferings are all their own fault (vv. 24–25). It is more reminiscent of Isaiah's vision 'in the year that King Uzziah died' (6:9–13) than the 'consolation chapters'. A modern suggestion is that this is God's response to Israel's complaint in Isa 40:27 (cf. Ps 44:9–12) (Westermann, Brueggemann). It is you that are blind, he says to Israel (Rashi); they have eyes and do not see, ears and do not hear' (cf. Isa 6:9–11; 43:8; Jer 5:21) (Cyril; Theodoret). The same applies to everyone who claims to be God's 'servant … or messenger' (v. 19) (Calvin), to popes and bishops as well as the Jews (Luther).

'Dedicated one' (RSV; Heb. *meshullam*), parallel to 'servant of the Lord' (v. 19), is obscure. Suggestions include 'the one who has been paid', that is, the one who has received his chastisements and been cleansed (Rashi; cf. Ibn Ezra), or the 'one who has been perfectly instructed' (Lowth, cf. Eusebius, AV) or 'the one who has been sold as a slave' (Vg *venundatus*; cf. Ps 104:17) (Jerome Aquinas). Others take it as a personal name, Meshullam (cf. 1 Chron 9:11; Ezra 8:16), applied to the Servant, like the name Jeshurun (Isa 44:2), but there is no explanation of why (Blenkinsopp). The grammar of verse 20 is difficult: 'there are many things to see but you do not observe them. I open your ears through the prophets, but no one listens' (Rashi; cf. AV). Most modern commentators emend to third person: 'he sees many things but does not observe them' (RSV).

In a tradition recorded twice in the Mishnah and remembered in the Jewish Daily Prayer Book, verse 21 is cited by Rabbi Hananiah to explain why God gave his people 'a copious law (Heb. *torah*) and many commandments': it was 'for his righteousness sake', that is, to enable them to acquire merit (m*Abot* 6:11; m*Makkot*.3:16; ADPB 528–529, 536–537). Verse 21 also appears in the *Qedushah de-Sidra* at the end of the morning service (cf. 26:4; 59:20–21; 65:24) (see on Isa 6:3; ADPB 138–139). Today *Yagdil Torah* ('he will magnify the law') is the name of a popular website (www.yagdiltorah.org), a Lubavitcher Yeshivah in Brooklyn and several other educational institutions. The verse also features on one of a set of five postage stamps (cf. Deut 4:44; Prov 3:16, 17, 18) issued in Israel in September 1967 (Plate 32). Modern critics note an affinity to the language of Psalm 119, in praise of the Torah, and they conclude that the verse must be a late insertion (Westermann). In LXX there is no reference to the law:

PLATE 32   'For his servant's vindication he will magnify and glorify his Torah' (Isa 42:21). Israeli postage stamp (1967). Reproduced with kind permission of Israel Philatelic Society, Israel Postal Company.

instead God 'wanted to justify Israel and make them greatly admired' (Eusebius). Many Christian interpreters, like the Jews, interpret the verse as stressing how privileged they are, having, alone among the nations, been given the Law (Calvin), while for Luther, citing Paul (Rom 7:4–6), the verse extols the New Law, 'the law of faith'.

God has always treated them with fairness and compassion: their sufferings are sent by God but are entirely their own fault (vv. 22–25) (Cyril). They were robbed and plundered, trapped in holes (AV, RSV; Heb. *ba-ḥorim*): this means the lowest dungeons (cf. Isa 11:8) (Ibn Ezra). Others read 'all their chosen youths (Heb. *baḥurim*)' (Vg, Rashi, Lowth). They are trapped by ungodly teachers like the scribes and Pharisees (Jerome), and confined by the Law of Moses, which is like a prison (cf. Gal 3:23) (Luther). Then they will confess that their forefathers were blind and had no understanding (v. 24) (Ibn Ezra, Rashi). Their sins were directed against the Lord, so he unleashed the fury of his anger against them and the 'might of battle' (v. 25; cf. v. 13), not only the war from without, but also the war that besieges their souls from within (Eusebius).

I Am Your Saviour (Isa 43:1–13)

The first part of this chapter contains another Salvation Oracle (cf. 41:8–10), singled out already at Qumran as a message of comfort (see comm. on Isa 40). In the triennial lectionary it is the haftarah accompanying the story of Jacob at Bethel (Gen 35) (Mann 1971: 1, 282–289). After the horrors of the people's disobedience and its consequences (Isa 42:18–25), 'but now' means 'despite all this' (Rashi) and signifies 'the beginning of a new opportunity' (Cyril; cf. Gal 3:25).

Isaiah Through the Centuries, First Edition. John F. A. Sawyer.
© 2018 John Wiley & Sons Ltd. Published 2020 by John Wiley & Sons Ltd.

God addresses his people in a very personal way, introducing himself as the one who created them (cf. 44:2; 45:9–11), redeemed them and called them by name, as he called Abraham (Westermann; cf. Ibn Ezra). Christians see here a reference to the Church as the 'workmanship' of God (Eph 2:10) (Calvin) and redemption through the blood of Christ (Eph 1:7–10) (Cyril). The liberation theologians note the close relationship between creation and liberation here and elsewhere (cf. Isa 44:2; 51:9–11) (Miranda 1977: 77–78).

Rashi finds in verse 2 a reference to Israel passing through the Red Sea on dry land, while Aquinas identifies four of the enemies of God's people: the 'waters' are Egypt, the 'rivers' Babylon, the 'fire' Greece and the 'flame' Rome (cf. Jerome, Ibn Ezra). Others believe it refers to the persecution of the godly as predicted by Paul (2 Tim 3:12) and Christ: 'you will have sorrow in the world' (John 16:22) (Procopius; cf. Calvin). But the Lord will be with them always (Matt 28:20) (Eusebius) and through faith they will be preserved: 'none of these trials shall do you harm' (Luther). Others take the 'fire' (v. 2) as a reference to the 'fire of immoderate desire' that burns the soul (Ambrose, *Letter* 15), or the flaming sword which, until the coming of Christ, prevented people from entering paradise (Gen 3:24) (Origen, *Homily on 1 Kings* 28.9.3). For Rashi it is the fire of judgement on the wicked (cf. Isa 33:12).

'I gave Egypt as your ransom … peoples in exchange for your life' (vv. 3–4) refers to the killing of the first born in Egypt (Rashi; cf. Henry) or to the Babylonians given up to Cyrus on Israel's behalf (Theodoret). God is prepared to pay any price to redeem Israel (McKenzie): 'what are Ethiopia and Seba … compared to the blood of Christ?' (Henry). Another possibility is that it refers to the way God stirred up Egypt and her allies, Ethiopia and Seba, to distract Sennacherib and save Jerusalem from destruction (cf. Isa 37:9) (Calvin, Lowth). Whatever the details of the process, verse 4 is about God's love for his people. This is no ordinary love when he says 'you are precious in my eyes and honoured [or glorious LXX, Vg] and I love you': it is the love of a God who sent his son to die for us (John 3:16) (Oecolampadius; cf Calvin). Verse 2 is quoted by the mother of the seven martyred sons (4 Macc 18:14). A number of modern hymns were inspired by this passage, of which probably the most popular is 'Do Not Be Afraid' ('When you walk through the waters') (*CH4* 191; *HON* 122) (*BiM* 68).

A second short 'Salvation oracle' (or a continuation of the first) (vv. 5–7) begins, like the first, with 'Fear not' (v. 5) and ends with the naming and creating of Israel (v. 7; cf. v. 1). But the main theme is different: now God will bring his people, men and women, young and old, 'everyone who is called by my name', from the four corners of the earth. To Jewish commentators this refers to the return of the exiles to Jerusalem, from Babylon, Egypt and elsewhere (Ibn Ezra, Rashi; cf. Calvin). In rabbinic discussion verse 7 is quoted to show that

God 'did not create anything that was created in his world that was not for his glory, as it is said, "All that is called by my name…" (Isa 45:7)' (*Aboth* 6:11). Christians see the passage as a prophecy about the formation of the Church: its members are called 'sons and daughters' (v. 6) having received 'the spirit of sonship' (Rom 8:15–17), and 'Christians' having been called by the name of Christ (v. 7) (Cyril; cf. Eusebius, Jerome, Oecolampadius). According to Luther verses 6–7 imply that, if the gospel is not accepted in Jerusalem, I will bring people from afar who do accept it.

Another trial scene follows (vv. 8–13) in which two sets of witness are called to testify: 'the people who are blind' (that is, Israel; cf. 42:18–21) and 'all the nations'. Jewish interpreters argue that the eyes of blind Israel were opened when they were freed from exile (cf. Isa 42:18; Ibn Ezra, Rashi). 'My servant' is the prophet (Ibn Ezra) or Jacob (Rashi). 'I am he' (v. 10), repeated many times in Deutero-Isaiah (cf. Isa 41:4; 43:13; 46:4; 48:12), is the 'sublimest expression of the unity of God' and the 'I' is repeated (v. 11) as if to say 'I do not change' (cf. Mal 3:6) (Ibn Ezra). It is one of the divine self-proclamation passages appropriated by Jesus in John's Gospel (cf. Isa 41:4; 46:9).

The mission of the early Church was motivated by these words (Acts 1:8; Pao 2000: 91–96), and the Jehovah's Witnesses took their name from them, following the example of Christ, 'the Amen, the faithful and true witness, the beginning of God's creation' (Rev 3:14) (McKinney 1963:29). In a comment on Psalm 123:1, the rabbis noted a connection here between 'you are my witnesses' and 'I am God' (vv. 12–13): 'When you are my witnesses, I am God; when you are not my witnesses, I am, as it were, not God'. His very existence depends, in some sense, on his people's actions (*MidrPs* 123:2). The words 'You are my witnesses' (cf. Isa 43:12; 44:8) are inscribed in white letters on a black wall in the US Holocaust Memorial Museum in Washington (see on Isa 56:5). The words also feature in the context of martyrdom in Stanford's oratorio *The Three Holy Children* (1885) (cf. Dan 3) (*BiM* 241).

The three verbs in verse 12 suggest three stages in the history of God's people: 'I declared to Abraham … and saved from Egypt … and proclaimed on Sinai' (Tg, cf. Ibn Ezra, Rashi). 'Before the day was' (v. 13 AV) refers to the beginning of time, literally before the creation of day (Gen 1:5) (Rashi, Ibn Ezra). Others read 'from the beginning' (LXX, Vg, Childs), 'from eternity' (Tg, NJB, McKenzie) and 'from henceforth' (RSV; Brueggemann).

Christians, for their part, say that the eyes of the people will be opened when they enter the kingdom of Christ, along with people from 'all the nations' (Eusebius, Cyril): then they will be witnesses (Acts 1:8), alongside 'my servant', that is, Christ, to the truth of the gospel (Aquinas, Luther, Calvin). Verses 10–13 contain the first of several emphatic statements of explicit monotheism (cf. 44:6–8; 45:5–7, 14–22) (cf. John of Damascus, *Exposition of the Orthodox*

Faith 1.5), and Christian theologians cite verse 10 ('after me there was no god') to prove that Christ is God (Oecolampadius) and that, although he was born after the Father, he is nonetheless not younger, but co-eternal (Chrysostom, *Homilies on John* 4). Verse 11 ('besides me there is no saviour') shows that Father and Son are of the same essence (Theodoret) and verse 13 that those whom Christ saves, no one can snatch from his hand (cf. John 10:28) (Cyril).

A New Exodus (Isa 43:14–28)

Verses 14–15 form a short prophecy, with its own introductory formula, interpreted in the Targum as a prophecy of judgement in the past tense beginning 'because of you [your sins] I sent [you] to Babylon' (cf. Rashi). But most take it as a description of the destruction of Babylon by Cyrus, whether as an event that has already happened (Vg, AV, Jerome, Luther, Lowth), or still in the future (LXX, Theodoret, Cyril, Ibn Ezra, Duhm, Childs, RSV, NJB). 'Bars' (RSV; Heb. *berihim*) (Luther, Westermann, Oswalt) is read as 'fugitives' (*berihim*) by some, and the Targum has 'with oars' (*barihim*). The reference to Chaldaean ships has been widely questioned, although some imagine a scene of sudden destruction during a Chaldaean celebration (Tg, Ibn Ezra), perhaps as they were glorying in their naval superiority (Lowth; cf. Jerome). Some favour the Septuagint reading in some manuscripts 'bound in chains' (Gk *kloiois* for *ploiois* 'ships') (McKenzie). Most modern commentators substitute 'lamentations' (Heb. *aniyot*) for 'ships' (Heb. *oniyot*): 'the shouting … will be turned to lamentations' (RSV, NRSV, NJB; cf. Brueggemann, Childs). The closing statement (v. 15) that God, the Holy One, is creator of Israel and their king, however absurd this claim might appear to a people without a homeland (Calvin), recalls the words of Cyrus: 'the Lord … has given me all the kingdoms of the earth' (2 Chron 36:23) (Kimhi, Oecolampadius).

In the next short prophecy (vv. 16–21), the prophet first reminds them that this is the God who brought them out of slavery in Egypt, through the Red Sea and across the Jordan (vv. 16–17; cf. Ps 114:5; 66:6) (Cyril; cf. Eusebius, Rashi, Calvin). Perhaps it also shows that the Babylonian fleet will be defeated (Ibn Ezra). Then he tells them to forget the 'things of old' and focus instead on something new that is going to happen (Cyril): the fall of Babylon, the escape of Israel and their safe journey home through the wilderness where God will provide water for them (Ibn Ezra). Even the animals will break into songs of thanksgiving at the unexpected refreshment (v. 20) (Lowth). 'This people have I formed for myself' (v. 21 AV; cf. Tg Rashi) refers to the returning exiles (Ibn Ezra).

Christian interpreters apply these verses to the coming of Christ, the repeal of the old law, and the formation of the Church, something new that cannot be compared to anything that has happened before (Clement, *Stromateis* 2.4.15.3; cf. Irenaeus, *Against Heresies* 4.13.14). The 'rivers in the desert' are the waters of baptism (Cyprian, *Letter* 62.8), or the apostles preaching to the gentiles like the twelve springs of water of Elim (Num 33:9) (Tertullian, *Against Marcion* 4:13). The 'beasts of the field' (v. 20) are the souls that have gone wild: they will be changed by the force of the water and start praising God (Eusebius). The 'chosen people' (vv. 20–21) are the Church (1 Pet 2:9–10) (Cyril), formed to 'teach and preach and praise God' (Luther). Calvin is reminded of verses from Zechariah's hymn (Luke 1:71–72), and another modern hymn based on this chapter is a paraphrase of vv. 1, 2, 4, 10 and 19–21 with the refrain 'Fear not, for I have redeemed you' (*HON* 136; cf. vv. 1–4). In a speech in 1902 Monseigneur Louis-Adolphe Pâquet applied v. 21 to the French Canadian people (*NCHB* 2.423).

After this vision of a new age, the prophet returns to the subject of the disobedience of his people in the past and their consequent destruction (vv. 22–28). They gave up prayers and sacrifices because they found them burdensome (vv. 22). Sacrifice should be a freewill offering not a tiresome obligation (v. 23) (Rashi). The Church Fathers find an allusion to the new covenant here, according to which true sacrifice is 'a broken and a contrite heart' (Ps 51:17) (Jerome): God does not delight in the blood of bulls (Isa 1:11) (Eusebius; cf. Cyril). Luther compares the frankincense and sweet cane (vv. 23–24) to the 'ceremonies, tonsures and cowls' of the unreformed Catholic Church. The Hebrew of the next sentence appears to mean 'you have made me to serve' (Vg, AV; cf. Jer 17:4): through their sins God was made to look like a slave in the eyes of the nations (Ibn Ezra; Luther; Westermann). This anthropomorphism is removed by many commentators: 'you have burdened me with your sins' (RSV, NRSV cf. Tg LXX; Brueggemann, Childs).

The emphatic statement that follows, 'I, I am He who blots out your transgressions' (v. 25), recalls the statement of monotheism in v. 11 and combines it with his compassion (cf. Isa 51:12). The words 'for my own sake' challenge the notion that God's people can earn forgiveness by their own merits or by the merits of their fathers (Rashi). Luther describes the verse as a 'great thunderbolt against all merits', and explains 'for my own sake' as meaning 'My grace is freely given'. God says 'I will not remember your sins' (v. 25), but this does not mean we can forget them: as David said, 'My sin is always before me' (Ps 51:3) (Chrysostom, *Homilies on Repentance and Almsgiving* 7.4.11–12; cf. Jerome).

In one more court scene (cf. Isa 41:1, 21–29), he calls upon Israel to look back over their history (vv. 26–28). The Church Fathers take verse 26 as a guide to prayer: 'first confess your sins, then you will be justified' (cf. Prov 18:17) (Jerome; cf. Clement, *Fragments* 11.3). But the Reformers believe this is 'vehement mockery' (Calvin; cf Luther) because the prophet goes on to argue that Israel's sins are their own fault, not God's: they go back to their 'first father'

(v. 27) (Theodoret). This is probably Jacob (cf. Hos 12:2–3), but Ibn Ezra says it refers to King Jeroboam who led Israel astray after the death of Solomon (1 Kgs 12). Others suggest Adam (Kimḥi, Luther) and Abraham (Josh 24:2) (Jerome, Aquinas, Calvin). The Septuagint has 'fathers' (plural), leaving the question open, like the 'mediators' (RSV) or 'intercessors' (Rashi) or 'interpreters' (NRSV, NJB) or 'scoffers' (cf. Ps 1:1), identified as Moses and Aaron (Jerome, Aquinas), Levitical priests (Ibn Ezra, Luther) and other interpreters of scripture (Tg). Even they were not without sin so that Israel cannot rely on them to intercede on their behalf (cf. v. 25; Rashi; cf. Aquinas). That is why they have been punished, their leaders profaned, and the people utterly destroyed and reviled (v. 28). The 'princes of the sanctuary' are the priests according to Ibn Ezra, but it could refer to Israel's kings as well, notably Manasseh who profaned the sanctuary (Ephrem). For Luther all the leaders of the Church, religious and secular, are included.

I Am Alpha and Omega: Besides Me There Is No God (Isa 44:1–8)

The chapter begins with another 'salvation oracle' addressed to God's servant Jacob, with the characteristic 'fear not' (vv. 1–5; cf. Isa 41:10, 14; 43:1, 5). 'But now' shows how God's anger (Isa 43:27–28) is mitigated by his mercy (Calvin; cf. Ibn Ezra). The servant in this poem is named, and Jewish scholars, such as Nahmanides in the famous Barcelona disputation in 1263, cite this text to prove that the 'servant of the Lord' in Isaiah refers to God's people Israel, not the

Isaiah Through the Centuries, First Edition. John F. A. Sawyer.
© 2018 John Wiley & Sons Ltd. Published 2020 by John Wiley & Sons Ltd.

Messiah, as Christians maintain, especially in regard to chapter 53 (Maccoby 1982: 113). God's special care for his people is expressed in the reference to his mother's womb (cf. v. 24; Isa 46:3; 49:1, 5, 15; 66:9): like Jeremiah (1:5) and Paul (Gal 1:15–16), they were set apart by God before they were born. Some believe there is an allusion here to the story of the twins Jacob and Esau fighting in their mother's womb (Gen 25:22–26; cf. Hos 12:3) (Jerome, Ibn Ezra) or to Jacob's blessing (Gen 49) (Mann 1971: 1, 349–357).

'Jeshurun', another name for Israel, occurs only here and in the poems at the end of Deuteronomy (Deut 32:15; 33:5, 26). It is translated as 'beloved' in the Septuagint (cf. Eusebius, Calvin), but the Hebrew probably means 'upright, honest' (cf. *yashar*), perhaps a corrective to 'Jacob', which means 'crooked' (Duhm), recalling the prophecy that the 'crooked shall be made straight' (Isa 40:4) (Goldingay).

Rashi explains the imagery in verses 3–5 by reference to the spirit of God making the Jewish nation grow by multiplying their descendants, making the repentant (those who write on their hand 'the Lord's') return and encouraging proselytes (those who 'adopt the name Israel') to join them (cf. Zech 8:23) (cf. Ibn Ezra). This gives hope to the exiles living in the spiritual desert of Babylon (Theodoret). The life-giving water is the Holy Spirit (cf. John 7:39) (Cyril) or the waters of baptism (Jerome). The prophecy refers to the growth and regeneration of the Church (Calvin), and particularly to gentile believers, now called by the name Jacob, who become 'Abraham's offspring', partakers in the inheritance (cf. Gal 3:29) (Luther). Verse 4 was printed as the heading of a poem by the Anglican John Keble, in which the 'willows' are to be interpreted as the believers (Blair 2007: 617).

A second prophecy (vv. 6–8) moves beyond the boundaries of Israel and repeats the now familiar themes of God's kingship and control of world history. The title 'Lord of hosts' recalls the song of the seraphim (Isa 6:3). The words 'I am the first and I am the last; besides me there is no god' (v. 6) are quoted in a Jewish midrash to show that God has no father (before him), no son (after him) and no brother (beside him) (ExodR II 5). Israel's God is unique: he alone controls all that is past ('the ancient people' AV) and all that is to come (v. 7). The 'things that are to come' include the destruction of the Temple, the Babylonian exile and the birth of Cyrus, correctly foretold by Isaiah over a hundred years before they happened (Rashi, Calvin). 'You are my witnesses' (see comm. on Isa 43:12): you have seen what I have done; you have seen my prophets; you have seen into heaven (Rashi).

In Christian tradition these verses are cited in support of the Christian doctrine that God is Three in One (Tertullian, *Against Praxeas* 18:3–19:6; Theodoret). In the form 'I am Alpha and Omega', verse 6 (cf. Isa 48:12) was applied to Christ already in the Book of Revelation (Rev 1:8; 21:6; 22:13) and became a popular motif in Christian art from the third century, often combined with the Chi-Rho monogram. It also features in the fifth-century hymn 'Of the Father's Love Begotten' (*EH* 613; *CH2* 60 *GtG* 108 *AM* 80) and in the fourteenth-century German macaronic carol *In dulci jubilo: Matris in gremio / Alpha es et O* (On a mother's lap, you are Alpha and O) (*SNOBC* 82) (*BiM* 109).

The Folly of Idol Worship (Isa 44:9–20)

In contrast to the witnesses of God's power (v. 8), the behaviour of craftsmen making idols out of wood and metal ('witnesses that neither see nor know') is described in great detail, in places almost comical (vv. 9–20) (Irenaeus, *Against Heresies* 3.6.3; Athanasius, *Against the Pagans* 13.4). There are parallels in the apocrypha (Wisd 13:11–19; Baruch 6), but nothing so powerful and elegant as this passage (Lowth). Commentators quote a satirical parallel from classical literature: 'Once I was a trunk of a fig-tree, a useless piece of wood, when a carpenter, uncertain whether to make a bench or a Priapus, preferred that I should be a god; and so I became a god' (Horace, *Satire* 1,8) (Jerome, Calvin, Lowth). The thirteenth-century *Bible Moralisée* shows Isaiah watching with scorn or even amusement as one of them, with an axe in his hand, kneels in awe before a statue of a young man carrying a huge sword (vv. 12–13). Another cuts a piece of wood in half, puts part of it on the fire to warm himself and makes the other piece into a god, his idol; then he falls down before it and worships it (vv. 15–19), without noticing how stupid it is (Justin, *First Apology* 9.1–3; cf. Cyril, Theodoret, Luther).

The Dutch painter J. Jordaens, who converted to Calvinism in later life, puts a great deal of Isaianic detail into his painting of the scene, but the centrepiece, a nude female idol with what appears to be a crown on her head, surrounded by a crowd of men, women and children with outstretched hands praying desperately to her, looks very like a statue of the Virgin Mary, despite arguments to the contrary (Benisovitch: 1953). Incidentally, Jewish commentators found a reference to a female idol in the words 'the beauty of a man' (v. 13), which they interpreted as 'a woman, the beauty of her husband' (Rashi). Isaiah's attack on idolaters is applied to purveyors of heresy, who make idols out of their erroneous doctrines and force innocent people to worship them, whether in the patristic period (Jerome) or the sixteenth century (Luther). Modern commentators see this as an attack on the self-delusion of those who think they can 'capture the divine in the stuff of this world' (Oswalt) or compare Feuerbach's argument that gods are 'human projections' and, like Isaiah, stress that their God is not like other gods (Brueggemann), while postcolonial commentators question the assumption that there is something fundamentally wrong with idol-worship (see comm. on Isa 2:7–8).

Jerusalem Shall Be Rebuilt (Isa 44:21–28)

'Remember these things ... do not forget me [Tg, LXX, Vg]' (v. 21) seems at first sight to be a warning to avoid the errors of the idolatrous craftsmen just described (Cyril, Rashi, Calvin). The last words, however, read, 'you will not be forgotten by me' in the Hebrew (Ibn Ezra, AV, RSV), and it is unlikely that 'these things' refers only to the pathetic behavior of the idol-worshippers. Modern scholars suggest that the reference is rather to statements about the unique power of Israel's God and the certainty of redemption (e.g. Isa 44:6–8; Duhm, Westermann). Ibn Ezra suggests that the repeated pronoun 'you' (Heb. *atta*) implies 'you alone are my servant', while some of the Christian commentators give the passage a christological interpretation by following the Greek version 'you are my son ... you are my son' (Gk *pais*) (Cyril, Jerome). Either way it is an emphatic declaration of God's unfailing loyalty to his people (cf. vv. 1–2).

The beautiful imagery for the forgiveness of sins in verse 22 caught the eye of Luther too, who pictures Christ as the sun whose business it is 'to sweep away clouds and mist ... so that day by day we walk in a stronger faith' (cf. Origen, *Homilies on Genesis* 13:4; cf. Cyril). Philip Doddridge elegantly translated it into the language of an English hymn:

> He spoke and all the clouds dispers'd,
> And heaven unveil'd its shining face;
> The whole creation smil'd anew,
> Deck'd in the golden gleams of Grace. (1794: CIII)

Burkhard also singled out these two verses for a prominent musical role in his oratorio *Das Gesicht Jesaja* (1936) (Berges 2012: 126).

'Sing O heavens' (v. 23; cf. Isa 49:13) means that through the redemption of Israel, the whole world will see the glory of God and rejoice (Ibn Ezra). The 'foundations of the earth' join in as well: 'let the foundations of the earth sound the trumpet' (LXX). Christian writers interpret the verse as referring to the prophets or the apostles on whose faith the Church was founded (cf. Eph 2:20) (Cyril, Jerome, Theodoret, Nicholas). Mountains and forests join the celebrations (cf. Isa 55:12), believed by some to be the rich and famous, on the one hand, and the poor and humble on the other (Nicholas). Or perhaps it just means people in every country wherever they are situated (Calvin).

The last prophecy in the chapter is introduced, like the first (v. 2), with a reference to God's special relationship to his people: 'your Redeemer, who formed you from the womb' (v. 24; cf. Isa 46:3). It consists of one main clause, 'I am the Lord' (cf. Isa 42:8; 43:3, 11, 15; 45:5, 6, 18) and a long series of relative clauses beginning 'who made all things', ending with a reference to the rebuilding of Jerusalem in the days of Cyrus (vv. 24–28). 'Who was with me?' (RSV, NJB; cf. LXX, Vg) recalls the beginning of John's Gospel (John 1:1–3) (Athanasius, *Against the Arians* 3.24.9; cf. Eusebius). The Targum has 'I suspended the heavens by my Memra [word]' (v. 24; cf. Prov 8:27). The 'liars ... diviners [AV] ... soothsayers ... augurs' (NJB, JPS) are 'star-gazers' or 'astrologers', for whom Babylon was renowned (Rashi, Calvin), and whose attempts to predict the future were futile in comparison with those of God's 'servant' Moses (Rashi) or, more likely, Isaiah, who correctly predicted the end of the Babylonian exile and the rebuilding of Jerusalem (Ibn Ezra, Theodoret), and his messengers, the other prophets. Christian interpreters identify the 'messengers' with the apostles whose words are full of wisdom and truth (Cyril, Eusebius).

Commentators point out that, even though Cyrus was an idolater, he fulfilled God's purpose by conquering Babylon and freeing Israel so that the Temple and the cities of Judah could be rebuilt (Cyril; cf. Luther). The great city of Babylon, described as the 'deep' (v. 27 LXX *abyssos*) because of the vast numbers of its citizens and the nations that it ruled over, will be dried up and become a desert (v. 27; cf. Isa 13:19–22) (Jerome). It could be that the reference to 'rivers' (cf. Ps 137:1) alludes to the historical fact that Cyrus is said to have changed the course of the Euphrates so that his army could enter Babylon along the riverbed (Herodotus, *Histories* 1.185, 190; Nicholas, Lowth; cf. Eusebius). The references here to what actually happened in the sixth century BCE are unusually specific (cf. Ezra 1:1–4; Josephus, *Antiquities* 10:1–2; Jerome) and much quoted in modern discussions of the date and authorship of the Book of Isaiah.

Others take verse 27 as a reference to the Exodus, recalling the psalm 'What ails you, O sea that you flee, O Jordan that you turn back?' (Ps 114:5) (Luther), or as a metaphor for the powers of Satan and 'the armies of his iniquity' (Ephrem). The last words of the prophecy explicitly refer to the rebuilding of the Temple, and may also point beyond ancient history: 'in the present day he does not thus recommend to us a temple of wood or stone, but living temples of God, which we are; for the Lord hath chosen his habitation in us (2 Corinthians 6:16)' (Calvin).

Cyrus the Lord's Anointed (Isa 45:1–8)

The first prophecy in this chapter is apparently addressed by the Lord to 'his anointed Cyrus' (v. 1). Reservations about this use of the term 'Messiah' (Heb. *mashiaḥ*; Gk *christos*; cf. Vg, Tg) are frequent (b*Megillah* 12a; cf. Rashi). Ibn Ezra admits the possibility that it refers to Cyrus but says it could refer to the prophet (cf. Isa 61:1). Some of the Church Fathers remove the problem by reading *kurio* 'Lord' for *kuro* 'Cyrus' (Irenaeus, *Demonstration of the Apostolic*

Isaiah Through the Centuries, First Edition. John F. A. Sawyer.
© 2018 John Wiley & Sons Ltd. Published 2020 by John Wiley & Sons Ltd.

Preaching 49; Isidore, *De fide catholica* 3, 2–3), while others see Cyrus as a fore-shadowing of Christ's messiahship (Cyril, Nicholas). Many point out that it was normal for kings to be anointed with oil, even pagan kings (Jerome, Cyril, Theodoret, Nicholas), and some refer to evidence that Cyrus wrote in praise of God (cf. Ezra 1:2) (Jerome, Aquinas). Calvin argues that, although the title belongs properly only to Christ, it is applied here for a brief period to the one who restored freedom to God's people, one described by Eusebius as 'a good servant of my plan' (cf. Isa 46:11) and by Luther as 'a godly man'. Cyrus had been specially called, even though he was a 'slave to the error of idolatry' (Theodoret), not for his own sake or for any other reason, but for the sake of God's servant Jacob (v. 4) (Ibn Ezra).

The striking imagery of opening gates and breaking in pieces doors of bronze (vv. 1–2) originally referred to Cyrus' conquest of Babylon and other cities, well documented in Herodotus, Xenophon, Josephus and others, and the 'hidden treasures … and hoards' are the immense wealth he is said to have acquired, most notably when he defeated the legendary Croesus, king of Lydia, regarded as the wealthiest king in the world (Lowth). This is how Tennyson used the imagery in his poem 'Babylon' (1827):

> Though thy streets be a hundred, thy gates be all brass.
> Yet thy proud ones of war shall be wither'd like grass;
> Thy gates shall be broken, thy strength be laid low.
> And thy streets shall resound to the shouts of the foe! (Tennyson 1969: 1.156)

Popular metaphorical interpretations applied these images to the freeing of hearts from the iron grip of Satan (Tertullian, *Answer to the Jews* 7), while the hidden treasures of true knowledge will be revealed when the gates of ignorance are broken down (John Cassian, *Institutes* 5.5.2). This is how the well-known nineteenth-century missionary hymn used the imagery, beginning 'Lift up your heads, ye gates of brass' (*EH* 549; *CH2* 385 *GtG* 93). The breaking down of the gates of bronze can also be applied to Christ's defeat of death (Chrysostom, *Homilies concerning the Statutes* 7.1), and this is how the verse was interpreted in the Gospel of Nicodemus from where it made its way into medieval representations of the Harrowing of Hell (Twycross 2006: 341).

There was a popular belief in the nineteenth century that America was a modern Cyrus to help restore the Jews to Zion (cf. 2 Chron 36:22–23) (Chancey, Meyers and Meyers 2014: 43). More recently the American messianic sect known as the Branch Davidians, based in Waco, Texas, whose leader David Coresh took his name from verse 1, used the uncompromising tone to author-ize the fortification of their base, known as Apocalypse Ranch, with a huge armoury of weapons and ammunition, which led to the violent and bloody showdown with the US forces of law and order in 1993.

Commenting on verse 3 ('that you may know that it is I…') Eusebius suggests that this is an appeal to Cyrus to give up his ancestral gods for the one true God, and it may be no coincidence that there are more statements of explicit monotheism in this chapter (vv. 5, 6, 14, 18, 21, 22), apparently addressed to Cyrus, than anywhere else in the Bible. Even though Cyrus does not worship Israel's God, his victories on behalf of God's people will show the world, 'from the rising of the sun and from the west' (v. 6), that there is no other God besides him (Ibn Ezra; cf. Aquinas). Christian commentators point out that this does not imply that Christ was not God: the Son is inseparable from the Father (Tertullian, *Against Praxeas* 18).

The next statement that God is creator of 'light and darkness … peace and evil' (v. 7 KJV) is much quoted in theological discussion. Some understand it as a reference to the way God treats the righteous and the wicked: he will strengthen Cyrus and weaken the king of Babylon (Ibn Ezra; cf. Rashi). God makes peace with those who repent, but for the wicked he prepares eternal fire and darkness (Matt 8:12) (Irenaeus, *Against Heresies* 4.40.1; cf. Eusebius). He is like a good physician who not only 'leads his patient to baths and pools of water and sets before him a well-furnished table … but also confines him to bed, deprives him of light and food … cuts and cauterizes and brings him bitter medicines' (Chrysostom, *Concerning the Power of Demons* 1.5). 'Light' allegorically means good fortune and prosperity, 'darkness' denotes misfortune (Luther; cf. Theodoret). Several writers quote Job's words: 'If we receive good at the hand of the Lord, should we not also receive evil?' (Job 2:10) (Gregory, *Morals on Job* 3.15–16; cf. Origen, *Against Celsus* 6.54–55).

The words 'creator of evil' (v. 7) were quoted by Marcion in support of his argument that the God of the Old Testament was not the supreme God but an evil fashioner of the corrupt world in which we live (Tertullian, *Against Marcion* 1.2). A Qumran reading of the text, 'maker of good (Heb. *ṭov*) and creator of evil', may reflect a similar background (Blenkinsopp 2006: 90). The suggestion was rejected emphatically by Christians who argued that the word 'create' (Gk *ktizo*) here doesn't mean 'create out of nothing' but 'rearrange' (Gk *metakosmeo*) (Basil, *Homily* 9.4; cf. Augustine, *Against an Enemy of the Law and the Prophets* 1.23.48) (see comm. on Isa 40:26). Calvin distinguishes 'the evil of punishment from the evil of guilt'. The ethical implications of this verse and other passages (e.g. Isa 6:9–10) are discussed in *Double Standards in Isaiah* (A. Davies 2000).

The verse is cited in rabbinic discussions of the origin of the evil inclination: it was created by God but at the same time the Torah was created as its antidote (*RA* 125–126). The verse is also quoted in the Jewish Daily Prayer-book though 'creator of all things' is substituted for 'creator of evil' (*ADPB* 62–63). It features also in Elgar's oratorio *The Kingdom* (1906), in a beautiful aria sung by Mary as she contemplates what has happened on the day after Christ's Ascension

(*BiM* 134). A modern attempt to find common ground between biblical religions and Buddhism cites this passage as an expression of the total rejection of dualism (Strolz 1992:107–110).

In medieval Christian tradition the Latin version of verse 8 became very popular, partly because the first word, *rorate* (send down dew), is more euphonious than its equivalent in most other languages, and partly because it translates the Hebrew word *yesha'* (salvation) as *Salvatorem* (saviour). It then becomes a prayer for the Holy Spirit to come down on Mary like dew so that she will conceive and bear the Saviour (cf. Isa 53:2). The verse appears on the first page of the *Biblia Pauperum* alongside Gideon's fleece (Judg 6:36–8) and other fore-shadowings of the Virgin Birth (Ps 72:6; Isa 7:14) (*BP* 50). The *words Rorate coeli desuper* are the first line in a macaronic poem 'On the Nativity of Christ' by William Dunbar (Conlee 2004: 25–26), and, in John Bale's play *God's Promises* (1538), are heard in a prayer recited by Isaiah (cf. Isa 66:1; 16:1):

> Open thou the heavens, and let the Lamb come hither
> Which will deliver the people all together.
> Ye planets and clouds! Cast down your dews and rain,
> That the earth may bear our healthful saviour plain. (Happé 1985–1986: 1.26–27)

The *Rorate* used to be sung as an introit during Advent (*MR* 9, 18; cf. *EH* 735). Verse 8 is still one of the 'Alleluia verses' sung on weekdays in Advent: 'send victory like a dew, you heavens' (*ORM*), and the passage is read on weekdays in Advent (Isa 45:6b–8, 18, 21b–25; RCL). In addition to motets by Byrd and Palestrina, and Haydn's early *Rorate Mass* (*c.*1750), Liszt's oratorio *Christus* (1873) opens with an orchestral arrangement of the plainchant melody, and there are modern settings by John Joubert and Thea Musgrave, the latter a setting of the Dunbar poem (*BiM* 199–200).

The image of the Virgin and of women in general, as parcels of land, however, has no appeal today, and there have always been alternative interpretations. Luther condemned the 'papist preachers' for twisting the passage. Shakespeare quotes it in a very different context: 'The quality of mercy is not strained / It droppeth as the gentle dew from heaven' (*Merchant of Venice* IV.1,183) (1598), as does the American Quaker John Greenleaf Whittier (1807–1892) in his hymn 'Dear Lord and Father of Mankind': 'Drop thy still dews of quietness …' (*EH* 383; *CH2* 245; *HON* 116 *AM* 621). In contemporary Christianity it has become a prayer for justice:

> Rain down justice,
> You heavens, from above;
> Let the earth bring forth for us
> The one who is to come. (*HON* 459)

According to Ibn Ezra, the 'heavens' and 'skies' in verse 8 are metaphors for the angels (cf. Dan 10:2), called upon to intervene and establish righteousness in the world through the agency of Cyrus (cf. Eusebius, Ephrem). Luther sees in the verse a reference to the prophet weeping over Jerusalem (cf. Theodoret) and praying that God would 'break the heavens and rain down righteousness ... to refresh and renew us by his gifts'. 'Let the earth open' is about hearts and minds receiving the Word of God and Calvin finds similar imagery in a Psalm: 'faithfulness will spring up from the ground and righteousness will look down from the sky' (Ps 85:11).

Will You Criticize the Creator? *(Isa 45:9–13)*

The 'woe oracle' that follows (vv. 9–13; cf. Isa 5:8; 10:1; 28:1), the only one in Deutero-Isaiah, appears to be addressed to Israel, when they complain about God's choice of saviour (v. 1) (Brueggemann). Rashi suggests that the prophet had Habakkuk in mind, whose words 'How long, O Lord?' (Hab 1:2; cf. v. 14), believed to have been uttered during the long oppressive reign of Nebuchadnezzar, became proverbial. Luther compares it to the cries of Job (Job 3:3), Jeremiah (Jer 20:14–15) and Christ (Matt 27:46) as an example of the temptation to doubt in times of crisis: 'we must not complain but rather pray 'Shower, O heavens, from above' and not say 'Woe!'. The image of clay in the hands of a potter is used by Jeremiah (Jer 18), Paul (Rom 9:20) and others (Isa 29:16): 'as the potter knows what to do with clay, so I know what to do with Israel, my son' (Ibn Ezra). God can mould us in any way he pleases, and we have no means of changing that, although, according to Augustine, 'the whole lump fell into condemnation because of the ... free choice of the first human being' (*Letter* 186:18).

Verse 10 is quoted by Jerome in defense of the doctrine that Christ is the Son of God and the Virgin Mary (cf. Gal 4:4). The comparison between God and a woman in childbirth has prompted feminist writers to include it among biblical texts about female aspects of God (cf. Isa 42:14; 66:7–14) (Trible 1978: 60–69). In verse 11 instead of 'things to come' (Heb. *ha'otiyyot*; AV, LXX, Vg, Tg) 1QIsa[a] has 'the signs' (Heb. *ha'otot*): God is 'creator of the signs' (cf. Rashi), and it has been suggested that this may be a reference to astrology, particularly in view of the discovery at Qumran of many astrological texts (Blenkinsopp 2006: 90).

The 'woe oracle' ends with the emphatic repetition that it is Cyrus who 'shall build my city and set my exiles free' (v. 13; cf. Isa 44:28) (Ibn Ezra). The rabbis cite the reference to 'my city' here to prove that God is a fellow citizen as well as a kinsman (Ps 148:14), a brother (Ps 122:8) and a father (Deut 32:6) (*MidrPs* 118.10). Calvin adds that Cyrus, being called by God 'in righteousness' (cf. Isa 41:2), acted in accordance with God's will, not 'for any price or reward' as other kings might do (see comm. on Isa 13:17). Christian interpreters see here, especially in the phrase 'raised up in righteousness' (AV), a prediction of the Resurrection (Eusebius; cf. Cyril).

God Is With You Only and There Is No Other (Isa 45:14–25)

The rest of the chapter (vv. 14–25) contains a series of prophecies on the theme of monotheism. The prediction that Egyptians, Ethiopians and Sabaeans will bring treasures to Jerusalem and adopt monotheism (v. 14) is interpreted by Rashi as having been fulfilled in Isaiah's own day because when Sennacherib and his army laid siege to Jerusalem, they were laden with the spoils of war having just returned from Ethiopia (Isa 37:9, 36), and, according to a rabbinic tradition, Sennacherib's prisoners converted to Judaism when Hezekiah released them from their chains. Others take it as a reference to Cyrus' victories (cf. Isa 43:3) (Jerome, Luther). Christian commentators apply the prophecy to the future admission of gentiles, even 'the most superstitious', into the Church (Cyril; cf. Eusebius, Lowth): the words 'God is in you' (AV; Heb. *bak*, feminine singular) acknowledge the unique role of the new Jerusalem, that is, the Church (Calvin). Others like Gregory of Nyssa ignore the gender of the Hebrew and cite the verse to prove the divinity of Christ (cf. Rom 9:5; Titus 2:13; 1 Tim 3:16) (*Against Eunomius* 3.15–16). The chains are the commandments of Christ (Aquinas).

The idea of 'a God who hides himself' (v. 15) has been much discussed. Ibn Ezra stresses that it cannot mean 'invisible', as some have argued, but refers to a deliberate move on God's part to hide himself (cf. Ps 18:11; Aquinas). The Targum paraphrases 'O God, you made your Shekinah dwell in the great height'. Some believe this means that God is hidden from the nations, and revealed to Israel (Rashi, Eusebius, Oecolampadius); the Septuagint imagines them saying, 'You are God, yet we knew it not' (Cyril). Some Christian theologians have suggested it refers to Christ's divinity hidden under the infirmity of human flesh: 'God's power is hidden in the weakness and vulnerability of the Cross' (Brueggemann).

Many find here a statement about faith in God in times of crisis: Isaiah calls him 'a hidden God' because those things which he promised are not immediately visible to our eyes (cf. Rom 8:24) (Calvin, cf. Luther). It is an important text for Thomas à Kempis (*Imitatio Christi* 4.13.2), Pascal (*Thoughts* 4.242; cf. Matt 11:27) and other Christian theologians (cf. Howard-Snyder and Moser 2002). Post-holocaust Jewish theologians have found in verse 15 a biblical formulation of the doctrine of *hester panim* 'the hiding of God's face' (Cf. Deut 31:17).

Most of the other passages where the notion is referred to are questions addressed to God by someone in distress: 'Why do you hide your face and count me as your enemy?' (Job 13:24; cf. Pss 10:1; 44:24; 88:14; 104:29). Only here is it addressed to God as a statement: 'Truly you are a God that hides himself, O God of Israel, the Saviour'. God's absence from human history is necessary so that humanity can exist properly, his presence is necessary so that evil will not ultimately triumph. Some find him in his 'absence', some miss him in his presence. Either way the God of Israel who hides himself from time to time is, in Isaiah's words, the 'Saviour' (Berkovits 1973: 63–65, 101).

A third 'fragment' (Westermann) returns to the contrast between idol-worshippers, 'put to shame and confounded', and Israel, 'saved by the Lord with everlasting salvation' (vv. 16–17). Cyril was inspired, perhaps with an allusion to this passage in the New Testament in mind (Heb 5:9), to end his commentary on these two verses with a doxology 'for ever and ever. Amen' (cf. NJB).

The rest of the chapter contains a series of powerful arguments intended to confirm the promises just made concerning Cyrus and the defeat of the Babylonians (Luther, Calvin). First God is the creator of heaven and earth and there is no other god (v. 18; cf. vv. 5, 6, 14, 21, 22). The statement that he formed the earth 'to be inhabited' is cited by the rabbis in their teaching on marriage: 'Was not the world created only for fruition and increase' (m*Gittin* 4:5; m'*Eduyot* 1:13). Then verse 19 refers to Sinai where God spoke openly to Moses, not in secret or 'in some dark corner of the underworld' (NJB), and gave us the Law to be a lamp to our feet and a light to our paths' (Ps 119:105) (*Mekh* on Exod 19:1–2; Lauterbach 1933: 294) (Rashi). For Christian commentators, how much more does this apply to the gospel of Christ! (cf. 2 Cor 4:3–4) (Calvin). For a Yiddish translator of the Bible, it referred to the 'prophet's democratic lack of privacy ... in contrast to the dark and mystical cults of idol worshippers' (cf. Deut 30:11–14) (Waldinger 1998: 321).

Verses 20–25 are cited in the early Church in support of universalism (cf. Isa 44:3–5; Acts 15:18; Blenkinsopp 2006: 133). God challenges the 'survivors of the nations' to present their case (vv. 20–25; cf. Isa 41:8–13). In verse 20 some say he is referring to the nations that escaped the sword of Nebuchadnezzar (Rashi), others that he is addressing the Babylonians, whose idolatry is the subject of the next chapter (Ibn Ezra; cf. Luther). Cyril, citing Paul (Eph 2:13, 17), imagines God calling to his scattered children, rescued from the power of Satan, to 'assemble', that is, to be bound together in one faith, while Calvin thinks of 'the rejected of the nations' rather than 'survivors', that is to say, the 'highest in wealth and rank and power among the gentiles ... of no value in the sight of God' (Luke 15:15). All are challenged to foretell the future as God did (v. 21) when he predicted that the pagan king Cyrus would be the one to save God's people (Luther) or that Christ would one day shine upon the peoples of the earth (Cyril). There is no other God besides me, a 'righteous God', that is, one who forgives our sins (Luther) and a 'saviour', that is, one who exerts his power on behalf of his people (Calvin). For a medieval Jewish polemical interpretation of verse 20, see comm. on Isa 30:7.

The call to 'turn to me, face me and be saved' is addressed to 'all the ends of the earth' (v. 22) and implies the breaking down of the partition wall between Jews and Gentiles (Eph 2:14) (Calvin). For Matthew Henry it recalls Jesus' reference to drawing all men to himself when he is lifted up (John 12:32) like the bronze serpent in the wilderness (John 3:14–15). The direct language of this verse made it the 'conversion verse' of the English revivalist preacher Charles Spurgeon, who, on hearing a sermon preached on it on a snowy day in London, turned to Christ for salvation: 'then and there the cloud was gone, the darkness rolled away, and that moment I saw the sun' (Spurgeon 1897: 112). A hymn by the Jesuit John Foley, inspired by Isa 12 and 51:4, 6, has the refrain 'Turn to me, O turn and be saved' (v. 22) (*HON* 771).

The first part of verse 23 is about the unfailing power of God's word spoken by his prophets: 'it shall not return to me empty' (cf. Isa 55:10–11) (Cyril, Aquinas, Calvin). For Luther 'from my mouth in righteousness has gone forth a word' refers to the gospel which 'teaches faith, grace and a way of justification'. The words were used by Pope Benedict XIII, as if they were his own, to assert his authority at the Tortosa Disputation in 1413–1414 (Maccoby 1982: 168). The second half of the verse is quoted by the rabbis in a comment on Psalm 100 ('All people that on earth do dwell'): this means that all the nations of the earth are to worship God, gentiles as well as Jews (*MidrPs* 100.1). The reference to language (Heb. *lashon*; RSV 'tongue') recalls for some the words of Zephaniah: 'at that time I will change the speech (Heb. *saphah*) of the peoples to a pure speech' (Zeph 3:9) (Rashi).

Calvin similarly quotes another prophecy to show that speaking a new language means giving up beliefs and practices expressed in an old language, as when Egyptians speak the language of Canaan (Isa 19:18). Others compare it with a comment by Paul on 'Greeks and barbarians' (Rom 1:14) (Eusebius). Paul quotes verse 23 twice, once with reference to judgment day, when all will be equal before God (Rom 14:11; cf. Augustine, *Catholic and Manichaean Ways of Life* 14.32), and once with reference to the universal appeal of Christ in all his glory, 'the name which is above every name' (Phil 2:10–11). The words 'every knee shall bow ... and every tongue confess that Jesus Christ is Lord' figure in a several popular hymns including 'At the Name of Jesus' by the English hymn writer Caroline Maria Noel (1870), often sung to a tune by Vaughan Williams (*EH* 368; *CH2* 178; *HON* 50 *AM* 593). Verse 25 declares that, even when gentiles are included, God's promise to his own people remains unbroken (cf. Rom 11:25–27) (Calvin). The Church Fathers, working from the Septuagint ('all the offspring of the sons of Israel') made a distinction between 'all Israel' and those who separated themselves from Israel to believe in Christ (cf. Rom 9:6) (Jerome, Theodoret): the 'sons of Israel' are the first preachers of the gospel and it is their offspring, 'a few survivors' (Isa 1:9), who shall be justified and glorified (Isa 1:9) (Eusebius).

The False Gods of Babylon (Isa 46:1–13)

The next two chapters together focus on the Babylonians, the first on their religion, the second on their downfall and humiliation (Aquinas, Childs, Brueggemann). Chapter 46 begins by ridiculing the Babylonian gods, 'crouching … cowering' (NJB), heavy burdens on the backs of beasts of burden, incapable of doing anything for themselves and carried off into captivity (vv. 1–2). Rashi takes the two verbs in verse 1 as euphemisms, 'squatting … soiling themselves',

Isaiah Through the Centuries, First Edition. John F. A. Sawyer.
© 2018 John Wiley & Sons Ltd. Published 2020 by John Wiley & Sons Ltd.

as though they were suffering from diarrhoea. The Fathers comment on the unbearable and diabolical burden of the error of idolatry (Eusebius) and the terror these great idols instilled in their worshippers who demanded human sacrifice (Hos 13:2) (Cyril). The Book of Daniel contains some well-known examples (Luther), including the apocryphal Bel and the Dragon (Dan 14). The association of idols and beasts reminds some that idols were often made in the form of animals and birds, especially in Egypt (Theodotion). The Septuagint has Dagon instead of Nebo, recalling a dramatic prefiguration of the Isaiah passage from the days of the Philistines (1 Sam 5:1–5) (Cyril). An illustration of the passage in the *Bible Moralisée* shows a great idol being cut down by two angels. The words 'Bel shall stoop and Nebo bow' (v. 1) feature in a trio beginning 'Loud proclaim the great salvation' that is sung by three Israelites near the end of Act 1 of Spohr's oratorio *The Fall of Babylon* (1842) (*BiM* 82–83). For a postcolonial interpretation, see comm. on Isa 2:7–8.

Verses 3–4, in striking contrast, are addressed to the 'remnant of the house of Israel' (cf. Isa 10:20–22; 37:31–32), those who survived the Babylonian exile (Oecolampadius) or those who remained faithful (Eusebius, Jerome), and it presents God as a mother who has carried them in her arms since the day they were born. Verse 4 is recited in some synagogues at the end of the ancient *Alenu* prayer with which morning worship concludes (*ADPB* 142–143). Jerome, citing Psalm 109:3 (LXX) compares the image to that of the good shepherd (John 10:11; cf. Isa 40:11), but Calvin, quoting Moses (Deut 32:11), emphasizes the female imagery: 'he has manifested himself to be both their Father and their Mother' (see comm.on Isa 42:14). Modern writers likewise cite this verse in their discussions of female images of God (Trible 1978: 38), and it figures in the Church of Scotland's *Motherhood of God* pamphlet (1984) and in the papal encyclical *Mulieris dignitatem* (1988). God's promise in verse 4 to care for his people 'even to old age … and to grey hairs' is quoted by Augustine more than once 'for our stability, when it is in you, is stability indeed' (*Confessions* 4.15.31; cf. 6.16.26). The verse also contains one of the divine self-proclamation passages appropriated by Jesus in John's Gospel (cf. Isa 41:4; 43:10). Verses 5–7 continue the ridicule of idol-worshippers from the previous chapter (Isa 45:20). While our God freely offers to carry us in his arms and save us in times of trouble, idols are expensive to make, have to be carried and are unable to hear our prayers (Eusebius, Theodoret).

Verse 8 contains a rare word (*hit'osheshu*) sometimes translated 'consider' (RSV, NRSV) or 'be strong' (Tg, Rashi, Luther, AV, Lowth, NJB), but perhaps better understood as 'groan' (LXX) or 'be ashamed' (Jerome; cf. Kimḥi, Calvin, Westermann). Many note the addition of the verb 'repent' (*metanoeo*) after 'groan' in LXX (Jerome, Eusebius, Aquinas), and Augustine quotes it a number of times, comparing Isaiah's 'Turn back to the heart' (Vg; cf. LXX, NJB) to the

Prodigal Son 'returning to himself' (Luke 15:17) (*Confessions* 4.12.18; *Sermon* 102.2). Remember all that God has done in the past (v. 9), that is, the Exodus and the Sinai covenant (Rashi), and the works of creation where we can see the 'splendours of his wisdom' (Sir 42:15–25) (Aquinas). The prophet urges his suffering people to look beyond present evils to better things beyond (Cyril; cf. Luther). 'All my pleasure I will do' (v. 10) is God's promise to lead his creatures to righteousness (cf. Isa 42:21; Ezek 33:11) (ExodR IX:1). For Christians it recalls the Lord's Prayer: 'thy will be done on earth as in heaven' (John Cassian, *Conferences* 9.20).

The 'bird of prey (Heb. *'ayiṭ*) from the east' (v. 11) is Cyrus, so called because of his speed and power (Luther; cf. Ibn Ezra), perhaps also because Cyrus' standard was a golden eagle (Lowth; cf. Xenophon, *Cyropedia* 7). Some say it refers to those 'winged creatures' sent forth at God's command to save his people (Heb 1:14; cf. Ps 104:4), while 'the man of my counsel' must be Christ (cf. Ps 40:8), called from the innermost part of Hades (Eusebius; cf. Jerome). Rashi finds another word for 'counsel' (Aram. *'eṭa*) (cf. Dan 2:14) here instead of the bird of prey (cf. Calvin), and takes it as a reference to Abraham (cf. Isa 41:2).

The chapter ends (vv. 12–13) with another call to the 'stout-hearted' (Heb. *abbire leb*; cf. Ps 76:5) (AV), that is, those who clung to their faith even in a foreign land (Rashi). Most commentators read 'stubborn of heart' (RSV; cf. Vg, Tg) or 'hardened in their hearts' (Ibn Ezra, Aquinas, Lowth, Duhm), an apt description of the Babylonians (Luther) or the Jews (Calvin). 'Those who have lost heart' (LXX) are people who have neglected to cultivate their spiritual life (Origen, *Dialogue with Heraclides* 22). Whatever the state of their hearts, salvation is not far off (v. 13; cf. Hab 2:3) (Procopius; cf. Cyril). This is about God's love: when Israel fell into the marsh of judgement, God dragged them out (Cyril; cf. Theodoret); can the faithlessness of men nullify the faithfulness of God? (Rom 3:3) (Calvin). The verse may have been in Matthew's mind in his account of the appearance of John the Baptist (Matt 3:1–3) (Blenkinsopp 2006: 157–159). 'Israel my glory' is best explained as 'Israel in whom I will be glorified' (cf. Isa 49:3) (Ibn Ezra).

Isaiah 47

The Fall of Babylon (Isa 47:1–15)

This chapter, addressed directly to the 'virgin daughter of Babylon', has been described as a 'song of triumph' (Duhm) or a 'mocking song' (Muilenberg), and it resembles the 'oracles against foreign nations' (cf. Isa 13–23). The image of Babylon as a woman commanded to climb down from her throne and sit 'in the dust' (v. 1) (Eusebius) recalls the fate of Judah described earlier in terms of wealthy, elegant women stripped of their jewelry and forced to work like slaves

Isaiah Through the Centuries, First Edition. John F. A. Sawyer.
© 2018 John Wiley & Sons Ltd. Published 2020 by John Wiley & Sons Ltd.

(Isa 3:26; cf. Lam 2:10) (Cyril). The image appears again later in a famous reversal of this horrific scene: 'Awake, awake … shake yourself from the dust arise, O captive Jerusalem' (Isa 52:2) (Lowth).

Although addressed to 'Babylon … daughter of the Chaldaeans' (vv. 1, 5), there is not one detail that refers explicitly to a city, nothing about walls or gates or sieges. She is described as a 'virgin' (v. 1) not because she was chaste but because she was dressed in the manner of a virgin, wanting to appear youthful (Eusebius, cf. Cyril). The 'tender and delicate' skin of a queen becomes rough like that of a slave working in a mill like Samson (Judg 16:21; cf. Matt 24:41) (Jerome, Luther). Her clothes are stripped off and she is dragged away captive 'through the rivers' where even more details of her undignified, helpless plight are given (vv. 2–3). In an aside, described by Lowth as a 'chorus' (v. 4), an explanation is given of why Babylon is being treated like this (cf. Isa 40:1–2) (Cyril). In the synagogue this verse is part of a blessing recited immediately before the *Amidah* (*ADPB* 74–75).

The reasons for Babylon's humiliating downfall are spelled out in a dramatic speech beginning 'Sit down. Be silent' (Vg) (LXX 'pierced with woe'), 'bury yourself in darkness' (NJB) (vv. 5–11). When they were asked to punish Israel, they showed no mercy (cf. James 2:13), not even to the aged (v. 6; cf. Lam 4:16) (Theodoret, Aquinas, Calvin). Like Nineveh (Zeph 2:15), they displayed arrogance and boastfulness, like a 'loathsome and lewd woman given to coquettish and dissolute behavior' (Cyril), daring to make the claim that she has no rival (vv. 8, 10), a claim which only God has the right to make (cf. Isa 46:9) (Calvin). For this she will suffer a sudden, terrible fate, the loss both of her husband and her children 'on one day … in full measure … nothing will remain' (Luther). In one blow Cyrus will kill your king and all your warriors (Cyril; cf. Eusebius). No amount of sorcery and enchantment can save you (v. 9). Babylon was renowned for its astrologers, but their legendary skills were misguided (v. 10): no one could have predicted what happened in Babylon (cf. Dan 5:30) (Calvin). There is nothing they can do to 'charm away' (NJB, RSV 'expiate') the impending disaster (v. 11). The word translated 'desolation' (AV) or 'ruin' (RSV) is *Shoah*, now a Hebrew loanword in English referring to the Nazi Holocaust (cf. Isa 10:3; Job 30:3; Ps 35:8).

Sarcastic mockery of Babylon's astrologers continues: 'perhaps they will be able to succeed … prevail … save you … predict the future' (vv. 12–13) (Theodoret). The translation 'prevail' (AV; Heb. *'araṣ*) is explained by reference to a more familiar word variously translated 'ruthless, tyrant' (Heb. *'ariṣ*) (Isa 25:3–5; 29:20; 49:25) (Ibn Ezra; cf. AV, Calvin, Duhm). Modern versions have 'inspire terror' (RSV). Their fate is compared to a stubble fire, not a fire of live coals which lasts a long time and gives heat to people sitting around it but a sudden conflagration that destroys everything near it (v. 14) (Luther; cf. Rashi).

Nor is it a wood fire, which can be of some use, but stubble which is 'light and useless' (Jerome, Calvin). The 'power of the flame' refers to the impending destruction of Babylon by Cyrus, king of the Persians (cf. Num 21:28) (Ibn Ezra; cf. Luther). A nineteenth-century preacher uses verse 14 in a description of hellfire (Spurgeon 1856–1916: 8.211–212).

Modern commentators are critical of the biblical use of images of the sexual abuse of women (vv. 2–3; cf. Ezek 16; Hos 1–2) (Weems 1995). But the 'whore of Babylon', described in details derived from this chapter and elsewhere (Jer 51; Ezek 27), has featured quite prominently in Western culture, starting with the Book of Revelation (Rev 17–18), where she fondly imagines she will never be a widow or see mourning, but 'her plagues shall come in a single day' (Rev 18:7–8; cf. Isa 47:8–9). In that context she represents Rome, built on seven hills (Rev 17:9), and this is how Luther, fifteen centuries later, interprets it too, comparing the evil, ineffectual activities of the Babylonian soothsayers, for example (vv. 9, 12, 13), to the 'processions and altars and intercessions of the Church of Rome'. In the same century the Elizabethan poet Edmund Spenser, in Book 1 of his allegorical poem *The Faerie Queen* (1590), created a loathsome female character called Duessa, representing Mary Queen of Scots (I. 8.46–48; cf. V.9). She wears the pope's triple crown, rides a chariot drawn by seven bestial sins (1.4) and is described as a 'scarlet whore', stripped naked, her skin 'rough as maple rind … Her nether parts the shame of all her kind / My chaster Muse for shame doth blush to write' (vv. 1–3). By contrast the language and imagery of Tennyson's poem 'Babylon' (1827), beginning 'Bow, daughter of Babylon, bow thee to dust!' (cf. Isa 47:1) are similarly drawn almost entirely from Isaiah (Tennyson 1987: 1,155–1,1557), but without any of the sexual imagery, focusing instead on the victories of Cyrus (Isa 45:1–3) and their devastating effect on the region (Isa 34:14) (see comm. on Isa 45:1–2). The first Act of Spohr's oratorio *The Fall of Babylon* (1842), which also leaves out most of the female imagery, ends with a mighty chorus calling on Babylon to 'Come down and in the dust be humbled' (Isa 47:1) and 'Hallelujah! He shall reign for ever, the Mighty God of Israel!'.

A Rebel from Birth (Isa 48:1–11)

Chapter 48 is about the 'unwearied forbearance' of a God who 'relieves our afflictions, and assists those who had been unworthy, and even who had insolently rejected his grace' (Calvin). Rashi finds a distinction between 'Israel', the Northern Kingdom destroyed by the Assyrians, and Judah in the south, who 'leaned on the God of Israel' (v. 2) in the days of Hezekiah (2 Kgs 18:5) and were not exiled except in the days of Nebuchadnezzar when they were rescued by Cyrus.

Isaiah Through the Centuries, First Edition. John F. A. Sawyer.
© 2018 John Wiley & Sons Ltd. Published 2020 by John Wiley & Sons Ltd.

At all events, the chapter concludes by reiterating Deutero-Isaiah's message of hope for the exiles, but it is clear that this was not in any way because of what they had done: it was 'for my own sake, for my own sake' (v. 11) (Luther).

The Church Fathers suggest that here the prophet was addressing the evil practices associated with the reign of Hezekiah's successor, Manasseh (2 Kgs 21). Some applied the prophet's harsh words to the Jews in the time of Christ, citing their own claim that 'We have Abraham as our father' (John 8:33) (Cyril) and imagining that Stephen had this passage in mind when he called the Jews 'stiff-necked' (Acts 7:51) (Theodoret). Their claim that 'the holy city' and its Temple are exclusively theirs also gives reason to interpret this passage as an attack on Jews in the time of Christ (Luther). Modern commentators have sought to explain the discrepancy between the harsh rhetoric of chapter 48 and chapters 40–47, by identifying elements that reflect conditions in the early Second Temple period: in verses 1b, 4, 8b, 17–19 and 22, for example, a later voice can be heard addressing the people's disobedience and corruption after the prophecies of salvation had ostensibly been fulfilled in the victories of Cyrus (Duhm, Westermann).

The 'loins (Heb.*me'e*) of Judah' (v. 1 RSV) requires a textual emendation: the Hebrew has 'waters' (*me* cf. Vg, AV, NJB), whether a euphemism for 'sperm' (Eusebius, Aquinas) or a poetic allusion to Balaam's prophecy (Num 24:5–7) (Rashi) or the 'fountain of Jacob' (Deut 33:28; cf. Ps 68:26) (Lowth). The phrase 'holy city' (Heb. *'ir ha-qodesh* v. 2), from which the Arabic name for Jerusalem (*al-Quds*) is derived, occurs twice in Isaiah (cf. Isa 52:1) and then quite frequently in Second Temple period texts (Neh 11;1, 18; Dan 9:14; Matt 4:5; 27:53; Rev 11:2; 21:2, etc.). The 'holy mountain' (Heb. *har ha-qodesh*) appears quite frequently with a similar meaning (Isa 11:9; 27:13; 65:11, 25; 66:20; etc.).

The prophet goes on to remind his people, addressed in the singular (vv. 4–11), like the servant in Isa 41:8, that whatever happens is entirely under the control of God: the 'former things' that he promised would happen 'suddenly … came to pass' (v. 3), like the Exodus from Egypt and the destruction of Sennacherib (Rashi). Isaiah's attacks on idol worship are now applied to Israel, who stubbornly refuses to listen to God's true prophets and claims that it was their idol that did all these things (v. 5), recalling the women in Jeremiah's time who claimed it was because they stopped burning incense to their idol, the queen of heaven, that disaster fell upon them (Jer 44:18) (Cyril). The image of a neck so hard that it does not respond to the yoke of God (v. 4) is familiar from other attacks on the obstinacy and stubbornness of a stiff-necked people (Exod 32:9; 33:3, 5) (Nicholas), and the image of a forehead of brass, unable to blush however wicked and shameful the deeds perpetrated, recalls the demeanour of a shameless prostitute cited by Jeremiah to shame his audience (Jer 3:3) (Theodoret).

The now familiar theme of the 'new things' (v. 6) that God is about to perform, that is, the destruction of Babylon by Cyrus and the liberation of the exiles (cf. Isa 43:19), is repeated, but here the fact that Israel did not listen to his prophets is turned into another attack on their treacherous and rebellious behaviour 'from birth' (v. 8). Moses used this language about his people (Deut 31:27) (Luther), as did Ezekiel, who records that they had to cast away their 'detestable things' on the day when God first made himself known to them in Egypt (Ezek 20:1–8) (Rashi). God will delay his anger but this has nothing to do with who they are or what they deserve (vv. 9–11) (Eusebius). God will free them for his name's sake, not for their name's sake, not because they are 'Israel' or the 'holy city' (cf. v. 1). Redemption is due exclusively to God's grace, not to human works: in Paul's words, 'if justification came through the Law, then Christ died in vain' (Gal 2:2) (Luther).

The metallurgical imagery in verse 10 recalls parallels in the Psalms (Ps 12:6) and elsewhere (Jer 9:7; Dan 11:35; Mal 3:3), but here refinement is not with the fire of Gehenna (cf. Isa 30:27; 66:24) but in the 'crucible of poverty', a reference to conditions for the exiles in Babylon (Rashi). 'Not like silver' means that the people never became as pure as silver: however much they were 'refined' some impurity always remained (Nicholas). Others read 'not for silver, not for a price' and take it as a reference to God's motivation in 'refining' his people: it was not for material gain (Eusebius, Cyril). The second part of the image, 'the crucible of poverty' (Tg, Vg, LXX; Rashi), often taken more generally as 'the furnace of affliction' (cf. Deut 4:20; Jer 11:4; AV, RSV) or 'adversity' (NRSV), prompts comments on the spiritual value of poverty (cf. 1 Tim 6:8) (Jerome, Theodoret, Aquinas) – not the poverty of monks, however, which can be a source of pride, but that 'inner lowliness' of which Mary speaks (Luke 1:48) (Luther).

He repeats once again that it is for his own name's sake that he protects his people lest the nations laugh at them in their troubles and profane his name, saying 'Where is their God?' (Ps 79:10) (Jerome). Moses also explained why the Lord was unwilling to destroy the whole nation: 'Lest perhaps their enemies should claim it for themselves, and say, It is our lofty hand, and not the Lord, that hath done all this.' (Deut 32:27.) (Calvin). This is what he means when he says 'My glory I will not give to another' (v. 11) (Rashi).

Go Forth from Babylon (Isa 48:12–22)

After this harsh rebuke come three short prophecies about divine providence (vv. 12–19). The first continues addressing 'Jacob … Israel' as a single person (vv. 12–13; cf. vv. 4–10). Verse 13 is cited by the rabbis to prove that God created the heavens and the earth at the same time, not consecutively, but Ibn Ezra argues that 'stand forth together' (v. 13) is about obedience, not creation, 'for all things are your servants' (Ps 119:91; cf. Isa 40:26). Christian theologians find a reference here (cf. Isa 41:4; 44:6) to Christ, named 'first and last', 'Alpha and Omega' in the Book of Revelation (Rev 1:8; 21:6; 22:13), and the 'right hand of God' (Exod 15:6; Ps 89:13) (Cyril). Eusebius adds that Christ was 'first' because he was 'the life' (John 1:4) and 'last' because he 'emptied himself ... and became obedient to the Father even unto death' (Phil 2:7–8).

The second prophecy (vv. 14–16), addressing a plural audience in familiar language (cf. Isa 41:2–4; 45:1–4), is about Cyrus, who shall perform God's purpose on Babylon and upon the Chaldeans (Rashi, Ibn Ezra, Luther). Some argue that this is about Abraham (cf. Isa 41:1–4) but Cyrus makes better sense of the references to Babylon and the Chaldaeans. God's assertion that he loves Cyrus (cf. Isa 45:1) is missing from the Septuagint, where it is apparently Cyrus who is speaking and saying, 'Because I love you, I have done your will', a statement picked up by Ambrose in a discussion of the difference between obedience motivated by fear and obedience motivated by love (cf. Ps 119:97; Deut 6:5; Mark 12:30) (*Homily 13.3 on Psalm* 118).

The apparent change of speaker in verse 16 has generated much discussion: who is announcing that 'the Lord God has sent me and his spirit?'. Rashi believes that the whole verse comes from the mouth of the prophet and compares 'from the beginning' to a rabbinic tradition that all the prophets 'stood at Sinai' (cf. Deut 29:14–15) (*Tanḥ 28:6.* Yitro 11, f.124a; cf. Calvin). 'His spirit' refers to an angel, sent to verify the words of the prophet (Ibn Ezra; cf. Isa 37:36). Others believe that it is Cyrus repeating his belief, expressed in the famous edict (Ezra 1:1–4), that his rescue of the Jewish exiles from Babylon was at God's command (Cyril; Eusebius, Luther). It has also been suggested that it is the voice of the servant, anticipating Isa 49:1–6 (Childs). Christian theologians recognize the voice of Christ in this verse and a clear reference to the mystery of the Trinity (cf. Isa 42:1; 61:1) (Jerome, Theodoret). There is ambiguity in the Hebrew as to whether it reads 'the Lord God and his Spirit hath sent me' (AV) or 'the Lord God has sent me and his spirit' (RSV). Origen cites New Testament evidence to prove that the Lord sent his Son first and then the Holy Spirit (*Against Celsus* 1.46; cf. Theodoret), but Augustine points out that Isaiah's prophecy may refer to the fact that the Holy Spirit came upon Mary before Jesus was born (Matt 1:18) (Augustine, *On the Trinity* 2.5.8).

The wistfulness of the next short prophecy (vv. 17–19) has been much commented on. It is a way of announcing the reward that awaits those who listen to the word of God (Ibn Ezra). The implication is that God will have mercy on his people even though they have despised his laws (Theodoret). The verses are in a modern Advent lectionary along with verses from Psalm 1 (*ORM*, RCL), and they are included in a series of biblical passages on social justice by twentieth-century liberation theologians (Miranda 1977: 153–154). For some the images of a 'river' recall the life-giving water offered by Christ (John 4:14; Ambrose, *On the Holy Spirit* 1.16.161–162) while for others the irresistible force of a raging torrent and the great waves of the sea crashing on to the rocks describe the invincible power available to those who obey God's word (Cyril). Eusebius takes the imagery of both verses together and suggests that it is about abundance, both the abundant river of peace and righteousness that flows through God's people and the teeming multitude of their descendants, more numerous than the sands of the sea. This is how verse 18 is interpreted in Frances Havergal's hymn beginning 'Like a river glorious / Is God's perfect peace' (*CH2* 443). Jerome suggests 'pebbles' (cf. AV 'gravel') (v. 19) for the word often translated 'grains' (RSV; Heb. *me'ot*), while others take it as 'innards' (cf. 2 Sam 20:10), that is, the innards of the sea referring to all the innumerable life forms that live in the sea (Lowth, Rashi) or more specifically to the roe of the fish (Ibn Ezra).

After the chastening tone of earlier verses, repeatedly reminding the people of their wicked ways, the chapter ends with a call for them to join in a new exodus, to celebrate their redemption and tell the world what the Lord has done for them (vv. 20–21) (Cyril). The return of the exiles from Babylon to Jerusalem is described in the Book of Ezra (Ezra 8:31–36), although there is no mention there of the miracle of water gushing from a rock (Kimhi; cf. Jerome; Lowth). Some of the Church Fathers suggest that the rock from which living water flowed refers to the voice of prophecy heard by the exiles in Babylon, but also, when they returned to Jerusalem, to the 'divine teaching' of Haggai, Zechariah and Malachi, not to mention Zerubbabel and Jeshua the High Priest, which was 'like water to the thirsty' (Theodoret).

Many recognized that, in a historical sense, this refers to the exiles' liberation from Babylon in the days of Cyrus, but they argued that the prophecy goes much further and has to be understood metaphorically (Jerome, Calvin). It speaks of freedom from a 'spiritual captivity', of a time when a saviour would come to 'preach good news to the poor, to proclaim release to the captives' (Luke 4:18; cf. Isa 61:1–2) (Eusebius). The Septuagint has future tenses in verse 21: 'he shall lead them through the desert'. Then the rock is Christ (1 Cor 10:4) from whom living water flows, 'welling up to eternal life' (John 4:14) (Eusebius), and 'Go forth from Babylon' is a call to flee from 'the city of this world, from the fellowship of wicked angels and wicked people' (Augustine, *City of God* 18.18; cf Aquinas).

'There is no peace for the wicked' (v. 22) refers to 'Nebuchadnezzar and his seed' according to some (Rashi; cf. Cyril), but most take it as a reference to 'those who live impiously' (Eusebius) or hypocrites and disbelievers (Calvin) in general or to the wicked in Israel in particular (Ibn Ezra; cf. Luther).

The Septuagint has 'There is no joy for the wicked' and Augustine discusses the verse at some length in a commentary on the words of the psalmist 'Rejoice in the Lord, O you righteous' (Ps 97:12), highlighting the distinction between true joy and the licentiousness and frivolity that the world calls joy (*Exposition on Psalm 96:16*). In Longfellow's 'New England Tragedy' *John Endicott* (1888) (Act 3, Scene 1), the Quaker Wenlock Christison uses the words to good effect when he is sentenced to be 'hanged until dead – dead – dead' at his trial in 1661.

The first half of chapter 49 seems to have played a key role in the history of Christianity from the very beginning (vv. 1–13), and it appears in lectionaries for both Advent and Holy Week (*ORM*, RCL). It is quoted at least a dozen times in the New Testament and appears to have been 'fundamental to the thought of Paul' (Lindars 1961: 223f). Eusebius observes that the Word begins afresh at this point, turning to address the gentiles and prophesying about the Advent of our Saviour. Luther comments that 'from this chapter to the end there is nothing but Christ': in this chapter it is Christ who is speaking (Calvin). Oecolampadius gives the sixth and last volume of his Isaiah commentary (49–66) the title

Isaiah Through the Centuries, First Edition. John F. A. Sawyer.
© 2018 John Wiley & Sons Ltd. Published 2020 by John Wiley & Sons Ltd.

'The Messiah'. By contrast verses 1–13 are conspicuous by their absence from Jewish lectionaries, although in no way lacking in rabbinic commentary. Modern scholarship also sees a new beginning here: there is no further mention of the Babylonians or Cyrus or a new 'Exodus', for example, and there is a new focus on the 'servant of the Lord', which suggests a different audience is being addressed, perhaps already back in Jerusalem. Verses 1–13 comprise the second 'Servant Song' (vv. 1–4) with additions (vv. 5–13) (Westermann, Childs).

A Light to the Nations (Isa 49:1–6)

Unlike the first 'Servant Song' (Isa 42:1–4), this one is in the first person singular (vv. 1–4; cf. 48:16b) and tells us that the speaker has been called by the Lord to be his servant. Jewish commentators assume this is the prophet himself speaking. While he was still in his mother's womb (v. 1), God thought the name 'Isaiah' (Heb. *yesha'yahu*) would be appropriate as he would prophesy 'salvation' (*yeshu'ot*) (Rashi), and he is called 'Israel' (v. 3) because 'in God's eyes he is worth all the Israelites put together' (Ibn Ezra). The poem is also about Israel and the rabbis compared this unique expression of God's love for Israel with Israel's love for God: the Psalmist says, 'Thou art the glory of their strength' (Ps 89:17) and the Lord says, 'Israel, in thee I will be glorified' (Isa 49:3) (*Mekh* on Exod 15:1; Lauterbach 1933: 2.23).

Christian commentators from the beginning show that the 'servant' here cannot simply refer to the prophet Isaiah. The one who is 'called from the womb' can be a prophet like Jeremiah (Jer 1:5) or a preacher like Paul (Gal 1:15), 'chosen before the creation of the world' (Eph 1:4) (Calvin). But here the naming of the servant while he was still in his mother's womb refers to the angel appearing to Joseph and naming the child 'Immanuel' (Matt 1:23) or to Gabriel's words to Mary, 'You shall call his name Jesus' (Luke 1:31) (Eusebius, Jerome, Cyril). The 'mouth like a sharp sword' recalls Jesus' words (Matt 10:34) (Eusebius) as well as descriptions of the Word of God that 'issues from his mouth to smite the nations' (Rev 19:15, 21) as 'sharper than any two-edged sword' (Heb 4:12) (Theodoret, Calvin). Christ is the one 'chosen arrow' (LXX, Vg; 'polished' AV, RSV), distinguished from all the other prophets and apostles (Jerome). This refers to the arrows that wound the souls of those who love him, those who cry out 'I am wounded by love' (Cant 2:5) (Theodoret; cf. Jerome). The arrow was hidden in the quiver of God's foreknowledge until the incarnation (Cyril), or made flesh in the quiver of a human body (Eusebius). In him God will be glorified (v. 3; John 17:1; Phil 2:10–11) (Cyril; cf. Calvin). The name 'Israel', the one who contended with God on our behalf and prevailed (Gen 32:28), can only be applied to Christ (Lowth).

In modern times the identity of the servant has been a source of lively debate ever since Duhm first isolated the four Servant Songs from their context (see comm. on Isa 42:1–4). For many the absence of the name 'Israel' (v. 3) from a Qumran manuscript (4QIsa^d) (Blenkinsopp 2006: 269) confirmed the view that it is a gloss, and there are many suggestions as to who the unnamed individual is. They include the prophets Moses and Jeremiah who interceded for their people and suffered at their hands, Cyrus described as the Lord's anointed in an earlier prophecy (Isa 45:1), and an unnamed future Messiah. Parallels with the Son of Man, 'hidden in the presence of the Lord' (1 Enoch 48:6) have been noted (Blenkinsopp 2006: 264). Collective interpretations include the people Israel, frequently described elsewhere in these chapters as 'the servant of the Lord', although the reference to his mission to Israel (v. 5) would require a distinction between the people as a whole and a righteous remnant within Israel. More recent scholarship tends to the view that the four songs should not be removed from their literary context, so that, for example, the first poem may be about a messianic figure (42:1–4; cf. 45:1; 61:1–3), this one about a prophet to the nations, and the last one about a people (Isa.52:13–53:12).

The failure of the servant (v. 4) recalls many passages about the blindness, stubbornness and unreceptiveness of Isaiah's audience, and the rabbinic tradition that, when Isaiah said, 'Here am I, send me', God warned him that he would be rejected by his people (see comm. on Isa 6:8). It also recalls Jesus' parable of the vineyard (Matt 21:33–41) (Cyril) and indeed the experience of every preacher from Jeremiah (Lam 2:20) and Paul (2 Tim 1:15) right down to our own times (Luther). 'Yet surely' expresses his confidence that he is doing what is right and will receive a reward for his work (Ibn Ezra). It is not his fault that he has failed (Rashi, Luther). Paul exhorts his readers with the assurance that their labour is not in vain (1 Cor 15:58). The verse is given a poignant setting in Mendelssohn's oratorio *Elijah* (1846), where the prophet, alone in the desert, sings an aria combining it with Isaiah 64:1–2 and ending with the words 'O that I now might die' (cf. 1 Kgs 19:4) (Rogerson 2006: 292).

In the first of what are often considered to be additions to the original poem, the servant tells us he thought his mission was to his own people, but the Lord tells him that is not enough: he is to be a light to the nations so that God's salvation 'may reach to the ends of the earth' (vv. 5–6). The prophecy that 'Israel might not be gathered' (v. 5 AV; cf. Luther, Calvin) follows the consonantal text which has the negative *lo'* (not), seemingly separating Jacob from Israel, although 'to be gathered' can mean 'to be taken away, die' (Luther, Calvin). The evidence from Qumran and Masoretic tradition (cf. Tg, Rashi, Ibn Ezra) removes the negative and confirms the reading 'to him' (Heb. *lo*) (RSV; Rashi, Ibn Ezra). 'Restore the tribes of Jacob' (LXX) is part of Elijah's mission in the Greek version of Ecclesiasticus (Sir 48:10), and this establishes an eschatological interpretation of the poem by the late second century BCE (Blenkinsopp 2006: 261). The verse appears as an editorial comment on the cover of a Yiddish journal with the title *Berit 'Am* (v. 8), published in Germany from 1893 to 1924.

We have met the term 'a light to the nations' already (Isa 42:6) and seen how it was applied to the mission of Christ and his early followers. It is this verse that Paul and Barnabas quoted on their mission to Pisidian Antioch, when the gentiles 'were glad and glorified the word of the Lord' (Acts.13:47), a 'major turning point' (Evans 1989: 127). The Church Fathers compared it to the 'true light that lightens everyone that comes into the world' (John 1:9; cf vv. 4–5) (Origen, *Comm. on John* 1.158–159) as well as to prophecies about light coming to Jerusalem (Isa 60:1–2) and the rising of the 'sun of righteousness' (Mal 4:2), fulfilled in Christ's own words 'I am the Light of the World' (John 8:15) (Cyril). Kimḥi notes that, while Assyria, Babylon, Moab and other foreign nations had been the objects of some of Isaiah's bitterest attacks, now he is calling to them (v. 1) and prophesying salvation to the ends of the earth (v. 6), while Rashi observes that it was the prophet's prediction of the destruction of Babylon that would bring joy to the whole world.

A Day of Salvation (Isa 49:7–13)

The Lord addresses the prophet as one who is 'deeply despised, abhorred by the nations' (cf. v. 4), and tells him that kings like Cyrus will rise up and worship God when they hear his words (Ibn Ezra). Others interpret the prophecy as addressed to the suffering people of God, whether Israel (Rashi) or the Church (Luther). The rapid reversal of fortune in this verse from suffering and humiliation to glorification becomes a frequent theme in the next chapters (cf. verse 23; Isa 60:10–11; 62:2), and also in early Christian apocalyptic (Blenkinsopp). The prophecy that the Jews would one day be free of foreign domination was not fulfilled until the Maccabaean period (1 Macc 13). Christians applied it to Christ, despised by the Jews, humiliated before Annas and Caiaphas, sent to Herod and Pilate to be crucified (Jerome), 'enfeebled for our iniquities and betrayed for our sins' (cf. Isa 53:5; Rom 5:8–9; John 10:11) (Cyril; cf. Augustine, *Christian Combat* 11.12). Kings shall see him and prostrate themselves when he comes in glory to judge the living and the dead (Matt 25:31) (Eusebius). The rabbis used the verse as a recommendation of humility (*RA* 473). Where the Hebrew has 'his Holy One, to one deeply despised' (AV, RSV), the Septuagint has 'Sanctify the one who despises his life' and provides scriptural authority for the notion that true holiness comes from humility (Cyril). In a soprano aria at the beginning of part 2 of Mendelssohn's *Elijah* (1846), verse 7 introduces the words 'I, I am he that comforteth.' (Isa 51:10–11).

The next prophecy, introduced by the formula 'Thus says the Lord' (vv. 8–13), is addressed to a single individual (cf. vv. 1–7), once again understood by some as the prophet (Ibn Ezra), by others as the people Israel (Rashi) or the Church (Luther), by others as Christ (Cyril) or his followers (2 Cor 6:2) (v. 8). The passage then opens up into a typical Deutero-Isaianic prophecy about the freeing of prisoners, the feeding of the hungry, the building of roads and the ingathering of the exiles from afar (vv. 9–12; cf. 61:1–4). 'A time of favour' (RSV; 'an acceptable time' AV) is understood by Rashi to mean a time when God is well-disposed towards his people, that is, when they seek his favour in prayer, but he adds that 'a day of salvation' means a time when they need his help. Paul makes it clear that for him 'the acceptable time is now … the day of salvation has come' (2 Cor 6:2) (cf. Cyril, Eusebius, Luther). When the words were first uttered, they referred to the year when Babylon was destroyed, but for us they refer to our Redemption in Christ (Calvin). The difficult term *berit ʿam* 'a covenant to the people' (RSV) was discussed earlier (see comm. on Isa 42:6).

Some authorities divide verse 8 into two parts: first, in the past tense, 'I have answered you … helped you', and then, in the future, 'I will keep you … give you for a covenant' (Rashi, AV). The rabbis quote verse 8 in the context of a discussion of the sufferings with which the Messiah is afflicted in every generation: 'but in that hour I will afflict you no more' (*PesR* 31.10). 'To establish a land' (Rashi; cf. RSV) or 'the earth' (LXX, AV) is translated by the Targum as 'to raise up the righteous who lie in the dust', a reference to the resurrection of the dead (cf. Isa 26:19; Dan 12:2–3). According to Rashi freeing the prisoners from captivity refers to the end of the Babylonian exile. Their journey home will be made easy for them: they will have plenty to eat and drink and they will be protected from scorching wind (cf. Isa 35:7) and sun (cf. Ps 121:6) (Ibn Ezra). Roads that were impassable before (Isa 33:8) will be repaired (v. 11) (Rashi); and there will be such crowds of people that some will be forced to go up on to the hills on either side of the road, but God will prepare a road for them there too (v. 11) (Ibn Ezra). People will come from all directions: 'afar' means east, the north is Babylon, the west is Assyria and Sinim is a land to the south of Egypt (Ibn Ezra; cf. Tg). Modern discoveries confirm that the reference here is to Syene (1QIsaᵃ *swenim*; Arab. Aswan) in Upper Egypt, the site of a Jewish settlement from the sixth century BCE (cf. Ezek 29:10; 30:6), perhaps also referred to in Isaiah 19:18. 'And I will make all my mountains a way' is portrayed on one of the first postage stamps issued by the State of Israel in February 1949 (Plate 33).

For Christians verse 8 refers to Christ's suffering in Gethsemane (Matt 26:39) and on the cross (Ps 22:1): that was before the 'day of salvation', but then God answered his prayers and helped him (Cyril, Eusebius). Paul applied the verse to his own call (2 Cor 6:2). The rest of the prophecy, introduced by the

PLATE 33   'And I will make all my mountains a way' (Isa 49:11). Israeli postage stamp (1949). Reproduced with kind permission of Israel Philatelic Society, Israel Postal Company.

words 'saying to the prisoners', is then applied to the work of Christ and his apostles preaching the saving word of God to all nations (Eusebius, Cyril, Luther), in 'a kind of new creation' (Calvin) (vv. 9–12). The freeing of the prisoners (v. 9) cannot refer to what Zerubbabel did (Theodoret): this is about freeing sinners from 'the ropes of their own sins' (Prov 5:22) and dispelling darkness with the light of the knowledge of Christ (Eph 5:8) (Eusebius; cf. Cyril, Jerome). According to Luther it is about freedom from 'Moses, the papacy, monasticism and evil traditions.'

The picture of God's people refreshed and guided through the mountains recalls Psalm 23 (Eusebius, Calvin). Verses 8–15 are read on the Eve of the Theophany in Orthodox tradition (*OSB*). The springs of water are the Old Testament and the New Testament (Eusebius) or the prophets, apostles and evangelists who draw water from the 'wells of salvation' (Isa 12:3) (Cyril). 'The way of the righteous is level and well-fashioned' (Isa 26:7; cf. 40:4) (Cyril). The highways will be raised up (v. 11) because they lead to the heavenly Jerusalem (Gal 4:26) (Eusebius). People will come from all over the world, 'from all walks of life' (Luther), to worship Christ, starting with the three wise men from the east (Matt 2:2, 11; cf. Ps 72:15) (Cyril). Christian missionaries enthusiastically interpreted Sinim (v. 12; MT, AV, NJB) as a reference to China, as, for example, in the American Quaker account of missions to China entitled *Ohio Friends in the Land of Sinim* (1924).

The hymn of praise in verse 13 can be understood as a kind of liturgical response to the good news of the preceding prophecy (cf. Isa 12:5–6; 42:10–13; 44:23). With Isa 62:1, v. 13 inspired a joyful chorus in Saint-Saëns' *Oratorio de Noel* (1858) (*BiM* 180). This is the language of the Psalms (Ps 69:34) (Aquinas). God will be praised in heaven and on earth, that is, by choirs of angels in heaven and by human choirs on earth (Jerome, Cyril), recalling the words of Christ 'There is joy in heaven when one sinner repents' (Luke 15:7) (Eusebius, Theodoret). Alternatively it could simply mean, when God lifts his hand, heaven and earth are moved (Calvin). Some take it figuratively as a reference to the purity of the air and the productivity of the fields as all nature celebrates God's victory (cf. Isa 35:1–2) (Ibn Ezra) or else 'heaven', 'earth' and the 'mountains' can mean all classes of people, mighty and humble, rich and poor (Cyril, Eusebius, Nicholas). The reason for celebration is contained in the two words 'comfort' (Heb. *naham*) and 'compassion' (Heb. *raham*): this is one of the ancient Jewish 'consolation' texts (*Tanhumim*) at Qumran (see. comm. on Isa 40). The object of God's compassion is given as 'the afflicted' (AV, RSV; Heb. *'ani*), that is, those who suffer for their faith (Jerome, Luther, Calvin). Others take it as another reference to humility (LXX, Cyril, Eusebius; cf. v. 7), while the rabbis cite this verse to prove that Israelite law is biased in favour of the poor (cf. Exod 22:25) (ExodR XXXI.5).

Doubting Zion (Isa 49:14–26)

The second part of the chapter is a poetic dialogue in which Zion expresses her doubt and disbelief (v. 15; cf. vv. 21, 24) and is answered by some very strong divine rhetoric intended to reassure her (vv. 14–26). In Jewish lectionaries one of the 'consolation' haftarot begins here (Isa 49:14–51:3; see comm. on Isa 40).

The female character of Zion was introduced in chapter 40 (vv. 2, 9; cf. 1:21–26; 37:22), but it is not till now that we hear her voice expressing doubts in the same way as Jacob and the servant of the Lord have done (Isa 40:27; 49:4). This is a 'turning point in the book' (Blenkinsopp), and from now to the end of the book she plays a more significant role, particularly after the last of the four servant songs (Isa 54:1–10; 60; 62; 66:7–14) (Sawyer 1989). 'The Lord has forsaken me' (v. 14): she thinks God had forgotten her (Rashi), her children had abandoned her (Cyril). According to some, the Zion who speaks here is the community of the saints (Ps 87:2), in a time of crisis, complaining that they have been deserted and forsaken by God (Jerome).

God's first answer is in two parts (vv. 15–20). First, he quotes an illustration from nature: 'Can a woman forget her baby?'. Several commentators note that the bond between mother and child goes beyond human beings and applies equally to wild animals (Calvin). Luther says that God is our mother (cf. Isa 42:14), but he also points out that God is more tender-hearted than even the most tender-hearted human mother, or, as Theodoret puts it, 'God is nearer to us than a father and mother because he is our Maker and Creator' (*Letter* 14). The image appears in several hymns, notably William Cowper's 'Hark My Soul' (1768) (*EH* 400; *CH2* 417; *AM* 654):

> Can a woman's tender care
> Cease toward the child she bare?

Modern hymns by Carey Landrey and Dan Schutte are also inspired by verse 14 (*HON* 265, 569). The apparent connection between the Hebrew words for 'compassion' (*raham*) and 'womb' (*rehem*) was noted by late twentieth-century feminist writers. God's 'compassion' (*raham*) is mentioned three times in the verses leading up to this comparison between God's compassion and a mother's 'womb-love' (*rehem*) (vv. 10, 13, 15) (cf. Isa 63:15; Jer 31:20): 'an organ unique to the female becomes a vehicle pointing to the compassion of God' (Trible 1978:38; cf. McFague 1982: 169–170).

The other image in this first answer of God to doubting Zion, is quite different: 'I have graven you on the palms of my hands' (v. 16). For many, it simply means that God keeps us in mind at all times: he sees us as though we are engraved on his hands, we are always in his sight (Cyril, Rashi, Ibn Ezra). Calvin compares it to 'having something at one's finger tips' (cf. Nicholas). Some suggest it refers to some kind of mark on the skin worn by pilgrims (cf. 44:5) (Lowth), although this was forbidden by law (Duhm). The Church Fathers saw here a reference to Christ's passion and the imprint of the nails in his hands (John 20:25–28), which meant 'security and an unbreakable wall for those who believe in him' (Cyril). This is also how Carey Landrey interprets it in his popular hymn:

> I will never forget you, my people;
> I have carved you on the palm of my hand. (*HON* 265)

The Septuagint has 'I have painted your walls on my hands' (cf. Tg), and it may be that this refers to an architect's plan (cf. Ezek 4:1), carefully drawn and held in the king's hands (Blenkinsopp). This would be confirmed by the reading 'your builders' (*bonayik*) in the next verse: 'your builders shall outstrip your destroyers' (RSV; cf. 1QIsaᵃ LXX, Vg). As the prophecy that Jerusalem would be rebuilt with miraculous speed was never fulfilled, it fits better the rapid triumph of the Church over the 'kings of the earth who formerly persecuted her' (Augustine, *Letter to the Catholics on the Donatists* 7.16). The three verses (vv. 14–16) taken together are set to music by several German composers, including Thomas Selle in a motet for five voices beginning *Zion spricht* (Zion speaks) (Berges 2012: 123). There is a Scottish metrical paraphrase of verses 13–17 beginning 'Ye heav'ns send forth your song of praise'.

The building theme is less obvious in MT which has 'your sons (*banayik*) shall make haste' (v. 17), suggesting a scene of children running home to their mother after the danger is past (AV, Rashi, Ibn Ezra, Childs), an image picked up from verse 15 and developed in the next few verses (vv. 18–23). Dejected Zion is invited to lift up her eyes and see for herself that her children are coming back to her (v. 18): a great number of children brought up in the Christian faith, worn as ornaments, that is, the true splendour of the Church, rather than the painted tables, statues, costly garments and precious stones of the papists (Calvin; cf. Gregory, *Morals on Job* 27.38; Bede, *Homilies on the Gospels* 1.24). The numbers returning will be so huge that there will not be enough room for them in the land (v. 19). Zion still cannot believe that her fortunes have changed: in the language of a destitute widow ('bereaved … barren … put away … alone') she asks 'Where have they come from?' (v. 21).

God's answer is that the nations of the world will bring them back at his command (v. 22). The coming of the nations to Zion was foretold in an earlier prophecy (Isa 2:3) (Cyril): now they are to bring the exiles back with them, carrying them in their arms or on their backs. The 'signal' (v. 22) must be the resurrection of Christ from the dead, 'the root of Jesse as an ensign to the peoples' (Isa 11:10) (Jerome), and the preaching of the apostles who lead others into the Church of God and instruct them in their infancy (1 Cor 3:2) (Eusebius; cf. Calvin). The role of the nations in the redemption of Zion's children is made more explicit in the image of kings serving as childminders and queens as wet nurses (v. 23), a figurative expression for the great honour that will be shown to Israel (Ibn Ezra) or to the Church (Cyril, Eusebius). According to some commentators, citing examples of ancient Near Eastern protocol, the same is true of the next sentence: 'with their faces to the ground they shall bow to you and lick the dust of your feet' (Lowth, Blenkinsopp). Others find the image offensive and omit it as a late gloss (Duhm). However that may be, the verse ends with the statement that 'those who wait for the Lord' will not suffer such humiliation. For Christians it acknowledges that the Queen (the Church) will feed Christ's little ones and lead them to maturity, but also that kings and queens will support the church with earthly works and lick the dust of her feet, that is, 'lap up its word' (Jerome).

The first part of verse 23 features in the final chorus of Handel's well-known anthem 'My Heart Is Inditing' (HWV 261) (*BiM* 163–164), composed for the coronation of George II and Queen Caroline in 1727. The words are derived from an anthem composed by Purcell for the coronation of James II in 1685, but whereas in the Purcell text, the Isaiah verse follows a call to 'Praise the Lord, O Jerusalem, Praise thy God, O Sion' (Ps 147:12), and clearly implies that kings and queens must serve the Church (Sion), as 'nursing fathers' and 'nursing mothers', in Handel's anthem there is no reference to Sion, and it becomes instead a celebration of the king's supremacy over other kings and queens. The anthem appears in the final chorus of Handel's oratorio *Esther* (1718) (*BiM* 78).

The chapter concludes with another objection: 'Shall the prey be taken from the mighty?' (v. 24). The speaker could be Zion again (cf. vv. 14, 21), but this is not stated and some assume it is Israel speaking (Ibn Ezra). There is a strong case for reading 'captives of a tyrant' (RSV; Heb. *'ariṣ* cf. 1QIsaᵃ, Vg, *Pesh*) instead of 'lawful captive' (AV, Heb *ṣaddiq*). God's robust reply is addressed to Zion (feminine singular) and begins by saying that no human tyrants can stand up to him: 'I will contend with them and save your children' (v. 25). 'Christ came into the house of the strong man … and transmitted the victory to us, as Paul says, "I can do all things through Christ who gives me strength" (Phil 4:13), making it possible for us to plunder the strong man, or the 'giant', namely Satan' (Cyril).

Commenting on verse 26, Jewish commentators envisage God leaving the flesh of the wicked to the beasts of the field and the birds of the air, 'so that the beasts of the field will be drunk with their blood' (Tg; cf. Rashi). Some think of desperate siege conditions which can lead to cannibalism (cf. Deut 28:47–57; 2 Kgs 6:24–31; Lam 2:20; 4:10). God will send a dividing spirit among the Babylonians so they will bite and devour their own kith and kin (Henry). The sudden change to 'all flesh shall know' (cf. Isa 40:5) highlights the contrast between humanity, torn to pieces by suffering and slaughter, and the Lord God, who is above it all, your Saviour and your Redeemer, the 'Mighty One of Jacob' (Eusebius, Calvin).

I Hid Not My Face from Shame and Spitting (Isa 50:1–11)

The formula 'Thus says the Lord' continues the dialogue from the previous chapter (Isa 49:14–26), trying to convince Zion's children that they have not been abandoned by God (vv. 1–3). He asks them 'Where is your mother's bill of divorce?'(Deut 24:1–4; Mark 10:2–4) and says that though their mother may seem to have been abandoned, that was not because I divorced her: it was because she chose to leave me (Cyril, Eusebius, Calvin, Lowth). Luther sees it as

Isaiah Through the Centuries, First Edition. John F. A. Sawyer.
© 2018 John Wiley & Sons Ltd. Published 2020 by John Wiley & Sons Ltd.

an attack on the Jews, who are like a woman whose unfaithful behaviour is all the worse because she is still married. On the apparent contradiction between Isaiah and Jeremiah, who says the Lord had 'sent her away with a decree of divorce' (Jer 3:8), Ibn Ezra explains that Jeremiah was speaking about the ten tribes that have already been destroyed (Amos 5:2) while Isaiah is speaking about Judah, the kingdom of the house of David, which will be restored by the Messiah. The second image is of a man in such desperate traits that he has to sell his children to survive (cf. 2 Kgs 4:1; Neh 5:1–5). Again the prophet rejects this: it was not God's fault that the people had been sold into slavery, they were 'sold under sin' (Rom 7:14) (Jerome, Cyril, Calvin).

The prophet goes on (v. 2) to the familiar theme of Israel's repeated rejection of God's approaches through all his prophets (Ibn Ezra) and so many other 'signs and wonders' (Deut 4:33) (Calvin). The Church Fathers interpret God's 'I came' as 'I took flesh and became manifest to the people of Israel' (Cyril), and take 'there was no man' literally because they were not men: they were a 'brood of vipers ... dogs ... (Matt 23:33)... ...swine (Matt 7:6)', and Herod was a 'fox' (Luke 13:32) (Jerome). Although at his rebuke he 'can dry up the sea ... and make the rivers a desert', and he could have summoned 'more than twelve legions of angels' to help him (Matt 26:53), he chose to suffer death on the cross for the redemption of his people (Jerome; cf. Cyril). The drying up of the sea and making rivers into a desert refer back to the miracles of the Red Sea and the Jordan; while the clothing of the heavens in blackness (v. 3) recalls the darkness that 'covered the whole earth from the sixth to the ninth hour' on the day of the crucifixion (Matt 27:45) (Eusebius, Jerome, Nicholas) but also the day of judgement when 'the sun will be darkened and the moon will not give its light' (Matt 24:29) (Theodoret).

Jerome ends Book 13 of his great Isaiah commentary with these words and begins the next book with what is known today as the 'Third Servant Song' (Isa 50:4–9) (Duhm) (cf. Isa 42:1–4; 49:1–6; 52:13–53:12). The passage is usually taken, along with 49:1–6, as the words of the prophet, whose suffering, culminating in his martyrdom under Manasseh, was an important theme in rabbinic tradition (see comm. on Isa 6:8). Modern scholars suggest that these passages reflect the experience of 'Deutero-Isaiah', who, like Jeremiah, may have suffered at the hands of his people (Westermann, Brueggemann).

For Christians from early times every detail was fulfilled in the life of Christ, though this is not yet explicit in the New Testament. In many Christian lectionaries the passage is read on Palm Sunday (*ORM*, RCL) and refers to the Passion: 'the tongue of those who are taught' refers to the power of his mighty word to refute the Pharisees and the scribes (Justin, *Dialogue with Trypho* 102), while 'a word in season' (AV, cf. LXX) refers to his ability to know when to speak and when to remain silent, as he did before his accusers (Mark 15:5) (Cyril).

'Morning by morning' refers to the tradition that he preached in the temple early in the morning (Luke 21:38) (Henry). His courage in the face of the beating and spitting (v. 6) inflicted on him by Pilate's unholy servants (Cyril) is noted by many (Eusebius, Jerome, Theodoret). This is what Paul is referring to when he speaks of Christ 'humbling himself ... to the point of death on a cross' (Phil 2:8) (Origen, *Comm.on Matthew* 113). The specific reference to 'them that plucked off the hair' (AV v. 6), although not cited in the New Testament (Nicholas), came to be a central motif. Isidore of Seville already included it in his scriptural collage (*De Fide Catholica* 1. 29,2), and in late northern European iconography it was associated with the image of a 'sheep before its shearers' (Isa 53:7) and elaborated to the point of repugnance (Marrow 1979: 68–94). In a more genteel context, linked with Isa 53:3, it supplied the words of a poignant alto aria in Handel's *Messiah* (1742).

Many apply the words of the poem not only to Christ himself but also to his disciples. The passage describes the process by which they are 'won over by the spirit and experience enlightenment of mind ... so they can give instruction ... and clarify the divine mysteries ... in the morning, that is, at the dawning of God's spiritual light in heart and mind' (Cyril). Bernard of Clairvaux comments, 'How happy the one who said, The Lord opened my ear', and he cites 'Hear O Israel' (Deut 6:4) and Samuel's 'Speak, Lord, your servant hears' (1 Sam 3:10) as illustrations of the kind of hearing God asks for (*Sermons on Song of Songs* 28.6). The word the apostles speak has the same power as the word that parted the Red Sea (Luther).

When they are abused and shamefully treated, they must withstand all attacks with a forehead of flint (v. 7) as the servant and other prophets did (Jer 1:18; Ezek 3:9) (Calvin). This is the context in which Paul apparently cites verse 8, drawing on the same Greek legal vocabulary: 'Who shall bring any charge against God's elect? It is God who justifies' (Rom 8:31–34) (Hays 1989: 59–60). Anyone who stands up against them will 'fall apart like moth-eaten clothes' (NJB), an image that for some recalls the day of judgement when you will see the 'dead bodies of the men that have rebelled against me, for their worm shall not die' (cf. Isa 51:6) (Jerome).

Like the second servant song (Isa 49:1–6), this poem is followed by a comment on reactions to the servant's teaching, beginning 'Who among you obeys the voice of the servant?' (vv. 10–11). Some take it as a single rhetorical question implying the answer 'nobody', the familiar picture of the servant 'despised and rejected by men' (Isa 53:3), who walks in darkness, that is, ignored by his people (Ibn Ezra; cf. Tg RSV). Others divide the verse into two separate clauses and take it as a call to trust in God: 'Whoever among you fears the Lord and obeys the voice of his servant ... let him trust in the name of the Lord' (Tertullian, *Against Marcion* 4.22; Theodoret, Eusebius; cf. LXX, Vg,

Rashi, AV, NJB). The relative clause 'who walks in darkness and has no light' here describes not ignorance but the afflictions that the children of God continually suffer (Calvin; cf. Rashi, Luther). In the Jewish triennial lectionary the passage (Isa 50:10–51:11) is read with the last part of the story of Joseph and his brothers (Gen 42:18–43:13) (Mann 1971: 1.320–321). This reading of the verse figures in several hymns including one by Augustus Toplady (1740–1778), beginning 'Your harps, ye trembling saints' (*CH2* 561).

Verse 11 describes the connection between wickedness and the fire of judgement. Those who reject the servant's teaching 'kindle a fire' that will destroy them as it says 'wickedness burns like a fire and consumes briars and thorns' (Isa 9:18) (Origen, *On First Principles* 2.1.4; cf. Jerome, Rashi). The prophecy was fulfilled when the Jews rebelled against Rome and kindled a fire that consumed their city and their nation (Jerome, Vitringa). 'You shall lie down in torment' refers to death (cf. 1 Kgs 2:10) (Ibn Ezra) or to the fire that awaits the wicked after death (cf. Isa 66:24): the 'eternal fire prepared for the devil and his angels' (Matt 25:41) (Jerome; cf. Gregory of Nazianzus, *On Holy Baptism, Oration* 40.36). According to a rabbinic tradition, when the wicked complain about their treatment after death, verse 11 will be addressed to them: 'You kindled these flames yourselves … you shall lie down in torment' (*Ecclesiastes R.* 3,9,1).

Look to the Rock from Which You Were Hewn (Isa 51:1–9)

In Jewish lectionaries one of the seven consolation haftarot ends at verse 3 (Isa 49:14–51:3) (*JSB*), and verses 22–23 also appear among the consolation readings at Qumran (see comm. on Isa 40). The chapter plays a less significant role in the Christian liturgy, although some of the language and imagery has had a significant afterlife in both Jewish and Christian tradition. In modern times there is a popular Jesuit hymn which paraphrases three verses from the

Isaiah Through the Centuries, First Edition. John F. A. Sawyer.
© 2018 John Wiley & Sons Ltd. Published 2020 by John Wiley & Sons Ltd.

chapter (vv. 4, 6, 12) (see above on Isa 45:22), and the chapter has been much quoted in the context of liberation theology (Miranda 1977).

The first part is a series of three prophecies about salvation addressed to the 'good people, who believe in the words of the prophets' (Ibn Ezra) (vv. 1–8). The words 'look to the rock' recall the miracle at Horeb when the Lord said to Moses, 'Look, I will stand before you there on the rock!' and water flowed out of the rock for the people to drink (Exod 17:6) (Ibn Ezra). Figuratively the 'rock from which you were hewn' is also Abraham and the 'quarry' Sarah, who suffered birth pangs, like Zion (Isa 66:8), to be your mother (v. 2). The image of a rock from which two men were cut, Abraham and his brother Nahor, as well as their two wives, is developed in Pseudo-Philo (23:4; *OTP* 2.332). Abraham was one man, and God blessed him and gave him many descendants (v2): the Lord will do the same now for his people (Rashi). 'The Lord will comfort Zion' with the multitude of her children (Ibn Ezra). The ruins of Zion will be 'like Eden and her desert the garden of the Lord' (v. 3).

Traditionally Christian interpreters have interpreted this as a continuation of chapter 50. It begins by singling out from the audience 'those who pursue righteousness' (AV; cf. LXX, Vg; RSV 'deliverance'), a way of speaking used by Paul in his discussion of who among the Jews will be saved (Rom 9:31–32). The rock is Christ for some (1 Cor 10:4) and, for others, a foreshadowing of the rock-cut tomb of Joseph of Arimathaea that welcomed his body (Eusebius; cf. Jerome). Out of that rock will come the risen Saviour who in his Church will be the father of innumerable children, as Abraham was. It will be another miracle like the miracle of Sarah conceiving in her old age (Eusebius, Theodoret). We need the faith of Abraham and Sarah (cf. Rom 4:19): 'as he comforted and helped them, so he can promote and expand the church, no matter how sterile and forsaken and lonely it may be, even in the depths of despair' (Luther, cf. Calvin). For the Lord will comfort Zion, that is, the Church (v. 3): 'the desolate one will have more children than her that has a husband' (Isa 54:1). In Zion, it will be like a return to the garden of Eden, where saints and angels join together in songs of joy and thanksgiving (Jerome). The role of the 'well-watered garden' image in Christian hymnography and in the origins and development of the monastic movement is discussed elsewhere (see comm. on Isa 35:1–2; 58:11). Verse 3 is set to music as a contralto solo at the centre of Patten's oratorio *Isaiah* (1898) (*BiM* 112–113).

In the next prophecy (vv. 4–8) God tells his people about his plan for the world: 'a law will go forth from me and my justice for a light to the peoples' (v. 4) (cf. Isa 49:6). 'Law' (Heb. *torah*) refers to the prophet's teaching. The Masoretic Text adds, 'I will give them rest' (Heb. *argia'*; cf. Isa 28:12; Jer 50:34) (Rashi, Ibn Ezra), but many modern commentators take the word with the next verse in the sense of 'act speedily' (RSV; cf. Heb. *rega'* 'a moment' Isa 47:9; 54:8). In a midrash on the Song of Songs, it is God who is speaking and the words 'Listen to me, my people ('*ammi*)' are read as 'Listen to me, my mother' (*immi*) to illustrate how God's love for his people can be compared to a baby's love for its mother, just as elsewhere he calls Israel 'my daughter' (Ps 45:10) and 'my sister' (Cant 5:2) (*CantR* III.11). By contrast, some commentators note that this is the only passage where the Hebrew word *le'um* (nation) is used of Israel and recommend emending the two nouns to plurals, 'you peoples … you nations', and reading the prophecy as addressed not to Israel but to the gentiles (Lowth, Westermann). This time they are told to look up at the heavens and consider the earth they are standing on because they will vanish like smoke and wear out like a garment while God's salvation is stronger and sturdier even than they are (Rashi): 'my salvation will be for ever' (v. 6). The last short prophecy gives them the same assurance: do not be afraid if people reproach you and revile you, for they will be destroyed like a garment eaten by moths (cf. 50:9), while 'my righteousness will be for ever and my salvation to all generations' (vv. 7–8).

'Listen to me, listen to me, my people' (v. 4) (LXX): the repetition is to teach us that we are to listen 'with the ears of our body and the understanding of our soul' (Jerome). Many Christian commentators identify the 'law' referred to here as the new law that comes from Zion, not from Sinai (Jerome; cf. Cyril), the 'new covenant' referred to by Jeremiah (31:31–32) (Justin, *Dialogue with Trypho* 11), the 'spiritual law which is the New Testament' (Ephrem; cf. Henry). In place of 'my righteousness … my salvation' (MT, Tg, LXX, AV) in verse 5, Jerome's Latin version has 'my righteous one … my saviour', on the authority of the aged Symeon, who applied the word 'my salvation' (Heb. *yeshu'ah*) to the baby Jesus (Heb. *yeshua'*) (Luke 2:30) (cf. Isa 45:8). 'The heavens will vanish' (v. 6): God created heaven and earth with great ease and can easily make them disappear again, but his 'salvation' and his 'righteousness' will be forever (cf. Ps 102:26–27) (Theodoret; cf. Calvin). Modern research suggests reading the word *ken* (louse, gnat) as a collective noun (cf. Exod 8:13; Ps 105:31) in verse 4: 'all who dwell in it will die like gnats (*kemo ken*)' (RSV; cf. NJB 'vermin') rather than the traditional 'will die in like manner (Heb. *kemo ken*)' (AV; cf. LXX Tg, Vg). 'Fear not the reproach of men and … their revilings' (vv. 7–8): these two verses recall the last beatitude (Matt 5:11–12) (Theodoret). In 1739 Jonathan Edwards preached a series of thirty sermons on verse 8 in his church at Northampton, Massachusetts, published in 1774 as *A History of the Work of Redemption* (Edwards 1989: 111–528).

Arm of the Lord, Awake (Isa 51:10–23)

The next short prophecy (vv. 9–11) is a prayer reminiscent of some of the psalms (Ps 44:23) or of Gideon's desperate question when oppressed by the Midianites: 'where are all God's wonderful deeds which our fathers told us about?' (Judg 6:13) (Henry). It is not that the prophet seriously believed God was asleep: 'though the flesh imagines that he is asleep ... faith rises higher and lays hold on his eternal power' (Calvin). The words inspired a popular nineteenth-century hymn beginning 'Arm of the Lord, awake, awake, / Put on thy strength, the nations shake', the original words of which contained references to 'Mahomet' and 'papal superstition', omitted in later versions although not out of sympathy with the violence of the Isaiah passage (*CH2* 369) (Moffatt 1927: 123).

Traditional commentators are agreed that 'Rahab' refers to Egypt (cf. Isa 30:7; Ps 87:4) and the 'dragon' to the Pharaoh (cf. Ezek 29:3) (Rashi, Theodoret), and that the drying up of the sea so that the redeemed could pass over (vv. 9–10) refers to the story of the exodus (Exod 15) (cf. Isa 48:21; 52:11–12) (Jerome). But the myth of a cosmic battle between God and the powers of evil, represented by Rahab and the dragon, along with Yam (sea, v. 10), Tehom (deep, v. 10; cf. Gen 1:2), Leviathan (cf. Isa 27:1) and other monsters, culminating in Yahweh's victory and enthronement as king (Pss 74:12–17; 93; 95–99), could also be applied to victory over the Assyrians (Theodoret), as well as to Christ's redeeming victory over sin and death (Jerome). The reference to a procession of God's people back to Zion (v. 11) appears first in Isa 35:10 where it concludes a description of a *via sacra* (Holy Way) through the desert, and functions as the literary climax to chapters 1–35. Here it is to be taken with 'Awake, awake' (v. 9), linking the miraculous crossing of the Red Sea with the return of the exiles to Zion (cf. Isa 48:21; 52:11–12) (Rashi, Ibn Ezra). Christian commentators see a reference to the saints processing to the heavenly Jerusalem (Heb 12:22) crowned with victory garlands like winners at the games (Eusebius).

The next prophecy (vv. 12–16), beginning 'I, I am the one who comforts you', is the first part of another of the 'consolation' haftarot (Isa 51:12–52:12) (see comm. on Isa 40). Ibn Ezra hears the voice of the prophet here, saying to his people, 'Have you forgotten the Lord your maker ...?' (v. 12). But most are agreed that these are the words of God, reminiscent of His words to Israel at Sinai (ExodR XXIX.9), and of words from the Book of Law (Lev. 26:9) which comforts Israel in times of distress, for 'if the Law had not been my delight, I would have perished in my affliction' (Ps 119:92; cf. Lam 3:21) (*PesK* 19.33). This is the 'God of all comfort who comforts us in all our affliction' (2 Cor 1:3–4) (Jerome, Aquinas). When you look up at the heavens and see his handiwork (cf. v. 6), what is there to be afraid of? (Eph 2:10) (Calvin). 'He who is bowed down' (v. 14), that is, captive in an oppressor's prison, will be freed and fed properly, unlike Micaiah (1 Kgs 22:27) and Jeremiah (Jer 37:21) (Ibn Ezra). The reference is to Cyrus freeing the captives in Babylon, but also to Christ who 'will not leave my soul in hell' (Ps 16:10 AV) (Jerome, Aquinas). God's control of the sea (v. 15) is described in terms of 'stirring up' (cf. Job 26:12) (RSV, Rashi), understood by some as a reference to the Exodus (AV 'divided'; cf. Calvin), and, by others, figuratively, as power to still the roar of suffering and oppression (Ibn Ezra). The juxtaposition in these two verses shows that, in God's eyes, giving someone bread to eat is as wonderful a marvel as dividing the Red Sea (*PesR* 33.5).

'I have put my words in your mouth' (v. 16) refers to the inspiration of prophets in all ages (cf. Jer 1:9) (Jerome, Calvin). Christians apply it to the disciples who are told not to be 'anxious about what to say ... because it is not you who speak but the spirit of your Father speaking through you' (Matt 10:19) (Eusebius), and also to Christ's claim that his teaching was not his own but came from his Father in heaven (John 7:16) (Nicholas). 'Planting the heavens' (MT; AV) means restoring the nations to their former happiness (Ibn Ezra) or perhaps 'making the people as numerous as the stars of the heavens ...' (Tg; cf. Gen 22:17). For Christians it refers to the repairing of the whole world, which had been ruined by the fall of man: this will be achieved through the agency of the Church and her ministers, named at the end as 'my people Zion' (Calvin; cf. Nicholas).

Following this reference to 'Zion' (v. 16), Jerusalem is addressed as a woman, in another dialogue beginning 'Rouse yourself, rouse yourself' (vv. 17–23; cf. Isa 49:14–26). Combined with another verse (Isa 60:1) the words are addressed to the Sabbath in 'Lekha Dodi' (see comm. on Isa 52:1–2). Her plight is compared to that of a woman overwhelmed first by drunkenness (v. 17) and second by being deserted by all her loved ones (vv. 18–20) (Luther). She has drunk from the cup of God's wrath (cf. Jer 25:15–16; cf. Ps 75:8) (Jerome, Theodoret). Or it could refer to a bitter medicine: 'the physician of souls applies vengeance to the soul to purge out disease' (Eusebius). On the notion of a twofold calamity (v. 19; cf. Isa 47:9), Theodoret remarks that a fall (LXX; RSV 'devastation') need not be accompanied by injury or destruction, while famine in a besieged city combined with military defeat constitutes a terrible double chastisement. God's question 'By whom [or How] will I comfort you?' (v. 19 AV) implies there is no one else he can point to who is suffering the same fate (Ibn Ezra). To avoid the anthropomorphism the text is frequently emended to 'Who will comfort you?' (RSV; cf. LXX, Vg, 1QIsaᵃ). The Targum has 'There is no one to comfort you but me.' After a reference to her sons fainting and lying in the street, the 'antelope in a net' (v. 20) (or 'wild bull' AV; cf. Rashi) adds the familiar notion of captivity to the description of Zion's plight (cf. Isa 42:7; 49:9), although at the expense of realism (Duhm). The Septuagint has an entirely different image: 'like a half-cooked beetroot', a reference to the indolence and laxness of one who 'floats between vices and virtues' (Jerome; cf. Theodoret).

The chapter ends with the announcement that the Lord, who 'pleads the cause of his people', has taken the cup of wrath from her and put it into the hands of her tormentors (vv. 21–23). This also is included in the anthology of consolation texts found at Qumran (see comm. on Isa 40). It recalls Zion's terrible humiliation in graphic language associated with the well-documented practices of victorious ancient Near Eastern military leaders (v. 23; cf. Josh 10:24) (Lowth). The image of bodies being stamped upon in the street found its way into late medieval representations of Christ's Passion (cf. Isa 50:6; 53:7) (Marrow 1979: 80). But Gregory the Great prefers the image of the 'soul' (AV; cf. LXX, Vg), that refuses to bend down to what is low but 'stands upright with its mind on the things of heaven so that evil spirits have no power over it' (*Forty Gospel Homilies*, 31.7).

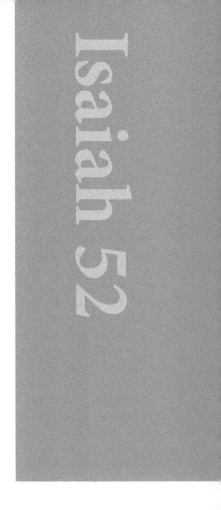

The Lord Has Comforted His People (Isa 52:1–12)

The first two verses are a continuation of the dialogue with Zion (vv. 1–2; cf. 51:17–23). She is encouraged to get up, shake off the dust and bonds of slavery, and, like a queen, put on fine garments and take her proper place on a throne. In Isa 51:9 the 'arm of the Lord' is called upon to 'awake, awake', and here the people are summoned to respond in 'joyous faith' (Oswalt). Verses 1–3 are among the 'comfort passages' listed at Qumran (see comm. on Isa 40) and

Isaiah Through the Centuries, First Edition. John F. A. Sawyer.
© 2018 John Wiley & Sons Ltd. Published 2020 by John Wiley & Sons Ltd.

alluded to, along with other passages from Isaiah's consolation prophecies (cf. Isa 40:5; 51:17; 54:3; 60:1; 62:5), in the popular sixteenth-century poem 'Lekha Dodi', traditionally sung to welcome in the Sabbath at sunset on Friday (*ADPB* 266–271; *BiM* 144). A musical setting of verse 1 features in Penderecki's choral *Symphony no.7: The Seven Gates of Jerusalem* (1996) (see comm. on Isa 26:2).

Most commentators understand the verses as addressed to the exiles in Babylon and apply the image of a queen, restored to her former glory, to the rebuilding of Jerusalem when they return from exile (Henry, Duhm, Westermann). For Ibn Ezra the prophecy goes beyond that and looks to the future when the Messiah will come, because only then will the city be free of the 'uncircumcised and the unclean'. Others apply it to the Church and a time when the 'uncircumcised and unclean', that is, irreligious people who corrupt the worship of God, will not be admitted (Calvin, Oecolampadius). The term 'holy city', rare in the Bible (see on Isa 48:2; cf. Neh 11:1, 18), describes a city free from ritual defilement caused by foreigners entering the sanctuary (Ezek 44:9; Ps 79:1) and made holy by the presence of God (v. 8). To Christian commentators it recalls the 'new Jerusalem coming down from heaven prepared as a bride for her husband' (Rev 21:2) and a church that is 'washed of every impurity and cleansed of every blemish ... and fortified with the grace of Christ against the assaults of the devil' (Cyril). It was the 'holy city' only after the resurrection (Matt 27:53) (Jerome).

In verse 2 the Targum explains the rather awkward 'Arise, sit down' (AV; LXX, Vg Heb. *shevi*) by inserting the words 'on the throne of glory' (cf. Rashi) and subsequent translations include 'ascend thy lofty seat' (Lowth) and 'sit enthroned' (Childs). Others read 'arise, O captive' (RSV, NJB; Heb. *sheviyyah*). The 'bonds' that held Jerusalem captive (cf. Isa 42:7; 49:9) may originally have referred to the chains of the Babylonian captivity, but for many down the ages they refer to the slavery of sin (cf. Prov 5:22) (Eusebius, Cyril, Aquinas), from which the gospel of Christ has rescued his people: 'If the Son makes you free, you shall be free indeed' (John 8:36) (Cyril). For some Christians it refers to the day when we will shake off the mortality of the flesh like dust (Tertullian, *On the Resurrection* 18), and, in Paul's words, 'put on the Lord Jesus Christ' (Rom 13:14), the 'most fitting garment for every holy person' (Cyril).

Verses 3–6 were treated as a 'late insertion' by many modern scholars, partly because they appear to be in prose unlike the rest of the passage (cf. RSV, NJB) and partly because they contain the only mention of the Assyrians in Isaiah 40–66 (Duhm, Westermann). More recently, however, its relevance in its present context has been appreciated (Beuken, Childs). The prophet seeks to encourage the exiles with three arguments: first, since nothing was paid when they were 'sold' into slavery, it will cost nothing to redeem them (cf. Isa 50:1), and, second, since Israel went down to Egypt of their own free will (Gen 46), there is no reason why the Assyrians (or the Babylonians) should oppress them because they have already paid the penalty (Kimḥi); and, third, since the sufferings of God's people make it look as though he is powerless and bring disgrace upon his name, he is bound to act. Jewish tradition associates this passage with the story of Joseph in Egypt (Gen 39–40; cf. Isa 29:8–19) (Mann 1971: 1,298–1,301). A modern interpretation of these verses (3–5) by an economist and former director of the international charity Christian Aid finds scriptural authority here for an emphasis on economic factors in biblical visions of a messianic age of justice and peace (C. Elliot 1985: 119f).

For Jerome and others 'redeemed without money' (v. 3) foretells the Church's doctrine of unmerited grace, that is to say, redemption by the precious blood of Christ, not by the payment of any money (Augustine, *Tractates on John* 41.4.3), and the 'howling oppressors' (v. 5) are the crowds shouting with one voice 'Crucify him! Crucify him!' (John 19:15) (cf. Eusebius). Paul cites this verse, with heavy irony, to shame the Jews for breaking their law (Rom 2:24; Grenholm and Patte 2000: 81).

The intimate anthropomorphism of verses 5–6 is striking. God says 'What am I doing here when my people are in need of my help? I will show them. I will say to them *hinneni* "Here I am!"' This is the first of three passages, unique to Isaiah, in which God uses a formula far more familiar from Isaiah's call vision (Isa 6) and normally associated with human beings offering their services to God (e.g. Gen 22:1,11; Exod 3:4; 1 Sam 3) than the other way round (see comm. on 58:9). Many commentators miss the significance of these words, but not all. Kimḥi adds, 'as I always have been, even when my people did not recognize me during the exile. I never change.' The divine 'Here I am' (v. 6) assumes special significance in the hands of Christian commentators. Some put a devotional slant on the words and stress the notion of the presence of God in prayer (Henry, Jones). Many understand the words as spoken by Christ (see on Isa 58:9; 65:1). Cyril, following the Septuagint, takes 'here am I' with the first few words of the next verse: 'therefore he [Christ] says, "Here I am like springtime upon the mountains": when the Only-Begotten appeared in the flesh … withered souls were brought back to life in him' (cf. Cant 2:10–12).

The next short passage (vv. 7–12) celebrates the news of victory, peace and divine triumph in language and imagery familiar from earlier chapters, particularly 35 and 49. At Qumran the passage was given an eschatological interpretation: the mountains are the prophets … the messenger is the Anointed One (11Q13.2; *DSSE* 533; Blenkinsopp 2006: 96–98). *Mashmia' yeshu'ah* ('announcing victory' JPS) is the title of one of Abravanel's three commentaries on messianic prophecy (cf. Isa 12:3) (Borodowski 2003: 6–7) and appeared with 'announcing happiness, heralding good fortune' on an Israeli postmark on 18 August 1967, the day after the Fast of the Ninth of Ab (see comm. on Isa 40) (Plate 34).

PLATE 34 'Announcing happiness, heralding good fortune, announcing victory'
(Isa 52:7 (JPS)). Israeli postmark (Jerusalem, August 1967). Reproduced with kind
permission of Israel Philatelic Society, Israel Postal Company.

A number of Jewish songs and hymns have been inspired by verse 7, including a
modern Israeli setting in Hebrew beginning *Ma navu* (1975). Verse 8 figures in the
Sabbath morning Torah Service alongside Isa 40:5 (*ADPB* 410–411).
The 'watchmen' are the prophets and seeing 'eye to eye' means that the spirit of
true prophecy, which ceased after the death of Haggai, Zechariah and Malachi,
will be restored (Kimḥi). In a new exodus (vv. 11–12), Israel will leave their place
of exile, peacefully, without fear of attack from their former oppressors, and bearing 'the vessels of the Lord' (v. 11), which means acts of divine loving kindness
and compassion, rather than swords and spears (Kimḥi).

In Christian tradition the verse beginning 'How beautiful are the feet' (cf.
Nah 1:15) is quoted or alluded to three times in the New Testament (Acts 10:36;
Rom 10:15; Eph 6:15). There is only one bringer of good news in the original
text as in the ancient versions and parallels (Isa 41:27; Nah 1:15; cf. Isa 40:9),
and some take it as a reference to the coming of Christ: 'Peace I leave with you,
my peace I give to you' (John 14:27) (Chrysostom, *Homilies on Matthew* 32:6;
cf. Cyril). But most follow Paul in reading the plural and seeing in the verse a
reference to preachers in general or the apostles in particular. Indeed the

Church Fathers tell us it refers to the washing of the disciples' feet at the Last Supper: 'once the feet of those proclaiming good news were ... washed and cleansed by Jesus' hands, they were able to walk on the holy way and travel on the One who said, "I am the Way"' (John 14:6) (Origen, *Comm. on John* 32.77–82; cf. Theodoret, Eusebius, Jerome). John Milton contrasted the beauty of the naked feet in this verse, 'shod with the equipment of the Gospel of peace' (Eph 6:15), with the 'gaudy glisterings' of the vestments worn by catholic priests who 'forsake the heavenly teaching of St Paul (Eph 6:15) for the hellish sophistry of Papism' (*The Reason of Church-Government Urged against Prelaty*, Patterson 1931: 247).

Among many musical interpretations of the verse, pride of place must go to the famous soprano aria 'How Beautiful Are the Feet of Them that Preach the Gospel of Peace' (Rom 10:15 AV) in Handel's *Messiah* (1742). The interpretation closely follows Paul and comes between choral settings of two verses from the Psalms: 'The Lord gave the word; great was the company of the preachers' (Ps 68:11) and 'Their sound is gone out into all lands, and their words unto the ends of the world' (Ps 19:4), the second of which is quoted by Paul in the same context (Rom 10:18). The three verses together beautifully provided authority and inspiration for the work of evangelical preachers in eighteenth-century England and no doubt contributed to the huge success of the aria, as well as the rest of Handel's *Messiah*, in churches and chapels throughout the land. Mention should also be made of Mendelssohn's lively choral setting of Paul's version of the text near the beginning of the second half of his oratorio *St Paul* (1836).

A popular modern hymn begins 'How lovely on the mountains' and has the refrain 'Our God reigns' (v. 7) (*HON* 224). A longer version by the same composer combines the passage with the Suffering Servant poem that follows (Isa 52:13–53:12) (*HON* 223). Isaac Watts' 'How Beauteous Are Their Feet' (1704) is also a paraphrase of verses 7–10, and Fanny Crosby's 'How Lovely on the Mountain' (1901), inspired no doubt by the words 'without money' in verse 3, combines them with the first verse of chapter 55. These three hymns all have the plural, following Paul. But an unusual interpretation appears in a hymn beginning 'In the crimson of the morning' by the American Presbyterian Lyman Whitney Allen. Not only does he go back to the singular of the original Isaiah, but he suggests that it was the sound of the messenger's feet approaching the waiting city that was beautiful, rather than what they looked like: 'I listen for the coming of his feet ... the sorrow ... the music ... the glory of the coming of his feet' (*HCL* 211).

The watchmen on the city walls will be the first to see for themselves ('eye to eye') the Lord returning to Zion (v. 8) (Rashi, Ibn Ezra). What they actually saw was the messenger approaching with the good news that Babylon had fallen (Aquinas, Lowth, Childs). The passage inspired a tenor solo in Bach's cantata

Wachet Auf (1599) (*BiM* 261) and an aria sung by the angel Gabriel in Elgar's oratorio *The Apostles* (1903) (*BiM* 18). It also provides the choral finale of Robert Starer's cantata *Ariel: Visions of Isaiah* (1963) (*BiM* 19).

For Luther, like Paul, the watchmen are ministers of the Word, pastors, stewards and bishops who have nothing but a voice with which 'harmoniously they proclaim joyful news' (cf. Cyril, Eusebius, Nicholas). 'The waste places of Jerusalem' means the whole city, which had been lying in ruins (Henry). Alternatively it was specifically the 'waste places' that are addressed (v. 9), that is, the poor who have good news preached to them (Matt 11:5): 'this kingdom belongs exclusively to those in tribulation' (Luther). 'The Lord has bared his holy arm before the eyes of all the nations' (v. 10) was quoted by Leo the Great in relation to the coming of the Magi to Bethlehem on the Feast of Epiphany when Christ first appeared to the world (*Sermon* 36.1). The general vision of 'the salvation of our God' reaching to the ends of the earth appears frequently in early Christian literature (Luke 2:30; 3:6; cf. Gal 1:16) (Theodoret, Eusebius).

The call to 'depart, depart, go out from there' (vv. 11–12) is addressed to those 'who bear the vessels of the Lord', that is, the people of God, bearers of the Law (Ibn Ezra). They are to leave their place of exile, purify themselves and set out, not 'in haste' as the Israelites did from Egypt (Exod 12:11; Deut 16:3) but in an orderly fashion as they did from Sinai (Num 10:11), with God as their leader and their rearguard (Num 10:25) (Rashi). Most commentators assume this is addressed to the exiles in Babylon (Nicholas, Calvin). Only Ibn Ezra argues that 'from there' is not specific, and that, as Babylon is not referred to by name in these chapters (cf. 48:20), we should take it as a call to exiles all over the world. Christians interpret it as a call to depart from the realm of sin and unbelief (2 Cor 6:17) (Origen, *Homilies on Leviticus* 11.1.5; cf. Aquinas, Luther). 'You who bear the vessels of the Lord', that is, priests and Levites, means all Christians who are called 'a royal priesthood' (1 Pet 2:9) and who carry the 'vessels' in their bodies, which are themselves 'temples of God' (1 Cor 6:19) (Calvin). Augustine uses this text in a discussion of how to avoid sin in our hearts without distancing ourselves from sinners who might profit from our company (*Sermon* 88.23, 25).

The Suffering Servant (Isa 52:13–53:12)

1QIsa[a] starts a new page at verse 13: 'Behold my Servant shall prosper'. At the same point Luther says 'Here we begin Chapter 53', and in some Greek and Latin manuscripts there is a heading such as *De Christi passione et glorificatione*. Ibn Ezra also ignores the chapter division, as do Calvin, Oecolampadius, Matthew Henry, Luzzatto and most modern scholars, who take the last three verses of chapter 52 with Chapter 53 as a single composition, known since Duhm as the 'Fourth Servant Song' (cf. 42:1–4; 49:1–6; 50:4–9). The passage is conspicuous by its absence from Jewish lectionaries, in which one haftarah ends at 52:12 and another begins at 54:1 (*JSB*). The striking omission is no doubt due to the dominant Christological interpretation of the passage (*RA* 544). William of Bourges (d. 1209), a convert from Judaism, recalls how as a child he was told to avoid it because it drew Jews away from the Law (*NCHB* 2.624).

The servant of the Lord here is not named as he is elsewhere (Isa 41:8; 44:1; 48:20; 49:3), but the fact that the people Israel are addressed in the passage immediately preceding the poem (52:11–12) as well as in the passage following it (54:1) suggests that the servant is Israel and his sufferings include the deaths of Jewish martyrs at the hand of gentiles (Rashi, Ibn Ezra). The larger context (52:13–56:8) is about the final exile of Israel and their future redemption (Luzzatto). This is the traditional Jewish interpretation, which was accepted by Andrew of St Victor (Smalley 1983: 164; *NCHB* 2.631). The Targum identifies the servant quite differently, however, by inserting the word 'Messiah' in verse 13, and, from the first century CE at the latest, the passage played a crucial role in the tradition of a suffering messiah (Rom 15:21; *Mart.Is.* 3:21; *OTP* 2.162–163) (Laato 2012).

Jewish suggestions for the identity of the Servant as an individual in this passage include a prophet like Moses (b*Soṭah* 14a), Jeremiah (Saadiya; cf. Jer 1:6; 11:19; 18:20; 40:5) (Driver and Neubauer 1877: 19, 152–154) and King Josiah (Abravanel) (Driver and Neubauer 1877: 187–197). Ibn Ezra argues that the servant is the prophet (cf. Isa 42:1; 49:6), in particular the author of chapters 40–66 (U. Simon 1985: 257–271). Bernhard Duhm proposed an unnamed rabbi with leprosy from the Second Temple period. Karl Barth suggests he may well be both an individual and the people, 'introduced as the partner of Yahweh in an eschatological encounter with the nations, the powerful witness of Yahweh in the midst of the nations' (*ChDogm* IV,1,29). There are many difficulties in the Hebrew text, described as 'unintelligible' in several places by commentators. This no doubt reflects uncertainty as to what it is about, and perhaps the 'opacity' that has generated so much debate was to some extent intentional (Clines 1976: 33). For present purposes it must suffice to listen to a small selection from innumerable interpretations of this unique passage. Every verse is of enormous exegetical interest.

The first three verses of the poem contain a summary of the story, beginning with a reference to its triumphant ending: 'he will be exalted and glorified exceedingly' (LXX; cf. Phil 2:8–9) (Eusebius). 'At the end of days' the righteous among God's people will prosper (v. 13) (Rashi). The Hebrew text can also be rendered 'shall deal prudently' (AV; cf. LXX, Ibn Ezra), a reference to the spirit of wisdom resting upon the Messiah (Isa 11:2) (Henry) or to the child Jesus in

Nazareth 'filled with wisdom' (Luke 2:40) (Eusebius). The relationship between practical wisdom and success was noted by Jesus when he advised his disciples to be 'wise as serpents' (Matt 10:16) (Luther). 'He will be exalted and lifted up and shall be very high' (LXX 'he will be glorified') refers to Christ's resurrection and ascension to heaven (cf. Ps 68:8; Eph 4:8–10 (Aquinas; cf. Nicholas; Isidore, *De Fide Catholica* 1.56.6). The phrase 'high and lifted up' tells us the Servant is God (cf. Isa 6:1; 57:15) (Cyril, Ephrem).

But first he must be rejected and humbled (v. 14) (cf. Phil 2:6–11) (Calvin). So disfigured was he by the 'shame and spitting' (Isa 50:6), the scourging and the crown of thorns, that he looked more like a worm than a man (Ps 22:6; cf. Isa 41:14) (Aquinas, Henry). Christian commentators say the 'astonished' onlookers are the Jews who could not believe such a helpless figure could be their Messiah, even though Isaiah had made it plain to them (cf. Isa 6:9) (Eusebius, Calvin). Medieval Jewish commentators applied the verse to racist attitudes towards them in their own day. These are the words of people who think Jews look strange and imagine that they are different from their fellow creatures: 'do they have eyes and mouths like the rest of us' (Ibn Ezra, Kimhi). When they say 'their form is beyond that of the sons of men', it is because they think their features are darker than those of other people (Rashi).

'He shall sprinkle many nations' (v. 15 AV) means 'he will scatter them' (Tg) or 'sprinkle their blood' (Ibn Ezra). The verb (Heb. *yazzeh*) is used with blood in a variety of contexts (Lev 6:20; cf. 2 Kgs 9:33; Isa 63:3). Some suggest that 'sprinkling' here refers to 'speaking, preaching' (cf. Ezek 21:2 AV) (Kimhi), a 'Hebraism' used by Peter (1 Pet 1:2) according to Luther (cf. Calvin). But an alternative explanation, supported by the Septuagint and accepted by most modern commentators, is 'he will make them jump' or 'give them a great shock' (Luzzatto; cf. RSV). This is confirmed by the context (vv. 14–15), which is about the amazement of people who look at Jews with such disdain at present and cannot believe Israel will ever be delivered (Ibn Ezra).

For many Christians it is about ritual cleansing (cf. Lev 14:7): he will cleanse the nations with his blood (cf. 1 Pet 1:2) or consecrate them to the service of God with the water of baptism (Heb 10:22) (Jerome; cf. Aquinas). The 'many nations' gives the verse a global context, welcomed by missionaries, as the following verse from a nineteenth-century hymn, contemporary with 'Fling Out the Banner' (see comm. on Isa 13:2), nicely illustrates:

> Saviour, sprinkle many nations,
> Fruitful let thy sorrows be;
> By thy pains and consolation
> Draw the Gentiles unto thee. (*EH* 551; *CH2* 382)

Moses' teaching dropped like gentle rain on one nation (Deut 32:2), Christ's on many nations (Henry). Paul cites the verse in the context of ensuring that the gospel is preached to all those who have not yet heard it (Rom 15:33). For Luther it is a celebration of the ultimate exaltation of Christ, the King before whom all other kings will be ashamed and shut their mouths (Luther).

The Suffering Servant (cont'd) (Isa 53:1–12)

Even if, as most believe, the original composition beginning at 52:13 has been interrupted by the present chapter division, the change of speaker provides an appropriate introduction to a new prophecy, linked to the previous one but independent (Whybray). The peoples of the world, referred to in the previous chapter ('many nations' 52:15), are now the speakers telling the story of the suffering servant with their interpretation of what it means to them. The chapter

Isaiah Through the Centuries, First Edition. John F. A. Sawyer.
© 2018 John Wiley & Sons Ltd. Published 2020 by John Wiley & Sons Ltd.

ends with an oracle in which God announces that his servant will be rewarded after his death because 'he bore the sin of many and made intercession for the transgressors' (v. 12).

It begins with a rhetorical question: 'Who has believed what we have heard?'. The nations of the world look at Israel and say, If we had not seen it for ourselves, we would not have believed it (Rashi) (v. 1). The Lord has revealed his greatness and his glory to Israel (Ibn Ezra). For Christian commentators from the beginning the implication of the two questions is that many people, especially among the Jews, did not believe in Christ even when 'the arm of the Lord was revealed' to them in the signs and wonders he performed (John 12:37–38; Rom 10:16; cf. Eusebius, Luther, Calvin). For Augustine the 'arm of the Lord' is Christ, who guides his people and leads them in the way of truth (cf. John 14:6; Ps 86:11) (*Sermon* 363.2; cf. Cyril, Aquinas).

The humble origins of God's people are described in the words 'He grew up before him like a young plant ... he had no form or comeliness' (v. 2) (Rashi). 'Before him' refers to God who watched over him as he grew up (Luzzatto). This repeats what has been said already in the previous chapter (Ibn Ezra) and some modern scholars relocate Isa 52:14b between verses 2 and 3 (Duhm). The root of a beautiful tree has no beauty although it contains within itself the potentiality for great beauty: so the prophet describes one who was spat upon, flogged, crucified and despised, and now you have the tree to look upon which has sprung up from that root and fills the whole world (Augustine, *Sermon* 44.1–2). The servant's disfigured countenance (L. *aspectus*) explains the choice of this verse to accompany the sixth Station of the Cross (Veronica wipes Christ's face) in a nineteenth-century Dutch Church (Sawyer 1996: 91–92). For Karl Barth the verse speaks of the true beauty of Christ, revealed in the self-abasing love of the servant (*ChDogm* II.1 665). The Targum suggests that his countenance will be holy, unlike that of any ordinary man. For some, verse 2 also recalls the 'stump of Jesse', and the 'dry ground' refers to the virgin birth (Eusebius, Jerome, Aquinas, Henry) (see comm. on Isa 11:1). This is how the verse is interpreted in the *Bible Moralisée*.

The 'physical pains' and 'sickness' in verses 3 and 4 (Matt 8:17 LXX, Vg) originally referred to the troubles that Israel had to suffer in exile (Luzzatto). They were like someone smitten by a terrible disease, leprosy according to Jerome (cf. Duhm), and covered themselves up in 'intense shame' not wanting people to see them (Rashi). Ibn Ezra reads 'as one from whom men hide their faces' (cf. LXX, Vg, AV, RSV), and, in another reference to contemporary anti-Semitism, comments, 'People turn away from a Jew in case they might have to help him' (cf. Isa 52:14).

The 'man of sorrows' (v. 3), also known as the *Imago Pietatis*, became one of the most familiar images in late medieval and renaissance Christian iconography.

It is a representation of the upper part of Christ's body, soon after the crucifixion, his hands crossed in front of him displaying his wounds, still alive and gazing at the viewer, or in some cases his head slumped on one side in death (Puglisi and Barcham 2013) (Plate 35). The term goes back to Jerome's Latin phrase *vir dolorum*, later translated into English in the Wycliffe Bible (1395). At that time 'sorrows' included physical pain, but taken up by the King James version (1611) the picture of 'a man of sorrows and acquainted with grief' changed from one of physical pain to one of sadness and deep sorrow (Sawyer 2013). In a sermon preached to comfort the bereaved at a funeral in 1627, John Donne described Christ as the one who 'fulfils in himself all types and images and prophecies of sorrows, who was (as the prophet calls him) *vir dolorum*' (Potter and Simpson 1956: 6.248), and in Handel's *Messiah* (1741), the 'man of sorrows' suffers scorn and mockery but little physical pain. In his commentary

PLATE 35   'Man of Sorrows (*Imago Pietatis*)' (cf. Isa 53:3). Oil painting by Giovanni Bellini (1460–1469) in the Museo Poldi Pezzoli, Milan.

on the verse Matthew Henry records the tradition that Jesus was never seen to smile (cf. Matt 26:38; Jerome).

'Man of Sorrows' in today's English is not a very appropriate title for the very physical *Imago Pietatis*, and in fact it was not until the late nineteenth-century that German art historians made the connection: before that neither the German term *Schmerzensmann*, which goes back to Luther's *voller Schmerzen und Krankheit* 'filled with pain and illness', nor the English 'Man of Sorrows' was used as an iconographic formula (Puglisi and Barcham 2013: 50). Modern scholars acknowledge the inaccuracy of the familiar phrase from the AV, and alternative translations include 'a man of suffering and acquainted with infirmity' (NRSV) and 'a man who suffered, no stranger to sickness' (Blenkinsopp), but the term survives in Hermann Melville's *Moby Dick* (1851), James Joyce *Portrait of the Artist as a Young Man* (1915) and elsewhere (*DBTEL* 476).

The physical nature of the suffering becomes still clearer in verse 4, where the 'sorrows' and 'griefs' are mentioned again, but this time along with the words 'stricken, smitten by God and afflicted'. The first term. 'stricken' (Heb. *nagua*'). is regularly applied to leprosy (Lev 13:22, 32; 2 Kgs 15:5) and is actually translated *leprosum* in the Vulgate (cf. Duhm). Leprosy sufferers by law had to 'cover their upper lip' (Lev 13:45), a practice perhaps alluded to in verse 3 'as one that hideth his face' (Lowth). According to St Bonaventure, in his *Life of St Francis*, it was this verse that prompted St Francis to 'visit lepers in their own homes, to give alms generously to them, to embrace them with the deepest compassion and to kiss their hands' (Bonaventure 2010: 5). The physical nature of the suffering continues into the next verse, which is quoted in the Gospels in relation to the healing miracles: 'he took our infirmities and bore our diseases' (Matt 8:17). Even more physical is the application of Isaiah 53 to Christ's circumcision in a scene depicted on the Klosterneuburg altar: 'Christ's flesh bore our wounds with a grievous wound' (Schiller 1971: 89).

Then the nations realize that the 'illnesses and pains' are theirs, not his, and confess their sins and their responsibility for the servant's sufferings (vv. 4–6). The first term, 'wounded' (Heb. *meholal*), implies fatal wounds (cf. *halal* 'corpse' Deut 21:1; Isa 22:2) (Ibn Ezra). In the gospel narrative the wounds, bruises and stripes mentioned here were because Christ had been 'scourged' (John 19:1), 'slapped' (Matt 26:67) and 'struck on the head with a reed' (Matt 27:30) (Eusebius).

Applied to the history of the Jewish people in exile, 'the chastisement of our peace was upon him' (v. 5 AV) means that Israel's suffering was so that there could be peace throughout the world (Rashi). So long as Israel is in exile, the gentiles will prosper, but at the time of our deliverance, there will be a time of trouble in the world (cf. Dan 12) (Ibn Ezra). They acknowledge that they have erred like lost sheep and that the Lord has laid on him their iniquity (v. 6), or the punishment for their iniquity (cf. 1 Sam 28:10; Lam 4:6) (Ibn Ezra, Kimḥi, Luzzatto).

The verb translated 'laid' in verse 6 (Vg, AV, RSV; Heb. *hipgia'*) is translated 'made intercession' in verse 12, and some commentators make that connection: the Lord shall accept the prayer of Israel that peace shall be on earth (Rashi). The Targum, which is more a paraphrase than a translation, places the emphasis on intercession, adding the word 'for his sake' (Aram. *bedileh*) three times: 'he shall pray on behalf of our transgressions and our iniquities shall be pardoned for his sake' (v. 4; cf. vv. 6, 12). Luther puts it this way: '*our, us* and *for us*' must be written in letters of gold. Verse 5 is quoted in Chaucer's *Parson's Tale* to remind people of their responsibility for Christ's agony (Chaucer 1980: 607).

Karl Barth finds a 'full-orbed, biblical understanding of the atonement' in the passage, even if it is not such a central theme in New Testament references to it (Matt 8:17; Luke 22:37; John 12:38; Acts 8:32–33; Rom 10:16; 15:21) (Gignilliat 2009:133). Only in I Peter is vicarious suffering explicitly referred to: 'by his bruises we were healed' (1 Pet 2:24). For the patristic writers this was to become the main point of the poem: 'this is a new and strange way of healing: the physician undergoes the operation and the patient obtains the healing' (Theodoret, Athanasius, *Against the Arians* 3.31; cf. Luther). On the phrase 'the chastisement of our peace' (v. 5 AV Heb. *shalom*) or 'by which our peace is effected' (Lowth) or 'that made us whole' (RSV), Calvin cites Paul's notion that Christ suffered so that we might 'have peace with God', that is, a clear conscience (Rom 5:1), but he prefers his own interpretation. For him 'peace' here denotes reconciliation: 'the wrath of God, which had been justly kindled against us, was appeased; and through the Mediator we have obtained peace by which we are reconciled.' 'All we like sheep have gone astray' (v. 6) means there are no exceptions: we are all guilty and the word 'many' later on in the poem (vv. 11, 12) reminds us that not all will be included in the redemption (Luther).

'Oppressed and afflicted' (v. 7) describes the fate of the Jewish people suffering from hard taskmasters and verbal abuse (Rashi). 'Oppress' (Heb. *nagas*) here recalls how ruthless creditors treat people, an activity expressly forbidden by law (Deut 15:2) (Luzzatto). In such situations a Jew dare not open his mouth, and in any case there is no one in authority who would help him (Ibn Ezra). Christian interpreters relate the verse to Christ's silence before Caiaphas (Matt 26:63) and Pilate (Matt 27:12–14; cf. Isa 50:4) (Cyril, Eusebius), or it could be taken more generally as implying that Christ did not even think of vengeance: 'when he suffered, he did not threaten' (cf. 1 Pet 2:23) (Luther).

Verse 7 played a macabre role in medieval iconography (Marrow 1979: 99–104). In portrayals of the *ductio Christi* 'the leading of Christ' (John 18:12–13) 'like a lamb to the slaughter' (cf. Jer 11:19), Christ is sometimes shown on all fours being kicked and struck and dragged with ropes along the stony path from the Mount of Olives to Jerusalem … through thistles and thorns (cf. Isa 5:6). The tradition that his persecutors pulled out his beard has already been referred to (cf. Isa 50:6), but the reference to 'shearers' here suggested that his hair and beard were completely pulled out so that he looked as if he had been shorn like a sheep. That is how 'Calvary' (*calvus* 'bald') came by its name (Marrow 1979: 163–164). According to Theodoret, Christ gave his fleece, that is, his humanity, to the shearers, while as God he remained alive (*On Divine Providence* 10.29–30).

The image of a 'lamb led to the slaughter' reminds us that the subject of this poem is the 'lamb of God that takes away the sins of the world' (John 1:29) (Origen, *Comm. on John* 6.273–281; Ambrose, *Letter* 69; Jerome, Calvin). In art the verse accompanies representations of *Agnus Dei* 'the lamb of God' (John 1:29) (Schiller 1972: 117–118). Francisco Zurbarán's painting in the San Diego Museum of Art, inscribed TANQUAM AGNUS (Acts 8:32), is a particularly striking example (Baticle 1987: 269) (Plate 36). Augustine, citing the Book of Revelation, observes that Christ is both a lamb and a lion (Rev 5:5): 'a lion because in being slain he slew death … a lamb because his innocence is everlasting' (*Sermon* 375A.1–2). In the Byzantine liturgy verse 7 is recited by the priest with reference to the bread of communion (Wybrew 1989:109–110).

For many the story of his suffering ends here and verse 8 is about his 'glorification' (Luther): 'taken (Heb. *laqaḥ*) from prison and from judgement' (AV) means 'redeemed' (Ibn Ezra, cf. Rashi) or 'rescued' (cf. Prov 11:8) (Aquinas; cf. Nicholas, Calvin, Oecolampadius, Henry). The verb can also have the sense of 'received' by God after death (cf. Gen 5:24; Pss 43:15; 73:24) (Duhm). But there is a completely different interpretation suggested already in the Septuagint ('in his humiliation his judgement was taken away'), and this has been adopted

PLATE 36   'Like a lamb led to the slaughter, or a sheep that before its shearers is silent' (Isa 53:7; cf. Acts 8:32). Oil painting by Francisco Zurbarán (1635–1640).

by modern commentators: 'by oppressive acts of judgement, he was led away' (Blenkinsopp; cf. Lowth, Westermann, Childs, RSV) or 'without authority and justice he was carried off' (Luzzatto).

'Who shall declare his generation [AV]?' is another rhetorical question (cf. v. 1) expressing amazement at all that happened in his lifetime (Rashi; cf. Luzzatto). Alternatively it implies that no one was concerned about him during his lifetime (Westermann). Another suggestion is that instead of 'generation' (Heb. *dor*) we should read 'fate' (cf. Akk. *duru*; Arab. *dawr*): 'Who could have imagined his future?' (NRSV; Blenkinsopp). Many Christian commentators find in this verse a reference to the miraculous, incomprehensible 'generation' of Christ, born of a Virgin (Augustine, *Sermon* 195.1; cf. Jerome, Cyril, Aquinas, Nicholas; see comm. on Isa 9:6). Others prefer the notion of a 'generation' of believers, born in Christ, which shall be permanent and eternal (Calvin; cf. Luther), and 'as the stars of the heaven for multitude' (Deut 1:11; Henry).

An explicit reference to the death of the servant, 'cut off from the land of the living', follows, with another comment that it was because of the 'transgressions of my people' (cf. v. 5) (Ibn Ezra). The verse ends apparently with the words 'a blow, a plague fell on them' (Heb. *nega' lamo;* cf. v. 4 *nagua'* 'stricken') (Rashi, Ibn Ezra; cf. Childs). Most commentators from ancient times down to the present, read the word as a verb, 'stricken', to which many add, following the Septuagint, 'to death' (*la-mawet*) (Vitringa, Lowth, Duhm, Westermann, Blenkinsopp NJB; cf. F. B. Watson 2009).

The story of the suffering servant ends with a reference to his burial alongside 'wicked men' and 'a rich man' (v. 9), a reference to Israel in exile among the wicked gentiles, who were rich in comparison (Ibn Ezra). On the relationship between 'wicked' and 'rich', commentators note how often it happens in this world that the rich are ungodly and their wealth is used for ungodly purposes (Luther; cf. Calvin). Scholars emend the word 'rich' (Heb. *'ashir*) to 'evil-doers, reprobates' (*'ose ra'*) (McKenzie, Westermann). The word translated 'in his death' (Heb. *bemotayw*) is understood by many as 'in his sepulchre' (cf. Heb. *bamah* 'high place'), parallel to 'his grave'. Lowth recalls Shebna's splendid tomb, carved from the rock, 'on the height' (Isa 22:16) (cf. Ibn Ezra, Oecolampadius, Duhm, Westermann, NRSV, NJB).

Christological interpreters read the verse as fulfilled in the story of Christ's burial in the tomb of Joseph, 'a rich man from Arimathaea' (Matt 27:57) (Isidore, *De Fide Catholica* 1.49,1), although the reference to 'his grave with the wicked' actually does not fit the gospel story, as the Jewish scholar Nahmanides pointed out in the Barcelona Disputation of 1263 (Maccoby 1982: 60). Finally the point is made once again that his suffering cannot have been owing to any 'violence' or 'deceit' of his own because he was innocent, for Christians a reference to the sinlessness and 'perfect innocence' of Christ (cf. 1 Pet 2:22)

(Calvin; cf. Eusebius, John of Damascus, *Exposition of the Orthodox Faith* 3.27; Aquinas).

The last three verses of the poem seek to explain the meaning of the suffering of the Lord's servant (vv. 10–12). It was the Lord's will that his people should suffer bruising and sickness, referring to the exile, because that will make them repent and they will offer him themselves as a guilt offering (v. 10) (Rashi). Then he and his children shall 'prolong their days ... and the will of the Lord shall prosper in his hands': this refers to the generation which will 'return to the law of God in the days of the Messiah when true religion will prosper and all nations will accept it' (Ibn Ezra). For Christian commentators it is a crucial reference to the atoning sacrifice of Christ on the cross. It is about 'turning the sorrow of the Cross into gladness' (cf. Eph 5:8) (Procopius). The reference to a 'sacrifice' recalls Christ's words that he had come to 'give his life as a ransom for many' and John the Baptist's statement that he is 'the Lamb of God that takes away the sins of the world' (John 1:29) (Henry). Like the good shepherd, he lays down his life for his sheep (John 10:11) (Aquinas). To explain how Christ can be a 'guilt offering' (Heb. *asham*), Calvin quotes Paul's statements about Christ becoming a curse for us 'that we might receive the promise of the spirit through him' (Gal 3:13–14; cf. 2 Cor 5:21).

Then 'he shall see his offspring' is a prophecy that after Christ's death his faithful followers will multiply in number (Nicholas, Calvin), recalling Jesus words, 'unless a grain of wheat falls into the earth and dies, it remains alone; but if it dies, it bears much fruit' (John 12:24) (Aquinas). Jerome cites the Parable of the Sower (Matt 13) and a verse from a royal Psalm: 'His seed shall endure for ever, and his throne as the sun before me' (Ps,89:36) (cf. Eusebius).

'Out of his anguish he shall see (light) and be satisfied' (NRSV) (v. 11). The word 'light' is not in the Hebrew but is added by modern commentators on the authority of the Septuagint and 1QIsaᵃ. A verse from Psalm 17 provides an interesting parallel which supports an eschatological interpretation: 'when I awake, I shall be satisfied' (Ps 17:15) (Sawyer 1973). According to Christian commentators 'he [Christ] will be satisfied' when he sees the spread of his Church throughout the world (Cyril, Aquinas).

'By his knowledge the righteous one, my servant, will make many righteous and bear the burden of their iniquities' (v. 11). 'His knowledge', that is, 'the knowledge of him' refers to 'faith in Christ': 'whoever will know and believe in Christ as bearing his sins will be righteous' (Luther; cf. Jerome, Aquinas). This is the righteousness of faith in Christ, who was a sacrifice for us and bore our sins, not the righteousness of the law: 'Christ is the end of the law that everyone who has faith may be justified' (Rom 10:4) (Calvin). Rashi applies the verse to his people in exile, citing the role of the sons of Aaron who 'bear iniquity' in the sanctuary (Num 18:1), while for Ibn Ezra it means that Israel will teach the nations how to live by the law and sympathize with them when they are in trouble.

The last verse is a short oracle of salvation, introduced by the conventional 'therefore' (cf. Isa 51:21; 52:6), in which the servant's sufferings are compared to a battle which is now over. Christ has conquered the principalities and powers, sin and Satan, death and hell, the world and the flesh, and our souls have been rescued from the devil (Henry; cf. Calvin, Oecolampadius). 'I will divide him a portion with the many (Heb. *rabbim*)' (NJB) suggested to Ephrem a picture of Christ distributing his body and blood in the Eucharist. The sharing out of the spoil was taken by Jewish commentators to mean that the reward for God's people who have died for their faith will be very great. Their merit is equal to that of the prophets ('the great') and the patriarchs ('the strong') (Ibn Ezra), 'in exchange for' (Heb. *taḥat asher*) pouring out their soul to death … and being treated as though they had transgressed … they made intercession for the transgressors'. Ibn Ezra also refers to Jeremiah's letter in which he urges the exiles to pray for the welfare of Babylon (Jer 29:7), and Christians find in this 'most noble text' a description of the One who bears and shoulders the burden of our sins but who also prays for his tormentors (Luke 23:34) (Luther; cf. Jerome, Aquinas). The words 'he was numbered with the transgressors' were fulfilled when Christ was crucified between two robbers (Mark 15:28) (Eusebius, Cyril, Henry) but could also refer to his 'shameful and accursed' death on a cross (Phil 2:8) (Calvin) and his descent into hell (cf. Ps 88:4) (Jerome, Aquinas).

The role of this poem in the history of passion iconography has been mentioned already. While in the early centuries Isaiah was mostly associated with the Nativity (Isa 1:3; 9:6) and the Virgin Mary (Isa 7:14), in the Middle Ages attention shifted dramatically to the Suffering Servant prophecy. A twelfth-century enamel plaque shows the prophet with the words 'Surely [he bore] our weaknesses' (Isa 53.4) (Sawyer 2013: 10), while in Claus Sluter's famous statue of the prophet in Dijon (1380–1400), he is holding a scroll with the Latin inscription 'Like a lamb before its shearers' (v. 7) (Sawyer 1996: 87–88). A particularly macabre painting of the Passion by Matthias Grünewald (1526) has the words 'Isaiah 53: He was beaten for our sins' written in German in large letters above it (Schiller 1972: 81–82). It features on two pages of the *Biblia Pauperum* (*BP* 95, 98), while in a more modern example from a church in Amsterdam, now demolished, three of the Stations of the Cross were accompanied by texts from Isaiah 53: Christ falls for the first time (v. 8), Veronica wipes his face (v. 2) and his crucifixion between two robbers (v. 12; cf. Luke 22:37) (Sawyer 1996: 92). As noted earlier in the chapter, paintings of the popular *Imago Pietatis*, known today as 'the Man of Sorrows' (v. 3), by Fra Angelico,

Bellini, Cranach the Younger, Dürer and many others, were not directly connected to Isaiah 53 before the nineteenth century.

In his painting *Still Life with open Bible* (1885) van Gogh juxtaposes the imagery of the suffering servant in Isaiah 53 with the story of Pauline Quenu, the young hero of Emil Zola's novel *La joie de vivre* (1884), who somehow found joy and satisfaction in her suffering (cf. v. 11) (O'Kane 2007:150–155). Chapter 53 also features in Phyllis Trible's study of four biblical texts, *Texts of Terror* (1984), where Hagar's epitaph is 'She was wounded for our transgressions' (v. 5) and Tamar's is 'A woman of sorrows and acquainted with grief' (v. 3). Mel Gibson's film *The Passion of the Christ* (2004) opens with the text of verse 5, 'an invitation to explore in lurid and lingering detail how a human body would look if pulped, pummelled and flogged' (Fredriksen 2006: 93): '1 Corinthians 1:18 would have been better' (S. Heschel 2006: 107); 'by his stripes were we healed' certainly does not apply to the Jews (Rubenstein 2006: 110).

Two of the hymns inspired by this passage have already been mentioned (see comm. on Isa 52:15 and 43:2). There are several others including one by Melchior Franck, *Fürwahr er trug unsre Krankheit* (Surely He Has Borne Our Sickness) (Isa 53:4–5) (1636), and another by Paul Gerhardt *O Haupt voll Blut und Wunden* (1656), which became popular in various English versions such as 'O Sacred Head Sore Wounded' and 'O Sacred Head surrounded / By crown of piercing thorn' (*EH* 102; *CH2* 107; *BiM* 176). It also figures five times in Bach's *St Matthew Passion* (1729), while much of Part 2 of Handel's *Messiah* (1742), after the chorus 'Behold the Lamb of God', consists of choral settings of verses 3–8 (cf. Isa 50:6), including 'And With His Stripes' and 'All We Like Sheep'. Less well known are Antonio Caldara's oratorio *Le profezie evangeliche d'Isaia* (1729) and a haunting setting of verses 2–5 for soprano solo in Willy Burkhard's *The Face of Isaiah* (1936) (Berges 2012: 127).

Zion and Her Children (Isa 54:1–17)

In the annual synagogue lectionary this chapter accompanies the second portion of the Torah (Gen 6:9–11:3), picking up the reference to Noah (v:9). Verses 1–10 are also the fourth of the 'consolation' haftarot, and verses 4–10 are among the *Tanḥumim* at Qumran (see comm. on Isa 40), declaring that one day Jerusalem will be stronger than ever. Muslim writers applied the passage to Mecca (Lazarus-Yafeh 1992: 86; Adang 1996: 273). In the Church the chapter

Isaiah Through the Centuries, First Edition. John F. A. Sawyer.
© 2018 John Wiley & Sons Ltd. Published 2020 by John Wiley & Sons Ltd.

provides Advent readings in most traditions (BCP, *ORM*, RCL), and a popular hymn composed in the 1970s by the American Catholic songwriter Dan Schutte has a verse beginning 'As he swore to your fathers / When the flood destroyed the land' and the refrain

> Though the mountains may fall
> And the hills turn to dust ...
> Yet the love of the Lord will stand. (*HON* 569)

Verses 11–14 inspired the Jewish poet Emma Lazarus, whose words, from her poem entitled 'The New Colossus' (1883), were inscribed on the Statue of Liberty in 1903, and the chapter played a significant role in the life of the African American Methodist, Julia A. J. Foote (*NCHB* 2.395).

The prophet addresses Zion again (cf. Isa 52:1), this time telling her to celebrate the news that, although she had thought she was barren, she is going to have more children than her that is married (v. 1; cf. Isa 49:14–21). In the triennial lectionary (Mann 1971: 1.106–116) chapter 54 is the haftarah for the story of Sarah and Hagar (Gen 16), and in a rabbinic midrash there is a tradition that Zion was the last of the seven barren matriarchs, beginning with Sarah, corresponding to the seven days of creation, who were raised from deprivation and humiliation to a state of being blessed and joyful (cf. Ps 113:9): on the seventh day God rested (Exod 20:11;) and desired Zion to be his resting place forever (Ps 132:14) (Callaway 1986: 117–120). Paul also connects the passage with the story of Hagar and Sarah, and claims that Christians are children of Sarah who had been barren (Gal 4:21–31). According to Philo this is an allegory for the soul (*De Praemiis et Poenis* 158–159), where barrenness, like virginity, is a state of availability and receptivity resulting in spiritual fruit (Callaway 1986: 98–100).

Jerusalem will have more citizens than Edom, says Rashi, probably thinking of Rome. Others say it refers to Babylon, but Ibn Ezra believes it refers to any nation that is 'married' (Heb. *be'ulah*; cf. Isa 62:4), a nation that has a husband, that is, its own king. Christian commentators observe that, after having spoken about the death of Christ in Chapter 53, the prophet moves on in chapter 54 to speak of the Church, just as in the Apostles Creed 'We believe in the Church' follows 'We believe in Jesus Christ' (Calvin). The image of the Church, the New Jerusalem, as a mother, and of God (or Christ) as her husband found its scriptural basis in Isaiah (Isa 50:1; 62:1–5; 66:10–11; cf. Rev 21:1–2; Gal 4:21–31). Just as a woman in childbirth is urged by nurses to cry out and shout aloud to help the birth, so the Church of the gentiles is told to shout with joy as she becomes the mother of countless people (Cyril). Luther, commenting on the sad state of the church in his own day ('barren, filthy and forsaken'), applies the verse to a time when, for example, 'there will be more Hussites than papists'.

'Enlarge the place of your tent' (v. 2) recalls the days when the patriarchs lived in tents (cf. Heb 11:9; Luther, Henry). Spaciousness is an important concept in biblical language about salvation, whether literally, as in the days of Abraham (Gen 26:22; cf. Deut 33:20) or metaphorically (Ps 4:1; Job 36:16; Ps 119:45) (Sawyer 1968). The words 'to the right and the left you shall burst forth' (v. 3) appear in the popular Jewish song 'Lekha Dodi' (see comm. on Isa 52:1–2). The Church Fathers contrasted the tabernacle in the wilderness (Exod 27:18) with the Church, built by God not man and much greater, and while there was only one tabernacle and only one Temple, there will be many churches (Cyril, Eusebius). Some noted that the Church is like a tent because it has no stable or permanent habitation and relies not on earthly forces and strength, but on the invincible power of God (Calvin). 'Your descendants [AV 'seed'] will inherit the nations' (v. 3) refers to the apostles and disciples who will spread the evangelical word among the gentiles like the sower in the parable (Matt 13) (Eusebius, Jerome), and then, when they have filled all the inhabited cities, will continue their mission into the uninhabited ('desolate') areas of the world (Cyril).

The missionary implications of these two verses inspired a famous sermon known by its title, 'Expect Great Things from God, Attempt Great Things from God', preached by William Carey on the occasion of the founding of the Baptist Missionary Society in Nottingham in 1792. It may be that Carey was himself inspired by William Cowper's hymn beginning 'Jesus, where'er thy people meet' (1779) (*EH* 422; *CH2* 247 *AM* 696), which has a somewhat ungainly paraphrase of verse 2, omitted in most modern hymnbooks:

> Behold at thy commanding word,
> We stretch the curtain and the cord;
> Come now and fill this wider space,
> And help us with a large increase.

In another striking anthropomorphism (vv. 4–10; cf. Isa 49:14), God appeals to the wife he had abandoned, like an apologetic husband promising he well never treat her like that again: 'In overflowing wrath for a moment I hid my face from you, but with everlasting love I will have compassion on you' (v. 8) (Sawyer 1989). For some 'the shame of your youth' (v. 4) refers to Israel's troubles in the old days, that is, the First Temple period when they lived in their own land, while 'the reproach of your widowhood' refers to the exile (Luzzatto; cf. Kimḥi). Others find a reference in the first expression to slavery in Egypt and, in the second, to the Babylonian exile (Lowth). Augustine applies the verse to the situation in his own day: in former days, he says, it was a disgrace and a stigma to be a Christian; but now 'you can forget your former shame' (LXX) (*Exposition of Psalm 58*, 1.10). You have nothing to fear because 'your husband is … the lord of hosts ... God of the whole earth' (v. 5), and so all nations will accept the divine Law (cf. Zeph 3:9) (Ibn Ezra). The word 'husband' is an unusual form in Hebrew (*bo'alayik*), suggesting 'one who will dominate you' (Vg), taken by Jerome as a reference to the reign of Christ over 'the whole earth', not just Jerusalem. He also describes himself as 'your maker', which suggests that, 'in Christ he will transform us ... into his own beautiful form so that others see us as different from the rest of humanity' (Cyril).

Israel's sufferings are compared to the plight of a young wife, 'forsaken and grieved in spirit ... cast off' by her husband (v. 6), all the more tragic because she is young (Luther). The nations pour scorn on them because they do not have a king of their own (cf. v. 4) (Ibn Ezra). God had forsaken his wife because she had behaved like a harlot and there was no going back (cf. Jer 3:1). On the notion of God 'hiding his face' (*hester panim*) (v. 8) see comm. on Isa 45:15. The Targum has 'I removed the presence of my Shekinah from you' and clearly has the Babylonian exile in mind when the Temple lay in ruins. This is how the expression is used in the Dead Sea Scrolls too (*CD* 1.3; cf. *CD* 2.8; *DSSE* 129–130; Blenkinsopp 2006: 243). But it was only for a moment (vv. 7–8): 'the days of the exile, though many, will be like a moment in comparison with the everlasting days of future happiness' (Ibn Ezra). In the words of St Paul, 'this slight momentary affliction is preparing for us an eternal weight of glory beyond all comparison (2 Cor 4:17)' (Cyril, Aquinas, Calvin). Lowth cites a Psalm: 'For his anger is but for a moment ... weeping may tarry for a night, but joy comes with the morning' (Ps 30:5).

'This is as the waters of Noah unto me' (v. 9 AV): Isaiah calls the Flood 'the waters of Noah' because Noah failed to stand up to God and plead for the world (*Zohar* 3:15a). The Babylonian captivity seemed like a flood that destroyed the whole earth (Isa 10:20–23) (Calvin). Others say the 'waters of Noah' here refer to the water of baptism (cf. 1 Pet 3:20–21) (Jerome). Modern commentators mostly follow the evidence of 1QIsaᵃ and the Targum (cf. Vg, RSV) in reading 'the days (Heb. *yeme*) of Noah', a parallel to 'the waters (Heb. *me*) of Noah' in the next line rather than a repetition. Either way, the verse compares God's promise to Jerusalem with his 'everlasting covenant' with Noah (Gen 9:16): he will never again be angry with her (cf. Gen 8:21). Zion's innocence is compared to that of Noah (Low 2013: 108).

His promise is also like the 'covenant of peace' between husband and wife who live together in peace and happiness (v. 10) (Ibn Ezra). God's steadfast love and compassion will never depart from his people even though 'the mountains may depart and the hills be removed'. The rabbis add that, even though 'the heavens vanish and the earth waxes old as a garment' (Isa 51:6)... ... 'the moon is confounded and the sun ashamed' (Isa 24:23)... ... 'and all the host of heaven be dissolved' (Isa 34:4), God will always have compassion on the righteous (b*Abodah Zarah* 17a). If we take this as a metaphor, the mountains are the patriarchs and the matriarchs and it means that, even if their merits come to nothing (Rashi), or, for Christians, even if the saints are shaken by a deluge of such a kind (Jerome), God's love for his people will never depart.

Verse 11 begins another of the 'consolation' haftarot (Isa 54:11–55:5) (see comm. on Isa 40). The poor little 'afflicted one [Vg *paupercula* ; cf. Isa 10:30; 51:21], storm-tossed and not comforted', is addressed again, now more as a city than a woman (cf. Isa 49:16–21): 'Behold I will set your stones in antimony' (vv. 11–12). Antimony (Heb. *puk*) is a black substance, itself precious (Ibn Ezra), used like mortar for setting precious stones (cf. 1 Chron 29:2). It was also used by women like mascara to make themselves look more beautiful (2 Kgs 9:30; cf. Jer 4:30), hence the name of Job's daughter, Kerenhappuch 'abundant mascara' (Job 42:14) (Luzzatto). The word thus suggests that the stones of the new building will be arranged with exceptional refinement and ornamentation. Translated into Greek as *anthrax* 'coal' (LXX), the word recalls the cleansing of Isaiah's lips (Isa 6:6) and implies that no stone in the new building will be unclean (Eusebius). To Jerome the 'coal' suggests something that ignites and enlightens those who believe, that is, the word of doctrine. The 'pinnacles' (RSV Heb. *shimshot*) or 'battlements' (LXX, NJB) are 'windows' in the Targum (cf. Rashi, Ibn Ezra, AV), no doubt by association with 'sun' (Heb. *shemesh*). A modern suggestion is 'shields' hung on the walls to make perfect your beauty (Ezek 27:11; Cant 4:4), and paired with 'sun' in the Psalms (Ps 84:11) (Blenkinsopp).

A commentator at Qumran interpreted the precious stones as referring to members of his community: the sapphires, for example, are 'the priests and the people that laid the foundations of the council of community' (4Q164; *DSSE* 500). This is also how Christians read the passage following Peter's words 'like living stones be yourselves built into a spiritual house' (1 Pet 2:5) (Gregory, *Homilies on Ezekiel* 2.6.3–4; cf. Calvin), and Paul when he says 'like a skilled architect I laid the foundation' (1 Cor 3:10) (Theodoret). The stones are worthy and precious souls … sapphire is the colour of heaven … as Paul says, 'Our citizenship is in heaven' (Phil 3:20). The battlements are those of strong faith who destroy every 'obstacle raised against the knowledge of God' (2 Cor 10:5). Gates of crystal (LXX) denote the clarity and purity of true faith, and the wall of special stones refers to those whose prayers surround and confirm the building (Eusebius; cf. Jerome, Aquinas, Nicholas). 'Every Christian is a jewel … some are more precious than others … there is a variety of gifts' (cf. 1 Cor 12:4) (Luther, Vitringa). This description of the New Jerusalem, which makes no mention of a Temple, influenced the author of Tobit (Tob 13:16–17) (Aquinas, Lowth) as well as John of Patmos (Rev 21:10–21) (Jerome).

In verse 13 the Targum makes it clear that the most precious stone in the new Jerusalem will be the study of the Torah, while for Christian interpreters the verse explains to her that the precious stones in the previous verses are her sons, and their only teacher is God, as Jesus said, 'call nobody on earth your teacher, for you have one teacher in heaven' (Matt 23:8) (Eusebius). Jeremiah put it another way: 'one shall not teach his neighbour, nor a man his brother; for all shall know me from the least even to the greatest, says the Lord' (Jer 31:34) (Calvin). Augustine applies the verse to 'all those who have been called according to God's purpose' (Rom 8:28), not through their own righteousness or free-will as Pelagians claim (*Grace of Christ and Original Sin* 1.13.14). It was a favourite verse of Luther who uses it, along with Isaiah 11:9, to give scriptural authority to his teaching on the priesthood of all believers as well to his passionate conviction that everyone, young and old must receive instruction in the Bible (*LW* 55 395). In a famous passage from the Babylonian Talmud, printed in the Daily Prayer Book, this verse is cited to illustrate the point that the effect of wise teaching is to bring peace into the world (cf. Ps 29:11) (b*Berakhot* 64a; *ADPB* 300–301).

'Righteousness', as defined by Paul, means good works (2 Tim 3:17) (Luther), and for Aquinas recalls the 'city of righteousness' in Isaiah 1:26. 'Go far from oppression' (MT, LXX, Tg, Vg) means 'stay far from oppressing other people' (Rashi), while Jerome takes it to mean you have nothing to fear if you keep away from injustice (Ps 48:6) (cf. Eusebius): 'the reformation of manners, the restoration of purity, the due administration of public justice, and the prevailing of honesty and fair dealing among men, are the strength and stability of any church or state' (Henry). Many interpret the verse, however, more as a continuation of the description of the New Jerusalem, taking 'in righteousness' (*bi-ṣedaqah*) as 'triumphantly' (cf. Isa 41:2) (Blenkinsopp), and emending the imperative 'go far from oppression' to 'you shall be far from oppression' (AV, RSV) or 'free from oppression' (NJB; cf. Calvin, Oecolampadius, Childs).

Following the reference to 'terror' in verse 14 and the warlike tone of verse 16, many take verse 15 as a description of foreign threats to Jerusalem and their failure: 'if anyone stirs up strife (Heb. *yagur*), it is not from me… and they shall fall' (RSV; cf. Luther; Rashi, Westermann). Some take the verb to mean 'gather together' (cf. Pss 59:3; 94:21 RSV): 'leagued together but not by my commend' (Lowth; cf Tg, AV). The commonest meaning of the word *yagur*, however, is 'to sojourn', from which the word *ger* (alien, proselyte) is derived, and this is how the verse is taken by many of the ancients, both Christian and Jewish: 'strangers shall come to you by me and shall sojourn with you' (LXX; cf. Vg Eusebius). Jerome explains it by reference to Christ's last words to his disciples (Matt 28:19), while Aquinas compares it with another passage about 'foreigners who join themselves to the Lord' (Isa 56:3–8). Ibn Ezra gives it a rather less generous slant: 'can there dwell a stranger in thy land except it be my will?' (Ibn Ezra).

Verses 16 and 17a seem to be unambiguously about the weapons of war and the invincibility of a city protected by the Lord. According to some commentators the 'smith' is the devil and the 'ravager' the archangel Michael in an apocalyptic vision, enhanced by the reference to fire at the beginning (Nicholas; cf. Jerome). But at Qumran the verse was used to show how the Lord had provided an interpreter of the Law as a 'tool for his work' (*CD* 6:3–8; *DSSE* 133–134). Ibn Ezra also suggests that the 'weapon' crafted by the Lord's blacksmith is not to be taken literally but is 'the tongue' with which every 'tongue that rises against you' can be confuted: 'no other weapon is so deadly and destructive' (Calvin). Jerome illustrates the passage with the story of how Paul overcame the evil magician Elymas by a powerful verbal attack (Acts 13:8–12). At his ordination the militant Protestant preacher and politician the Reverend Ian Paisley tells us he was armed by his mother with this verse. The whole prophecy is summed up in the last words: 'this is the heritage of the servants of the Lord'. The 'heritage' could be the Law (cf. Ps 119:111) or the Land (Ibn Ezra), or life in the world to come (Eusebius). 'Their righteousness is of me' (AV) is understood as 'their vindication' (RSV) or 'their just reward' (cf. Matt 25:34–35) (Theodoret; cf Rashi).

Come to Me, All You Who Thirst (Isa 55:1–13)

Whether or not modern scholars since Duhm were right to think of chapters
40–55 ('Deutero-Isaiah') as a distinct literary unit, it cannot be denied that
chapter 55 has a certain independence (Westermann) and the elements of a
climax (Childs). There is no introductory formula like 'Thus says the Lord', and
in contrast with the preceding chapters those being addressed are not named:
'everyone who thirsts … those who have no money'. In the Jewish lectionary
verses 1–5 are part of the third 'consolation' haftarah (see comm. on Isa 40)

Isaiah Through the Centuries, First Edition. John F. A. Sawyer.
© 2018 John Wiley & Sons Ltd. Published 2020 by John Wiley & Sons Ltd.

(*JSB*), and verses 6–13 the first part of a reading for Public Fast Days (55:6–56:8 JSB). Kimḥi tells us it refers to a time after the war of Gog and Magog. For Aquinas 'This is the heritage of the servants of the Lord' (Isa 54:17; cf. Ps 16:5–6), referring to 'an everlasting covenant' (v. 3) and 'an everlasting sign which shall not be cut off' (v. 13). Luther describes it as 'an exhortation which is not less necessary than doctrine'.

The prophet portrays the Lord issuing an invitation reminiscent of Lady Wisdom's invitation: 'Come eat of my bread and drink of the wine I have mixed' (Prov 9:5). It refers to the wisdom of the Torah: the soul needs wisdom as the body needs food (Ibn Ezra; cf. Rashi). The rabbis explained that the words of the Torah are compared to water because, 'just as water flows from high places to low places, so the words of the Torah leave those that are haughty and stay with those that are humble' (b *Ta'anit* 7a). They are compared to wine and milk because they serve as both food and drink (Ibn Ezra).

The passage is alluded to in an ancient apocalypse (1 Enoch 48:1; *OTP* 1.35), and Christian interpreters believe it foreshadows Christ's invitation: 'If anyone thirst, let him come to me and drink' (John 7:37) (Cyril). It is an invitation to the banquet of God's word: sacred scripture is like food to be broken up for people to eat (cf. Lam 4:4) (Gregory, *Morals on Job* 1.29). Buying 'without money and without price' is a strange way to buy, but it can be explained by the fact that wisdom is beyond price (Prov 8:19; 16:26) and any price that had to be paid was paid in full by Christ, not with money but with his own blood (Henry; cf. Jerome, Cyril). Some say it refers to his instructions to the disciples to 'baptize all nations in the name of the Father' (Matt 28:19) (*Bible Moralisée*; cf. Theodoret). The wine is for the adults and the milk for children (Luther). Some refer to the custom in Eastern Churches of giving newborn babies wine and milk at their baptism (Jerome, Eusebius). In a figurative sense, the redness of wine and the whiteness of milk, foretold by Jacob on his deathbed (Gen 49:11–12), recall Christ's passion (Jerome).

The Septuagint has 'wine and fat' (cf. Isa 1:11; 43:24), interpreted by some as a reference to the 'richness and nourishment of spiritual food in Christ' (cf. John 6:53) (Eusebius, Cyril). 'Wine, milk, bread and water' are all that is necessary for the spiritual life (Calvin). Wasting money and effort on worldly pursuits (v. 2) is condemned and contrasted with the 'good things to come' (cf. Heb. 10:1) (Eusebius). 'Fatness' (cf. Isa 30:23; Job 36:16) is 'the happiness that the soul enjoys after its separation from the body by death' (Ibn Ezra). 'Come to me … that your soul may live' (v. 3) means you will live for ever after the death of your body (Ibn Ezra).

The 'everlasting covenant' (v. 3) recalls the covenant made with David (Ps 89:1–4, 28–29) and here refers to the Davidic Messiah in the future as the following verses make clear: 'nations that knew you not shall run to you … for he has glorified you' (Ibn Ezra). The Church Fathers contrasted the old covenant, which was not everlasting, with the new (cf. Heb. 8:7–13) (Cyril; cf. Eusebius, Jerome).

'The sure mercies of David' (AV) or 'the sacred and faithful things of David' (LXX) are the things promised to David (cf. RSV 'my steadfast, sure love for David') and fulfilled in Christ (cf. Ps 89:1) (Tertullian, *Against Marcion* .20.10). In Acts the expression is cited along with two texts from the Davidic Psalms (Ps 2:7; 16:10) to demonstrate the certainty of Jesus' resurrection from the dead (Acts 13:34) (Berges 2012: 103). The Messiah is described as a 'witness to the peoples' (v. 4; cf. Rev 3:14), that is, one who will testify that there is no other ruler of the world than God (Ibn Ezra), recalling the role of the disciples in the world (Matt 24:14) (Jerome). Under the leadership of the Messiah, 'nations that have not known you shall call upon you' (v. 5): recalling an earlier messianic prophecy beginning 'the people that walked in darkness' (Isa 9:1) (Jerome). This is why Zion was told to 'stretch out and enlarge her tent' (Isa 54:2) (Eusebius). This is what happens when the Holy One of Israel 'glorifies his people' (cf. Isa 26:15; 49:3; 60:9) (Jerome). God's 'option for the poor' is to become a model for all nations (cf. 42:3–4, 6; 49:6; 51:4–5) (Lohfink 1987: 224).

'Seek the Lord while he may be found' (v. 6) begins the second part of this great exhortation (vv. 6–11). It is the first part of the Jewish haftarah for fast days (Isa 55:6–56:8), and there is a note of urgency in the appeal (Ibn Ezra). Luther quotes Jesus' words: 'Walk while you have the light lest the darkness overtake you' (John 12:35) (cf. Aquinas). 'If you ask when is the opportune time to seek the Lord, the simple answer is all your life' (Gregory of Nyssa, *Homily 7 on Ecclesiastes*). 'Seek' means 'draw near to God' (cf. Ps 73:28; Jer 23:23) (Jerome), originally in the physical sense of visiting a sacred place but later given a spiritual interpretation (Amos 4:4–5; cf. Matt 7:7). For the Reformers 'drawing near to God' means listening to the preaching of the gospel (Rom 10:8; cf. Phil 4:5) (Calvin). Verse 7 is another explanation of verse 6 (Ibn Ezra): to seek God means forsaking the 'former road of ungodliness and immorality' (cf. Theodoret). The image of life as a way or a journey is frequent in the later chapters of Isaiah (Isa 53:6; 56:11; 57:10, 18; 58:13; 59:10; 65:2; 66:3) and familiar from the Dead Sea Scrolls (1QS 9:17; 1QM 14:7; *DSSE* 111, 180) and the New Testament (Matt 22:16; Mark 12:14; Luke 20:21; John 14:6; cf. Isa 30:20–21) Blenkinsopp 2006: 178–185). The promise of abundant forgiveness for those who 'return to the Lord' is a 'golden text' according to Luther, reminiscent of Psalm 32:1 (Jerome): 'even if things are incurable according to your own abilities, they are not incurable with me' (Eusebius).

Two famous verses expand on the notion of divine forgiveness (vv. 8–9). 'You thought I would punish you even after you returned to me; but your thoughts are not mine' (Ibn Ezra). In a human court whoever pleads guilty is punished; but with me, whoever confesses and gives up his evil ways, is granted clemency (cf. Prov 28:13) (Rashi). If we take back servants who have offended us when they promise to improve … how much more does God act thus (Chrysostom, *Letter to the Fallen Theodore* 1.15; cf. Calvin). There is as vast a distance between heaven and earth as there is between God and humanity: 'you are intent on rebelling against me while I am intent on bringing you back' (Rashi; cf. Luther). But this also means that God's love is beyond human comprehension (cf. Ps 103:11) (Calvin, Lowth). In the words of the Latin poet Prudentius, 'ascend to heaven and banish cares of earth' (*Against Symmachus* 2.123–140).

But Moses had told his people that there is no need to ascend to heaven to find God's Word: 'it is very near you; it is in your mouth and in your heart' (Deut 30:11–14), and the next passage is about its unfailing power in the world: 'as the rain and the snow come down from heaven … so shall my word be that goes forth from my mouth' (vv. 10–11) (Calvin; cf. Jerome). 'I shall fulfil all that I spoke through the prophets' (Ibn Ezra; cf. Rashi). As the rain can achieve everything for the earth, so also my Word accomplishes everything: this is spoken partly for the confutation of the stubborn, and partly for the consolation of the weak (Luther). The chapter ends with a joyful chorus (vv. 12–13) in which the mountains, the hills and the trees of the field join in, and thorns and briers are replaced by cypresses and myrtles – a wilderness turned into a paradise (Lowth) as an 'everlasting sign' of God's love for his people. 'The whole world and all the angels … will be watching us as we fight for Christianity' (cf. 1 Cor 4:9) (Origen, *Exhortation to Martyrdom* 18).

The chapter is read on Holy Saturday in some Christian traditions (*ORM*, RCL) and the Eve of the Theophany in others (*OSB*). George Herbert's poem 'The Invitation' (1633) focuses on its universality: five of the six stanzas begin 'Come ye hither all' and urgently summon the faithful to the Eucharist: 'save your cost … taste and fear not ,… Here is love, which having breath / Ev'n in death, / After death can never die'. The last stanza, addressed by an Anglican priest to his God, explains why:

> For it seems but just and right,
> In my sight,
> Where is all, there all should be. (Herbert 2007: 246)

By contrast, A. E. Housman's poem 'Ho, Everyone that Thirsteth' (1936), drawing on Proverbs (Prov 9:17) as well as Isaiah 55, is about getting the most out of life before it is too late: 'Come to the stolen waters, / Drink and your soul shall live.' A nineteenth-century example is in a hymn by the prolific Scottish hymn writer Horatius Bonar:

> I heard the voice of Jesus say,
> Behold I freely give
> The living water: thirsty one,
> Stoop down and drink and live. (*EH* 574; *CH2* 410 *AM* 669)

Mendelssohn's oratorio *Elijah* (1846) ends with a musical setting of verses 1, 3 for a soprano, alto, tenor, bass quartet between two great choruses (Isa 41:25; 58:8) (*BiM* 75), and there is an evocative choral setting of verse 12 in the last movement of Randall Thompson's *Peaceable Kingdom* (1936) (*BiM* 185–186).

PLATE 37 'Instead of the thorn shall come up the fir-tree, the myrtle instead of the brier' (Isa 55:13). Copper engraving from Johann Jacob Scheuchzer, *Physica Sacra* (Augsburg and Ulm, 1735). Reproduced with kind permission of David Gunn.

More recent compositions include hymns inspired by the first few verses (*HON* 741), in one case combined with Matthew 11:28–30 (*HON* 400). The last part of the chapter inspired a musical paraphrase of verses 10–13 by N. T. Wright (*AM* 222) and 'The trees of the field', a popular setting of verse 12 by Stuart Dauermann with the refrain 'And the trees of the field shall clap their hands' (*CH4* 804; *GtG* 80; *AM* 484) (Plate 37).

A House of Prayer for All Nations (Isa 56:1–8)

After the climax of chapter 55, chapter 56 seems to break new ground and the last eleven chapters of the book, known since Duhm as 'Third Isaiah' or 'Trito-Isaiah', are believed by most scholars to be a distinct literary unit. Few would argue that 'Trito-Isaiah' can be thought of as a single author, but there are clear indications that these chapters reflect a later period when the struggling community in Judah faced new problems referred to in texts like Haggai, Jonah,

Isaiah Through the Centuries, First Edition. John F. A. Sawyer.
© 2018 John Wiley & Sons Ltd. Published 2020 by John Wiley & Sons Ltd.

Ezra-Nehemiah and Daniel. Hopes of a mass return of the exiles from Babylon, for example, had not materialized, there was opposition to the building of the Temple, and relations between Jews and gentiles in the Persian Empire raised new problems. The fact that these chapters consciously allude to phrases and themes in 40–55 has suggested to some that they are the work of a class of scholars (*schriftgelehrte Prophetie*) whose task was to interpret earlier prophetic texts in the light of the new situation in which they found themselves (Williamson 1994: 19–21; Berges 2012: 20–22).

The Jewish haftarah for fast days (Isa 55:6–56:8), however, ignores the chapter division, beginning 'Seek the Lord while he may be found' (Isa 55:6) and ending with the inclusion of foreigners and the 'outcasts of Israel' (Isa 56:8). 'Keep justice and do righteousness' (v. 1) is cited by the rabbis to show that, like Jesus (Matt 22:34–40), Isaiah reduced the 613 Commandments to two (b*Makkot* 23b–24a). Here as elsewhere (Pss 15:2; 106:3; Isa 26:9), 'justice' really means 'every virtue' (Jerome). 'Soon my salvation will come' (v. 1) implies it is still delayed because of Israel's sins (Ibn Ezra), but, on the other hand, the rabbis noticed that God says 'my salvation, not your salvation, which means that, even if you have no merit, I will nevertheless do it for my own sake' (ExodR XXX.24). For Christian commentators 'my salvation' means Christ (Jerome, Luther); and, as Paul says, 'our salvation is nearer than we thought' (Rom 13:11) (Calvin). 'My righteousness' (Heb. *ṣidqati*) (Tg, Vg, AV) implies 'saving justice' (NJB), 'deliverance' (RSV) and even 'mercy' (LXX).

Sabbath observance, criticized by the prophets along with other festivals before the exile (Isa 1:13; Hos.2:11), became, in the early Second Temple period, an aspect of Judaism more important than circumcision in creating a strong ethnic consciousness (cf. Isa 58:13; 66:23; Jer 17:24–27; Neh 10:28–31; 13:15–22) (Blenkinsopp). Christian commentators interpret 'sabbath' here as a figure of speech denoting a cessation from iniquity and call for a 'perpetual Sabbath' (Jerome; cf. Calvin), or a 'spiritual Sabbath' when we would avoid worldly cares and worship God with holy vigour (Cyril; cf. Theodoret, Nicholas). Others point out that the seventh day of the week (Exod 20:8–11) has been replaced in Christian practice by the first day, that is, the day of the resurrection (John 20:1) (Aquinas).

Verses 3–5 explain that the terms 'man' and 'son of man' ('mortal' NRSV; 'anyone' NJB) mean everybody that keeps the Sabbath and avoids evil (v. 2), even foreigners and eunuchs. This attitude to proselytes was anticipated in Solomon's prayer at the dedication of the Temple in Jerusalem (1 Kgs 8:41) (Ibn Ezra) and in another remarkable verse from earlier in the book (Isa 14:1) (ExodR XIX.4). A rabbinic tradition suggests that Isaiah had in mind the foreigner who says, like Abraham, 'When can I become a proselyte and dwell beneath the wings of the Shekinah?': that is the true proselyte (*RA* 578).

Christians, quoting Paul (Eph 2:12–13), interpret it as being fulfilled in Christ (Calvin). The word translated 'eunuch' (Heb. *saris*) is elsewhere applied to court officials of various types, including Potiphar (Gen 39:1; cf. Esth 2:3,14) but is defined here by reference to the inability to beget children and is usually understood to be included in the Mosaic law banning such people from the 'assembly of the Lord', although the actual term is not used there (Deut 23:1) (Nicholas). Now those people who feel disgraced and shut out from the promise to 'Abraham and his seed for ever', are told to imitate Abraham 'who did not look either at his own decayed body or the barren womb of Sarah ... but hoped above all hope' (Rom 4:18) (Calvin). Some of the Church Fathers, to Luther's disgust, cite the case of the Ethiopian eunuch (Acts 8:27) and interpret this welcome of eunuchs into the Church as scriptural encouragement for virgins, celibate priests and all those who choose to be holy in body as well as spirit, 'making themselves eunuchs for the sake of the kingdom of heaven' (Matt 19:12). Instead of having sons and daughters they will have a place prepared for them in heaven (Clement, *Stromateis* 3.91, 98; Augustine, *Holy Virginity* 24–25; cf Jerome, Cyril). A modern discussion of the Ethiopian's handling of Isaiah in Acts 8 coins the term 'Eunuch's Bible' with reference to this passage (cf. Isa 18:1; 45:14) (Parsons 1998: 111–113), while another suggests that the term for 'eunuch' here includes homosexuals (*NCHB* 2.648).

In a second oracle beginning 'For thus says the Lord', God promises to give them 'a monument and a name' (Heb. *yad va-shem*) (vv. 4–7). The usual meaning of the Hebrew word *yad* is 'hand' but it can be applied to a stone monument as in the case of 'Absalom's monument' (2 Sam 18:18). This seems unlikely in the present context ('in my house'), and it has traditionally been understood as 'place' (cf. Num 2:17; Deut 23:12) (Tg, Vg, Rashi, AV, Delitzsch), taken by some with 'name' (cf. Prov 22:1) as a hendiadys: 'an honourable place' (LXX Oecolampadius). The comparison implied by 'better than sons and daughters' (v. 5) prompted Luther to paraphrase God's promise as 'I would rather have a pious Turk than a wicked Christian'.

It is to be an 'everlasting name', picking up a theme introduced at the end of the previous chapter (Isa 55:13): everlasting because it will be written in heaven so that in the presence of angels we will be reckoned children of God (Calvin). The words inspired a well-known nineteenth-century hymn beginning 'The head that once was crowned with thorns':

> To them the cross with all its shame
> With all its grace is given;
> Their name an everlasting name,
> Their joy the joy of heaven. (*EH* 147; *HON* 524; *CH4* 438)

In the second half of the twentieth century the 6,000,000 victims of the Nazi holocaust, most of them Jews, were included in Isaiah's promise when the name Yad Vashem was chosen for the Holocaust Memorial, established in Jerusalem in 1953, as the world centre for documentation, research, education and commemoration (cf. Isa 43:10).

The sacrifices of strangers will be accepted on the altar at Jerusalem (vv. 6–7), a remarkable prophecy illustrated by Westall and Martin (1835: 147–149). 'The house of prayer' must be the Temple (Ibn Ezra, Kimḥi; cf. Matt 21:13; Mark 11:17; Luke 19:46), although scholars have suggested that the words 'within my walls' (v. 5) are a gloss suggesting that it does not refer to the actual Temple building, but to the Temple precinct (Duhm). Some say it refers to the 'heavenly Jerusalem' (Eusebius), and the 'house of prayer for all nations' became a popular way of describing the Church (Jerome, Ephrem; Cassiodorus, *Exposition of Romans* 3). It also came to be one of the commonest words for synagogue, especially in Hellenistic Greek (Acts 16:13). The rabbis quoted this verse to prove that God himself prays (b*Berakhot* 7a; cf. LXX 'the house of my prayer'), and it is inscribed in Hebrew above the entrance to the Great Synagogue in Turin (1880) (Plate 38), as well as on other nineteenth-century synagogues,

PLATE 38   'For my house shall be called a house of prayer for all peoples' (Isa 56:7). Hebrew inscription on the façade of the Great Synagogue of Turin (1880).

including those in St Petersburg (1893) and Cardiff (1896–1897; demolished in 1989) (Kadish 2010: 280–282).

A third short prophecy repeats the promise that proselytes will join the returning exiles (v. 8) (Rashi, Ibn Ezra) in words recited daily in the *Shmoneh esreh* ('Eighteen Benedictions'): 'Blessed are you, Lord, who gathers the dispersed of his people Israel' (*ADPB* 84; cf. Deut 30:4; Mic 4:6; Ps 147:2). To Christians the 'outcasts of Israel' are the scattered Church, and these words are intended to reassure them that they will increase and multiply (Calvin; cf. Aquinas). Earlier commentators saw a connection between verses 8 and 9, recalling a scene of scattered sheep at the mercy of wild beasts (cf. Jer 50:17; Ps 74:19), and the words of Jesus, the good shepherd (John 10:16) (Jerome). The animals and creatures of the forest invited to 'come and eat' (v. 9) are the proselytes (Rashi), including all who live a godly life, now gathered together in Israel (Eusebius). Even creatures captured by the devil and under his tyranny for a long time, God calls to his spiritual banquet to eat the bread of life and rejoice (Procopius).

Corruption in High Places (Isa 56:9–57:13)

For most commentators there is a sharp break between verses 8 and 9 (Calvin, Lowth, Luzzatto). After three glowing salvation oracles (Isa 56:1–8), verses 9–12 begin a typical judgement prophecy (Duhm, Westermann). Luzzatto suggests that verses 8–12 are a funeral dirge composed for the death of Isaiah during the reign of the idol-worshipping Manasseh. It is a fierce attack on corrupt leaders, compared to useless watchmen, hungry dogs, stupid shepherds and drunkards (vv. 10–12). The wild beasts are the idolatrous wicked nations summoned to come and devour the wicked in Israel like wild beasts that devour each other (Ibn Ezra). There is a close parallel in Jeremiah: 'Go, assemble all the wild beasts; bring them to devour' (Jer 12:9) (Lowth). The prophet is foretelling the Roman destruction of Jerusalem in 70 CE (Theodoret).

The Church Fathers compare some of Christ's attacks on religious leaders in his own time: 'Woe to you, blind guides … you blind fools' (Matt 23:16, 17; cf. 15:14) (Chrysostom, *Discourses against the Jews* 4.6.3; cf. Jerome, Eusebius). The watchmen are the false prophets in Israel (cf. Ezek 3:17) (Rashi, Ibn Ezra). The shepherds without understanding are the bishops who read the words of the gospel and do not understand it themselves (Aquinas, Luther). The reference to drunkenness (v. 12) recalls other passages in Isaiah (Isa 22:13) and Paul's famous teaching on the subject (1 Cor 15:32) (Jerome). Calvin observes that the prophet's closing condemnation of those who say 'Come let us get wine' is not concerned about drunkenness for its own sake, but because it 'buries reflection … that no shame or fear, no reverence for God or men, might disturb their repose'.

Corruption in High Places (cont'd) (Isa 57:1–13)

Before the second part of his long bitter attack on corruption in Israel (Isa 56:9–57:13), the prophet turns aside to mourn the fate of the righteous in such an evil world, 'devout men taken away and no one understands' (vv. 1–2). The language recalls passages from the Psalms (e.g. Ps 12) and Micah (Mic 7:2). The odd vacillation between singular and plural, 'the righteous man/devout men/ the righteous man [v. 1] … he enters into peace/they rest [v. 2]', may be explained

Isaiah Through the Centuries, First Edition. John F. A. Sawyer.
© 2018 John Wiley & Sons Ltd. Published 2020 by John Wiley & Sons Ltd.

by positing an intertextual link with 'the righteous one, my servant' in chapter 53 (Isa 53:11), whose story has obvious parallels (Blenkinsopp). The term translated 'devout men' (RSV) or 'the faithful' (NJB), literally 'men of devotion' (Heb. *anshe ḥesed*), refers to those who display *ḥesed* 'faithful love, loyalty' both to man and to God (Calvin; cf. Neh 13:14). It seems to be a synonym of the word *ḥasidim* (Gk *Hasidaioi*), which came to be applied to specific groups of devout Jews in the Maccabaean period (1 Macc 7:13; 2 Macc 14:6) and the rabbinic literature (b*Berakhot* 5a) (Duhm). The use of the semi-technical term *ne'asap* (be gathered, taken away) twice in this context (cf. Gen 25:8; 2 Kgs 22:20) suggests that the author of the Damascus Document may have had Isaiah 57:1–2 in mind when he wrote of the death of the Teacher of Righteousness (Blenkinsopp 2006: 191), while Christian interpreters identify 'the Righteous Man' with Christ (Theodoret, Nicholas).

Verse 2 continues 'they shall enter into peace; they shall rest in their beds, each one walking in his uprightness' (vv. 1–2 AV). The righteous shall not witness the evil that is going to befall Israel and the holy city: they shall die in peace like Abraham (Gen 15:15) (Ibn Ezra). Josiah is a good example (cf. 2 Kgs 22:20) (Rashi). According to Gregory the Great, however, not all the elect will be removed from the world, because sinners would never turn to repentance if there were no good examples to inspire them (*Dialogues* 3.37). This is about the peace promised to the faithful by Christ (John 14:27), the man of peace whose apostles rest in their beds (Jerome). Rabbi Meir said 'God has given no more beautiful gift to the righteous than peace: when they die three companies of ministering angels recite this verse' (NumR XI.7). The words 'May he rest in his bed' are inscribed, in Hebrew, on a family tomb in the Church of S. Ambrogio in Florence (1480), and the verse was later selected by Luther, along with three other texts, as suitable for use as an epitaph (see comm. on Isa 25:7–9). An ancient Greek parallel, almost certainly inspired by this text, beginning 'But the souls of the righteous are in the hand of God' (Wisd 3:1–9), is a regular reading at funerals and Masses of the dead in Christian lectionaries (*ORM*, RCL).

The second part of the prophet's attack on his people takes the form of another trial scene (vv. 3–13; cf. Isa 41:1–7; 43:8–13): the accused are summoned 'to the judgement seat of God' (Calvin) (v. 3), their crimes are graphically enumerated (vv. 4–11) and sentence passed on them (vv. 12–13). The people are addressed as 'sons of the sorceress ... children of transgression' (vv. 3–5). They cannot claim to be the children of Abraham and Sarah because, if they were Abraham's children, they would do what Abraham did (John 8:39) (Eusebius). They 'enjoy themselves' (Heb. *hit'anneg*) and mock the prophets instead of 'taking delight in the Lord' (Heb. *hit'anneg*) (Isa 58:14) (Rashi). 'You who burn with lust' (Heb. *ha-neḥamim*) (cf. 1 Cor 7:9) refers to the passion of misguided idol-worshippers which can lead to child-sacrifice (Rashi, Luther), and the 'oaks' (RSV; Heb. *elim*) to sacred groves where such activities were practised (Hos 4:12–13; Deut 16:21). An alternative suggested by the Vulgate (cf. *Pesh*) is 'you who seek consolation [cf. *nahamu* Isa 40:1] with the shades of the dead' (cf. 1 Sam 28:13; Isa 8:19–20) (Blenkinsopp).

Then they are compared to a harlot since 'the faithful city has become a whore' (Isa 1:21) (Eusebius), addressed once more in the second person feminine singular (vv. 6–13; cf. Isa 54; 60). 'Smooth stones' (v. 6), like the stones used by David in his sling (1 Sam 17:40), would be shaped into idols (Ibn Ezra). Rashi suggests that 'their portion' means that the fate of the wicked in Jerusalem would be to be stoned with them. Calvin observes that, when their portion should have been the Lord (Ps 16:5; cf. Num 18:20; Ps 73:26), they chose the smooth stones of idol worship (cf. Jerome). They flaunt their disobedience by building altars on high places (cf. 2 Kgs 17:10; Jer 2:20; 3:6–10), like a harlot that commits adultery in public (Ibn Ezra) (v. 7). The implied contrast with 'my holy mountain' (v. 13) is unmistakeable.

The description of Zion's behaviour in verse 8 is unclear and has been interpreted in different ways. 'You have set up a symbol (*zikron*)' (RSV) places the emphasis on cultic practice, perhaps contrasting a pagan 'memorial' (LXX, Vg, Tg; cf. AV) with the Jewish *mezuzah* 'doorpost' (Deut 6:9) (Eusebius, Lowth). Others stress the erotic elements in the scene taking *zikron* in the sense of 'perfume' (cf. *azkarah* Lev 2:2) (Ibn Ezra), for example, and *yad* (hand, monument) (NJB 'sacred symbol') in an obscene sense (Duhm; cf. RSV 'nakedness'). According to Rashi, Israel is compared to an adulterous woman, lying beside her husband but directing her thoughts (Heb. *zikron*) to the door and the doorpost, and imagining how she will open the door and come out to meet her lovers waiting outside.

Her evil ways extended far beyond her home: she sends envoys as far as Sheol. Though wearied by a long journey, she did not give up, fired by such enthusiasm for her idolatrous activities (vv. 9–10). Rejecting advice to go along the 'king's highway ... turning neither to the right nor to the left' (Num 20:17; cf. John 14:6), she chose a winding road where it is forbidden to walk (Jerome; cf. Eusebius). Though well aware it is the wrong road, she obstinately persists, like the fools ridiculed by Jeremiah (Jer 18:12) (Calvin). 'Going to the king' (Heb. *melek*) (AV, Tg) is usually interpreted as a reference to 'those who go down to Egypt for help and rely on horses' (Isa 31:1; cf. 2 Kgs 16:8; 17:4) (Ibn Ezra, Luther), or to playing the harlot with Egyptians, Assyrians and Chaldaeans (cf. Ezek 16:26–29) (Jerome). But a popular alternative finds a reference to the well-documented cult of the pagan god Molech (RSV, NJB), which involved child-sacrifice and was practised on a high place called the Tophet in the Valley of Hinnom (Heb. *gehinnom*) on the outskirts of Jerusalem (cf. Jer 32:35; Lev 20:1–5) (RSV, NJB; Childs).

The climax of the passage (vv. 11–13) perhaps contains echoes of an earlier prophecy condemning those who made a covenant with death and made lies their refuge (Isa 28:15). Instead of remembering God and fearing him they were in awe of some other power. 'Whom did you dread and fear?' recalls Jeremiah's question 'Where are your gods? Let them arise if they can save you' (Jer 2:28). Instead of chanting 'The Lord is my light and my salvation: whom shall I fear?' (Ps 27:1), they lied and did not give him a thought (Jerome). For 'lied' (Heb. *kizzeb*) some commentators read 'failed' (cf. Isa 58:11) (Rashi). The irony of the prophet continues: 'their righteousness' (v. 12) means their sin under the guise of godliness' (Luther; cf. Calvin). 'Your collection of idols' (RSV), literally 'collections' (Heb. *qibbuṣim*), is explained as 'your idols and all their auxiliary forces' (Luther; cf. Rashi, Childs). Other suggestions include 'companies, troops' (AV, Kimhi, Calvin, Lowth), 'gatherings' in the sense of synagogues (Symmachus, Eusebius, Jerome) and 'gathered ones, i.e. dead ancestors' (Blenkinsopp). Whoever or whatever you turn to for support will be blown away in the wind and no one will hear your cry. 'But he who takes refuge in me shall possess the land and shall inherit my holy mountain' (v. 13). For some Christians this reward for the faithful was fulfilled when the Emperor Hadrian decreed that Jews could no longer live in the rebuilt city of Jerusalem but Christians could (Nicholas). For others it refers to 'Mount Zion … the city of the living God, the heavenly Jerusalem' (Heb 12:22) (Jerome): 'we are going to rise again and be the holy mountain of God' (Augustine, *Sermon* 45.3–5).

Peace, Peace to the Far and to the Near (Isa 57:14–21)

In the Jewish lectionaries the haftarah read on the morning of Yom Kippur begins at verse 14 (Isa 57:14–58:14) (*JSB*). But 'and he shall say' (MT *we'amar*) suggests that 'he who takes refuge in me' (v. 13) tells others to 'prepare the way of the Lord' (Isa 40:3), like a preacher whose 'first message is to teach penitence, remove offences, proclaim the Law and humiliate and terrify sinners' (Luther; cf. Symmachus, AV). 1QIsaᵃ has 'build up, build up the highway' (cf. Isa 11:16; 40:3). Some read 'And I shall say' (Heb. *we'omar*) (Vg, Lowth), anticipating God's next prophecy (v. 15), but most read it as impersonal, 'and it shall be said' (RSV) or 'they shall say' (LXX). Modern scholars recognize in vv. 15–19 an 'oracle of salvation', the first in Trito-Isaiah (Westermann), or a prophecy of comfort for mourners (v. 18), trying to make sense of God's anger (v. 16) and the 'hiding of his face' from them (v. 17: cf. Isa 46:15) (Blenkinsopp 2006: 217).

After the call to 'prepare the way', recalling Chapter 40, the prophecy is introduced by a formula which goes back even further to Isaiah's vision 'in the year that King Uzziah died': 'thus says the one who is high and lifted up [Isa 6:1], who inhabits eternity, whose name is Holy' (v. 15). In 1QIsa[a] and the ancient versions, verse 15 continues in the third person: 'the one who dwells in a high and holy place and also with those who are of a contrite heart' (LXX, Vg, Tg), making verse 16 the first words of the prophecy. But in the MT and most commentaries (Rashi, Calvin, Lowth, Luzzatto; cf. AV, RSV) the prophecy begins with the words 'I dwell in the high and holy place and also with those who are of a contrite heart'. This is the language of the Psalms: 'though the Lord is high, he regards the lowly' (Ps 138:6; cf. Ps 113:5–9) (Jerome). Verse 15 is quoted at the beginning of the Sabbath morning service (*ADPB* 366–367).

It has been pointed out that 'dwelling' with them, in the sense of being enthroned, is unparalleled (Westermann), but for the rabbis this is one of seven verses from scripture, one from the Torah (Deut 10:17–18), two from Isaiah (cf. Isa 66:1–2) and four from the Psalms (Pss 138:6; 10:16–18; 68:4–5; 146:5–7), in which God equates himself with those of a humble heart (*Tanḥ*. Gen 4:3). The Septuagint pictures God 'resting with the saints, giving patience to the faint-hearted and new life to the broken hearted' (Eusebius), and this prompts Jerome to add that the Holy One actually 'dwells in saints and in those of a contrite heart', which means that saints are raised to heaven (cf. Ps 30:1). 'God descends even to the lifeless, that he may breathe new life into them and form them anew' (Calvin).

Verse 15 requires five stanzas to unpack its imagery metrically, both in the Scottish paraphrase beginning 'Thus speaks the high and lofty one' (1742) (*CH2*, Paraphrase 21), and in Charlotte Elliott's hymn (1819) beginning 'There is a holy sacrifice' with the refrain 'The contrite heart' at the end of each verse (*CH2* 408). Rudyard Kipling's famous hymn 'God of our Fathers', composed for Queen Victoria's diamond jubilee in 1897, contains cautionary words from the same scripture source:

> Still stands thine ancient sacrifice,
> An humble and a contrite heart.
> Lord of hosts, be with us yet,
> Lest we forget, lest we forget. (*EH* 558; *CH2* 637)

Verse 16 has been interpreted in various ways. God makes the 'outstanding and dynamic promise' (Luther) that his anger will not last forever: 'for the spirit should fail (Heb. '*aṭap*) before me' (AV). According to Jerome this means that it would not be right for creatures created and sustained by God's spirit to perish forever as Job says, 'the spirit of God has made me and the breath of the Almighty gives me life' (Job 33:4; cf. Gen 2:7; Ps 150:6) (Jerome, Eusebius). 'As a father pities his children … he remembers we are dust' (Ps 103:13–14; cf. Ps 78:38–9) (Calvin). The rabbis used wordplay in the second clause 'not for ever [*lo la-neṣaḥ*] will I be angry'. In post-biblical Hebrew *neṣaḥ* can also mean 'victory' (cf. 1QM 4:13; *DSSE* 170), and they explained 'my anger does not lead to victory' as 'when I conquer I lose, and when I am conquered I gain': for example, in my anger I conquered the generation of the flood but lost almost all the inhabitants of the earth, while in the story of the Golden Calf my anger was defeated by Moses' intercessions and I gained the survival of my people (*PesR* 9.3). Others take it as a reference to the coming of the Holy Spirit: 'from me proceeds the spirit' (RSV, LXX, Vg) (cf. Zech 12:10; cf. Num 11:29; Joel 2:28) (Jerome, Eusebius), the Paraclete to comfort and console (John 14:16; 15:26) (Luther). The Targum interprets it as an additional promise that God will restore the spirits of the dead and the souls that he has made. Others make the promise conditional, citing the Psalm of 'one afflicted, when he is humble' (*'aṭap*) (Ps 102:1): 'I will not be angry forever when a spirit before me humbles himself' (Rashi; cf. Ibn Ezra).

The next verse goes back over the story of Israel's disobedience and God's anger (v. 17). Their sin is described as 'covetousness', where a part is taken for the whole as 'the love of money is the root of all evils' (1 Tim 6:10) (Calvin). Some Christian commentators identify the sinners as Pharisees, 'lovers of money' (Luke 16:14), or suggest that 'God struck them in his anger' refers to the Roman army in 70 CE (Nicholas). God turned his face away from them, that is, for Jews, he removed his Shekinah from them and hurled them away (Tg), for Christians it means 'withdrew his Word and grace from them' (Luther; see comm. on Isa 45:15). But they went on backsliding (RSV), rebelliously following the imagination of their hearts (cf. Gen 8:21) (Tg Ibn Ezra), wandering like sheep without a shepherd (Aquinas). The Greek fathers softened this harsh message, influenced perhaps by an earlier prophecy (Isa 54:7–8): 'for a little while, because of human weakness, I grieved and struck them, as a father disciplines his children (Prov 3:12). But once you felt my discipline, you were grieved with a godly grief (2 Cor 7:9) and went on sorrowful in your ways' (cf. LXX) (Eusebius).

When he saw 'their ways' (v. 18) can be taken as a reference to them humbling themselves and repenting (Eusebius, Jerome, Rashi). But more often it is interpreted as God's promise to heal and comfort his people in spite of their evil ways: 'I have pity on them in their calamity out of regard for my mercy, not their works' (Luther; cf. RSV Nicholas, Calvin). This is how the verse is interpreted in the *Biblia Pauperum*, where it serves as a comment on the Doubting Thomas story (John 20:24–31; cf. Jer 31:18) (*BP* 114). The words 'requite with comfort' (RSV; cf. Isa 40:1; 52:9) suggest a departure from strict principles of justice, and 'mourners' are not the same as repentant sinners. Rashi observes that the verb translated 'lead' (Heb. *hinḥah*) is an expression of rest and tranquility (cf. LXX, Tg), perhaps with the noun *menuḥah* 'rest' in mind (cf. Isa 28:12; Ps 23:2). Others suggest it means 'leading back' (Vg *reduxi*), that is, towards repentance as 'no chastisements, however severe, will drive us to repentance if the Lord does not quicken us by his spirit' (Calvin). In the MT verse 18 ends with the words 'comfort for him and his mourners' (cf. Tg, Vg, AV, NJB), that is, for the people of Israel and their friends 'who usually begin to mourn when they see a sick friend dying' (Ibn Ezra; cf. Rashi).

'I create the fruit of the lips' (v. 19), that is, speech (Ibn Ezra). Elsewhere the expression refers to a sacrifice of praise (cf. Heb 13:15) (Lowth), and Rashi suggests that here it means a new manner of speech: instead of insulting and degrading him, they will call 'Peace, peace'. Luther translates 'distended lips' and imagines a preacher like Paul with broad lips that can project the preaching of the Word to the whole world (cf. Mark 16:15). Modern commentators mostly take 'for his mourners' with this phrase: 'putting words of praise on the lips of those among them who mourn' (cf. Matt 5:4; Blenkinsopp; cf. RSV, Westermann, Childs).

'Peace, peace to the far and to the near' (v. 19) referred first to the edict of Cyrus (Ezra 1) but was later quoted by Paul in a spiritual sense (Eph.2:17) (Nicholas, Luther). By 'peace' the prophet means reconciling men to God (2 Cor 5:20), made clear by the addition of the words 'and I will heal him': the full and perfect happiness of God's people is absolutely the gift of God (Calvin). For Christian interpreters 'the far … and the near' nicely refers to Gentiles and Jews, in order of preference (Jerome, Nicholas). But the verse was also popular among the rabbis who quote it a number of times to show that God gives peace to the penitent, that is to say, those who were far off but have come near (NumR XI.7), or that he gives peace to those who are far off, including proselytes, before he gives it to the near (NumR VIII.4). Another Jewish interpretation of the verse is that it refers first to the aged who have kept the Torah all their lives, and then to those who have come to it recently (Rashi, Tg).

The Israeli prime minister Yitzhak Rabin quoted these words to express commitment to peace at his historic meeting with Yasser Arafat, Chairman of the Palestine Liberation Organization, in Washington on 14 September 1993. The verse also inspired one of Philip Doddridge's *Hymns Founded on Various Texts in the Holy Scriptures*, in which he interprets 'the far and the near' as follows:

> Receive the tidings with the delight,
> Ye Gentile nations from afar;
> And you, the children of his love,
> Whom grace hath brought already near. (1794: CXIV)

Not all are included in the promise: the 'wicked' are defined as those who will never know that peace (vv. 20–21). They will be tossed about like a stormy sea, thundering against the righteous (1QH 10:15; *DSSE* 262), recalling the image of Leviathan making 'the deep boil like a pot' (Job 41:31) (Aquinas). Just as each wave breaks on the shore against its will, and the next wave sees it but cannot turn back, so the wicked man sees his friend being punished but does not turn back (Rashi), or, like a stormy and troubled sea in which the billows dash against each other with terrible violence, so the wicked are tormented by evil thoughts and pangs of conscience (Calvin). Their evil works are compared to the 'mire and dirt' churned up by the sea, in contrast to the works of the godly, which are like gold and silver and precious stones (cf. Phil 3:19) (Luther). With this vivid image in mind, the chapter concludes, like an earlier chapter, with the proverb 'There is no peace for the wicked', but here instead of 'says the Lord' (Isa 48:22), we have the more personal 'says my God', a bold declaration of war against all those who falsely boast of his name (Calvin).

Is Not This the Fast That I Choose? (Isa 58:1–14)

The next chapter ends with a beautiful account of the peace and joy of the Sabbath, which refers, not only to Judaism's most popular and distinctive institution (Deut 5:12–15) but also to the fast of Yom Kippur (cf. Lev 16:31; 23:32). In the synagogue lectionary Isa 57:14–58:14 has been the haftarah for the morning service on Yom Kippur from the rabbinic period down to modern times (*JSB*; cf. b*Megillah* 31a). Isaiah 58 was to be read as an admonition to the

Isaiah Through the Centuries, First Edition. John F. A. Sawyer.
© 2018 John Wiley & Sons Ltd. Published 2020 by John Wiley & Sons Ltd.

community at the beginning of every fast, not just Yom Kippur (*Tos*Ta'anit 1:8), and is cited frequently in the Zohar. In Western Christianity verses 1–12 (or Joel 2:1–2, 12–17) are traditionally read on Ash Wednesday (RCL) or the Saturday after Ash Wednesday (*ORM*), while in the Greek Orthodox lectionary verses 1–11 is the reading prescribed for the Wednesday of the Sixth Week of Great Lent (*OSB*).

The passage contains echoes of Isa 40:1–11 and ends with the distinctive Isaianic 'For the mouth of the Lord has spoken' (cf. Isa 1:20; 40:5; Williamson 1994: 81, 153). Historical critics suggest that the prophecy, or the original core of the prophecy to which later material has subsequently been added, was uttered in Jerusalem in the early years of the Second Temple period when fasting was apparently a controversial issue (Zech 8:19; cf. Ezra 8:21–23, Joel 1:14) and the Sabbath was becoming an increasingly important institution (Neh 13:15–22) (Duhm, Cheyne, Westermann).

Rabbi Judah ben Ilai identifies 'my people' in verse 1 as the learned whose sins are regarded as presumptuous and the 'house of Jacob' as the untutored whose sins are unwitting, thus ensuring that everyone is included (b*Baba Metziah* 33b). Rashi compares the long litany of his people's sins in Psalm 78, in particular verse 36: 'but they flattered him with their mouths and lied to him with their tongues(cf. Kimhi). Christian commentators recognize in verse 1 a call to preachers to speak out boldly against ritualism and hypocrisy in their own day, whether among the Jews (Jerome), the papists (Luther), ordinary churchgoers (Henry) or all three (Calvin). Preaching should be like the sound of trumpet (Heb. *shofar*) (Luther). According to Jerome, the trumpet also announces the Last Judgement on God's rejected people, while for Aquinas it heralds the resurrection of the dead (1 Cor 15:52).

Christian writers cite the prophecy at length as providing the scriptural standard for the understanding of fasting (EpBarn 3; Justin, *Dialogue with Trypho* 15) (Horbury 1998: 136–138). Some cite examples of true fasting from the Psalms (e.g. Pss 35:13–14; 110:9) and compare this to circumcision of the heart (Jer 4:4; Col.2:11) (Jerome). Calvin, unlike most Protestant scholars, cites a verse from the Vulgate (not in the best Greek manuscripts) in which Jesus apparently recommends prayer and fasting as essential to faith (Matt 17:21; cf. Mark 9:29).

Several commentators compare the complaints of the wicked that God did not accept their rituals (v. 3) to the anger of Cain when the Lord had regard for his brother Abel's sacrifice but not for his (Gen 4:4–5) (Cyril), and their 'voice' (v. 4) to the blood of Abel crying for vengeance from earth to heaven (Gen 4:10) (Luther). The noise and unseemly disorder explains why God hates their 'fasting and their holidays and feasts' (Isa 1:13–14) (Eusebius). They should listen again to what Moses said about Yom Kippur: 'every soul that does not humble itself shall be cut off from the people' (Lev 23:29; Athanasius, *Festal Letters* 1.4). Aquinas quotes Joel: 'rend your hearts and not your garments' (Joel 2:13).

There is some debate among Jewish commentators on exactly what actions are 'acceptable to the Lord' (vv. 6–7). The word translated in most English versions as 'yoke' (Heb. *mota*) is pointed differently by Rashi, following the Targum: 'untie the bands of perverseness' (Heb. *mutteh*; cf. Ezek 9:9 'injustice'). Ibn Ezra recalls the Exodus tradition when the Lord freed Israel from slavery in Egypt and 'broke the bars (Heb. *motot*) of your yoke and made you walk upright' (Lev 26:13). The word often translated 'homeless, cast out' (Heb. *merudim*; AV, RSV, NJB; Ibn Ezra) (v. 7) is understood by Rashi as 'moaning' (cf. Lam 3:19; Ps 55:3). Most Jewish commentators understand 'your own flesh' in verse 7 as 'your own kin' (Tg, Rashi, JPS), but the Baal Shem Tov quotes this verse in support of his rejection of ascetic practices: 'Do not remain indifferent to your own flesh, that is, your own body's needs' (A. J. Heschel 1973: 27).

In Luke 4:18 the words 'let the oppressed go free' (v. 6) are added to the quotation from Isa 61:1–2 preached on by Jesus in Nazareth, and Jerome compares it to a 'real jubilee' (*jubilaeus verus*) when, on the day of atonement, to the sound of a loud trumpet, liberty shall be proclaimed to all the inhabitants of the land (Lev 25:9–10). Calvin rejects the view of some that the 'bonds of the wicked' are sinful thoughts (cf. Acts 8:23) and stresses that this is a passage about the actual abuse of the poor. Several writers point out that 'your own flesh' (v. 7) need not mean only one's own family: it refers to all human beings since we are all of one flesh (Cyril). In a modern Catholic lectionary verses 6–11 are read at special Masses 'for the starving people of the world' (*ORM*), and they are quoted by feminists and liberation theologians as one of the clearest and most unequivocal appeals for social justice in the Bible (Ruether 1985: 202–205; Miranda 1977: 48, 56, 100–101). It has been observed that this call for social justice is made in the context of a discussion of fasting: 'when fasting makes the wealthy poor in spirit and the poor impart to the wealthy their attitude of humble waiting upon God, then God will answer' (Stuelmuller).

'Break your bread with anyone who is hungry' (L. *Frange esurienti panem tuum*) (v. 7) is cited in an attack on debauchery and gluttony in the medieval English poem *Piers Plowman* (Langland 1959:153), and there is a setting of the same text for two voices by the French Flemish composer Pierre de la Rue. Verses 7–8, in Luther's German, also provided the words for the opening chorus of a Bach Cantata, *Brich dem Hungrigen dein Brod* (*BWV* 39), first performed in June 1726 on behalf of Protestant refugees from Salzburg who were seeking asylum in Leipzig (Whittaker 1959: 688). The passage features in a recent liberationist study of the hermeneutic of the hungry which seeks to locate interpretive centres in the experiences of 'the hungry' in our world (McGinn, Ngan and Calderón Pilarski 2014).

Verse 8 is interpreted by many as a reference to the resurrection of the dead. An early commentary on the Song of the Sea (Exod 15) includes verse 8 in a list of passages beginning with the word 'then' (Heb. *az*) (Isa 35:5, 6; 58:8; 60:5; Jer 31:12; Ps 126:2) and implies that they all, including Exodus 15, refer to the resurrection of the dead (*Mekh* on Exod 15:1 Lauterbach 1933: 169). The verse also provides scriptural authority for the belief that, when people perform a *mitzvah* 'a good deed' in this life, it will precede them and herald their arrival in the world to come, as it is said: 'righteousness shall go before you' (*Sotah* 6b; Maimonides 1956; 391). Verse 8 figures prominently in Mendelssohn's oratorio *Elijah* (1846): after Elijah is taken up by a whirlwind to heaven, the final chorus (*andante maestoso*) begins with the dignified, perhaps triumphant words of Isaiah 58:8: 'And then shall your light break forth as the light of morning breaketh', immediately followed by a lively fugue on the first verse of Psalm 8 ('Lord, our Creator, how excellent thy name is in all the earth'), which provides a kind of doxology to Mendelssohn's musical interpretation of the Elijah story (*BiM* 75).

There is a remarkable rabbinic interpretation of the next clause: 'the glory of the Lord shall gather you up'. On this is based the belief that God will honour the righteous by collecting up their bones (Heb. *asap*; cf. Isa 57:1) and burying them himself when they die, as he did for Moses (cf. Deut 34:6) (m*Sotah* 1:9; cf. Tg, Vg). This is actually closer to the original Hebrew than the traditional translation, 'the glory of the Lord will be your rearguard', which involves emending the text (*BHS*; cf. Isa 52:12).

'Then you shall call and the Lord will answer you' (v. 9) is cited by the rabbis as the reward for those who 'love their neighbours, look after their relations ... and lend money to the poor in distress' (b*Sanhedrin* 76b). It is the second of the three divine 'Here I am' sayings in Isaiah (cf. Isa 52:6; 65:1) in which God 'gives a practical declaration that he is near and reconciled to us' (Calvin; cf. Chrysostom, *Homilies on Matthew* 54.8). God here places himself at our disposal in a remarkable act of condescension recalling Deuteronomy 4:7: 'What great nation is there that has a god so near to it as the Lord our God is to us?' (Henry). Westermann, citing Buber, sees it as a definition of salvation, 'not described as a state of bliss, but as the constancy of the dialogical relationship between man and God'.

Three examples of evil conduct and two of good are next listed as the conditions for salvation (vv. 9a–10b). The 'yoke' is the 'shackles of sin' (cf. v. 6; Acts 8:23), that is, evil conduct in general (Jerome). The 'pointing of the finger' is a gesture interpreted as indicating the abuse of authority on the part of those in power: Matthew Henry imagines the finger with a signet ring on it, symbol of authority (cf. Dan 6:18; Hag 2:23). Others take it with 'speaking evil' in the sense of false accusations and defamatory speech directed at fellow citizens (Calvin), although speaking evil against God may also be included (Eusebius).

'Pouring oneself out' reminds us that acts of kindness to the hungry and afflicted must be done with warmth and affection: in Paul's words 'If I give all my goods to the poor and have not love, I am nothing' (1 Cor 13:3) (Calvin).

The image of 'light rising in the darkness' (v. 10b) is picked up from verse 8 and developed. The Targum elaborates the imagery of life in the world to come: 'and your body shall enjoy everlasting life and your soul shall be filled with delights' (v. 11). Maimonides in his comments on the verse, however, explicitly states that the delights of the world to come are not like bodily pleasures (1956: 391). The Church Fathers also identified the watered garden with paradise (Gen 2:8–10) (Jerome; cf. Luther) and saw the Church as the 'garden of Christ' (Cyril) where the faithful are nourished by the living water of the Holy Spirit (cf. Ps 36:8–9; John 4:7–15).

Brueggemann compares the image of God leading his people 'by still waters' to the familiar words of Psalm 23, while Childs observes that, whereas elsewhere in Isaiah the wilderness is transformed into a garden (Isa 51:3; 61:11), here it is the people themselves who are to become 'like a watered garden, like a spring whose waters do not fail.' The same image is used to good effect by Charles Wesley in one of his hymns invoking the power of the Holy Spirit: 'Make our hearts a watered garden, / Fill our spotless souls with God' (*MHB* 525). Luther adds that in such a paradise the faithful will bear fruit, 'doing good to all in word and deed', and notes that the subject in verse 12 is singular, implying that that one good man, whether a preacher or a pastor or a ruler, can single-handedly rebuild a state. The images of ancient ruins and foundations, building fences ('repairer of the breach' AV, RSV) and restoring streets (v. 12) are applied to the Church by several Christian commentators (cf. 1 Cor 3:10; Jerome, Aquinas, Calvin, Luther), but they are taken literally by many, either with reference to building works in general (Henry) or, more specifically, the rebuilding of Jerusalem after the exile (cf. Isa 44:26–28) (Aquinas, Duhm).

The concluding verses on the Sabbath naturally have special significance in Jewish tradition (vv. 13–14). The instruction to call the Sabbath 'a delight' (Heb. *'oneg*) gives the word particular rich associations (cf. *hit'anneg* 'to take delight' v. 14). 'The delight of the Sabbath' (Heb. *'oneg shabbat*) in popular idiom came to be applied to festivities and other activities traditionally enjoyed in Jewish families and communities on Saturday afternoons (Plate 39). In the Warsaw Ghetto *Oyneg Shabbos* (as they pronounced it there) was the code name of a group of Polish Jews led by the historian Emmanuel Ringelblum who met up on Saturday afternoons from 1940 to 1943 to collect archival material which they hid in milk cans and buried in the ground to be dug up many years later. The custom of wearing one's best clothes on the Sabbath 'to honour it, not going your own ways or seeking your own pleasure' (v. 13), likewise derives its scriptural authority from this passage (Sawyer 2003: 247). The rabbis deduced from verse 14

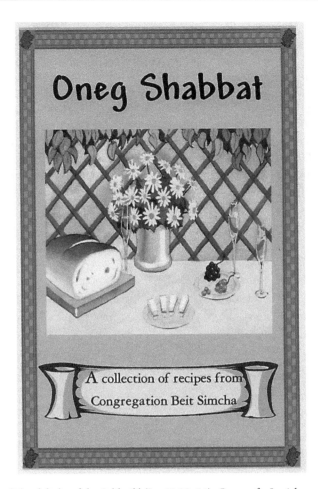

PLATE 39 'The delight of the Sabbath' (Isa 58:13–14). Cover of a Jewish cookbook (Beit Simcha, Glen Gardner NJ). Reproduced with kind permission of Sue Levy, Beit Simcha, Glen Gardner, NJ.

(cf. Ps 37:4) that 'all who take delight in the sabbath will receive their hearts' desire', interpreting 'delight (Heb. *hit'annag*) in the Lord' as referring to the Sabbath (b*Shabbat* 118b; *Zohar* 2:88b). 'Riding upon the heights of the mountains' (cf. Deut 33:13) and 'feeding on the heritage of Jacob' refers to the return to the promised land, if not in this world, then in the next (Kimḥi).

The Church Fathers interpreted the reference to the Sabbath in verses 13–14 in the light of Hebrews 4:10: 'so then there remains a Sabbath rest for the people of God, for whoever enters God's rest also ceases from his labours as God did from his' (Jerome). Like 'circumcision of the heart' (Rom 2:29) it means spiritual, not literal rest (Cyril), and the 'heritage of Jacob' means the heavenly Jerusalem, not the city rebuilt by Cyrus and destroyed by the Romans (cf. Heb 11:16; Jerome). The reformers maintain that the true Sabbath is self-denial (Calvin), abstaining from our own works and 'doing the works of God, hearing the Word, praying and doing good in every way to the neighbour' (Luther). To 'ride upon the heights of the earth' (cf. Deut 32:13) is understood by many to refer to regaining control of the fortified cities, built on a hill like Jerusalem (Vitringa, Calvin), higher than any other city in the world (Kimḥi), and therefore in control and able to prevail over all your ills and calamities (Luther). Others see it as a reference to our journey to heaven (Henry; cf. Eusebius).

Estrangement from God (Isa 59:1–21)

Described by C. C.Torrey as a 'great poem *de profundis*' (cf. Ps 130 Vg), in which sin has separated the people from their God and darkness prevails, chapter 59 begins with a stern warning to the people that this lamentable situation is their own fault (vv. 1–8) and their own heart-rending confession (vv. 9–14), but it ends with a promise of redemption for 'those in Jacob who turn from transgression' (vv. 15–21). Paul Hanson also compares the bitterness, anger, violence and radical imagery of chapter 59 (cf. 63:1–6; 66:15–16, 24) to

Isaiah Through the Centuries, First Edition. John F. A. Sawyer.
© 2018 John Wiley & Sons Ltd. Published 2020 by John Wiley & Sons Ltd.

conditions in our own society: 'the rhetoric of militant blacks, strident feminists, revolutionary pacifists and radical pacifists whose apocalyptic picture is not the illusion of a sick mind but the moral dread arising in the face of a human dereliction that threatens all life on our planet' (Hanson 1995: 100). Modern scholars have struggled to explain unexpected changes of tense and speaker in the chapter, but there is general agreement that it reflects conditions in the early years of the Persian Period (Westermann, Childs).

The rebuke starts with an emphatic challenge: 'No (Heb. *hen*), the arm of the Lord is not too short to save' (NJB); his power is limitless and he is 'always ready to be reconciled and lend a willing ear' (Calvin). His hand is not shortened (cf. Num 11:23); 'even before they call, he answers' (Isa 65: 24) (Henry). It is not that 'his ear is dull and he cannot hear', like the people Isaiah was sent to preach to (Isa 6:10; cf. Zech 7:11). The 'separation' (AV, RSV) or 'gulf' (NJB) between them and their God is their own fault: it is caused by their sins (v. 2), like Paul's 'dividing wall of hostility' (Eph 2:14), to be broken down by Christ (Eusebius), and the closed door into paradise with the flaming sword (Gen 3:24), extinguished by the blood of Christ, so that the robber might hear the words 'This day you shall be with me in paradise' (Luke 23:43) (Jerome). The image of God deliberately hiding his face like 'a man covering his face and closing his ears when he does not want to see or hear' (Ibn Ezra), goes back to Moses (Deut 32:20; cf. Isa 57:17) (Aquinas).

The passage contains an astonishingly rich and diverse 'vocabulary of sin' (Muilenberg): 'iniquities … sins (v. 2) … blood … lies … wickedness (v. 3) … empty words … falsehood … trouble… evil (Heb. *aven*) (v. 4) … violence (v. 6) … evil (Heb *ra'*) (v. 7) … crooked (v. 8)'. Their crimes include murder, dishonesty and corruption (Ibn Ezra). The 'blood on their hands' (v. 3) reminded the Church Fathers of the notorious response of the crowd to Pilate (Matt 27:24; cf. Isa 1:15) (Eusebius, Jerome), and their lies are the 'Jewish myths and commands by men who reject the truth' condemned by Paul (Titus 1:14) (Eusebius). 'They make haste to shed innocent blood' (v. 7) refers to the shedding of the blood of Christ and his apostles (Nicholas). Luther thinks instead of the blood of the prophets (cf. Matt 23:30), while Calvin takes the reference to blood guilt as metaphorical: 'he calls them murderers because they cruelly harassed the innocent, and seized by force and violence the property of others'.

The image of vipers and their eggs (vv. 5–6) was used by a sectarian writer at Qumran (*CD* 5:13–14; *DSSE* 133), John the Baptist (Matt 3:7) and Jesus (Matt 23:33) in attacks on their opponents (Blenkinsopp 2006: 140). Not only are their own deeds evil but they beget evil children … the adder's eggs denote poison and iniquity, the spider's webs weakness (Ishodad) (cf. Job 8:14). All their work fails to produce either a vestment for Christ or a covering to protect the soul (Jerome). Gregory of Nyssa applied the verse to the insubstantiality of heretical teaching, which may look like something woven but breaks at the touch of a finger (*Against Eunomius* 2.7). No part of their body is free from crime: hands, tongues and feet (vv. 3, 7) are all equally 'proficient in every kind of villainy' (Calvin).

Verses 7 and 8 are quoted in full by Paul to show that everyone, Jew and gentile alike, is under the power of sin (Rom 3:15–17) (Calvin). 'Desolation and destruction are in the highways ... they have made their roads crooked' (v. 8). Jerome is reminded of Christ's words: 'Jerusalem, Jerusalem, killing the prophets and stoning those who are sent to you ... Behold your house is forsaken and desolate!' (Matt 23:37). In all this there is no one who is just and honest (v. 4; cf. Isa 57:1–2) (Eusebius). The one missing is Christ 'whom God made our wisdom, our righteousness and sanctification' (1 Cor 1:30) (Nicholas). 'The way of peace' (v. 8; cf. Luke 1:79; John 14:6) is Christ but they do not know him: in Him alone one must believe and simply commit oneself to his mercy (cf. Ps 55:22) (Luther; cf. Eusebius, Jerome).

The prophet represents the people Israel in exile as speaking (Ibn Ezra): and 'therefore' introduces their communal confession of sin (vv. 9–15a), answering the charges made against them (vv. 1–8) (Westermann) and presenting the response of faith as the repentance that precedes divine intervention (Childs). First they describe what it is like to be rejected by God: 'the ungodly are crushed by a double devastation, inwardly by a terrified conscience and outwardly by calamity ... like Ahab (1 Kgs 22)' (Luther) or Paul (Rom 7:24) (Oecolampadius; cf. Henry). The absence of justice, righteousness (v. 9) and salvation (v. 11) is compared to the absence of light: 'we look for light and behold darkness' (cf. Isa 5:30; 42:19; Job 5:14) (Aquinas). The repetition of the word 'grope' (Heb. *gishshesh*) (v. 10) has 'a poverty and inelegance extremely unworthy of the prophet' (Lowth) and a synonym 'feel one's way' (Heb. *mishshesh*; cf. Deut 28:29; Job 5:14) has been proposed (*BHS*; cf. Lowth, Blenkinsopp). The verse is quoted in the prologue to the Damascus Document (*CD* 1:8–9; *DSSE* 129) with reference to the period of disorientation in the community before the arrival on the scene of the Teacher of Righteousness (cf. vv. 5–6; Blenkinsopp 2006: 93). Christian commentators have identified the situation with that of Jews and others who do not recognize their saviour in Jesus, the light of the world (Eusebius, Nicholas).

The phrase 'like dead men in desolate places' (Heb. *ashmanim*) (AV, Calvin), recalling Ezekiel's valley of dry bones (Ezek 37:12) (Henry), is unknown elsewhere and has been much discussed. Rashi and most modern commentators take it to mean 'like dead men among the healthy' (cf. Heb. *shemanim* 'fat'). Other suggestions include 'in gloomy darkness' (Jerome), 'in graves' (Kimḥi; cf. Tg) and 'amongst the fat ones', that is the heathen (Ibn Ezra). They desperately call for help like a bear robbed of her young (2 Sam 17:8) (Eusebius; cf. Ibn

Ezra) and moan pitifully like doves (cf. Isa 38:14; Ezek 7:16; Nah 2:7) (Calvin, Henry). Jerome has 'meditating doves' and, quoting another prophet's words, 'Ephraim is a dove, silly and without sense' (Hos 7:11; cf. Matt 10:16), applies the image to those who recite only the words of scripture, without understanding.

In a painful self-analysis familiar from Psalms (Pss 8:4; 40:12) and the prayers of Ezra (Ezra 9:6–7), Daniel (Dan 9:4–19) and others (vv. 12–15a), the sinners repeat that their sufferings were not God's fault (cf. v. 1): it was their own life of iniquity that deprived them of his care and concern (Theodoret). The graphic image of truth stumbling in the public square (v. 14 NRSV), used again in the apocalyptic account of the Seleucid persecution of the Jews (Dan 8:12), refers to the condemnation and killing of preachers of the truth (Luther). It was used to good effect in David Lyndesay's famous *Satyre of the Three Estates* (1540), where 'Truth', in the stocks because she has been found to be carrying a copy of the New Testament in the vernacular, remembers Isaiah as the prophet who would best understand her suffering in a corrupt society:

> The prophecy of the prophet Esay
> is practised Alas! on me this day
> who said that veritie should be trampled down
> amid the street and put in strong prison. (Happé 1979: 489)

Truth is lacking and he who departs from evil, like Job (Job 1:1), 'makes himself a prey' (Heb. *hishtolel*; Tg, Vg, AV, RSV) (v. 15), that is, he is at the mercy of the wicked like a sheep among wolves (Calvin). Rashi, citing Micah 1:8 (cf. Ps 76:5), has 'he who departs from evil is thought to be mad' (cf. LXX Ibn Ezra).

The second half of verse 15, beginning 'The Lord saw it', is considered by most modern commentators to be the start of new section, turning from human failings and wickedness to divine providence: 'although they have grievously offended ... still the Lord will have regard for his people' (Calvin). He is depicted as trying to find a just person who could intervene on their behalf (cf. Isa 50:2) (Jerome). But there was no one and God was 'appalled' (cf. Jer 2:12; Ezek 3:15; Job 18:20) (Rashi, NRSV). The anthropomorphism is omitted by the Septuagint and the Targum, but Jerome uses the word *aporiatus* (bewildered), and most commentators take it literally as a measure of the extent of the ungodliness in the world: just as when he came down to see what was going on in Babel (Gen 11:8), God himself could hardly believe it (Luther). Only his own arm could save them and 'his righteousness' (AV, RSV; Heb. *ṣedaqah*), translated 'saving justice' (NJB) or 'triumphant power' by modern commentators (Blenkinsopp), and 'mercy' (Gk *eleemosune*) in the Septuagint. The Greek Fathers interpreted 'his arm' as the just recompense that God demands while 'his mercy' teaches us the usefulness of discipline (Theodoret). Some of the Jewish commentators interpret righteousness as 'judgement on the wicked and salvation for the good' (Luzzatto).

The 'armour of God' combines 'righteousness' and 'salvation' with 'vengeance' and 'fury' (v. 17). The passage is alluded to in the Wisdom of Solomon (Wisd 5:18) and was certainly in Paul's mind when he described the 'whole armour of God' designed to withstand the wiles of the devil (Eph 6:14–17; cf. 1 Thess 5:8) (Jerome). Paul called it 'the armour of God' because God wore it first and fitted it for us, but he kept the 'garments of vengeance and the cloak of fury' for himself (Henry). God will wreak vengeance on the enemies of his people wherever they are, on the islands as well as on the continent (v. 18) (Ibn Ezra). Some Christian commentators included the Jews among God's enemies because they rejected the Messiah and take the reference here to be to the Roman legions that destroyed Jerusalem in 70 CE (Eusebius, Jerome, Nicholas). Luther, by contrast, thinks of Sennacherib and the Assyrians, and Calvin observes that, 'although none but mortal men are mentioned, still we must begin with Satan, who is their head'.

Verse 19 is one of several references to the global relevance of Isaiah (cf. Isa 43:5–6; 45:6; 49:12) given prominence in early Christianity (Matt 8:11; Luke 13:29): the fear of the Lord (Pss 33:10; 112:1) and the glory of God will spread to all the nations of the world (Eusebius). Aquinas compares this with the decree of Darius 'that in all my dominion men tremble and fear before the God of Daniel' (Dan 6: 25–27). The meaning of the next two clauses is unclear. For the first, Rashi has 'distress (Heb *ṣar*) shall come like a river'. Others have 'oppressors will come like the flooding of the river Euphrates' (Tg; cf. Isa 8:7; 11:15), or 'the enemy (Heb *ṣar*) shall come as a flood' (AV; cf. Calvin), a reference to the Roman army (Nicholas). The Septuagint has 'the wrath of the Lord will come like a mighty river' and most modern interpreters have 'he will come like a pent-up (Heb *ṣar*) torrent' (NRSV, NJB; cf. Vg, Luther). Ibn Ezra paraphrases it as follows: 'And there shall be a time of trouble such as has never been seen before' (cf. Dan 12:1) (Ibn Ezra). The second clause is usually interpreted as 'which the wind [or spirit] of the Lord drives' (Heb. *nosesah*) (Vg, Luther, RSV) or 'puts to flight' (Kimḥi). The Church Fathers found a reference to the rushing mighty wind at Pentecost (Acts 2:2–4) (Eusebius, Jerome). By association with the popular Hebrew word *nes* (ensign, flag) (cf. Isa 5:26; 11:10–12; 49:22; 62:10), the verse was taken by some to mean 'the spirit of the Lord will lift up a standard against him' (AV). In post-biblical Hebrew *nes* came to mean 'miracle' (m*Berakhot* 9:1), and Rashi suggests 'the spirit of the Lord works wonders'. The verse features, with Isa 60:1–2, in the final chorus of Penderecki's choral Symphony *The Seven Gates of Jerusalem* (1996) (*BiM* 232).

'And he will come to Zion as Redeemer' (v. 20): Calvin observes that Zion refers to 'captives and exiles who, however far from their homeland, still must have carried the temple in their hearts' (Calvin). It refers to the coming of the Messiah and those who turn from transgression are 'all those whose names are written in the book' (Dan 12:1) (Ibn Ezra). The phrase is alluded to more than once in the sectarian literature from Qumran (*CD* 6:5; 8:16; 19:29), where it can be taken as 'those who returned from Israel' as well 'the penitents of Israel' (Blenkinsopp 2006: 212–216). The Targum interprets the prophecy to mean that the Messiah 'will turn the rebellious ones in the house of Jacob to the law' (cf. LXX). In the synagogue verses 21–22 are recited in the *Qedushah de-Sidra* at the end of the morning service (cf. Isa 26:4; 42:21; 65:24) (see on Isa 6:3; *ADPB* 138–139).

The passage is quoted by Paul to prove that, despite the present hardening of their hearts, in the end 'all Israel will be saved' (Rom 11:26–27) and gathered into one fold (John 10:16) (Calvin). For Christian commentators the 'Redeemer', the kinsman (Heb. *go'el*) of Israel, is Christ who will redeem them with his own blood (Num 35:19) (Luther; cf. Jerome). 'Zion' is the Church, and 'those that turn from iniquity' are converts (Eusebius) or penitent Christians (Jerome). The refrain of the Advent hymn 'O come, O come, Immanuel' probably alludes to this famous verse:

> Rejoice! Rejoice! Immanuel
> Shall come to thee, O Israel.

Verse 21 has its own formula, 'saith the Lord', and is considered by many to be a prose addition to the main prophecy. It adds the promise that the spirit of prophecy will never depart from the hearts of the Israelites (cf. Joel 2:28–29) (Ibn Ezra, Aquinas). The choice of the word 'covenant' points to 'the greatness and excellence of this promise' and anticipates the 'new covenant' established in Christ (Calvin), recalling an earlier promise 'the Word of the Lord abides for ever' (Isa 40:8) and the words of Christ himself, 'I am with you always even to the end of the world' (Matt 28:20) (Luther). The Church Fathers also saw this as foretelling the coming of the Holy Spirit (John 20:22–23), a 'key part of the mystery' (Eusebius, Jerome). Paul quotes a Greek version of verses 20–21 towards the end of his discussion of the place of the Jews in God's divine plan: 'the deliverer will come from Zion, he will banish ungodliness from Jacob and this will be my covenant with them' (Rom 11:26–27). Paul was at pains to show how the Jews have been rejected but at the same time some are saved (Luther).

Arise, Shine for Your Light Is Come (Isa 60:1–14)

Chapters 60–62 are considered by most modern scholars to be a distinctive literary unit at the heart of 'Trito-Isaiah' (Isa 56–66). On the one hand, there are no references in these three chapters to the wicked and their fate, which are such a conspicuous feature of the other chapters, while, on the other, the language and imagery bring them particularly close to 'Deutero-Isaiah' (Isa 40–55) (Westermann, Childs). Aquinas also takes the three chapters together as a single promise of salvation containing prosperity (60), the joy of the spirit of

Isaiah Through the Centuries, First Edition. John F. A. Sawyer.
© 2018 John Wiley & Sons Ltd. Published 2020 by John Wiley & Sons Ltd.

the Lord (61) and the glorification of Zion (62). The striking continuity between chapter 40 and chapter 60 is beautifully employed in Handel's *Messiah*, where, in the context of the Nativity, verse 1 is interwoven with Isa 40:9–10 in the contralto aria: 'O Thou that tellest good tidings to Zion … Arise shine for thy light is come'. The chorus continues, 'Say unto the cities of Judah, Behold your God' (Butt 2011: 299). Verse 2, combined with Isa 9:2, provides the text for the bass recitative and aria that follow, 'For behold darkness shall cover the earth … The people that walked in darkness', leading into the chorus 'For unto us a child is born' (Isa 9:6). The same continuity is reflected in a stained glass window in St Peter's Church Lampeter, illustrating Matthew 4:12–20 (Isa 9:2), with Isaiah, 'the spirit of prophecy', and the words of verse 1 in the tracery at the top (Bowe 2010: 211–212).

In the Jewish lectionary, chapter 60 is one of the seven 'consolation' haftarot (see comm. on Isa 40), and the first words, 'Arise, shine for your light is come', figure in 'Lekha Dodi' (see comm. on Isa 52:1–2). Imagery from the chapter is evident also in the popular Israeli song *Jerusalem of Gold* (1967). *Qumi Ori* (Arise, Shine) is the title of a Zionist tract published by the ultra-orthodox rabbi Yeshayahu Margolis in 1925 (Ravitzky 1996: 53–57) and of the biography of the Israeli artist Aviva Uri written by her daughter, Rachel. The title reflects the fact that Uri's Ukrainian parents, young Zionists, had the name Licht (light) before fleeing to Palestine in 1921.

In Christian lectionaries verses 1–6 are most often associated with Epiphany thanks to the image of people coming from afar on camels with 'gold and frankincense' (v. 6; cf. Matt 2:11) (*ORM*, RCL). Verse 1 has been particularly popular in Christian tradition from the patristic period down to the present day. John of Damascus applies the Greek version to the resurrection: 'Shine, shine, O new Jerusalem, for the glory of the Lord has risen over you' (*Canon of Pascha, Ninth Ode*; Wybrew 2001: 37–39). Eusebius says that this prophecy was only partially fulfilled at the first coming of the Saviour: the darkness when 'the sun shall be no more by day, nor the moon by night' (v. 19) refers to his second coming, when the true light, 'the sun of righteousness', will replace them (cf. John 1:9; Mal 4:2; 1 Thess 4:16). Ibn Ezra notes that the words translated 'come' (Heb. *bo*) and 'arise' (Heb. *zaraḥ*) often have an astronomical meaning (cf. v. 20; Gen 28:11), and he takes 'your light has come' in the sense of 'your light has set', while in its place 'the glory of the Lord will rise over you (like the sun)' (cf. vv. 19–20). The repetition of 'upon you' suggests 'upon you alone', because, when the Messiah is revealed, all the other nations of the world will be in darkness and will be attracted by your light (*PesR* 36.2).

In the medieval *Biblia Pauperum*, it is one of the four biblical texts accompanying the illustration of the Transfiguration (Matt 17:1–9): 'Jerusalem, your light has come and the glory of the Lord has risen over you' (*BP* 71). As in the other three texts (Ps 45:2; Mal 4:2; Hab 3:4), the emphasis is on the light and beauty of the 'glorified son of God' (Henry). Luther takes it in a more general sense, like Paul's 'Awake and Christ shall give you light' (Eph 5:14; cf. Eph 5:8). Many point out that 'Jerusalem' here must refer to the heavenly Jerusalem, that is the Church, and the light is the light of Christ who 'called you out of darkness into his marvellous light' (1 Pet 2:9) (Jerome, Cyril, Aquinas, Oecolampadius). There are several sixteenth-century settings of the passage (L. *Surge illuminare*), including a motet by Palestrina (1581), and an impressive modern one in John Tavener's *Veil of the Temple* (2003) (*BiM* 251–252).

The coming of the nations from the darkness to 'your light' (v. 3) reminds us that the prophecy begins with the imperative, 'Arise, shine', and means that Jerusalem is called upon to give light to the nations in the sense of cleansing them from their sins with the 'power of the divine mysteries' (Eusebius, Cyril; cf. Ambrose, *On Theodosius* 52). In a thirteenth-century stained glass window in Canterbury Cathedral the verse is illustrated by Isaiah pointing with one hand to the star over the magi and with the other to the gates of Jerusalem (Caviness 1977: 120–121).

'Lift up your eyes and look around' recalls Christ's words to his disciples (John 4:35) and the scene of people from many countries receiving the word of God at Pentecost (Acts 2) (Jerome). Jerusalem's children will come back to her, her sons strong enough to come on their own feet, their daughters carried 'on the hip' (v. 4). The word 'carried' (Heb. *'aman*) elsewhere refers specifically to nursing (Ibn Ezra; cf. Esth 2:7; Ruth 4:16), and Jerome, citing Peter (1 Pet 2: 2; cf. Gal 4:19; 1 Thess 2:7), finds in the words 'your daughters shall be nursed' (AV; cf. NRSV) a reference to Christian souls receiving the 'pure spiritual milk' of the apostles (cf. Cyril). The joy that fills the heart of Jerusalem (v. 5; cf. Zeph 3:14; Zech 2:10–11) (Jerome) recalls 'the joy in heaven over one sinner that repents' (Luke 15:7) (Eusebius) but uses the striking language of trembling to 'express the astonishment and even amazement of the Church ... when she perceives she has been elevated to so high a rank of honour' (Calvin; cf. Jer 33:9 Lowth). 'Anxiety is mixed with rejoicing' because of the sheer scale of the multitude that will come to Jerusalem (Ibn Ezra).

Verse 5 describes the abundance of the sea, that is, the wealth of the west (Tg) coming to Jerusalem, and the 'wealth of the nations' (RSV), that is, their possessions (Rashi, cf. Duhm), or the power of money (Luther). This is now the commonest interpretation of the phrase going back to the Septuagint (cf. Lowth, Luzzatto, Westermann, Childs), and probably where the founder of modern economics, Adam Smith, found the title of his famous work *The Wealth of Nations* (1776). Not everyone, however, accepts an interpretation of the verse that describes the arrival of the material wealth with which the new city will be built (vv. 10–11). Instead of 'wealth' (Heb. *ḥayil*) Ibn

Ezra has 'land armies' (cf. Nicholas) and Matthew Henry envisages the 'forces of the gentiles' (AV) who had been against her, now at peace (cf. Prov 16:7) and fighting for her. The Vulgate gives a third possibility, *fortitudo*, explained by Jerome as 'the strengthened faith (*roborata fide*) of the nations', with reference to Paul's 'I can do all things through Christ who strengthens me' (Phil 4:13; cf. Eusebius). Aquinas similarly observes that their true strength is spiritual, citing Job: 'the Almighty is your gold and your precious silver' (Job 22:25).

From the east 'a multitude of camels' (Vg *inundatio*) will come, bringing gold and frankincense, and will 'proclaim the praise of the Lord' (v. 6). This continues the scene of great riches arriving in Jerusalem to make it the most beautiful city in the world (Jerome). But taken with the next verse, where 'the flocks of Kedar ... and the rams of Nebaioth will minister to you' (v. 7), the focus once again switches from material wealth to something spiritual. The animals 'shall be at your service' (Heb. *sharet*) like the furnishings of the tabernacle (Exod 35:19) (Ibn Ezra) and 'will be offered up on my altar' (Tg; cf. Rashi). Calvin observes that the 'camels, gold, frankincense and sheep ... are what each country produces', and this means that we cannot be truly converted to the Lord without offering all our faculties as 'spiritual sacrifices' (1 Pet 2:5; Rom 12:1). Frankincense represents the spiritual fragrance of worship and gold stands for physical abundance (Eusebius; cf. Jerome). Some commentators point out that it is the animals that are depicted as coming to worship the Lord: for 'it is easier for a camel to go through the eye of a needle than for a rich man to enter the kingdom of heaven' (Matt 19:24) (Eusebius; cf. Theodoret). They are willing victims (Vitringa).

The passage beginning 'Arise, shine for your light is come' (v. 1) was applied by the Fathers to the coming of light into the world (Gk *Epiphania*) when Christ was born (cf. Matt 4:16; Luke 1:79; John 1:9). Images of the Magi coming from afar with camels and gifts of gold and frankincense (Matt 2:11) go back to these verses. The tradition that the three wise men were kings comes from this passage (v. 3; cf. Ps 72:10–11), and early Christian art portrayals of the Adoration of the Magi show the camels in fulfilment of Isaiah's prophecy (v. 6) (cf. Nicholas, Luther) (Schiller 1971: 101, Plate 147) (Plate 40). The camels also appear in the *Bible Moralisée*. In music, the best known setting is Bach's Cantata *Sie werden aus Saba alle kommen* ('They will all come from Sheba') (*BWV* 65), composed for Epiphany in 1724 (Plate 41). The opening chorus is a setting of verse 6b, with horn signals and oboes perhaps to give an oriental sound, and a fugue suggesting the gathering of a great crowd. The bass and tenor solos add the personal comments of a pious worshipper: 'Gold from Ophir [Isa 13:12] is too slight ... having thee, I must / The most abundant store of wealth / One day above in heav'n inherit'.

PLATE 40   'The young camels of Midian shall come … all those from Sheba …
bringing gold and frankincense' (Isa 60:6). Fourth-century Roman sarcophagus.

PLATE 41   'A multitude of camels will overwhelm you' (Isa 60:6). Copper
engraving from Johann Jacob Scheuchzer, *Physica Sacra* (Augsburg and Ulm, 1735).
Reproduced with kind permission of David Gunn.

Another part of the story of the return of Jerusalem's 'sons from afar' depicts her looking round (v. 4), and when she sees what look like clouds scurrying across the sky or doves flying home, she asks in amazement, 'Who are these …?' (vv. 8–9; cf. Isa 63:1). These are her children, the exiles of Israel coming home (Tg). Christian interpreters take it as a reference to the apostles (Nicholas) or converts to Christianity (Eusebius, Jerome, Aquinas). Ambrose applies the image to the souls of the righteous unencumbered by any earthly weight (*On Virginity* 17.108), while for Luther the clouds are preachers sending down rain on the people and their sermons are like pigeons that do not fly at random but to explicit places. Some of Christopher Columbus' contemporaries interpreted his name as meaning 'dove' (L. *columba*; Heb. *yonah* 'Jonah'), and saw a reference not only to Jonah, who embarked for Tarshish in the distant west (Jon. 1:3), but also to the flying doves in this passage. Later Jonathan Edwards also found here a clear reference to America (Edwards 1972: 128–133), while in 1792 William Carey, founder of the Baptist Missionary Society, quoted it as scriptural authority for the idea of combining Christianity and commerce in the East India Trading Company (cf. Isa 54:2–3): 'ships of Tarshish … to bring thy children from afar, their silver and their gold with them, unto the name of the Lord thy God' (Smith 1906: 25). Nicholas quotes the tradition that some of the first Christians sold their possessions and laid the proceeds at the apostles' feet (Acts 4). Others suggest a metaphorical interpretation whereby silver is the eloquence and gold the wisdom offered by new converts to the Church (Aquinas, Luther).

In a passage alluded to in the War Scroll (1QM 12:13–14; *DSSE* 178), the foreign nations, who had previously oppressed and despised Israel, will build up the walls of Jerusalem and 'bring to you the wealth of the nations … and bow down at your feet' (vv. 10–14). God's anger, which had made them suffer so much, will give way to compassion (Isa 54:8) (Aquinas); 'in wrath he remembers mercy' (Hab 3:2) (Calvin; cf. Luther). Applied to the Church, several commentators point out that Christ first employed a few apostles to start building, but soon they were joined by foreigners and princes from all over the world who had converted to Christianity (Jerome, Nicholas). Calvin used this verse to prove that kings (vv. 10, 11, 16) are still kings when they submit to Christ, in opposition to the papists who claim that the Pope has supreme power over kings and princes. Other Christian interpretations include the idea that the Word is the wall of the Church and the foreign builders are preachers like Augustine, Jerome and Cyprian (Luther). In the Book of Revelation verse 11 is cited in the description of the heavenly Jerusalem (Rev 21:25–26). The gates will always be open because there will be no more danger from outside: all the nations that will not serve you shall have perished (vv. 11–12). The 'open gates' are the teachers who will admit all the elect from among the nations to worship God (Eusebius).

'The glory of Lebanon' refers to the 'best trees' (Ibn Ezra), like those used in the building of Solomon's Temple (2 Chron 2:16; Ps 74:5–6) (Jerome). There is scholarly disagreement as to what the trees referred to are: fir, pine, box (AV; cf. Vg); cypress, pine, box (JPS); or cypress, plane and pine (RSV). For Christian readers this new temple will be more splendid than the old because Christ will come to it (Mal 3:1) (Henry), a 'spiritual temple' (Eph.2:21) of which we are the 'living stones' (1 Pet 2:5) (Calvin). 'The place of my feet' refers to the ark, elsewhere called 'his footstool' (Ezek 43:7; Pss 99:5; 132:7) (Aquinas, Henry), or perhaps it just means the place where God can be found, not in all his majesty, which could not be confined in a small space, but in such a way as to raise our eyes to heaven (Isa 66:1) (Nicholas; cf. Calvin). Then they shall call you the 'city of the Lord' because there will be one city and one people when 'the full number of the gentiles come in and all Israel will be saved' (Rom 11:25–26) (Eusebius; cf. Jerome). 'The Zion of the Holy One of Israel' (AV, RSV) is a striking expression found only here, questioned by some (*BHS*, Luzzatto) and avoided in the Targum, which has 'Zion, in which the Holy One delights'.

Your Sun Shall Set No More (Isa 60:15–22)

The image of Zion as a deserted city to be transformed into something majestic and a joy forever (v. 15) is followed immediately by the image, familiar from an earlier passage (Isa 49:23), of Zion as a baby girl at her mother's breast (v. 16): 'you shall suck the milk of nations'. This time the image of 'sucking the breast of kings', described by modern commentators as 'repugnant' (Duhm), 'inelegant' (Zimmerli) and a 'gender mistake' (Sherwood 2007: 300), is avoided by the Septuagint and the Targum (cf. Duhm, NJB); Ibn Ezra explains that 'the milk of nations' means their money: the kings themselves will bring their treasures to Jerusalem (Luzzatto). For the Church Fathers the kings are the teachers of the Church and their milk is the doctrine that nourishes newly born converts (cf. v. 4; 1 Pet 2:2) (Jerome, Aquinas). 'And you shall know that I, the Lord' echoes chapter 49 as well.

'Instead of bronze I will bring gold' introduces the last part of this prophecy, describing in still greater detail the miraculous transformation that is to come (vv. 17–22). It describes a society in which your money will be returned to you (Rashi) and tax collectors will act peacefully and fairly (v. 17) (Ibn Ezra). According to the Church Fathers the prophecy that 'wood will be turned into bronze and stone into iron' refers to the conversion of useless, stupid people into men who will be strong and useful, 'God's fellow workers', employed in building the city (Eusebius, Jerome, Aquinas) or the spiritual temple (Calvin). Luther recalls that Augustus said he found Rome wooden and left it golden. The prophecy that the new leaders who are to bring peace and righteousness are called 'overseers' and 'taskmasters' (Gk *episkopoi*) was applied by Christian authorities from as early as the first century to the role of bishops and deacons in the Church (Clement of Rome, *Letter to the Corinthians* 42:1–5; cf. Irenaeus, *Against Heresies* 4.26.5).

Verse 20 was the inspiration for a hymn by the English clergyman Geoffrey Thring, who applies Isaiah's imagery, as John of Patmos does (Rev 22:13; 23:5), to heaven 'Where saints are clothed in spotless white / And evening shadows never fall' (*EH* 279; *CH2* 279; Moffatt 1927: 98). In Jewish tradition too, verse 19 is one of three passages from Isaiah (cf. Isa 66:13; 25:8) which conclude the liturgy of consolation recited in the house of mourning after a funeral (see comm. on Isa 66:13), and in the Mishnah verse 21 is quoted in a famous discussion of who will have a share in the world to come (m*Sanhedrin* 10:1–2). It is also one of the verses cited to illustrate the belief that God is both prosecutor and counsel for the defence at the same time: 'The same mouth which said 'A people laden with iniquity' (Isa 1:4) said also 'My people shall all be righteous (Isa 60:21)' (cf. Isa 26:2; 65:24; 66:23) (*ExodusR* Mishpatim 30.24). Verse 21 is quoted over thirty times in the Zohar.

The Biluim (see comm. on 2:5) chose verse 22a as their motto to express the hope that their pioneering efforts, initially on a relatively small scale, would eventually lead to the establishment of 'a mighty nation'. The Church Fathers recalled the good servants in the parable 'who shall have authority over five or ten cities' (Luke 19:17, 19) and Paul, 'the least of all the saints' (Eph 3:8) who, by the grace of God, will become the princes of a great nation in heaven (Eusebius, Jerome). Luther also applied the prophecy to the miraculous expansion of the Church, quoting the endless number of disciples Paul, Augustine and others produced, as well as examples from his own day, including some who were burnt at the stake.

'I am the Lord; in its time I will hasten it' (v. 22 RSV): this means, if they are worthy, I will act swiftly, but if they are not worthy, their salvation will come in its own time (Rashi). Some read 'in his time' and refer it to the coming of Christ (Jerome). The Hebrew actually has 'in her time', that is, at the time when the Church (feminine) is to be delivered (Calvin). The Greek has 'I will gather them' recalling Christ's promise that, when the trumpet sounds, the elect will be gathered 'from one end of heaven to the other' (Matt 24:31) (Eusebius).

Good News for the Poor (Isa 61:1–11)

The appearance of one anointed by the Lord, on whom the spirit of the Lord rests, recalls references to the Davidic messiah (Isa 11:2) (Eusebius, Jerome), the Servant of the Lord (Isa 42:1–4) (Torrey, Rudolph) and even Cyrus (Isa 45:1) (Blenkinsopp). But most assume it is the prophet himself speaking, like Micah who claimed he was 'filled with the spirit of Yahweh' (Mic 3:8) (Westermann). 'Anointing' is rarely used of prophets (1 Kgs 19:16; Ps 105:15) (Ibn Ezra), and it may be used here in a non-technical sense, a synonym

Isaiah Through the Centuries, First Edition. John F. A. Sawyer.
© 2018 John Wiley & Sons Ltd. Published 2020 by John Wiley & Sons Ltd.

for 'send' or 'appoint' (Duhm), or 'nothing but an expression of nobility and greatness' (Rashi). 'Bringing good news' is already familiar (Isa 40:9; 41:27; 52:7) and the 'year of the Lord's favour' recalls the 'day of the Lord's favour' (Isa 49:8; 58:5), but 'binding up the broken-hearted' and 'proclaiming liberty to the captives' appear only here in Isaiah and make this passage strikingly original and much quoted. The word 'liberty' (Heb. *deror*) from the law of the Jubilee (Lev 25:10) occurs only here and in Jeremiah 34:8, 15, 17.

Along with Isa 52:7, these verses are the subject of an eschatological midrash found at Qumran in which 'the year of the Lord's favour' (RSV) or 'the acceptable year of the Lord' (AV) is the final day of judgement on the Day of Atonement in the Jubilee year (Lev 25:10), when a mysterious heavenly figure known as Melchizedek will proclaim liberty to the captives, forgiving them all their iniquities (11Q13; *DSSE* 532–534). It is applied to the Messiah in the 'resurrection fragment' (4Q521; *DSSE* 412–413), and Christians since the very beginning applied it to the coming of Christ. In the West, the chapter features in the lectionary for Epiphany (*ORM*, RCL); in Orthodox tradition on Holy Saturday (*OSB*). Indeed the christological interpretation of the passage became so pervasive in Christian Europe that, although the passage was apparently in the sabbath lectionary in the days of Christ (Luke 4:17–18), and had some significance in the Qumran community, it is conspicuous by its absence from Jewish lectionaries in use today (*JSB*). The sixth consolation haftarah (Isa 60:1–22) is followed by the seventh (Isa 61:10–63:9), omitting 61:1–9 entirely (see comm. on Isa 40).

In Luke's Gospel Jesus' public ministry begins when he comes to Nazareth 'in the power of the spirit' (Luke 4:1–16) and reads this passage in the synagogue: 'Today, he said, this passage has been fulfilled in your hearing' (Luke 4:21). The reference to the spirit of God being upon him recalls the dove in the baptism story (Luke 3:22) (Jerome) and the 'anointing' makes the reference to Christ explicit, reminding us that he is the Messiah, both king and priest (Luther), 'anointed' with the gifts of the spirit which dwell in him (Rom 8:22; cf. 1 Cor 12:4) (Calvin). Jesus alludes to this verse according to Matthew's Gospel as well (Matt 11:5), and the Church Fathers observe that the tasks assigned to the prophet nicely correspond to Christ's teaching, for example, in the Beatitudes: 'Blessed are the poor in spirit' (Matt.5:3) ... 'those who mourn' (Matt.5:4) ... 'those who weep' (Luke 6:21) (Eusebius, Jerome). The Luke passage follows the Septuagint closely with 'good news to the poor' rather than 'meek' (AV) or 'afflicted' (RSV) or 'poor in spirit' (cf. Matt 5:3), and it adds 'recovery of sight to the blind', both variations that highlight ways in which Christ fulfils the prophecy (cf. Luke 6:20; 7:21–22).

Luther, quoting Paul (1 Cor 15:56), suggests that the 'brokenhearted' are those crushed by the Law, the 'captives' are those held under the power of sin, and 'those who are bound' refers to those under the sentence of death. By contrast many modern commentators point out that in Luke's interpretation of the passage the emphasis is on socio-economic issues, not spiritual, and that Christ chooses widows and lepers (Luke 4:25,27) to illustrate the meaning of Isaiah's words, not sinners (Ruether 1983: 32; Lohfink 1987: 71–72). At the end of the twentieth century, relief organizations such as 'Make Poverty History', under the title 'Jubilee 2000', derived from Leviticus 25:1 and Isaiah 61:1–2, succeeded in achieving the cancellation of a vast amount of Third World debt (Tate 2006: 530).

Numerous hymns have been inspired by verse 1, notably 'Hark the Glad Sound!', one of Philip Doddridge's best known paraphrases:

> He comes the broken hearts to bind,
> The bleeding souls to cure;
> And with the treasures of his grace
> To enrich the humble poor. (*EH* 6; *CH2* 40; *AM* 36)

A modern Catholic hymn book contains seven modern examples (*HON* 84, 106, 183, 295, 548, 549, 774), to which one by Luke Connaughton beginning 'The voice of God goes out to all the world' may be added (*CH4* 283). Other musical settings include the prologue to Elgar's oratorio *The Apostles* (1903) (*BiM* 18), and a bass solo preceding the final chorus in Burkhard's *The Face of Isaiah* (1936), which celebrates the spread of peace like an overflowing stream (Isa 66:12) and the creation of a new heaven and a new earth (Isa 65:17) (Berges 2012: 127).

The 'year of the Lord's favour' (v. 2) means the year in which he revealed his glory dwelling among us (Cyril). It is the 'time of fullness' referred to by Paul (Gal 4:4; cf. 2 Cor 6:2) (Calvin). It will be an 'agreeable year' for the afflicted but a terrible 'day of vengeance' for the ungodly (Luther). Some suggest that it refers to the First Coming of Christ, while 'the day of vengeance' (v. 2) refers to his Second Coming (Theodoret). Some modern scholars find the mention of 'vengeance' here discordant and seek to remove it either by textual emendation or by proposing a less negative meaning such as 'recompense' (cf. Isa 35:4) (Westermann). The Greek *antapodosis* 'reward' (cf. Ps 19:11; Col 3:24) lends some support to this.

Comfort for 'those who mourn for Zion' (v. 3 LXX) is described in terms of transforming traditional rituals of fasting (cf. Isa 58; Jon 3:6; Zech 7:1–7) into a celebration of some happy event (cf. Jud 10:3): a garland on their heads instead of dust and ashes, a body freshly treated with oil and a mantle of praise or 'festal attire' (NJB) instead of sackcloth or torn clothes (Jer 41:5) (Lowth). 'The oil of joy' which makes the face shine comes from the oil with which Christ himself was anointed (Heb 1:9) (Henry). An elegant wordplay on 'garland' (Heb. *pe'ar*) and 'dust' (Heb. *'eper*) is noted by many commentators (Calvin, Lowth, Duhm). Instead of stooping, faint and dispirited, they will stand up like great oak-trees, 'the planting of the lord' (cf. Eph 1:4; 1 Cor 3:7) (Calvin). Jerome takes the oaks of righteousness and the 'planting of the Lord' with verses 4 and 5, and envisages a scene of rebuilding and pastures new, described by Paul as 'God's field, God's building' (1 Cor 3:9), where the shepherds will no longer be scribes and pharisees but the apostles of Christ called upon to feed his sheep (John 21:17).

'But you shall be called the priests of the Lord' (v. 6): this means that the other nations will be like the Israelites, while the Israelites will be like the sons of Aaron and receive the wealth of the nations as their tithes (Num 18:24). You shall glory in their riches (Ibn Ezra, Kimḥi, Vg). Christian commentators recall that all God's people are called 'a kingdom of priests' (Exod 19:6; cf. 1 Pet 2:9) and interpret the verse as a call to commitment and self-sacrifice (Luther, Calvin). 'If you want to exercise the priesthood of your soul, never let the fire go out on your altar' (Lev 6:12) (Origen, *Homilies on Leviticus* 4.6). The 'strength of the nations' (LXX) refers to the martyrs of God who 'strove even to death for the truth' (Sir 4:28) (cf. Isa 60:5) (Eusebius).

Instead of shame and dishonour they will receive a double portion of the land, and their joy will be everlasting (v. 7). After suffering 'double for all her sins' (Isa 40:2), now she is going to receive a double reward as Job did (Job 42:10) (Henry). If they did not, it would be robbery, and the Lord hates robbery (v. 8) (Ibn Ezra). The Hebrew text, followed by the Vulgate, has 'I hate robbery with a burnt offering' (Heb. *'olah*; cf. AV, JPS, Childs) and this has prompted comments on hypocrisy in worship (cf. Hos 6:6; Matt 9:13; 23:23) (Calvin, Henry). Most modern commentators, however, with 1QIsaᵃ, LXX and the Targum, read 'robbery and wrong-doing' (Heb. *'avla*; cf. Pss 58:2; 64:6) (RSV, NJB, Westermann, Blenkinsopp, Oswalt). The sentence 'I the Lord love justice' is quoted a number of times in the rabbinic literature: God loves Israel more than the other nations and he loves justice; so he said I will give the thing that I love to the people that I love' (DeutR V.7). The universal acknowledgement among the nations that Israel are a people whom the Lord has blessed (v. 9) will be demonstrated when they all come up to Jerusalem year after year to worship the King, the Lord of hosts, at the Feast of Sukkot (Zech 14:16) (Ibn Ezra).

In Jewish lectionaries verses 10 and 11 begin the last of the seven 'consolation' haftarot (61:10–63:9) (see comm. Isa 40). Verse 10 is about Israel's love for God, as a queen for her king. The speaker is Jerusalem (cf. Tg) and there is a midrash explaining that, when her sons and daughters return home from far (cf. Isa 60:4), she says, 'What is that to me?', but when she hears that her king is coming, she will say, 'Now there is complete rejoicing' as it is said, 'Rejoice greatly, O daughter of Zion' (Zech 9:9) and 'I will greatly rejoice in the Lord'

(Isa 61:10) (*CantR* I.1–2). She wears the 'garments of salvation' and the 'robe of righteousness' (or 'victory'; cf. Luther), prepared to greet him like a bride or a bridegroom adorned for their wedding. The Church Fathers interpret the 'garment of salvation' as the resurrection body which Christians put on at baptism (Theodoret). We shall no longer dwell in a 'body of death' (Rom 7:24): the new birth described in verse 11 refers to the fruit of the union between the bride (the Church) and the bridegroom (the Word) (Eusebius, Cyril). Others envisage the 'earth bringing forth its shoots' as the Word sown and bearing fruit in the churches planted throughout the world by the first Christians (Bede *Retractations on the Acts* 8.4).

The image of the bride and bridegroom rejoicing in their festal garments and jewellery has been popular in Christian tradition. Already in the Book of Revelation it is applied to the 'new Jerusalem coming down out of heaven from God' (Rev 21: 2). Verse 10 is quoted twice in the *Biblia Pauperum*, first in relation to the joy of Mary Magdalene when she meets the risen Christ in the garden (John 20:11–17) and, on the last page, to describe Christ putting the crown of eternal life on the head of his bride, the Church (*BP* 110, 127). In modern times, before the Second Vatican Council, verse 10 was sung as an introit on the Feast of the Immaculate Conception (*MR* 583), and in some liturgical traditions the last two verses of chapter 61 are taken with the first few verses of chapter 62 as a Lesser Canticle or a reading celebrating the Feast of Virgins (Mearns 1914:92; Harper 1991: 257).

For Zion's Sake I Will Not Keep Silent (Isa 62:1–12)

After an introduction (vv. 1–2), the chapter continues the nuptial celebrations started at the end of the previous chapter. The ancient versions interpret verse 1 in various different ways, taken up by the commentators. The Targum has 'I will give no rest to the peoples … no quiet to the kingdoms until …'. Rashi also implies that the prophet's silence is directed against those responsible for Zion's suffering: 'I will not be silent about what they did to her'. Today the first words *Lema'an Zion* (For Zion's sake) is the name of a website which addresses

Isaiah Through the Centuries, First Edition. John F. A. Sawyer.
© 2018 John Wiley & Sons Ltd. Published 2020 by John Wiley & Sons Ltd.

religious and political issues of concern to Jews and friends of Israel, and verses 1–2a in Hebrew are set to music in a popular Hasidic folk song (1973). It also recalls Jeremiah's compulsion to speak out (Jer 4:19) and Paul's 'Woe to me if I do not preach the Gospel' (1 Cor 9:16) (Aquinas, Luther). The medieval French writer Walter of Chatillon used verse 1 in a satirical poem lamenting the state of the Church in his day: 'For Zion's sake, I will not keep silent … I will weep for the ruins of Rome' (Traill 2013: 262–263).

The silence of God in times of trouble is a powerful theme in biblical theology (cf. Isa 42:14; 57:11; 64:12; 65:6; Pss 28:1; 83:2). But the Vulgate gives the two verses an explicitly messianic meaning (cf. Isa 45:8; 62:11): 'until her Righteous One comes forth as a bright light … her Saviour as a burning torch'. Jerome and others point out that it is Jesus who is the light of the world (John 8:12) (Cyril). The chapter is read in many churches on Christmas Day (*ORM*, RCL). The 'new name' of the city (v. 2), according to Christian interpreters, would be 'Church', not synagogue (Cyril, Aquinas, Nicholas); and its citizens would be called Christians, instead of Israel (Jerome, Theodoret, Luther). Calvin suggests it means no more than that the multitude of persons scattered among the Babylonians were now to become one people again, and a broken body, once more united, would regain the 'name' of which they had long been deprived. With Isa 49:13, verse 1 inspired a joyful chorus in Saint-Saens' *Oratorio de Noel* (1858) (*BiM* 180).

'The crown of beauty … and the royal diadem' (v. 3) seems to pick up the theme of wedding celebrations from Isa 61:10, but 'in the hand of the Lord' puzzled some commentators. Ibn Ezra tells us that in some countries people wear 'crowns' on their hands. Some suggest it refers to a reward for the saints and martyrs (Eusebius, Jerome) and remind us that God protects those he loves 'in the shadow of his hand' (Isa 51:16): 'no one is able to snatch them out of the Father's hand' (John 10:29) (Cyril). The names given to Zion, however (v. 4), make it clear that this is about the marriage of God to his beloved (cf. Isa 54) or Christ to the Church (Eph.5:32) (Jerome). No longer 'Forsaken' and 'Desolate', she will be called Hephzibah ('My delight is in her') and Beulah ('Married') because the Lord delights in her. Hephzibah was the mother of Manasseh, one of the wickedest kings of Judah, who put the prophet Isaiah to death (cf. 2 Kgs 21:1–2). But it is the meaning of her name that is so appropriate here (cf. Prov 5:19) (Henry). It means the initiative is entirely God's, as Hosea puts it: 'I will betroth you to me in mercy and compassion' (Hos 2:19) (Calvin). The name is rare in literature. She is one of the characters in Antonio Caldara's oratorio *Le Profezie evangeliche d'Isaia* (1729), and little Eppie in George Eliot's novel *Silas Marner* (1861) is another example: she found Hephzibah too difficult to pronounce. It is also the name of a kibbutz in modern Israel, founded in 1922, the site of the celebrated sixth-century Beth Alpha synagogue.

Her other name will be Beulah ('Married') because 'your land shall be married'. This is explained in the next verse: 'your sons shall marry you' (v. 5), which is to be understood figuratively as meaning 'your sons shall dwell in you' (LXX, Vg, Nicholas) or 'your kingdom shall be restored to you' (Ibn Ezra). Her sons figure frequently in these prophecies (cf. 41:9; 43:5–6; 49:20–21; 54:1), and the verb *ba'al* can mean 'rule over, possess' as well as marry. The sons are the apostles, the priests and the righteous ones who are 'like husbands to the Church' (Ephrem). An alternative is to emend 'your sons' (*banayik*) to 'your Builder (*bonek*)', that is, God (cf. Ps 147:2), the subject of the rest of the passage, which would certainly fit the immediate context very well (Lowth). It concludes 'as the bridegroom rejoices over the bride, so shall the Lord rejoice over you' (v. 5) words addressed to the Sabbath in the popular song 'Lekha Dodi' (see comm.on Isa 52:1–2).

It was Bunyan who first used the name Beulah, in his *Pilgrim's Progress* (1678), to refer to a peaceful land on the way to paradise. Later, in the writings of William Blake, Beulah is a land of flowers and beautiful maidens and can also represent a spiritual union between mankind and the Saviour (Damrosch 1980: 220–233). Robert Louis Stevenson in his essay 'On Falling in Love' (1921) parodies the name as a land 'upon the borders of Heaven and within sight of the City of Love'. As a biblical synonym for heaven or the promised land, it also features in gospel songs like 'Beulah Land' by Edgar Page Stites (1876) and 'Sweet Beulah Land' by Squire Parsons (1973).

The next passage continues the theme of refusing to be silent until 'he establishes Jerusalem and makes it a praise in all the earth' (vv. 6–7). The 'watchmen' are the angels, apostles and ministers of the gospel who defend the Church from the attacks of Satan (Jerome, Calvin). An illustration in the *Bible Moralisée* portrays them as two trumpeters, high on the city wall, playing their instruments as the prophet instructs them. Their intercessions never cease (cf. 1 Thess 5:17) (Aquinas; cf. Eusebius), as Moses raised his hands and kept them steady until Israel had obtained victory over Amalek (Exod 17:10, 12) (Henry). Jewish interpreters find a reference here to the doctrine of the merits of the fathers: 'the righteous works of your fathers, O Jerusalem, are ... before me day and night' (Tg; cf. Rashi). Ibn Ezra, by contrast, suggests that the watchmen are those who mourn for Zion day and night to remind God of Zion's plight.

God promises to answer their prayers, first by driving out the enemy from their land (vv. 8–9) and second by freeing the captives (vv. 10–12) (Aquinas). He swears 'by his right hand and his mighty arm' to indicate his power to overcome any enemies of Israel (Ibn Ezra, Calvin). They will be able to eat the fruit of their labours (Ps 128:2); it is a special blessing when everyone is able to eat under their own vine and their own fig tree (1 Kgs 4:25; Mic 4:4) (Calvin). 'They shall eat and praise the Lord ... in the courts of my sanctuary' (v. 9) adds the image of temple worship to the picture of future bliss (cf. Deut 12:18) (Calvin). The Church Fathers found a reference to the Eucharist here (John 6:52–58) and eternal salvation (Mark 14:25) (Jerome, Nicholas; cf. Eusebius). The 'daughter of Zion' from this passage features as narrator in an early Protestant passion oratorio by Reinhard Keiser (1704) (*BiM* 35).

The last verses of the chapter beginning 'Go through, go through the gates' (vv. 10–12) conclude the extended prophecy Isaiah 60–62 (see on Isa 60:1) and recall the conclusion of 40–48 (Isa 48:20–21). In Christian iconography verses 10–11 accompany scenes of Christ's entry into Jerusalem (cf. Zech 9:9; Matt 21:5) (Schiller 1972: 18–21). 'Prepare the way' goes back further to chapter 40 (Aquinas), where the last part of verse 11 appears verbatim (Isa 40:10) and the 'highway' (Heb. *mesillah*; cf. 40:3) recalls earlier prophecies of salvation (Isa 11:16; 35:8; 36:2; cf. Isa 19:23;57:14). The words are addressed to the people returning from exile to their city (Ibn Ezra). Some Christian commentators believe it refers to the heavenly city (Heb 12:22) and the people addressed are angelic beings, charged with removing all impediments, whether ill will or envy, demons or evil spirits, from the path of the righteous (Eusebius). Others tell us the words are addressed to the faithful, telling them to prepare the way of the Lord as John the Baptist did, by repenting and removing the stones, that is, their sins, that make them stumble (Jerome). This is how the Jewish Targum interprets the verse: 'Turn the heart of the people into the right way ... clear away any stone of stumbling such as the evil inclination' (cf. Rashi). Nicholas of Lyra and others take it as a call to pass through the gates of baptism into the Church. The words 'Build up, build up the highway' appeared on a postage stamp in 1996 celebrating 75 years of the Israeli Public Works Department (Plate 42).

The 'ensign over the peoples' is a banner intended to attract the attention of the exiles (Rashi). In an earlier messianic prophecy it was identified as the 'root of Jesse' (Isa 11:10), and Christians take it to mean the cross of Christ (Nicholas) or the Word, 'a fighting word ... by teaching it one wages war against the ungodly' (Luther). In place of 'Behold your salvation (Heb. *yish'ek*) comes', the Septuagint, the Vulgate and the Targum, have 'Behold your saviour comes' (cf. v. 1; 45:8), and it is in this form that the words are quoted, along with Zechariah 9:9, in Matthew's account of Christ's entry into Jerusalem (Matt 21:5). Jerome comments that this is how Gabriel and Joseph understood the Hebrew word (Matt 1:21). 'His reward is with him' (cf. 40:10; 61:8) encourages the faithful, reassuring them that they will be rewarded (Lowth): 'God is not mocked for whatever a man sows, that he will also reap' (Gal 6:7) (Aquinas). Even the thief on the cross would receive a reward for his faith (Luke 23:43) (Cyril).'Recompense' (RSV Heb. *pe'ulah*) is rendered 'wages' by some (cf. Isa 61:8; Ibn Ezra). To some it suggests the Second Coming of Christ, when he will

PLATE 42   'Build up, build up the highway' (Isa 62:10). Israeli postage stamp celebrating 75 years of the Public Works Department (1996). Reproduced with kind permission of Israel Philatelic Society, Israel Postal Company.

be revealed as the Judge and Giver of rewards (Eusebius). It has been suggested by modern scholars that the scene envisaged is analogous to the *parousia* in Hellenistic and Roman literature reflecting ceremonies associated with the arrival of the emperor on an official visit to a provincial city (Blenkinsopp).

The prophecy concludes with the giving of new names to the people and the city (v. 12; cf. v. 4). 'They shall call them the Holy People' (MT, Tg, Vg, AV) implies that it will be evident to the whole world that God has been faithful to his covenant with Abraham (cf. Exod 19:6) (Calvin), a nuance omitted by many modern commentators (Duhm, Westermann; cf. RSV, NRSV, NJB). The city will be 'Sought after' and 'Not Forsaken' because the one who 'came to seek and to save what is lost' (Luke 19:10) found it and saved it (Eusebius). Before it had been 'Forsaken' and 'Desolate' (Matt 23:38; cf. Jer 12:7) (Cyril). The Church Fathers apply these words to the Church, sanctified by Christ so that she may be holy and without blemish (Eph 5:25–27) (*Acts of the Council of Carthage* 3.258).

The Grapes of Wrath (Isa 63:1–6)

The next prophecy returns to another theme expounded earlier, the 'great slaughter in the land of Edom … a day of vengeance, a year of recompense' (Isa 34:5–8) (Rashi, Lowth). The Edomites were always among Israel's bitterest enemies, remembered, for example, for exulting in the Babylonian destruction of Jerusalem (Ps 137:7) (Calvin). There have been other attempts to explain why Edom should be the object of this particularly graphic and bloody prophecy, from the Talmud (cf. Rashi) down to modern times

Isaiah Through the Centuries, First Edition. John F. A. Sawyer.
© 2018 John Wiley & Sons Ltd. Published 2020 by John Wiley & Sons Ltd.

(Beuken, Childs) (see comm. on Isa 34:6). For Ibn Ezra 'Edom' stands for the empires of Rome and Constantinople because they adopted the Christian religion; for Luther it is the 'ungodly synagogue'. Another suggestion is to remove 'from Edom (Heb. *me'edom*) … from Bozrah (Heb. *mi-boṣrah*)' (v. 1) from the text by emending it to 'stained with red (Heb. *me'oddam*) … redder than a vine-dresser (Heb. *mi-boṣer*)' (de Lagarde, Duhm).

But the most widespread interpretation, going back to New Testament times, is that Edom, both here and in chapter 34, is the scene of the great battle in which God finally destroys the nations of the world: they are his victims (vv. 3, 6), not the inhabitants of Edom. This is how the texts are used in the Book of Revelation (Rev 6:13–14; 19:11–15) (cf. Eusebius) and the apocalyptic nature of the passage is now widely recognized (Westermann). It was from Edom, also known as Seir, that Yahweh entered history in the beginning (Deut 33:2; Judg 5:4), and it was there that his last battle would be fought (Blenkinsopp).

The extraordinary scene portrays the return of Yahweh to Jerusalem after the battle. He is unrecognizable, in bloodstained garments, strong and glorious, but 'bowed down' (Heb. *ṣo'eh*; cf. Isa 51:14; Jer 2:22), 'stooping' (NEB) or 'swaying' (Childs). 'Marching' (RSV, NRSV, NJB, Duhm, Westermann) comes from an emended text (Heb. *ṣo'ed*). Others, influenced by post-biblical usage where it is applied to gypsies, take it to mean 'travelling' (Kimḥi, AV; Sawyer 1993). The watchmen on the city wall (cf. Isa 62:6) ask, 'Who is this that comes from Edom?'. The Church Fathers identified the figure as Christ, his true glory revealed in the bloodstained garments, symbols of his passion (Cyril; Tertullian, *Against Marcion* 4.40). The questioners are the angels greeting Christ when he returned to glory after his passion, recalling the Psalm: 'Who is the king of glory …? Lift up your heads, O gates … that the king of glory may enter in' (Ps 24:7–10) (Origen, *Commentary on John* 6.287–292; Cyril). For Jerome it describes the resurrection, while in the medieval *Bible Moralisée* and the *Biblia Pauperum* it is associated with the Ascension (*BP* 115). The notion that the angels did not recognize Christ when he rose from the dead and approached the gates of heaven (cf. Ps 24:10) (Ambrose, *On the Mysteries* 7.36) is questioned by Augustine and others (cf. Eph 3:5) (*Sermon* 372.2; cf. Aquinas). The reformers rejected this christological interpretation as a 'violent distortion of the chapter' (Calvin) and subsequent Christian interpreters have taken it as describing the Passion of God, not Christ: 'it is not the Messiah or the Servant of Jehovah, who is here pictured, but Jehovah himself' (Smith; cf. Luther, Duhm, Westermann, Childs).

The first answer, whether interpreted as the words of God or of Christ, is a succinct statement about the relationship between 'righteousness' (Heb. *ṣedaqah*) and salvation (Heb. *hoshia'*): 'It is I that speak in righteousness, mighty to save'. Rashi explains that it refers not only to the righteousness of God but also to the righteousness (good deeds) of the patriarchs and the righteous persecuted in Israel (cf. *RA* 311). Others say it simply means that the saving God is true to his word (Tg, cf. Calvin) or that he is a just God who will 'proclaim liberty to the captives, freedom to those that are bound' (Isa 61:1) (Jerome). In the synagogue lectionary verses 1–9 are the last part of the seventh 'consolation' haftarah (Isa 61:10–63:9) (see comm. on Isa 40).

The second question reminded some commentators of a Scottish ballad in which a mother asks her son on his return home, 'Why does your sword so drop with blood, Edward, Edward?' (Herder, Westermann). It also introduces the striking image of a wine press (v. 2), and it is answered with the words 'I have trodden the wine press alone' (cf. v. 6), recalling Jeremiah's lament over God's violent treatment of Judah (Lam 1:15) (Eusebius, Aquinas). 'Alone' means unassisted by any angel or archangel (Jerome) or anyone from the peoples (Heb. *'ammim*) of the world, any human agent like Cyrus (Henry). 1QIsa^a has 'from my own people' (Heb. *'ammi*; cf. NJB), which implies a criticism of Israel, developed in verse 5: 'I looked but there was no one to help ... I was appalled' (cf. Isa 59:16) (cf. Aquinas). Many Christians applied the words to the loneliness of Christ's Passion when all the disciples forsook him and fled (Matt 26:56; cf. Jerome, Henry). This is the 'day of vengeance' (v. 4) referred to in the earlier account of the slaughter in Edom (34:8) (Aquinas), but it is also 'my year of redemption', the jubilee year when the captives will be freed and the people redeemed by the precious blood of the lamb (Rev 12:11) (Jerome).

In Anglican tradition the whole chapter used to be prescribed to be read on the Monday before Easter (BCP), while in the Roman missal verses 1–7 (with Isa 62:11) were read on the Wednesday of Holy Week (*MR* 235–236). In some modern lectionaries verses 1–9 are still read on the Wednesday of Holy Week (RCL) and Passion Sunday (BCO). Augustine cites the passage in his commentary on Psalm 56:1–2 ('my enemies trample on me all day long') to explain that Christ was the 'first cluster of grapes', pressed in the wine press of tribulation (*Exposition of Psalm* 56.4). The Church Fathers noted the appropriateness of the image in the context of the Eucharist (Matt 26:27–29): Isaiah helps us to see in wine an ancient figure for blood (cf. Gen 49:11) (Cyril, Jerome). They identified the blood as Christ's own blood and imagined him trodden on and pressed down by the violence of the Passion, like grapes in a wine press (Cyprian, *Letter* 63.6–7), 'obedient to the Father even unto the press of the cross which he trod alone' (Bernard of Clairvaux, *Apology to Abbot William* 3.5–6) (Marrow 1979: 83–94; Duffy 1992: 251–253.

This bizarre image has had a particularly long and colourful afterlife in Christian tradition from the 'winepress of the fury of the wrath of God' in the Book of Revelation (Rev 19:15) and images of the cross modified to look like a wine press in medieval iconography (Schiller 1972: 229, fig.810) to Steinbeck's great novel *The Grapes of Wrath* (1939). It is developed by George Herbert, particularly in 'The Bunch of Grapes' in *The Temple* (1633):

> Who of the Law's sour juice sweet wine did make,
> Ev'n God himself being pressed for my sake.

Gerald Manley Hopkins in 'Barnfloor and Winepress' (1903) applies the image more explicitly to the wine of the Eucharist:

> Terrible fruit was on the tree
> In the acre of Gethsemane:
> For us by Calvary's distress
> The Wine was rackèd from the press;
> Now, in our altar-vessels stored,
> Lo, the sweet Vintage of the Lord!

The scene is depicted very frequently in Christian iconography. A painting from about 1500 in the Bavarian National Museum in Munich shows Christ carrying the cross, which is attached to the giant wooden screw of a wine press, and his bleeding feet are trampling on a great wooden vat of grapes, while in the foreground half a dozen labourers are collecting and processing the fruit of the grapes in a variety of wooden containers (Schiller 1972: 229, Figure 810). Another early sixteenth-century example by the French artist Jean Bellegambe, shows a fairly conventional crucifixion scene, except that at the top, above Christ's head, is the inscription TORCULAR CALCAVI SOLUS ('I trod the winepress alone') (Marrow 1979: 84, Plate v). A sixteenth-century window in the Church of Sainte-Foi in Conches shows a wine press with Christ standing alone inside it, the wine being gathered in a tub beneath his feet, but the overall effect is to depict a crucifixion rather than a scene of wine-pressing (Lee, Seddon and Stephen 1976: 140). Very different in style and conception is *The Wine Press* (1864), a painting in the Tate Gallery by the English painter John Roddam Spencer Stanhope, showing Christ in royal garments with a crown on his head, holding on to a wooden bar above his head with a clean white arm, his bare feet hardly soiled by the grapes he is trampling on (1864) (Plate 43).

There are motets entitled *Quis est iste qui venit* (v. 1 Vg) by Melchior Franck (*c.*1579–1639) and Giovanni Gabrieli, combining verses 1–3 with Ps 24:7,8,10, and a poignant setting of verses 1–9 for soloists and chorus in Patten's *Isaiah* (1898) contrasting the violence of God's fury (vv. 1–6) with the mention of his loving kindness (vv. 7–9) (*BiM* 112). Two modern compositions focus less on Christ's passion and more on judgement: 'Who Is This with Garments Gory' by Arthur Cleveland Coxe (*EH* 108) and Julia Ward Howe's 'Battle Hymn of the

PLATE 43   *The Wine Press* (Isa 63:3) by John Roddam Spencer Stanhope (1864),
Tate Gallery, London.

Republic' (1861) (*CH2* 155, *HON* 349, *GtG* 354). In Catholic liturgical tradition
the connection between the wine press and Christ's Passion was further eroded
when it was decided at the Second Vatican Council (1962–1966) to remove the
passage from the Holy Week lectionary.

Our Father in Heaven (Isa 63:7–19)

A change of speaker and subject matter in verse 7 marks the beginning of a long
psalm-like passage similar in form and style to what scholars call a 'community
lament' (Isa 63:7–64:12; cf. Pss 44, 60, 74, 79, 80, 83, 85, 89, 90, 94; Lam 5).

Witnessing the fate of other nations (vv. 1–6), 'the wise in Israel will then acknowledge the great number of acts of loving kindness bestowed upon them by the Lord, when they left Egypt, during the exile and when he saved them and brought them back to their land' (Ibn Ezra). According to the Targum, it is the prophet speaking. The heavenly judge will not let Israel go unpunished but rather he will mingle his wrath with loving kindness, as he said, 'I have borne and raised sons' (Isa 1:2) (Cyril). God loved his people so much he could not believe they would deal falsely (v. 8) (Ibn Ezra), or at least thought of them as innocent, and 'in his love and his pity redeemed them' (v. 9) (Rashi).

'In all their affliction he was afflicted' (v. 9) (Heb. *lo ṣar*) concludes the last of the seven 'consolation readings' in Jewish lectionaries (Isa 61:10–63:9) (see comm.on Isa 40), and is much quoted in the rabbinic literature. One discussion cites the example of slavery ('when Israel is enslaved, the Shekinah is enslaved with them') and adds that this applies equally to an individual Israelite, as it is said, 'I will be with him [singular] in distress' (Ps 91:15) (*Sifre Num* Beha'aloteka para 85, f.22b). It is also quoted in a midrash on the burning bush story: God said to Moses, 'Know from the place whence I speak to you, from the midst of thorns, it is as if I stand in their distresses' (ExodR II.5). Some commentators point out that, while God cannot suffer, his sympathy with us in our troubles is so great that he 'assumes and applies to himself human passions' (Calvin; cf. Kimḥi, Henry). Others point to how Christ identified human suffering with his own as, for example, on the Damascus Road: 'Saul, Saul why are you persecuting me' (Acts 9:4; cf. Luke 10:16) (Luther).

A completely different interpretation goes back before the rabbinic tradition to the consonantal Hebrew text which has the negative (*lo'*) instead of 'to him' (*lo*): 'In all their affliction, he did not afflict them (*lo' ṣar*)', that is, he did not make them suffer as they deserved (Rashi; cf. Tg). The Septuagint takes the first phrase with the previous verse ('he became their saviour from all their afflictions') and then reads *ṣir* (ambassador, messenger) for *ṣar* (affliction): it was no messenger or angel but his presence that saved them (cf. Lowth, Duhm, Westermann, NRSV, NJB).

Either way, the verse continues with an emphatic statement of God's unceasing love for his people whom he 'saved … redeemed … lifted up … and carried all the days of old', recalling the images of an eagle (Deut 32:11) and a shepherd (Isa 40:11) (Calvin). But before developing this theme in some beautiful nostalgic language (vv. 11–14), there is a chilling reminder of Israel's disobedience and the divine anger it caused: 'they rebelled and grieved his Holy Spirit and he turned to be their enemy' (v. 10). 'Rebellion' (Heb. *marah*) is a recurring theme in the story of Israel's journeyings in the wilderness (cf. Deut 1:26, 43; 9:23; Ps 78:8, 17, 40, 56), and is illustrated most vividly by the story of the golden calf (cf. Acts 7:41) (Eusebius). This is the only place, apart from Psalm 51:11, where the term 'Holy

Spirit' appears in the Hebrew Bible. Here it may be another term for a mediator between God and the world, like 'angel' and 'presence' in verse 9, and the rabbinic terms *Shekinah* (presence) and *Memra* (word). Ibn Ezra describes it as a figurative expression for God. In rabbinic tradition it came to be understood as the spirit of prophecy: 'when the last prophets, Haggai, Zechariah and Malachi, died the Holy Spirit departed from Israel' (b*Yoma* 9b). This is how Kimhi understood it here: 'the words of his holy prophets' (cf. Tg). The Church Fathers relate it both to the third person of the Trinity and to 'the holy and disciplined spirit that flees from deceit' at the beginning of the Wisdom of Solomon (Wisd 1:5) (Jerome). Some say the Holy Spirit is 'above the angels ... he is Lord and God' (Cyril; cf. Athanasius, *Letter to Serapion* 1.12), while others believe 'spirit' is just another name for 'angel' (cf. Ps 104:4; Heb 1:14) (Jerome).

'Then he remembered the days of old, Moses and his people' (v. 11): that is, God remembered how Moses had interceded for his people (Exod 32:31–32) (Jerome, Aquinas). He was moved to intervene, not so much by our cries as by the promises he had made to Abraham, Moses and David (Luther). Others believe that 'he' refers to the people: 'then they remembered ...' (Rashi, Calvin, Westermann). 'Moses, his people' (Heb. *moshe 'ammo*) is problematical and has been explained in a variety of ways: some commentators supply 'and' (Calvin, Childs; AV). Others emend to 'Moses his servant' (*moshe 'abdo*) (Syriac, Lowth, Westermann, RSV); while some omit the phrase altogether (LXX Duhm). For Rashi 'his people' is the subject of the sentence ('his people remembered'), while Ibn Ezra suggests that here the name Moses (Heb. *moshe*) has its lexical meaning of 'the one who draws his people out of the water' (cf. Exod 2:10).

In verses 11–14 the exiles wistfully recall the stories of the Exodus when God led his people out of slavery through the depths of the sea: in those days the Lord placed his spirit within them to teach them the statutes and ordinances (Rashi); 'his glorious arm' went before them in the form of an angel (Exod 14:19) (Ibn Ezra); they did not stumble (v. 13); they had a leader (v. 14) (Jerome). 'The spirit of the Lord gave them rest' (v. 14 AV, RSV). This is the normal meaning of the Hebrew (*tenihennu*), although the ancient versions and commentaries, both Jewish and Christian, up to the sixteenth century, have 'the spirit of the Lord was their leader' (*tanhennu*). Luther reads 'the spirit of the Lord gave us rest' and modern commentators universally add this image of the people reaching the 'rest' (Heb. *menuhah*) of the promised land (cf. Deut 12:9; 1 Kgs 8:56). In a midrash on Psalm 44:1 verse 12 is quoted to illustrate the rabbinic doctrine that God's mighty acts on behalf of Israel were not for their own sake but so that his 'everlasting' (v. 12) and 'glorious' (v. 14) name would be made famous among the nations (*MidrPs* 44.1).

The lament continues with a plea to God to 'look down from heaven' and remember his children with compassion: 'for you are our father' (vv. 15–19).

The striking description of heaven as a 'holy and glorious habitation' (Heb. *zebul*) occurs several times in the Scrolls (e.g. 1QM 12:1; 1QS 10:3). The meaning of the word is explained by reference to the story of how Zebulun got his name: 'Leah said, My husband will dwell (Heb. *zabal*) with me': hence *zebul* 'a dwelling' (Ibn Ezra; cf. AV). Modern scholars, on the basis of Ugaritic and Akkadian cognates, believe that the verb means 'to exalt, honour' (cf. Beelzebul Matt 10:25), and the noun 'an exalted house' (1 Kgs 8:13; cf. RSV; NJB). The word translated 'your heart' in the RSV (Heb. *me'eka*) or 'your mercy' (LXX, Vg, cf. Rashi) elsewhere refers to 'bowels' (AV), in particular the womb (Isa 48:19), and some modern commentators have argued that this is an example of female imagery applied to God: 'the trembling of thy womb and thy compassion' (cf. Isa 42:14; 46:3–4; 49:15; 66:13) (Muilenberg). Trible points out (1978: 38) that while a human mother's love for her baby can fail, God's 'womb-love' for his people will never fail.

This is one of the very few places in the Hebrew Bible in which God is addressed as 'our father' (Heb. *abinu*) (v. 16; cf. 64:8; 1 Chron 29:10). Isaiah uttered the inspiration of 'Our Father' long before either Church or 'Christian Europe' (Rosenzweig quoted by Waldinger 1998: 316). He is 'father' in the sense of creator of all things (Jerome) and occasionally acknowledged to be father of Israel (Exod 4:22; Deut 32:6). The notion of God as 'father' (Heb. *ab*) also appears in some personal names like Abijah, Abihu and Joab. But it seems as though it was avoided in Israel, even as a metaphor, until the exilic period at the earliest, probably because of its association with pagan practices (cf. Jer 2:27) (Childs). God's fatherly love for his people is contrasted with the role of the patriarchs, Abraham and Israel (that is, Jacob; cf. Gen 32:28): they are dead and unaware of their children's needs (cf. Job 14:21), or else we are so degenerate and corrupt that they would not own us, but here 'our father' in pardoning us is God, not man (Hos 11:9) (Henry). The Targum paraphrases the verse to make this point even more clearly: 'for you are he whose compassion for us is more than that of a father towards his children'.

The verse is quoted by the rabbis to distinguish between a father who merely begets and a true father who brings you up and is a good and faithful guardian (ExodR XLVI.5). Elsewhere, in an argument between God and the patriarchs about this verse, Isaac says to God, 'are they not also your children? Did you not call Israel your "first born son"'? (Exod 4:22) (b*Shabbat* 89b). Prayers addressed to 'our Father' began to be widespread in Second Temple period Judaism (cf. Tobit 13:4; Sir 23:1, 4; Wisd 14:3; 3 Macc 5:7) and later normal in both Jewish and Christian liturgy, as for example, *Abinu malkenu* ('our God our father), a prayer attributed to Rabbi Akiba (*ADPB* 98–103), and the Lord's Prayer (*Paternoster* 'Our Father') (Matt 6:9–15).

Blaming God for their sins (v. 17) recalls the hardening of Pharaoh's heart (Exod 10:1, 20, 27) (Eusebius, Theodoret) and Paul's comments about God driving people into error (2 Thess 2:11; cf. Rom 1:28) (Calvin). Augustine argues that sin is itself punishment for previous sins (*Against Julian* 5.3.12), while others suggest that there was so much sin there already that they deserved to become worse and be punished accordingly (Isidore of Seville, *Sententiarum tres libri* 2.19.5–6). Ibn Ezra suggests that it refers to the experience of those so overwhelmed by their inclination to sin that they believe it must be God's will to prevent them from repenting (cf. m*Aboth* 5:18). One version has 'Why leave us to stray from your ways…?' (NJB).

'Return' (Tg 'send back your Shekinah to us') is the cry of a people who feel they have been abandoned by God, their city destroyed (vv. 18–19). For some it recalls the final words of Lamentations: 'Restore us to yourself, O Lord … renew our days of old' (Lam 5:21) (Aquinas). The Hebrew of verse 18 is problematical: one solution is to emend the text and read 'Why have the wicked made light of your holy place?' (Duhm, Westermann). But as it stands, it appears to say, 'For only a short time your holy people possessed it' (AV; cf. RSV), and commentators explain that the twenty-eight generations from Abraham to the captivity (Matt 1:17) were 'but a little while' when compared with eternity (Gen 17:8) (Henry): it is wonderful that people should call it 'a short time' (cf. Ps 102:23–24) (Calvin). Now they are dispossessed, under foreign rule and indistinguishable from people who are not called by God's name (v. 19). It is as if they were back in the desert 'without prophets, priests and kings' (Hos 3:4; Lam 2:9) (Eusebius). The Targum takes it as a continuation of the negatives: 'not (Heb. *lo*') for them did you bow the heavens and reveal yourself … as you did when you saved us from the Egyptians' (Rashi). But most commentators ignore the verse division in the Hebrew text, and take the second half of verse 19 as the beginning of chapter 64 (Ibn Ezra; cf. Eusebius, Jerome, Aquinas, Calvin, Lowth).

O Lord, You Have Hidden Your Face from Us (Isa 64:1–12)

'If only (Heb. *lu*) you would tear open the heavens and come down, then the mountains would flow down at your presence' (v. 1). The rare image of mountains turning to liquid (Heb. *nazal*) at the appearance of the Lord (cf. Judg.5:5) (Vg, AV, Luther, Lowth) recalls the fire that rained down on the Egyptians (Exod 9:24) and 'the fire of the Lord' that came down from heaven in answer to Elijah's prayer on Mount Carmel (1 Kgs 18:38) (Rashi): 'for the Lord is a consuming fire' (Deut 4:24) (Jerome). The Hebrew in verse 2 is difficult and the

Isaiah Through the Centuries, First Edition. John F. A. Sawyer.
© 2018 John Wiley & Sons Ltd. Published 2020 by John Wiley & Sons Ltd.

Septuagint develops the image with a reference, not in the Hebrew, to wax melting in the fire (v. 2; cf. Ps 97:5) (Theodoret, Jerome). Some point out that in his great love, God spread out the heavens to shield us from his unapproachable power (cf. Exod 33:20) (Cyril). Some suggest that 'mountains' here is an image for 'kings who sit in safety' and would 'melt before God' as 'the nations tremble at his presence' (v. 2) (Ibn Ezra). 'Pharaoh, who was a most haughty mountain, flowed like water' (Luther). Calvin explains the image as describing how the presence of God breaks down insurmountable obstacles to make a way for his people to pass through (Calvin).

The text goes on to say that God did come down from heaven (v. 3) and Christian writers have applied the language about the heavens opening to the baptism of Jesus (Matt 3:16), when 'the Word was made flesh and dwelt among us' (John 1:14; cf. Matt 1:23) (Jerome). The passage is read in Advent in some churches (*ORM*, BCO) and at Epiphany in others (RCL). A connection was seen between this passage about the heavens opening to let the saviour come down to earth, and the two Advent chants, *Emitte agnum* (Isa 16:1) and *Rorate coeli* (Isa 45:8).

Verse 4 celebrates the uniqueness of God: 'no one has ever seen a god who performs such wonders for those who wait for him as you do' (Rashi). Paul seems to cite this verse in his letter to the Corinthians (1 Cor 2:9), 'not word for word ... but expressing the truth of its meaning' (Jerome), and the Church Fathers believed he was referring to life after death (cf. Matt 25:34) (Augustine, *Sermon on Ps 35.5*; Leo the Great, *Sermon* 95.8). Luther rejects this otherworldly interpretation and applies it to the mystery of faith here and now: 'faith is the assurance of things hoped for and the conviction of things not seen' (Heb 11:1). Calvin comments that the original Isaiah text was about 'blessings of a temporal nature', while Paul applies it to spiritual blessings. Some suggest that the verse may also allude to Isaiah's own experience when he saw the glory of God in a way that no one else did (*Mart.Isa* 8:11–12; 11:34; *OTP* 2.168, 176) (Hilary, *On the Trinity* 5.33; cf. Jerome, Lowth). 'You come to meet those who are happy to act uprightly' (v. 5; NJB): the verb 'meet' (Heb. *paga*') recalls Moses 'standing in the breach' (Ps 106:23) and the servant interceding for the transgressors (Isa 53:12) (Ibn Ezra). 'Even when you were angry and we sinned, you saved us': Luther takes this as a continuation of the description of how things were in the past and how merciful God had been to his people. In the Jewish tradition too this is about God's anger and how Israel was saved in spite of it: the words 'by them' (Heb. *bahem*) refer to the merits of the fathers from of old (Heb. *'olam*) (Tg, Ibn Ezra).

The Hebrew of verse 5 is difficult, however, and Christian commentators have interpreted it quite differently. Several of the Church Fathers want to reverse the two clauses and read 'because we sinned, you are angry with us', not the other way round (Eusebius; cf. Cyril). The words 'in them' (Heb. *bahem*) mean 'in our sins', where we have been for a long time ('*olam*): and yet through the compassion of God we shall be saved (Jerome). Modern solutions include making the last clause a question 'and shall we be saved?' (RSV, Childs) or emending it to 'we have been rebellious' (Heb. *wa-nipsha'*) (cf. LXX; Lowth) or 'wicked' (Heb. *wa-nirsha'*) (Duhm). Even more radical is the emendation 'when you hid yourself' (Heb. *be-hit'allemka*), a common theme in prayers of this kind (cf. Ps 10:11; 13:1; 27:9; 30:7), and picked up again in verse 7: 'When you were angry, we sinned; when you hid yourself, we were rebellious' (cf. Isa 8:17; 45:15; 57:17; 59:2) (Blenkinsopp).

This sense of estrangement and alienation from God is further elaborated in the images of an unclean rag, polluted garments (cf. Lam 1:17) and a faded leaf blowing in the wind (v. 6). Christian commentators note that the prophet defines the polluted garments as 'our righteous acts' and describes 'our iniquities' as the wind that blows us away: in comparison with the purity of the gospel, the righteousness of the law is called uncleanness, like 'the rags of a beggar or a menstrual rag' (cf. Phil 3:7–8) (Jerome; cf. John Cassian, *Conferences* 23.4). According to Gregory the Great, sin carries us away like the wind because 'since we are not steadied by any weight of virtue, it lifts us up to a state of vain pride' (*Morals on Job* 11.60). John Bunyan alludes to this verse in the opening scene of *The Pilgrim's Progress* (1678).

No one calls upon God's name (v. 7): so it is with good reason that he hid his face from them (cf. Isa 45:15) (Eusebius) and 'caused us to wander (Heb. *temugenu*) through our iniquities' (Rashi) or 'consumed us with our iniquities' (AV) or 'melted us with our sins' (cf. Exod 15:15; Ibn Ezra, Childs). Most modern commentators emend to 'handed them over [Heb. *temaggenenu*; cf. Gen 14:20] to their iniquities' (Tg LXX RSV; Lowth, Duhm, Brueggemann).

The long prayer, which began in Isa 63:7, ends with a final impassioned appeal to God to intervene on behalf of his people: their city is in ruins, their temple burned by fire (vv. 8–12) (Rashi). Once again they address God as their Father (cf. v. 16), a Father whose love is greater than that of any human father (Tg). Like Moses (Deut 32:6), the prophet Isaiah encourages us to call God 'Father' (Cyril, *Catechetical Lecture* 7.8), as does Paul (Rom 8:15; Gal.4:6) and Jesus (Matt 5:9). Verse 8 is quoted in the *Tahanun*, a long private prayer of intercession that follows the *Amidah* and *Avinu malkenu* prayers at daily worship (*ADPB* 106–107). Creatures of clay in the hands of a potter (cf. Isa 29:16; 45:9) suggest 'fragile earthenware vessels good for nothing but to be broken apart and shattered' (Eusebius). According to a Rabbinic tradition, the evil inclination (Heb. *yeṣer ha-ra'*) in human beings was a flaw left by the potter (Heb. *yoṣer*) in the original clay (cf. Gen 8:21), and in the world to come God will remove it (ExodR XLIV.4). Luther believes this will happen in this world: 'we are the clay of the Potter … thrust into the lump, that is the Babylonian captivity … he will shape us and turn us into a fine little jug again' (cf. Jer 18) (Luther). With this optimistic interpretation, verse 8 provides the refrain of the hymn 'Abba, Abba, Father' by Carey Landry:

> Mould us, mould us and fashion us
> Into the image of Jesus your Son,
> Of Jesus your Son. (*HON* 1)

Verses 9–10 return to the theme of God's anger and the terrible price his people have paid for their iniquity: 'Be not exceedingly angry, O Lord … your holy cities have become a wilderness' For most readers the 'holy cities' are all the cities in the Holy Land (Ibn Ezra, Calvin, Luzzatto), but for some they recall the Psalmist's lament 'they have burnt up all the synagogues in the land' (Ps 74:8 AV) (Henry). The Greek and Latin versions have the singular 'the city of your holy one' which, taken with verse 11, originally referred to the Temple, destroyed by Nebuchadnezzar and later by the Romans (Cyril, Theodoret), but applicable figuratively to 'the soul of a holy person when the Father, the Son and the Holy Spirit dwell within it' (cf. 1 Cor 3:16–17): when shame is expelled and the flame of desire rages in it (v. 11), all that once was glorious is destroyed (Jerome).

William Byrd's setting for five voices a cappella is in two parts *Ne irascaris, domine* (v. 9) and *Civitas sancti tui* (v. 10), often performed separately. It was composed not long after the martyrdom of Edmond Campion (1581) and it is not hard to recognize bitter allusions to the destruction of the Roman Catholic Church in Elizabethan England: 'Behold, we are all your people … The city of your holy one has become a desert' (Kerman 1981: 42–44). In the Septuagint verse 12 continues in the past tense and concludes that what has already happened is due to the silence of God: 'and for all these things, O Lord, you have been silent' (cf. Isa 62:1, 6). But for most commentators the prayer ends with a passionate plea to God: 'will you keep silent and afflict us sorely?' (MT, Tg). Will you not hasten to save us (Ibn Ezra)? Can you contain yourself at these things (cf. Ps 83:1; 109:1) (Henry)?

The Sheep and the Goats on Judgement Day (Isa 65:1–16)

The Book of Isaiah ends, like the Book of Revelation, with a prophecy that there will be a new heaven and a new earth, and the righteous and wicked will finally receive their just reward. Chapter 65 answers the prayer in the preceding chapter by saying that God will separate the sheep from the goats (vv. 1–6; cf. Matt 25) and a New Jerusalem will be created in which people will be live in peace and happiness, and 'the wolf and the lamb shall feed together' (vv. 17–25). Chapter 66 contains further details of the new city, concerning the role of the

Isaiah Through the Centuries, First Edition. John F. A. Sawyer.
© 2018 John Wiley & Sons Ltd. Published 2020 by John Wiley & Sons Ltd.

temple in particular (cf. Rev 21:22) and the global influence of Jerusalem, together with one last appearance of the familiar maternal image of the 'daughter of Zion' (vv. 7–12), and of God as a mother comforting her children (v. 13).

Jewish tradition understands verse 1 as a response to the long prayer in the preceding chapters (63:7–64:12) (Ibn Ezra). Even when they turned their backs on God, he was still ready to help, waiting for them to return. He said to them *hinneni* (here I am), words far more often used by human agents offering to serve God than the other way round (see comm. on Isa 58:9). The daring anthropomorphism is omitted by the Targum but commented on by Rashi and Kimḥi, who say it means 'ready to welcome them back', and by Maimonides who paraphrases the Hebrew as 'I offered myself to be sought by them' (1956: 207). Even more striking is the image of God holding out his hands to them 'in an extraordinary gesture' (v. 2) (Sommer), like a devout worshipper in the act of prayer (1 Kgs 8:22, 38), or someone waving to a friend to attract his attention (Altschuler). Again the Targum changes this image of God's unceasing efforts to call the people back to the more orthodox 'I sent my prophets all day long to a rebellious people' (cf. 2 Kgs 17:13; Jer 29:19–20) (cf. Ibn Ezra).

According to Paul's interpretation (Rom 10:20–21), verse 1 refers to the gentiles and verse 2 to the Jews, with the consequence that the 'sheep and the goats' in the rest of the passage are Christians and Jews. This is how most Christian interpreters down to modern times have understood it (Jerome, Calvin, Henry, Wesley), and the result is that Isaiah 65:1–16 has been one of the most popular sources of anti-Semitic propaganda in the Bible, condemning the Jews for their rebellious and stubborn behaviour (vv. 2–3) and gloating over the history of their sufferings down the ages (vv. 13–15). To this day the words of verses 2–3a are inscribed on the façade of a church facing the Great Synagogue in Rome. The church, originally built in 1729 overlooking the entrance to the ghetto, was refurbished in 1858 after the ghetto was destroyed, and the inscription added on the orders of Pope Pius IX, in Hebrew as well as Latin, so that the Jews could understand it (Sawyer 2004: 394–395).

Paul's interpretation of these verses, however, is rejected by virtually all modern scholars (Duhm, Westermann, Childs), and the history of their reception in Christianity is not all one-sided and malign. Commenting on verse 1, for example, some quote the Magi (Irenaeus, *Against Heresies* 3.9.2) and the centurion (Matt 8:10) or the Syro-Phoenician woman (John 4) (Jerome) as fulfilling the prophet's words. For some Isaiah's statement that God revealed himself to those who did not seek him recalls the words of John: 'Let us love for He first loved us' (1 John 4:19) (Leo the Great, *Sermon* 12.1). Some commentators compare the image to that of the father in the parable opening his arms to welcome home the prodigal son (Sawyer; cf. Wesley on Isa 64:5; Calvin on Rom 10:21).

Many interpret the words as spoken by Christ, the twice repeated divine 'Here I am' symbolizing his closeness to those who call upon him in spirit and in truth (Athanasius, *On the Incarnation* 38.2), and his hands outstretched on the cross so that he might embrace the ends of the earth (Cyril), as he says 'Father forgive them' (Luke 23:34) (Jerome) (Sawyer 2011b). This third and last 'Here I am' passage (cf. Isa 52:6, 58:9), in which he offers himself to us as Isaiah offered himself to God (6:8), has a theological significance similar to Pilate's *Ecce Homo* 'behold the man' (John 19:5) (Sawyer 2007). Without quoting Isaiah, the German Jewish poet Hilde Domin also appears to be alluding to this passage in a short poem entitled '*Ecce Homo*', which ends with the words

> Nur der Gekreuzigte
> beide Arme
> weit offen
> der Hier-Bin-Ich

'Only the man on the Cross, his arms wide open, the *Here-I-Am*' (Domin 1987: 345). The suggestion appears to be that the true meaning of *Ecce Homo* is revealed only when the Man on the Cross himself says, 'Yes, here I am. I am the One.' Clearly the poet's *Hier-Bin-Ich* recalls the responses of Abraham (Gen 22:1), Moses (3:4), the boy Samuel (1 Sam 3:4, 5, 6, 9, 11), Isaiah (6:8) and other servants of the Lord who, like Jesus, were prepared to answer God's call wherever it should lead them. But does it also recall the words of Isaiah 65? The 'here I am' beside 'his arms wide open' certainly suggests that it does, while the title of the poem clearly points to Christ. Can we interpret the words 'Here-I-am' in Hilda Domin's poem as addressed to us both by the Man on the Cross, and at the same time, in fulfilment of Isaiah's prophecy, by God? The Jewish poet would more than likely have rejected such a theology, as Elie Wiesel rejected belief in a God hanging from the gallows in Auschwitz (2006: 65). But for Christian theologians, Christ is both man and God, and the words of Isaiah, addressed to us, beautifully express this although it was the Jewish poet who pointed it out by bringing the *Ecce Homo* and the 'Here I am' together. In Christ's 'Here I am', as in the *Ecce Homo*, 'the declaration *ho logos sarx egeneto* ('the Word was made flesh' John 1:14) has become visible in its extremest consequence' (Bultmann 1971: 659).

The list of the people's crimes (vv. 3–7) has attracted little comment except to refer to the laws banning them (e.g. Lev 11:7) and narratives where their ancestors are described as committing them (e.g. 2 Kgs 12:3; 23:8; Judg 6:19–20). Sacred groves or gardens (v. 3) are referred to elsewhere in Isaiah (Isa 1:29; 66:17), and communication through mediums with the spirits of dead ancestors was widespread (1 Sam 28; cf. Lev 19:31; 20:6, 27;

Deut 18:11). To these must be added a reference to star worship or astrology in verse 11 where 'Fortune' (Heb. *gad*) and 'Destiny' (Heb. *meni*) are believed to be the names of stars (Rashi, Ibn Ezra). Gad appears in biblical place names (Josh 11:17; 15:37) and Meni may be identical with Manat, one of the pre-Islamic deities mentioned in the Qur'an (Sura 53:20) (Westermann). Elsewhere the smoke of sacrifice can be a 'pleasing odour to the Lord' (Lev 1; cf. Gen 8:21), but here it kindles his wrath (cf. Heb. *ap* 'nostril, wrath'), which 'burns all the day', that is, an everlasting fire like the fire kept burning continually on the altar (Lev 6:13: cf. Altschuler). The sense is then that the punishment of the wicked affects their children and their children's children (Kimḥi; cf. v. 7), or that it will continue after their death (cf. Isa 66:24) (Jerome).

Jerome finds a reference in verse 3 to contemporary pagan practices such as those associated with the cults of Adonis and Asclepius, but it also prompts him to quote a famous verse about the transience of human endeavours (Isa 40:6). Modern scholars suggest that spending the night in cemeteries and secret places (v. 4) probably refers as much to the practice of necromancy as to ancestor worship (Childs), in any case, a practice totally against the strict Jewish legislation forbidding all contact with dead bodies (Num 19:11–13). The words 'holier than thou' (AV v. 5) were coined by Coverdale (1539), and through the influence of the Authorized Version (1611) they entered the English language as a popular description of self-righteousness. Some commentators predictably refer to the scribes and Pharisees of the New Testament in their comments on this verse (Henry; cf. Augustine, *Sermon* 99.8), while others, like Charles Spurgeon, use the words to condemn self-righteous attitudes among their contemporaries (1856–1916: 25.553–556). More recently the American Heavy Metal group Metallica published an angry lyric entitled 'Holier Than Thou', with the refrain 'Judge not lest ye be judged yourself' (Matt 7:1) (1991).

Several commentators find in the 'fire that burns all the day' (v. 5) a reference to hellfire, quoting a verse from the Song of Moses: 'a fire is kindled by my anger and it will burn to the depths of hell' (Deut 32:22) (Jerome; cf. Aquinas). The Book of Isaiah ends with another reference to the unquenchable flames of eternal judgement awaiting the wicked (66:24), and this scéne is alluded to, according to ancient commentators, in the reference to a written record of their sins in verse 6 (cf. Dan 7:10) (Jerome). Calvin and most modern scholars reject the eschatological interpretation of the verse and compare the rhetoric of Jeremiah: 'the sin of Judah is written with an iron pen and with the nail of a diamond' (Jer 17:1).

The image of new wine as a symbol of the saving remnant (v. 8), recalls the role of Noah in rescuing humanity from God's wrath (Tg; Rashi; cf. Gen 9:20).

The chosen ones will inherit the land (v. 9) and build houses ... and plant vines' in it (vv. 21–22; cf. Isa 5:10). The fertile plain of Sharon, along the coast between Haifa and Tel Aviv, is synonymous with peace and beauty (Cant 2:1; Isa 35:2) and marks the western boundary of the promised land, while the Valley of Achor near Jericho on the east will also become, in Hosea's words, a 'door of hope' (Heb. *Petaḥ Tikvah*) (Hos.2:15) for the redeemed (Ibn Ezra, Kimḥi). The wicked are told to their faces that they will suffer and die for their sins (vv. 11–12).

While 'my servants ... my chosen', that is, the 'righteous' (Rashi), eat, drink and rejoice, the wicked will starve, wail and cry out in pain (vv. 13–16). The fate of the Jews who believed is set against the fate of those who persisted in unbelief, as life and death, good and evil, the blessing and the curse (Henry). A dramatic musical interpretation of verse 14, taken with Isaiah 3:10–11, forms the opening of Randall Thompson's choral work *The Peaceable Kingdom* (1936) (*BiM* 185–186). The righteous will acquire a new name in the world, a reputation (cf. Prov 22:1) unsullied by the sins of their ancestors, and worship 'the God of truth' (AV RSV) or 'the true God' (LXX JPS). The Hebrew word translated 'true' is *amen*, which in rabbinic tradition 'implies an oath' (Num.5:22), 'a promise' (Deut:27:26) and 'a prayer' (Jer 28:6) (b*Shevuot* 36a). Here it is interpreted as 'the living God' (Tg), the one true God, 'faithful and sure' (Isa 25:1; Ibn Ezra). The prophet predicts the 'moral improvement of our nation to such a degree that we shall be a blessing on the earth and the previous troubles will be forgotten' (Maimonides 1956: 208).

Christian commentators identify the righteous remnant, described here as 'my chosen ... my servants' (cf. Isa 41:8–9; 42:1; 44:1) with members of the Church. Eating, drinking and rejoicing (v. 13) then refers to the Eucharist (Jerome) and the 'new name' (v. 15; cf. Isa 62:2, Rev 2:17) is 'Christian' (Cyril, Theodoret) or 'Jesus' (Aquinas). It also includes 'children' (Isa 8:18), 'little ones' (Matt 10:42), 'chicks' (Matt 23:37) and 'lambs' (Isa 40:11) (Clement of Alexandria, *Paedagogus* 1.5.12–24). This is the 'new name' which is given to those who are victorious and is known only to them, written on a white stone (Rev 2:17) (Jerome). Eating and drinking are important signs of God's compassion towards the righteous, as in the Feeding of the Five Thousand (Luke 9:16) and the parable of the Great Supper (Luke 14:16–17), while famine is a just punishment for wickedness (Amos 8:11) (Origen, *Commentary on John* 13.220–225).

On the new name of God, literally 'the God of Amen' (Heb. *elohe amen*) in verse 16, many commentators say nothing about the oddness of the use of the word 'amen' here and take it as simply a variant of the usual words *emet* (truth) or *emunah* (faithfulness) (AV, RSV, Calvin, Childs, Otwell) or emend it to read *omen* (truth) (cf. Isa 25:1) 'the God of truth' (Duhm, Cheyne). Luther says 'God

is Amen, that is, faithful'. The name 'Amen', however, is given to Jesus in the
Book of Revelation 3:14, and it may have special significance here. One modern
commentator, for example, noting that virtually all other occurrences of the
word 'Amen' are liturgical responses by human speakers to God, suggests that
what is meant is that 'the faithfulness of God and the truthfulness of men will
answer to one another' (Jones). The twice-repeated *Amen* in the new name by
which God is henceforth to be known would then contain another anthropomorphism, not dissimilar to the twice-repeated 'Here I am' and the outstretched
hands at the beginning of the chapter. Rashi in a different context depicts the
deity in imagery strikingly similar and may have had this remarkable passage in
mind: 'God nods his head as though to acknowledge my blessing and says
"Amen"' (b*Berakhot* 7a).

A New Creation (Isa 65:17–25)

Jerome, followed by many modern scholars (Duhm, Westermann), takes the
'Amen' (v. 16a) as concluding a section, and begins his commentary on the vision
of a new heaven and a new earth (vv. 17–25) with the words 'For the former
troubles have been forgotten and are hidden from my eyes', anticipating a similar
comment in verse 17b and recalling the proverb 'In a day of prosperity, adversity
is forgotten' (Sir 11:25) (cf. Eusebius). In his great mercy God remembers only
the good done by his people, not the evil (*RA* 65). Jewish commentators also
emphasize that this is a prophecy about renewal and restoration in this world, in
particular in Jerusalem (vv. 18, 19, 25), not about a new creation or about the
world to come: it will be as if a new heaven and a new earth are created when
Zion comes home (cf. Isa 51:16) (Kimḥi, Luzzatto); 'new heavens' means a new
atmosphere where people will be healthy and enjoy a long life and 'a new earth'
refers to increased productivity in the soil (Ibn Ezra). 'Create' (Heb. *bara*'; cf. Isa
40:26; 42:5; 43:1) does not mean to produce something out of nothing, but 'to
restore, renew' (Ibn Ezra).

Rashi, quoting Isaiah 66:22, seems to take it more literally, with reference to
the world to come, and this is how Christian commentators have interpreted
the passage, starting with Peter and John of Patmos: 'the heavens will be kindled
and dissolved ... but according to his promise we wait for new heavens and a
new earth in which righteousness dwells' (2 Pet 3:13; Rev 21:1–2). Like John's
vision, Isaiah's has the new Jerusalem at its centre' (v. 18). The notion of a new
heaven and a new earth also appears in apocalyptic works like 1 Enoch 45:4–5
(cf. 91:16, *OTP* 1.34, 73; *Apocalypse of Elijah* 5:38, *OTP* 1.753). The Church
Fathers speculated on the nature of the new world: it cannot mean that bodily
nature will be entirely destroyed (Origen, *On First Principles* 1.6.4), but it

certainly means a change for the better for the old heavens will be worn out like an old garment (cf. Ps 102:25–26) (Jerome). Theodoret interprets the passage as describing how people will perceive all that is in heaven and in earth as God's creation. Calvin argues that it refers to the 'new age' (Heb 2:5), that is the whole reign of Christ from his first coming to his last. Luther stresses that it is about physical renewal as well as spiritual: on Judgement Day we will say 'What a dark sun and what small stars we used to have!' Christopher Columbus applied the vision to his discovery of the New World (Boitani 1994: 63–68), while Willy Burkhard's choral setting of verses 17–18a provides the conclusion of his oratorio, *The Face of Isaiah*, first performed in Switzerland on the eve of the Second World War. 'The new heaven and the new earth' (v. 17) are combined with the 'peaceable kingdom' imagery (v. 25; cf. 2 Pet 3:13) in a war memorial window in the Reformed Church in Spaarndam, Holland (Sawyer 1996: 238).

'Be glad and rejoice for ever' (v. 18) is addressed to the chosen people, safely back in their city. Christian commentators, following the Greek version, take it as a reference to the everlasting joy of those who have found Christ, whether in the Church today or on Judgement Day in the future (2 Pet 3:13) (Cyril). God shares in the joy of his people like the bridegroom with his bride (cf. Isa 62:5), and there will be no more weeping or crying (v. 19) because never again will children die young or old men die before they have lived a full life (vv. 20–22). It will be like the old days, from the days of Adam to Noah, when everyone lived for hundreds of years (Ibn Ezra). The problem in this world, where the innocent die young and sinners live to a ripe old age, will be resolved in the next: 'a child shall live to a hundred, but a sinner who lives to a hundred will be cursed' (v. 20 AV, Lowth). Unbelievers will be unhappy in life, however long they live (Henry): 'old age is not honoured for length of time … a blameless life is ripe old age' (Wisd 4:8–9) (Aquinas). Some modern scholars understand the verb *ḥaṭa* (to sin) in the sense of 'to miss the mark' (cf. Job 5:24; Prov 19:2) and remove the notion of reward and punishment: 'he who falls short of a hundred, will be considered accursed' (NRSV; cf. Westermann, Blenkinsopp).

The vision of a world where enemy invasion no longer interferes with daily life and people can enjoy the fruits of their labours (vv. 21–22) cancels earlier prophecies of doom (Deut 28:30) (Calvin). The language recalls Deuteronomic legislation for war (Deut 20:5–6), which will no longer be relevant (Nicholas). The Church Fathers took these verses to refer to a time when everyone will have experienced the resurrection and will reach 'mature manhood to the measure of the stature of the fullness of Christ' (Eph 4:13); the prophet is clearly speaking about eternal and immortal life here (Eusebius). This is the heavenly Jerusalem (Aquinas). Some consider the reference to building and planting in such a world to be inappropriate and suggest that 'the houses and vineyards' (v. 21) are metaphors for virtuous deeds (cf. Gal.6:7–8; 2 Cor 9:6) (Theodoret).

Long life is compared to 'the days of a tree' (v. 22), perhaps recalling the well-known image from Psalm 1 of a 'tree planted by streams of water ... whose leaf does not wither' (Ps 1:3). Lowth refers to a common belief that oak trees last for a thousand years, and Matthew Henry suggests that Isa 6:13 might help us understand the use of a tree as an image for survival. Both the Septuagint and the Targum add a reference to the 'tree of life', that is, the tree planted in the garden of Eden, out of reach of Adam and Eve (Gen 3:22–24) but now attainable to all in Christ who is the Wisdom of God, 'the tree of life to all who embrace her' (Prov 3:18) (Augustine, *City of God* 20:26.1–2; cf. Jerome). Others say the tree is the cross of salvation and 'those who put forth their hands to take its fruit will have eternal life' (Theodoret).

Their children will not die because God has blessed the parents and blessed the children so they will remain with their parents (v. 23) (Ibn Ezra). Jewish liturgical tradition associates this passage (Isa 65:23–66:8) with the birth of Jacob and Esau (Gen 25:19–26) (Mann 1971: 1, 200–204). Their prosperity will remain with their children and their inheritance to their children's children (Sir 44:11) (Aquinas; cf. Calvin). 'They shall not bear children for calamity', while the ungodly will have a miscarriage (cf. Ps 7:14) (Luther). The reference to procreation prompts some commentators to point out that, according to Jesus, 'in the resurrection they neither marry nor are given in marriage for they will be like angels of God in heaven' (Matt 22:30 Vg, AV), and the 'children' referred to are disciples born again in Christ 'by the washing of regeneration' (Tit 3:5) (Nicholas). Although verbal correspondences are absent, some also find an allusion to the Genesis story here (cf. v. 25) and suggest that in this new world the curse of Eve (Gen 3:16) will be replaced by a blessing (Eusebius).

The rabbis quoted verse 24 in a discussion of how God is both prosecutor and counsel for the defence: 'the same mouth which said "Though you make many prayers, I will not hear" (Isa.1:15) said "Before they call, I will answer" (Isa.65:24)' (ExodR XV 29). In the synagogue the verse is included in the *Qedushah de-Sidra* at the end of the morning service (cf. Isa 26:4; 42:21; 59:21–22) (see on Isa 6:3; *ADPB* 138–139). Aquinas reminds us of an earlier passage where Isaiah makes a similar prophecy (Isa 30:19), while Calvin compares Paul's teaching on access to God the Father through Christ (cf. Eph 2:18; 3:12). The verse, which he describes as 'a very lovely promise', inspired Luther to write a long paragraph on prayer: 'God will answer my prayer on a far higher level than I can imagine' (cf. John 15:7).

The vision of a new heaven and a new earth ends with an allusion to the peaceable kingdom, where 'the wolf and the lamb shall feed together' (cf. Isa 11:6–9). This is a figurative expression for 'peace will be established': God will remove the voracious nature of wild animals such as the lion which will eat straw ... even the snake will be harmless (Ibn Ezra). The animals refer to different kinds of people who will spend their life together in blessedness on God's holy mountain (Eusebius). When wolves like Paul, of the tribe of Benjamin (Gen 49:27), who had fiercely persecuted the Christians, come into the fold with them (cf. John 10:16), then 'the wolf and the lamb can feed together' (Henry). Calvin sees here a comparison between Adam and Christ: in paradise before the Fall even the fiercest animals 'bowed cheerfully to the dominion of man' and with the coming of Christ the 'world shall return to its first origin', and even the serpent, satisfied with his dust, will be harmless. Others consider the serpent here to be Satan, who continues in the curse, in wrath, in hell and so on (Luther; cf. Nicholas), but is trampled under foot and crushed by the wood of the cross (Theodoret).

Literary and artistic allusions to the peaceable kingdom imagery are mostly based on Isaiah 11:6–9. But a poem entitled 'On Falling Asleep by Firelight' by the American poet William Meredith alludes to verse 25 (Atwan and Wieder 1993: 406–407):

> Around the fireplace pointing at the fire
> As in the prophet's dream of the last truce
> The animals lie down; they doze or stare,
> Their hoofs or paws in comical disuse...
>   ...the heat
> Turns softly on the hearth into that dust
> Isaiah said would be the serpent's meat.

Sacrifices Acceptable to the Lord (Isa 66:1–6)

'Heaven is my throne and the earth my footstool': the first words of the chapter recall many texts extolling God's universal sovereignty (Deut 4:39; 1 Kgs 8:27; Ps 33:6–7; Jer 23:24) (Jerome), and are quoted in a great hymn sung in heaven at the beginning of Enoch's Book of Dreams (1 Enoch 84:2; *OTP* 1.62). They also appear, sometimes with Isaiah 6:1, on Isaiah's scroll in medieval representations of *Christus Pantocrator* (Kirschbaum 1970: col. 358; Berges 2012: 122, 143). Augustine, in a lighter vein, ridicules the literal interpretation of the verse: if

Isaiah Through the Centuries, First Edition. John F. A. Sawyer.
© 2018 John Wiley & Sons Ltd. Published 2020 by John Wiley & Sons Ltd.

God can weigh the heavens in the palm of his hand (Isa 40:12 Vg), how can he also sit on them? It must mean all the saints in heaven, and all the people on earth (cf. Ps 66:4) (*Sermon* 53:13–14). Eusebius points out that there will be a new heaven and a new earth and no remembrance of the physical mountain or the earthly Jerusalem (Isa 65:17). The chapter as a whole contains a variety of largely unconnected material, some of it directly alluding to earlier passages in the book, and some of it, such as the last verse (cf. Dan 12:2), probably from a later period. It has been suggested that verses 7–14 have been added as an epilogue to Third Isaiah (Isa 56–66), verses 15–21 as an epilogue to Second Isaiah (Isa 40–66) and verses 22–24 as an epilogue to the whole book (Beuken 1991).

After the first few words, the chapter as a whole returns to the theme of judgement: 'the prophet again rebukes the wicked people' (Ibn Ezra). His opening words mean 'I do not need your temple'; the Shekinah once dwelt there when the poor and humble hastened to do his bidding (v. 2), 'but now I have no desire for you' (Rashi). 'They chose their own ways' (v. 3) refers to Israel's ancestors (Ibn Ezra). There is hope for a new Jerusalem (vv. 7–14; 18–21; cf. Isa 65:18–19), but the chapter ends with hellfire for those who rebel against God (v. 24) (Rashi, Kimḥi). Christian commentators use the chapter to condemn Jewish legalism and disbelief (Jerome, Theodoret, Nicholas, Luther): their sacrifices are an abomination to him (cf. Prov 15:8) (Henry). They quote verses 1–3, sometimes along with verses from chapter 1 (Isa 1:10–17) and Jeremiah (Jer 7:18, 21–22), in relation to the abrogation of the old covenant and all its institutions, and the punishment of the people who abused them (Theodoret; Athanasius, *Festal Letters* 19.2; Isidore, *De Fide Catholica* 2.6.4). Some quote the case of Stephen, who died at the hands of the Jews with Isaiah's words on his lips (Isa 66:1–2; Acts 7:49–50) (Jerome; cf. Henry).

God's apparent rejection of the belief that the Temple in Jerusalem is his 'house and … the place of his rest' (v. 1) would go against traditions clearly expressed several times in Israel's liturgical texts (2 Chron 6:41; Ps 132:14) as well as earlier in the Book of Isaiah (Isa 11:10) (Calvin). Similar language was actually used by Solomon when he inaugurated the First Temple (1 Kgs 8:27), and in a rabbinic midrash Moses quotes this verse, along with a parallel from Jeremiah (Jer 23:24), when he asks why God would want to 'dwell among his people' (Exod 25:8). God replies that it has nothing to do with his own capacity but with the capacity of his people (NumR XII.3). It is therefore most unlikely that the passage is an attack on the Jewish institution *per se* (cf Hag 1) Calvin). It is more likely to be part of a final attack by the prophet on those who mock their creator, delighting in all manner of abominations (v. 3) and hating the poor and needy (vv. 2, 5). There is an ancient Jewish tradition that Isaiah addressed these words to Manasseh on the day that he brought the idol into the Temple (2 Chron 33:7) (*PesR* 4:3; Berges 2012: 109–110).

The rhetoric of verse 2 is noted by commentators: 'though heaven is my throne, I will look to the one who is poor and of a contrite spirit'. 'I will look to' is the opposite of 'I will turn my face away from' (cf. Isa 1:15) (Ibn Ezra), and in a midrash this is one of seven texts where God 'equates himself with those of a humble heart' (see on Isa 57:15). Jerome comments that God refuses to be contained in an earthly temple and chooses a person who is humble and meek to dwell in (cf. 1 Cor 3:16) (cf. Clement of Rome, *Letter to the Corinthians* 13:3; cf. Theodoret) while Ambrose quoted this verse in his funeral oration in praise of the Emperor Theodosius with reference to the emperor's famous act of public penance after a massacre in Thessalonica (*On Theodosius* 33) (cf. Isa 60:3). In a remarkable thirteenth-century German wall-painting the verse is cited along with other texts (e.g. Hos 1:19; 1 Sam 15:21) in an array of virtues attributed to the Virgin Mary (Schiller 1971: 24).

A paraphrase of verses 1 and 2 by the American Jewish poet David Rosenberg, highlights the word 'poor' (Heb. *'ani*):

> But I look at man especially
> for the man or woman oppressed
> poor or powerless
>
> when he knows he is
> brokenhearted and
> filled with humility
>
> his body trembling with care
> open to others
> to my words (Rosenberg 1991:299–300).

Some would argue that 'poor' (AV, ASV) here means 'poor in spirit, humble' (LXX, RSV, NJB; cf. Matt 5:3) (Jerome, Calvin, Westermann), but many would agree with Rosenberg in applying the verse to powerless and marginalized members of society (cf. Isa 3:14–15; 10:2; 58:7; Luke 6:20) (Luther, Duhm, Blenkinsopp, Childs).

The violent language of verse 3 recalls the 'hands full of blood' condemned in chapter 1 (Isa 1:15) where the prophet first attacks those who abuse the rituals (cf. Isa 58) (Calvin; cf. Athanasius, *Festal Letters* 19.2). If sacrifices are not done properly, the worshipper is as guilty as if he were a murderer, whether his offering is an ox or a lamb, a cereal offering or incense (Ibn Ezra). Unlike the sacrifices of Abel and Abraham (cf. Heb 11:4, 8), which are the ways of God, these people 'have chosen their own ways' and their sacrifices are made without faith and without fear (Luther). As well as homicide, references to 'a dog's neck,' 'swine's blood' (cf. Isa 65:4) and 'blessing an idol' focus on the ritual aspects of their behaviour (cf. Ezek 23:39) (Lowth) as well as the moral (cf. Hos 6:6) (Jerome). The verse has also been quoted as scriptural authority for vegetarianism as it implies that 'animal murder is equal to human murder'(Skriver 1990: 100). 'I will choose to mock them' (NRSV; cf. LXX, Vg, AV, NJB) (v. 4), because they mocked me (cf. Num 22:29) (Rashi). Others prefer to take the word 'mockeries' (Heb. *ta'alulim*) as related to a more general term for 'charges' (Ibn Ezra) or 'afflictions, punishments' (RSV; Westermann).

Verse 5 is addressed to 'those who tremble at my word' (v. 5; cf. v. 2). They are the remnant of God's people, who remain faithful to him when the majority have gone astray. They are hated by their brothers, mocked and 'cast out for my name's sake', but the prophet reassures them that 'it is they who will be put to shame' (AV, RSV, Lowth, Westermann). The ancient versions are slightly different, and the Church Fathers found a parallel to the commandment to love your enemies (Matt 5:44): 'speak, our brothers, to those who hate you' and when they see this, they will 'glorify your Father in heaven' (Matt 5:16) (Eusebius; cf. Jerome). The verse is quoted in discussions of early Jewish sectarianism (Blenkinsopp 2006: 71–72).

The term 'those who tremble' (Heb. *haredim*), (cf. 'Quakers'), who hasten with quaking to hear God's words (Rashi), appears only here (vv. 2, 5) and in the Book of Ezra (Ezra 9:4; 10:3), where, without being a technical term, it appears to describe an identifiable subgroup within the Jewish community struggling to redefine itself after the exile (Oswalt). Today the 'Haredi Jews', especially in New York and Israel but increasingly elsewhere in Western Europe, are Jews who dissociate themselves from other modern forms of Judaism and claim to preserve the true essence of Judaism in their beliefs and lifestyle. The title of a Haredi newspaper, *yated ne'eman*, has been mentioned (Isa 22:23).

Verse 6 adds a colourful footnote about the impending doom of God's enemies: there will be a huge noise and news of their punishment will spread everywhere (Ibn Ezra). Christian commentators apply it to the destruction of Jerusalem by the Romans in 70 CE, in particular an incident described by Josephus when a man cried, 'A voice from the east, a voice from the west, a voice from the four winds, a voice against Jerusalem and the holy house' (*War* 6:301) (Henry; cf. Jerome, Nicholas).

Mother Zion and Her Children (Isa 66:7–16)

The vivid image of a woman having a baby without labour pains (vv. 7–9), which immediately follows, indicates that the exiles will return to their homeland without trouble: it will be as if Zion had conceived and born her children on one day (cf. Isa 49; 54) (Ibn Ezra; cf. Rashi, Eusebius, Luther, Calvin). This was fulfilled in the rapid successes of Cyrus and the fall of Babylon, but also in the growth of the Church of Christ when the spirit was poured forth and multitudes were converted in a short time (cf. Ps 110:3) (Henry; cf. Calvin). The miraculous childbirth (cf. Ps 113:9) is about new creation, as Paul says, 'If anyone is in Christ, he is a new creature: the old has passed away, the new has come' (2 Cor 5:17) (Jerome; cf. Eusebius, Cyril). The absence of labour pains suggests a return to paradise (cf. Isa 51:3) (Ackerman 1992: 166). The image of childbirth has been used a number of times in relation to the fate of Zion (cf. Isa 49:14–26; 54:8; 60:4, 9; 62:4–5): this final example adds a miraculous element (v. 7) and is immediately followed by a description of her children blissfully sucking at her 'consoling breasts' (v. 11), the climax of the 'daughter of Zion' story (Sawyer 1989).

She was delivered of a son, not a daughter (v. 7) because 'Christians are man-like, courageous and strong' (Luther; cf. Calvin). There is a reference to Zion's labour pains (v. 8), to take account of her sufferings, but, as the Targum puts it, she is 'about to be comforted'. Rhetorical questions typical of these chapters of Isaiah (cf. 40:21; 42:19, 23–24; 45:11; 53:1, etc.) further highlight the unprecedented miraculous nature of what has happened (v. 8) and the infinite power of God to bring about a happy outcome after a period of pain (v. 9), such as the birth of a child to a woman in labour (cf. John 16:21). Luther adds that this is about spiritual birth: God desires to have children even though they should be persecuted because the blood of martyrs is the seed of Christians. Some of the Church Fathers cite verse 7 in support of the Doctrine of the Virgin Birth: 'the most holy virgin mother, therefore, escaped entirely the manner of women' (Methodius, *Oration concerning Simeon and Anna* 3); 'where pleasure had not preceded, pain did not follow' (John of Damascus, *Exposition of the Orthodox Faith* 4.14).

The miraculous birth of a son is celebrated in a short hymn of thanksgiving followed by an oracle of salvation (vv. 10–14). All who love Jerusalem and mourn over her are now exhorted to rejoice with her and be glad for her (vv. 10–11; cf. Isa 12:4–6; 65:18–19). The *Bible Moralisée* shows the prophet conducting a small band of musicians, Jews and Gentiles, celebrating in the New Jersualem (Plate 44). 'Consolations' (v. 11 AV Heb. *tanḥumim*) picks up the word 'comfort' (Heb. *naḥmu*) from Chapter 40 (see comm.), but it now means simply 'fullness of joy' as there is no longer any need for comfort or consolation (Ibn Ezra). They will now be like babies who 'enjoy their mother with every advantage, and hang on her breasts' (Calvin). The Church Fathers expand this image in a variety of ways: her milk is the spiritual milk referred to by Paul (1 Cor 3:2) (Cyril), which flows from her two breasts, that is, from the Old Testament and the New Testament (Eusebius). Many also cite the Song of

PLATE 44   'Rejoice with Jerusalem and be glad for her, all you who love her' (Isa 66:10). *Bible Moralisée* (Paris 1233). Reproduced with kind permission of the Warburg Institute London.

Solomon: 'your breasts are better than wine' (Cant 1:2 LXX) (Cyril, Jerome, Aquinas). The Targum by contrast avoids the maternal imagery entirely and reads: 'that you may be satisfied with the spoil of consolations; that you may drink and be drunk with the wine of her glory'.

In another curious elaboration of this theme the English writer Frances Quarles wrote a poem headed 'Isaiah 66:11. You may suck, but not be satisfied with the breast of her consolation'. It picks up from the text the theme of unrestrained physical pleasure, but turns it into an attack on gluttony: 'Thou tak'st a surfeit where thou should'st but taste, / And mak'st too much not half enough to please thee' (Quarles 1777: 44–45). The reference to 'knees' (v. 12) led to the inclusion of this verse in a medieval poem about the seven 'Limbs of our Jesus' (*Membra Jesu Nostri*) (cf. Nah 1:15; Zech 13:6; Cant 2:13–14; 1 Pet 2:2–3; Cant 4:9; Ps 31:16), set to music as a cycle of seven cantatas by Buxtehude (1689) (*BiM* 155–f).

The oracle of salvation (vv. 12–14), beginning with the formula 'For thus says the Lord', is rich in imagery: 'I will extend peace [Heb. *shalom*] to her like a river and the wealth of the nations like an everflowing stream'. The nations of the world will bring their property to Jerusalem (cf. Isa 60:5, 11; 61:6) (Ibn Ezra). The ancient versions have 'river of peace' and the Church Fathers compare this to passages in the Psalms about 'the river of God' (Ps 65:9) and the 'streams that make glad the city of God' (Ps 46:4) (Eusebius, Jerome), sometimes identifying the river with Christ (Cyril). The verse inspired the young English poet Frances Ridley Havergal to write the well-known hymn beginning 'Like a river glorious / Is God's perfect peace' (*CH2* 443), and Willy Burkhard chose the same verse, along with Isaiah 65:17–18, to conclude his oratorio *The Face of Isaiah* (1936) (Berges 2012: 127).

The rare image of God as a mother comforting her children is taken up by the author of a hymn found among the Dead Sea Scrolls (4Q434 fr.2,6; *DSSE* 446). In a medieval representation of verse 13, in the context of the story of Lazarus being carried by the angels to Abraham's bosom (Luke 16:22), Christ is shown holding newborn souls in a napkin: 'there is tenderness, then, in heaven' (*Biblia Pauperum* 1987: 126). There are several choral settings of the words, beginning *Laetare Hierusalem* 'Rejoice Jerusalem' (Isa 66:11; Ps 122) and focusing on the mother–child imagery, including one by the sixteenth-century Italian Andrea Rota and another by the contemporary British composer Robert Hugill. In Brahms' *German Requiem* (1857–1868) it provides the words for a chorus sung in dialogue with the soprano solo 'You Who Now Have Sorrow' (John 6:22). A sixteenth-century Bohemian Brethren hymn contains the line 'With a mother's tender hand, God gently leads the chosen band' (*GtG* 645). Since the Second Vatican Council verses 10–14 are read at the Feast of our Lady of Lourdes (*ORM*). Verse 13 also features in a number of official church pronouncements on the motherhood of God (see comm. on Isa 46:3–4). In Jewish tradition the verse is the first of three passages recited in the concluding paragraph of 'Prayer in a house of mourning' (cf. Isa 25:8; 60:19; *ADPB* 842–845).

The prophecy continues with a reference to a joyful heart and 'bones flourishing like the grass' (v. 14), which reminded Calvin of a proverb about dried bones (Prov 17:22), but for Theodoret, perhaps with Ezekiel's famous vision of the valley of dry bones in mind (Ezek 37), it foretold the resurrection of the dead. It ends, however, with a reference to the Lord's 'indignation against his enemies', which is vividly expanded in the last part beginning 'Behold the Lord will come in fire' (vv. 15–16). Fire normally accompanies the coming of the Lord (cf. Ps 97:3) (Nicholas), and his chariots were twenty thousand when he came from Sinai (cf. Ps 68:17) (Cyril). Perhaps originally the 'chariots like a whirlwind' here were Nebuchadnezzar's chariots that punished Jerusalem in 586 BCE (Jer 4:13) (cf. Aquinas). But here the fire is the fire of Gehenna (cf. Ezek 38:22) (Rashi), and the chariots are the angels and powers that surround him when he comes to judge the living and the dead (2 Tim.4:1; cf. Matt 16:27) (Eusebius, Jerome, Nicholas). The sword is the sword with which the wicked are punished (Ps 7:12; Amos 9:10), the sword with which Leviathan was slain (Isa 27:1) (Jerome). This is apocalyptic language about judgement day recalling the carnage in Edom: 'the Lord has a sword: it is sated with blood' (Isa 34:6; cf. 63:1–6), but here it affects 'all flesh' (v. 16) (Aquinas). In a graphic visual commentary taking verses 16 and 23 together, the *Bible Moralisée* depicts the day of judgement on three levels, with angels in heaven, terrified human beings on earth listening to the prophet and suffering souls in torment in hell beneath: in the centre, dominating the scene, is the Lord, enthroned over heaven and earth, the book of life open in his hand.

A New Heaven and a New Earth (Isa 66:17–24)

The last part of the chapter is divided into four short prophecies separated by the formula 'says the Lord' (17, 18–21, 22–23, 24), all in prose except verses 22–23. The first of these is a prophecy of judgement (v. 17), which singles out for special mention those guilty of taking part in idolatrous rituals 'in the gardens' (cf. Isa 1:29; 65:3) and breaking the Jewish dietary laws by eating pork, mice and other 'abominations' (Heb. *sheqeṣ*) (cf. Lev 11:7–8, 29). Some have suggested emending 'abomination' (Heb. *sheqeṣ*) to 'creeping things' (Heb. *shereṣ*; cf. Lev 11:21, 41–44) (Duhm). Christian commentators stress that it is their idolatrous behaviour that is at fault rather than what they eat (Eusebius, Luther), and some add that sexual orgies were involved (Jerome, Aquinas). The phrase 'behind one in the midst' (Heb. *ahar ahat ba-tavek*) has been much discussed: probably it refers to a tree, perhaps an Asherah (Ibn Ezra) or some other idol (Henry), set up in the middle of the garden for worshippers to process or dance round, 'one after the other' (cf. Tg, *Pesh*).

The second prophecy (vv. 18–21) has been interpreted in various ways. According to Jewish tradition the passage refers to the war of Gog and Magog (Ezek 38) or the scene described in the last chapter of Zechariah where the nations gathered round Jerusalem are smitten by a terrible plague (Zech 14:12). Ibn Ezra explains verse 18 ('I their works and their thoughts ... it has come...') as follows: 'when they intend to rebel against me (cf. Ps 2:2), then the time is come to gather all the nations around Jerusalem'. Most will be destroyed: that is what is meant by 'they will see my glory' (vv. 18–19) (Rashi). But there will be some survivors (v. 19) and it will be their task to go out into the world, marked with some 'sign of reproach' like the loss of an eye (Ibn Ezra), to tell the nations about God's glory and the plague with which they had been smitten (Rashi). Then they will provide horses, chariots, waggons, mules and dromedaries (Heb. *kirkarot* RSV Ibn Ezra; AV "swift beasts") (v.20) to bring back the Jews from exile to Jerusalem. They will come with singing and dancing (cf. 2 Sam 6:14; Tg, Rashi), like Israelites bringing offerings to the Temple in clean vessels. Among them will be priests and Levites and they will be able to resume their duties (v. 21) (Rashi).

Christian interpreters take the passage in a very different way. Verses 18–19 may have helped to shape the understanding of mission among the early Christians (Blenkinsopp 2006:133). In some manuscripts of the Septuagint, verse 18 reads, 'for I know their works and their thoughts and I am coming to gather all nations and tongues and they shall come and see my glory' (cf. Vg, RSV). This then becomes a prophecy about the day when 'the Son of Man comes in the glory of the Father and all the angels with him and they will gather all the nations' (Matt 25:31–33) (Eusebius). Those who are saved from among the nations will have the 'sign' of baptism on their foreheads, like the Tau in Ezekiel's vision (Ezek 9:4; cf. Exod 12:7; Isa 7:14; Pss 60:4; 86:17), as the Lord, before he ascended to the Father, instructed his disciples (Matt 28:19) (Jerome, Calvin). 'The servants of our God have been sealed upon their foreheads' (Rev 7:3) (Henry): they shall go to peoples that have not heard my name or seen my glory (cf. Isa 65:1) (Eusebius). As Paul said to the Jews of Antioch, since you do not want to hear, we will turn to the gentiles (Acts 13:46) (Nicholas, Luther).

The list of 'nations and tongues' (v. 19) (cf. Ezek 27:10, 12–13; Gen 10:2–5, 6–12) recalls the miracle of Pentecost (Acts 2) (Theodoret). Tarshish was often identified with Tarsus in Asia Minor; Pul (or Put LXX RSV), a son of Ham (Gen 10:6), was in Africa and Lud was probably Lydia (Jerome). 'Those who draw the bow' have often been identified with the Parthians, noted for their archery skills (Luther). Tubal and Javan were traditionally located in Italy and Greece respectively and 'the islands' denote unknown countries (Calvin). The Greek version has Meshech in place of 'those who draw (Heb. *mashak*) the bow', and this probably refers to the Moschi, a people located in a region south-east of the Black Sea (Lowth; cf. Jerome). Along with Tubal and Javan, Meshech is a descendant of Noah's son Japheth (cf. Ezek 27:13), as is Tarshish (Gen 10:4; cf. Ezek 27:12), nowadays usually identified with Tartessus, a Phoenician port on the Mediterranean coast of Spain (Duhm, Westermann).

The nations of the world are called 'your brothers' (v. 20), that is, 'brothers of the saints and patriarchs through the hearing of the Word' (Luther). They shall be brought to Jerusalem as an offering to the Lord, that is, instead of animal sacrifices brought to the temple in the earthly Jerusalem, this is about a new kind of sacrifice described by Paul in his letter to the Romans (Rom 15:16) (Calvin). It is not about people journeying to the earthly Jerusalem: it is about the presence of Christ 'where two or three are gathered together in his name' (Nicholas). The horses and chariots refer to angelic powers that will carry them up to heaven (1 Thess 4:17) (Eusebius) as they carried Elijah (2 Kgs 2) (Jerome). The Church Fathers take the next two verses together and argue that, when heaven is new and earth is new (v. 22), there will be a new priesthood (v. 21) which will not follow a genealogy but an order of faith (Jerome, Eusebius) (v. 21). It is not clear whether this refers to the priesthood of all believers (1 Pet 2:9; Rev 1:6; 5:10) or to the special office of ministers and teachers of the gospel who offer spiritual sacrifices to God by the gospel (Calvin). Either way this is about the calling of the nations, the election of the apostles and the whole world worshipping Christ (Cyril).

Such Christian interpretations of the passage highlight references to a mission to the gentiles and the apparent appointment of priests and Levites from among them. There are precedents in Isaiah (Isa 56:3–7; 60:4–9; 61:6; 64:2), but the emphasis on this one Isaianic theme and its climactic position in the book have raised doubts about its date and authorship. Many scholars identify signs of late editorial activity on the part of the Jewish authorities in the Second Temple period, for example, in the insertion of verse 20, which limits the role of gentiles to providing sacrificial material (Westermann). Others stress the continuity within the book which culminates in a similar 'terrifying paradox' to the one at the end of the New Testament (Rev 20:11, 13; 21:1–4; 22:15) (Childs).

The second reference to 'the new heavens and the new earth' (v. 22; cf. 65:17) is God's promise to his people that their descendants and their name will endure for ever, while the reference to 'all flesh' (v. 23) implies that this is not just about Israel: 'the book ends on a highly universal note' (Sommer). Christian commentators apply the prophecy to the Church, citizens of the heavenly Jerusalem (Irenaeus, *Against Heresies* 5.36.1), the assembly of the firstborn who are enrolled in heaven (Heb 12:22–23) (Eusebius; cf. Calvin). 'From new moon to new moon, from sabbath to sabbath' means that the Church will shine like the moon and find true sabbath rest (cf. Isa 56:4,6; Col 2:16–17), and 'the light of the moon will be as the light of the sun and the light of the sun will be sevenfold (Isa 30:26; Cant 6:9) (Jerome). With Joel (Joel 2:28), Zechariah (Zech.2:13; 14:16) and others (Pss 65:2; 86:9) the prophet declares that 'all flesh shall come to worship before me, says the Lord' (cf. Isa 40:5) (Jerome). The whole passage (vv. 18–22) features prominently (with Dan 10:19; Hag 2:9; Mic 4:3; Lev 26:6; Pss 85:10; 118:19; Isa 43:9) in a passionate chorus towards the end of Vaughan Williams' cantata *Dona nobis pacem* (1936) (*BiM* 69).

The final verse concludes that, in the new age, when the whole of humanity is saved (vv. 22–23), they will go forth and look on the corpses of those who had rebelled against God, eaten by worms and burnt in the eternal fire of Gehinnom (v. 24). Jesus alludes to this (Mark 9:47–48) and the Church Fathers discuss it length: Augustine begins with Jesus' words: 'it is better for you to enter the kingdom of God with one eye than to keep both eyes and be consigned to hellfire' (Augustine, *City of God* 21.9). The righteous will go out to witness the fate of the wicked (Ps 58:10) (Aquinas). The worm is the conscience that eats away at them day and night (cf. Ps 32:4 Vg; Prov 4:30) (Jerome, Eusebius, Luther). If the worm of sinners does not die, how shall the flesh of the just perish? (Ambrose, *On Satyrus* 2.87). The verse is quoted in Chaucer's *Parson's Tale* to remind people of hellfire (cf. Isa 14:11) (Chaucer 1980: 603), and it played a significant role in the development of medieval images of hell (cf. Isa 14:15–20; Ezek 32:18–25; Wisd 17; Kirschbaum 1970: col. 313; Bernstein 1993: 28–29). Whether this final prophecy refers to the destruction of Jerusalem by the Romans or to the Last Judgement, 'Christ will deliver us from all these things' (Cyril).

The verse attracted much discussion in Jewish tradition as well. Rabbi Jose cited it to prove that Gehenna exists for ever (*Tos*Berakhot 5.31). According to some rabbinic authorities it describes only the fate of the worst offenders, such as heretics, atheists who repudiate the law and those who deny the resurrection of the dead (b*Rosh ha-Shanah* 17a), while others argue, on the basis of verse 23 (from new moon one year to the same month next year) that the punishment of the wicked in hell is limited to twelve months (m*Eduyot* 2:10; cf. Ibn Ezra). The Targum also softens the horrific image somewhat in a paraphrase of the verse: 'and the wicked shall be judged in Gehenna until the righteous say, "We have seen enough"' (cf. LXX, Vg). In the Jewish annual lectionary, chapter 66 is the haftarah read when the sabbath coincides with the new moon (cf. v. 23), but verse 24 is considered so terrible that it is the custom to end the reading with the words of verse 23 repeated a second time after it (Sommer).

Glossary

Alexandria: capital of Egypt in the third century BCE; city where the Septuagint was translated. Famous for allegorical exegesis of the Bible.

Allegory: method of interpretation that seeks figurative meanings of spiritual or moral import.

Amidah: Jewish communal prayer consisting of the 'Eighteen Benedictions' recited standing (Heb. *'amidah*).

Antioch: Syrian city; home of early Church Fathers who used a more historical and literal approach than the Alexandrians.

Antiphon: a short sentence sung or recited before and after a psalm or canticle.

Aramaic: Semitic language, originally of Syria and later the official language of Persia.

Isaiah Through the Centuries, First Edition. John F. A. Sawyer.
© 2018 John Wiley & Sons Ltd. Published 2020 by John Wiley & Sons Ltd.

Bible Moralisée: type of medieval illustrated commentary on the Bible.

Biblia pauperum: medieval pictorial commentary portraying scenes of the life of Jesus accompanied by scenes and texts from the Old Testament.

Darby Bible: original translation of the whole Bible by John Nelson Darby (1800–1882), one of the original Plymouth Brethren, published in 1890.

Dead Sea Scrolls: manuscripts of the Bible and other texts discovered at Qumran and elsewhere in the Judaean desert from 1948 onward.

Deutero-Isaiah (Second Isaiah): Isaiah 40–55 or the supposed author of Isaiah 40–55.

Dies irae (L. 'day of wrath'): thirteenth-century hymn sung at Requiem Masses.

Falashas or **Beta Israel**: the Jews of Ethiopia, many now settled in Israel.

Gematria: An exegetical method based on the numerical value of the twenty-two letters of the Hebrew alphabet.

Geneva Bible: sixteenth-century translation of the Bible by English Protestants who fled to Geneva from persecution under Mary Tudor.

Glossa Ordinaria: influential medieval collection of marginal glosses from the Church Fathers.

Haftarah (Heb. *haftarah*): a passage from the Hebrew Prophets accompanying each liturgical reading from Torah.

Historical criticism: exegetical approaches concerned with the date, authorship, sources and original meaning of the biblical text.

Jehovah's Witnesses: millennarian sect founded in Pittsburg in 1872.

Kaaba: huge granite cube at the heart of Islam's most sacred site in Mecca.

Kabbalah: system of Jewish mysticism originating in twelfth-thirteenth century Europe and reinterpreted in sixteenth century Palestine.

Kethib: Masoretic term for the written text of scripture.

Lambeth Bible: twelfth-century illuminated manuscript from romanesque England.

Lectionary: list of selected scripture readings arranged for liturgical use. See **Haftarah**.

Lives of the Prophets: collection of Jewish legends, probably from first century CE.

Maḥzor: Jewish prayer book for annual festivals and fasts.

Masoretic Text (MT): standard Hebrew text of the Bible produced by Jewish grammarians in the sixth to tenth centuries CE, with vowel points, accents and marginal notes for copyists.

Mekhilta (**of Rabbi Ishmael**): third- or fourth-century CE halakhic Midrash to Exodus.

Midrash Rabbah: third- to fifth-century rabbinic commentary on the Five Books of Moses (Genesis Rabbah, etc.) and the Five Scrolls (Ruth Rabbah, etc.).

Miqra'ot Gedolot ('Rabbinic Bible'): influential edition of Masoretic text with Targum and commentaries by Rashi, Ibn Ezra, Kimhi and others. First printed in Venice in 1524–1525.

Mishnah: collection of rabbinic sayings attributed to Rabbi Judah ha-Nasi arranged thematically in Six Orders and 63 Tractates. See **Talmud**.

Mormons: members of the Church of Jesus Christ of Latter Day Saints, founded in the 1820s. Their centre is in Utah and their sacred text the Book of Mormon.

Olney Hymns (1979): collection of evangelical hymns by John Newton and William Cowper

Paris Psalter: tenth-century Byzantine illuminated manuscript.

Passover Haggadah: Jewish text laying out the order (Heb. *seder*) of the annual feast in the family home, celebrating the beginning of Passover.

Peshitta: first-century CE Syriac translation of the Hebrew Bible, later with New Testament added, monopolized by Christians.

Pesikta de Rav Kahana: sixth-century collection of Midrashic stories and homilies.

Pesikta Rabbati: ninth-century compilation of Midrashic material.

Pseudepigrapha: generic name given to non-canonical Jewish texts, mostly written between 200 BCE and 150 CE.

Pseudo-Matthew: seventh-century apocryphal 'Infancy Gospel'.

Qere: Masoretic term for the vocalized text of scripture where it differs from Kethib.

Qumran: location of a Jewish sectarian monastic settlement north-west of the Dead Sea, where the first of the Dead Sea Scrolls were discovered.

Rastafarians: messianic cult originating in Jamaica in 1930.

Requiem: traditional Roman Catholic Mass for the dead.

Scottish Paraphrases: vernacular English translations of biblical passages, apart from Psalms, commissioned by the Church of Scotland in 1742.

Second Vatican Council (Vatican 2) (1962–1965): ecumenical council, initiated by Pope John XXIII, for the spiritual renewal of the Roman Catholic Church.

Septuagint (LXX): ancient Greek translation of the Hebrew Bible ordered by Ptolemy Philadelphus (285–246 BCE) for Greek-speaking Jews in Egypt.

Shofar: wind-instrument made from a ram's horn, sounded at Jewish New Year.

Sibylline Oracles: collection of sacred Greek writings, mostly pre-Christian, attributed to female prophets or 'Sibyls'.

Sukkot, Feast of (Tabernacles, Booths): autumnal Jewish feast commemorating the wilderness period between the Exodus and settlement in the Promised Land.

Talmud: vast collection of rabbinic sayings in the form of a commentary on the Mishnah; preserved in the Palestinian Talmud (*Yerushalmi*) (fourth century) and the Babylonian Talmud (*Bavli*) (fifth century).

Tanakh Hebrew Bible: Law (*Torah*), Prophets (*Nevi'im*) and Writings (*Ketuvim*).

Tanḥuma: midrash on the Torah, named after the fourth-century CE Rabbi Tanḥuma bar Abba.

Targum: Aramaic translation of the Hebrew Bible, used in Jewish worship from fifth century BCE (cf. Ezr 4:7). Targum Onkelos (Torah) and Targum Yonatan (Prophets) *c.*100–200 CE.

Tiberius Psalter: eleventh-century illustrated manuscript depicting the lives of David and Christ.

Tosefta: rabbinic commentary compiled at about the same time as the Mishnah.

Trito-Isaiah (Third Isaiah): Isaiah 56–66, or the supposed author of Isaiah 56–66.

Utrecht Psalter: Carolingian Psalter, made between *c.*820–835 CE at Benedictine monastery at Hautvilliers near Eperny.

Vulgate: fourth-century Latin translation of the Bible by Jerome; designated the only authentic Latin Bible at the Council of Trent (1545–1563).

Wycliffe Bible: first complete translation of the Bible into English; named after John Wycliffe.

Yeshivah: Jewish institution of higher education.

York Plays: cycle of medieval 'mystery' plays performed on Corpus Christi Day.

Zohar ('Book of Splendour'): thirteenth-century work of Kabbalah mysticism; written in Aramaic.

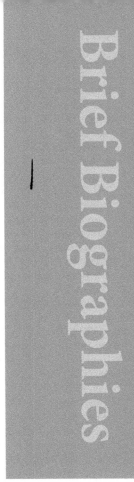

Brief Biographies

Abravanel (Isaac ben Judah) (1437–1508): Portuguese-born Jewish exegete, exiled many times because of his Jewish identity.

Aelred (1109–1167): Cistercian monk and Abbot of Rievaulx.

Aḥad Ha'Am (Asher Ginsberg) (1856–1927): Zionist thinker and Hebrew writer.

Akiba, Rabbi (c.50–c.135): leading teacher of the Torah. 'Chief of the Sages'.

Alexander (d. 329): Bishop of Alexandria and fierce opponent of the Arian heresy.

Allen, Lyman Whitney (1854–1930): American Presbyterian pastor and hymn writer.

Altschuler, David (seventeenth century): Jewish Bible commentator, author of *Metzudat David* and *Metzudat Tziyon* in rabbinic Bibles (*Miqra'ot Gedolot*).

Isaiah Through the Centuries, First Edition. John F. A. Sawyer.
© 2018 John Wiley & Sons Ltd. Published 2020 by John Wiley & Sons Ltd.

Ambrose (*c*.333–397): bishop of Milan and teacher of Augustine; fought Arianism and defended Church independence against the Western Roman emperors.

Andrew of St Victor (d. 1175): biblical exegete, following literal method of Hugh of St Victor.

Angelico, Fra Beato (*c*.1400–1455): Italian Dominican and religious artist.

Anselm (1033–1109): archbishop of Canterbury. Foremost scholastic thinker.

Aquila (second century CE). Jewish scholar and author of a literalistic Greek translation of the Hebrew Bible

Aquinas, Thomas (*c*.1225–1274): a Dominican and the Christian church's major systematic theologian.

Armes, Philip (1836–1908): English organist and composer.

Arnold, George Benjamin (1832–1902): English organist and composer.

Athanasius (*c*.296–373): bishop of Alexandria; advocated the adoption of the books of the Old Testament and the New Testament as canon; wrote and fought against the Arians.

Augustine of Hippo (354–430): the most influential theologian of Western Christianity, author of *The City of God*.

Baal Shem Tov (1698–1750): Jewish mystic. Founder of Hasidism.

Bach, Johann Sebastian (1685–1750): German Lutheran organist and composer. Music director at St Thomas' Church, Leipzig from 1723.

Bale, John (1495–1563): English churchman, controversialist and playwright.

Barth, Karl (1886–1968): Swiss Protestant theologian.

Bartolommeo, Fra (1475–1517): Italian painter of the High Renaissance.

Basil the Great (*c*.330–79): anti-Arian bishop of Caesarea, called Basil the Great; helped organize Eastern monasticism.

Bede, The Venerable (early eighth century): chronicler of English Christianity.

Bellegambe, Jean (*c*.1470–*c*.1536): Flemish religious painter.

Bellini, Giovanni (1430–1516): greatest Venetian artist of his day.

Bennett, William Sterndale (1816–1875): English pianist and composer.

Bernard of Clairvaux (1090–1153): a monastic reformer and abbot of one of the chief centres of the Cistercian order.

Bickersteth, Edward (1786–1850): English evangelical clergyman and hymn writer.

Biruni, Abū Rayhān Muhammad ibn Ahmad 'Al-Biruni' (973–1048): Iranian scholar and polymath.

Blake, William (1757–1827): an English artist, poet and visionary on the fringe of radical movements in London at the time of the French Revolution.

Bonar, Horatius (1808–1889): Scottish Free Church minister and hymn writer.

Bonaventure, St (1221–1274): Franciscan biographer of St Francis.

Bosch, Hieronymus (*c*.1450–1516): Dutch painter best known for his ghoulish nightmarish paintings of hell.

Botticelli, Sandro (1444–1510): Florentine painter of religious subjects, but best known for *The Birth of Venus* and *Primavera*.

Bowring, John (1792–1872): English politician and hymn writer.

Brahms, Johannes (1833–1897): German composer. After earning a living by playing in taverns in Hamburg, in 1862 he settled in Vienna, where he devoted his life to composing mainly orchestral works.

Britten, Benjamin (1913–1976): English composer. Apart from a few orchestral works and some chamber music, most of Britten's compositions were inspired by words.

Browning, Robert (1812–89): an English poet who, like Blake, reacted against the effects of higher criticism of the Bible.

Bruckner, Anton (1824–1896): Austrian composer. He was appointed cathedral organist in Linz from 1855 and, in 1868, professor at the Vienna Conservatory, where he spent the rest of his life.

Buber, Martin (1878–1965): Jewish religious thinker and writer, author of *I and Thou* (1923).

Bultmann, Rudolf (1884–1976): German New Testament scholar and theologian.

Bunyan, John (1628–1688): author of *Pilgrim's Progress* (1679), preacher and member of an independent congregation in Bedford, imprisoned for his beliefs.

Burkhard, Willy (1900–1955): Swiss composer.

Buxtehude, Dietrich (*c*.1637–1707): German organist and composer, admired by Bach.

Byrd, William (1543–1623): English Catholic composer. Probably the greatest of the Tudor composers, prosecuted several times for recusancy.

Byron, George Gordon, Lord (1788– 1824): Romantic poet and adventurer.

Caldara, Antonio (1670–1736): Italian composer, born in Venice moved to Vienna.

Calvin, John (1509–1564): French Reformer; wrote major works of theology and biblical commentary, and led a theocratic regime in Geneva.

Carey, William (1761–1834): Baptist missionary, orientalist and bible translator.

Carissimi, Giacomo (1605–1674): Italian organist and composer.

Cassian, John (*c*.360–*c*.435): monk who trained in Egypt and settled in Marseilles.

Cassiodorus (*c*.490–*c*.585): Roman historian, politician, and monk.

Chaucer, Geoffrey (1343/4–1400): translator and narrative poet.

Cheyne, Rev T. K. (1841–1915): Oxford scholar, author, editor.

Chrysologus, Peter (*c*.400–450): bishop of Ravenna.

Chrysostom, John (*c*.347–407): bishop of Constantinople; often considered the greatest preacher of the patristic era.

Clement of Alexandria (*c*.150–*c*.215): head of the catechetical school of Alexandria.

Clement of Rome (64–96): bishop of Rome; one of the Apostolic Fathers.

Coleridge, Samuel Taylor (1772–1834): an English poet and theologian.

Columbus, Christopher (1451–1506): Genoese explorer. Discovered the New World in 1492.

Connaughton, Luke (1917–1979): English Catholic journalist and hymn writer.

Constantine (d. 337): first Christian emperor, moved capital from Rome to Byzantium in 324.

Cosin, John (1594–1672): bishop of Durham. Contributed to the 1661 Prayer Book.

Costa, Lorenzo (*c*.1460–1535): Italian renaissance painter.

Coverdale, Miles (1488–1568): Augustinian friar and translator of the Bible into English.

Cowley, Abraham (1618–1667): English poet.

Cowper, William (1731–1800): English poet and hymn writer. Collaborated with **John Newton** in the production of the **Olney Hymns**.

Coxe, Arthur Cleveland (1818–1896): American Episcopalian bishop, scholar and poet.

Cranach, Lucas, the Elder (1472–1553): German painter, illustrator of Luther's Bible (1522).

Cranach, Lucas, the Younger (1515–1586): German painter, second son of Cranach the Elder.

Crosby, Fanny (1820–1915): Protestant hymn writer, venerated by the US Episcopal Church.

Cyprian (d. 258): bishop of Carthage. Author of some important treatises.

Cyril of Alexandria (d. 444): patriarch of Alexandria, champion of orthodoxy against the Antiochene Nestorius and author of a complete commentary on Isaiah.

Cyril of Jerusalem (*c*.315–387): bishop of Jerusalem, author of catechetical works on baptism.

Daly, Mary (1928–): American theological writer and post-Christian feminist.

Dante Alighieri (1265–1321): Italian poet and political theorist, author of the *Divina Commedia* (1314).

Dauermann, S. (1944–): American Messianic Jewish musician.

De La Rue, Pierre (*c*.1452–1518): Franco-Flemish Renaissance singer and composer.

Didymus the Blind (*c*.313–398): Head of catechetical school in Alexandria. His writings, including biblical commentaries, which are mostly lost, are influenced by Origen.

Diemer, Emma Lou (1927–): American composer.

Doddridge. Philip (1702–1751): Nonconformist divine and hymn writer.

Döderlein, Johann Christoph (1745–1792): German biblical scholar; early proponent of the exilic dating of Isaiah 40–66.

Domin, Hilde (1909–2006): German lyric poet and writer.

Donne, John (1571–1631): Dean of St Paul's London and metaphysical poet.

Doré, Gustave (1832–1883): French artist and book illustrator.

Drayton, Michael (1563–1631): English poet.

Dürer, Albrecht (1471–1528): German printer and engraver.

Duhm, Bernhard (1847–1928): German Old Testament scholar noted for his Isaiah commentary.

Dunbar, William (*c*.1460– *c*.1520): Scottish poet.

Dylan, Bob (1941–): American singer and songwriter. His poetry for a time reflected an evangelical Christian faith and later found inspiration in his Jewish origins.

Ecclestone, Alan (1904–1992): Radical inner-city parish priest and writer.

Edwards, Jonathan (1703–1758): North American Puritan preacher and revivalist.

Eichhorn, Johann Gottfried (1752– 1827): German Old Testament scholar.

Elgar, Sir Edward (1857–1934): English organist and composer. Appointed Master of the King's Music in 1929.

Eliot, George (1819–1880): English novelist.

Eliot, T.S. (1888–1965): American poet and critic. Awarded Nobel Prize for Literature in 1948.

Ephraim of Bonn (1132–1200): German Jewish poet.

Ephrem Syrus (*c*.306–373): Syrian writer and poet, author of numerous hymns and biblical commentaries.

Eusebius of Caesarea (*c*.260–*c*.339): bishop of Caesarea, author of a Life of Constantine, a history of the Church and a complete commentary on Isaiah.

Faber, Johannes (*c*.1455–1536): French Catholic humanist condemned for heresy in 1525. Translated Bible into French.

Fleeson, Mary (1959–): English religious artist and calligrapher, living on Holy Island since 1997.

Foley, John (1939–): American Jesuit priest and hymn writer.

Foote, Julia A.J. (1823–1901): the first African American woman deacon in the Methodist tradition.

Francis of Assisi, St (1182–1226): Italian Roman Catholic friar and preacher, founder of the Franciscan order.

Franck, Melchior (*c*.1579–1639): German composer of Protestant church music.

Gabrieli, Giovanni (*c*.1555–1612): Italian composer who exploited the acoustic effects of St Mark's Venice.

Gerhardt, Paul (*c*.1607–1676): German Luthean hymn writer.

Gesenius, H. F. W. (1786–1842): German lexicographer and grammarian.

Gibbons, Orlando (1583–1625): English organist and composer.

Gibson, Mel (1956–): American actor and film maker.

Goethe, Johann Wolfgang von (1749–1832): German poet, novelist, and playwright, regarded by many as his country's greatest literary figure.

Goldschmidt, Otto (1829–1907): German pianist, composer and conductor.

Gray, G. B. (1865–1922): English Hebrew and biblical scholar.

Gregory of Nazianzus (Gregory the Theologian) (330–389): one of the Cappadocian Fathers, eloquent champion of orthodoxy.

Gregory of Nyssa (333–395): one of the Cappadocian Fathers, brother of Basil. Outstanding orator, exegete and ascetical writer.

Gregory the Great (*c*.540–604): pope from 590, one of the Doctors of the Church and father of the medieval papacy.

Gressman, Hugo (1877–1927): German Old Testament scholar at Berlin.

Grünewald, Matthias (*c*.1475–1528): German painter noted for cruel realism.

Gunkel, Hermann (1862–1932): German Biblical scholar, professor, developed the study of biblical literary forms ('form criticism').

Hadrian (76–138): Roman emperor from 117 CE. Remembered as a just ruler and patron of the arts.

Handel, George Frideric (1685–1759): German composer. His religious compositions, notably *Messiah* (1741) and the 'Israelite oratorios', were first performed in England, where he settled in 1710.

Hanson, Paul D. (1939–): American biblical scholar at Harvard University.

Harbison, John (1938–): American composer.

Harnack, Adolf (1851–1930): German theologian and patristics and New Testament scholar.

Harris, Robert (1951–1993): Australian poet.

Hartog, Jan de (1914–2002): Dutch playwright and novelist. Moved to the United States in the 1960s and became a Quaker.

Hauerwas, Stanley (1940–): American theologian and ethicist at Duke University.

Havergal, Frances (1836–1879): English hymn writer, daughter of a composer.

Haydn, Franz Joseph (1732–1809): Austrian composer.

Heber, Reginald (1783–1826): bishop of Calcutta, author of some well-known hymns.

Hegel, Georg Wilhelm Friedrich (1770–1831): immensely influential German idealist philosopher.

Henry, Matthew (1662–1714): non-conformist minister, author of a popular commentary on the whole Bible.

Herbert, George (1593–1633): Welsh-born Anglican priest and poet.

Herder, Johann Gottfried (1744–1803): German rationalist philosopher and literary critic.

Herodotus (*c*.485–425): Greek historian and traveller. 'Father of history'.

Heschel, Abraham Joshua (1907–1972): Jewish American scholar and philosopher.

Hicks, Edward (1780–1849): American Quaker minister and folk painter.

Hoffmann, Daniel (1923–2013): American poet.

Holland, Henry Scott (1847–1918): English theologian and preacher, founder of Christian Social Union (1889).

Hopkins, Gerald Manley (1844–1889): English Roman Catholic poet.

Housman, A. E. (1859–1936): English classical scholar and poet.

Howe, Julia Ward (1819–1910): writer, reformer and feminist.

Hugill, Robert (1955–): English composer.

Hugo, Victor (1802–1855): French novelist.

Hus, Jan (*c*.1370–1415): Czech reformer put to death at the Council of Constance.

Hussar, Bruno (1911–1996): Dominican priest of Egyptian Jewish origins.

Ibn Ezra, Abraham (1092/3–1167): Jewish poet, grammarian, philosopher and biblical exegete.

Irenaeus (*c*.120–*c*.200): bishop of Lyons, fierce opponent of Gnosticism.

Isidore of Seville (560–636): Spanish bishop, Doctor of the Church and encyclopedist.

Jackson, Mahalia (1911–1972): African American gospel singer. 'Queen of gospel music'.

James, Henry (1843–1916): American novelist.

Jerome (*c*.340–420): biblical scholar. Educated in Rome. Spent most of his life as head of a monastery in Bethlehem. Best known for his translation of the Bible into Latin (Vulgate) and his biblical commentaries.

John of Damascus (*c*.650–750): Greek theologian, who lived in Syria and Palestine. Author of several influential works including the *Fount of Wisdom*.

Jordaens, Jakob (1593–1678): Flemish painter influenced by Rubens.

Josephus, Flavius (*c*.37–*c*.100): Jewish politician and soldier, author of the *Jewish War* and *Jewish Antiquities*.

Joubert, John (1927–): British composer, born in South Africa.

Joyce, James (1882–1941): Irish novelist, author of *Ulysses* (1922) and *Finnegans Wake* (1939).

Justin Martyr (*c*.100–*c*.165): Christian theologian and apologist. Born in Palestine. Moved to Ephesus and Rome where he was martyred along with other Christians.

Käsemann, Ernst (1906–1998): German evangelical New Testament scholar.

Kara, Joseph (1488–1575): Jewish lawyer and mystic. Head of Yeshivah at Safed from 1536.

Keble, John (1792–1866): Anglican priest, scholar and poet. Leading member of the Oxford Movement.

Keiser, Reinhard (1674–1739): German composer.

Kellogg, Daniel (1976–): American composer.

Kempis, Thomas à (*c*.1380–1471): German ascetic, writer and preacher. Author of the *Imitation of Christ*.

Kierkegaard, Søren (1813–1855): Danish philosopher. His works, especially *Philosophical Fragments* (1844) and *Sickness unto Death* (1849), influenced Barth, Heidegger and others.

Kimḥi, David (also known as Radak) (*c*.1160–*c*.1235): Jewish lexicographer, grammarian and Bible translator.

Kipling, Rudyard (1865–1936): English novelist and poet, much influenced by his years in India under British rule.

Knox, John (*c*.1513–1572): influential Scottish preacher, writer and reformer.

Koresh, David (Vernon Howell) (1959–1993): leader of the Branch Davidians, killed when the sect's compound was stormed by US federal troops in 1993.

Kuhnau, Johann (1660–1722): German scholar, writer and composer.

Landrey, Carey (1944–): American Catholic composer.

Langland, William (*c*.1330–1400): English author of *Piers Plowman*.

Langton, Stephen (d. 1228): archbishop of Canterbury. Studied in Paris. Author of scholarly works on theology and the Bible.

Lawrence, D. H. (1885–1930): An English novelist who devoted the later years of his life to the study of the Apocalypse.

Lazarus, Emma (1849–1887): American poet and essayist.

Leo the Great (d. 461): Doctor of the Church. Pope from 440 during the Council of Chalcedon (451) and the sack of Rome by the Vandals (452).

Levinas, Emmanuel (1906–1995): French philosopher of Lithuanian Jewish ancestry.

Liddell, Eric (1902–1945): Scottish athlete and missionary to China.

Liszt, Franz (1811–1886): Hungarian pianist and composer.

Longfellow, Henry Wadsworth (1807–1882): American poet best known for *Hiawatha* (1855).

Lowth, Robert (1710–1787): bishop of London and Oxford professor of poetry.

Lucan (39–65): Roman poet, author of the epic *Pharsalia*.

Lucretius (*c*.99–55 BCE): Roman poet and philosopher, author of *De Rerum Natura*.

Luther, Martin (1483–1546): German Augustinian monk and university teacher. Leader of the Reformation in Germany. Commented extensively on the Bible.

Luzzatto, Samuel David (1800–1865): Italian historian, theologian and biblical exegete.

Lyndesay, David (*c*.1486–1555): Scottish poet, politician and reformer.

McKenzie, John L. (1910–1991): American Jesuit biblical scholar.

MacMillan, Sir James (1959–): Scottish classical composer and conductor.

Maimonides, Moses (Rambam) (1135–1204): influential Jewish philosopher and physician. Author of a commentary on the Mishnah and *The Guide for the Perplexed*.

Mallea, Eduardo (1903–1982): Argentinian writer.

Mantegna, Andrea (1431–1506): Italian painter and engraver.

Marcion (d. 160): heretic with a large following throughout the Roman Empire; fiercely opposed by Irenaeus, Tertullian and others.

Marley, Bob (1945–1981): Jamaican singer, guitarist and composer.

Marlowe, Christopher (1564–1593): English dramatist.

Martin, John (1789–1854): English painter.

Maurois, André (1885–1967): French novelist and biographer.

Maxwell Davies, Sir Peter (1934–2015): English composer. From 1970 lived in Orkney.

Meir, Rabbi (second century CE): leading Jewish scholar, who features prominently in the Mishnah.

Mellers, Wilfrid (1914–2008): English music critic and composer.

Melville, Herman (1819–1891): an American novelist.

Mendelssohn, Felix (1809–1847): German composer. Produced his oratorio *Elijah* in Birmingham, England (1846).

Meredith, William (1919–2007): American poet.

Metallica (1981–): American heavy metal band.

Methodius of Olympus (d. 311): bishop in Lycia. Martyred under Diocletian.

Meynell, Alice (1847–1922): English essayist and poet.

Michelangelo di Lodovico Buonarroti (1475–1564): Italian renaissance artist, best known for his paintings of creation, the Last Judgement and the prophet Isaiah in the Sistine Chapel.

Milton, John (1609–1674): poet, nonconformist and anti-monarchist. Inspired interpreter of the Bible, his works include *Samson Agonistes* and, his greatest work, *Paradise Lost*.

Monteney, Georgette de (1540–1581): French Calvinist artist.

Monteverdi, Claudio (1567–1643): Italian composer, master of music in St Mark's Venice from 1613.

Morales, Cristobal de (*c*.1500–1553): Spanish priest and composer.

More, Thomas (1478–1535): English lawyer, politician and intellectual. Beheaded for opposing Henry VIII and canonized by Pius XI in 1935.

Morison, John (1750–1798): Scottish minister and author of metrical paraphrases.

Musgrave, Thea (1928–): Scottish composer, living in the United States since 1972.

Nahmanides (Rabbi Moses ben Nahman or Ramban) (1194–1270): wrote a famous commentary on the Torah and numerous other works on Jewish law.

Neale, John Mason (1818–1866): Anglican author and hymn writer.

Newton, Isaac (1642–1727): English mathematician who looked in biblical prophecy for evidence of providential arrangement in history.

Newton, John (1725–1807): English evangelical clergyman and hymn writer. Captain of a slave-trading ship, converted to Christianity and, with **William Cowper**, published the **Olney Hymns**.

Nicholas of Cusa (1401–1464): German cardinal and philosopher.

Nicholas of Lyra (*c*.1270–1349): Franciscan scholar. Studied the Bible's literal meaning with a vast knowledge of patristic, rabbinic and medieval texts.

Noel, Caroline Maria (1817–1877): English hymn writer.

O'Connor, Sinead (1966–): Irish singer/songwriter, and campaigner for social justice.

Oecolampadius, John (1482–1531): German reformer, author of large commentary on Isaiah.

Origen (*c*.185–235): leading theologian and exegete, moved from Alexandria to Caesarea, where he was a victim of Decian persecution.

Otto, Rudolph (1869–1937): Protestant theologian, author of *The Idea of the Holy* (1923).

Owen, Wilfred (1893–1918): English war poet killed in France in 1918.

Pachomius (*c*.290–346): Egyptian founder of communal monasticism and author of the earliest extant rules for the monastic life.

Paisley, Rev. Ian (1926–2004): Northern Ireland Protestant clergyman and politician.

Palestrina, Giovanni Pierluigi da (*c*.1525–1594): Italian composer of religious music. From 1571 choirmaster of St Peter's Rome.

Pâquet, Monseigneur Louis-Adolphe (1859–1942): influential French Canadian theologian.

Parsons, Squire (1948–): American gospel singer and songwriter.

Pascal, Blaise (1623–1662): French theologian and mathematician.

Patten, Willard (1853–1924): American musician and composer.

Pelagius (*c*.360–418): British theologian and exegete. Condemned as a heretic chiefly because in his travels to Rome and Palestine he rejected the doctrine of original sin.

Penderecki, Krzysztof (1933–): Polish composer whose *Dies irae* (1967) is a memorial to the victims at Auschwitz.

Philo of Alexandria (*c*.20–*c*.50): Greek-speaking Jewish philosopher of Hellenistic Judaism.

Pliny the Elder (23–79): Roman writer and natural historian.

Pope, Alexander (1688–1744): English poet and satirist.

Praetorius, Michael (1571–1621): German musician, composer and writer.

Procopius of Caesarea (mid-sixth century): Byzantine historian.

Prudentius, Aurelius Clemens (348–*c*.410): Latin Christian poet and hymn writer.

Pseudo-Philo, name given to the author of a first-century history from Adam to Saul's death.

Purcell, Henry (1659–1695): English composer of religious music.

Quarles, Francis (1592–1644): English religious poet, popular among Puritans but a Royalist politically.

Rabanus Maurus (776–856): archbishop of Mainz. Learned theologian and poet.

Rabin, Yitzhak (1922–1995): Israeli politician, twice prime minister. Assassinated in 1995.

Raffaellino del Garbo (*c*.1470 –1527): Early Renaissance Italian painter.

Raphael, Sanzio (1483–1520): Italian painter of the High Renaissance.

Rashi, Rabbi Shlomo ben Isaac (1040– 1105): French Jewish exegete who combined literal reading and spiritual interpretation.

Richard of St Victor (1123–1173): successor to Hugh as the prior of the Abbey of St Victor, Paris.

Ringelblum, Emmanuel (1900–1944): Polish Jewish historian and social activist.

Romanos the Melodist (mid-sixth century CE): Greek Christian poet and composer of kontakia (metrical sermons).

Rosenberg, David (1943–): American poet and biblical translator.

Rossetti, Christina Georgina (1830–94): English Pre-Raphaelite poet, sister of **Dante Gabriel Rossetti**.

Rossetti, Dante Gabriel (1828–1882): English Pre-Raphaelite poet and painter.

Rota, Andrea (*c*.1553–1597): Italian renaissance composer.

Rubens, Peter Paul (1577–1640): Flemish Baroque painter, influenced by Italian art.

Rufinus (*c*.345–410): Italian monk, historian and translator. Studied in Alexandria.

Saadiya Gaon (882–942): prominent Talmudist, biblical exegete and philosopher.

Saint-Saëns, Camille (1835–1921): French organist and composer.

Scott, Sir Walter (1771–1832): Scottish novelist and poet.

Shakespeare, William (1564–1616): English poet and dramatist.

Scholem, Gershom (1897–1982): German scholar, foremost expert on Jewish mysticism.

Schubert, Franz (1797–1828): Austrian composer, perhaps best known for his song cycles.

Schutte, Dan (1947–): American songwriter and composer of Catholic liturgical music.

Schütz, Heinrich (1585–1672): German composer. Influenced by Gabrieli in Venice.

Schwarz-Bart, André (1928–2006): French novelist of Polish Jewish origins.

Selle, Thomas (1599–1663): German baroque composer.

Shelley, Percy Bysshe (1792–1822): one of the major English Romantic poets.

Silkin, Jon (1930–1997): English poet from a Jewish immigrant family.

Simone, Nina (1933–2003): American singer/songwriter and civil rights activist.

Sitwell, Osbert (1892–1969): English writer.

Sluter, Claus (*c.*1340–1405): Early Dutch sculptor.

Smart, Christopher (1722–1771): English poet, author of sacred poems, epigrams and translations from the Bible. Died insane.

Smith, Adam (1723–1790): Scottish economist and philosopher. Author of *Wealth of Nations*.

Smith, George Adam (1856–1942): Scottish Free Church professor, widely travelled.

Smith, Joseph (1805–1844): Mormon. Founder of the Church of Jesus Christ of Latter-day Saints.

Spencer-Stanhope, John Roddam (1829–1908): Pre-Raphaelite artist.

Spenser, Edmund (1552–1599): English Protestant poet, author of *The Faerie Queene*.

Spohr, Louis (1784–1859): Early Romantic German violinist, composer and conductor.

Spurgeon, Charles (1834–1892): English Baptist preacher and author.

Stainer, John (1840–1901): English organist and composer.

Stanford, Charles Villiers (1852–1924): Irish composer who influenced English church music.

Stanton, Elizabeth Cady (1815–1902): American social activist and driving force in the US women's rights movement.

Starer, Robert (1924–2001): Austrian-born American composer and pianist.

Steinbeck, John (1902–1968): American novelist, awarded Nobel Prize for Literature 1962.

Stevenson, Robert Louis (1850–94): Scottish novelist, essayist and poet.

Stites, Edgar Page (1836–1921): American Methodist hymn writer.

Sweelinck, Jan Pieterszoon (1562–1621): Dutch composer, organist and harpsichordist.

Symmachus (late second century CE): Greek translator of the Hebrew Bible, probably Jewish.

Tallis, Thomas (*c.*1505–1585): English composer. Known as 'father of English cathedral music'.

Tate, Nahum (1652–1715): Irish Protestant poet, author and hymn writer.

Tavener, John (1944–2013): English composer, best known for his use of Russian and Greek Orthodox tradition.

Tennyson, Alfred, Lord (1809–1892): English poet. Poet Laureate from 1850.

Tertullian (*c.*160–*c.*220): early Christian theologian, writing in Latin.

Theodore of Mopsuestia (*c.*350–428/9): Antiochene theologian and biblical interpreter.

Theodoret of Cyr (*c.*393–*c.*458): Syrian bishop and biblical interpreter in the Antiochene tradition.

Theodotion (second century CE): Jewish scholar and author of a Greek translation of the Hebrew Bible which was popular among Christians.

Thompson, Randall (1899–1984): American composer.

Thring, Geoffrey (1823–1903): English clergyman and hymn writer.

Tiepolo, Giovanni Battista (1696–1770): major Italian rococo artist.

Toplady, Augustus Montague (1740–1778): English author and hymn writer, influenced by John Wesley.

Torrey, C. C. (1863–1956): controversial American biblical scholar.

Trible, Phyllis (1932–): feminist biblical scholar, seminary professor.

Tristram, Ernest (1882–1952): British art historian, artist and conservator.

Tutu, Desmond (1931–): the first black Anglican archbishop of Cape Town; he won the Nobel Peace Prize in 1984 for his pacifist fight against apartheid.

Twain, Mark (1835–1910): American writer, best known for *Tom Sawyer* and *Huckelberry Finn*.

Uri, Aviva (1922–1989): Israeli artist.

Van Gogh, Vincent (1853–1890): Dutch post-Impressionist painter.

Vaughan Williams, Ralph (1872–1958): English composer.

Verdi, Giuseppe (1813–1901): Italian composer.

Virgil (Publius Virgilius Maro) (70–19 BCE): Roman poet much respected by Christian writers.

Vitringa, Campegius (*c*.1659–1722): Dutch scholar, author of a two-volume commentary on Isaiah.

Walter of Chatillon (twelfth century): French theologian and poet.

Walton, William (1902–1983): English composer. Composed music for official occasions. Knighted in 1951.

Ward Howe, Julia (1819–1910): poet, reformer and author of 'The Battle Hymn of the Republic'.

Watts, Isaac (1674–1748): English hymn writer. After studying at a Dissenting Academy, he became pastor of an Independent parish in London.

Wesley, Charles (1707–1788): English Methodist hymn writer.

Wesley, John (1707–1788): Anglican priest and evangelist. Founder of Methodism.

Wesley, Samuel Sebastian (1810–1876): English organist and composer.

West, Benjamin (1738–1820): American-born British painter.

Westall, Richard (1765–1836): English painter and illustrator.

Whittier, John Greenleaf (1807–1892): American Quaker poet.

Wiesel, Elie (1928–2016): novelist and activist; Holocaust survivor. Awarded the Nobel Peace Prize in 1986.

William of Bourges (*c*.1155–1209): French Cistercian ascetic.

Williams, Roger (*c*.1604–1683): English Reformed theologian. Founder of first Baptist Church in the United States.

Wither, George (1588–1667): English poet and pamphleteer.

Wright, N. T. (1948–): British New Testament scholar. Bishop of Durham 2003–2010.

Wolcott, John Truman (1869–1925): American composer.

Wycliffe, John (*c*.1330–1384): English philosopher and theologian, forerunner of the Reformation. Inspired the first English translation of the Vulgate.

Xenophon (*c*.430–*c*.350 BCE): Greek military commander and historian.

Yannai (? sixth century CE): Jewish poet living in Palestine.

Zola, Emil (1840–1902): French novelist.

Zurbarán, Francisco (1598–1662): Spanish religious painter.

Abbreviations

Note: References to authors without details of date or page are references to commentaries listed separately in a subsection of the bibliography.

1QH	The Thanksgiving Hymns from Qumrn *DSSE* 249-305
1QIsaᵃ	The Isaiah Scroll A from Qumran
1QM	The War Scroll from Qumran *DSSE* 163–185
1QS	The Community Rule from Qumran *DSSE* 97–117
AB	Anchor Bible
ADPB	S. Singer, ed., *Authorised Daily Prayer Book of the United Hebrew Congregations of the British Commonwealth of Nations* (4th edn, J. Sacks). London, 2007

Isaiah Through the Centuries, First Edition. John F. A. Sawyer.
© 2018 John Wiley & Sons Ltd. Published 2020 by John Wiley & Sons Ltd.

AEH	*Anglican and Episcopal History* (1987–)
AM	*Ancient and Modern: Hymns and Songs for Refreshing Worship*, 9th edn, 2013
ASTI	*Annual of the Swedish Theological Institute*. Jerusalem
ASV	*American Standard Version* (revised version, American Edition), 1901
ATWAT	'As Those Who Are Taught': The Interpretation of Isaiah from the LXX to the SBL (Symposium Series), ed. C. M. McGinnis and P. K. Tull. Atlanta: Society of Biblical Literature, 2006
AV	King James' Authorized Version of the Bible (1611)
b	*The Babylonian Talmud*, ed. I. Epstein, 35 vols. London: Soncino, 1935–1948
BCE	Before the Common Era
BCO	The Book of Common Order. Edinburgh: St Andrew Press, 1979
BCP	Book of Common Prayer (1662). American Theological Library Association, 1913
BHS	*Biblia Hebraica Stuttgartiensis* (critical edn of the Masoretic text of the Hebrew Bible). Stuttgart: Deutsche Bibelgesellschaft, 1983
BiM	*Bible in Music: A Dictionary of Songs, Works and More*, S. Dowling Long and J. F. A. Sawyer. Lanham, MA: Rowman and Littlefield, 2015
BP	*Biblia Pauperum: A Facsimile and Edition*, ed. A. Henry. London: Scolar Press, 1987 (see Bibliography: Websites)
BWV	*Bach-Werke Verzeichnis*, catalogue of J. S. Bach's works by Wolfgang Schnieder
CantR	Song of Songs in *MidrRab*, Vol. 9
CD	*Cairo Damascus Document*, DSSE 127–45
CE	Common Era
CELR	*Concise Encyclopedia of Language and Religion*, ed. J. F. A. Sawyer and J. M. Y. Simpson. Amsterdam/New York/Oxford: Elsevier, 2001
CGL	*The Coptic Gnostic Library: A Complete Edition of the Nag Hammadi Codices*, ed. J. M. Robinson. Institute for Antiquity and Christianity. Leiden: Brill, 2000
CH2	*The Church Hymnary*. Rev. edn (with metrical psalms and paraphrases). London/Glasgow: Oxford University Press, 1929
CH4	*The Church Hymnary*, 4th edn. Canterbury Press, 2005
ChDogm	K. Barth, *The Church Dogmatics*, ed. G. W. Bromiley and T. F. Torrance. Edinburgh: T&T Clark, 1936–1977
CML	*Canaanite Myths and Legends*, ed. J. C. L. Gibson. Edinburgh: T&T Clark, 1978
DBLF	C. Jullien, *Dictionnaire de la Bible dans la littérature française: Figures, thèmes, symboles, auteurs*, 2003
DBTEL	*Dictionary of Biblical Tradition in English Literature*, ed. D. L. Jeffrey, Grand Rapids, MI, 1992
DCH	*Dictionary of Classical Hebrew*, ed. D. J. A. Clines, 9 vols. Sheffield: Sheffield Academic Press, 1993–2016
DeutR	Deuteronomy in *MidrRab*, Vol. 7
DSSE	*The Complete Dead Sea Scrolls in English*, ed. G. Vermes (50th anniversary edn). London: Penguin, 2011

EBR	*Encyclopedia of the Bible and its Reception*, ed. D. C. Allison, Jr, C. Helmer, C.-L. Seow, H. Spieckermann, B. D. Walfish and E. Ziolkowski, 30 vols. Berlin: de Gruyter 2012–
EH	*English Hymnal*, eds. W. J. Birkbeck, P. Dearmer, R. Vaughan Williams and others. London 1906
EJ	*Encyclopedia Judaica*, 16 vols, 2nd edn. Jerusalem, 2007
EM	*Encyclopedia of Mormonism*, ed. D. H. Ludlow. 4 vols. New York: Macmillan, 1992
EpBarn	Epistle of Barnabas in *Apostolic Farthers*, 1989
EstherR	Esther in *MidrRab*, Vol. 9
ExodR	Exodus in *MidrRab*, Vol. 3
GenR	Genesis in *MidrRab*, Vols 1 and 2
Glossa	*Glossa Ordinaria. PL*, Vols. 113–114
GtG	*Glory to God: The Presbyterian Hymnal.* Louisville, KY: Westminster John Knox Press, 2013
Gk	Greek
HCL	*Hymns of the Christian Life: A Book of Worship in Song Emphasizing Evangelism, Missions, and the Deeper Life.* Harrisburg, PA: Christian Publications, 1962
Heb.	Hebrew
HON	*Hymns Old and New, with Supplement*, ed. K. Mayhew. Avon: Bath Press 1989
JBL	*Journal of Biblical Literature*
JJS	Journal of Jewish Studies
JPS	Jewish Publication Society *Tanakh Translation.* New York, 1999
JSB	*The Jewish Study Bible*, ed. A. Berlin, A. Brettler and M. Z. Brettler Oxford: Oxford University Press, 2004
JSNT	*Journal for the Study of the New Testament*
JSOT	*Journal for the Study of the Old Testament*
L.	Latin
LamR	Lamentations in *MidrRab*, Vol. 7
LevR	Leviticus in *MidrRab*, Vol. 4
LW	*Luther's Works*, ed. J. Pelikan *et al.*, 55 vols. St Louis and Philadelphia, 1955–
LXX	*Septuaginta*, ed. A. Rahlfs and R. Hanhart. Stuttgart: Deutsche Bibelgesellschaft, 2006
m	*The Mishnah*, trans. H. Danby. Oxford: Oxford University, 1933
Maḥzor	*The New Maḥzor for Rosh Hashanah and Yom Kippur*, ed. S. Greenberg and J. D. Levine. Bridgeport, CT: Media Judaica, 1978
Mart.Isa	*Martyrdom and Ascension of Isaiah*, ed. M. A. Knibb in *OTP* 2, 143–76
Mekh	*Mekhilta de-Rabbi Ishmael*, ed. J. Z. Lauterbach. Philadelphia: Jewish Publication Society, 1933
mg	margin, footnote
MHB	*Methodist Hymn Book.* London, 1904
MidrPs	*The Midrash on Psalms*, 2 vols, trans. W. G. Braude. New Haven, CT: Yale University Press, 1959
MidrRab	*Midrash Rabbah*, 10 vols, ed. H. Freedman and M. Simon. London: Soncino Press, 1939

MR	*Missale Romanum ex decreto SS.Concili Tridentini.* Ratisbon, 1924
MT	Masoretic Text. See *BHS*
NCHB	*The New Cambridge History of the Bible*, 4 vols. New York: Cambridge University Press, 2012–2015
NEB	*New English Bible*. Oxford/Cambridge, 1970
NJB	*New Jerusalem Bible*. London, 1985
NRSV	*New Revised Standard Version*. Oxford, 1991
NumR	Numbers in *MidrRab*, vols 5 and 6
ORM	*Lectionary: Order of Readings for Use at Mass (Reader's Edition)*. London: Geoffrey Chapman, 1970
OSB	*The Orthodox Study Bible*, ed. J. N. Sparks. Nashville, TN: Thomas Nelson, 2008
OTP	*Old Testament Pseudepigrapha*, 2 vols, ed. J. H. Charlesworth. New York/London: Doubleday, 1985
Pesh	*The Old Testament in Syriac: Peshitta Version*. Pt. III, fasc.1. Isaiah, ed. S. P. Brock. Leiden: E. J.Brill, 1987
PesK	*Pesikta de Rav Kahana: An Analytical Translation*, ed. J. Neusner. Atlanta, GA: Scholars Press, 1987
PesR	*Pesikta Rabbati: Discourses for Feasts, Fasts, and Special Sabbaths*, trans. W. G. Braude. New Haven: Yale University Press, 1968
PG	J.-P. Migne, *Patrologiae cursus completus: Series Graeca*, 166 vols. Paris: Migne, 1857–1886
PL	J.-P. Migne, *Patrologiae cursus completus: Series Latina*, 221 vols. Paris: Migne, 1844–1864
RA	*Rabbinic Anthology*, ed. C. Montefiore and H. Loewe. New York: Meridian Books, 1963
RCL	*Revised Common Lectionary in NRSV*. London: Mowbray, 1997
RSV	*Revised Standard Version*, Ecumenical Edition. London, 1973
SBSA	*The Songbook of the Salvation Army*. London: Salvation Army, 1986
SC	*Sources Chrétiennes*. Paris: Editions du Cerf 1948–
Sib.Or	*Sibylline Oracles*, ed. J. J. Collins in OTP 1, 472
SNOBC	*The Shorter New Oxford Book of Carols*, ed. H. Keyte and A. Parrott. Oxford/New York: Oxford University Press, 1993
STSM	*Sacred Texts and Sacred Meanings*, J. F. A. Sawyer. Sheffield: Phoenix Press, 2011
SVT	Supplements to *Vetus Testamentum*
Tanḥ	*Midrash Tanḥuma*, ed. J. T. Townsend and S. Buber. Hoboken, NJ: Ktav Publishing House, 1989
Tg	Targum Jonathan. *The Bible in Aramaic*. Vol. 3, *The Latter Prophets According to Targum Jonathan*, ed. A. Sperber. Leiden: Brill, 1962
TLev	*Testament of Levi*, ed. H. C. Kee in OTP 1, 788–795
Tos	*The Tosefta: Translated from the Hebrew*, ed. J. Neusner. New York: KTAV, 1977–1986
TSol	*Testament of Solomon*, ed. D. C. Duling in OTP 1, 935–987
Vg	The Vulgate, ed. R. Weber. Stuttgart: Deutsche Bibelgesellschaft, 1994
VT	*Vetus Testamentum*
ZAW	*Zeitschrift für die Alttestamentliche Wissenchaft*

Bibliography

Note: References to the verse-by-verse commentaries listed separately below, are by author's name only, other bibliographical details being unnecessary.

Many of the patristic texts cited or referred to are available in translation in the Isaiah volumes of the *Ancient Christian Commentary on Scripture* series (McKinion 2004; M. W. Elliott 2007) or the *Church's Bible* (Wilken 2007). Other texts can be found in *Ancient Christian Writers* (1946–), *Apostolic Fathers* (1965), *Fathers of the Church* (1948–) and other series.

A number of websites which readers may find helpful, are listed at the end of the bibliography.

Isaiah Through the Centuries, First Edition. John F. A. Sawyer.
© 2018 John Wiley & Sons Ltd. Published 2020 by John Wiley & Sons Ltd.

Commentaries

Achtemeier, E. 1982. *The Community and Message of Isaiah 56–66: A Theological Commentary* (Minneapolis, MN: Augsburg Publishing House).

Ackerman, S. 1992. 'Isaiah', in *Women's Bible Commentary* (ed. C. A. Newsom and S. H. Ringe; London: SPCK).

Altschuler, D. 1959. *Metzudat David*, in *Miqra'ot gedolot* (Tel Aviv: Schocken).

Aquinas, Thomas. 1974. *Expositio super Isaiam ad litteram. Opera Omnia*, vols 18, 19. (Rome: Ed. di San Tommaso).

Basil the Great. 2001. *Commentary on Isaiah* (trans. N. A. Lipatov; Cambridge: Cicero).

Beuken, W. 2003–2007. *Jesaja 1–27* (2 vols; Freiburg am Breisgau: Herder).

Beuken, W. 2000. *Isaiah 28–39* (Leuven: Peeters).

Blenkinsopp, J. 2000–2003. *Isaiah* (3 vols; New Haven, CT/London: Yale University Press).

Bonnard, P.-E. 1972. *Le Second Isaïe: Son disciple et leurs éditeurs. Isaïe 40–66* (Paris: J. Gabalda).

Brueggemann, W. 1998. *Isaiah 1–39* (Louisville, KY).

Brueggemann, W. 1998. *Isaiah 40–66* (Louisville, KY).

Calvin, J. 1979. *Commentary on the Book of the Prophet Isaiah* (Grand Rapids, MI: Baker).

Cheyne, T. K. 1895. *Introduction to the Book of Isaiah* (London: Adam and Charles Black).

Childs, B. S. 2001. *Isaiah: A Commentary (OTL)* (Louisville KY: Westminster John Knox).

Chrysostom, John. 1983. *Commentary on Isaiah*, Chs 1:1–8:10. (ed. Jean Dumortier; SC 304 Paris: Editions du Cerf).

Clements, R. E. 1980. *Isaiah 1–39* (Grand Rapids, MI/London: Wm. B. Eerdmans).

Cyril of Alexandria. 2008–. *Commentary on Isaiah: Vol.1. Chapters 1–14. Vol.2. Chapters 15–39.* Vol. 3, *Chapters 40–50* (trans. R. C. Hill; Brookline, MA: Holy Cross Orthodox Press).

Delitzsch, F. 1889. *Commentar über das Buch Jesaia* (Leipzig: Dörffling & Franke; 4th edn) [Eng. trans. 1980.]

Dillmann, A. 1890. *Der Prophet Jesaja* (Leipzig: S. Hirzel).

Duhm, B. 1892. *Das Buch Jesaia, übersetzt und erklärt* (Göttingen:Vandenhoeck and Ruprecht). [3rd edn 1914].

Elliott, M. W., ed. 2007. *Ancient Christian Commentary on Scripture: Old Testament.* Vol. 11, *Isaiah 40–66* (Downers Grove, IL: InterVarsity Fellowship).

Ephrem the Syrian. 1882–1902. *Sancti Ephraem Syri hymni et sermones*, vol. 2 cols. 3–214 (commentary on Isa 43–66; ed. T. J. Lamy; Mechelen, Belgium).

Eusebius of Caesarea. 2013. *Commentary on Isaiah* (trans. J. J. Armstrong; Downers Grove, IL: Intervarsity Press).

Gesenius, H. F. W. 1821. *Philologisch-Kritiker und historiker Kommentar über den Jesaia* (3 vols; Leipzig: F. C. W.Vogel).

Goldingay, J. and D. F. Payne. 2006. *A Critical and Exegetical Commentary on Isaiah 40–55* (London; New York: T&T Clark).

Gray, G. B. 1912 *A Critical and Exegetical Commentary on the Book of Isaiah I–XXVII* (Edinburgh: T&T Clark).

Hanson, P. D. 1995. *Isaiah 40–66* (Louisville, KY: John Knox Press).

Henry, M. 2003. *Commentary on the Whole Bible in One Volume: Genesis to Revelation* (ed. L. F. Church; London: Thomas Nelson).

Ibn Ezra. 1877. *The Commentary of Ibn Ezra on Isaiah* (ed. M. Friedländer; London).

Jerome. 2015. *Commentary on Isaiah: Origen homilies 1–9 on Isaiah* (trans. and with an introduction by T. P. Scheck; Mahwah: Paulist Press).

Jones, D. R. 1962. 'Isaiah II and III', in *Peake's Commentary on the Bible* (ed. M. Black and H. H. Rowley; London: Nelson), 516–536.

Kaiser, O. 1972, 1974. *Isaiah 1–39: A Commentary (OTL)* (2 vols; London: SCM Press/ Phildelphia: Westminster).

Kimḥi, Rabbi David (Radak), 1926. *The Commentary of David Kimḥi on Isaiah* (ed. Louise Finkelstein; New York: Columbia University Press).

Lowth, R. 1857. *Isaiah: A New Translation with a Preliminary Dissertation and Notes, Critical, Philological and Explanatory* (London; 15th edn).

Luther, M. 1969. *Luther's Works*. Vol. 16, *Lectures on Isaiah Chapters 1–39* (ed. J. Pelikan; St Louis: Concordia Publishing House).

Luther, M. 1969. *Luther's Works*. Vol. 17, *Lectures on Isaiah Chapters 40–66*, ed. H. C. Oswald; St Louis: Concordia Publishing House).

Luzzatto, S. D. 1970. *Perush Shadal 'al sefer Yesha'yah* (S. D. Luzzatto's commentary to the book of Isaiah; Tel Aviv: Devir).

Manly, J., ed. 1995. *Isaiah through the Ages* (Menlo Park, CA: Monastery Books).

Marti, K. 1900. *Das Buch Jesaja* (Tübingen: Mohr).

Mauchline, J. 1962. *Isaiah 1–39 (TBC*; New York: Macmillan).

McKenzie, J. L. 1968. *Second Isaiah: Introduction, Translation and Notes* (Anchor Bible; New York: Doubleday).

McKinion, S. S., ed. 2004. *Ancient Christian Commentary on Scripture. Old Testament.* Vol. 10, *Isaiah 1–39* (Downers Grove, IL: InterVarsity Fellowship).

Miscall, P. D. 1993. *Isaiah: Readings. A New Biblical Commentary* (Sheffield: Sheffield Academic Press).

Muilenberg, J. 1951–1957. 'Isaiah Chapters 40–66'in *The Interpreter's Bible*, vol. 5 (New York: Abingdon Press) 381–773.

Nicholas of Lyra. 1992. *Biblia Sacra cum Glossa Ordinaria* (4 vols; ed. K. Froehlich and M. J. Gibson; Turnhout: Brépols).

North, C. R. 1964. *The Second Isaiah: Introduction, Translation and Commentary to Chapters XL–LV* (Oxford: Oxford University Press).

Oecolampadius, J. 1558. *In Jesaiam prophetam, hypomnematon, hoc est, commentariorum, Ioannis Oecolampadij libri sex.* (Geneva).

Oswalt, J. N. 1986–1998. *The Book of Isaiah* (2 vols; Grand Rapids MI/Cambridge: Eerdmans).

Paul, S. 2012. *Isaiah 40–66* (Grand Rapids MI/Cambridge: Eerdmans).

Procopius of Gaza. *Catena in Isaiam. PG* 87b, cols. 1817–2715.

Rashi (Rabbi Shlomo ben Isaac). n.d. *The Complete Tanach with Rashi's Commentary* (trans. A. J. Rosenberg).

Roberts, J. J. 2015. *First Isaiah: A Commentary* (Hermeneia; Minneapolis, MN: Fortress Press).

Sawyer, J. F. A. 1984, 1986. *Isaiah* (2 vols; Edinburgh: St Andrew Press/Louisville KY: Westminster John Knox Press).

Seitz, C. R. 1994–2004. 'The Book of Isaiah 40–66', in *The New Interpreter's Bible*, vol. 6 (Nashville: Abingdon Press) 309–552.

Simon, U. 1953. *A Theology of Salvation: A Commentary on Isaiah XL–LV* (London: SPCK).

Skinner, J. 1896. *The Book of the Prophet Isaiah: Chapters I–XXXIX* (Cambridge: Cambridge University Press).

Slotki, I. W. 1949. *Isaiah* (London: Soncino).

Smith, G. A. 1888–1890. *The Book of Isaiah* (2 vols; London: Hodder and Stoughton).

Sommer, B., 'Isaiah', in *JSB*; 780–916.

Stuhlmueller, C. 1989. 'Deutero-Isaiah and Trito-Isaiah', in *The New Jerome Biblical Commentary* (ed. R. E. Brown, J. A. Fitzmyer and R. E. Murphy; London: Chapman).

Sweeney, M. 1996. *Isaiah 1–39, with an Introduction to Prophetic Literature* (Forms of Old Testament Literature series; Grand Rapids, MI: Eerdmans).

Theodoret of Cyr. 1981–1984. *Commentaire sur Isaïe* (ed. J.-P. Guinot; SC 276, 295, 315; Paris: Editions du Cerf).

Torrey, C. C. 1928. *The Second Isaiah: A New Interpretation* (Edinburgh: T&T Clark).

Vermeylen, J. 1977–1978. *Du prophète Isaïe à l'apocalyptique. Isaïe I–XXXV*, 2 vols (Paris: J. Gabalda).

Vitringa, Campegius. 1714–1720. *Commentarius in librum prophetiarum Jesajae*, 2 vols (Leeuwarden: F. Holma).

Watts, J. D. W. 1985. *Isaiah 1–33* (WBC; Waco, TX: Word Books).

Watts, J. D. W. 1987. *Isaiah 34–66* (WBC Waco, TX: Word Books).

Wesley, John. 1987. *Wesley's Notes on the Bible* (ed. G. Roger Schoenhals; Grand Rapids, MI: Francis Asbury Press).

Westermann, C. 1969. *Isaiah 40–66: A Commentary* (OTL; London: SCM Press).

Whybray, R. N. 1983. *The Second Isaiah* (Sheffield: JSOT Press).

Wildberger, H. 1972–1982. *Jesaja 1–39 (BKAT)* (3 vols; Neukirchen-Vluyn: Neukirchener Verglag). [Eng. trans. 1991– 2002. Minneapolis: Fortress press.]

Wilken, R. L., ed. 2007. *The Church's Bible: Isaiah Interpreted by Early Christian and Medieval Commentators* (Grand Rapids MI/Cambridge: Wm. B. Eerdmans).

General Bibliography

Ackroyd, P. 1995. *Blake* (London: Sinclair-Stevenson).

Adang, C. 1996. *Muslim Writers on Judaism and the Hebrew Bible: From Ibn Rabban to Ibn Hazm* (Leiden: E. J. Brill).

Alexander, P., ed. 1983. '3 (Hebrew Apocalypse of) Enoch', in *The Old Testament Pseudepigrapha*, vol. 1 (ed. J. H. Charlesworth; New York: Doubleday) 223–315.

Ancient Christian Writers: The Works of the Fathers in Translation (Mahwah, NJ: Paulist Press 1946–).

Anti-Nicene Fathers. 1885–1896 (eds. A. Roberts and J. Donaldson; 10 vols; Buffalo NY).

Apostolic Fathers. Vol. 2, *First and Second Clement.* 1965 (ed. R. M. Grant; New York/London: Thomas Nelson).

Apostolic Fathers. Vol. 3, *Barnabas and the Didache.* 1965 (trans. R. A. Kraft; New York/London: Thomas Nelson).

Atwan, R. and Wieder, L. 1993. *Chapters into Verse: A Selection of Poetry in English Inspired by the Bible.* Vol.1, *Genesis to Malachi* (Oxford: Oxford University Press).

Augustine. 1990–. *Works of St. Augustine: A Translation for the 21st Century* (Brooklyn NY: New City Press).

Baer, D. A. 2006. 'It's All About Us!' Nationalistic Exegesis in the Greek Isaiah (Chapters 1–12)', in *ATWAT*; 29–47.

Barth, H. 1977. *Die Jesaja-Worte in der Josiazeit (WMANT 48)* (Neukirchen-Vluyn: Neukirchener Verlag).

Baticle, J., ed. 1987. *Zurbarán* (New York: The Metropolitan Museum of Art).

Beadle, R. and P. M. King, eds. 1999. *York Mystery Plays: A Selection in Modern Spelling* (Oxford: Oxford University Press).

Beal, T. K. and T. Linafelt, eds. 2006. *Mel Gibson's Bible: Religion, Popular Culture, and The Passion of the Christ* (Chicago/London: University of Chicago Press).

Benisovitch, M. N. 1953. 'Un dessin de Jacob Jordaens à la E. B.Crocker Gallery (Sacramento)', *Oudholland* 68: 56–57.

Berges, U. F. 2012. *Isaiah: The Prophet and his Book* (Sheffield: Phoenix Press).

Berkovits, E. 1973. *Faith after the Holocaust* (Ktav: New York).

Bernstein, A. E. 1993. *The Formation of Hell: Death and Retribution in the Ancient and Early Christian Worlds* (London: UCL Press).

Beuken, W. A. M. 1991. 'Isaiah Chapter 65–66: Trito-Isaiah and the Closure of the Book of Isaiah', *Congress Volume: Leuven 1989* (ed. J. A. Emerton; Leiden: E. J. Brill) 204–221.

Bevan, E. R. and C. Singer, eds. 1927. *The Legacy of Israel* (Oxford: Clarendon Press).

Bible Moralisée 1911–1927 (ed. A. de Laborde, Paris) (see Glossary and under Websites).

Biblia Pauperum: A Facsimile and Edition. 1987 (ed. A. Henry. London: Scolar Press) (see Glossary and under Websites).

Birnbaum, P., ed. 1976. *The Birnbaum Haggadah* (New York).

Biruni, Muḥammad ibn Aḥmad. 1879. *The Chronology of Ancient Nations: An English Version of the Arabic Text of the Athâr-ul-bâkiya of Albîrûnî, or 'Vestiges of the Past* (London: W. H. Allen for Oriental Translation Fund).

Blair, K. 2007. 'Keble and *The Christian Year*', in Hass, Jasper and Jay 2007; 607–623.

Blake, W. 1966. *Complete Writings* (ed. G. Keynes; Oxford: Oxford University Press).

Blenkinsopp, J. 2006. *Opening the Sealed Book: Interpretations of the Book of Isaiah in Late Antiquity* (Grand Rapids MI/Cambridge UK: Wm. B. Eerdmans).

Boitani, P. 1994. *The Shadow of Ulysses: Figures of a Myth* (Oxford: Clarendon Press).

Boitani, P. 2011. 'Dante and the Bible: A Sketch', in Lieb, Mason and Roberts 2011; 282–293.

Bonaventure. 2010. *The Life of St Francis: From the Legenda Sancti Francisci* (ed. Cardinal Manning; repr. Charlotte, NC: Tan Books). [Original edition 1867.]

Borodowski, A. F. 2003. *Isaac Abravanel on Miracles, Creation, Prophecy, and Evil: The Tension between Medieval Jewish Philosophy and Biblical Commentary* (New York: Peter Lang).

Borts, B. 1994. 'Lilith', in *Hear Our Voice: Women Rabbis Tell Their Stories* (ed. S. Sheridan; London: SCM Press) 98–109.

Bowe, N. G. 2010. 'Interpreting the Bible through Painted Glass: The Harry Clark Studios and Wilhelmina Geddes (1887–1955)', in O'Kane and Morgan-Guy 2010; 206–215.

Boyarin, D. 2000. 'Israel Reading in 'Reading Israel', in Grenholm and Patte 2000; 246–250.

Boyer, P. 1992. *When Time Shall be No More* (Cambridge, MA: Harvard University Press).

Bright, J. 1981. *A History of Israel* (London: SCM Press).

Brooke, G. J. 2006. 'On Isaiah at Qumran', in *ATWAT*; 69–85.

Broyles, C. C. and C. A. Evans, eds. 1997. *Writing and Reading the Scroll of Isaiah* (*SVT* 70/2; 2 vols; Leiden: E. J. Brill).

Buber, M. 1994. *Scripture and Translation* (Bloomington, IN: Indiana University Press).

Bultmann, R. 1971. *The Gospel of John: A Commentary* (English trans. G. R. Beasley-Murray; Oxford: Blackwell).

Burckhardt, J. 1950. *Recollections of Rubens* (London: Phaedon Press).

Butt, J. 2011. 'George Friedric Handel and the Messiah', in Lieb, Mason and Roberts 2011; 294–306.

Callaway, M. 1986 *Sing, O Barren One: A Study in Comparative Midrash* (Atlanta, GA: Scholars Press).

Carmi, T., ed. 1991. *The Penguin Book of Hebrew Verse* (London: Allen Lane).

Caviness, M. H. 1977. *The Early Stained Glass of Canterbury Cathedral, Circa 1175–1220* (Princeton: Princeton University Press).

Cassel, J. D. 2006. 'Patristic Interpretation of Isaiah', *ATWAT* 145–170.

Chancey, M. A., C. L. Meyers and E. M. Meyers. 2014. *The Bible in the Public Square: Its Enduring Influence in American Life* (Atlanta, GA: SBL Press).

Chaucer, G. 1980. *The Canterbury Tales* (ed. N. F. Blake. London: Arnold).

Chilton, B. 1982. *The Glory of Israel: The Theology and Provenience of the Isaiah Targum* (Sheffield: JSOT Press).

Chilton, B. 1987. *The Isaiah Targum: Introduction, Translation, Apparatus and Notes* (Edinburgh: T&T Clark).

Clines, D. J. A. 1974. 'The Evidence for an Autumnal New Year Festival in Pre-exilic Israel Reconsidered', *JBL* 93 (22): 40.

Clines, D. J. A. 1976. *I, He, We and They: A Literary Approach to Isaiah 53* (JSOT Suppl 1; Sheffield: JSOT Press).

Coggins, J. J. and J. H. Han. 2011. *Six Minor Prophets Through the Centuries* (Malden, MA: Wiley Blackwell).

Cohen R. and R. Westbrook, eds. 2008. *Isaiah's Vision of Peace in Biblical and Modern International Relations: Swords into Plowshares* (New York: Palgrave Macmillan).

Conlee, J. W. 2004. *William Dunbar: The Complete Works* (Kalamazoo, MI: Medieval Institute Publications, Western Michigan University).

Conrad, E. 1991. *Reading Isaiah* (Minneapolis, MN: Fortress Press).

Corpus Christianorum. 1953– (Series Latina; Turnhout Belgium: Brepols).

Cowan, J. 1979. *Rose Windows* (London: Thames and Hudson).

Cowley, A. 1967. *The Complete Works in Verse and Prose of Abraham Cowley* (ed. A. B. Grosart; 2 vols; New York: AMS Press).

Daly, M. 1973. *Beyond God the Father: Towards a Philosophy of Women's Liberation* (Boston: Beacon Press).

Damrosch, L. 1980. *Symbol and Truth in Blake's Myth* (Princeton: Princeton University Press), 220–233.

Danby, H., ed. 1933. *The Mishnah* (Oxford: Oxford University).

Dante Alighieri. 1995. *The Divine Comedy: Inferno. Purgatorio. Paradiso* (trans. A. Mandelbaum; London: Dent).

Darr, K. P. 1994. *Isaiah's Vision and the Family of God* (Louisville, KY: Westminster/John Knox Press).

Davies, A. 2000. *Double Standards in Isaiah: Re-evaluating Prophetic Ethics and Divine Justice* (Leiden: Brill).

Davies, A. 2013. 'What Does it Mean to Read the Bible as a Pentecostal?', in *Pentecostal Hermeneutics: a Reader* (ed. L. R. Martin; Leiden: Brill) 249–262.

Davies, A. 2007. 'Oratorio as Exegesis: The Use of the Book of Isaiah in Handel's *Messiah*', in *Retellings: The Bible in Literature, Music, Art and Film* (ed. J. Cheryl Exum; Leiden/Boston: Brill) 114–134. [*Biblical Interpretation*, 15 (2007): 464–484.]

Davies, W. D. 1988. *A Critical and Exegetical Commentary on the Gospel According to Saint Matthew*, vol. 1 (Edinburgh: Clark).

Déclais, J.-L. 2001. *Un récit musulman sur Isaïe* (Paris: Editions du Cerf).

Del Olmo Lete, G. 2014 *Canaanite Religion: According to the Liturgical Texts of Ugarit* (trans. W. G. E. Watson; Münster: Ugarit-Verlag).

de Wald, E. T., ed. 1933. *The Illustrations of the Utrecht Psalter* (Princeton: Princeton University Press).

Dijkstra, B. 1986. *Idols of Perversity: Fantasies of Feminine Evil in Fin-de-Siècle Culture* (New York/Oxford: Oxford University Press).

Dille, S. J. 2004. *Mixing Metaphors: God as Mother and Father in Deutero-Isaiah* (London: T & T Clark International).

Doddridge, P. 1794. *Hymns Founded on Various Texts in the Holy Scriptures* (London: J. Hodges, W. Millar, R. Tonson, T. French, J. Ottridge, G. Wade, and J. Wren).

Dodwell, C. R., ed. 1960. *St Alban's Psalter* (London: Warburg Institute).

Domin, H. 1987. *Gesammelte Gedichte* (Frankfurt: S. Fischer).

Dowling Long, S. and J. F. A. Sawyer 2015. *Bible in Music: A Dictionary of Songs, Works and More* (Lanham, MA: Rowman and Littlefield).

Driver, S. R. and A. Neubauer. 1877. *The Fifty-third Chapter of Isaiah According to the Jewish Interpreters*, vol. 2 (Oxford: J. Parker).

Duffy, E. 1992. *The Stripping of the Altars: Traditional Religion in England* (New Haven, CT: Yale University Press).

Dunbar, W. 1958. *Poems* (ed. J. Kinsley; Oxford: Clarendon Press).

Dussel, E. 1964. 'Universalismo y mision en los poemas del Siervo de Yaveh', *Ciencia y Fe* 20: 419–464.

Edwards, J. 1972. *The Works*. Vol. 4. *The Great Awakening…* (ed. C. C. Goen; gen. ed. J. E. Smith. New Haven, CT: Yale University Press).

Edwards, J. 1989. *The Works.* Vol. 9, *A History of the Work of Redemption* (ed. J. F. Wilson; gen. ed. J. E. Smith; New Haven, CT: Yale University Press).

Elbogen, I. 1993. *Jewish Liturgy: A Comprehensive History (Die jüdische Gottesdienst in seiner geschichtlichen Entwicklung)* (trans. R. P. Scheidlin; Philadelphia: Jewish Publication Society). [German original, Frankfurt 1913.]

Elliot, C. 1985. *Praying the Kingdom: Towards a Political Spirituality* (London: Darton, Longman and Todd).

Elliott, J. K. 1993. *The Apocryphal New Testament a Collection of Apocryphal Christian Literature in an English Translation* (Oxford: Clarendon).

Elsig, F. 2004. *Jheronimus Bosch: la question de la chronologie* (Genève: Droz).

Epstein. I., ed. 1935–1948. *The Babylonian Talmud* (35 vols; London: Soncino).

Eskenazi, T. C., G. A. Phillips and D. Jobling, eds. 2003. *Levinas and Biblical Studies* (Semeia Series; Atlanta, GA: SBL Press).

Ettlinger, L. D. and H. S. Ettlinger. 1987. *Raphael* (Oxford: Phaidon).

Evans, C. A. 1989. *To See and Not Perceive: Isaiah 6:9–10 in Early Jewish and Christian Interpretation* (Sheffield: JSOT Press).

Exum, J. C. 1982. 'Whom Will He Teach Knowledge? A Literary Approach to Isaiah 28', in *Art And Meaning: Rhetoric in Biblicsal Literature* (ed. D. J. A. Clines et al.; Sheffield: JSOT Press), 108–139.

Exum, J. C. and E. Nutu, eds. 2007. *Between the Text and the Canvas: The Bible and Art in Dialogue.* Sheffield: Sheffield Phoenix Press.

Fackenheim, E. 1990. *The Jewish Bible after the Holocaust* (Bloomington, IN: Indiana University).

Fathers of the Church: A New Translation 1947–.(Washington, DC: Catholic University of America Press).

Fekkes, J. 1994. *Isaiah and Prophetic Traditions in the Book of Revelation: Visionary Antecedents and their Development* (JSNT Suppl. 93) (Sheffield: Sheffield Academic Press).

Flannery, A., ed. 1981. *Vatican Council II: The Conciliar and Post Conciliar Documents* (Dublin: Dominican Publications; rev. edn). [Original 1975.]

Fouts, D. M. 1991. 'A Suggestion for Isaiah 26:16', *VT* 41: 472–475.

Fredriksen, P. 2006. 'No Pain No Gain', in Beal and Linafelt 2006; 91–98.

Gadamer, H.-G. 1975. *Truth and Method* (London: Sheed & Ward).

Ghose, J. C. 1982. *The English Works of Raja Rammohun Roy*, vol. 3 (New Delhi: Cosmo).

Gibson, J. C. L., ed. 1978. *Canaanite Myths and Legends* (Edinburgh: T&T Clark). [Originally edited by by G. R. Driver, 1956.]

Gignilliat, M. S. 2009. *Karl Barth and the Fifth Gospel: Barth's Theological Exegesis of Isaiah* (Farnham, UK: Ashgate).

Gill, Andy. 1998. *Classic Bob Dylan (1962–69): My Back Pages* (London: Carlton).

Ginzberg, L. 1954. *The Legends of the Jews* (7 vols; Philadelphia: Jewish Publication Society).

Ginzberg, L. 1975. *The Legends of the Bible* (Philadelphia: Jewish Publication Society).

Gorringe, T. 2006. 'Politics', in Sawyer 2006; 414–431.

Goulder, M. D. 2004. *Isaiah as Liturgy* (Aldershot/Burlington, VT: Ashgate).

Gregory of Nyssa. 1960–1972. *Gregorii Nysseni Opera* (ed. W. Jaeger et al.; Leiden: Brill).

Grenholm, C. and D. Patte, eds. 2000. *Reading Israel in Romans: Legitimacy and Plausibility of Divergent Interpretations* (Harrisburg, PA: Trinity Press International).

Gressmann, H. 1929. *Der Messias (FRLANT 43*; Göttingen: Vandenhoeck and Ruprecht).

Gruber, M. I. 1992. *The Motherhood of God and Other Studies* (Atlanta, GA: Scholars Press).

Gundry, R. H. 1982. *Matthew: A Commentary on his Literary and Theological Art* (Grand Rapids, MI: Wm. B. Eerdmans).

Gunkel, H. 1924. 'Jesaja 33, eine prophetische Liturgie', *ZAW* 42: 177–208.

Gutiérrez, G. 1974. *A Theology of Liberation: History, Politics and Salvation* (London: SCM Press).

Haitovsky, D. 1994. 'A New Look at a Lost Painting: The Hebrew Inscription in Lorenzo Costa's Presentation in the Temple', *Artibus et Historiae*, 15 (29): 111–120.

Hammond, G. 1982. *The Making of the English Bible* (Manchester: Carcanet New Press).

Happé, P., ed. 1979. *Four Morality Plays* (Harmondsworth: Penguin).

Happé, P., ed. 1985–1986. *The Complete Plays of John Bale* (2 vols; Cambridge: Brewer).

Harnack, A. von. 1893. *Dogmengeschichte* (Freiburg im Breisgau: J.C.B. Mohr).

Harper, J. 1991. *The Forms and Orders of Western Liturgy from the Tenth to the Eighteenth Century* (Oxford: Clarendon Press).

Harris, R. 1986. *The Cloud Passes Over* (London: Angus & Robertson).

Harris, R. A. 2006. 'Structure and composition in Isaiah 1–12: A Twelfth-century Northern French Rabbinic perspective' in *ATWAT* 171–188.

Harrisville, R. A. and W. Sundberg. 2002. *The Bible in Modern Culture: Baruch Spinoza to Brevard Childs* (Grand Rapids, MI: Wm. B. Eerdmans; 2nd edn).

Hartman, D. 1997. *A Living Covenant: The Innovative Spirit in Traditional Judaism* (Woodstock, VT: Jewish Lights Publishing).

Hass, A., D. Jasper and E. Jay, eds. 2007. *Oxford Handbook of English Literature and Theology* (Oxford: Oxford University Press).

Hays, R. B. 1989. *Echoes of Scripture in the Letters of Paul* (New Haven, CT: Yale University Press).

Hayward, C. T. R. 1982. 'The Jewish Temple at Leontopolis: A Reconsideration', *JJS* 33: 429–443.

Heitz, P. and W. L. Scheiber. 1903. *Biblia pauperum: Nach dem einzigen Exemplare in 50 Darstellungen* (Strassburg: n.p.).

Hengel, M. 1989. *The Zealots: Investigations into the Jewish Freedom Movement in the Period from Herod I until 70 A.D.* (Edinburgh: T&T Clark).

Herbert, G. 2007. *The English Poems* (ed. H. Wilcox; Cambridge: Cambridge University Press).

Herodotus. 1972. *Histories* (trans. A. de Selincourt. Harmondsworth: Penguin; 2nd edn).

Hertzberg, A., ed. 1997. *The Zionist Idea: A Historical Analysis and Reader* (Philadelphia: Jewish Publication Society).

Heschel, A. J. 1962. *The Prophets* (New York: Jewish Publication Society).

Heschel, A. J. 1973. *A Passion for Truth* (New York: Farrar, Straus and Giroux).

Heschel, S. 2006. 'Christ's Passion: Homoeroticism and the Origins of Christianity', in Beal and Linafelt 2006; 99–108.

Heylin, C. 1991. *Dylan: Behind the Shades* (Harmondsworth: Penguin).

Hoffmann, D. 1981. *Brotherly Love* (New York: Vintage Books).

Hopkins, G. M. 1990. *The Poetical Works* (ed. N. H. MacKenzie; Oxford: Oxford University Press).

Hopkins, J. 2006. 'Nicholas of Cusa's Intellectual Relationship to Anselm of Canterbury', in *Cusanus: The Legacy of Learned Ignorance* (ed. P. Casarella; Washington, DC: Catholic University of America Press) 54–73.

Horbury, W. 1998. *Jews and Christians in Contact and Controversy* (Edinburgh: T&T Clark).

Housman, A. E. 1995. *Collected Poems* (Penguin Books).

Howard-Snyder, D. and P. K. Moser, eds. 2002. *Divine Hiddenness: New Essays* (Cambridge/New York: Cambridge University Press).

Hussar, B. 1989. *When the Cloud Lifted: The Testimony of an Israeli* (Eng. trans. Alison Megroz; Dublin: Veritas Publications).

Isidore of Seville, *De fide catholica contra iudaeos. PL* 83. 450–537.

Isidore of Seville, *Sententiarum tres libri. PL* 83. 537–738.

Jauss, H. R. 1982. *Toward an Aesthetic of Reception* (trans. T. Bahti; Minneapolis, MN: University of Minnesota Press).

Jeremias, J. 1969. *Jerusalem in the Time of Jesus* (London: SCM Press).

Jones, D. R. 1955. 'The Traditio of the Oracles of Isaiah of Jerusalem' *ZAW* 67, 226–246.

Josephus, Flavius. 1937. *Jewish Antiquities* (Loeb Classical Library; 4 vols; trans. R. Marcus; London: Heinemann).

Josephus, Flavius. 1928. *The Jewish War* (Loeb Classical Library; 2 vols; trans. H. St J. Thackeray; London: Heinemann).

Joyce, P. and D. Lipton. 2013. *Lamentations Through the Centuries* (Blackwell Bible Commentary Series) (Oxford: Wiley Blackwell).

Kadish, S. 2010. 'The Jewish Presence in Wales: Image and Material Reality', in O'Kane and Morgan-Guy 2010; 272–289.

Katzenstein, H. J. 1997. *The History of Tyre, from the Beginning of the Second Millenium B.C.E. until the Fall of the Neo-Babylonian Empire in 539 B.C.E.* (Jerusalem: BenGurion University of the Negev Press).

Kerman, J. 1981. *The Masses and Motets of William Byrd* (London: Faber).

Kessler, F. 1982. *The Falashas: The Forgotten Jews of Ethiopia* (London: Allen & Unwin).

Kipling, Rudyard. 2013. *Poems* (3 vols., ed. T. Pinney; Cambridge: Cambridge University Press).

Kirschbaum, E., ed. 1970. *Lexikon der christlichen Ikonographie*, vol. 2 (Rome: Herder).

Knibb, M. 1985. 'Martyrdom and Ascension of Isaiah', in *OTP*, vol. 1; 143–176.

Kovacs, J. and C. Rowland. 2004. *Revelation* (Blackwell Bible Commentaries; Oxford: Blackwell).

Kreitzer, L. 1994. *The Old Testament in Fiction and Film: On Reversing the Hermeneutical Flow* (Sheffield: Sheffield Academic Press).

Laato, A. 1988. *Who Is Immanuel? The Rise and the Foundering of Isaiah's Messianic Expectations* (Winona Lake, IN: Eisenbrauns).

Laato, A. 2012. *Who Is the Servant of the Lord? Jewish and Christian Interpretations of Isaiah 53 from Antiquity to the Middle Ages* (Studies in Rewritten Bible 4; Winona Lake, IN: Eisenbrauns).

Labanow, Cory E. 2009. *Evangelicalism and the Emerging Church: A Congregational Study of a Vineyard Church* (Aldershot: Ashgate).

Lambden, S. N. 2006. 'Islam', in Sawyer 2006; 135–157.

Lampe, G. W. H. 1961. *A Patristic Greek Lexicon* (Oxford: Clarendon Press).

Landy, F., 'The Covenant with Death', in Linafelt 2001; 220–232.

Lange, A., and M. Weigold, 2011 *Biblical Quotations and Allusions in Second Temple Jewish literature* (Göttingen/Oakville, CT.: Vandenhoeck & Ruprecht).

Langland, W. 1959. *Piers the Ploughman* (ed. J. F. Goodridge; Harmondsworth: Penguin Books).

Lauterbach, J. Z., ed. 1933. *Mekhilta de-Rabbi Ishmael* (Philadelphia: Jewish Publication Society).

Lavik, M. H. 2001. 'The "African" Texts of the Old Testament and their African Interpretations', in *Interpreting the Old Testament in Africa* (ed. M. N. Getui, K. Holter and V. Zinkuratire; New York/Oxford: Peter Lang).

Lawrence, D. H. 1974. *Apocalypse* (London: Penguin).

Lazarus-Yafeh, H. 1992. *Intertwined Worlds: Medieval Islam and Bible Criticism* (Princeton: Princeton University Press).

Lee, L., G. Seddon and F. Stephen. 1976. *Stained Glass* (New York: Crown).

LeMarquand, G. 2006. 'Bibles, Crosses, Songs, Guns and Oil: Sudanese Readings of the Bible in the Midst of Civil War,' *AEH* 75 (4): 553–79.

Lieb, M., E. Mason and J. Roberts, eds. 2011. *The Oxford Handbook of the Reception History of the Bible* (consultant ed. C. Rowlands; Oxford: Oxford University Press).

Lightbrown, R. 1986. *Mantegna* (Oxford: Phaidon).

Linafelt, T. 2000. *Surviving Lamentations: Catastrophe, Lament amd Protest in the Afterlife of a Biblical Book* (Chicago & London: University of Chicago Press).

Linafelt, T., ed. 2001. *Strange Fire: Reading the Bible after the Holocaust* (New York: New York University Press).

Lindars, B. 1961. *New Testament Apologetic: The Doctrinal Significance of the Old Testament Quotations* (London: SCM Press).

Lindblom, J. 1958. *A Study on the Immanuel Section of Isaiah (Is 7:1–9:6)* (Lund: Gleerup).

Lohfink, N. 1987. *Option for the Poor: The Basic Principles of Liberation Theology in the Light of the Bible* (Berkeley: Bibal Press).

Longfellow, H. W. 1893. *The Complete Poetical Works* (ed. H. E. Scudder; Boston/New York: Houghton, Mifflin & Co.).

Louth, A. 2003. *The Wilderness of God* (London: Darton Longman & Todd).

Low, M. 2013. *Mother Zion in Deutero-Isaiah: A Metaphor for Zion Theology* (New York: Peter Lang).

Lowenherz, R. J. 1959. 'Roger Williams and the Great Quaker Debate', *American Quarterly* 11 (1): 157–165.

Lucan. 2012. *The Civil War (Pharsalia)* (trans. M. Fox; London: Penguin).

Lucas, St J., ed. 1957. *The Oxford Book of French Verse* (Oxford: Clarendon Press).

Lucretius. 2001. *On the Nature of the Universe* (trans. M. F. Smith; Indianapolis: Hackett Publishing).

Luz, U. 2007. *Matthew 1–7: A Commentary* (Minneapolis, MN: Fortress Press).

Maccoby, H. 1982. *Judaism on Trial: Jewish Christian Disputations in the Middle Ages* (London and Toronto: Associated University Presses).

Magnusson, S. 1981. *The Flying Scotsman: A Biography* (London/New York: Quartet Books).

Maimonides, M. 1956. *The Guide for the Perplexed* (ed. M. Friedländer; New York: Dover Publications; 2nd edn).

Mango, C. A. and Scott, R. 1997. *The Chronicle of Theophanes Confessor: Byzantine and Near Eastern History a.d. 284–813* (Oxford: Clarendon Press).

Mann, J. 1971. *The Bible as Read and Preached in the Old Synagogue: A Study in the Cycles of the Readings from Torah and Prophets, as well as from Psalms, and in the Structure of the Midrashic Homilies* (2 vols; New York: Ktav Publishing House).

Manuel, F. 1992. *The Broken Staff: Judaism through Christian Eyes* (Cambridge, MA/London: Harvard University Press).

Marley, B. 1973. 'Small Axe', *Burnin'* (Island Records).

Marlow, H. 2007. 'The Lament over the River Nile: Isaiah xix 5–10 in Its Wider Context', *VT* 57 (2): 229–242.

Marlow, H. and J. Barton. 2009. *Biblical Prophets and Contemporary Environmental Ethics: Re-Reading Amos, Hosea and First Isaiah* (Oxford: Oxford University Press).

Marrow, J. H. 1979. *Passion Iconography in Northern European Art in the Late Middle Ages and Early Renaissance: A Study of the Transformation of Sacred Metaphor into Descriptive Narrative* (Brussels: Van Ghemmert).

McFague, S. 1982. *Metaphorical Theology: Models of God in Religious Language* (London: SCM Press).

McGinn, S. E., L. L. E. Ngan and A. Calderón Pilarski, eds. 2014. *By Bread Alone: The Bible through the Eyes of the Hungry* (Minneapolis, MN: Fortress).

McGinnis, C. M. and P. K. Tull, eds. 2006. '*As Those Who Are Taught*': *The Interpretation of Isaiah from the LXX to the SBL* (Symposium Series; Atlanta, GA: Society of Biblical Literature).

McKinney, G. D. 1963. *The Theology of the Jehovah's Witnesses* (London/Edinburgh: Marshall, Morgan & Scott).

Mearns, J. 1914. *The Canticles of the Christian Church: Eastern and Western, in Early and Medieval Times* (Cambridge: Cambridge University Press).

Melamed, Y. Y. 2016. 'Ma'oz Tzur and the "End of Christianity"'at http://thetorah.com/maoz-tzur-and-the-end-of-christianity/ (accessed 23 June, 2017).

Mesters, C. 1990. *The Mission of the People who Suffer: The Songs of the Servant of God* (Cape Town: Theology Exchange Programme).

Mettinger, T. N. D. 1983. *A Farewell to the Servant Songs* (Lund: Gleerup).

Meynell, Alice. 1927. *Poems* (London: Burns and Oates).

Milton, J. 1998. *The Complete Poems: John Milton* (ed. J. Leonard; London: Penguin).

Miranda, J. P. 1977. *Marx and the Bible: A Critique of the Philosophy of Oppression* (London: SCM Press).

Miscall, P. D. 1999. *Isaiah 34–35: A Nightmare/A Dream* (Sheffield: Sheffield Academic Press).

Moffatt, J. 1924. *The Bible in Scots Literature* (London: Hodder and Stoughton).

Moffatt, J. 1927. *Handbook to the Church Hymnary* (Oxford: Oxford University Press).

Montefiore, C. and H. Loewe, eds. 1963. *Rabbinic Anthology* (New York: Meridian Books).

Moracchini-Mazel, G. 1967. *Les Monuments paléochrétiens de la Corse* (Paris: Klincksieck).

Moyise, S. and M. J. J. Menken, eds. 2005. *Isaiah in the New Testament* (London/New York: T&T Clark).

Myers, C. 2012. 'From Capital to Community: Discipleship as Defection in Jesus' Parable', in *Radical Christian Voices and Practice. Essays in Honour of Christopher Rowland* (ed. Z. Bennett and D. Gowler; Oxford: Oxford University Press) 51–67.

Nabholz, J. 1958. 'The Covenant with Hell in Klinger's "Faust"', *Monatshefte* 50 (6): 311–319.

New Cambridge History of the Bible. 2012–2016 (Vol. 1, ed. J.C. Paget and J. Schaper; Vol. 2, ed. R. Marsden and E.A. Matter; Vol. 3, ed. E. Cameron; Vol. 4, ed. J. Riches; Cambridge: Cambridge University Press).

Newton, I. 1733. *Observations upon the Prophecies of Daniel, and the Apocalypse of St. John* (Part 1; London: n.p.).

Nicene and Post-Nicene Fathers, A Select Library of the. 1887–1894 (28 vols. ed. P. Schaff et al.; Buffalo, NY: Christian Literature).

O'Dea, T. F. 1957. *The Mormons* (Chicago: University of Chicago Press).

O'Kane, M. 2007. *Painting the Text: The Artist as Biblical Interpreter* (Sheffield: Sheffield Phoenix Press).

O'Kane, M. and J. Morgan-Guy, eds. 2010. *Biblical Art from Wales* (Sheffield: Sheffield Phoenix Press).

Olitzky, K. M. 1996. *The American Synagogue: A Historical Dictionary and Sourcebook* (Westport, CT/London: Greenwood Press).

Orlinsky, H. M. 1941. 'Yehoash's Yiddish Translation of the Bible', *JBL* 60: 73–177.

Otto, R. 1950. *The Idea of the Holy: An Inquiry into the Non-rational Factor in the Idea of the Divine and its Relation to the Rational* (Oxford: Oxford University Press).

Owen, W. 1994. *Poems* (ed. J. Stallworthy; London: Chatto and Windus).

Pao, D. W. 2000. *Acts and the Isaianic New Exodus* (WUNT.2 130; Tübingen: Mohr Siebeck).

Parsons, M. C. 1998. 'Isaiah 53 in Acts 8', in *Jesus and the Suffering Servant: Isaiah 53 and Christian Origins* (ed. W. H. Bellinger and W. R. Farmer, Harrisburg, PA: Trinity Press) 104–119.

Pascal, B. 1910. *Thoughts* (ed. O. W. Wight, M. L. Booth and W. F. Trotter; New York: P. F. Collier & Son).

Patterson, F. A., ed. 1931. *The Works of John Milton.* Vol. 3, Pt. 1. *The Reason of Church-Government Urged against Prelaty* (New York: Columbia University Press). [Original 1641.]

Pauw, A. P. 2006. '"Becoming a part of Israel": John Calvin's Exegesis of Calvin', in *ATWAT*; 201–222.

Percy, Lord Eustace. 1937. *John Knox* (London: Hodder and Stoughton).

Pope, A. 1978. *Poetical Works* (ed. H. Davies; Oxford: Oxford University Press).

Potter, G. R. and E. M. Simpson, eds. 1953–1962. *The Sermons of John Donne* (Berkeley: University of California Press).

Puglisi, C. R. and W. L. Barcham 2013. *New Perspectives on the Man of Sorrows* (Kalamazoo, MI: Medieval Institute Publications, Western Michigan University).

Quarles, F. 1977. *Emblems Divine and Moral: Together with Hieroglyphics of the Life of Man* (London: H. Trapp).

Ravitzky, A. 1996. *Messianism, Zionism and Jewish Religious Radicalism* (Chicago: University of Chicago Press).

Réau, L. 1956. *Iconographie de l'art chrétien: 2 Iconographie de la Bible. 1 Ancien Testament* (Paris: Presses universitaires de France).

Rendtorff, R. 1984. 'Zur Komposition des Buches Jesaja', *VT* 34: 295–320.

Ricks, C. and J. McCue, eds. 2015. *The Poems of T.S. Eliot* (London: Faber & Faber).

Rogerson, J. W. 2006 'Music', in Sawyer 2006; 286–298.

Romanos, Melodus. 1995. *On the Life of Christ: Kontakia* (Engl. trans. Ephrem Lash. San Francisco: HarperCollins Publishers).

Rossetti, C. G. 1904. *Poetical Works, with a Memoir and Notes by William Michael Rossetti* (London: Macmillan).

Rubenstein, R. L. 2006. 'Mel Gibson's Passion', in T. K. Beal and T. Linafelt 2006; 109–120.

Ruether, R. R. 1983. *Sexism and God-Talk: Towards a Feminist Theology* (London: SCM Press).

Ruether, R. R. 1985. *Womanguides: Readings toward a Feminist Theology* (Boston: Beacon Press).

Russell, J. 1987. *The Mosaic Inscriptions of Anemurium* (Vienna: Verlag der Österreichischen Akademie der Wissenschaften).

Sawyer, J. F. A. 1964.'The Qumran reading of Isaiah 6:13', *ASTI* 3: 111–114. [*STSM* 130–132.]

Sawyer, J. F. A. 1968. 'Spaciousness in Biblical Language about Salvation', *Annual of the Swedish Theological Institute* 6: 20–34 (STSM 270–280).

Sawyer, J. F. A. 1973. 'Hebrew Terms for the Resurrexion of the Dead', *VT* 23: 218–234 [*STSM* 256–269.]

Sawyer, J. F. A. 1986. 'Blessed be Egypt, My People: A Commentary on Isaiah 19.16–25', in *A Word in Season* (ed. J. D. Martin; Sheffield: *JSOT* Press) 21–35. [*STSM* 138–50.]

Sawyer, J. F. A. 1989. 'Daughter of Zion and Servant of the Lord in Isaiah: A Comparison', *Journal for the Study of the Old Testament* 44: 89–107. [*STSM* 67–83.]

Sawyer, J. F. A. 1993. 'I Have Trodden the Wine-press Alone: Radical Images of YHWH in Isaiah 63', in *Among the Prophets: Language, Image and Structure in the Prophetic Writings* (ed. P. R. Davies and D. J. A. Clines; Sheffield: *JSOT* Press) 72–82. [*STSM* 184–193.]

Sawyer, J. F. A. 1996. *The Fifth Gospel: Isaiah in the History of Christianity* (Cambridge: Cambridge University Press).

Sawyer, J.F.A. 2003. 'Isaiah and Zionism', in *Sense and Sensitivity: Essays on Biblical Prophecy, Ideology and Reception in Tribute to Robert Carroll* (ed. P. R. Davies and A. G. Hunter; Sheffield: Sheffield Academic Press) 246–269. [*STSM* 231–244.]

Sawyer, J. F. A. 2004. 'Isaiah and the Jews: Some Reflections on the Church's Use of the Bible', in *Reading from Right to Left: Essays in Honour of David J. A. Clines* (ed. J. C. Exum and H. G. M. Williamson; Sheffield: Sheffield Academic Press) 390–401 (STSM 220–230).

Sawyer, J. F. A., ed. 2006. *The Blackwell Companion to the Bible and Culture* (Oxford: Blackwell).

Sawyer, J. F. A. 2007. 'Anthony van Dyck's Birmingham *Ecce Homo* "Behold the Man!"', in O'Kane 2007; 122–144.

Sawyer, J. F. A. 2008. 'Immanuel', in *The New Interpreter's Dictionary of the Bible*, vol. 3 (ed. K. D. Sakenfeld; Nashville, TN: Abingdon Press). (*STSM* 133–137).

Sawyer, J. F. A. 2011a. 'Interpreting Hebrew Writing in Christian Art', in *A Critical Engagement: Essays on the Hebrew Bible in Honour of J. Cheryl Exum* (ed. E. Van Wolde and D. J. A. Clines; Sheffield: Phoenix) 372–390.

Sawyer, J. F. A. 2011b. 'The Divine "Here I am" (*hinneni*) in Isaiah', in *STSM*; 194–206.

Sawyer, J. F.A. 2012. 'A Critical Review of Recent Projects and Publications', *Hebrew Bible and Ancient Israel* (special issue on Reception History, ed. Carol Newsom) 1 (3): 298–326.

Sawyer, J. F. A. 2013. '"A Man of Sorrows and Acquainted with Grief": The Biblical Text and its Afterlife in Christian Tradition', in Puglisi and Barcham 2013; 7–18.

Schiller, G. 1971. *Iconography of Christian Art*. Vol. 1, *Christ's Incarnation. Childhood. Baptism. Temptation. Transfiguration. Works and Miracles* (Eng. trans. Janet Seligman; London: Lund Humphries).

Schiller, G. 1972. *Iconography of Christian Art*. Vol. 2, *The Passion of Jesus Christ* (Eng. trans. Janet Seligman; London: Lund Humphries).

Schmidt, H. 1925. *Der Mythos vom wiederkehrenden König im Alten Testament* (Giessen: A. Töpelmann).

Scholem, G. 1965. *On the Kabbalah and its Symbolism* (New York: Schocken Books).

Scholem, G. 1971. *The Messianic Idea in Judaism and Other Essays on Jewish Spirituality* (New York: Schocken Books).

Scholem, G. 2007. 'Lilith' in *EJ* 11,245–249.

Schwartz, H. 1998. *Reimagining the Bible: The Storytelling of the Rabbis* (New York/ Oxford: Oxford University Press).

Seiferth, W. S. 1970. *Synagogue and Church in the Middle Ages: Two Symbols in Art and Literature* (New York: Ungar).

Seitz, C. R., ed. 1988. *Reading and Preaching the Book of Isaiah* (Philadelphia: Fortress Press).

Sicker, M. 1992. *Judaism, Nationalism, and the Land of Israel* (Boulder, CO: Westview Press).

Simone, N. 1965. 'Sinnerman'. *Pastel Blues* (Phillips Records).

Sherwood, Y. 2007. 'Prophetic Literature', in Hass, Jasper and Jay 2007: 289–306.

Simon, L. 1960. *Ahad Ha-Am: Asher Ginsberg. A Biography* (London: East & West Library).

Simon, U. 1985. 'Ibn Ezra between Medievalism and Modernism', in *Congress Volume: Salamanca 1983* (SVT 36) (ed. J. A. Emerton; Leiden: E. J. Brill) 257–271.

Skriver, C. A. 1990. *The Forgotten Beginnings of Creation and Christianity* (Denver, CO: Vegetarian Press).

Slapak, O., ed. 1995. *The Jews of India: A Story of Three Communities* (Jerusalem: Israel Museum).

Smalley, B. 1983. *The Study of the Bible in the Middle Ages* (Oxford: Basil Blackwell).

Smith, G. 1906. *The Life of William Carey: Shoemaker and Missionary* (London: J. M. Dent).

Soares-Prabhu, G. 1995. 'Laughing at Idols: The Dark Side of Biblical Monotheism', in *Reading from This Place*, vol. 2 (ed. F. Segovia and M. Tolbert; Minneapolis, MN: Fortress Press) 109–131.

Spiegel, S. 1979. *The Last Trial: On the Legends and Lore of the Command to Abraham to offer Isaac as a Sacrifice* (Eng. trans. J. Goldin; New York: Behrman).

Spier, J. 2008. *Picturing the Bible: The Earliest Christian Art* (New Haven, CT and London: Yale University Press).

Spinks, B. D. 1991. *The Sanctus in the Eucharistic Prayer* (Cambridge: Cambridge University Press).

Spurgeon, C. H. 1897. *Autobiography, Compiled from His Diary, Letters*, vol. 1 (London: Passmore and Alabaster).

Spurgeon, C. H. 1856–1916. *The Metropolitan Tabernacle Pulpit: Sermons Preached and Revised* (55 vols; London: Passmore & Alabaster).

Stanton, E. C. 1985. *The Woman's Bible: The Original Feminist Attack on the Bible* (Edinburgh: Polygon Books).

Stenning, J. F., ed. 1949. *The Targum of Isaiah* (Oxford: Clarendon Press).

Strolz, W. 1992. 'The Incomparability of God as Biblical Experience of Faith', in *On Sharing Religious Experience: Possibilities of Interfaith Mutuality* (ed. J. D. Gort et al.; Amsterdam: Editions Rodopi/Grand Rapids, MI: Wm. B. Eerdmans) 106–115.

Sugirtharajah, R. S., ed. 1995. *Voices front the Margin: Interpreting the Bible in the Third World* (Maryknoll, NY: Orbis Books, new edn).

Sweeney, M. J. 2006. 'On the Road to Duhm: Isaiah in Nineteenth Century Critical Scholarship' *ATWAT* 243–261.

Tate, A. 2006. 'Postmodernism', in Sawyer 2006; 515–533.

Tennyson, Alfred Lord. 1969. *The Poems of Tennyson* (3 vols; ed. C. Ricks; London: Longman).

Terry, R.R. 1932. *A Medieval Carol Book* (London: Burns Oates & Washbourne).

Traill, D. A., ed. 2013. *Walter of Châtillon, the Shorter Poems: Christmas Hymns, Love Lyrics, and Moral-Satirical Verse* (Oxford: Oxford University Press).

Trible, P. 1984. *Texts of Terror: Literary Feminist Readings of Biblical Narratives* (Philadelphia: Fortress Press).

Trible, P. 1978. *God and the Rhetoric of Sexuality* (Philadelphia: Fortress Press).

Tull, P. K. 2006. 'One Book, Many Voices: Conceiving of Isaiah's Polyphonic Message', in *ATWAT*; 279–314.

Tutu, D. 1991. *Church and Prophecy in South Africa Today* (University of Essex: Centre for the Study of Theology).

Twain, M. 1980. *The Innocents Abroad* (New York: New American Library).

Twycross, M. 2006. 'The Theatre', in Sawyer 2006; 339–364.

Uffenheimer, B. 1971. 'The Consecration of Isaiah in Rabbinic Exegesis', *Scripta Hierosolymitana* 22 (Jerusalem), 234–246.

van der Kooij, A. 1981. *Die alten Textzeugen des Jesajabuches: ein Beitrag zur Textgeschichte des Alten Testaments* (Göttingen: Vandenhoeck & Ruprecht).

van der Kooij, A. 1988. *The Oracle of Tyre: The LXX of Isaiah 23 as Version and Vision* (Leiden: E. J. Brill).

van der Kooij, A. 2006. 'Interpretation of the Book of Isaiah in the Septuagint and in Other Ancient Versions', *ATWAT* 49–68.

Vermeylen, J. 1989. 'L'unité du livre d'Isaïe', in *The Book of Isaiah* (ed. J. Vermeylen; Leuven: Leuven University Press) 11–53.

Vogel, D., ed. 1996. *Early Mormon Documents* (Salt Lake City: Signature Books).

von Rad, G. 1965. 'The City on the Hill', in *The Problem of the Hexateuch and Other Essays* (Engl. trans; Edinburgh and London: Oliver & Boyd) 232–242. [*Evangelische Theologie* 8 (1949) 211–215.]

Wagner, J. R. 2006. 'Moses and Isaiah in Concert: Paul's Reading of Isaiah and Deuteronomy in the Letter to the Romans', in *ATWAT*; 87–105.

Waldinger, A. 1998. 'A Prophecy for the Jews: Isaiah in Yiddish and German', *Babel* 44 (4): 316–335.

Watson, A. 1934. *The Early Iconography of the Tree of Jesse* (Oxford: Oxford University Press).

Watson, F. B. 2009. 'Mistranslation and the Death of Christ: Isaiah 53 LXX and its Pauline Reception', in *Translating the New Testament: Text, Translation, Theology* (ed. S. Porter and M. J. Boda; Grand Rapids, MI: Wm. B. Eerdmans).

Weems, R. J. 1995. *Battered Love: Marriage, Sex, and Violence in the Hebrew Prophets* (Minneapolis, MN: Fortress Press).

Wesley, J. 1984–1987. *The Works of John Wesley. Sermons*, vols 1–4 (ed. A. C. Outler; Nashville, TN: Abingdon Press).

Westall, R. and J. Martin.1835. *Illustrations of the Bible*, vol. 2 (London: n.p.).

Whittaker, W. G. 1959. *The Cantatas of Johann Sebastian Bach: Sacred and Secular* (London: Oxford University Press).

Wiesel, E. 2006. *Night* (Engl. trans. M. Wiesel; New York: Hill and Wang). [French original: Paris, 1958.]

Williams, R. 1963. *The Complete Writings of Roger Williams (1604–83)* (7 vols; New York: Russell & Russell).

Williamson, H. 1994. *The Book Called Isaiah: Deutero-Isaiah's Role in Composition and Redaction* (Oxford: Clarendon Press).

Wolff, H. W. 1959. *Immanuel: das Zeichen dem widersprochen wird* (Neukirchen-Vluyn: Neukirchener Verlag).

Wright, D. F., ed. 1988. *The Bible in Scottish Life and Literature* (Edinburgh: The St Andrew Press).

Wybrew, H. 1989. *The Orthodox Liturgy: The Development of the Eucharistic Liturgy in the Byzantine Rite* (London: SPCK).

Wybrew, H. 2001. *Risen with Christ: Eastertide in the Orthodox Church* (London: SPCK).

Zohar: the Book of Enlightenment. 1983 (ed. D. C. Matt; London: SPCK).

Websites

Babylonian Talmud: large selection of texts in English. www.come-and-hear.com/talmud/.

The Bible and the Arts: new website dedicated to the promotion, enjoyment and understanding of the Bible in literature, painting, sculpture, film, music and opera, theatre and performance, publishing, translation, digital and mass media. www.thebibleandthearts.com.

Bridgeman Images: huge searchable collection. www.bridgemanimages.com/en-GB/.

Christian Classics Ethereal Library: Church Fathers, commentaries, sermons and hymns,searchable by author, biblical reference, etc. www.ccel.org/.

Early Christian Writings: Apostolic Fathers, Gnostics, etc. www.earlychristianwritings.com/.

Early Jewish Writings: Pseudepigrapha, Josephus, Philo, etc. www.earlyjewishwritings.com/.

The Great Isaiah Scroll from Qumran (1QIsaa): http://dss.collections.imj.org.il/.

Hebrew Songs inspired by texts from Isaiah: hebrewsongs.com/search.asp?PageNo=&KW=isaiah&SF=All&OrderBy=New&TLT=ALL.

Hymnary.org: A comprehensive index of over 1 million hymns searchable by title, biblical text, composer, etc. https://hymnary.org/.

IMSLP Petrucci Music Library: scores and recordings searchable by composer, title, etc.: imslp.org/wiki/Main_Page.

Israel Philatelic Federation: Israeli stamps, searchable by biblical book, historical event, etc.: israelphilately.org.il/en.

Legends of the Jews, ed. L. Ginzberg (1909): www.sacred-texts.com/jud/loj/index.htm.

Pitts Theology Library Digital Image Archive: huge collection of biblical illustrations, portraits of religious leaders, etc. pitts.emory.edu/dia/.

Rashi's Commentary on Isaiah: www.chabad.org/library/bible_cdo/aid/15932#showrashi=true.

Warburg Institute Iconographic Database: large selection of illuminated manuscripts, printed books, stained glass, sculptures, etc., searchable by biblical text. https://iconographic.warburg.sas.ac.uk/vpc/VPC_search/subcats.php?cat_1=14&cat_2=28.

Web Gallery of Art: searchable database of European fine arts and architecture (eighth–nineteenth centuries). www.wga.hu/index.html.

Wiley Blackwell Bible Commentary series website contains bibliographies and other valuable reception history resources: www.bbibcomm.info.

Index of Biblical and Other Ancient References

Isaiah Through the Centuries, First Edition. John F. A. Sawyer.
© 2018 John Wiley & Sons Ltd. Published 2020 by John Wiley & Sons Ltd.

General Index

Isaiah Through the Centuries, First Edition. John F. A. Sawyer.
© 2018 John Wiley & Sons Ltd. Published 2020 by John Wiley & Sons Ltd.